Financial Accounting and Reporting

L. Murphy Smith, D.B.A., CPA
Murray State University

Katherine Taken Smith, D.B.A.
Murray State University

Shannon Knight Deer, CPA
Texas A&M University

.CCH
a Wolters Kluwer business

EDITORIAL STAFF
Editor: Sandra Lim
Production: Jennifer Schencker, Kathie Luzod
Cover Design: Kathie Luzod

ISBN: 978-0-8080-3133-8

Printed in the United States of America

SUSTAINABLE FORESTRY INITIATIVE

Certified Chain of Custody
Promoting Sustainable Forestry
www.sfiprogram.org
SFI-01268

SFI label applies to the text stock

Dedication

To Don Chamberlain, Terry Holmes, Tim Todd, and Glynn Mangold, who blazed the trail for us to Kentucky.

— LMS and KTS

To Ryan Deer, who makes it possible for me to accomplish so much more professionally and personally, including our contributions to this book.

— SKD

About The Authors

L. MURPHY SMITH, D.B.A., CPA

Dr. L. Murphy Smith, CPA, is the David and Ashley Dill Distinguished Professor of Accounting at Murray State University. Dr. Smith's academic record includes numerous professional journal articles, research grants, books, and professional meeting presentations in the United States and abroad. His work has been cited in various news media, including *Fortune*, *USA Today*, and *The Wall Street Journal*. He has received numerous teaching and research awards, including the Outstanding Educator Award from the Texas Society of CPAs and Outstanding Researcher Award from the American Accounting Association Strategic and Emerging Technologies Section. He ranks in the top one percent of authors on Social Sciences Research Network (SSRN.com) by downloaded articles. During his career, he has held a number of leadership positions in academic and professional organizations such as President of the American Accounting Association Gender Issues and Work-Life Balance Section.

KATHERINE T. SMITH, D.B.A.

Dr. Katherine T. Smith, D.B.A., is a business professor at Murray State University. Previously, she taught at Texas A&M University, University of Mississippi, and Louisiana Tech University. She has been recognized for both outstanding teaching and outstanding research. Her research has appeared in major academic journals. She is in the top five percent of authors on Social Sciences Research Network, based on downloaded articles. She serves on five journal editorial boards, and has co-authored several books. In addition, she has made numerous presentations at professional meetings in the United States and abroad. She has received the Outstanding Educator Award from the Academy of Educational Leadership.

SHANNON KNIGHT DEER, CPA

Shannon Knight Deer, CPA, is the Assistant Department Head in the Accounting Department at Texas A&M University. She gained experience in public accounting prior to entering academia. She teaches financial reporting at the principles and intermediate levels and stays abreast of emerging issues through consulting work and teaching a CPA review course. Her accomplishments include departmental- and university-level teaching awards.

Acknowledgments

We express our sincere gratitude to the many instructors and students who provided suggestions to make this textbook more engaging, understandable, and practical to those who study financial accounting and reporting. Our goal is to continue to make improvements with future editions. In this regard, we welcome and appreciate any comments, criticisms, or suggestions you may have about the book.

— L. Murphy Smith, Katherine Taken Smith, and Shannon Knight Deer

Preface

LOADED WITH OUTSTANDING FEATURES

Financial Accounting and Reporting covers the fundamentals of financial accounting that are essential to preparers and users of accounting information. Topics include basic accounting principles, accounting transaction processing, financial statements, assets, liabilities, accounting for the corporation, financial statement analysis, ethics, and internal control. Students will learn how to use accounting information to answer key questions about a company's financial situation and prospects. In addition, the book addresses contemporary accounting issues related to ethics, international financial reporting, information technology, and global commerce. This book benefits from numerous helpful comments and suggestions contributed by highly experienced instructors who reviewed the book and from students who used the book in the classroom.

The textbook is especially designed to present financial accounting in a one-sequence course in two-year or four-year colleges. The book can also be effectively used in a graduate-level financial accounting course for MBA students who are from non-business major backgrounds.

CROSS-FUNCTIONAL APPROACH

While presenting the fundamentals of financial accounting and reporting, a cross-functional approach is used to demonstrate the relevance of accounting information to the various business functional areas (e.g., marketing, finance, and production). This approach motivates learning by making the subject matter relevant to all majors. Accounting majors will appreciate how accounting information contributes to the success of the firm and the decision-making of every member of the management team. Non-accounting majors will understand how they will use accounting information in their future jobs. Cross-functional applications are interwoven into the presentation of accounting fundamentals in each chapter. In addition, the book engages students regarding contemporary issues such as ethics, international financial reporting, information technology, and global commerce. The book features a chapter, as well as observations throughout the book, on International Financial Reporting Standards (IFRS) and how they differ from U.S. generally accepted accounting principles (GAAP).

FOCUS ON BUSINESS

To complement the cross-functional aspects of the book, each chapter focuses on general business issues. Each chapter opens with a "Focus on Business" box that applies the chapter's topics to a real company. The box is designed to pique the student's interest and preview what will be learned in the chapter. For example, Chapter 1's Focus on Business brings up the debate for taste preference between Pepsi and Coca-Cola and uses that as a segue to explain how an investor would use financial reports to choose a company in which to invest.

A small company is created and used throughout the book to illustrate accounting transactions. Seeing a company start from scratch and apply financial accounting in the process enables students to connect better with accounting concepts.

While the focus throughout the book is on the accounting impact of business decisions, this book also teaches students about general business principles. This is critical, as accounting is often the first business course that students take. For example, the book helps students understand why a company would sell goods on credit, rather than solely teaching them how to calculate the accounts receivable balance.

OTHER SPECIAL FEATURES

- **Student-Friendly:** Chapters are organized in an easy-to-follow manner and contain features to create an interest in accounting. The colloquial writing style is appealing to students and easy to read.
- **Teacher-Friendly:** Detailed PowerPoint slides facilitate a smooth and structured flow of concepts in teaching. A variety of homework assignments is provided along with a test bank. An 'A' and 'B' set of assignments are provided for use in alternating semesters.

- **Real-World Examples:** Throughout the text, well-known companies are used as examples to clarify and reinforce accounting concepts. Interesting and relevant company information is presented to engage the student.
- **Application:** Each major section within a chapter ends with a thought question that encourages students to apply a chapter topic to their real-life situation.
- **Ethics:** In addition to Chapter 5 that focuses on ethics and internal control, ethics issues are incorporated into the book when ethical dilemmas arise in connection to the chapter content.
- **Global Commerce:** Modern business is international in scope. Thanks to the Web and e-business, all firms compete in a global marketplace. This concept is interwoven throughout the book where applicable.
- **International Accounting:** Differences between U.S. generally accepted accounting principles (GAAP) and International Financial Reporting Principles (IFRS) are described in the book's final chapter. In addition, IFRS are mentioned, where appropriate, in other chapters of the book.
- **Information Technology:** Except for Chapter 1, each chapter includes a boxed-insert explaining an Excel function that relates to the chapter. Students will recognize the efficiency of Excel in preparing financial analyses. Optional Excel assignments are provided at the end of each chapter. In addition to Excel, other technology issues will be presented, such as use of Web resources, computer security, and e-commerce.
- **Website:** A website (*http://www.cchgroup.com/FINAR*) contains optional student working paper files.
- **Tying It All Together:** Each chapter's opening box, entitled "Focus on Business," contains an accounting question or problem that will be answered in that chapter. At the end of the chapter is a section entitled "Concluding Remarks" that refers back to the initial question and the student's new knowledge pertaining to it. This section also links chapter material with upcoming information in the next chapter in order to give the student an understanding of how the information ties together.

END OF CHAPTER MATERIAL

Each chapter typically includes:

- 16-26 discussion questions
- 12-28 short exercises designed to build accounting skills*
- 12-24 problems designed to apply accounting knowledge*
- 3-6 cross-functional discussion questions and one cross-functional case designed for individual or team projects
- 5-10 Excel assignments
- 3-8 Web assignments
- Test Prepper containing 10 true/false questions and 10 multiple-choice questions.

* The exercises and problems are separated into Sets A and B so that the sets can be assigned in alternating semesters.

ANCILLARY MATERIALS

Solution Manual, Test Bank, PowerPoint Slides, Website, and Optional Student Working Papers. The website (*http://www.cchgroup.com/FINAR*) includes the optional student working papers and supplementary information, such as current news events, example Excel files, and other helpful information.

Table of Contents

CHAPTER 5   CASH, INTERNAL CONTROL, AND ETHICS

CHAPTER 6   ACCOUNTS RECEIVABLE AND NOTES RECEIVABLE

CHAPTER 7   ACCOUNTING FOR THE MERCHANDISING FIRM

CHAPTER 8   PLANT ASSETS, INTANGIBLES, AND LONG-TERM INVESTMENTS

CHAPTER 10 ACCOUNTING FOR THE CORPORATION

CHAPTER 12 THE STATEMENT OF CASH FLOWS

Chapter

1

The Accounting Information System

LEARNING OBJECTIVES

After studying Chapter 1, you should be able to do the following:

1. Describe how accounting is used by people within and outside the firm.
2. Explain how accounting affects everyone, including you.
3. Understand the difference between management accounting and financial accounting and explain how an accounting information system contributes to the firm.
4. List the three basic forms of business and describe the owner's financial liability in each case.
5. Understand the role of GAAP and IFRS.
6. Explain how to apply the following accounting concepts to the recording of business transactions— economic entity assumption, monetary unit assumption, relevance and faithful representation characteristics, measurement principle, and going-concern assumption.

CHAPTER CONTENTS

The Accounting Information System

Focus on Business — Pepsi vs. Coke: Using Accounting Information to Make Decisions

FOCUS ON BUSINESS

Pepsi vs. Coke: Using Accounting Information to Make Decisions

The eternal debate between Pepsi and Coca-Cola was around before companies were required to file their financial statements with the Securities and Exchange Commission (SEC). Beyond the debate for taste preference, investors have been faced with deciding between investing in Pepsi or Coca-Cola for many years. Many investment decisions are made based on the information in a company's financial statements. For example, PepsiCo experienced approximately a 34% increase in revenue one year, while Coca-Cola Company's revenue only increased 13% during the same time period. Someone looking to invest in the soft drink industry would make that comparison, along with many others, to determine which company gives them the best chance of growing their money. These comparisons would not be possible if companies were using different rules for preparing their financial data.

In the same way, it would be impossible to judge who won a game if one team was playing soccer while the other team was playing football. Can you imagine the LA Galaxy playing soccer against the San Diego Chargers while they were playing football? The teams would be playing different games with different rules and different scoring systems. One touchdown would equal seven points for the Chargers, while a goal would only be one point for the Galaxy.

In order to compare Coca-Cola and Pepsi it is important they prepare their financial statements with the same general rules. In this chapter we will explore some of the accounting rules that impact a company's score sheet—their financial statements. We will also further explore the importance of a common set of accounting standards.

*Source: *www.pepsico.com* and *www.coca-cola.com*

¶101

Cross-functional refers to the teamwork among people in different departments, using accounting information and applying their specialized skills to achieve company goals.

Applications to People Within and Outside the Firm

LEARNING OBJECTIVE 1: Describe how accounting is used by people within and outside the firm.

You can tell if a business is popular in the marketplace by noticing how many people are buying its products or using its services. But how can you tell if the firm is flourishing financially? The economic activities and financial conditions of a company are captured using accounting. Persons within (internal users) and those outside the company (external users) make use of this information for a variety of decisions. An internal user is directly involved in the day-to-day decision making of the firm; an external user is not.

¶101.01

INTERNAL USERS

At PepsiCo, various managers are the internal users of accounting information. Managers need timely and accurate accounting information for planning and controlling company operations. Managers are people specialized in marketing, production, human resources, finance, data processing, accounting, and other functional areas within the company. Managers must work together across their various functional areas to enable the business to be successful. The term **cross-functional** refers to the teamwork among people in different departments, using accounting information and applying their specialized skills to achieve company goals.

For example, the marketing manager of the Gatorade division at PepsiCo might make the case that because demand for the product in foreign countries has increased, it would be profitable to expand distribution in those countries by adding more shipping routes. The additional cost of expansion would be offset by increased sales. Using sales figures from marketing and cost estimates from shipping, the accounting department can predict how long it will take to recoup proposed expansion costs and forecast the amount of profits generated from the additional sales. This illustrates the use of accounting information in a cross-functional effort to profit the company.

¶101.02

If you were loaning your money to a business firm, what financial information would you like to know about the business firm?

EXTERNAL USERS

People outside the firm who make use of a firm's accounting information include the government, stockholders, lenders, suppliers, and customers. An example of an external user would be a financial institution that uses PepsiCo's financial information in deciding whether to lend the company money to expand its shipping department. The lending institution must predict whether PepsiCo can pay back the loan; this decision depends on accurate accounting information contained in financial reports.

¶102

Accounting and You

> **LEARNING OBJECTIVE 2:** Explain how accounting affects everyone, including you.

Accounting is the recording, summarizing, and reporting of the economic activity and events of an organization.

Whether shopping at your local grocery store, picking up a movie from Redbox, or buying your first shares of stock in Google, you are affected by accounting on a daily basis. Consider the price you were charged for milk or the rental fee for your movie. Both were established as a result of extensive analysis of financial information generated from the processes of accounting. **Accounting** is the recording, summarizing, and reporting of the economic activity and events of an organization. Before making investments in companies like Google, potential investors routinely review the company's financial statements—another product of accounting. The success or failure of your favorite Italian bistro depends on a skilled chef, effective management, friendly staff, and, of course, an accurate assessment of the financial health of the business. Imagine if you were asked to analyze the viability of a new manufacturing facility in China or determine the best location for an international distribution center. Accounting plays a critical role in these decisions.

While a career in accounting may or may not be in your immediate plans, a solid understanding of accounting brings with it a foothold into many managerial jobs. You will be more effective throughout your career, if you know how to use accounting information.

¶103

The Accounting Information System (AIS)

Do you ever need accounting information to evaluate your personal finances?

> **LEARNING OBJECTIVE 3:** Understand the difference between management accounting and financial accounting and explain how the AIS contributes to the firm.

The accounting information system (AIS) provides financial information to internal and external users. The AIS involves sales, purchases, cash receipts and disbursements, and other financial processes.

To effectively communicate with someone, you must speak the same language. The language of business transactions is accounting. People in every department at PepsiCo, such as marketing, production, finance, and human resources, use accounting information to improve the quality of departmental activities, as well as the overall goals of the company. Like other businesses, PepsiCo's goals include providing a useful product or service to customers, making a reasonable profit, and helping employees progress in their careers.

A typical **accounting information system (AIS)** involves sales, purchases, cash receipts and disbursements, and other financial processes. The AIS has two principal objectives: (1) to provide all of the financial information needed internally by management for business decision making and (2) to provide financial information to various external users concerned with the financial activities of the organization. The accounting information system contributes to developing a sound organizational structure, ensuring that employees are accountable for their actions, and maintaining cost effective business operations.

¶103.01

MANAGEMENT ACCOUNTING

Management accounting is the part of the AIS that provides information to management.

Management accounting is the part of the accounting information system that provides information to management—the internal user of accounting information. Managers in marketing, personnel, production, and other departments, often rely on information from accounting to make optimum decisions. For example, at Coca-Cola, Inc., decisions such as these might be made:

- Marketing managers use cost information to decide which drinks and related products the firm will sell and what prices to charge.
- Purchasing managers use accounting reports from suppliers to select the most cost-effective providers of raw materials, packaging materials, and other items used in their business.
- Human resource managers, also called "personnel managers," use accounting information concerning available funds for salaries and benefits to help make decisions about the number of employees to hire at each level within the Coca-Cola organization.
- Production managers use information regarding cost and depreciation to decide what equipment to acquire for production line use and whether to convert existing machinery to accommodate changes in a product.
- Finance managers decide how Coca-Cola will finance its operations, what the projected costs and profits are of a new drink flavor, and whether it is profitable to buy out a small competitor.
- The board of directors uses information about labor costs, distribution costs, taxes, and currency to decide which countries will manufacture and distribute its products.

Managers include top level managers, such as the vice president of human resources, and lower level managers, such as a shop supervisor in a manufacturing firm or a loan officer in a bank. Whatever their organizational level, all managers use data provided by the accounting information system. Even though information requirements may vary substantially between organizations, management accounting usually includes similar kinds of financial analysis and internal documents and reports, such as sales invoices, purchase orders, and budgets. The basic guidelines for preparing these internal documents and reports are widely accepted.

A firm's success is dependent upon the ethical integrity of its employees, especially its management. A company will not survive unchecked employee theft, fraudulent financial reporting, or corrupt business practices. Because every employee cannot be monitored every hour of the workday, the company's productivity depends on the honesty of individuals as they perform their jobs. Unethical behavior in business dealings will damage the firm as a whole. Enron is an example of a company in which top management used questionable accounting practices, resulting in the downfall of the company and loss of trust from business partners, customers, and investors. Even if questionable activities occur at a lower level of management, top management will ultimately be accountable.

The image of many great sports heroes today has been tarnished by performance enhancing drugs. All of the homeruns hit and championships won by those individuals are no longer respected, because those accomplishments were obtained by breaking the rules. A sports hero's role is to win championships and to do so within the code of conduct set by his or her league. An accountant's role is to report financial details and provide financial analyses. The accountants, along with all authoritative positions within a firm, have the responsibility of being accurate and honest in performing their duties. Heroes in the business world are people who act according to high ethical values and personal integrity. A company that does not live up to that expectation tarnishes its reputation permanently.

FOCUS ON ETHICS

Institute of Management Accountants' Ethics Code

The Institute of Management Accountants (IMA) provides formal standards of ethical conduct for its members. The standards relate to personal competence, confidentiality, integrity, and objectivity. To cite a few examples, members have a responsibility to: (1) refrain from using confidential information acquired in their work for unethical or illegal advantage, (2) refuse any gift or favor that would influence their actions, and (3) refrain from engaging in or supporting any activity that would discredit the profession. Members of the IMA have an obligation not to commit acts contrary to the standards of ethical conduct or condone such acts by others within their organizations. The IMA also provides an online ethics hotline for members who have an ethical dilemma.

¶103.02   FINANCIAL ACCOUNTING

Financial accounting is the part of the AIS that supplies information focused on external users.

The part of the accounting information system that supplies information focused on external users is **financial accounting.** Financial accounting involves accumulating, classifying, and summarizing data to prepare reports on the financial matters of the firm. External users of accounting information can be categorized into two major groups. The first group includes organizations requiring information to be reported to them, like federal, state, and local government agencies. For example, the Social Security Administration requires regular reporting of payroll information, including the amount of social security taxes withheld from employees' pay and matched by employers. The Internal Revenue Services (IRS) requires the filing of an annual tax return as well as the submission of other financial information throughout the year, such as federal income tax withholdings from employees' pay.

The government requires publicly-traded corporations to provide annual financial statements to stockholders. This information is filed with the Securities and Exchange Commission (SEC) on Form 10-K. The same financial statements are widely used by other external users for a variety of purposes.

In addition to the group of external users that require certain information to be reported, there is a second group of external users who may not *require* financial information, but they *expect* certain information to be provided to them. For example, PepsiCo was granted a $2.6 billion revolving line of credit. Before granting the loan, the bank probably asked PepsiCo to provide certain financial information, including the most recent financial statements. Since PepsiCo is publicly traded, its statements are already prepared for stockholder use. Financial statements help a lender assess the borrowing firm's ability to meet its financial obligations, specifically the ability to pay back a loan. Naturally, the lender will likely assess other factors as well, such as management's competence and general economic conditions. However, the financial statements, or information derived from them, may be the most important factor in the lender's loan decision.

In many cases, external accounting information is prepared in a particular format. For example, the IRS requires tax-related information to be prepared on specific IRS forms and according to specific procedures.

Other external groups that use accounting information include credit-rating agencies, vendors (suppliers), employees, and customers. Exhibit 1.1 lists external users and the type of information with which they are typically concerned.

Exhibit 1.1 EXTERNAL USERS OF ACCOUNTING INFORMATION	
External User	**Information Required or Expected**
1. Governmental Units	Federal, state, and local government require specified financial information, much of which is connected to or derived from financial statement information. The IRS, for example, requires an annual tax return.
2. Lenders	Financial statement information may be requested, specifically information concerning ability to meet financial obligations.
3. Vendors (Suppliers)	Financial statement information may be requested, specifically information regarding ability to pay for purchases made on credit. Also, the vendor will often receive financial documents from the customer/firm.
4. Credit-Rating Agencies	Similar to information required by lenders and vendors, financial statement information may be requested. Lenders and vendors often purchase reports that assess credit-worthiness from assessment agencies.
5. Stockholders (Investors)	Stockholders (investors) are generally interested in financial statement information as well as details concerning stock and dividend transactions.
6. Customers	Customers are provided financial information such as billing statements, sales invoices, amounts owed, account status, date due, and product information.
7. Employees	Individuals expect payment of wages and specific payroll information, such as payroll deductions for social security, insurance, and retirement plans. Employee groups, such as labor unions, may want aggregate information, such as profits, payroll expense, and pension funding and liability.

¶103.03   LIMITATIONS OF ACCOUNTING

As you know, the AIS provides the financial information needed internally by management and externally by various external users, such as government agencies and stockholders. However, not all information needed internally by management or externally by external users is financial in nature. Additionally, not all information can be accessed by external users when needed.

For example, McDonald's may plan to introduce a new food item, but the marketing department should first perform marketing research to determine whether consumers will purchase the new product. Tastes and preferences of consumers are essential information that the marketing system must obtain for management's decision purposes. Thus, while the AIS provides crucial information, it does not provide all the information needed by management.

The MIS provides all of the information, financial and non-financial, needed by management for decision-making.

The **management information system (MIS)** provides all of the information, financial and non-financial, needed by management for its decision-making purposes. Therefore, the MIS can be thought of as the aggregation of all the organization's information sources. These information sources are based on functional areas, such as accounting, marketing, and personnel. An example of MIS composition is illustrated in Exhibit 1.2.

Exhibit 1.2 COMPONENTS OF THE MANAGEMENT INFORMATION SYSTEM

Each of the MIS components generates specific types of information. For example, the marketing system generates information concerning marketing research, customer relations, sales, product development, and advertising. The personnel department provides information associated with recruiting, job descriptions, employee retention, and training and development.

As previously mentioned, external users rely on the information in the 10-K and other reports companies file with the Securities and Exchange Commission. Companies are only required to file their financial statements quarterly. However, investment decisions occur constantly by many different external users who do not have access to updated financial information. The nature of the data is another issue. Financial statements reflect a company's past performance. It can be challenging for investors to predict a company's future performance with information about the past.

As with internal users, external users need to consider many factors in their investment decisions some of which are not financial. For example, most of Apple Inc.'s value comes from its employees developing the best new gadget. However, the financial reports filed with the Securities and Exchange Commission will not assign a value to Apple's employees, because it is too difficult to objectively value their expertise and creativity.

¶103.04   ACCOUNTING'S CONTRIBUTION TO THE FIRM

While accounting information may have some limitations, it is still critical to a company. Accounting provides financial information and services to the other functional systems in the firm. Services of the accounting information system (AIS) include financial record keeping and various types of financial analysis. For example, the AIS of Barnes and Noble receives sales information from marketing and then records the sales amounts, maintains customer accounts, bills customers, tracks inventory movement, and provides reports. One example of a report provided by the AIS is a sales analysis, sorted by product, by customer, or by salesperson.

If you are a decision maker within an organization, how is the AIS helpful?

In the case of the personnel (human resources) system, the AIS handles a number of critical record keeping chores. The AIS maintains the payroll files that include information on employee pay rates, federal income tax withholding rates, social security tax, and other deductions. The AIS processes the payroll information that is used to prepare paychecks, which are ultimately distributed by the other departments.

¶104   Forms of Businesses

> **LEARNING OBJECTIVE 4:** List the three basic forms of business and describe the owner's financial liability in each case.

A business is set up as a sole proprietorship, partnership, or corporation. A sole proprietorship has the simplest accounting system, while a corporation usually has a more complex system.

¶104.01   SOLE PROPRIETORSHIP

The sole proprietor of a business owns all the assets and is personally liable for all the firm's debts.

A **sole proprietorship** is a firm with one owner who usually manages its operations. The sole proprietor owns all the assets and is personally liable for all the firm's debts. Sole proprietorships are mostly small local businesses. Typical sole proprietorships include businesses such as dry cleaners, lawn service firms, and flower shops.

¶104.02   PARTNERSHIP

In a partnership, partners jointly own the assets and are personally responsible for all partnership debts.

A **partnership** is a form of business in which two or more persons co-own the business. The partners jointly own all the firm's assets, much like a sole proprietorship. In addition, each partner is personally responsible for all the partnership debts. This means each partner is subject to legal obligations that other partners create, not just a proportionate share but 100 percent of the obligation. For example, assume that three accountants, Joe, Bill and Mike, form a partnership and borrow $300,000 to purchase a building. If Joe and Bill become bankrupt, then Mike alone must pay back the $300,000. Obviously, partners need to have a high degree of confidence in each other, as they are at risk for each other's business decisions.

¶104.03   CORPORATION

The owners of a corporation are stockholders.

A **corporation** is a form of business in which ownership is represented by shares of stock. Thus, the owners are called "**shareholders**" or "**stockholders.**" A corporation has its own legal identity, separate from its owners. The biggest advantage of a corporation to its owners is that they are not personally liable for the debts of the firm. The most the owners can lose is the amount they paid for the stock.

Board of directors — determines corporate policies and selects corporate officers.

Corporations account for most of the business activity in the United States. Examples of the largest and most well-known corporations include Disney, Microsoft, and McDonald's. Stockholders control the corporation according to their shares of stock. One share generally equals one vote. Usually at an annual meeting, the stockholders elect the **board of directors** who determine corporate policies and select corporate officers, such as the chief executive officer (CEO).

Think of your favorite store or restaurant. Is it a sole proprietorship, partnership, or corporation?

A public corporation acquires money by selling stock in the company. The corporate form of business facilitates business activity; the sale of stock produces the money needed for business operations. Once stockholders receive their shares of stock, they may decide not to keep the stock but to sell it to other investors. A **stock exchange** is where people buy and sell shares of stock. While there are several exchanges throughout the world in cities such as London and Tokyo, the New York Stock Exchange, which began in 1792, is the largest and most prestigious.

¶105 Accounting Standard Setting

> **LEARNING OBJECTIVE 5:** Understanding the role of GAAP and IFRS.

A key aspect of accounting is recording business transactions, which are the economic activities of the firm. Identifying the appropriate accounting treatment for a particular transaction or event is sometimes a complex process requiring careful examination. When recording transactions, accountants must abide by specific rules. By using a standard set of rules, it is easier to compare the financial statements of different companies. As stated in the introduction to this chapter, both Pepsi and Coca-Cola need to follow the same rules so that investors can compare their financial performance.

¶105.01 FASB AND GAAP

When recording transactions, accountants must abide by specific rules, known as "GAAP."

The **Financial Accounting Standards Board** (FASB) is the primary source of a common set of accounting standards for U.S. companies known as **"generally accepted accounting principles"** (GAAP). The FASB is a private organization that writes GAAP for U.S. companies.

Since GAAP is constantly evolving, financial accountants must be careful to stay abreast of current developments. All authoritative guidance issued by the FASB is stored in the Codification. This is like the "Google of GAAP" — a sophisticated search engine for accounting rules. The Codification stores the procedures for dealing with specific accounting problems.

¶105.02 ROLE OF THE SEC

Once standards are set, it is important that they are also enforced. The Securities and Exchange Commission (SEC) enforces accounting standards in the U.S. As previously mentioned, all companies with stocks publicly traded in the U.S. must file their financial statements with the SEC. The SEC would notify companies of any noted deviations from GAAP.

Additionally, the SEC has the authority to set standards or to give that authority to another organization. Currently, the SEC chooses to share that authority with the FASB. However, the SEC is considering adoption of the **International Financial Reporting Standards** (IFRS) set by the **International Accounting Standards Board** (IASB).

¶105.03 IASB AND IFRS

Over 100 countries across the world use IFRS. For many years, the FASB and the IASB have been working together on developing new standards and revising old standards to make the two sets of rules more similar. The two organizations continue to work together on joint projects. However, key differences remain that leave the potential for very different results in a company's financial statements.

The SEC currently allows foreign-based companies with stock traded on the U.S. stock exchange to file their financial statements prepared according to IFRS. The differences between IFRS and U.S. GAAP have caused the SEC to explore requiring the same for U.S. companies. Having one set of global accounting standards would provide better comparability for investing purposes in a business environment that is already global. However, many constituents have concerns about making a change this significant as it will result in many challenges. For example, it would be extremely costly for companies to educate U.S. accountants and to change their accounting information systems to abide by the new standards.

¶106

Accounting Concepts

> **LEARNING OBJECTIVE 6:** Explain how to apply the following standards to the recording of business transactions: economic entity assumption, monetary unit assumption, relevance and faithful representation, measurement principle, and going-concern assumption.

This book presents basic elements of GAAP while also pointing out some of the key differences between GAAP and IFRS. The ultimate goal is that you will be able to understand the basis upon which financial statements are prepared and then use the accounting information to make effective business decisions. To understand accounting standards, you must first become acquainted with several basic accounting concepts that guide how GAAP is set and applied.

¶106.01 ECONOMIC ENTITY ASSUMPTION

The economic entity assumption states that a business is a separate entity from its owners, employees, creditors, and customers.

The **economic entity assumption** states that a business is distinct from its owners, employees, creditors, and customers — it is a separate entity. The business activities of one entity are separate and distinct from other entities. For example, the president of Google owns a home, car, boat, and various other personal possessions. These assets are the president's alone and do not affect the accounting records of Google. The corporation has its own assets and liabilities, separate and distinct from those of its president. The president and Google are separate and distinct entities.

¶106.02 MONETARY UNIT ASSUMPTION

The monetary unit assumption states that the currency's purchasing power is relatively unchanging.

The dollar is the currency of the United States and the unit of measure for financial statements. For accounting purposes, the dollar's buying power is assumed to be stable. The **monetary unit assumption** is based on the assumption that the currency's purchasing power is relatively unchanging. Inflation reduces purchasing power and is defined as a persistent increase in the level of prices. In the United States, there has been relatively little inflation. If this were not the case, the monetary unit assumption would not apply.

¶106.03 RELEVANCE AND FAITHFUL REPRESENTATION

Relevance states that accounting information must be useful for decision-making. Faithful representation states that information must accurately reflect a company's financial position.

Accounting information should be both relevant and faithfully represented so that users can rely on the information in their decision-making process. In order for information to be relevant, it must impact a user's decision-making. For example, accounting information from two years ago may no longer impact a decision an investor needs to make today.

Additionally, to be useful, accounting information must be represented faithfully, meaning that the accounting information fairly represents the events that impact a company's financial position. For example, a company should not report $100 in advertising expense if they actual incurred $500 in advertising expenses that period. To ensure that accounting information is faithfully represented, the information can be verified by an independent person. For example, a canceled check for $500 written to an advertising agency provides verification that the accountant should record advertising expense of $500.

Sometimes relevance and faithful representation can work against each other. We have already established in this chapter that accounting information is not perfect. This conflict with relevance and faithful representation can sometimes be the cause. For example, in order for data to be relevant, it has to be timely (received when it is needed to make a decision). However, it takes time to verify and review accounting information in order to ensure faithful representation. Reviewing data compromises relevance, but releasing accounting information that is not properly reviewed compromises faithful representation. Companies constantly have to balance the tradeoffs between these two characteristics.

¶106.04

The measurement principle states that some acquired assets should be recorded at their original cost, while other assets should be recorded at the current value.

The historical cost of an asset includes the price paid plus any expenditure necessary to prepare the asset for use.

MEASUREMENT PRINCIPLE

The **measurement principle** states that some acquired assets should be recorded at their original cost while other assets should be recorded at the current value, also referred to as "historical cost" and "fair market value" respectively.

Historical cost is the price paid at the time of the transaction plus any expenditure necessary to prepare the asset for use. For example, Google might purchase a building for $10 million. Five years later, the building might have an appraised value of $12 million. According to U.S. GAAP, the building will be shown in the accounting records at its original cost of $10 million. Thus, the balance sheet does not show the current value of the building. Original cost can be verified by evidence created at the time of the transaction. The price paid, or original cost, is verified by the agreement of two parties, the buyer and the seller.

GAAP allows other assets to be recorded at **fair market value** or the price at which they could be bought or sold today. U.S. GAAP limits such treatment primarily to financial instruments. For example, Google might purchase a share of another company's stock for $50. Five years later, the stock is now worth $100. At the time of the purchase, Google could record the asset at the purchase price of $50. However, over time, as the value of the stock changes, the asset balance would also change to reflect the new fair market value. This accounting treatment is referred to as "mark-to-market accounting."

Concerns about mark-to-market accounting result from the challenges of determining a market value for some assets. The value of a stock is easy to verify, because it is traded on a stock exchange. If you needed to know the value of Apple's stock, at any time you could go online and find it. Determining the value of many other assets can be more subjective. In the previous example with the building, the $12 million appraisal value was an estimate made by an expert. Another expert may determine another value for that building.

This is another example of a tradeoff between relevance and reliability. Fair value may be more relevant to investors, because it reflects the most current value of an item. However, if that value is subjective, it may not faithfully represent the true value of the item. The original purchase price of an item (historical cost) is easy to verify, and therefore may be a more faithful representation of the item.

¶106.05

The going-concern assumption states that a firm will continue operating in the future.

GOING-CONCERN ASSUMPTION

The **going-concern assumption** is the assumption that a business will continue operating in the future. Accountants assume that Google Corporation will remain in business and thus continue to use its resources, such as buildings and equipment. In this way, the going concern concept supports the application of the cost principle. If going concern was not assumed and the firm was considered "going out of business," then the assets should be reported at liquidation values.

In addition to the concepts already discussed, the revenue recognition and expense recognition principles are key principles that will be discussed in chapter two along with the definition of revenue and expense.

¶107

Can you imagine the difficulty of comparing or using other firm's accounting records if generally accepted accounting principles (GAAP) did not exist?

Concluding Remarks

You learned how the accounting information system assists every department within a company by providing financial information that is useful in decision-making. Now you understand the importance of a common set of accounting standards. You learned the standard-setting body in the U.S. and internationally. The basic accounting concepts explored in this chapter will help you tackle the next chapter, which will start to cover the four financial statements. You will learn the purpose and components of the four financial statements. Additionally, you will start to understand how the statements interact with each other, and why they would be helpful to all departments within a company as well as to external users.

¶108

Chapter Review

LEARNING OBJECTIVE 1

Describe how accounting is used by people within and outside the firm.

Persons within a company (internal users) and those outside the company (external users) use accounting information for a variety of decisions. Company managers must work together across their various functional areas to enable the business to be successful. The term "cross-functional" refers to the teamwork among people in different departments, using accounting information and applying their specialized skills to achieve company goals. Outside users, like government agencies or lenders, use accounting information to assess the financial position or profitability of the business.

LEARNING OBJECTIVE 2

Explain how accounting affects everyone, including you.

You are affected by accounting on a daily basis. Accounting is the recording, summarizing, and reporting of the economic activity and events of an organization. The prices you pay for products and services are determined from analyses of financial information generated from the processes of accounting.

LEARNING OBJECTIVE 3

Understand the difference between management accounting and financial accounting and explain how an accounting information system contributes to the firm.

Accounting is called the "language of business" because accounting provides the information that people need to make effective business decisions. Accounting is the recording, summarizing, and reporting of the economic activity and events of an organization. Management accounting is the part of the accounting information system that provides information to management, the internal user of accounting information. The part of the accounting information system that supplies information primarily to external users is financial accounting. Financial accounting reports are the financial statements.

LEARNING OBJECTIVE 4

List the three basic forms of business and describe the owner's financial liability in each case.

A business is set up as a sole proprietorship, partnership, or corporation. The sole proprietor owns all of the assets and is personally liable for all of the firm's debts. A partnership is a form of business in which two or more persons participate as co-owners. Each partner is personally responsible for all of the partnership debts. A corporation is a form of business in which ownership is represented by shares of stock. A corporation has its own legal identity, separate from its owners; thus, the owners are not personally liable for the debts of the firm.

LEARNING OBJECTIVE 5

Understand the role of GAAP and IFRS.

Accountants must abide by specific rules when recording transactions. In the U.S., these rules are called "generally accepted accounting principles (GAAP)." Approximately 100 countries use International Financial Reporting Standards (IFRS).

LEARNING OBJECTIVE 6

Explain how to apply the following accounting concepts to the recording of business transactions — economic entity assumption, monetary unit assumption, relevance and faithful representation characteristics, measurement principle, and going-concern assumption.

To understand GAAP, you must first become acquainted with several basic accounting concepts, including the economic entity assumption, monetary unit assumption, relevance and faithful representation measurement principle, and going-concern assumption.

The economic entity assumption states that a business is distinct from its creditors, customers, and owners—it is a separate entity. The monetary unit assumption is based on the assumption that the currency's purchasing power is relatively unchanging. Relevance states that accounting information should be useful in decision making. Additionally, the information should faithfully represent the company's financial position. The measurement principle requires that some acquired assets and services be recorded at their original cost (historical cost), while others are recorded at current value (fair market value). The going-concern assumption is the assumption that a business will continue operating in the future.

¶109

Glossary

Accounting

Accounting is the recording, summarizing, and reporting of the economic activities and events of an organization.

Accounting information system (AIS)

An AIS typically has two principal objectives: (1) to provide all the financial information needed internally by management for business decision making, and (2) to provide financial information to various external users concerned with the financial activities of the organization.

Board of directors

The board of directors is elected by the stockholders of the corporation. The board determines the policies of a corporation and selects corporate officers.

Codification

A compilation of all authoritative generally accepted accounting principles (GAAP) maintained by the Financial Accounting Standards Board, which provide the procedures for dealing with specific accounting problems.

Corporation

A corporation is a form of business in which ownership is represented by shares of stock. The owners are called "shareholders" or "stockholders."

Cross-functional

Cross-functional refers to the teamwork among people in different departments, using accounting information and applying their specialized skills to achieve company goals.

Economic entity assumption

The economic entity assumption states that a business is distinct from its owners, employees, creditors, and customers — it is a separate entity. The business activities of one entity are separate and distinct from other entities.

Fair market value (also: fair value)

Fair market value is the value that could be obtained by selling an asset in a normal market.

Faithful representation

Financial information should represent the events that impact the company's financial position as fairly as possible.

Financial accounting

The part of the accounting information system that supplies information primarily to external users is financial accounting. Financial accounting reports are the financial statements.

Financial Accounting Standards Board (FASB)

The Financial Accounting Standards Board is the primary source of generally accepted accounting principles (GAAP).

Generally accepted accounting principles (GAAP)

GAAP are the rules by which financial statements are prepared.

Going-concern assumption

The going-concern assumption is the assumption that a business will continue operating in the future.

Historical cost

The historical cost of an asset includes the price paid plus any expenditure necessary to prepare the asset for use.

International Accounting Standards Board (IASB)

The International Accounting Standards Board is the primary source of International Financial Reporting Standards (IFRS).

International Financial Reporting Standards (IFRS)

IFRS are the rules by which financial statements are prepared for many companies outside of the U.S.

Management accounting

Management accounting is the part of the accounting information system that provides information to management — the only internal user of accounting information.

Management Information System (MIS)

The MIS provides all of the information, financial and non-financial, needed by management for its decision-making purposes. The MIS can be thought of as the aggregation of all of the organization's information sources.

Measurement principle

The measurement principle states that assets (and liabilities) are measured based on their attributes. Measurement methods include historical cost or market value.

Monetary unit assumption

The monetary unit assumption is used for accounting purposes and is based on the assumption that the currency's purchasing power is relatively unchanging.

Partnership

A partnership is a form of business in which two or more persons co-own the business. Each partner is personally responsible for all the partnership debts.

Relevance

The financial information could make a difference in users' decision making.

Shareholder

A shareholder owns one or more shares of stock in a corporation and thus is a part owner of the corporation.

Sole proprietorship

A sole proprietorship is a business with only one owner. The sole proprietor owns all the assets and is personally liable for all the firm's debts.

Stock exchange

A stock exchange is where people buy and sell shares of stock in a corporation.

Stockholder

A shareholder owns one or more shares of stock in a corporation and thus is a part owner of the corporation.

¶110   # Chapter Assignments

QUESTIONS

1. **[Obj. 1]** Describe the external users of accounting information.

2. **[Obj. 2]** What is the definition of accounting? Why is it vital for an accountant to be honest and trustworthy?

3. **[Obj. 3]:** What are the two principal objectives of the accounting information system (AIS)?

4. **[Obj. 3]** What is management accounting?

5. **[Obj. 3]** What is financial accounting?

6. **[Obj. 4]** Briefly describe the three forms of business.

7. **[Obj. 4]** What are the benefits and liabilities of being the sole proprietor of a business?

8. **[Obj. 4]** Who determines corporate policies and selects corporate officers in a corporation?

9. **[Obj. 4]** How does one become part of the board of directors for a corporation?

10. **[Obj. 5]** What are generally accepted accounting principles (GAAP)?

11. **[Obj. 5]** What are international financial reporting standards (IFRS)?

12. **[Obj. 6]** What is the economic entity assumption?

13. **[Obj. 6]** What is the monetary unit assumption?

14. **[Obj. 6]** What are relevance and faithful representation?

15. **[Obj. 6]** What is historical cost?

16. **[Obj. 6]** What is fair value?

17. **[Obj. 6]** What is the going-concern assumption?

SHORT EXERCISES — SET A

Building Accounting Skills

1. **[Obj. 1]** Internal Users of Accounting Information: Business managers throughout a company use accounting information. Consider the following managers at General Motors and list the accounting information that they might use.
    a. Marketing
    b. Purchasing
    c. Human resources

2. **[Obj. 1]** External Users of Accounting Information: What accounting information is required or expected by the following external users?
    a. Governmental units
    b. Lenders
    c. Vendors (Suppliers)

3. **[Obj. 6]** Knowing the Accounting Standards: Match each accounting standards with the correct description.
    a. Going-concern assumption
    b. Historical cost
    c. Faithful representation
    d. Economic entity assumption
    e. Monetary unit assumption
    f. Fair value
    g. Relevance

    ___ A currency's purchasing power is relatively unchanging.
    ___ A firm is a separate entity.
    ___ Accounting information is based on the most reliable data available.
    ___ Assets are recorded at original cost.
    ___ Firms continue operating into the future.
    ___ Assets are recorded at the current value.
    ___ Accounting information is useful in decision making.

4. **[Obj. 6]** Economic Entity Assumption: Define the entity concept and explain why it is important to financial reporting. Give an example.

5. **[Obj. 6]** Monetary Unit Assumption: Define the stable currency concept and explain why it is important to financial reporting.

6. **[Obj. 6]** Relevance and Faithful Representation: Define relevance and faithful representation and explain why they are important to financial reporting. Give an example of how to verify accounting information.

7. **[Obj. 6]** Measurement Principle: Define the measurement principle and explain why it is important to financial reporting. Give an example. Discuss the types of assets than must be recorded at historical cost and those recorded at fair value.

8. **[Obj. 6]** Going-Concern Assumption: Define the going-concern assumption and explain why it is important to financial reporting. Give an example.

SHORT EXERCISES — SET B

Building Accounting Skills

1. **[Obj. 1]** Internal Users of Accounting Information: Decision makers throughout a company use accounting information. Consider the following people at Intel Corporation and list the accounting information that they might use.
    a. Board of directors
    b. Production
    c. Finance

2. **[Obj. 1]** External Users of Accounting Information: What accounting information is required or expected by the following external users?
    a. Credit-rating agencies
    b. Stockholders (Investors)
    c. Customers
    d. Employees

3. **[Obj. 6]** Knowing the Accounting Standards: Match each accounting standards with the illustration.
    a. Monetary unit assumption
    b. Economic entity assumption
    c. Faithful representation
    d. Historical cost
    e. Going concern assumption
    f. Fair value
    g. Relevance

    ___ Ten dollars today has the same value as $10 next year.
    ___ The amount paid for a building ten years ago is the amount shown on the balance sheet this year.
    ___ Use the most reliable data available.
    ___ The owner's personal debt doesn't affect company liabilities.
    ___ A financial instrument purchased five years ago is on the balance sheet at its current sales price.
    ___ Assume the company will not go out of business.
    ___ Provide information on a timely basis so investors can use it to make decisions.

4. **[Obj. 6]** Going Concern Assumption: Define the going concern assumption and explain why it is important to financial reporting. Give an example.

5. **[Obj. 6]** Measurement Principle: Define the measurement principle and explain why it is important to financial reporting. Discuss the types of assets than must be recorded at historical cost and those recorded at fair value.

6. **[Obj. 6]** Relevance and Faithful Representation: Define relevance and faithful representation and explain why they are important to financial reporting. Give an example of how to verify accounting information.

7. **[Obj. 6]** Monetary Unit Assumption: Define the monetary unit assumption and explain why it is important to financial reporting. Give an example.

8. **[Obj. 6]** Economic Entity Assumption: Define the economic entity assumption and explain why it is important to financial reporting. Give an example.

CROSS-FUNCTIONAL PERSPECTIVES

Discussion Questions

1. **[Obj. 3]** Why is accounting called the language of business? How does accounting impact other departments within a business?

2. **[Obj. 3]** Business managers in marketing, personnel, production, and other departments rely on accounting information to make optimum decisions. What are some examples of decisions for which an accountant provides information?

3. **[Obj. 3]** The accounting information system (AIS) is one part of the management information system (MIS). The AIS provides the financial information needed internally by management and externally by various external users, such as government agencies and stockholders. Describe some nonfinancial information provided by other departments in the MIS.

4. **[Obj. 3]** Describe the management information system (MIS). How do all the departments with a business, including accounting, contribute to the MIS?

5. **[Obj. 3]** What sort of information processing does accounting provide for the marketing system? For the personnel (human resources) system?

Cross-functional Case: New International Manufacturing Facility

PepsiCo's Chief Operations Officer (COO) is trying to determine whether or not the company should open a new manufacturing facility in China. The company is interested in expanding its operations in Asian markets. The company wants to ensure the new facility will increase the company's profit.

Required: With which departments within the company should the COO schedule a meeting? What issues should the COO discuss with each department to determine whether the manufacturing facility will increase the company's profitability?

WEB ASSIGNMENTS

1. **[Obj. 1]** Go to the website for PepsiCo. What accounting jobs are currently available within the company?

2. **[Obj. 3 & 5]** Go to the website for PepsiCo. Within their Worldwide Code of Conduct, which rules pertain specifically to the accounting department? (Hint: To find PepsiCo's Worldwide Code of Conduct, look under Company.)

3. **[Obj. 3 & 5]** Use a Web search tool (e.g. Google.com) and find information on accounting ethics. Prepare a one-page report. Use at least three Web sources. Cite your sources, including Web addresses, in your report.

¶111

Test Prepper

Use this sample test to gauge your comprehension of the chapter material.

True/False Questions

___ 1. Accounting generates information used for decision-making by internal users and external users.

___ 2. An external user of a firm's accounting information is directly involved in the day-to-day decision making of the firm.

___ 3. Management accounting is the part of the accounting information system that provides information to external users.

___ 4. Financial accounting involves accumulating, classifying, and summarizing data to prepare reports on the financial matters of the firm.

___ 5. The stockholders of a corporation elect the board of directors who determine corporate policies and select corporate officers.

___ 6. The financial statements of publicly-traded companies must be prepared according to GAAP.

___ 7. The going-concern assumption requires that acquired assets and services be recorded at their original cost, also referred to as historical cost.

___ 8. The Codification is the single source of authoritative U.S. GAAP.

___ 9. The AIS provides all financial and non-financial information needed by management for decision making.

___ 10. The IASB sets U.S. accounting standards.

Multiple-Choice Questions

___ 1. Which of the following is an external user of a firm's accounting information?
   a. the government
   b. stockholders
   c. lenders
   d. customers
   e. all of the above

___ 2. Accounting is not the
   a. recording of a firm's economic activity and events
   b. summarizing of a firm's economic activity and events
   c. reporting of a firm's economic activity and events
   d. manipulating of a firm's economic activity and events
   e. language of business

__ 3. An objective of an accounting information system (AIS) is to
   a. provide all the financial information needed internally by management for business decision making
   b. provide financial information to various external users concerned with the financial activities of the organization
   c. provide background information on employees.
   d. a. and b.
   e. a. and c.

__ 4. Under which form of business are the owners not personally liable for the debts of the firm?
   a. sole proprietorship
   b. partnership
   c. corporation
   d. all of the above
   e. none of the above

__ 5. Who is the primary developer of U.S. generally accepted accounting standards (GAAP)?
   a. International Accounting Board (IAB)
   b. The Accounting Review (AR)
   c. Financial Accounting Standards Board (FASB)
   d. Financial and Reporting for Business (FRB)
   e. The government

__ 6. Which of the following requires that accounting information to be based on the most reliable data available?
   a. monetary unit assumption
   b. faithful representation
   c. going-concern assumption
   d. economic entity assumption
   e. measurement principle

__ 7. Assets on the financial statements should be reported at which value(s)?
   I. Historical cost
   II. Fair value
   a. I only
   b. II only
   c. Either I or II, based on the type of asset
   d. Both I and II
   e. Neither I or II

__ 8. The benefits of the U.S. adopting or converging with IFRS include all but which of the following?
   a. facilitate international trade and business
   b. increase comparability of U.S. and international companies' financial statements on the U.S. stock exchange.
   c. increase efficiencies in global audits since all auditors will be trained in the same accounting practices
   d. benefit the U.S., because the initial costs of training U.S. accountants will be low.
   e. Neither b. nor d. are benefits

__ 9. Which piece of information could not be obtained by management through the AIS?
   a. Total sales per customer
   b. Probability a product in the testing phase will succeed
   c. Salaries paid to each employee
   d. Inventory on hand
   e. Company's ability to repay a loan

__10. Which of the following accounting concepts states a purchase made by a company's owner should not affect the company's financial statements?
   a. monetary unit assumption
   b. faithful representation
   c. going-concern assumption
   d. economic entity assumption
   e. measurement principle

Chapter

2

The Financial Statements

LEARNING OBJECTIVES

After studying Chapter 2, you should be able to do the following:

1. Describe how people within and outside the firm use financial statements.
2. Identify the purpose and components of the four types of financial statements.
3. Describe the relationship among the four financial statements.
4. Evaluate a company's financial statements.

CHAPTER CONTENTS

FOCUS ON BUSINESS

Apple, Inc.: Profit or Loss?

There are millions of iPhone users in the U.S. alone. Does that mean Apple is a profitable company? It certainly means Apple has sold a large number of iPhones since the device was first released in 2008. However, sales are only one piece of profitability and the iPhone is only one of several product lines developed by Apple.

In order to determine whether or not Apple is profitable we would have to look at its financial reports. Before we can determine if Apple made a profit, we must know what expenses Apple incurred. This is where the income statement comes into play. The income statement reveals how much money a firm has earned or lost by subtracting expenses from revenues. We can guess Apple's revenues are high by the number of people who own an iPhone. However, if Apple did not effectively manage its expenses, its would not be as profitable or could operate at a loss.

Apple has not always been a profitable company. In 2001, Apple reported a net loss of $25 million. Its biggest loss was reported in 1997, totaling over $1 billion. The company attributed the loss in 2001 to $2.6 billion or 33% decline in net sales from 2000 to 2001. Prior to the end of 2001, Apple's sales came from desktop and PowerBook sales. At the very end of 2001, Apple released the iPod. The device was released too late in 2001 to make the company profitable for the year, but the iPod, iPhone and iPad have catapulted the company into profitability. Ten years later, the company reported over $14 billion in net income.

For Apple, staying on the cutting edge of technology by developing the next best device is critically important. Prior to developing the iPod, Apple's product line was fairly narrow and its competitors had similar products that were more widely used. Apple will need to stay ahead of its competition to remain profitable.

For example, Google's release of the Android operating system for smartphones and tablets may again challenge Apple's profitability. Understanding a company's financial statements is critical in learning more about its financial position. The details of financial statements, along with Apple's financial condition, will unfold within this chapter.

*Source: *Investor.Apple.com*

¶201

Applications to People Within and Outside the Firm

LEARNING OBJECTIVE 1: Describe how financial statements are used by people within and outside the firm.

The economy of the United States is built on free enterprise, which is typified by individual ownership of property, the profit motive to encourage production, competition to guarantee efficiency, and the forces of demand and supply to guide the production of goods and services. The United States free enterprise system has facilitated the greatest and most widely distributed accumulation of wealth in the history of the world. Thanks to the success of the country's economy, the average American enjoys a very high standard of living. The largest businesses are corporations, which are owned by numerous individual stockholders. The stock of a corporation is bought and sold on a stock market. The largest stock market, or exchange, in the world is the New York Stock Exchange, often referred to simply as the "NYSE." The NYSE was formed in 1792, near the beginning of the United States. On a daily basis, billions of dollars of stock are bought and sold on the NYSE.

Within a business firm, the managers of the business are the internal users of the financial statements and related accounting information. The financial statements help the managers assess their management performance. Outside the firm are many external users of financial statements. Investors are one type of external user. How do people decide which stock to buy or which stock to sell? The decision to buy or sell a corporation's stock is frequently based on the accounting information contained in the corporation's financial statements. Financial statements are like windows that enable individuals to see into the corporation's financial situation: whether the business had a profit or loss, how much the business owned or owed, and how much cash it received or paid out. When corporate financial statements report favorable financial results, this increases people's interest in buying the stock of that corporation. On the other hand, if corporate financial statements reveal a deteriorating financial condition, stockholders may decide to sell their stock and invest their money in a different corporation, one with more favorable prospects.

¶201.01　INTERNAL USERS

Financial statements are extremely meaningful to the internal users, that is, business managers. Financial statements, along with related accounting information, provide a basis for planning and controlling business activities. Business managers need to know their company's financial situation, so that efforts can be made to maintain a good financial situation or correct a bad financial situation. If a company's sales revenue is increasing year-by-year, this is good news to the marketing managers. If a company has adequate cash to pay off its debt, this is good news to financial managers. Financial statements are a kind of scorecard that tells managers whether they are managing well or not.

¶201.02　EXTERNAL USERS

How would financial statement information help you know if you wanted to invest in a company's stock?

Investors and lenders are two key external users of financial statements. Investors often compare the financial statements of many different corporations before deciding which are the better investments. As will be described later in this book, the information in financial statements is analyzed in various ways to determine if the business is doing well or doing poorly. Just as the financial statements are a kind of scorecard that informs business managers of their personal performance, financial statements help inform investors which corporations are performing well and thereby providing their stockholders with better returns on their investments.

In the same way that investors use financial statements to decide whether a corporation is a good investment, bankers and other lenders examine a corporation's financial statements to decide whether to lend money to a corporation. The lender must determine whether the corporation is financially sound and has good future prospects. The financial statements include critical information such as whether the corporation is earning a profit and accumulating cash necessary to pay back the loan, along with interest.

¶202　Financial Accounting Reports: The Four Financial Statements

LEARNING OBJECTIVE 2: Identify the purpose and components of the four types of financial statements.

Financial Statements

Income Statement

Statement of Retained Earnings

Balance Sheet

Statement of Cash Flows

Accounting is called the "language of business" because it provides the information that people need to make effective business decisions. The most important reports produced by the accounting information system are the set of **financial statements**. For a corporation, these financial statements are:

- Income statement
- Statement of retained earnings
- Balance sheet
- Statement of cash flows

Together, these four statements represent a business in financial terms. Each statement corresponds to a specific date or a designated time period, such as a year. Together, the four financial statements reveal how much the firm has earned or lost, the change in retained earnings, the firm's ending financial position, and how much cash was generated and spent.

¶202.01 INCOME STATEMENT

The income statement summarizes the revenues earned and the expenses incurred by a business over a period of time.

Income Statements

| Revenues |
| – Expenses |
| Net Income |

The income statement answers the question "How much income did the firm earn or lose during the period?" The **income statement** summarizes the revenues earned and the expenses incurred by a business over a period of time. The result is a net income or net loss. Knowing whether or not the firm made a profit is of great interest to the owners and managers of a company. As we get into the specifics of the income statement, you will see how internal users can use accounting information to assess whether company goals have been met. For example, the income statement reports sales revenue, which can be compared to the targeted sales goals of the marketing department. The purchasing department is interested in the cost of those goods sold, which is also reported on the income statement. External users of the income statement are lenders and creditors who are interested in a company's net income to determine if the company will be able to pay its bills.

A firm's net income or net loss is determined as follows:

Revenues – Expenses = Net Income (or Net Loss)

The term "net" indicates the result after a subtraction has occurred. Thus, **net income** is the amount of income after subtracting expenses from the revenues. In accounting, "net income" is used interchangeably with the word "profit." A **net loss** occurs when expenses are greater than revenues and thus, there is a negative result from the subtraction.

An example income statement is shown in Exhibit 2.1. Let's look at this income statement for Fashion Company line by line. Net Sales Revenue is the first line item. During 20Y2, Fashion Company had net sales revenue of $600 million. The term "net sales revenue" is used because merchandise that was returned by customers and the discounts taken by customers were subtracted from total sales. Fashion Company's income statement reports operating results for two years in order to show trends in the amounts listed. As you can see, net sales revenue increased from 20Y1 to 20Y2. This is good news for investors and lenders. Inside the company, it's good news for the marketing manager.

Exhibit 2.1 FASHION COMPANY CONSOLIDATED STATEMENT OF INCOME

		Year Dec 31, 20Y2 ($ Millions)	Year Dec 31, 20Y1 ($ Millions)
1	Net Sales Revenue	$ 600	$ 550
2	Cost of Goods Sold	(340)	(330)
3	Operating Expenses	(160)	(145)
4	Income Tax	(40)	(35)
5	Total Expenses*	(540)	(510)
6	Net Income	$ 60	$ 40

*Sum of lines 2 through 4.

A revenue is an increase in assets that results from operating a business.

A **revenue** is an increase in assets that results from operating a business, such as selling goods, performing services, or performing other business activities (e.g., rent and interest income). In order for revenue to be recognized, two criteria of the **revenue recognition principle** must be met. First, revenue must be realized or realizable. This means that cash must have already been received or is expected to be received in the future. The second requirement is that revenue must be earned. This means that the seller must satisfy its obligation to the buyer by providing the buyer with the good or service purchased. Once both criteria are met, a company can record revenue on its income statement. For most companies revenue is recorded at the time of the sale. For example, if you go to the store and pay cash for jeans the retail company can record revenue for the sale. In the transaction described you paid for the jeans (cash was realized) and the seller provided you with the jeans (revenue is earned).

Apple has numerous sources of revenue, including the sale of Apple's popular devices like iPads and iPhones. For some of Apple's devices, like an iPod Shuffle purchased at a store, Apple would recognize revenue at the time of the sale—like the jeans transaction. However, for other Apple products, revenue recognition is much more complicated. When Apple sells an iPhone, it is not just selling an electronic device. The device also comes with software. When a customer purchases an iPhone, he or she receives the device and the software necessary for the device to function. That seems similar to the sale of the jeans or the iPod Shuffle previously discussed. It may seem like Apple should record revenue at the time of the sale since it provided the customer with the iPhone and the software. The complication is that Apple also promises to provide customers with software upgrades in the future. This means that Apple has not provided 100% of its obligation to the customer at the time of the sale of the device and necessary software. Based on this, it is appropriate for Apple to recognize some revenue at the time of the sale and wait to recognize some of the revenue from the sale over time as the company provides updates. It is important for companies to recognize revenue as it is earned. However, it can be challenging to determine how much revenue to recognize when goods or services from a sale are delivered at different times.

Over the life of the iPhone, total revenue will be the agreed-upon price for the iPhone that was purchased by the customer, regardless of when the revenue is recorded. The reason it is so important to recognize revenue at the appropriate time relates to the fact that financial information is broken up into time periods. So, it is important to recognize only the revenue that is earned in the period reported. If Apple recorded all of the revenue from the sale of an iPhone at the time of the sale, it would be overstating revenue during that period, which would mislead investors.

An expense is a decrease of assets due to manufacturing and selling products, rendering services, or carrying out other activities that comprise the firm's ongoing operations.

Still referring to Exhibit 2.1, expenses are listed immediately after net sales revenue. An **expense** is a decrease of assets due to manufacturing and selling products, rendering services, or carrying out other activities that comprise the firm's ongoing operations. The first item under expenses is cost of goods sold (line 2) which is also referred to as "cost of sales." **Cost of goods sold** is the cost to Fashion Company of the products it sold to customers. Cost of goods sold is the largest expense of merchandising firms such as Macy's, Best Buy, or Kroger. The next expense listed, "operating expenses," is a wide category for expenses directly associated with operations. In the case of Fashion, this pertains to expenses such as insurance, utilities, employee wages, and office supplies. The next expense is income tax, which is the tax on earnings that Fashion must pay to the government.

Cost of goods sold is the cost of the products a firm sells to its customers.

Expense recognition principle states that expenses must follow revenue. This means there are times when a purchase may not be recorded as an expense immediately. Instead, the company would wait to record an expense until the item purchased is used to generate revenue for the company. For example, if Macy's buys a shirt from a designer it will not expense the cost of the shirt purchased until Macy's sells the shirt to its customer. A transaction like this would be recorded as cost of goods sold, as referenced above.

Revenue recognition and expense recognition will be further discussed along with accrual basis accounting in Chapter 3. At that time, we will explore the timing of recognizing revenues and expenses.

The bottom line of the income statement is the company's net income. Fashion Company's net sales revenue increased from 20Y1 to 20Y2. Fashion's net income increased from $40 million in 20Y1 to $60 million in 20Y2. This upward trend in net income was good news for the firm's managers and investors. Net income is used in the computation in the company's statement of retained earnings described in the next section.

¶202.02 STATEMENT OF RETAINED EARNINGS

Retained earnings is equity of the stockholders generated from operations and reinvested into the company.

Retained earnings is the part of the equity of the stockholders generated from operations and kept for use in future operations. In other words, retained earnings is income earned from company operations and reinvested into the company. The **statement of retained earnings** is simple. It shows: (1) the starting balance for retained earnings, (2) additions and reductions to retained earnings, and (3) the ending balance of retained earnings. The statement of retained earnings answers the question, "In what way did retained earnings change?" Net income increases retained earnings. Net losses and the payment of dividends decrease retained earnings. A **dividend** is a distribution of a corporation's earnings, usually in cash, to its stockholders. The statement of retained earnings represents the equation:

A dividend is a distribution of a corporation's earnings to it stockholders.

Beginning retained earnings + Net income – Dividends = Ending retained earnings

Stockholders are very interested in the statement of retained earnings because it reports on their investment. Company management uses the statement of retained earnings to gauge how well the company is increasing that investment.

Let's look at Fashion Company's statement of retained earnings shown in Exhibit 2.2. The first line shows that Fashion's retained earnings at the beginning of 20Y2 is $590 million. Fashion's net income of $60 million in 20Y2 (as previously discussed) is an addition to retained earnings.

Retained Earnings

Beg. Retained Earnings
+ Net Income
– Dividends

Net Income

Exhibit 2.2 FASHION COMPANY CONSOLIDATED STATEMENT OF RETAINED EARNINGS		
Retained Earnings	**Year Ended Dec 31, 20Y2 ($ Millions)**	**Year Ended Dec 31, 20Y1 ($ Millions)**
1 Balance, beginning of year	$590	$580
2 Net income for the year*	60	40
3 Less: cash dividends declared	(50)	(30)
4 Balance, end of year	$600	$590**

* From Income Statement.
** Ending Balance becomes Beginning Balance of the next year.

Owners' equity is the residual interest in the assets of a business that remains after deducting liabilities. Stockholders' equity is the owners' equity in a corporation.

When a firm has net income, the board of directors must decide how much to keep and how much, if any, to pay as cash dividends to the owners (i.e., stockholders). In both 20Y2 and 20Y1, Fashion declared dividends (line 3). Dividends decrease retained earnings.

The ending balance of retained earnings in year 20Y1 becomes the starting balance in year 20Y2, as you can see in Exhibit 2.2. Placing parentheses around an amount indicates a negative amount, or in this case, a reduction to retained earnings. The ending balance of retained earnings is used in the balance sheet, described in the next section, as a component of owners' equity. **Owners' equity** is the residual interest in the assets of a business that remains after deducting liabilities. In other words, owners' equity is an owner's investment in the business. For a corporation, owners' equity is replaced by the term **stockholders' equity**, since stockholders are the owners.

¶202.03

A balance sheet lists the balances of the asset, liability, and owners' equity accounts of a business on a specific date.

BALANCE SHEET

A **balance sheet** lists the balances of the asset, liability, and owners' equity accounts of a business on a specific date. A balance sheet answers the question, "What is the firm's financial position at a designated point in time (i.e., 12 midnight on the balance sheet date)?" A firm's financial position is what the firm owns (assets), owes (liabilities), and the residual interest of the owners on a specified day. The balance sheet is different from the other three financial statements that are period statements because the balance sheet accumulates results of activities that occur throughout the accounting period. All balance sheet accounts start with a beginning balance, which is the prior period ending balance. Current period activity is added to that balance to come up with a new ending balance. In contrast, income statement accounts always start with a balance of zero.

The balance sheet is also referred to as the "statement of financial position." Company managers use the balance sheet to assess the financial position of the company. For example, is the company financially strong enough to expand or start a new product-line? Does the company have enough assets to allow it to take on additional liabilities for buying land or equipment?

Let's look at Fashion Company's balance sheet in Exhibit 2.3. The balance sheet for Fashion Company is dated December 31, 20Y2, the last day of the firm's accounting period. As you can see, it lists company accounts under three categories: assets, liabilities, and stockholders' equity. Each category will be discussed in the following paragraphs.

Balance Sheet

Assets
Liabilities
Owner's Equity

Exhibit 2.3 FASHION COMPANY CONSOLIDATED BALANCE SHEET

	ASSETS	Dec 31, 20Y2 ($ Millions)	Dec 31, 20Y1 ($ Millions)
1	Cash	$100	$90
2	Accounts Receivable	220	180
3	Inventory	180	200
4	Equipment	1,200	1,130
5	Total Assets*	$1,700	1,600
	LIABILITIES		
6	Accounts Payable	$80	30
7	Income Taxes Payable	40	40
8	Long-Term Debt	480	440
9	Total Liabilites**	600	510
	STOCKHOLDERS' EQUITY		
10	Common Stock	500	500
11	Retained Earnings	600	590
12	Total Stockholders' Equity	1,100	1,090
13	Total Liabilities & Stockholders' Equity***	$1,700	$1,600

* Sum of lines 1 and 4.
** Sum of lines 6 through 8.
*** Total liabilities plus total stockholders equity should always equal total assets.

¶202.03.01 Accounting Equation

Accounting equation: Assets = Liabilities + Owners' Equity

The accounts on the balance sheet relate to each other in the following manner, known as the "**accounting equation**":

Assets = Liabilities + Owners' Equity

Fashion's total assets equal total liabilities plus total stockholders' equity, as they should according to the accounting equation.

¶202.03.02 Assets

Assets are the economic resources owned by the firm.

Assets are the first item listed on the balance sheet. **Assets** are the economic resources owned by the firm. Fashion Company's assets are cash, accounts receivable, inventory, and equipment. Accounts receivable is the amount owed to the firm from customers.

¶202.03.03 Liabilities

Liabilities are the debts of the firm.

After assets, the balance sheet presents the firm's liabilities. **Liabilities** are the debts or economic obligations of the firm. Fashion Company's liabilities are accounts payable, income taxes payable, and long-term debt.

¶202.03.04 Owners' Equity (Stockholders' Equity)

The last part of the balance sheet is owners' equity. As already stated, owners' equity is the residual interest in the assets of the firm after subtracting the liabilities. The equation for owners' equity is as follows:

Owners' Equity = Total Assets – Total Liabilities

You'll recall that a business is set up as a sole proprietorship, partnership, or corporation. Accounting for the transactions of the firm will be somewhat different depending on its form. The main difference in accounting concerns the treatment of owners' equity. Shown below are the different owners' equity accounts pertaining to the three forms of business.

Business Form	Owners' Equity Accounts	($ Millions)
Sole Proprietorship	Jean Deaux, Capital	$1,100
Partnership	Robyn Lindblade, Capital	$550
	Rusty Biles, Capital	550
	Total Partners' Equity	$1,100
Corporation	Common Stock	$500
	Retained Earnings	600
	Total Stockholders' Equity	$1,100

Total stockholders' equity for Fashion Company is $1,100 million (line 12 of Exhibit 2.3) at December 31, 20Y2. Fashion's stockholders' equity is in the form of common stock and retained earnings. Common stock consists of the shares that the firm has sold to stockholders. You'll recall that a retained earnings of $600 million was computed previously on Fashion's 20Y2 statement of retained earnings.

At the bottom of the balance sheet, total liabilities and stockholders' equity are added together. As noted previously, this amount is the same amount as total assets. As the name says, the balance sheet should always balance total assets with an equal combination of total liabilities plus stockholders' equity.

FOCUS ON GLOBAL TRADE

Apple Goes Around the World

Apple is not only an iconic company in the United States; a love for Apple products is shared around the world. Apple has flagship stores in Tokyo, Osaka, London, Sydney, Perth, Palo Alto, Montreal, Munich, Frankfurt, Zurich, Paris, Beijing, Glasgow, Shanghai, and Hong Kong. International operations continue to grow substantially. In one year, Apple experienced 160% growth in net sales in its Asia-Pacific markets (Asia and Australia) compared to 29% in North, Central and South America combined. Apple is certainly focused on international markets.

Source: *Investor.Apple.com*

¶202.04 STATEMENT OF CASH FLOWS

The statement of cash flows shows the company's inflows and outflows of cash.

The **statement of cash flows** shows the company's cash receipts and cash payments, that is, the inflows and outflows of cash. The statement of cash flows answers the question, "How much cash was taken in and paid out during the period?" The statement of cash flows classifies cash inflows (receipts) and cash outflows (payments) under three categories of business activities: operating activities, investing activities, and financing activities. These three activities will be discussed in detail in Chapter 12. A net increase or decrease in cash is calculated by summing the totals of the three activities.

Company managers use the statement of cash flows to determine sources and uses of cash during a period. This helps management plan for future cash needs and monitor how cash is used. External users such as suppliers and creditors can view the statement of cash flows to see if the company has enough cash to pay its bills or whether the company is drowning in debt. Investors can determine if the company is utilizing its cash effectively.

Let's look at the statement of cash flows for Fashion Company as shown in Exhibit 2.4. (Parentheses around an amount indicate a cash outflow or payment.)

Exhibit 2.4 FASHION COMPANY CONSOLIDATED STATEMENT OF CASH FLOWS

	CASH FLOWS FROM OPERATING ACTIVITIES	Year Ended Dec 31, 20Y2 ($ Millions)	
1	Cash received from customers	$560	
2	Cash paid to suppliers and employees	(430)	
3	Cash paid for income tax expense	(40)	
4	Net cash provided by operating activities*		$90
	CASH FLOWS FROM INVESTING ACTIVITIES		
5	Sale of equipment	$170	
6	Purchase of equipment	(200)	
7	Net cash used for investing activities		(30)
	CASH FLOWS FROM FINANCING ACTIVITIES		
8	Cash dividends paid	$(50)	
9	Net cash used for financing activities		(50)
10	Net increase (decrease) in cash**		$10
11	Cash at beginning of year		90
12	Cash at end of year***		$100

* Sum of lines 1 through 3. Net cash means cash received minus cash paid.
** Sum of lines 4, 7, and 9.
*** Matches cash on Balance sheet.

Statement of Cash Flows

Cash receipts and payments from:
• Operating activites
• Investing activities
• Financing activites

? *In keeping track of your personal finances, how might you use one of the four types of financial statements?*

For Fashion Company, cash flows resulted in an increase in cash of $10 million (line 10). This amount is added to Fashion's $90 million in cash it began the year with (line 11). Thus, Fashion's cash amount at the end of the year is $100 million (line 12).

¶203   Relationship Among Financial Statements

LEARNING OBJECTIVE 3: Describe the relationship among the four financial statements.

? *Each financial statement answers one of four key questions:*

How much did the firm earn or lose from operations during the period?

In what way did the firm's retained earnings change during the period?

What is the firm's financial position at a designated point in time?

What amount of cash was generated and spent during the period?

Can you think of a way that one of the questions connects to another?

In review, there are four essential questions that are answered by the four financial statements. These are summarized in Exhibit 2.5. The construction of each financial statement will be discussed in more detail in later chapters.

Exhibit 2.5 Fundamental Financial Questions and Answers

Financial Statement	Question	Answer
Income Statement	How much did the firm earn or lose from operations during the period?	Revenues – Expenses Net income (or Net loss)
Statement of Retained Earnings	In what way did the firm's retained earnings change during the period?	Beginning retained earnings + Net income (or – net loss) – Dividends Ending retained earnings
Balance Sheet	What is the firm's financial position at a designated point in time?	Assets = Liabilities + Owners' Equity
Statement of Cash Flows	What amount of cash was generated and spent during the period?	Operating cash flows + Investing cash flows + Financing cash flows Increase (or decrease) in cash during the period

Exhibit 2.6 illustrates the relationships between certain accounts within the four financial statements. For example, the net income figure from the income statement is included on the statement of retained earnings. Ending retained earnings is shown on the statement of retained earnings and the balance sheet.

The amount of cash on the balance sheet corresponds to the ending cash amount computed in the statement of cash flows.

Exhibit 2.6 FASHION COMPANY RELATIONSHIPS AMONG FINANCIAL STATEMENTS

Income Statement — For the Year Ended (FYE) December 31, 20Y2 (Details Given in Exhibit 2.1)

Revenues	$600
Total Expenses	540
Net Income	$60

Statement of Retained Earnings — FYE December 31, 20Y2 (Details Given in Exhibit 2.2)

Retained Earnings, Beginning of the Year	$590
Net Income	60
Cash Dividends	(50)
Retained Earnings, End of the Year	$600

Balance Sheet — December 31, 20Y2 (Details Given in Exhibit 2.3)

ASSETS	
Cash	$100
All Other Assets	1,600
Total Assets	$1,700
LIABILITIES	
Total Liabilities	$600
STOCKHOLDERS' EQUITY	
Common Stock	500
Retained Earnings	600
Total Liabilities and Stockholders' Equity	$1,700

Statement of Cash Flows — FYE December 31, 20Y2 (Details Given in Exhibit 2.4)

Net Cash Flows Provided by Operating Activities	$90
Net Cash Flows Used for Investing Activities	(30)
Net Cash Flows Used for Financing Activities	(50)
Net Increase (Decrease) in Cash	$10
Beginning Cash	90
Ending Cash	$100

¶204 A Case Study: Financial Statements of Apple Inc.

LEARNING OBJECTIVE 4: Evaluate a company's financial statements.

Let's now consider the financial statements of Apple Inc. shown in Exhibits 2.7 to 2.10. Apple's financial statements are more complex than Fashion Company's financial statements. For example, Apple's income statement includes more accounts than Fashion Company's. Yet, both companies' income statements show revenues and expenses, and the resulting net income. Apple's income statement, entitled "Consolidated Statements of Operations," is shown in Exhibit 2.7.

Exhibit 2.7 APPLE INC. CONSOLIDATED STATEMENTS OF OPERATIONS (ADAPTED)

	Years ended September 25,		
	20Y3 **($ Millions)**	**20Y2** **($ Millions)**	**20Y1** **($ Millions)**
Net sales	$65,225	$42,905	$37,491
Cost of goods sold	39,541	25,683	24,294
Gross margin	25,684	17,222	13,197
Operating expenses:			
Research and development	1,782	1,333	1,109
Selling, general and administrative	5,517	4,149	3,761
Total operating expenses	7,299	5,482	4,870
Operating income	18,385	11,740	8,327
Other income and expenses	155	326	620
Income before income tax expense	18,540	12,066	8,947
Income tax expense	4,527	3,831	2,828
Net income	$14,013	$8,235	$6,119

Apple is a parent firm, which means it owns other firms called "subsidiaries." To provide a full accounting of all of the resources that Apple controls, the amounts shown on the financial statements include figures for both Apple and its subsidiaries. The financial statements for most companies show the consolidation of the parent firm and its subsidiary firms and use the word "consolidated" in financial statement titles.

You will note that Apple's income statement shows three years' data for comparative purposes. What is the trend? Apple has experienced dramatic increases in net income each year. The other financial statements should be reviewed to further understand how this income was generated and used.

Apple's Statement of Shareholders' Equity is shown in Exhibit 2.8. Having an increase in retained earnings for three years in a row is also a good sign for Apple. Retained earnings went from $9.1 billion in the beginning of 20Y1 to over $37 million in 20Y3.

Exhibit 2.8 APPLE INC. CONSOLIDATED STATEMENTS OF RETAINED EARNINGS (ADAPTED)

	Years ended September 25,		
	20Y3 **($ Millions)**	**20Y2** **($ Millions)**	**20Y1** **($ Millions)**
Beginning retained earnings	$23,353	$15,129	$9,111
Net income	14,013	8,235	6,119
Dividends	(197)	(11)	(101)
Ending retained earnings	$37,169	$23,353	$15,129

Current assets are those that will be used up, sold, or converted to cash within the year.

Current liabilities are those debts that are payable within the year.

Apple's balance sheet includes data for two years, as shown in Exhibit 2.9. Apple's assets are categorized into current assets and long-term assets. **Current assets** are those that will be used up, sold, or converted to cash within the year, or the normal operating cycle if longer than one year. All other assets are referred to as "long-term assets."

Apple's liabilities are also categorized into current and long-term. **Current liabilities** are those debts that are payable within one year, or within the firm's normal operating cycle if more than one year. All other debts are referred to as "long-term liabilities." Categorizing assets and liabilities into current and long-term is necessary for all companies.

Did the company's financial position improve or decline? From 20Y2 to 20Y3, Apple's total assets increased by approximately $27.7 million. Total liabilities increased by $11.5 million. Stockholders' equity decreased by over $16 million. This information, along with the large increases in income has made Apple an appealing investment for many.

Exhibit 2.9 APPLE INC. CONSOLIDATED BALANCE SHEETS (ADAPTED)		
	Years ended September 25,	
	20Y3 ($ Millions)	20Y2 ($ Millions)
ASSETS		
Current assets:		
Cash and cash equivalents	$11,261	$5,263
Short-term marketable securities	14,359	18,201
Accounts receivable, net	5,510	3,361
Inventories	1,051	455
Other current assets	9,497	4,275
Total current assets	41,678	31,555
Long-term marketable securities	25,391	10,528
Property, plant and equipment, net	4,768	2,954
Goodwill	741	206
Acquired intangible assets, net	342	247
Other assets	2,263	2,011
Total assets	$75,183	$47,501
LIABILITIES AND STOCKHOLDERS' EQUITY		
Current liabilities:		
Accounts payable	$12,015	$5,601
Accrued expenses	5,723	3,852
Deferred revenue	2,984	2,053
Total current liabilities	20,722	11,506
Deferred revenue — non-current	1,139	853
Other non-current liabilities	5,531	3,502
Total liabilities	27,392	15,861
Stockholders' Equity:		
Common Stock	10,668	8,210
Retained earnings	37,169	23,353
Accumulated other comprehensive income	(46)	77
Total stockholder's equity	47,791	31,640
Total liabilities and stockholder's equity	$75,183	$47,501

Apple's statement of cash flows provides data for multiple years, as shown in Exhibit 2.10. Apple has experienced an increase in cash flow from operations each year. The company's overall cash balance has fluctuated over the three years due primarily to investing decisions. The statement illustrates the company's ability to use its cash to continue ongoing operations and to consider new ventures. By reviewing the statement of cash flows, along with the other financial statements, the top management of Apple can assess the company's financial situation. They can make plans to achieve company goals, such as increasing sales and reducing expenses. For external users, such as investors and lenders, financial statements help them assess the likelihood of a good return on their investment or repayment of their loans.

Exhibit 2.10 APPLE INC. CONSOLIDATED STATEMENTS OF CASH FLOWS (ADAPTED)

	Years ended September 25,		
	20Y3 ($ Millions)	20Y2 ($ Millions)	20Y1 ($ Millions)
Net cash provided by operating activities	$ 18,595	10,159	9,596
Net cash used in investing activities	(13,854)	(17,434)	(8,189)
Net cash provided by financing activities	1,257	663	1,116
Net increase (decrease) in cash	5,998	(6,612)	2,523
Cash and cash equivalent at beginning of year	5,263	11,875	9,352
Cash and cash equivalent at end of year	11,261	5,263	11,875

Would you recommend Apple as an investment?

Preparing financial statements requires entering data, making calculations, and presenting information in a readable format. To help with this formidable task, spreadsheet software, such as Microsoft Excel, is extremely useful. The boxed insert, "Focus on Technology," shows how to prepare an income statement using Microsoft Excel.

FOCUS ON TECHNOLOGY

Using Microsoft Excel: Preparing an Income Statement

Using Excel, we will create Exhibit 2.11, Atomic Motor Company's income statement. If you have not used Excel before, please refer to the Excel information in the appendix.

1. Open your spreadsheet program; you will see a blank worksheet. Using the Save As command on the File menu, name the file atomic.xls.
2. File Identification Area: Create the file identification area by typing in the information shown in cells A1 through A5 of Exhibit 2.11. Use the Enter or arrow key to move from row to row. You'll note that the words are longer than the cell width and will automatically run into the adjoining cell. This is not a problem as long as there is not any data in the adjoining cell.

Exhibit 2.11 EXAMPLE EXCEL WORKSHEET: INCOME STATEMENT

	A	B	C	D	E
1	**IDENTIFICATION AREA:**				
2	File name:				
3	Designer:				
4	File created:				
5	File modified:				
6					
7	Input Required				
8		a. Net sales amount			
9		b. Cost of goods sold as a % of sales			
10		c. Operating expenses			
11					
12	Output Required:		Income Statement		
13					
14	**INPUT AREA:**				
15	Net sales ($):				1000
16	Cost of goods sold as a % of sales:				60%
17	Operating expenses ($):				100
18					
19	**OUTPUT AREA:**				
20		Atomic Motor Company			
21		Income Statement			
22		For the year Ended December 31, 20Y1			
23					
24	Sales			$1000	
25	Cost of goods sold			600	
26	Gross Profit			400	
27	Operating expenses			100	
28	Net Income			$300	
29					
30					
31	*Formulas Used:*				
32	*Sales (cell D24)*			=E15	
33	*Cost of goods sold (cell D25)*			=D24*E16	
34	*Gross profit (cell D26)*			=D24–D25	
35	*Operating expenses (cell D27)*			=E17	
36	*Projected net income (cell D28)*			=D26–D27	
37					

FOCUS ON TECHNOLOGY (CONTINUED)

3. In Cell A7, add the label "Input Required". In Cells B8, B9, and B10, enter the information as shown in Exhibit 2.11.
4. Input Area: As shown in the exhibit, three items are selected for input: net sales amount, cost of goods sold as a percentage of sales, and operating expenses. Enter these labels into cells A15-A17.
5. Enter the input values 1000, 60%, and 100 into cells E15, E16, and E17, respectively.
6. Output Area: Refer to Exhibit 2.11 and type the heading of the income statement (lines 20-22) onto your worksheet. Optional: To center each line of the heading across several columns, first highlight the cells where you want the words to appear. For Atomic Motor Company, highlight cells A20 – D20. Next, click on the icon with the boxed-in "a" (merge and center icon) at the top of the tool bar. Instead of using the icon, you can follow the menu bar commands: Format – Cells – Alignment tab. Under Horizontal, select Center. Click on the Merge cells box to unite the cells.
7. To list the names of the items within the income statement, enter the information shown in cells A24 through A28. Do not enter their corresponding numbers; they will be computed using formulas in the next step.
8. Formulas: Remember that for Excel to recognize data as a formula, the formula must be preceded by an equal sign (=), and the equal sign must be the first item in the cell (no spaces or characters preceding it). For example, to tell Excel to multiply cells D24 and E16, you would enter the following: =D24*E16. When a cell contains a formula, the resulting value will appear in the cell.
9. Refer to the bottom of Exhibit 2.11, which shows the formulas used to compute the values for each item within the income statement. You'll note that the formula for sales is =E15. Thus, to enter the formula for sales, type =E15 into cell D24. This tells Excel that sales equal the amount shown in cell E15 (which is the location of net sales within the input area). To enter the formula for cost of goods sold, enter =D24*E16 into cell D25. This tells Excel that Cost of goods sold equals the value in cell D24 (sales) multiplied by the value in cell E16 (60%). Type the remaining formulas into their designated cells.

The formulas are displayed at the bottom of the exhibit simply for teaching purposes; you do not need to duplicate that section onto your worksheet. To view the formula used in computing a value within a specific cell, click on the cell and the formula will appear in the formula bar at the top of the worksheet. If you wish to show a formula in a cell rather than its value, simply put a space before the equal sign, Excel will treat it as text.

¶205   Concluding Remarks

We began this chapter with the question: What is Apple's current financial situation? Thanks to the income statement, we learned that Apple is making a profit. Would you like to know the financial status of a particular company? Now you understand how to evaluate a company's financial situation by reading its financial statements. The financial statements are useful to people within and outside the company.

You are now ready to tackle the next chapter, which looks at the specific accounts listed in the four financial statements. You will learn how an accountant evaluates a business transaction and records the correct amount in the appropriate account.

¶206 Chapter Review

LEARNING OBJECTIVE 1

Describe how people within and outside the firm use financial statements.

Within a business firm, the managers of the business are the internal users of the financial statements and related accounting information. Information contained in the financial statements assist managers in assessing their management performance. Outside the firm are many external users such as investors and lenders. Deciding whether to buy or sell a corporation's stock is frequently based on the accounting information contained in the corporation's financial statements. In the same way, deciding whether to lend money to a corporation is frequently based on the information provided in the corporation's financial statements.

LEARNING OBJECTIVE 2

Identify the purpose and components of the four types of financial statements.

The most important reports produced by the accounting information system are the financial statements. The financial statements include the income statement, statement of retained earnings, balance sheet, and statement of cash flows. The four statements describe a business in financial terms. Each statement corresponds to a specific date or a designated time period, such as a year. Together, the four financial statements reveal how much the firm has earned or lost, the change in retained earnings, the firm's ending financial position, and how much cash was generated and spent.

Components of the income statement include the firm's revenues, expenses, and net income or net loss for the period. The statement of retained earnings shows the beginning balance, changes to, and ending balance of retained earnings. A balance sheet provides a "snapshot" of a firm's financial position at a designated point in time. The balance sheet shows three types of accounts: assets, liabilities, and owners' (stockholders') equity. The statement of cash flows presents cash inflows (receipts) and outflows (payments) under three categories of business activities: operating, investing, and financing.

LEARNING OBJECTIVE 3

Describe the relationship among the four financial statements.

Accounts within the financial statements are interrelated. For example, the net income figure from the income statement is included on the statement of retained earnings. Ending retained earnings is shown on the statement of retained earnings and the balance sheet. The amount of cash on the balance sheet corresponds to the ending cash amount computed in the statement of cash flows.

LEARNING OBJECTIVE 4

Evaluate a company's financial statements.

Financial statements can be evaluated to determine a company's financial situation by providing answers to four important questions. The income statement answers the question: How much did the firm earn or lose from operations during the period? The statement of retained earnings answers the question: In what way did the firm's retained earnings change during the period? The balance sheet answers the question: What is the firm's financial position at a designated point in time? The statement of cash flows answers the question: What amount of cash was generated and spent during the period? In evaluating financial statements, having financial statements for multiple years is helpful in assessing the financial trends of a company, such as whether profit is going up or down.

¶207   Glossary

Accounting equation

Assets = Liabilities + Owners' Equity

Assets

Assets are the economic resources owned by the firm.

Balance sheet

A balance sheet lists the balances of the asset, liability, and owners' equity accounts of a business on a specific date. The balance sheet is also known as the "statement of financial position."

Cost of goods sold

Cost of goods sold is the cost of the products a firm sells to its customers.

Current assets

Current assets are those assets that will be used up, sold, or converted to cash within the year, or the normal operating cycle if more than a year.

Current liabilities

Current liabilities are those debts that are payable within one year, or within the firm's normal operating cycle if more than one year.

Dividend

A dividend is a distribution of a corporation's earnings, usually cash, to its stockholders.

Expense

An expense is an outflow or using up of assets from manufacturing products, rendering services, or carrying out other activities that comprise the firm's ongoing operations.

Expense recognition principle

Expenses should follow revenues.

Financial statements

Financial statements include the income statement, statement of retained earnings, balance sheet, and statement of cash flows. They are produced by the accounting information system.

Income statement

The income statement shows the firm's revenues, expenses, and net income or net loss for the period.

Liabilities

Liabilities are the debts or economic obligations of the firm.

Net income

Net income is the amount by which revenues exceed expenses.

Net loss

A net loss occurs when expenses are greater than revenues.

Owners' equity

Owners' equity is the residual interest in the assets of a business that remains after deducting liabilities.

Retained earnings

Retained earnings is the equity of the stockholders generated from operations and kept for use in future operations.

Revenue

A revenue is an increase of assets that result from operating a business, such as selling goods, performing services, or performing other business activities.

Revenue recognition principle

Revenue should be recognized when it is realized or realizable and earned.

Statement of cash flows

The statement of cash flows presents cash inflows (receipts) and outflows (payments) under three categories of business activities: operating, investing, and financing.

Statement of retained earnings

The statement of retained earnings shows the beginning balance for retained earnings, additions and reductions to retained earnings, and the ending balance of retained earnings.

Stockholders' equity

Stockholders' equity is the owners' equity in a corporation — the residual interest of the owners in the assets of the firm after subtracting the liabilities. Corporations label owners' equity as stockholders' equity because the stockholders are the owners.

¶208 Appendix: Using Spreadsheets for Financial Statement Preparation and Analysis

Preparing financial statements requires entering data, making calculations, and presenting information in a readable format. To help with this formidable task, spreadsheet software, such as Microsoft Excel, is extremely useful. This appendix explains how to prepare and use the three parts of a worksheet: identification area, input area, and output area.

Spreadsheet software is second only to word processing software in terms of availability and use. The most widely used spreadsheet software is Microsoft Excel. Financial data can be entered into a spreadsheet file. In Microsoft Excel, a spreadsheet is called a worksheet. Several worksheets can be contained within one workbook file. Accountants in firms such as Apple Inc. use spreadsheet software to analyze financial information. The job description for an accounting position at Apple includes creating Excel spreadsheets for special projects.

A worksheet is arranged in rows and column, with columns designated by letters (A, B, C, etc.) and rows designated by numbers (1, 2, 3, etc.). Thus, a specific location, or cell, has an address containing a letter and number. For example, the top left-most cell is A1. Each cell may contain text or numeric data, including formulas.

One of the greatest benefits of using spreadsheet software is the ability to do sensitivity analysis, also called "what-if" analysis. Sensitivity analysis measures the impact of a change in one variable upon other variables. For example, suppose the income statement of a company is entered into a worksheet. If the worksheet is properly designed, what-if analysis can be used to facilitate decision-making. You can change the amount of sales, or any other figure in the input area, and immediately ascertain its impact on net income in the output area.

Spreadsheet software, such as Microsoft Excel, simplifies the process of creating financial reports. Uniformity and thoroughness in design is very helpful in creating useful reports via Excel worksheets. A worksheet is more user friendly if the information it contains is complete and laid out in a uniform manner. A worksheet should have three parts: identification area, input area, and output area. These parts will be discussed in the following sections.

¶208.01 IDENTIFICATION AREA

The identification area appears at the top of the worksheet. The first purpose of the identification area is to provide facts about the file itself, such as:

- Filename
- Designer of the file
- Date file was created
- Date file was modified

The second purpose of the identification area is to identify the worksheet requirements. What data is necessary to solve the problem at hand? What is the output result? The worksheet requirements consist of the information needed as input and the resulting information that is desired as output. These requirements are outlined in the identification area. For example, assume you are asked to create a worksheet for Atomic Motor Company that provides the end of the year balance for retained earnings, in other words, a statement of retained earnings. In this case, the required input is the beginning of the year balance for retained earnings, the net income for the year, and the amount of cash dividends declared. The output requirement would be the statement of retained earnings, which includes the end of the year balance. At the top of Exhibit 2.A, you can see an example of an identification area.

¶208.02   INPUT AREA

The input area is the second part of the worksheet. The items that go into the input area have already been outlined in the identification area. These items are typed into a column along with their respective values. As you'll note from the exhibit, the input items were listed in column A and their values were typed into column D, specifically, D11 to D13. The location or cell address of these values will then be used in writing formulas for the output area, as described in the next section.

¶208.03   OUTPUT AREA

The output area is the final part of the worksheet and contains the desired results, which is the statement of retained earnings in this case. The great benefit of using good worksheet design is that you do not have to manually compute the values in the output area. A formula was entered for each of the output items in our example. For example, the formula for end of the year balance is: beginning balance + net income – cash dividends. This formula is typed into the output area using the cell addresses for beginning balance (D11), net income (D12), and cash dividends (D13). (The boxed insert on Excel provides more detailed instruction for writing formulas.)

Since formulas within the output area are based upon values in the input area, the user can modify any value in the input area and instantly see how the change affects the output. For example, if you changed the amount of dividends declared, you would instantly see the revised end of the year balance in the output area.

Exhibit 2.A displays the statement of retained earnings in the output area along with the formulas that were used. As shown, Atomic Motor Company started the year with $150 in retained earnings and ended the year with $350.

Exhibit 2.A EXCEL WORKSHEET

	A	B	C	D	E	F	G
1	**IDENTIFICATION AREA:**						
2	File name:						
3	Designer:						
4	File created:						
5	Input Required		a. Retained earnings, beginning of year balance				
6			b. Net income for the year				
7			c. Cash dividends declared				
8	Output Required:		Statement of retained earnings				
9							
10	**INPUT AREA:**						
11	Balance, beginning of year			150			
12	Net income for the year			300			
13	Cash Dividends declared			100			
14							
15	**OUTPUT AREA:**						
16		Atomic Motor Company					
17		Income Statement					
18		For the year Ended December 31, 20Y1					
19	Retained Earnings:						
20	Balance, beginning of year			$150			
21	Net income for the year			300			
22	Less: Cash dividends declared			100			
23	Balance, end of year			$350			
24							
25	*Formulas used:*						
26	Balance, beginning of year			=D11			
27	Net income for the year			=D12			
28	Cash dividends declared			=D13			
29	Balance, end of year			=D20+D21−D22			

Chapter Assignments

QUESTIONS

1. **[Obj. 1]** What are some ways that internal users benefit from financial statements?

2. **[Obj. 1]** What are some ways that external users benefit from financial statements?

3. **[Obj. 2]** Briefly describe the income statement.

4. **[Obj. 2]** Briefly describe the statement of retained earnings.

5. **[Obj. 2]** Briefly describe the balance sheet.

6. **[Obj. 2]** Briefly describe the statement of cash flows.

7. **[Obj. 2]** What are some ways that external users benefit from information in the income statement?

8. **[Obj. 2]** What is the meaning of net income and net loss?

9. **[Obj. 2]** How do you define revenue?

10. **[Obj. 2]** What are the two requirements of the revenue recognition principle?

11. **[Obj. 2]** How do you define expense?

12. **[Obj. 2]** Describe cost of goods sold.

13. **[Obj. 2]** What is the expense recognition principle?

14. **[Obj. 2]** What is a dividend?

15. **[Obj. 2]** Define owner's equity and stockholders' equity.

16. **[Obj. 2]** Describe the accounting equation.

17. **[Obj. 3]** What are the four essential questions that are answered by the four financial statements?

18. **[Obj. 3]** Describe relationships between accounts within the four financial statements.

19. **[Obj. 4]** What does it mean that one business firm is a 'parent' firm and other business firms are 'subsidiary' firms?

20. **[Obj. 4]** Why do corporate financial statements include financial statements for more than one year?

SHORT EXERCISES – SET A

Building Accounting Skills

1. **[Obj. 2]** Identifying Financial Statements: Classify each of the following items as to whether they would be shown on the income statement (I), balance sheet (B), or statement of cash flows (CF).
    ___ Inventory
    ___ Long-Term Debt
    ___ Cash Dividends Paid
    ___ Cost of Goods Sold
    ___ Cash
    ___ Net Income
    ___ Buildings & Equipment
    ___ Income Taxes Payable
    ___ Operating Expenses
    ___ Retained Earnings

2. **[Obj. 2]** Balance Sheet Accounts: Using these abbreviations, classify each of the following account titles as to what section of the balance sheet they would appear.
    CA – Current Assets
    LTA – Long-Term Assets
    CL – Current Liabilities
    LTL – Long-Term Liabilities
    SE – Stockholders' Equity
    ___ Cash
    ___ Retained Earnings
    ___ Accounts Receivable
    ___ Buildings and Equipment
    ___ Common Stock
    ___ Taxes Payable
    ___ Inventory
    ___ Long-Term Debt
    ___ Accounts Payable

3. **[Obj. 2]** Computing: Fill in the blanks:

ASSETS	
Cash	$25,000
Accounts Receivable	50,000
Inventory	75,000
Buildings & Equipment	260,000
Land	40,000
Total Assets	$_____ a
LIABILITIES AND STOCKHOLDERS' EQUITY	
Accounts Payable	$40,000
Income Taxes Payable	25,000
Long-Term Debt	b
Common Stock	75,000
Retained Earnings	175,000
Total Liabilities and Stockholders' Equity	$_____ c

4. **[Obj. 2]** Preparing Statement of Retained Earnings: Southwest Gym Company started the year 20Y1 with $800,000 in retained earnings. Net income for the year is $240,000. The company declared and paid $140,000 in dividends during the year.
    a. Determine the amount of retained earnings at the end of the year.
    b. Prepare a statement of retained earnings for the year-ended 20Y1.

5. **[Obj. 3]** Relationships Among Financial Statements: Given the following information, fill in the missing items.

Income Statement	
Revenues	$7,000
Total Expenses	a
Net Income	$2,000
Statement of Retained Earnings	
Retained Earnings, Beginning of the Year	$12,000
Net Income	2,000
Cash Dividends	b
Retained Earnings, End of the Year	$13,000
Balance Sheet	
ASSETS	
Cash	$16,000
All Other Assets	c
Total Assets	$50,000
LIABILITIES	
Total Liabilities	$ d
STOCKHOLDERS EQUITY	
Common Stock	10,000
Retained Earnings	13,000
Other Equity	7,000
Total Liabilities and Stockholders Equity	$ e
Statement of Cash Flows	
Net Cash Flows Provided by Operating Activities	$8,000
Net Cash Flows Used for Investing Activities	4,000
Net Cash Flows Provided by Financing Activities	1,000
Net Increase (Decrease) in Cash	13,000
Beginning Cash	f
Ending Cash	$16,000

6. **[Obj. 3]** Knowing the Financial Statements: What financial statement answers the following question?
    a. How much did the firm earn or lose from operations during the period?
    b. In what way did the firm's retained earnings change during the period?
    c. What is the firm's financial position at the designated point in time?
    d. What amount of cash was generated and spent during the period?

SHORT EXERCISES – SET B

Building Accounting Skills

1. **[Obj. 2]** Identifying Financial Statements: Classify each of the following items as to whether they would be shown on the income statement (I), balance sheet (B), or statement of cash flows (CF).
   ___ Land
   ___ Income Taxes Payable
   ___ Interest Expense
   ___ Retained Earnings
   ___ Net Income
   ___ Prepaid Expenses
   ___ Cash Dividends Paid
   ___ Cost of Goods Sold
   ___ Cash
   ___ Inventory

2. **[Obj. 2]** Balance Sheet Accounts: Using these abbreviations, classify each of the following account titles as to what section of the balance sheet they would appear.
   CA – Current Assets
   LTA – Long-Term Assets
   CL – Current Liabilities
   LTL – Long-Term Liabilities
   SE – Stockholders' Equity
   ___ Taxes Payable
   ___ Inventory
   ___ Long-Term Debt
   ___ Accounts Payable
   ___ Land
   ___ Common Stock
   ___ Cash
   ___ Retained Earnings
   ___ Accounts Receivable
   ___ Buildings and Equipment

3. **[Obj. 2]** Computing: Fill in the blanks:

ASSETS	
Cash	$15,000
Accounts Receivable	40,000
Inventory	75,000
Buildings & Equipment	160,000
Land	40,000
Total Assets	$ a
LIABILITIES AND STOCKHOLDERS' EQUITY	
Accounts Payable	$30,000
Income Taxes Payable	25,000
Long-Term Debt	85,000
Common Stock	b
Retained Earnings	125,000
Total Liabilities and Stockholders' Equity	$ c

4. **[Obj. 2]** Preparing Statement of Retained Earnings: Pizza Galleria started the year 20Y1 with $400,000 in retained earnings. Net income for the year was $120,000. The company declared and paid $70,000 in dividends during the year.
   a. Determine the amount of retained earnings the company had at the end of the year.
   b. Prepare a statement of retained earnings for the year-ended 20Y1.

5. **[Obj. 3]** Relationships Among Financial Statements: Given the following information, fill in the missing items.

Income Statement	
Revenues	$17,000
Total Expenses	a
Net Income	$7,000
Statement of Retained Earnings	
Retained Earnings, Beginning of the Year	$14,000
Net Income	7,000
Cash Dividends	b
Retained Earnings, End of the Year	$9,000
Balance Sheet	
ASSETS	
Cash	$15,000
All Other Assets	c
Total Assets	$60,000
LIABILITIES	
Total Liabilities	$ d
STOCKHOLDERS EQUITY	
Common Stock	34,000
Retained Earnings	9,000
Other Equity	7,000
Total Liabilities and Stockholders Equity	$ e
Statement of Cash Flows	
Net Cash Flows Provided by Operating Activities	$8,000
Net Cash Flows Used for Investing Activities	4,000
Net Cash Flows Provided by Financing Activities	1,000
Net Increase (Decrease) in Cash	13,000
Beginning Cash	f
Ending Cash	$15,000

6. **[Obj. 3]** Knowing the Financial Statements: What accounting formula provides the answer to the following questions?
   a. How much did the firm earn or lose from operations during the period?
   b. In what way did the firm's retained earnings change during the period?
   c. What is the firm's financial position at a designated point in time?
   d. What amount of cash was generated and spent during the period?

PROBLEMS – SET A

Applying Accounting Knowledge

1. **[Obj. 2]** Preparing a Balance Sheet: The following account information is for Mercury Flying Shoe Company. Account balances are as of December 31, 20Y1. The accounts are listed in random order:

Accounts Receivable	$40,000
Common Stock	30,000
Accounts Payable	23,000
Retained Earnings	175,000
Inventory	75,000
Buildings & Equipment	140,000
Cash	25,000
Long-Term Debt	52,000

    Required:
    a. Prepare a balance sheet for Mercury Flying Shoe Company.
    b. Evaluate: How would you describe Mercury's financial position on Dec. 31, 20Y1?

2. **[Obj. 2]** Preparing a Balance Sheet: The following account is for Ocean Shipping Company. Account balances are as of December 31, 20Y1. The accounts are listed in random order:

Accounts Receivable	$17,000
Common Stock	206,000
Accounts Payable	59,000
Retained Earnings	87,000
Inventory	91,000
Ships & Equipment	394,000
Cash	64,000
Long-Term Debt	214,000

    Required:
    a. Prepare a balance sheet for Ocean Shipping Company.
    b. Evaluate: How would you assess the financial position of Ocean Shipping on Dec. 31, 20Y1?

3. **[Obj. 2]** Preparing a Balance Sheet: Same as Problem A2, except the account balances for cash and retained earnings are different. Account balances for Ocean Shipping Company are as of December 31, 20Y1. The accounts are listed in random order:

Accounts Receivable	$17,000
Common Stock	206,000
Accounts Payable	59,000
Retained Earnings	73,000
Inventory	91,000
Ships & Equipment	394,000
Cash	50,000
Long-Term Debt	214,000

    Required:
    a. Prepare a balance sheet for Ocean Shipping Company.
    b. Evaluate: How would you assess the financial position of Ocean Shipping on Dec. 31, 20Y1?

4. **[Obj. 2]** Preparing an Income Statement: Use the following account information to prepare an income statement for Armstrong Tire Company. Account balances are as of December 31, 20Y1. The accounts are listed in random order.

Cost of Goods Sold	$100,000
Net Sales	220,000
Income Tax Expense	20,000
Operating Expenses	87,000

    Required:
    a. Prepare an income statement for Armstrong Tire Company.
    b. Evaluate: How much did the firm earn or lose from operations during the period? How would you assess the financial position of Armstrong Tire?

5. **[Obj. 2]** Preparing an Income Statement: Same as Problem A4, except the account balances for cost of goods sold and income tax expense are different. Use the following account information to prepare an income statement for Armstrong Tire Company. Account balances are as of December 31, 20Y1. The accounts are listed in random order.

Cost of Goods Sold	$90,000
Net Sales	220,000
Income Tax Expense	25,000
Operating Expenses	87,000

Required:
a. Prepare an income statement for Armstrong Tire Company.
b. Evaluate: How much did the firm earn or lose from operations during the period? How would you assess the financial position of Armstrong Tire?

6. **[Obj. 2]** Preparing the Financial Statements: Start with the Fashion Company financial statements (Exhibits 2.1 to 2.4) and change the following account balances for 20Y2:
  ■ Sales to $700 million
  ■ Cash on 12/31 to $200 million
  ■ Cash received from customers to $660 million
  ■ Cash on 1/1 to $90 million

Required:
a. Prepare an income statement for 20Y2 (one year only).
b. Prepare a statement of retained earnings for 20Y2.
c. Prepare a balance sheet for 20Y2.
d. Prepare a statement of cash flows for 20Y2.
e. Evaluate: How would you assess the company's financial situation?

7. **[Obj. 3]** Relationships Among Financial Statements: Prepare an exhibit, similar to Exhibit 2.6, showing the relationships among the financial statements from Problem A6.

8. **[Obj. 4]** Interpreting the Financial Statements: Refer to the Apple financial statements, shown in Exhibits 2.7 to 2.10. Answer the following questions.

Required:
a. What was net income for the most recent year?
b. Did the most recent year's net income increase or decrease from the prior year?
c. Was the change in net income because of an increase/decrease in revenue, an increase/decrease in expenses, or both?
d. What was the largest expense in the most recent year?
e. How much was income tax expense in the most recent year?
f. Which current asset is the largest at the end of the most recent year?
g. Comparing the two most recent years, what was the change in total liabilities?
h. What is the largest asset amount in the balance sheet at the end of the most recent year?
i. Comparing the two most recent years, how much did total stockholders' equity increase/decrease?
j. Comparing the two most recent years, did "net cash provided by operating activities" increase or decrease?
k. Evaluate: What is your evaluation of Apple's current financial situation and future?

PROBLEMS – SET B

Applying Accounting Knowledge

1. **[Obj. 2]** Preparing a Balance Sheet: The following account information is for Einstein Computers. Account balances are as of December 31, 20Y1. The accounts are listed in random order:

Accounts Receivable	$80,000
Common Stock	60,000
Accounts Payable	46,000
Retained Earnings	350,000
Inventory	150,000
Buildings & Equipment	280,000
Cash	50,000
Long-Term Debt	104,000

Required:
a. Prepare a balance sheet for Einstein Computers.
b. Evaluate: How would you describe the financial position of Einstein Computers on Dec. 31, 20Y1?

2. **[Obj. 2]** Preparing a Balance Sheet: The following account is for Keep-on-Trucking Company. Account balances are as of December 31, 20Y1. The accounts are listed in random order.

Accounts Receivable	$8,500
Common Stock	103,000
Accounts Payable	29,500
Retained Earnings	43,500
Inventory	45,500
Trucks & Equipment	197,000
Cash	32,000
Long-Term Debt	107,000

Required:
a. Prepare a balance sheet for Keep-on-Trucking Company.
b. Evaluate: How would you assess the financial position of the Keep-on-Trucking Company on Dec. 31, 20Y1?

3. **[Obj. 2]** Preparing a Balance Sheet: Same as Problem B2 regarding Keep-on-Trucking Company, except the account balances for cash and retained earnings are different. Account balances are as of December 31, 20Y1. The accounts are listed in random order:

Accounts Receivable	$8,500
Common Stock	103,000
Accounts Payable	29,500
Retained Earnings	36,500
Inventory	45,500
Trucks & Equipment	197,000
Cash	25,000
Long-Term Debt	107,000

Required:
a. Prepare a balance sheet for Keep-on-Trucking Company.
b. Evaluate: How would you assess the financial position of the Keep-on-Trucking Company on Dec. 31, 20Y1?

4. **[Obj. 2]** Preparing an Income Statement: Use the following account information to prepare an income statement for Dynasty Jewelry. Account balances are as of December 31, 20Y1. The accounts are listed in random order.

Cost of Goods Sold	$200,000
Net Sales	440,000
Income Tax Expense	40,000
Operating Expenses	174,000

Required:
a. Prepare an income statement for Dynasty Jewelry.
b. Evaluate: How much did the firm earn or lose from operations during the period? How would you assess the financial position of Dynasty Jewelry?

5. **[Obj. 2]** Preparing an Income Statement: Same as Problem B4 regarding Dynasty Jewelry, except the account balances for cost of goods sold and income tax expense are different. Account balances are as of December 31, 20Y1. The accounts are listed in random order.

Cost of Goods Sold	$180,000
Net Sales	440,000
Income Tax Expense	50,000
Operating Expenses	174,000

Required:

a. Prepare an income statement for Dynasty Jewelry.

b. Evaluate: How much did the firm earn or lose from operations during the period? How would you assess the financial position of Dynasty Jewelry?

6. **[Obj. 2]** Preparing the Financial Statements: Start with the Fashion Company financial statements (Exhibits 2.1 to 2.4) and change the following account balances for 20Y2:
   - Sales to $800 million
   - Cash on 12/31 to $300 million
   - Cash received from customers to $760 million
   - Cash on 1/1 to $90 million

Required:

a. Prepare an income statement for 20Y2 (one year only).

b. Prepare a statement of retained earnings for 20Y2.

c. Prepare a balance sheet for 20Y2.

d. Prepare a statement of cash flows for 20Y2.

e. Evaluate: How would you assess the company's financial situation?

7. **[Obj. 3]** Relationships Among Financial Statements: Prepare an exhibit, similar to Exhibit 2.6, showing the relationships among the financial statements prepared in Problem B6.

8. **[Obj. 4]** Interpreting the Financial Statements: Refer to Fashion Company's financial statements shown in Exhibits 2.1 to 2.4. Answer the following questions.

Required:

a. What was net income for the most recent year?

b. Did the most recent year's net income increase or decrease from the prior year?

c. Was the change in net income because of an increase/decrease in revenue, an increase/decrease in expenses, or both?

d. What was the largest expense in the most recent year?

e. How much was income tax expense in the most recent year?

f. Comparing the two years, what was the change in total liabilities?

g. What is the largest asset amount in the balance sheet at the end of the most recent year?

h. Comparing the two years, how much did total stockholders' equity increase/decrease?

i. Evaluate: What is your evaluation of Fashion Company's current financial situation and future?

CROSS-FUNCTIONAL PERSPECTIVES

Discussion Questions

1. **[Obj. 1]** Why does the marketing department pay close attention to the income statement?

2. **[Obj. 1]** Why does the finance department pay close attention to the statement of retained earnings?

3. **[Obj. 1]** Why is the finance department especially interested in the balance sheet?

4. **[Obj. 1]** Which departments are interested in the statement of cash flows and why?

Cross-functional Case: New Project Team

New Project Team Proposal: Suppose the creative team at Apple has developed a new iPad with 3-D technology. The iPad 3-D is faster, can store more data and the 3-D technology screen is much clearer and more impressive than that current model. The Apple team would like to introduce the iPad 3-D into the market next year. They propose advertising the iPad 3-D on the Web, television, and in trade magazines. They also propose using product give-aways, mail-outs, 3-D displays, and posters for distributors. Additional personnel, including 3-D specialists, must be hired to carry out its plan.

The Players: The proposal is presented in a meeting with the chief executive officer and top managers from marketing, production, finance, human resources, and accounting. Each department serves a unique function in contributing to the company's success. Like positions on a football team, each player carries out a distinctive task to successfully run each play. Teamwork is essential for success.

The Decisions: Should Apple go forward with the iPad 3-D? Let's consider some information that top management must assimilate to make the decision. First, the production manager must estimate the staff needed and time required to develop the new device and software. If additional staff is to be hired, the human resources manager must determine how and when this can be accomplished.

The marketing department must survey Apple's customers to assess their response to the iPad 3-D and then develop a suitable promotional plan. Marketing needs to provide accounting with an estimate of market demand, including a sales forecast. Using the sales forecast, accountants can develop a budget of expected revenues and expenses. The accountants will also project cash inflows and outflows, plus assess profitability. If additional cash is needed to fund the development and promotion of the iPad 3-D, the financial specialist must ascertain the sources and terms of additional financing.

Additional Information:

- The cost to develop and produce 1,000,000 new devices and necessary software is $150,000,000.
- Spending on advertising and promotional items is estimated at $30,000,000.
- Forecasted sales revenue is $200,000,000.
- Distribution costs are estimated at $4,000,000.
- Salaries for necessary additional personnel are $15,000,000.
- A short-term loan of $15,000,000 is necessary to cover initial production and marketing costs. Interest expense on the loan would be $1,000,000.

Required:

a. Assume you are the accountant on the new project team. Using the facts given, prepare an analysis of revenues and costs. What is your projected net income on the new iPad 3-D?

b. Assume you are the chief executive officer at Apple. Based on the accountant's analysis, would you recommend going forward with the new product?

c. Assume you are the marketing advisor on the new project team. After further analysis, you think that advertising and promotional expenditures can be cut in half, without decreasing the sales forecast. How does this affect the profitability of the new product? Do you recommend going forward with the iPad 3-D?

d. Assume you are the production manager. After additional analysis, you believe that development and production costs can be cut in half. What would you recommend regarding the proposed product?

EXCEL ASSIGNMENTS

Refer to the Appendix in this chapter for instructions on using Microsoft Excel.

1. **[Obj. 2]** Preparing an Income Statement: Using Microsoft Excel, prepare an income statement for Fashion Company for the year ended December 31, 20Y1. Design the worksheet with an identification area, input area, and output area. Type "Net Sales Revenue" into the input area with the value of $10,000. In the output area, create a formula for cost of goods sold so that it is always 48 percent of net sales revenue. Create a formula for income tax so that it is always 18 percent of net sales revenue. Operating expenses is a fixed amount of $3,000. Consequently, if net sales revenue is $10,000, then net income is $400.

    Required:
    a. Prepare an Excel worksheet similar to the income statement shown in Exhibit 2.1 for Fashion Company, but using the amounts described above. Print your worksheet.
    b. On your worksheet, change net sales revenue in the input area from $10,000 to $11,000. What is net income? If you designed your worksheet file properly, you can change the net sales revenue amount in the input area and net income is automatically computed in the output area. Print the revised worksheet.

2. **[Obj. 2]** Preparing an Income Statement: Same as Excel assignment 1, except change net sales revenue to $20,000.

    Required:
    a. Prepare an Excel worksheet similar to the income statement shown in Exhibit 2.1 for Fashion Company. Print your worksheet.
    b. On your worksheet, change net sales revenue in the input area from $20,000 to $30,000. What is net income? Print the revised worksheet.

3. **[Obj. 2]** Preparing a Balance Sheet: Using Microsoft Excel, prepare a balance sheet for Mercury Flying Shoe Store. On your Excel worksheet, set up an identification area, input area, and output area. Include all accounts in the input area. The output area contains the balance sheet. The output area should be formula-driven based on the amounts entered in the input area. Account balances are as of December 31, 20Y1. Use the following information, which is in no particular order, pertaining to Mercury Flying Shoe Company.

Accounts Receivable	$50,000
Common Stock	50,000
Accounts Payable	20,000
Retained Earnings	175,000
Inventory	75,000
Buildings & Equipment	140,000
Cash	25,000
Long-Term Debt	45,000

Required: Use Excel to prepare a balance sheet for Mercury Flying Shoe Company using the directions above. Print your worksheet.

4. **[Obj. 2]** Preparing a Balance Sheet: Same as Excel assignment 3, except change accounts receivable to $43,000 and retained earnings to $168,000.

    Required: Prepare a balance sheet for Mercury Flying Shoe Company using Excel. Print your worksheet.

5. **[Obj. 2]** Preparing a Balance Sheet: Using Microsoft Excel, prepare a balance sheet for Argonaut Shipping Company. On your Excel worksheet, set up an identification area, input area, and output area. Include all accounts in the input area. The output area contains the balance sheet. The output should be formula-driven based on the amounts entered in the input area. Account balances are as of December 31, 20Y1. Use the following information, which is in no particular order, pertaining to Argonaut Shipping Company.

Accounts Receivable	$17,000
Common Stock	23,000
Accounts Payable	42,000
Retained Earnings	67,000
Inventory	15,000
Ships & Equipment	132,000
Cash	7,000
Long-Term Debt	39,000

Required: Use Excel to prepare a balance sheet for Argonaut Shipping Company. Print your worksheet.

6. **[Obj. 2]** Preparing a Balance Sheet: Same as Excel assignment 5, except change Cash to $15,000, Accounts Receivable to $40,000, Long-Term Debt to $18,000, and Retained Earnings to $119,000.

Required: Prepare a balance sheet for Argonaut Shipping Company using Excel. Print your worksheet.

7. **[Obj. 2]** Preparing an Income Statement: Using Microsoft Excel, prepare an income statement for Argonaut Shipping Company. On your Excel worksheet, set up an identification area, input area, and output area. Include all accounts in the input area. The output area contains the income statement. The output should be formula-driven based on the amounts entered in the input area. Account balances are as of December 31, 20Y1. Use the following information, which is in no particular order, pertaining to Argonaut Shipping Company.

Cost of Goods Sold	$125,000
Net Sales	250,000
Income Tax Expense	20,000
Advertising Expense	34,000
Depreciation Expense	26,000
Other Operating Expenses	18,000
Interest Expense	10,000

Required: Use Excel to prepare an income statement for Argonaut Shipping Company. Print your worksheet.

8. **[Obj. 2]** Preparing an Income Statement: Same as Excel assignment 7, except change Net Sales to $280,000 and Cost of Goods Sold to $150,000.

Required: Prepare an income statement for Argonaut Shipping Company using Excel. Print your worksheet.

9. **[Obj. 2]** Preparing the Financial Statements: Prepare Dugout Canoe Company's financial statements for the year ended December 31, 20Y1. For examples, refer to Exhibits 2.1 to 2.4. Set up an identification area, input area, and output area. Include all accounts in the input area. The output area will contain the financial statements. The output area should be formula-driven based on the amounts entered in the input area. Use the following information, which is in no particular order. Account balances at December 31, unless otherwise indicated. (Amounts are in thousands.)

10. **[Obj. 3]** Relationships Among Financial Statements: Build on Excel assignment 9.

    Required: Using Excel, prepare an exhibit, similar to Exhibit 2.6, showing the relationships among the financial statements.

Net Sales Revenue	25,600	Income Taxes Payable	300
Cost of Goods Sold	7,700	Long-Term Debt	13,900
Operating Expense	3,830	Common Stock	11,535
Income Tax Expense	200	Cash Received from Customers	10,000
Retained Earnings, Jan. 1	6,935	Cash Paid to Suppliers & Employees	6,330
Cash Dividends Declared	250	Cash Paid for Income Tax Expense	200
Cash, December 31	2,900	Cash from Sale of Equipment	1,020
Accounts Receivable	22,500	Cash Paid for Purchase of Equipment	2,790
Inventory	16,840	Cash Dividends Paid	700
Equipment	13,150	Cash, January 1	1,900
Accounts Payable	9,100		

Required: Use Excel to prepare each of the following for Dugout Canoe Company. Print your worksheets.
  a. income statement
  b. statement of retained earnings
  c. balance sheet
  d. statement of cash flows

WEB ASSIGNMENTS

1. **[Obj. 1]** Go to the website for the American Institute of CPAs and prepare a brief report on the requirements to become a Certified Public Accountant.

2. **[Obj. 4]** Go to the website for Apple Inc. or do a search on Google to find the company's financial statements. Did the firm show a profit or loss in the most recent year?

3. **[Obj. 4]** Go to the website for Apple Inc. or do a search on Google to find an accounting-related news item from the past year, such as Apple reporting on its financial results, issuing stock, or paying off a bank loan. Give a one-paragraph summary of the news item.

¶210 # Test Prepper

Use this sample test to gauge your comprehension of the chapter material.

True/False Questions

___1. A balance sheet lists the balances of the asset, liability, and owners' equity accounts of a business on a given date.

___2. Long-term assets are those that will be used up, sold, or converted to cash within the year.

___3. The statement of cash flows answers the question: "How much cash was taken in and paid out during the period?"

___4. The income statement includes revenue and expenses. These balances are also included on the balance sheet as part of retained earnings.

___5. Assets must always equal liabilities minus stockholders' equity.

___6. Revenue should be included on the balance sheet as an asset.

___7. Net income increases retained earnings.

___8. Accounts payable should be classified as a liability on the balance sheet.

___9. Cash should be listed before land on the balance sheet.

___10. The balance sheet will tell you how much the firm earned or lost during the period.

Multiple-Choice Questions

___1. Which of the following financial statements summarizes the revenues earned and the expenses incurred by a business over a period of time?
   a. income statement
   b. balance sheet
   c. statement of cash flows
   d. statement of retained earnings
   e. statement of owners' equity

___2. The accounting equation is
   a. Liabilities = Assets + Owners' equity
   b. Assets = Liabilities + Owners' equity
   c. Owners' equity = Assets + Liabilities
   d. Assets = Cash − Expenses
   e. Revenue − Expenses = Net Income

___3. Which of the following is the residual interest in the assets of the firm after subtracting the liabilities?
   a. current assets
   b. depreciation
   c. owners' equity
   d. liabilities
   e. net assets

___4. The statement of cash flows classifies cash inflows (receipts) and cash outflows (payments) under which category of business activities?
   a. operating activities
   b. investing activities
   c. financing activities
   d. all of the above
   e. none of the above

___5. Which of the following is a liability?
   a. Common stock
   b. Building and equipment
   c. Inventory
   d. Retained earnings
   e. Long-term debt

___6. Which of the following financial statements would be impacted by the current period net income?
   I. Balance Sheet
   II. Income Statement
   III. Statement of Stockholders' Equity
   IV. Cash Flow Statement

   a. II only
   b. I and II only
   c. II and III only
   d. I, II, III only
   e. I, II, III, IV

__7. Which of the following forms of business would have common stock instead of a capital account for each owner?
   a. Sole proprietorship
   b. Partnership
   c. Corporation
   d. all of the above
   e. none of the above

__8. What would an income statement with the following account balances (listed in random order) tell an investor about a company's operations?

Cost of Goods Sold	$150,000
Net Sales	200,000
Operating Expenses	75,000

   a. The company is profitable this period
   b. The company is operating at a loss this period
   c. The company broke even this period
   d. The company has always been profitable
   e. The company has always operated at a loss

__9. Which criteria must be met in order for revenue to be recorded?
   a. Cash must have been received.
   b. The company must expect cash to be received in the future.
   c. The company must have provided the customer with a good or service.
   d. Both a. and c. must occur in order to record revenue.
   e. Either a. or b. must occur along with c. in order to record revenue.

__10. Fashion Forward, a fashion magazine sells one-year subscriptions. The customers pay for all twelve issues when they sign up for the subscription. When should Fashion Forward record revenue for the sale of a subscription?
   a. When the customer pays for the subscription.
   b. When the first magazine is provided to the customer.
   c. At the end of the year when all magazines have been provided.
   d. A portion of the revenue should be recorded each month as the magazines are provided.
   e. Either a. or b.

Chapter

3

Accounting Transaction Processing

LEARNING OBJECTIVES

You should be able to do the following after studying "Part I: Recording Business Transactions":

1. Describe how an understanding of accounting transaction processing is beneficial to people within and outside the firm.
2. Implement the steps of recognition, valuation, and classification in processing a business transaction.
3. Understand the relationships among the accounts in the chart of accounts.
4. Record 10 basic accounting transactions and comprehend how each affects the accounting equation: Assets = Liabilities + Stockholders' Equity.

You should be able to do the following after studying "Part II: Double-Entry Accounting":

5. Understand the rationale behind double-entry accounting and the tools used to apply it.
6. Describe how to record a business transaction in the general journal.
7. Explain the function of the general ledger.
8. Prepare a trial balance.

CHAPTER CONTENTS

FOCUS ON BUSINESS

McDonald's: Accounting for Business Transactions on a Global Scale

Where can you go when you have a craving for a chat pata chicken roll, an order of alloo fingers, and a large coke? McDonald's in Pakistan, of course! Entering the Pakistan market in 1998, McDonald's now has 20 restaurants in four major Pakistani cities. If you crave a Big Mac made with mutton instead of beef, get a Maharaja Mac™ in India. Because of the religious sentiments of the population, McDonald's does not include beef or pork products in the menu.

McDonald's is the world's leading foodservice retailer with over 30,000 restaurants serving nearly 46 million people a day in more than 100 countries. How does McDonald's keep track of its sales in the U.S. and abroad? Each McDonald's restaurant must keep its own records regarding its local business. How does the corporate office assimilate this accounting information from around the world? Fortunately, there is a common method of recording transactions used throughout the world called double-entry accounting. The introduction of double-entry accounting was one of the notable achievements of the Renaissance period in Europe. Based on the idea of balance, there are two aspects of every transaction using double-entry accounting: every transaction debits one or more accounts and credits one or more accounts. This chapter will delve deeper into the mechanics of double-entry accounting.

Source: *www.mcdonalds.com*

¶301 Applications to People Within and Outside the Firm

LEARNING OBJECTIVE 1: Describe how an understanding of accounting transaction processing is beneficial to people within and outside the firm.

Learning the accounting process helps people within and outside a firm better understand the organization's operations. In the case of a business, revenues and expenses can be evaluated and plans to improve profits can be formulated. For government agencies or nonprofit organizations, accounting information can be used to develop strategies to make more effective use of resources and to better serve constituents.

Accounting has a long history, dating back to ancient Mesopotamia, Egypt, and Rome. Later, during the European Renaissance, the double-entry system was invented. The modern-day double-entry accounting system facilitates effective business operations by accounting for business transactions such as acquiring assets, buying and selling merchandise, receiving customer payments, and paying for expenses. In learning the rationale behind the double-entry system, you will understand the impact of various business dealings. You will more firmly grasp the connection between a firm's assets, liabilities, stockholders' equity, revenues, and expenses. Understanding accounting can help you make significant contributions to the company or organization for which you work.

¶301.01 INTERNAL USERS

When business transactions are complicated by credit sales, subsidiary firms, and e-commerce, how does a business keep track of daily operations? While the company carries out business activities, such as purchasing merchandise from suppliers and then selling that merchandise to customers, the company's accountants track and report these transactions. Managers from the various functional areas of a company can benefit from understanding the steps in accounting for a business transaction. Understanding basic transactions enables managers to see the big picture – how all departments within a firm contribute to the successful completion of a business transaction.

Assume McDonald's purchases a large shipment of beef. Where does the money come from to pay the bill; to which account is the expenditure assigned? How is the purchase recorded so that McDonald's can keep track of how much beef is bought from each supplier and what the prices were? What if McDonald buys the beef on credit? Understanding the different aspects of a transaction and the different accounts involved helps a person understand the cash flows of the company and whether the company is profitable. It's like organizing your closet and knowing exactly where everything is. Double-entry accounting is a standardized system that enables people to keep track of amounts associated with business transactions. When employees are familiar with how business transactions are processed and recorded, they do a better job managing business activity.

¶301.02

Have you ever wondered how a large international company, such as McDonald's, keeps track of its assets, liabilities, and numerous business transactions?

EXTERNAL USERS

You don't have to be the accountant within a company to appreciate a well-run business or the value of a good investment. If a company's accounting transaction processing is efficient and reliable, this will lead to financial statements that are accurate and dependable. A general knowledge of the accounting process helps the average investor know what to look for in choosing companies that will be good investments. Accounting transaction processing is critical for company financial reporting, which is the basis for many important activities such as raising capital for business expansion and making good lending decisions. An awareness of how accounting works will also enhance your understanding of the operations of the national economy, which is the aggregation of all the individual businesses, large and small.

Part I: Recording Business Transactions

¶302

Evaluating a Business Transaction

We depend on accountants to provide truthful and accurate financial statements.

LEARNING OBJECTIVE 2: Implement the steps of recognition, valuation, and classification in processing a business transaction.

Business transactions are economic events that affect the financial situation of the firm.

In the accounting transaction process, the accountant determines when the transaction occurred, the dollar amount of the transaction, and how to categorize the transaction.

Financial statements report on the economic matters of a business. Managers and external users depend on financial statements for the information they need to make decisions. As described in Chapter 2, the basic financial statements are the income statement, statement of retained earnings, balance sheet, and statement of cash flows. Financial statements chiefly consist of accounts and the dollar amounts in those accounts. For example, the balance sheet shows how much cash a firm has. The Cash account includes all cash available for use by the firm, which includes cash on hand, in cash registers, and in bank accounts. Obviously, it is very important for the dollar amount stated on the financial statement to be truthful and accurate; this is consistent with the concept of relevance and faithful representation that you learned in Chapter 1. The accountant is responsible for maintaining accurate financial records.

The amount (balance) in an account such as Cash is the end result of many business transactions. **Business transactions** are economic events that affect the financial situation of the firm. Business transactions can be as large as the merger of Chevron and Texaco, or as small as the local grocery store purchasing a truckload of watermelons to sell.

The **accounting transaction process** is the evaluation of business transactions. In evaluating a business transaction, the accountant determines: (1) when the transaction occurred, (2) the dollar amount of the transaction, and (3) which accounts are affected by the transaction.

¶302.01

Recognition is the determination of when a transaction occurred and, thus, must be recorded.

RECOGNITION

Determining when a transaction occurred is called "**recognition**." Once a transaction is recognized, it must be recorded. For example, suppose that McDonald's orders, receives, and sends payment to Texas Beef Corporation for an order of frozen beef patties. When should the transaction be recorded? Recording the transaction involves decreasing the amount of cash and increasing the amount of food inventory. At which of the following points should the purchase be recorded (recognized)?

1. When McDonald's sends the purchase order to Texas Beef.
2. When McDonald's receives the beef patties.
3. When McDonald's sends payment.

A purchase transaction is recorded when ownership (title) of the merchandise passes from the supplier to the buyer, creating an obligation to pay. In the example above, McDonald's records the purchase when they receive the beef patties. At the same time, the accountants at Texas Beef would record the transaction as a sale.

Accurate recognition requires the cooperation of various departments within McDonald's. For instance, the receiving department must notify the accounting department when merchandise has been received. To ensure that the goods received were actually ordered, the receiving report is compared to the purchase order, which was previously prepared by the purchasing department.

¶302.02

Valuation involves determining the dollar amount of a business transaction.

VALUATION

Determining the dollar amount of a business transaction is called "**valuation**." Generally accepted accounting principles (GAAP) requires most transactions to be recorded at original cost, also called "historical cost." The original cost of an item is the price paid at the time of the transaction. As you recall from Chapter 1, this is the measurement principle.

Over time, more transactions under both U.S. GAAP and IFRS are allowed to be recorded at fair market value. The fair value of an item is the price someone would pay for that item today. At the time of a transaction the cost and fair value are the same, because someone would only be willing to buy an item today for what it is worth, not more. The same is true for the seller. The seller is only willing to sell something today for what it is worth, not less. Over time the original purchase price (historical cost) and the value today (fair value) may not be equal. While what you paid for an item will never change, the current market value can fluctuate. For example, the market value of a stock is almost constantly changing. When one company purchases another company's stock as an investment, the company would record it at fair market value rather than the original purchase price. This means that the value on the financial statements could change every period to represent the new market value, rather than always represent the original purchase price.

A source document is a document that serves as evidence that a transaction has occurred.

To help ensure accurate accounting, the amount of a transaction should be supported by source documents such as legal contracts or cancelled checks. A **source document** is evidence that a transaction has occurred, such as a sales invoice for sales revenue or a bill from a utility company for utilities expense. For example, a loan transaction is supported by a signed promissory note. The value of a stock referenced above could be supported by the current stock price according to the New York Stock Exchange on a specific date.

It can be more challenging to support the fair value of an item without a quoted market price. For example, a building is not traded on an exchange. An expert can estimate the fair value of a building by comparing it to similar buildings. However, two experts may estimate a different fair value of the same building. Ultimately, the fair value of a building will be the agreed-upon sales price. Prior to actually selling the building, the fair value can be a somewhat subjective number. The valuation of a fixed asset such as a building will be further discussed in Chapter 8.

Source documents sometimes provide an interface between departments. For example, the sales invoice is an interface between marketing and accounting. A customer places an order with a salesperson in the marketing department of Tracy's Toys. The order is received verbally, on a printed document, or online. A sales invoice is then prepared in the marketing department. The **sales invoice** contains information regarding the customer, items ordered, price, and delivery. An example sales invoice is shown in Exhibit 3.1. Before the order is fully processed, the customer is approved for credit.

Exhibit 3.1 SALES INVOICE

SALES INVOICE

Tracy's Toys 99 Whippoorwill Oxford, MS 84655		Invoice:	#120
Customer Account Number:	359	Salesperson:	#27
Order Number:	1003	Order Date:	6-20-Y1
Customer Name:	Texas Hobby Store		
Billing Address:	420 Camelot Houston, TX 79012		
Shipping Address:	Same		
Terms of Sale:	2/10, net 60	Date Delivered:	7-02-13

Item #	Description	Quantity	Unit Price	Total
2237	Butterfly Kite	40	$3.25	$130.00
8012	Bug Catcher	20	6.00	120.00
4990	Peek-a-Boo Book	50	2.83	141.50
	Shipping Total			$391.50

Multiple copies of the sales invoice are prepared and used for various purposes. One copy of the sales invoice serves as a bill and is sent to the customer by the accounting department. Another copy of the sales invoice is included with the shipment, and is referred to as the "packing slip." Exhibit 3.2 shows the interface between marketing and accounting in this sales process.

Exhibit 3.2 INTERFACE BETWEEN MARKETING AND ACCOUNTING

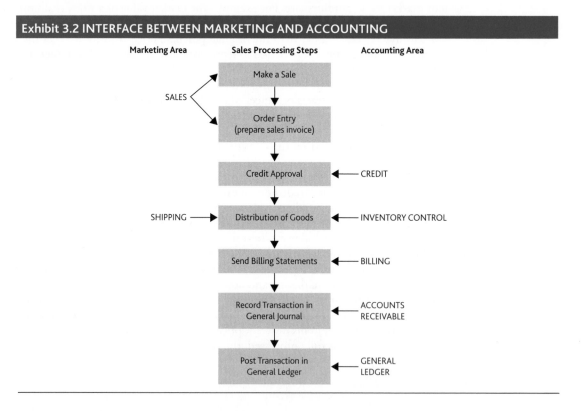

¶302.03   CLASSIFICATION

Classification is assigning transactions to the appropriate accounts.

Determining which categories or accounts are affected by a business transaction is called "**classification**." In other words, the dollar amount of the transaction must be placed into appropriate accounts. For example, if Hobby Lobby pays $100 cash for office supplies, an accountant decreases the Cash account by $100 and increases the Supplies account by $100. Some transactions are more intricate and require more consideration. For example, if Hobby Lobby borrows money from a bank, a portion of the debt may be classified as short-term and a portion as long-term, depending on the date it must be paid back to the lender.

¶303 Relationships Among Accounts

When you pay your phone bill, you are trusting the accountant to process that transaction accurately and honestly.

Your credit card charge slips, phone bill, and cancelled rent checks are all examples of source documents. How do they help ensure that businesses process transactions properly?

Accounts are the storage units for accounting data and are used to accumulate amounts for similar transactions.

The general ledger contains all the accounts for a business.

The chart of accounts is a list of account numbers and their corresponding names.

LEARNING OBJECTIVE 3: Understand the relationships among the accounts in the chart of accounts.

As you can imagine, recording the business transactions of a company requires the accumulation of vast amounts of data. Data must be stored in a retrievable form so that it can be used later for calculations, financial reporting, or other purposes. **Accounts** are the storage units for accounting data and are used to accumulate amounts for similar transactions. Every asset, liability, and stockholders' equity item (including revenues and expenses) has a unique account. For example, all sales of merchandise are accumulated in the Sales Revenue account.

All the accounts for a business are collected together in the **general ledger**. Prior to computers, the general ledger was a book. In computer systems, the general ledger is a computer file. To make data storage and account retrieval more efficient, the accounts in the general ledger may be assigned a unique number. The list of account numbers and corresponding names is called the "**chart of accounts**." Exhibit 3.3 shows the chart of accounts for JK Productions.

Exhibit 3.3 BASIC CHART OF ACCOUNTS FOR JK PRODUCTIONS

Account Number	Account Name	Description
Assets		
101	Cash	Money such as coins, currency, checks, postal and express money orders, and money on deposit in a bank.
102	Accounts Receivable	Amounts due from others for revenues or credit sales.
103	Office Supplies	Office supplies purchased and not used.
104	Land	Property owned for use in the business.
105	Buildings	Structures owned for use in the business.
Liabilities		
201	Accounts Payable	Money owed to others for purchases of products or services on credit.
202	Unearned Videography Fees	Cash received in advance for videography services to be provided in the future.
203	Wages Payable	Money owed to employees for wages earned and not paid.
204	Income Taxes Payable	Money owed to the government for income taxes due and not paid.
Stockholders' Equity		
301	Common Stock	Stockholders' investments in a corporation.
302	Retained Earnings	Stockholders' claims against company assets resulting from profitable operations.
303	Dividends	Distributions of assets (normally cash) that reduce retained earnings.
304	Additional Paid-in Capital	When investors acquire stock for amounts that exceed the par value of the stock.
Revenues		
401	Videography Fees Revenue	Revenues derived from performing videography services.
Expenses		
501	Wages Expense	Money earned by employees.
502	Advertising Expense	Amount for advertisements.
503	Office Supplies Expense	Amount for office supplies used.

FOCUS ON GLOBAL TRADE

What's in a Name?

Around the globe, an account name in one company's chart of accounts may have a different meaning from the same account name in a different country. This is particularly true when different languages are used. However, even when a common language is used, two countries may have different meanings for the same word. For example, in the United States, the account name "Stock" refers to ownership shares, but in the United Kingdom it strictly means inventory.

Accounts are classified as follows: assets, liabilities, stockholders' equity, revenues, and expenses. The accounting equation shows the relationship of these accounts:

Assets = Liabilities + Stockholders' Equity*

*Stockholders' equity includes revenues and expenses

In the next section, we review the accounting procedure for 10 basic business transactions. When a business transaction occurs, you must determine which accounts are affected. The accounting equation must always stay in balance: Assets = Liabilities + Stockholders' Equity. Do not make the mistake in thinking that every transaction involves an increase to one account and a decrease to another account. This only occurs if accounts on just one side of the equation are affected. For example, the collection of an account receivable involves accounts only on the Asset side of the equation: Cash is increased and Accounts Receivable is decreased. This is shown in the next section, Basic Transactions, as transaction number 7.

Do you have a chart that helps you keep track of names and numbers – perhaps a list of passwords and their corresponding uses?

If a business transaction affects accounts on both sides of the equation, then there may be a decrease to all affected accounts. Likewise, there could be an increase to all affected accounts. An example of this is the purchase of supplies on credit; Supplies (asset) is increased and Accounts Payable (liability) is increased.

¶304   Basic Transactions

LEARNING OBJECTIVE 4: Record 10 basic accounting transactions and comprehend how each affects the accounting equation.

We will now examine 10 basic business transactions and how they affect the accounting equation (Assets = Liabilities + Stockholders' Equity). Take notice that the accounting equation will always stay in balance after each transaction. An example small business will be used to illustrate proper accounting. Basic transactions include: setting up a business, purchasing assets by paying cash, purchasing assets with debt financing, paying a liability, earning revenues, receiving payment on customer account, incurring expenses, and paying dividends.

¶304.01   TRANSACTION 1: SETTING UP A BUSINESS

A young married couple, Jay and Kay Morgan, decide to start a videography company called "JK Productions." Jay and Kay have been providing videography services for a couple of years, but only on a limited basis in addition to their regular jobs. Jay has a business degree and Kay has an accounting degree. Combining their skills, they decide to operate their videography business full-time. Jay and Kay set up the business as a corporation to protect their personal assets from any liabilities related to the corporation. This limited liability feature is a major advantage of the corporate form of business. The couple invests $10,000 of their own savings. Friends and relatives invest an additional $90,000 in the business. Thus, JK Productions (business entity) starts up with $100,000 cash.

In return for the $100,000 investment, JK Productions issues 10,000 shares of $1 par value stock; 1,000 shares go to Jay and Kay, with the remaining 9,000 shares going to friends and relatives. When a firm sells stock, the stock may be assigned a par value. **Par value** is an arbitrary amount assigned by the company to each share of stock. Many states require that stocks have a par value to provide a baseline or

When a corporation sells stock for more than its par value, the amount over par is called "additional paid-in capital."

a minimum amount of legal capital to pay creditors. Stock usually sells for more than its par value; the amount over par value is called "**additional paid-in capital**" or "**paid-in capital in excess of par.**" The transaction is recorded as an increase in Cash of $100,000, an increase in Common Stock of $10,000 at par value, and an increase in Additional Paid-In Capital of $90,000.

On the date of incorporation, the balance sheet of the company would show the asset Cash and the contributed capital, Common Stock and Additional Paid-In Capital:

	Assets	=	Stockholder's Equity (SE)	
	Cash		**Common Stock**	**Additional Paid-In Capital**
bal.	0	=	0	0
1.	$100,000		$10,000	$90,000
bal.	$100,000	=	$10,000	$90,000

At this point, the balance sheet is very simple. There are only three accounts: one asset account (Cash) and two stockholders' equity accounts (Common Stock and Additional Paid-In Capital). There are no liability accounts at this time.

For other actions that Jay and Kay were required to take in order to start a new business, see the insert "Three Steps to Starting a Business."

FOCUS ON BUSINESS

Three Steps to Starting a Business

1. **Structure and Name:** Determine the legal structure of the business and properly file the business name with the state and/or county. Jay and Kay's video business is set up as a corporation with the name JK Productions. They registered the corporation with the Secretary of State and filed an Assumed Name Certificate with their local county clerk.

2. **Tax Responsibilities:** Determine the potential tax responsibilities of the new business on the federal, state, and local levels. Taxation of a corporation varies depending on the type of corporation formed. In order to pay the required state sales tax on the videos they sell, Jay and Kay went to their state's website to obtain a corporate sales tax number.

3. **Licenses and Permits:** Determine necessary licenses and permits for a business. A corporation is monitored by federal, state, and local agencies, and thus, entails more paperwork than other forms of organization.

 For more information, go to the small business website (*sba.gov*) and your official state website.

¶304.02 TRANSACTION 2: PURCHASING ASSETS BY PAYING CASH

JK Productions specializes in video recording children's athletic events, such as soccer and football. The customized video will include highlights of the games along with interviews of the coaches and players of an individual team. The video will be sold to team members. The company needs a place of business where they can conduct business and where athletes can come to be interviewed. Jay and Kay find a prime location with a small building that will meet their needs. The land costs $40,000 and the building costs $30,000. JK Productions pays for the land and the building with cash; thus, $70,000 is deducted from the Cash account. The balance sheet would now appear as follows. Note that total assets still equal total stockholders' equity.

	Assets			=	Stockholder's Equity (SE)	
	Cash	Land	Building		Common Stock	Additional Paid-In Capital
bal.	$100,000			=	$10,000	$90,000
2.	– 70,000	+ $40,000	+ $30,000			
bal.	$30,000	$40,000	$30,000	=	$10,000	$90,000

| | $100,000 | | | | $100,000 | |

¶304.03 TRANSACTION 3: PURCHASING ASSETS ON CREDIT

Acquisition of assets does not always require a cash outlay. A firm can purchase assets on credit. Buying on credit means that the company agrees to pay the amount at a later date to the seller. For example, Jay purchases $1,000 of video supplies on credit for the business. Consequently, an asset account (Supplies) increases and a liability account (Accounts Payable) is increased. The balance sheet would appear as follows:

	Assets				=	Liabilities	+	Stockholder's Equity (SE)	
	Cash	Supplies	Land	Building		Accounts Payable		Common Stock	Additional Paid-In Capital
bal.	$30,000		$40,000	$30,000	=			$10,000	$90,000
3.		+ $1,000				+ $1,000			
bal.	$30,000	$1,000	$40,000	$30,000	=	$1,000		$10,000	$90,000

| | $101,000 | | | | | $101,000 | | | |

Following the purchase of supplies on account, total assets now equal $101,000. Total liabilities plus total stockholders' equity equal $101,000.

¶304.04 TRANSACTION 4: PAYING A LIABILITY

JK Productions sends in payment of $500 for one-half of the amount owed for the supplies. Consequently, assets (Cash) are reduced by $500 and liabilities (Accounts Payable) are reduced by $500. Supplies remain unchanged at $1,000.

	Assets				=	Liabilities	+	Stockholder's Equity (SE)	
	Cash	Supplies	Land	Building		Accounts Payable		Common Stock	Additional Paid-In Capital
bal.	$30,000	$1,000	$40,000	$30,000	=	$1,000		$10,000	$90,000
4.	– $500					– $500			
bal.	$29,500	$1,000	$40,000	$30,000	=	$500		$10,000	$90,000

| | $100,500 | | | | | $100,500 | | | |

Following the payment, total assets are $100,500. Total liabilities plus total stockholders' equity equal $100,500.

¶304.05 TRANSACTION 5: RECORDING REVENUES RECEIVED IN CASH

Revenues are recorded when they are earned. JK Productions earns its revenues by selling customized videos to customers. The videos are usually paid for in cash immediately upon delivery.

Let's consider a case in which JK Productions is hired to document the highlights of a weeklong football camp. The participants of the camp order 200 videos at a total fee of $5,000. The participants pay cash for the full amount. Assets (Cash) are increased by $5,000 and stockholders' equity (Retained Earnings) is increased by $5,000 from videography fees revenue. The amount was placed into Retained Earnings because revenues increase stockholders' equity while expenses decrease stockholders' equity. Later, you will learn how to use separate accounts for various revenues and expenses, rather than increasing and decreasing retained earnings. As always, total assets equal total liabilities plus stockholders' equity.

	Assets				=	Liabilities	+	Stockholder's Equity (SE)		
	Cash	Supplies	Land	Building		Accounts Payable	Common Stock	Additional Paid-In Capital	Retained Earnings
bal.	$29,500	$1,000	$40,000	$30,000	=	$500	$10,000	$90,000	
5.	+ $5,000								+ $5,000*
bal.	$34,500	$1,000	$40,000	$30,000	=	$500	$10,000	$90,000	$5,000
			$105,500					$105,500	

*Videotaping fees revenue of $5,000.

¶304.06   TRANSACTION 6: RECORDING REVENUES RECEIVED ON CREDIT

In some cases, customers arrange to make payment in the future. When this occurs, the company records the revenues when earned, even though payment has not been received. For example, a dance studio arranges for JK Productions to video its recital. The owner of the dance studio requests 320 copies of the video for a fee of $8,000. Instead of paying cash upon delivery, this customer arranges to make payment in 90 days. Assets and stockholders' equity would both increase. However, cash is not increased; instead, a different asset account, Accounts Receivable, would be increased.

	Assets					=	Liabilities	+	Stockholder's Equity (SE)		
	Cash	Accounts Receivable	Supplies	Land	Building		Accounts Payable	Common Stock	Additional Paid-In Capital	Retained Earnings
bal.	$34,500		$1,000	$40,000	$30,000	=	$500	$10,000	$90,000	$5,000
6.		+ $8,000								+ $8,000*
bal.	$34,500	$8,000	$1,000	$40,000	$30,000	=	$500	$10,000	$90,000	$13,000
			$113,500						$113,500	

*Videotaping fees revenue of $8,000.

After the videos are sold on account (on credit), total assets are $113,500; total liabilities are $500; and total stockholders' equity is $113,000.

¶304.07   TRANSACTION 7: RECEIVING PAYMENT ON CUSTOMER ACCOUNT

When the owner of the dance studio in Transaction 6 above sends in a payment, the amount of the customer's accounts receivable would be reduced accordingly. Assume that the customer sends in $4,000, half of the amount owed. As a result, Cash increases by that amount and Accounts Receivable decreases. Thus, total assets remain the same since only one side of the equation was affected. Stockholders' equity is unaffected by this transaction because revenue was recognized when earned (Transaction 5).

	Assets					=	Liabilities	+	Stockholder's Equity (SE)		
	Cash	Accounts Receivable	Supplies	Land	Building		Accounts Payable	Common Stock	Additional Paid-In Capital	Retained Earnings
bal.	$34,500	$8,000	$1,000	$40,000	$30,000	=	$500	$10,000	$90,000	$13,000
7.	+ $4,000	− $4,000								
bal.	$38,500	$4,000	$1,000	$40,000	$30,000	=	$500	$10,000	$90,000	$13,000
			$113,500						$113,500	

¶304.08

TRANSACTION 8: RECORDING EXPENSES PAID WITH CASH

When an expense is incurred, retained earnings is reduced by the amount of the expense. If the expense is paid in cash, then the cash account is decreased. If the expense is financed with credit, then a liability account is increased.

JK Productions pays wages in cash of $2,000 to the employees. Employees include Jay and Kay. This transaction would decrease assets (Cash) and stockholders' equity (Retained Earnings).

		Assets				=	Liabilities	+	Stockholder's Equity (SE)		
	Cash	Accounts Receivable	Supplies	Land	Building		Accounts Payable	Common Stock	Additional Paid-In Capital	Retained Earnings	
bal.	$38,500	$4,000	$1,000	$40,000	$30,000	=	$500	$10,000	$90,000	$13,000	
8.	– $2,000									– $2,000*	
bal.	$36,500	$4,000	$1,000	$40,000	$30,000	=	$500	$10,000	$90,000	$11,000	
			$111,500						$111,500		

*Wages Expense of $2,000

¶304.09

TRANSACTION 9: RECORDING EXPENSES PAID ON CREDIT

Jay and Kay decide to advertise their company's services on the radio. JK Productions incurs $200 in advertising expenses. Instead of paying for this expense immediately, Kay arranges to pay in the future (i.e., buys on credit). As a result, JK Productions would reduce stockholders' equity (Retained Earnings) and increase liabilities (Accounts Payable).

		Assets				=	Liabilities	+	Stockholder's Equity (SE)		
	Cash	Accounts Receivable	Supplies	Land	Building		Accounts Payable	Common Stock	Additional Paid-In Capital	Retained Earnings	
bal.	$36,500	$4,000	$1,000	$40,000	$30,000	=	$500	$10,000	$90,000	$11,000	
9.							+ $200			– $200*	
bal.	$36,500	$4,000	$1,000	$40,000	$30,000	=	$700	$10,000	$90,000	$10,800	
			$111,500						$111,500		

*Advertising Expense of $200

Note that the asset accounts were not affected by this credit transaction. Total liabilities increased by $200 and total stockholders' equity decreased by $200. Total liabilities and total stockholders' equity still equal total assets.

¶304.10

A dividend is the distribution of a corporation's earnings, usually cash, to its stockholders.

TRANSACTION 10: RECORDING DIVIDENDS

A **dividend** is the distribution of a corporation's earnings, usually in cash, to its stockholders. JK Productions declares and pays a dividend of $1,000. As a result, $1,000 in cash is removed from the company bank account and paid to the stockholders. Assets (Cash) are decreased and stockholders' equity (Retained Earnings) is decreased.

		Assets				=	Liabilities	+	Stockholder's Equity (SE)		
	Cash	Accounts Receivable	Supplies	Land	Building		Accounts Payable	Common Stock	Additional Paid-In Capital	Retained Earnings	
bal.	$36,500	$4,000	$1,000	$40,000	$30,000	=	$700	$10,000	$90,000	$10,800	
10.	– $1,000									– $1,000*	
bal.	$35,500	$4,000	$1,000	$40,000	$30,000	=	$700	$10,000	$90,000	$9,800	
			$110,500						$110,500		

*Dividends of $1,000.

Following distribution of the dividends, total assets equal $110,500; total liabilities equal $700; and total stockholders' equity equals $109,800. Dividends decrease Retained Earnings just as expenses decrease Retained Earnings. However, dividends are not considered an expense because they have a different purpose. Expenses are payments for goods and services that help generate revenues for the firm. Dividends are distributions of earnings in the form of assets (Cash) to stockholders.

¶304.11   RECAP

A recap of the 10 basic transactions is shown in Exhibit 3.4. To help you understand the transactions, they are shown horizontally according to the accounting equation.

Being a consumer, have you participated in any of these basic transactions?

Exhibit 3.4 RECAP OF BASIC TRANSACTIONS OF JK PRODUCTIONS

	Assets					=	Liabilities	+	Stockholder's Equity (SE)		
	Cash	Accounts Receivable	Supplies	Land	Building		Accounts Payable	Common Stock	Additional Paid-In Capital	Retained Earnings	
1.	100,000					=		10,000	90,000		
2.	− 70,000			+ 40,000	+ 30,000						
bal.	30,000			40,000	30,000	=		10,000	90,000		
3.			+ 1,000				+ 1,000				
bal.	30,000		1,000	40,000	30,000	=	1,000	10,000	90,000		
4.	− 500						− 500				
bal.	29,500		1,000	40,000	30,000	=	500	10,000	90,000		
5.	+ 5,000									(a) + 5,000	
bal.	34,500		1,000	40,000	30,000	=	500	10,000	90,000	5,000	
6.		+ 8,000								(b) + 8,000	
bal.	34,500	8,000	1,000	40,000	30,000	=	500	10,000	90,000	13,000	
7.	+ 4,000	− 4,000									
bal.	38,500	4,000	1,000	40,000	30,000	=	500	10,000	90,000	13,000	
8.	− 2,000									(c) − 2,000	
bal.	36,500	4,000	1,000	40,000	30,000	=	500	10,000	90,000	11,000	
9.							+ 200			(d) − 200	
bal.	36,500	4,000	1,000	40,000	30,000	=	700	10,000	90,000	10,800	
10.	− 1,000									(e) − 1,000	
bal.	35,500	4,000	1,000	40,000	30,000	=	700	10,000	90,000	9,800	

Notes: (a) Videography fees revenue of $5,000. (b) Videography fees revenue of $8,000. (c) Wages expense of $2,000. (d) Advertising expense of $200. (e) Dividends of $1,000.

Part II: Double-Entry Accounting

¶305   Debits, Credits, and the T Account

LEARNING OBJECTIVE 5: Understand the rationale behind double-entry accounting and the tools used to apply it.

T accounts are tools to help you visualize how accounts are affected by business transactions. The activity in any account can be displayed through a T account. The T account contains three components: (1) the account title, (2) the left side, and (3) the right side. The T account is so named because it resembles the letter T, as shown:

Account Title	
Debit	Credit

The terms debit and credit are used to specify the left and right sides of an account, respectively.

The terms **debit** and **credit** are used to specify the left and right sides of an account, respectively. Do not confuse the meaning of credit with the common definition: "an amount placed at a person's disposal." In accounting, credit is simply the right side of an account. An entry made to the right side of a T account is a credit, while an entry to the left side is a debit. Do not confuse the meaning of debit with the function of a debit card. Accountants use "debit" and "credit" to mean "left" and "right," nothing more.

To illustrate the use of a T account, refer to the transactions in Exhibit 3.4. The transactions affecting the Cash account are recorded as follows:

Cash	
(1) 100,000	(2) 70,000
(5) 5,000	(4) 500
(7) 4,000	(8) 2,000
	(10) 1,000
109,000	73,500
Bal. 35,500	

The difference between the debits and credits in an account is its balance.

The numbers in parentheses are the transaction numbers from the recap. For example, Transaction 1 – an investment of $100,000 in JK Productions in exchange for 10,000 shares of $1 par value stock – is a debit of $100,000 to Cash. In the above Cash account, total debits equal $109,000 and total credits equal $73,500. The difference between the debits and credits in an account is its **balance**; thus the balance of the Cash account is a debit balance of $35,500.

¶305.01   DOUBLE-ENTRY ACCOUNTING

Sometime during the Middle Ages, in an epiphany, an accountant devised the system of double-entry accounting. This system was then described in a book written by a Franciscan friar, Luca Pacioli, the "Father of Accounting." **Double-entry accounting** is based on the idea of balance; there are two aspects of every transaction. Each transaction will be recorded with at least one debit and at least one credit, such that the total dollar amount of debits equals the total dollar amount of credits. Rather than denoting transactions as multiple increases, multiple decreases, or a combination of increases and decreases, accountants use the terms "debit" and "credit." In accounting, debits must always equal credits. Depending on the account, a debit may mean an increase or decrease. The same holds true for a credit. The German philosopher, Goethe, described double-entry accounting as one of the greatest inventions of the human mind.

To illustrate the concept of double-entry accounting, assume McDonald's pays cash for a supply of paper cups; the Cash account is decreased and the Supplies account is increased. The use of debits and credits may appear a little confusing at first. Just remember: Debits and credits are simply a system of ensuring that when a transaction occurs, the impact of the transaction is recorded on at least two accounts.

Remember, for double-entry accounting, you must always keep in mind the following two things:

- The accounting equation: Asset = Liabilities + Stockholders' Equity
- The double-entry rule: Total Debits = Total Credits

For a more thorough explanation of how double-entry accounting came into being, read the boxed insert on the history of accounting.

Double-entry accounting is based on balance: for every transaction, the total dollar amount of debits equals credits.

FOCUS ON ACCOUNTING

History of Accounting

Double entry bookkeeping developed in Italy between 1200-1350. An Italian Franciscan friar, **Luca Pacioli**, wrote the first book about double entry accounting, printed in 1494. Friar Luca did not invent the double-entry system, but his book was instrumental to the spread of double entry accounting around the world. Pacioli became known as the "Father of Accounting." Later in life, he collaborated with and sometimes traveled with Leonardo da Vinci. Pacioli's famous book included most of the accounting cycle as we know it today. For example, he described the use of journals and ledgers, and he warned that a person should not go to sleep at night until the debits equaled the credits!

Early accountants played key roles in the progress of cities and nations. Accountants participated in the development of money and banking, plus developing confidence in capital markets, which were necessary for western capitalism. Today accountants are fundamental to the information revolution that is transforming the modern global economy.

¶305.02 RECORDING INCREASES AND DECREASES TO AN ACCOUNT

When the accounting system was invented hundreds of years ago, the rules for increasing and decreasing different types of accounts were also established. An increase to an asset is always recorded as a debit. A decrease to an asset is recorded as a credit. Remember the accounting equation: Assets = Liabilities + Stockholders' Equity. Because Liabilities and Stockholders' Equity accounts are on the opposite side of the equation from Assets, increases and decreases are treated differently. This is shown through the following illustration:

Assets		=	Liabilities		+	Stockholder's Equity	
Debit Increases (+)	Credit Decreases (−)		Debit Decreases (−)	Credit Increases (+)		Debit Decreases (−)	Credit Increases (+)

As you can see, the T accounts for Liabilities and Stockholders' Equity still have the debit column on the left and the credit column on the right. However, what increases and decreases the account's value is reversed from that of an Asset account. A debit in a liability or stockholders' equity account represents a decrease. A credit in these accounts represents an increase.

Debits increase an asset account and credits decrease an asset account.

As already stated, an increase to an asset account is a debit and a decrease is a credit. If you can remember this rule for asset accounts, you can remember that the opposite holds true for the accounts on the other side of the equation: liabilities and stockholders' equity.

¶305.03 STOCKHOLDERS' EQUITY ACCOUNTS

As you recall, stockholders' equity consists of stockholders' contributions and retained earnings. Accounts relating to contributions from stockholders are Common Stock and Additional Paid-in Capital. Accounts relating to earnings retained by the firm are Retained Earnings, revenues, expenses, and Dividends. Revenue and expenses affect stockholders' equity by increasing or decreasing retained earnings. The difference between revenues and expenses is net income (or net loss), which ultimately increases (or decreases) retained earnings.

The relationships among stockholders' equity accounts are shown in Exhibit 3.5. As you can see in Exhibit 3.5, revenue and expense accounts are shown on the income statement. The resulting net income is a component of the statement of retained earnings.

Exhibit 3.5 RELATIONSHIPS AMONG STOCKHOLDERS' EQUITY ACCOUNTS

INCOME STATEMENT

Revenues
– Expenses
_____
Net Income

STATEMENT OF RETAINED EARNINGS

Beginning balance of Retained Earnings
+ Net Income
– Dividends
_____
Ending balance of Retained Earnings

BALANCE SHEET

Assets
Liabilities
Stockholders' Equity
   * Common Stock
   * Additional Paid-in Captial
   * Retained Earnings

Investments by stockholders.

(Assets = Liabilities + Stockholders' Equity)

Retained earnings is essentially the sum total of net income (revenues minus expenses) less dividends for all the years in which a firm operates. Dividends is a type of stockholders' equity account that appears only on the statement of retained earnings. Dividends are payments to stockholders. Usually dividends are payments of cash, known as "cash dividends." Dividends may also be payments of additional shares of stock (known as "stock dividends") or property or investments of a firm (known as "property dividends").

The ending balance of Retained Earnings is a component of stockholders' equity on the balance sheet. Besides Retained Earnings, stockholders' equity is comprised of investments by stockholders plus Common Stock and Additional Paid-in Capital.

In review, stockholders' equity accounts include Common Stock, Additional Paid-in Capital, Retained Earnings, Dividends, revenues, and expenses. These accounts will be discussed with regard to double-entry accounting in the following paragraphs.

Revenues increase stockholders' equity. Thus, the rule for recording increases and decreases to a revenue account is the same as that for stockholders' equity:

- A decrease to revenue is a debit.
- An increase to revenue is a credit.

Expenses have the reverse effect on stockholders' equity; expenses decrease stockholders' equity. Thus, the rule for recording expenses is the reverse from that for revenues and stockholders' equity:

- An increase to expense is a debit.
- A decrease to expense is a credit.

Like expenses, dividends decrease stockholders' equity. Thus, the rule for recording dividends is the same as for expenses. The rules for revenue, expense, and dividend accounts can be illustrated as follows:

Revenues		Expenses		Dividends	
Debit	Credit	Debit	Credit	Debit	Credit
Decreases	Increases	Increases	Decreases	Increases	Decreases
(–)	(+)	(+)	(–)	(+)	(–)

Note that in the equation below dividends and expenses are the only accounts that are subtracted from stockholders' equity. Expenses and dividends are accounts that reduce stockholders' equity and thus have a reverse rule from the other stockholders' equity accounts. The other stockholders' equity accounts include common stock, additional paid-in capital, and retained earnings. Including all these accounts in the accounting model would result in the following equation:

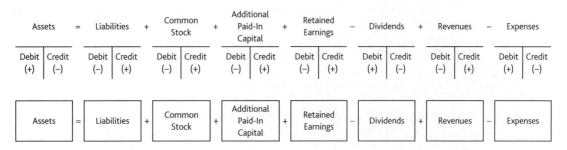

Assets	=	Liabilities	+	Common Stock	+	Additional Paid-In Capital	+	Retained Earnings	–	Dividends	+	Revenues	–	Expenses
Debit (+) | Credit (–)		Debit (–) | Credit (+)		Debit (–) | Credit (+)		Debit (–) | Credit (+)		Debit (–) | Credit (+)		Debit (+) | Credit (–)		Debit (–) | Credit (+)		Debit (+) | Credit (–)

Assets	=	Liabilities	+	Common Stock	+	Additional Paid-In Capital	+	Retained Earnings	–	Dividends	+	Revenues	–	Expenses

Incorporating the impact of debits and credits into the equation, we can show the relationships as follows:

Thus far we have used debit and credit referring to the left and right side of an account. Depending on the account, these sides represent an increase or decrease to the account. We will now make the transition of referring directly to that increase or decrease when using the terms "debit" and "credit." For example, the debit side of an expense account represents an increase to the expense. Thus, if we were to say "debit expense $100," that means the expense account is increased by $100.

¶305.04

APPLYING DOUBLE-ENTRY RULES

To illustrate the implementation of double-entry rules, assume that a McDonald's franchise obtains a $1,000 cash loan from its bank to pay for landscaping. The loan is in the legal form of a promissory note ("promise to pay"). The transaction increases assets (Cash) by $1,000 and also increases liabilities (Notes Payable) by the same amount. To record this transaction, the firm debits (increases) the Cash account for $1,000 and, at the same time, credits (increases) the Notes Payable, a liability account. In T accounts, the transaction is recorded as follows:

	Assets	=	Liabilities	+	Stockholder's Equity

Cash	=	Notes Payable
1,000		1,000

Remember that debits are always listed on the left and credits on the right. As shown, the total debits (in this case, to Cash for $1,000) are equal to total credits (in this case, to Notes Payable for $1,000). The accounting equation, Assets = Liabilities + Stockholders' Equity, remains in balance because the assets and liabilities were each increased by the same amount, $1,000. Stockholders' equity was not affected by this transaction.

When the McDonald's franchise repays its loan to the bank, the payment of $1,000 will reduce the Cash account by $1,000 and reduce the Notes Payable account by the same amount. The transaction is recorded in the T accounts by a credit (decrease) to Cash of $1,000 and a debit (decrease) to Notes Payable of $1,000. The result of the two transactions, the loan and its repayment, are recorded in the accounts as follows:

Cash		Notes Payable	
(1) 1,000 | (2) 1,000		(2) 1,000 | (1) 1,000	

(1) Borrow $1,000 from bank.
(2) Repay $1,000 to bank.

As before, the accounting equation remains in balance with total debits equaling total credits.

Business transactions are recorded as they occur. This enables a business firm to consider and analyze the impact of ongoing business operations. People working throughout the firm, in various departments such as marketing, finance, and production, can review the accounting records to see the financial status of the company and thereby plan for the future. The accounting records enable a firm to analyze whether a new venture or product is financially successful. For example, when McDonald's introduced a new line of salads served with chicken and Newman's Own salad dressing, management kept a close watch on accounting records to discern if sales revenue was high enough to cover the costs associated with the new salads. Since space is limited within the McDonald's restaurant for storage and preparation of food items, management may set a specific profit requirement for a new food item in order to keep it on the menu.

The new line of salads at McDonald's requires an outlay of cash for initial advertising and start-up costs, such as seeking new suppliers, developing new packaging, and possibly additional tools for food preparation. Thus, it may take months before these start-up costs are recovered and for the new product to yield a profit. Several people within McDonald's will review the accounting records regarding the new salad line. For one, top management will be looking for an upward trend in sales revenue to discern whether the new line has the potential to earn a profit and help bring in customers. Second, the marketing department will view sales transactions to determine if the new line needs additional promotion. Third, the production department will analyze the accounting records to determine if the new line's distribution system is cost efficient and if the budgeted amount of ingredients is being purchased.

One way that production uses accounting data is to compare budgeted and actual costs. For example, if tomato purchases are in excess of the amount budgeted, the predicted profit target may not be met. Excessive use of tomatoes may be caused by incorrect preparation of the salad; thus, the personnel department may be called upon to improve employee training. Or, there could be unnecessary waste of tomatoes due to improper storage, in which case management would need to improve storage facilities. As you can see, several departments within a firm make use of the accounting records of business transactions for various reasons.

Now that we have looked at the reasoning behind the double-entry accounting system, let's examine the format for recording a business transaction.

> *Balance is a part of everything in life, including accounting: Debits = Credits. Do you ever struggle to keep things in balance?*

¶306 Recording General Journal Entries

LEARNING OBJECTIVE 6: Describe how to record a business transaction in the general journal.

> *A general journal entry, or journal entry, records a transaction by showing both the debit and credit.*

As previously stated, when a business transaction occurs, the first step is to evaluate the transaction in order to identify when it occurred (recognition), the dollar amount (valuation), and accounts affected (classification.) The next step is to record the transaction in the general journal, sometimes referred to as the "book of original entry." A **general journal entry**, often simply called a "**journal entry**," is a means of recording a transaction, showing both the debit and credit in one place. Do not confuse the general journal with the general ledger, previously described as containing all of a company's accounts. The general journal is a simpler journal used to record all transactions chronologically so that individual transactions and errors can be more easily identified. The process of recording journal entries is called "**journalizing**."

Journalizing is carried out using the following steps:

1. Write the date of the transaction in the date column.
2. Write the title of the account to be debited and the amount of the debit on the first line. This may take more than one line if there is more than one account to debit.
3. Indent and write the title of the account and the amount to be credited on the next line. Again, more than one line will be needed if more than one account is to be credited.
4. Beneath the debit and credit lines, write a short explanation of the transaction.

For example, a $1,000 bank loan on April 1 is recorded as a general journal entry as follows:

> *You may currently have your own version of "journalizing" your inflows and outflows of money. Why is it important to keep a record?*

		Debit	Credit
April 1	Cash	1,000	
	Notes payable		1,000
	Loan received from bank.		

The next step in processing a business transaction is to post the transaction into the general ledger.

¶307

Posting to the General Ledger

LEARNING OBJECTIVE 7: Explain the function of the general ledger

Posting is the act of transferring information from the general journal to the general ledger.

Periodically, the amounts in the journal entries are transferred to their corresponding accounts in the general ledger. This step of transferring information from the general journal to the general ledger is referred to as "**posting**." To learn more about the process of posting, see the Appendix to this chapter.

The general ledger contains a running balance of each account. The general ledger includes all accounts: assets, liabilities, stockholders' equity, revenues, and expenses. Periodically, the balances of all the general ledger accounts are listed in an accounting report called the trial balance.

¶308

Creating a Trial Balance

LEARNING OBJECTIVE 8: Prepare a trial balance.

The trial balance lists the balances of all accounts to determine if total debits equal total credits.

Just as its name suggests, the **trial balance** is a "trial" (or test) listing of accounts to determine if the debits equal the credits. The trial balance helps ensure the accuracy of the accounting records prior to preparation of the financial statements. All accounts are included in the trial balance; account balances are obtained from the general ledger. The accounts on the trial balance are listed in the same order as they are listed in the chart of accounts and general ledger: assets, liabilities, stockholders' equity, revenues, and then expenses.

A trial balance does not guarantee accuracy of all the accounting records; it only guarantees that total debits equal total credits. For example, if McDonald's loan of $1,000 in the prior illustration were erroneously recorded as a $100 debit to Cash and a $100 credit to Notes Payable, then debits still equal credits. The trial balance would still be in balance, but the total would be incorrect by $900. However, if the debit to Cash were entered as $1,000 and the credit to Notes Payable incorrectly entered as $100, then debits would not equal credits. The trial balance would reveal an error because total debits would be $900 more than total credits.

The steps in the double-entry accounting process, from evaluating the transaction to preparing the trial balance, are shown in Exhibit 3.6. The format of a general journal and a general ledger can vary to some degree depending on the preferences or needs of the firm. The exhibit shows a simple format for both the general journal and general ledger.

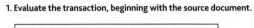

Exhibit 3.6 STEPS IN THE ACCOUNTING PROCESS

1. Evaluate the transaction, beginning with the source document.

AT&T TELEPHONE BILL	
Feb. 9, 20Y1	
AT&T rate plan	$35
Taxes and surcharges	5
Total amount due	40

2. Record the transaction in the General Journal.
Follow the rules of double-entry accounting:
* Assets = Liabilities + Stockholders' equity
* Total Debits = Total Credits

GENERAL JOURNAL

Date	Description	Debit	Credit
20Y1			
Feb. 9	Phone Expense	40	
	Cash		40
	Payment of phone bill.		

3. Post the journal entry into the General Ledger.

GENERAL LEDGER

Cash   Account No.   101

				Bala	nce
Date	Item	Debit	Credit	Debit	Credit
20Y1					
Feb. 3	Customer Payment	160		160	
9	Phone Bill		40	120	

GENERAL LEDGER

Phone Expense   Account No.   207

				Bala	nce
Date	Item	Debit	Credit	Debit	Credit
20Y1					
Jan. 8	Monthly Bill	40		40	
Feb. 9	Monthly Bill	40		80	

4. Prepare the Trial Balance.

TRIAL BALANCE

Account	Date	Debit	Credit
Cash		XX	
A/R		XX	
Stock			XX
Dividends		XX	
Phone Exp.		XX	
		XX	XX

The steps in the double-entry accounting process can be performed manually on paper documents or they can be done in a computerized accounting system. A general journal book and a general ledger book can both be purchased from an office supply store. Accounting software, such as QuickBooks or Peachtree, can also be purchased and used to record accounting transactions. These software products are described in the insert on Accounting Software. A simple accounting system can even be set up in an Excel spreadsheet.

FOCUS ON TECHNOLOGY

ACCOUNTING SOFTWARE

QuickBooks

Manufactured by Intuit, QuickBooks accounting software is customized for different types of users. For example, QuickBooks: Pro provides accounting tools for small business financial management; QuickBooks: Contractor Edition is specialized for building contractors; and QuickBooks Premier: Accountant Edition is customized to help accountants serve their clients. More information about QuickBooks can be obtained from their website.

Peachtree

Manufactured by Best Software, Peachtree is easy-to-use accounting software for all types of businesses ranging from 1 to 50 employees. Using a double-entry accounting system, Peachtree is designed to enable people with very limited accounting knowledge to set up and use an accounting system. The software provides a complete set of accounting functions, including payroll, inventory, job costing, and time and billing. For larger firms, Peachtree has a special edition available. Additional information is available on its website.

¶308.01 NORMAL ACCOUNT BALANCES

The normal balance of an account is its usual balance in regard to being a debit or a credit.

The **normal balance** of an account is its usual balance in regard to being a debit or a credit. The side (debit or credit) that increases the account determines what the normal balance is. For example, an asset is increased with a debit, thus the normal balance for an asset account is a debit balance. For liability accounts, the normal balance is a credit balance since a liability account is increased with a credit. For stockholders' equity accounts, the normal balance is a credit balance.

¶308.02 CORRECTING ERRORS

The trial balance helps ensure the accuracy of the accounting records in two ways. The trial balance enables you to check for a definite error or a possible error. There is a definite error if the total debits do not equal total credits. There is a possible error if an account does not have a normal balance. Note, this is only a possible error, as there are occasions when legitimate, but unusual, business transactions result in abnormal account balances.

In the case where debits do not equal credits, you should perform the following steps, until you find the error:

- First, re-add the columns to ensure that a simple addition error is not to blame.
- Second, double-check that the general ledger account balances are correctly shown in the trial balance.
- Third, re-compute the balances in the general ledger to ensure that they are computed correctly.
- If you still have not found the cause of the error after the first three steps, review all journal entries and corresponding postings, looking for the journal entry where the debit portion does not equal the credit portion.

FOCUS ON TECHNOLOGY

Using Microsoft Excel: Preparing a Trial Balance

Using Excel, we will create Exhibit 3.7, the trial balance for JK Productions. If you need further instruction at any point, refer to the Excel information in the Appendix in Chapter 2.

1. **Identification Area:** In an Excel worksheet, set up an identification area like the one in Exhibit 3.7.
2. **Input Area:** Enter the account names and numbers from the input area shown in Exhibit 3.7.
3. **Output Area:** Type the trial balance heading shown in the exhibit onto your worksheet using the merge and center command. (Refer to the "Using Excel" box in Chapter 1, if needed.) Be sure to also type in the column headings, Debit and Credit.
4. **Account Names:** Instead of manually retyping the account names, they can be copied and pasted from the Input Area. **Note:** do not copy the numbers. To copy and paste, highlight the cells containing the account names, then click on the copy icon. Next, click on the cell within the output area in which you want the first account to appear, and then click on the paste icon.
5. **Account Values:** Remember, we want the output area to be formula driven so it can be manipulated by changing values within the input area. Thus, use formulas to compute the values for each account. For instance, the formula for Cash (=D12) should be typed into cell D31.
6. **Automatic Sums:** We want to sum each column in the trial balance to confirm that debits equal credits. Excel will automatically sum the numbers within cells you select. To do so, highlight the cells in the Debit column (cells D31 through D43) and click on the autosum icon (Σ). Instead of using the icon, you can type in a formula. The formula to add up the numbers within the Credit column is: =sum(F36:F40).

A balance of debits and credits in the trial balance helps ensure, but does not guarantee, that journal entries are accurately recorded. Do you know why this is true?

Exhibit 3.7 EXAMPLE WORKSHEET: TRIAL BALANCE

	A	B	C	D	E	F	G	H
1	**IDENTIFICATION AREA:**							
2	File name: Trial Balance.xls							
3	Designer: B. Quick							
4	File created:							
5	Input Required		Cash, Accounts Receivable, Supplies, Land, Building,					
6			Accounts Payable, Common Stock, Additional Paid-In Capital,					
7			Retained Earnings, Videography Fees Revenue, Wages Expense,					
8			Advertising Expense, and Dividends					
9	Output Required:							
10								
11	**INPUT AREA:**							
12	Cash			35,000				
13	Accounts Receivable			4,000				
14	Supplies			1,000				
15	Land			40,000				
16	Building			30,000				
17	Accounts Payable			700				
18	Common Stock			10,000				
19	Additional Paid-In Capital			90,000				
20	Retained Earnings			0				
21	Videography Fees Revenue			13,000				
22	Wages Expense			2,000				
23	Advertising Expense			200				
24	Dividends			1,000				
25								
26	**OUTPUT AREA:**							
27			JK Productions					
28			Trial Balance					
29			June 30, 20Y1					
30				**Debit**	**Credit**			
31	Cash			$35,000				
32	Accounts Receivable			4,000				
33	Supplies			1,000				
34	Land			40,000				
35	Building			30,000				
36	Accounts Payable				$700			
37	Common Stock				10,000			
38	Additional Paid-In Capital				90,000			
39	Retained Earnings				0			
40	Videography Fees Revenue				13,000			
41	Wages Expense			2,000				
42	Advertising Expense			200				
43	Dividends			1,000				
44	TOTAL			$113,700	$113,700			

¶308.02

¶309

Concluding Remarks

We began this chapter with the question: How does McDonald's keep track of all the business transactions generated by its restaurants around the world? Thanks to a standardized accounting system entitled double-entry accounting, that's how. You learned how to record a business transaction using the double-entry system. These transactions were recorded in the general journal and posted to the general ledger. You learned about various accounts and the relationships between them.

Now that you've learned how transactions affect different accounts, you are ready to see the final steps in the accounting process that result in the financial statements. That is the focus of the next chapter.

¶310

Chapter Review

LEARNING OBJECTIVE 1

Describe how an understanding of accounting transaction processing is beneficial to people within and outside the firm.

While the company carries out business activities, such as purchasing merchandise from suppliers and then selling that merchandise to customers, the company's accountants track and report these transactions. The modern-day double-entry accounting system facilitates effective business operations by accounting for business transactions. Understanding basic transactions enables managers to see the big picture – how all departments within a firm contribute to the successful completion of a business transaction. A general knowledge of the accounting process helps the average investor know what to look for in choosing companies that will be good investments. Accounting is critical for company financial reporting, which is the basis for many important activities such as raising capital for business expansion, making good lending decisions, and selecting companies in which to invest.

LEARNING OBJECTIVE 2

Implement the steps of recognition, valuation, and classification in processing a business transaction.

The accounting transaction process is the measurement of business transactions. The accountant determines when the transaction occurred (recognition), the dollar amount of the transaction (valuation), and how to categorize the transaction (classification).

LEARNING OBJECTIVE 3

Understand the relationships among the accounts in the chart of accounts.

All the accounts for a business are in the general ledger; each account is assigned a unique number. The list of account numbers and corresponding names is called the "chart of accounts." Accounts are classified as assets, liabilities, stockholders' equity, revenues, and expenses. The accounting equation shows the relationship of these accounts: Assets = Liabilities + Stockholders' Equity. The accounting equation must always stay in balance.

LEARNING OBJECTIVE 4

Record 10 basic accounting transactions and comprehend how each affects the accounting equation.

Basic accounting transactions include: setting up a business, purchasing assets by paying cash, purchasing assets with debt financing, paying liabilities, recording revenues, receiving payments on customer accounts, recording expenses, and recording dividends. The chapter goes through a step-by-step example showing how these 10 transactions affect the accounting equation.

LEARNING OBJECTIVE 5

Understand the rationale behind double-entry accounting and the tools used to apply it.

The double-entry system of accounting was described in a book written by Luca Pacioli in 1494. The terms "debit" and "credit" are used to specify the left and right sides of an account, respectively. An entry made to the right side of an account is a credit, while an entry to the left side is a debit. Rules for making debits and credits can be illustrated as follows:

Assets		Liabilities		Stockholder's Equity	
Debit Increases (+)	Credit Decreases (−)	Debit Decreases (−)	Credit Increases (+)	Debit Decreases (−)	Credit Increases (+)

¶310

LEARNING OBJECTIVE 6

Describe how to record a business transaction in the general journal.

After a business transaction occurs, it is recorded as a general journal entry. A general journal entry, often simply called a "journal entry," is a means of recording a transaction, showing both the debit and credit in one place. The process of recording journal entries is called "journalizing."

LEARNING OBJECTIVE 7

Explain the function of the general ledger.

Periodically, the amounts in the journal entries are transferred to their corresponding accounts in the general ledger. This step is referred to as "posting," which is transferring information from the general journal to the general ledger. The general ledger contains a running balance of each account.

LEARNING OBJECTIVE 8

Prepare a trial balance.

Intermittently, the balances in all the general ledger accounts are listed in an accounting report called the "trial balance." Just as its name suggests, the trial balance is a "trial" (or test) listing of accounts to determine if the debits equal the credits. The trial balance helps ensure the accuracy of this equality in the accounting records prior to preparation of the financial statements.

¶311

Glossary

Accounting transaction process

The accounting transaction process is the evaluation of business transactions.

Accounts

Accounts are the storage units for accounting data and are used to accumulate amounts for similar transactions.

Additional paid-in capital

When a corporation sells stock for more than its par value, the amount paid over par value is called "additional paid-in capital" or "paid-in capital in excess of par."

Balance

The difference between the debits and credits in an account is its balance.

Business transactions

Business transactions are economic events that affect the financial situation of the firm.

Chart of accounts

The chart of accounts is a list of all of a firm's account numbers and their matching names.

Classification

Classification is determining which categories or accounts are affected by a business transaction.

Credit

A credit is an entry to the right side of an account.

Debit

A debit is an entry to the left side of an account.

Dividends

A dividend is the distribution of a corporation's earnings, usually cash, to its stockholders.

Double-entry accounting

Double-entry accounting is based on the idea of maintaining two key aspects of balance for every transaction. One of these is that each transaction must be recorded with at least one debit and one credit, and the second aspect holds that the total dollar amount of debits equals the total dollar amount of credits.

General journal entry

A general journal entry, also called a journal entry, is a means of recording the transactions of a firm in terms of debits and credits.

General ledger

A general ledger contains all the accounts for a business firm.

Journal entry

A journal entry, also called a "general journal entry," is a means of recording the transactions of a firm in terms of debits and credits.

Journalizing

Journalizing is the process of recording journal entries.

Luca Pacioli

Luca Pacioli is called the "Father of Accounting." He wrote the first book on double-entry accounting. He lived from 1447-1517.

Normal balance

The normal balance of an account is its usual balance in regard to being a debit or a credit. The side (debit or credit) that increases the account determines what the normal balance is.

Par value

Par value is an arbitrary amount assigned to each share of stock. Many states require that stocks have a par value to provide a baseline or a minimum amount of legal capital to pay creditors.

Posting

Posting involves transferring transaction information from the general journal to the accounts in the general ledger. Posting updates the account balances in the general ledger.

Real accounts

The asset, liability, and stockholders' equity accounts are called "real" or "permanent" accounts because the balances in these accounts at the end of one accounting period appear in the balance sheet and are carried forward to the subsequent period.

Recognition

Recognition is determining when a business transaction occurred.

Sales invoice

The sales invoice documents information regarding the customer, items ordered, price, and delivery.

Source document

A source document is evidence that a transaction has occurred, such as a sales invoice or a bill.

Trial balance

The trial balance is a trial listing of accounts to determine if the total debits equal the total credits.

Valuation

Valuation involves determining the dollar amount of a business transaction.

¶312

Appendix: A Case Study of Double-Entry Accounting

This appendix provides a case study on journalizing and posting using the ten basic accounting transactions. For each transaction, you will see the corresponding general journal entry and how the entry is posted to the general ledger.

¶312.01

CASE STUDY: JOURNALIZING AND POSTING

In review, a business transaction is evaluated to determine when it occurred, the dollar amount involved, and which accounts are affected. Transactions are recorded in the general journal and then posted to the general ledger.

An up-to-date general ledger is immensely helpful to business executives for the purpose of managing company operations. For example, the marketing manager can evaluate sales-to-date by checking the balance in the sales revenue account in the general ledger. Current year sales can be compared to prior year sales for the same date. The manager can answer the question: Is the firm doing better or worse than last year?

¶312.01.01

Transaction 1: Setting Up a Business.

As described earlier, Jay and Kay Morgan set up a business with an investment of $100,000 in JK Productions on June 1. In return stockholders received 10,000 shares of $1 par value common stock. The general journal entry for JK Productions is recorded as follows:

		Dr.	Cr.
June 1	Cash	100,000	
	Common Stock		10,000
	Additional Paid-In Capital		90,000
	Initial investment in the corporation.		

This entry is later posted to the general ledger as follows. We will use a very simple general ledger format for our illustrations.

Cash				Account No. 101	
				Balance	
Date		Debit	Credit	Debit	Credit
June	**1**	**100,000**		100,000	

Common Stock				Account No. 301	
				Balance	
Date		Debit	Credit	Debit	Credit
June	**1**		**10,000**		10,000

Additional Paid-In Capital				Account No. 305	
				Balance	
Date		Debit	Credit	Debit	Credit
June	**1**		**90,000**		90,000

As shown, Cash is debited for $100,000. Cash is an asset and a debit to an asset account represents an increase. Common Stock, a stockholders' equity account, is credited for $10,000 (10,000 shares at $1 par value each). Remember that a credit to a stockholders' equity account represents an increase. The other stockholders' equity account, Additional Paid-In Capital, is credited (increased) for $90,000, which is the difference between the paid amount of $100,000 and the par value of $10,000.

Knowing how much money the company started with is imperative to investors. This amount must be kept separate from the earnings that are reinvested in the company. Many small businesses fail each year due to starting with insufficient funds.

¶312.01.02   ## Transaction 2: Purchasing Assets by Paying Cash

On June 2, JK Productions purchases land for $40,000 and a building for $30,000. Land is debited (increased) for $40,000 and the building account is debited (increased) for $30,000. Cash is paid for both assets. Consequently, Cash is credited (reduced) for $70,000. Note that land, buildings, and cash are all assets. The journal entry is recorded as follows:

	Dr.	Cr.
June 2 Land	40,000	
Building	30,000	
Cash		70,000
Purchase of land and building.		

The entry for June 2 is posted to the general ledger as follows:

Cash				Account No. 101	
				Balance	
Date	Debit	Credit	Debit	Credit	
June	1	100,000		100,000	
June	2		70,000	30,000	

Land				Account No. 108	
				Balance	
Date	Debit	Credit	Debit	Credit	
June	2	40,000		40,000	

Building				Account No. 111	
				Balance	
Date	Debit	Credit	Debit	Credit	
June	2	30,000		30,000	

As shown, the Land account and the Building account in the general ledger are posted with a debit (increase) of $40,000 and $30,000, respectively. The Cash account is posted with a credit (decrease) of $70,000.

Keeping track of assets owned by the company is critical for operations. This is especially useful for managing operations. Managers can answer vital questions such as: How much cash is available for use?

¶312.01.03   ## Transaction 3: Purchasing Assets on Credit

On June 6, JK Productions purchases supplies on credit for $1,000. Thus, the asset account, Supplies, is debited (increased) for $1,000 and the liability account, Accounts Payable, is credited (increased) for $1,000. The journal entry is as follows:

	Dr.	Cr.
June 6 Supplies	1,000	
Accounts Payable		1,000
Purchase of supplies on credit.		

The entry for June 6 is posted to the general ledger as follows:

Supplies					Account No. 105	
					Balance	
Date		Debit	Credit	Debit	Credit	
June	**6**	**1,000**		1,000		

Accounts Payable					Account No. 201	
					Balance	
Date		Debit	Credit	Debit	Credit	
June	**6**		**1,000**		1,000	

Company managers need to know the amount of supplies on hand so they can order more when supplies run low. Managing accounts payable is also important. Knowing how much the company owes and paying off debts is essential for maintaining a good credit record.

¶312.01.04   Transaction 4: Paying a Liability

On June 9, JK Productions pays $500 of the amount owed on the accounts payable. Cash is credited (decreased) and Accounts Payable, a liability, is debited (decreased). The journal entry is recorded as follows:

		Dr.	Cr.
June 9	Accounts Payable	500	
	Cash		500
	Payment on accounts payable.		

The entry for June 9 is posted to the general ledger as follows:

Cash					Account No. 101	
					Balance	
Date		Debit	Credit	Debit	Credit	
June	1	100,000		100,000		
	3		70,000	30,000		
June	**9**		**500**	29,500		

Accounts Payable					Account No. 201	
					Balance	
Date		Debit	Credit	Debit	Credit	
June	6		1,000		1,000	
June	**9**	**500**			500	

¶312.01.05   Transaction 5: Recording Revenues Received in Cash

On June 12, JK Productions earns $5,000 by video recording a football camp. The customers pay $5,000 in cash to JK Productions. The transaction is recorded with a debit (increase) to Cash and a credit (increase) to Videography Fees Revenue. The journal entry is as follows:

		Dr.	Cr.
June 12	Cash	5,000	
	Videography Fees Revenue		5,000
	Receipt of cash for services provided		

The entry for June 12 is posted to the general ledger as follows:

Cash				Account No. 101	
				Balance	
Date		Debit	Credit	Debit	Credit
June	1	100,000		100,000	
	3		70,000	30,000	
	9		500	29,500	
June	12	5,000		34,500	

Videography Fees Revenue				Account No. 401	
				Balance	
Date		Debit	Credit	Debit	Credit
June	12		5,000		5,000

Keeping track of revenues provides marketing managers with the knowledge of which areas of the business are lucrative. High revenues may result in more company resources and emphasis being put on that area which is bringing in sales. Low revenues may point to an area of the business that needs revitalization in order to increase sales, or perhaps downsizing in order to decrease costs. Keeping track of revenue is also of great interest to investors who want to know whether the company is growing or not.

¶312.01.06 Transaction 6: Recording Revenues Received on Credit

On June 13, JK Productions provides videos of a dance recital. The owner of the dance studio arranges to pay at a future date. In other words, the services are provided on credit. Selling on credit is also called "on account," meaning that an account receivable must be established. The fee is $8,000 and the general journal entry shows a debit (increase) to Accounts Receivable and a credit (increase) to Videography Fees Revenue.

		Dr.	Cr.
June 13	Accounts Receivable	8,000	
	Videography Fees Revenue		8,000
	Videography services provided on credit.		

The entry for June 13 is posted to the general ledger as follows:

Accounts Receivable				Account No. 102	
				Balance	
Date		Debit	Credit	Debit	Credit
June	13	8,000		8,000	

Videography Fees Revenue				Account No. 401	
				Balance	
Date		Debit	Credit	Debit	Credit
June	12		5,000		5,000
June	13		8,000		13,000

Company managers must keep track of amounts owed by customers. Based on this information, bills requesting payment are periodically sent to customers.

¶312.01.07   Transaction 7: Receiving Payment on Customer Account

On June 14, the owner of the dance studio, with the $8,000 account receivable, sends in payment of $4,000. Consequently, Cash is debited (increased) and Accounts Receivable is credited (decreased). The result is that the customer now owes only $4,000. You should note that this transaction has no effect on revenues because Videography Fees Revenues was previously recorded on June 13. The journal entry for the customer payment is as follows.

		Dr.	Cr.
June 14	Cash	4,000	
	Accounts Receivable		4,000
	Customer payment received on account.		

The entry for June 14 is posted to the general ledger as follows:

Cash				Account No. 101	
				Balance	
Date		Debit	Credit	Debit	Credit
June	1	100,000		100,000	
	3		70,000	30,000	
	9		500	29,500	
	12	5,000		34,500	
June	**14**	**4,000**		38,500	

Accounts Receivable				Account No. 102	
				Balance	
Date		Debit	Credit	Debit	Credit
June	13	8,000		8,000	
June	**14**		**4,000**	4,000	

Maintaining up to date customer accounts is crucial. If a customer fails to pay off amounts owed, then the company must stop selling on credit to that customer.

¶312.01.08   Transaction 8: Recording Expenses Paid with Cash

On June 15, JK Productions pays wages of $2,000 to employees. This expense is recorded in the general journal as a debit (increase) to Wages Expense and a credit (decrease) to Cash. Wages Expense is an expense account because it represents a payment necessary for business operations, and results in a decrease in stockholders' equity.

		Dr.	Cr.
June 15	Wages Expense	2,000	
	Cash		2,000
	Employees wages are paid.		

The entry for June 15 is posted as follows:

Cash				Account No. 101	
				Balance	
Date		Debit	Credit	Debit	Credit
June	1	100,000		100,000	
	3		70,000	30,000	
	9		500	29,500	
	12	5,000		34,500	
	14	4,000		38,500	
June	15		2,000	36,500	

Wages Expense				Account No. 501	
				Balance	
Date		Debit	Credit	Debit	Credit
June	15	2,000		2,000	

Managers must know at all times how much cash is available for paying bills and purchasing items necessary for company operations. This requires meticulous attention to cash inflows and outflows.

¶312.01.09   Transaction 9: Recording Expenses Paid with Credit

On June 29, JK Productions receives a bill of $200 for advertising. Jay arranges to pay this bill in the future. Consequently, JK Productions must show a liability for the amount owed to the radio station for advertising. In the general journal, JK Productions records a debit (increase) to Advertising Expense and a credit (increase) to Accounts Payable.

		Dr.	Cr.
June 29	Advertising Expense	200	
	Accounts Payable		200
	Advertising purchased on credit.		

The entry for June 29 is posted to the general ledger as follows:

Advertising Expense				Account No. 509	
				Balance	
Date		Debit	Credit	Debit	Credit
June	29	200		200	

Accounts Payable				Account No. 201	
				Balance	
Date		Debit	Credit	Debit	Credit
June	6		1,000		1,000
	9	500			500
June	29		200		700

¶312.01.10　Transaction 10: Recording Dividends

On June 30, JK Productions declares and pays a dividend of $1,000. This transaction is recorded in the general journal with a debit (increase) to Dividends and a credit (decrease) to Cash. Dividends is a stockholders' equity account.

		Dr.	Cr.
June 30	Dividends	1,000	
	Cash		1,000
	Payments of dividends.		

The entry for June 30 is posted to the general ledger as follows:

Cash				Account No. 101	
				Balance	
Date		Debit	Credit	Debit	Credit
June	1	100,000		100,000	
	3		70,000	30,000	
	9		500	29,500	
	12	5,000		34,500	
	14	4,000		38,500	
	15		2,000	36,500	
June	**30**		**1,000**	35,500	

Dividends				Account No. 303	
				Balance	
Date		Debit	Credit	Debit	Credit
June	**30**	**1,000**		1,000	

The owners (stockholders) of a company are concerned with how much money is paid to them through dividends. Stock listings on financial websites, such as Yahoo!Finance (finance.yahoo.com), typically show the dollar amount of a company's dividend along with the dividend as a percentage of stock price.

¶312.02 CASE STUDY: GENERAL LEDGER BALANCES

After posting all the general journal entries of JK Productions, previously described, the T accounts in Exhibit 3.A summarize the balances in the general ledger accounts.

Exhibit 3.A T ACCOUNTS REPRESENTING THE GENERAL LEDGER OF JK PRODUCTIONS

ASSETS

Cash

June 1	100,000	June 2	70,000
June 12	5,000	June 9	500
June 14	4,000	June 15	2,000
		June 30	1,000
	109,000		73,500
Bal.	35,500		

Accounts Receivable

June 13	8,000	June 14	4,000
Bal.	4,000		

Supplies

June 6	1,000	
Bal.	1,000	

Land

June 2	40,000	
Bal.	40,000	

Building

June 2	30,000	
Bal.	30,000	

LIABILITIES AND STOCKHOLDER'S EQUITY

Accounts Payable

June 9	500	June 6	1,000
		June 29	200
	500		1,200
		Bal.	700

Common Stock

	June 1	10,000
	Bal.	10,000

Additional Paid-In Capital

	June 1	90,000
	Bal.	90,000

Retained Earnings

	Bal.	0

Videotaping Fees Revenue

	June 12	5,000
	June 13	8,000
	Bal.	13,000

Wages Expense

June 15	2,000	
Bal.	2,000	

Advertising Expense

June 29	200	
Bal.	200	

Dividends

June 30	1,000	
Bal.	1,000	

¶312.03   CASE STUDY: TRIAL BALANCE

As previously described, the trial balance is prepared periodically to ensure that total debits equal total credits. The trial balance is not a trial "balance sheet." A trial balance prepared for JK Productions on June 30 is shown in Exhibit 3.B.

Exhibit 3.B JK PRODUCTIONS TRIAL BALANCE JUNE 30, 20Y1		
	Debit	**Credit**
Cash	$35,500	
Accounts Receivable	4,000	
Supplies	1,000	
Land	40,000	
Building	30,000	
Accounts Payable		$700
Common Stock		10,000
Additional Paid-In Capital		90,000
Retained Earnings		0
Videography Fees Revenue		13,000
Wages Expense	2,000	
Advertising Expense	200	
Dividends	1,000	
	$13,700	$13,700

As shown in Exhibit 3.B, each account is listed on the left side in the first column. Debit amounts and credit amounts are shown in the second and third columns, respectively. For JK Productions, total debits equal total credits equal $113,700. At this time, Retained Earnings has a zero balance. The account balance will not remain zero. Retained Earnings will be increased later by the amount of the firm's net income or decreased by the amount of a net loss. This is described in Chapter 4.

¶313 # Chapter Assignments

QUESTIONS

1. **[Obj. 1]** When was the double-entry system invented as a method of accounting?

2. **[Obj. 2]** What is the function of financial statements?

3. **[Obj. 2]** Define business transactions.

4. **[Obj. 2]** What does the accountant determine in the accounting transaction process? What are the ethical implications of these responsibilities?

5. **[Obj. 2]** Describe the three steps in the accounting transaction process.

6. **[Obj. 2]** Why are shipping terms important in the accounting transaction process?

7. **[Obj. 2]** What is a source document?

8. **[Obj. 3]** What is the definition of accounts?

9. **[Obj. 3]** What is the chart of accounts?

10. **[Obj. 3]** What are some differences you may find in comparing charts of accounts from different countries?

11. **[Obj. 5]** When you subtract expenses from revenues, what is the difference called and how does it affect stockholders' equity?

12. **[Obj. 5]** Describe the components of a T account.

13. **[Obj. 5]** What do the terms debit and credit mean?

14. **[Obj. 5]** How do you calculate the balance of an account?

15. **[Obj. 5]** What is double-entry accounting?

16. **[Obj. 5]** List the stockholders' equity accounts and explain how they are related to stockholders' equity.

17. **[Obj. 6]** Describe the journal entry process.

18. **[Obj. 6]** Describe the function of the general ledger.

19. **[Obj. 6]** What is the purpose of the trial balance?

20. **[Obj. 7]** Does the trial balance guarantee the accuracy of the accounting records?

SHORT EXERCISES – SET A

Building Accounting Skills

1. **[Obj. 5]** Writing Equations: Write the two fundamental equations that are pertinent to double-entry accounting.

2. **[Obj. 5]** Preparing T Accounts: Use T accounts to illustrate how debits and credits increase or decrease assets, liabilities, and stockholders' equity accounts.

3. **[Obj. 5]** Showing the Relationship Among Accounts: Create an equation that shows the relationship of the following items:
   a. additional paid-in capital
   b. assets
   c. common stock
   d. dividends
   e. expenses
   f. liabilities
   g. retained earnings
   h. revenues

4. **[Obj. 5]** Posting to T Accounts: Assume that a firm borrows $1,000. Set up T accounts for Cash and Notes Payable and post the transaction to the T accounts.

5. **[Obj. 6]** Recording a Transaction: Assume that a firm borrows $1,000. How would this transaction be recorded in the general journal?

6. **[Obj. 6]** Recording a Transaction: On April 1, Johnny Skywalker set up a business by investing $180,000. In return he received 1,000 shares of $100 par value common stock. How would this transaction be recorded in the general journal?

7. **[Obj. 6]** Recording a Transaction: On April 15, Skywalker Shoe Company paid $90,000 cash for a building that cost $50,000 and office equipment that cost $40,000. How would this transaction be recorded in the general journal?

8. **[Obj. 6]** Recording a Transaction: Today, you buy a car for $15,000. You pay $1,500 in cash and finance the rest on credit. How would this transaction be recorded in the general journal?

9. **[Obj. 6]** Recording a Transaction: On June 1, you pay $1,000 of the amount owed on the car you purchased in Ex-A8. (Thus, you are reducing your accounts payable.) How would this transaction be recorded in the general journal?

10. **[Obj. 6]** Recording a Transaction: On Nov. 30, your friend, Joe, pays back the $50 he borrowed from you at the beginning of the semester. Assume you had set up a general journal account in your friend's name when he originally borrowed the money, how would you record the receipt of his payment?

SHORT EXERCISES – SET B

Building Accounting Skills

[Obj. 4] Recording Transactions: The following exercises relate to the first 10 business transactions of Mike's Muffler Company, a small corporation that provides automobile muffler repairs. For each transaction, show how the transaction affects the accounts in the accounting equation. Use the format shown in Exhibit 3.4, Recap of Basic Transactions.

1. Mike Elliot sets up a corporation, Mike's Muffler Company. He invests $200,000 in cash into the corporate checking account. He received 10,000 shares of $12 par value stock.

2. The company pays $50,000 in cash for land and $70,000 in cash for buildings.

3. The company purchases muffler supplies for $2,000 on credit.

4. The company sends in payment of $500, part of the amount owed for supplies.

5. The company makes muffler repairs for customers who pay cash for the full amount, $6,000.

6. The company makes muffler repairs of $9,000 for customers who arrange to make payment in 30 days.

7. The customers in the previous transaction send in partial payment of $5,000.

8. Mike's Muffler Company pays wages of $2,000 to employees.

9. Mike's Muffler Company incurs $200 in advertising expense. Instead of paying immediately, the company arranges to pay in the future.

10. The company declares and pays a dividend of $1,000.

PROBLEMS – SET A

Applying Accounting Knowledge

1. **[Obj. 5]** Posting to T Accounts: Rambo Smith sets up a corporation with $50,000 cash. In return, Rambo received 10,000 shares of $1 par value stock. Next, the business pays $25,000 cash for a building. Third, the company acquires equipment with a loan (promissory note) of $5,000.

   Required: Use T accounts to illustrate these three transactions.

2. **[Obj. 5]** Posting to T Accounts: Shiny Shoe Repair Company engaged in the following transactions during March 20Y1, its first month of operations:

   Mar. 1 Joe Jones invested $50,000 of cash to set up the corporation, Shiny Shoe Repair Company. He received 1,000 shares of $20 par value stock.
   2 Purchased office supplies of $200 on account.
   4 Paid $40,000 cash for a building to use as a future office.
   6 Performed service for customers and received cash, $2,000.
   9 Paid $100 on accounts payable.
   17 Performed service for customers on account, $1,600.
   23 Received $1,200 cash from a customer on account.
   31 Paid the following expenses: salary, $1,200; rent, $500.

   Required: Set up T accounts and post the above transactions.

   Use the following accounts: Cash; Accounts Receivable; Office Supplies; Building; Accounts Payable; Common Stock; Additional Paid-In Capital; Service Revenue; Salary Expense; and Rent Expense. Compute the ending balance for each account. Show dates by each entry.

3. **[Obj. 8]** Preparing Trial Balance:

   Required:
   a. From the general ledger balances prepared in Problem A2, prepare a trial balance of Shiny Shoe Repair Company at March 31, 20Y1.
   b. Evaluate: How would you describe the company's financial situation on March 31, 20Y1?

4. **[Obj. 6]** Recording Journal Entries: Following are transactions of the Michelle Hannah Consulting Company:

   Jan. 1: Michelle Hannah set up a corporation, Michelle Hannah Consulting Company, with a $10,000 deposit into the firm's checking account. She received 5,000 shares of $1 par value common stock.
   Jan. 2: Borrowed $4,000 with a note payable to purchase a computer (Office Equipment).
   Jan. 3: Purchased office supplies on credit for $800.
   Jan. 10: Provided consulting services on account for $3,200.
   Jan. 12: Provided consulting services on account for $1,200.
   Jan. 15: Received partial payment of $1,600 for services rendered on account on January 10.
   Jan. 20: Provided consulting services on account for $2,000.
   Jan. 25: Paid telephone bill of $375.
   Jan. 26: Paid electric bill of $225.
   Jan. 31: Paid January rent of $1,500.
   Jan. 31: The firm paid dividends of $4,000.

   Required: Make general journal entries for the above transactions.

5.   **[Obj. 5]** Posting Transactions to General Ledger:

     Required: Using the general journal transactions prepared in Problem A4, set up general ledger accounts and post the January transactions for the Michelle Hannah Consulting Company. Use the following accounts: Cash; Accounts Receivable; Office Supplies; Office Equipment; Accounts Payable; Notes Payable; Common Stock; Additional Paid-In Capital; Dividends; Consulting Fees Earned; Rent Expense; Utilities Expense; and Telephone Expense. Compute the ending balance for each account. Show dates by each entry.

6.   **[Obj. 8]** Preparing Trial Balance:

     Required:
     a.   From the general ledger balances prepared in Problem A5, prepare a trial balance of Michelle Hannah Consulting Company at January 31, 20Y1.
     b.   Evaluate: How would you describe the company's financial situation on January 31, 20Y1?

PROBLEMS – SET B

Applying Accounting Knowledge

1.   **[Obj. 5]** Posting to T Accounts: Bee Hive sets up a corporation with $100,000 cash. In return, Bee received 20,000 shares of $1 par value stock. Next, the business pays $50,000 cash for a building. Third, the company acquires equipment with a loan (promissory note) of $10,000.

     Required: Use T accounts to illustrate these three transactions.

2.   **[Obj. 5]** Posting to T Accounts: Beethoven's Music Company engaged in the following transactions during March 20Y1, its first month of operations:

Mar. 1	Mary Beethoven invested $100,000 of cash to set up the corporation, Beethoven's Music Company. She received 2,000 shares of $20 par value stock.
Mar. 2	Purchased office supplies of $400 on account.
Mar. 4	Paid $80,000 cash for a building.
Mar. 6	Gave private music lessons to customers and received cash, $4,000.
Mar. 9	Paid $200 on accounts payable.
Mar. 17	Gave private music lessons to customers on account, $3,200.
Mar. 23	Received $2,400 cash from a customer on account.
Mar. 31	Paid the following expenses: salary, $2,400; rent, $1000.

     Required: Set up T accounts and post the above transactions.

     Show dates by each entry. Compute the ending balance for each account. Use the following accounts: Cash; Accounts Receivable; Office Supplies; Building; Accounts Payable; Common Stock; Additional Paid-In Capital; Service Revenue; Salary Expense; and Rent Expense.

3. **[Obj. 6]** Preparing Trial Balance:

   Required:
   a. From the general ledger balances prepared in Problem B2, prepare the trial balance of Beethoven's Music Company at March 31, 20Y1.
   b. Evaluate: How would you describe the company's financial situation on March 31, 20Y1?

4. **[Obj. 6]** Recording Journal Entries: Following are transactions of the Jacob Lawrence Sports Consultants:

   Jan. 1:   Jacob Lawrence set up a corporation, Jacob Lawrence Sports Consultants, with a $20,000 deposit into the firm's checking account. He received 10,000 shares of $1 par value common stock.
   Jan. 2:   Borrowed $8,000 with a note payable to purchase a computer (Office Equipment).
   Jan. 3:   Purchased office supplies on credit for $1,600.
   Jan. 10: Provided consulting services on account for $6,400.
   Jan. 12: Provided consulting services on account for $2,400.
   Jan. 15: Received partial payment of $3,200 for services rendered on account on January 10.
   Jan. 20: Provided consulting services on account for $4,000.
   Jan. 25: Paid monthly payment of $750 on auto loan for company car.
   Jan. 26: Paid utility bill of $450.
   Jan. 31: Paid January rent of $3,000.
   Jan. 31: The firm paid dividends of $8,000.

   Required: Make general journal entries for the above transactions.

5. **[Obj. 5]** Posting Transactions to General Ledger:

   Required: Using the general journal transactions prepared in Problem B4, set up general ledger accounts and post the January transactions for the Jacob Lawrence Sports Consultants. Use the following accounts: Cash; Accounts Receivable; Office Supplies; Office Equipment; Accounts Payable; Notes Payable; Common Stock; Additional Paid-In Capital; Dividends; Consulting Fees Earned; Rent Expense; Utilities Expense; and Auto Loan Expense. Compute the ending balance for each account. Show dates by each entry.

6. **[Obj. 6]** Preparing Trial Balance:

   Required:
   a. From the general ledger balances prepared in Problem B5, prepare a trial balance of Jacob Lawrence Sports Consultants at January 31, 20Y1.
   b. Evaluate: How would you describe the company's financial situation on January 31, 20Y1?

CROSS-FUNCTIONAL PERSPECTIVES

Discussion Questions

1. **[Obj. 1]** List users of financial information within a firm and describe what kinds of information is useful to them.

2. **[Obj. 1]** Who are some people outside of a firm who rely on the firm's financial statements?

3. **[Obj. 2]** List examples of source documents and the company department or outside source each originates from.

4. **[Obj. 2]** Source documents sometimes provide an interface between departments. Give examples of this.

5. **[Obj. 2]** In a sales transaction, what is the function of the marketing department and accounting department?

Cross-functional Case: Too Much E-Commerce?

Suppose you are the new marketing manager at McDonald's. You propose a new way to sell McDonald's products: Customers will order a Big Mac meal or a salad at home using the Web instead of using the drive-thru lane. When the customer arrives, the meal will be hot and fresh. Each restaurant location would be equipped with a computer workstation and satellite link to the Web. The McDonald's website would be updated to include a menu and order form. Customers could access their local restaurant website and place orders for pick-up. Delivery might also be available at some locations. To determine whether this kind of e-commerce website could be profitable will require analyses from accounting, finance, human resources, marketing, and production. Besides projecting revenues and expenses, logistical issues must be considered. Will this process save customers time? How will orders be prepared so that they will be fresh at pick-up? How will the store keep Web order separate from in-store orders?

Required: Answer the question, "What issues must be addressed to make this proposed e-commerce website work?" from the perspective of each of the following departments:
a. Accounting
b. Finance
c. Human resources (personnel)
d. Marketing
e. Production (food preparation)

EXCEL ASSIGNMENTS

1. **[Obj. 8]** Preparing Trial Balance: On your worksheet, put the general ledger account balances in the input area and the trial balance in the output area. The worksheet should be designed so that the output area automatically inserts the account balances from the input area. Use the general ledger account balances, shown below, of Booster Supply Company as of June 30, 20Y1.

Required: Prepare a trial balance for Booster Supply Company using Excel. Print your worksheet.

Cash	$18,230
Accounts Receivable	26,890
Office Supplies	12,266
Office Equipment	44,000
Accounts Payable	7,800
Notes Payable	5,000
Common Stock	25,000
Additional Paid-In Capital	35,000
Dividends	2,500
Consulting Fees Earned	34,780
Rent Expense	2,450
Utilities Expense	956
Telephone Expense	288

2. **[Obj. 8]** Preparing Trial Balance: On your worksheet, put the general ledger account balances in the input area and the trial balance in the output area. The worksheet should be designed so that the output area automatically inserts the account balances from the input area. Use the general ledger account balances, shown below, of Reliable Laser Corporation as of September 30, 20Y1.

Cash	$16,555
Accounts Receivable	24,890
Office Supplies	3,400
Office Equipment	88,000
Accounts Payable	22,300
Notes Payable	500
Common Stock	10,000
Additional Paid-In Capital	40,000
Dividends	13,000
Consulting Fees Earned	81,425
Rent Expense	6,600
Utilities Expense	1,220
Telephone Expense	560

Required: Prepare a trial balance for Reliable Laser Corporation using Excel. Print your worksheet.

3. **[Obj. 5 & 6]** Preparing T Accounts and Trial Balance: On your worksheet, show T accounts in the input area and the trial balance in the output area. Use the following accounts: Cash; Accounts Receivable; Office Supplies; Building; Accounts Payable; Common Stock; Additional Paid-In Capital; Service Revenue; Salary Expense; and Rent Expense. Compute the ending balance for each account. Start with a zero balance in all general ledger accounts and enter the following transactions of March 20Y1.

Mar. 1 Joe Jones invested $50,000 of cash to set up the corporation, Shiny Shoe Repair Company. He received 1,000 shares of $20 par value stock.

Mar. 2 Purchased office supplies of $200 on account.

Mar. 4 Paid $40,000 cash for a building to use as a future office.

Mar. 6 Performed service for customers and received cash, $2,000.

Mar. 9 Paid $100 on accounts payable.

Mar. 17 Performed service for customers on account, $1,600.

Mar. 23 Received $1,200 cash from a customer on account.

Mar. 31 Paid the following expenses: salary of $1,200; rent of $500.

Required: Prepare T accounts and a trial balance using Excel. Print your worksheet.

4. **[Obj. 5 & 8]** Preparing T Accounts and Trial Balance: Assume the same transactions presented in Excel-3, except for the following:
   ■ The investment on March 1 was for $60,000 of cash not $50,000.
   ■ The services performed on March 17 were for $5,600 not $1,600.

Required: Prepare T accounts and a trial balance using Excel. Print your worksheet.

5. **[Obj. 7]** Posting to General Ledger: In order to design a worksheet that enables the user to record transactions in general ledger accounts, use the following format for the general ledger in the *output* area:

Account Number and Title			
Date	Debit	Credit	Balance
Entry 1	xx		xx
Entry 2		xx	xx
Ending Balance			xx

The balance column should show the running balance in the account. Use the following accounts: Cash; Accounts Receivable; Office Supplies; Office Equipment; Accounts Payable; Notes Payable; Common Stock; Additional Paid-In Capital; Dividends; Consulting Fees Earned; Rent Expense; Utilities Expense; and Telephone Expense. Compute the ending balance for each account. Start with a zero balance in all general ledger accounts. The following transactions of January 20Y1 should be entered into the input area in journal fashion and then posted to the general ledger in the output area. After all entries have been made, print your worksheet.

Jan. 1   Becky Smith set up a corporation, Becky Smith Consulting Company, with a $10,000 deposit into the firm's checking account. She received 5,000 shares of $1 par value common stock.

Jan. 2   Borrowed $4,000 with a note payable to purchase a computer (Office Equipment).

Jan. 3   Purchased office supplies on credit for $800.

Jan. 10   Provided consulting services on account for $3,200.

Jan. 12   Provided consulting services on account for $1,200.

Jan. 15   Received partial payment of $1,600 for services rendered on account on January 10.

Jan. 20   Provided consulting services on account for $2,000.

Jan. 25   Paid telephone bill of $375.

Jan. 26   Paid electric bill of $225.

Jan. 31   Paid January rent of $1,500.

Jan. 31   The firm paid dividends of $4,000.

Required: Design a worksheet that enables the user to record transactions in general ledger accounts.

6. **[Obj. 8]** Preparing Trial Balance: Start with the worksheet you created for Excel-5 in order to prepare the trial balance. Set up your worksheet so that the trial balance is automatically computed from the ending balances in the general ledger accounts.

Required: Prepare the trial balance of Becky Smith Consulting Company at January 31, 20Y1 using Excel. Print your worksheet.

7. **[Obj. 7]** Posting to General Ledger: Assume the same transactions presented in Excel-5, except for the following:
   - On January 2, the firm borrowed $6,000 to buy office equipment, not $4,000.
   - On January 31, the firm paid dividends of $2,000, not $4,000.

Required: Design a worksheet that enables the user to record transactions in general ledger accounts.

8. **[Obj. 8]** Preparing Trial Balance: Start with the worksheet from Excel-7 in order to prepare the trial balance. Set up the worksheet so that the trial balance is automatically computed from the ending balances in the general ledger accounts.

Required: Prepare the trial balance of Becky Smith Consulting Company at January 31, 20Y1 using Excel. Print your worksheet.

WEB ASSIGNMENTS

1. **[Obj. 1]** Go to the website for McDonald's. What accounting jobs are currently available within the company?

2. **[Obj. 5]** Use a Web search tool (e.g. Yahoo. com) and find information on double-entry accounting. Prepare a one-page report. Use at least two Web sources. Cite your sources, including their Web address, in your report.

3. **[All Obj]** Go to the website for McDonald's or do a search on Google to find an accounting-related news item from the past year pertaining to McDonald's. Give a one-paragraph summary of the news item. (Hint: You must go to the Corporate page to find accounting-related items.)

4. **[Technology]** Search the Web for information on two accounting software packages, such as QuickBooks and Peachtree. How much does the software cost? What are the system requirements?

5. **[Career]** Jay and Kay Morgan must pay self-employment tax. What is self-employment tax and how is it computed? In order to give an answer to these questions, go to the IRS website (IRS.gov) and look under employment taxes for small businesses, or do a search on Google.

6. **[Ethics]** Go to McDonald's website or do a search on Google to find out how McDonald's allocates the money contributed to Ronald McDonald House Charities and the World Children's Day.

¶314

Test Prepper

Use this sample test to gauge your comprehension of the chapter material.

True/False Questions

___ 1. Business transactions are economic events that affect the financial situation of the firm.

___ 2. The general ledger contains all of the company's accounts arranged in the same order as the chart of accounts.

___ 3. Once a transaction is recognized, it must be recorded.

___ 4. The term "debit" is used to specify the right side of an account.

___ 5. Every transaction is recorded with at least one debit and one credit, such that the total dollar amount of debits equals the total dollar amount of credits.

___ 6. A decrease to an asset is always recorded as a debit.

___ 7. Revenues decrease stockholders' equity.

___ 8. A decrease to a stockholders' equity or liability account is recorded as a debit.

___ 9. Transferring information from the general journal to the general ledger is referred to as "posting."

___ 10. The balance sheet is a test listing of accounts to determine if the revenues equal the expenses.

Multiple-Choice Questions

___ 1. In evaluating a business transaction, the accountant determines
   a. When the transaction occurred.
   b. The dollar amount of the transaction.
   c. Accounts are affected by the transaction.
   d. all of the above
   e. both b and c, but not a

___ 2. Determining the dollar amount of a business transaction is called
   a. Recognition
   b. Valuation
   c. Evaluation
   d. Classification
   e. all of the above

___ 3. The list of account numbers and corresponding names is called the
   a. general ledger
   b. general journal
   c. chart of records
   d. chart of accounts
   e. account properties

___ 4. In a T account, what do you call the difference between the sum of the debits and the sum of the credits?
   a. account total
   b. debit
   c. credit
   d. product
   e. balance

___ 5. An increase to an asset is always recorded as a
   a. debit
   b. credit
   c. memorandum entry
   d. charge-back
   e. debit or a memorandum entry

___ 6. Accounts relating to stockholders' equity are
   a. retained earnings
   b. revenues and expenses
   c. dividends
   d. all of the above
   e. a and b

___ 7. Stockholders' equity accounts do not include
   a. common stock and additional paid-in capital
   b. retained earnings
   c. revenues and expenses
   d. dividends
   e. prepaid expenses

___ 8. Which of the following is an increase to an asset account?
   a. debit
   b. credit
   c. balance
   d. increment
   e. zap

___ 9. Which of the following is a decrease to a liability account?
   a. debit
   b. credit
   c. balance
   d. increment
   e. zap

___ 10. After a business transaction has been evaluated, the next step is to record the transaction in the
   a. T account
   b. general ledger
   c. general journal
   d. chart of accounts
   e. statement of stockholders' equity

Measuring Profitability and Financial Position on the Financial Statements

LEARNING OBJECTIVES

After completing "Part I: Accounting for the Business Cycle, Adjustments, and Closing the Books," you should be able to:

1. Describe how the measurement of profitability and the assessment of financial position are valuable to people within and outside the firm.
2. Describe the activities that comprise the business cycle.
3. Explain the key steps in the accounting process.
4. Implement accrual basis accounting.
5. Make the four basic types of adjusting journal entries.
6. Prepare an adjusted trial balance.
7. Close the books.

You should be able to do the following after studying "Part II: Financial Reporting and Ethics":

8. Prepare the financial statements from an adjusted trial balance.
9. Be able to use either of the two formats for the income statement and for the balance sheet.
10. Understand the ethical issues associated with accrual accounting.

CHAPTER CONTENTS

Measuring Profitability and Financial Position on the Financial Statements

FOCUS ON BUSINESS

JC Penney Company: Towels Clean Up

JC Penney Company is one of America's largest department store retailers. Suppose that the local Penney's store purchases a large quantity of bathroom towels in August to sell to the college students who move back into town that month. Payment for the towels isn't due to the supplier until September.

The manager wants an income statement prepared for August stating the revenues and expenses for the month. Should the towels be listed as an expense on the August income statement even though there has not been an actual payment of cash and payment is not due until September? Accounting principles require expenses to be recorded in the accounting period in which they are used to generate revenue. The towels sold in August generated revenue in August. Following this principle, the cost of the towels is reported as an expense in August. Accounting principles require the reporting of expenses when incurred, even if cash is not disbursed. You will learn more about the accrual basis of accounting in this chapter.

¶401 Applications to People Within and Outside the Firm

LEARNING OBJECTIVE 1: Describe how the measurement of profitability and the assessment of financial position are valuable to people within and outside the firm.

Profit can be viewed as the reward that business owners receive for risking their money on an investment. A business must make a profit to survive, but profit is not guaranteed. There is a reasonable possibility that a business will be unprofitable. In fact, many small businesses fail their first year because they lack cash to pay monthly expenses.

As the business world becomes more complex and competitive, the need for measurement of profitability has never been more important. Companies are larger, methods of product delivery more varied, payment options are expanding, and reporting regulations are more stringent. Both internal and external users require financial information for critical business decisions.

¶401.01 INTERNAL USERS

At JC Penney Company, top management is responsible for formulating plans and controlling operations for one of the largest department store retailers. Management measures profitability and financial strength to determine if business operations are meeting company goals. Ultimately, accountants gather information from the other departments and prepare financial statements that enable management to evaluate the company's success or failure. Understanding the intricacies of what increases and decreases a firm's profit is helpful knowledge for any businessperson. As you will see from the chapter, financial reporting is essential for managing business operations.

Nothing reveals the successful teamwork of the functional areas more than a healthy profit. For a profit-oriented company, profit is the end result of a successful business cycle. The four operating cycles that make up the business cycle draw attention to the interrelated activities of a company. From acquiring funds for operations in the financial cycle, to selling goods and services in the revenue cycle, accountants provide managers with information necessary for decision-making and for evaluating the success or failure regarding company operations.

¶401.02 EXTERNAL USERS

There are a host of external users who are interested in the financial viability of JC Penney Company. Investors are keenly interested in whether the company is profitable, and thus, generating a return on their

From personal observation, you can judge if a local store seems to be doing a large volume of sales. Why do you need the company's financial statements to determine if it is actually making a profit?

investment. Vendors and manufacturers who sell merchandise to JC Penney Company are also users of financial data. Manufacturers sell their merchandise on credit to retail firms, who then sell the merchandise to customers. For example, if Martha Stewart receives a large purchase order from JC Penney, Martha must evaluate the financial viability or credit risk of JC Penney before selling the products on credit. If JC Penney seeks to borrow money to build a new store, the lending institution must examine the company's financial statements and assess JC Penney's ability to pay back the loan.

Investors, suppliers, lenders, and other external users must have the financial reports of JC Penney to evaluate its profitability and financial strength. Profitability and financial strength result from successful business operations.

Part I: Accounting for the Business Cycle, Adjustments, and Closing the Books

¶402

The Business Cycle

> **LEARNING OBJECTIVE 2:** Describe the activities that comprise the business cycle.

The business cycle converts cash into goods and sells these goods, thus converting resources back into cash.

The **business cycle** is the process of converting cash into goods and services for sale and then selling these goods and services in order to convert resources back into cash. The idea of course is to make a profit by taking in more cash from selling goods and services than is disbursed to pay for materials, labor, and overhead. All businesses have a business cycle.

The business cycle can be broken down into four basic operating cycles:

- **Expenditure cycle** — includes purchasing of goods and services, plus payroll processing.
- **Conversion cycle** — involves the transformation of a firm's resources into products or services that are then sold to customers.
- **Revenue cycle** — encompasses the marketing-related activities of the firm, such as sales; also called the "marketing cycle."
- **Financial cycle** — concerns financing and investing activities, plus financial reporting.

The relationship among the four cycles is illustrated in Exhibit 4.1.

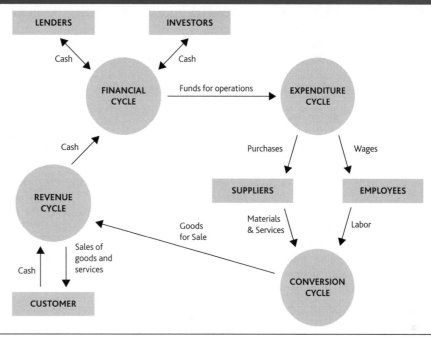

Exhibit 4.1 OPERATING CYCLES OF THE BUSINESS CYCLE

Successful business operations depend on skilled people in the various functional areas such as marketing, purchasing, production, finance, human resources, information management, and accounting. Frequently, people working in different functional areas are called to work together in teams to solve business problems and make plans for future operations. For example, the marketing department at JC Penney provides sales forecasts to the purchasing department so that the appropriate number of products can be purchased from suppliers.

Using the sales forecasts and estimated purchase costs, accountants prepare budgets based on anticipated revenues and costs. In a small business, perhaps a local gift shop, the owner may personally carry out all cycle activities. Many small businesses hire an independent accountant to perform accounting tasks such as bookkeeping, payroll, and tax preparation.

¶402.01 EXPENDITURE CYCLE

The expenditure cycle includes purchasing of goods and services, plus payroll processing.

Through the expenditure cycle, the firm acquires the goods and services necessary for operations to carry out business. Effective business operations depend on the availability of goods such as fixed assets, various types of supplies, and assorted inventory items. Necessary services include items such as utility services, delivery services, and repair services. The accounting department plays an active role in the expenditure cycle since it is responsible for recording all the expenses incurred and reporting expenses on the income statement. The expenditure cycle also includes the payroll function, in which the firm pays wages and salaries of employees.

¶402.02 CONVERSION CYCLE

The conversion cycle transforms resources into products or services that are sold later to customers or clients.

The conversion cycle involves the transformation of a firm's resources into products or services that are later sold to customers or clients. The quality of those goods and services is a key factor in the success or failure of the firm. In a manufacturing firm, the conversion cycle is sometimes referred to as the "production cycle." While the conversion cycle is mostly associated with a manufacturing firm, the cycle concepts also apply to service firms, retail firms, and nonprofit organizations.

In a service firm, the conversion cycle involves the conversion of labor and office expenditures into services. In this respect, service firms are less complicated than manufacturing firms that convert materials, labor, and factory expenditures into a finished product. For example, during the production process at General Motors, control must be maintained over parts inventory, work in process, finished goods, labor hours, and factory overhead. Accounting accumulates the costs of automobile assembly within each stage of the production process. When production is completed, the costs of completed automobiles must be transferred to the finished goods account. Management uses the accounting information generated during the conversion cycle (production) to plan and control conversion activities.

¶402.02

¶402.03

The revenue cycle encompasses the marketing-related activities of the firm.

REVENUE (MARKETING) CYCLE

Marketing generates the revenue that sustains a business. The development, promotion, selling, and distribution of goods and services are coordinated through the marketing department. The marketing concept of running a business is to focus all efforts on satisfying the customer while still making a profit. An old saying is: "You can build a better mouse trap, but no one will buy it unless the consumer knows about it and believes it's better."

Marketing strategy is intertwined with the firm's strategy. Company executives and marketing management are required to examine consumer needs and assess the company's ability to satisfy those needs at a profit. Company strategy involves marketing variables such as market share, product development, competition, and sales volume. Thus, planning requires up-to-date information. Without an information base, executives can only rely on intuition—not a reliable method in today's competitive and fast-changing business world.

E-commerce has added a new dimension to the revenue (marketing) cycle. For example, JC Penney sells to the global market mainly through e-commerce. JC Penney Catalog, which includes e-commerce, is the nation's largest catalog merchant of general merchandise. The company launched its online store on the Internet in 1998, with year-end sales totaling $15 million. Since then, JCPenney.com sales have soared to over $300 million. (**Source:** *JCPenney.com*)

In accounting terms, the revenue cycle is a transaction-oriented cycle that utilizes information from the accounting system while also generating important input for the accounting system. The main accounting-related functions pertaining to the revenue (marketing) cycle are as follows:

- Document sales orders
- Verify customer credit
- Document the distribution of goods
- Bill the customer and update customer files
- Record cash receipts

¶402.04

The financial cycle involves financing and investing activities, as well as financial reporting.

When you work for a company, you will be assisting in at least one of the business cycles: marketing, expenditure, conversion, or financial. Which do you think is the most interesting?

FINANCIAL CYCLE

The purpose of the financial cycle is to process business transactions that have not been processed by other cycles. These include the following:

- Record adjusting entries
- Record closing entries
- Generate the financial statements and various performance reports

The financial cycle is the culmination of the accounting activities of an organization, from both an external reporting perspective and an internal management perspective.

The financial cycle produces information for a number of financial reports for a business organization. Some of the objectives associated with the financial cycle include the following:

- All appropriate business transactions are recorded correctly and on a timely basis.
- All recorded transactions are posted to the proper accounts.
- Equality between total debits and total credits in all account balances is maintained.
- All necessary adjusting journal entries are processed.
- All necessary financial reports are prepared on a timely basis.

¶403

The accounting process starts with recording transactions and finishes with the financial statements.

The Accounting Process

LEARNING OBJECTIVE 3: Explain the key steps in the accounting process.

The **accounting process**, illustrated in Exhibit 4.2, involves the steps in which accountants assimilate financial data for the purpose of producing the firm's financial statements. The accounting process starts with recording transactions and produces the financial statements. The accounting process consists of the following steps, which occur each period:

1. Record transactions in the general journal
2. Post transactions to the general ledger
3. Prepare the trial balance
4. Record adjusting journal entries and post to the general ledger
5. Prepare the adjusted trial balance
6. Record closing journal entries and post to the general ledger
7. Prepare the post-closing trial balance
8. Prepare financial statements

Exhibit 4.2 Key Steps in the Accounting Process

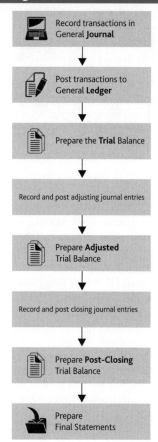

The periodicity concept requires that accounting information be reported in regular intervals.

A fiscal year is an accounting period of twelve months.

An interim period is an accounting period of less than a year.

¶403.01 PERIODICITY CONCEPT

Revenue recognition principle states that revenue should be recognized when earned as long as cash has been received or is expected to be received. The expense recognition principle states that expenses must be recorded in the period in which they generated revenue.

The **periodicity concept** requires that accounting information regarding a firm's business cycle be reported in regular intervals. Financial statements are prepared for specific time periods. The basic accounting period is one year. Business firms usually prepare annual financial statements based on their **fiscal year**. A fiscal year can be any 12-month time period. The fiscal year for most business firms is the calendar year from January 1 to December 31. Some firms use a fiscal year ending on a date other than December 31. For example, the fiscal year for the University of California runs from July 1 to June 30. Organizations often choose a fiscal year that corresponds to their primary cycle of operations.

Financial statements can be prepared for time periods of less than a year. Managers and investors may need to measure the company's performance before the end of the year. Accounting periods of less than a year are called "**interim periods**." Many companies prepare financial statements once a quarter (every three months) or even monthly. Most of the discussion in this text is based on the annual accounting period.

¶403.02

Can you see how the reporting of academic grades follows the periodicity principle and expense recognition principle?

REVENUE AND EXPENSE RECOGNITION PRINCIPLES REVIEWED

Revenues and expenses could be accounted for on a cash basis, that is, when cash is received and disbursed. This is usually the basis that an individual uses to prepare his or her tax return. However, the cash basis does not provide a complete and accurate accounting for all revenues and expenses. Revenues can be earned even though cash is not received and expenses can be incurred without an outlay of cash. As stated in Chapter 3, accounting follows the revenue recognition and expense recognition principles which state that revenues are recorded when earned and expenses are recorded when they are used to generate revenue.

¶404

Accrual Basis Accounting

The accrual basis of accounting records the financial effects of transaction in the periods in which those transactions occur.

The cash basis of accounting records revenues only if cash is received, and records expenses only if cash is disbursed.

> **LEARNING OBJECTIVE 4:** Implement accrual basis accounting.

The **accrual basis of accounting** records the financial effects of transactions in the periods in which those transactions occur rather than only in the periods in which cash is received or paid by the company. The accrual basis of accounting applies the revenue and expense recognition principles in two ways: by recording revenues when earned, and recording expenses when incurred. In contrast to the accrual method, the **cash basis of accounting** records revenues only if cash is received, and records expenses only if cash is disbursed. Since the accrual method records revenues and expenses even if no cash is received or disbursed, it is more complete, and therefore, more accurate than cash basis accounting. Accrue means "to come into existence."

Assume that JK Productions performs services for a customer in March, but the customer's payment of $3,000 is not due until April. Should this account receivable be recorded as an asset? At the end of March, using the cash basis of accounting, the company would not show the asset because the cash has not been received. Under the accrual basis of accounting, JK Productions would record the account receivable (an asset), along with the revenue earned.

In addition, suppose JK Productions owes $700 on accounts payable at the end of March. This amount is a real liability that must be paid in April; thus, under accrual basis accounting, the liability should be recorded. Cash basis accounting fails to include these significant items.

Accrual basis accounting records non-cash transactions such as the following:

- Sales on account (on credit)
- Purchases on account (on credit)
- Expenses incurred, but not yet paid
- Usage of supplies, insurance, and prepaid rent

Accrual accounting also records cash transactions, including the following:

- Collecting payments from customers
- Obtaining money from loans
- Paying back loans
- Paying wages, utilities, and other expenses
- Receiving cash from issuing stock

¶404.01   REVENUE RECOGNIZED WHEN EARNED

Revenue is an inflow of assets from delivering products, providing services, or other activities that comprise the firm's ongoing operations. Under accrual basis accounting, revenues are to be recorded when they are earned. Most of the time, revenue is earned when the firm has delivered a product or service to a customer. The firm has done all that is necessary to earn the revenue by delivering the product or service to the customer.

Exhibit 4.3 provides guidance on when and when not to record revenue. Scenario A shows that intent does not justify the recording of a revenue. The transaction has not yet occurred; thus, the journal entry should not yet be recorded. Scenario B shows that when a seller has shipped an order and title has transferred to the buyer, it is time to record a revenue. A transaction has occurred and the journal entry should be recorded.

Exhibit 4.3 When Revenue Should Be Recorded

Scenario A: No transaction — Do not record revenue.

A customer is thinking about using our firm to ship materials.

Scenario B: Transaction has occured — Record revenue.

Our firm has shipped materials per the customer's order.

¶404.02

EXPENSE RECOGNIZED WHEN INCURRED

As you learned in Chapter 1, an expense is an outflow or using up of assets as a result of manufacturing products, rendering services, or carrying out other activities that comprise a firm's ongoing operations. Expenses are to be recorded when they are incurred. For example, if a company places an advertisement for its services in a newspaper in January, the expense is incurred in January no matter when the company pays the bill.

To illustrate this concept, here's an example using JK Productions: On July 1, JK Productions receives its utility bill for $100; the expense is recognized as both having been incurred and as helping generate revenue. If the bill were paid immediately, the journal entry would be as follows:

July 1	Utility Expense	100	
	Cash		100
	To record utility bill.		

Alternatively, if the bill were not paid immediately, the journal entry would be:

July 1	Utility Expense	100	
	Accounts Payable		100
	To record utility bill.		

In keeping track of your personal finances, do you use accrual or cash basis accounting?

Whether the utility bill is paid immediately or at a future time, the expense is incurred, and therefore must be recorded. The reason for recording an expense is its occurrence, not the payment of cash.

In summary, revenue is recognized when earned and expenses are recognized when incurred. To measure net income, incurred expenses follow recognized revenues (expense recognition principle).

¶405

Adjusting Journal Entries

LEARNING OBJECTIVE 5: Make the four basic types of adjusting journal entries.

Accrual accounting applies the revenue and expense recognition principles through the use of adjusting journal entries. Accounts are adjusted or updated at the end of an accounting period to ensure that all previously unrecorded revenues and expenses are recorded in the period in which they are earned (revenue recognition) and incurred (expense recognition). In other words, adjusting journal entries are necessary when cash is exchanged either before or after it is actually earned.

At the end of an accounting period, a business prepares financial statements. Before the financial statements are produced, a trial balance is prepared. The trial balance is called the "unadjusted" trial balance because the accounts are not ready for the financial statements. However, the title "unadjusted" is often omitted and the document is simply called the "Trial Balance." Exhibit 4.4 is the trial balance of JK Productions.

Exhibit 4.4 JK PRODUCTIONS
Unadjusted Trial Balance June 30, 20Y1

	Dr.	Cr.
Cash	$40,900	
Accounts Receivable	4,000	
Supplies	1,000	
Prepaid Expenses	600	
Land	40,000	
Building	30,000	
Accounts Payable		$700
Unearned Videography Fees		6,000
Common Stock		100,000
Dividends	1,000	
Videography Fees Revenue		13,000
Wages Expense	2,000	
Advertising Expense	200	
Total	$119,700	$119,700

All accounts must be up-to-date because managers and investors use the financial statements to determine how well the firm performed and to evaluate the firm's financial position. Did the firm make a profit or loss? How much in assets does the firm own? How much does the firm owe? All accounts must be up-to-date; consequently, some accounts need adjustment. The adjusting process begins with the trial balance, like the one shown in Exhibit 4.4.

How can you tell which accounts need adjustment? An adjustment is needed if the business transactions of the period did not provide all the data necessary for the account to be up-to-date. For example, let's consider the supplies account. During the month of June, JK Productions used labels, containers, and other supplies to provide videography services to customers. Each time the firm packaged a video, Kay did not record a journal entry for the supplies used. Instead, the firm accounts for all supplies used up at the end of the month. Using supplies is an expense of doing business. An adjusting journal entry updates the Supplies Expense account and the Supplies account. After adjustment, these accounts are ready to be shown in the June financial statements.

Looking at the trial balance, which accounts may need adjustment? All accounts whose balances are not up-to-date must be adjusted at the end of the period. **Deferrals** are adjustments made to accounts when the firm either receives or pays cash in advance. In other words, the exchange of cash occurs first. **Accruals** are adjustments made to accounts when the firm incurs an expense before paying cash, or earns revenue before receiving cash payment. In other words, the exchange of cash occurs later.

The basic categories of adjustments are as follows.

- Expenses: Deferred Expense – a prepaid expense

   Accrued Expense – an expense incurred but not yet paid for

- Revenues: Deferred Revenue – unearned revenue (the customer prepaid)

   Accrued Revenue – revenue earned but not yet received (customer has not yet paid)

Deferrals are adjustments made to accounts when the firm either receives or pays cash in advance.

Accruals are adjustments made to accounts when the firm incurs an expense before paying cash, or earns a revenue before receiving cash payment.

¶405.01   DEFERRED (PREPAID) EXPENSE

A **deferred expense** is a prepayment for an item that will become an expense in the future. Deferred expenses are also called "prepaid expenses." For example, if a firm prepays three months' rent of $3,000 on January 1, then the firm would record an asset called "Prepaid Rent." Prepaid Rent is an asset because it represents an economic resource; in this case, it is the right to use a building for three months into the future. The journal entry would increase the Prepaid Rent account and decrease the Cash account by $3,000:

Jan. 1	Prepaid Rent	3,000	
	Cash		3,000
	Paid three months' rent in advance.		

The rent "expense" is deferred, or delayed, until a future time. A deferred (prepaid) expense is actually an asset, not an expense.

At the end of one month, one-third of the prepaid expense is used and thus has become an expense. The adjusting journal entry would increase Rent Expense and decrease the Prepaid Rent account by $1,000 ($3,000 × 1/3). The remaining $2,000 in Prepaid Rent is an asset. The adjusting entry for deferred expenses reduces the value of the asset account and increases an expense account by the same amount.

A deferred expense is prepaid.

In the following paragraphs, let's look at JK Productions' first month of operations to provide some examples of deferred expenses.

¶405.01.01   Supplies

Supplies are a deferred expense. When JK Productions purchases supplies, in effect the firm is prepaying its Supplies Expense. JK Productions purchased $1,000 of supplies on June 6 and made this entry:

June 6	Supplies	1,000	
	Cash		1,000
	Paid cash for supplies.		

The amount of supplies used during June is the supplies expense. To determine supplies expense, the firm counts supplies on hand at the end of the month. The count reveals $300 is on hand. Subtracting the $300 remaining from the supplies available ($1,000) calculates the supplies expense as $700. The June 30 adjusting entry debits the expense account (Supplies Expense) and credits the asset account (Supplies), as shown:

June 30	Supplies Expense	700	
	Supplies		700
	To record supplies used.		

After posting this entry to the general ledger, the Supplies and Supplies Expense accounts are as follows:

	Supplies		
June 6	1,000	June 30	700
Bal.	300		

	Supplies Expense	
June 30	700	
Bal.	700	

The Supplies account thus begins the month of July with a $300 balance, and the adjustment process continues month after month.

¶405.01.02   Prepaid Insurance

Prepaid Insurance is another example of a deferred expense, which is an asset account, not an expense account. Insurance is paid in advance. The prepayment creates an asset for the insured.

Suppose JK Productions prepays six months insurance on June 1. The entry would be as shown:

June 1	Prepaid Insurance	600	
	Cash		600
	Paid six months' insurance in advance.		

After posting, the Prepaid Insurance account appears as follows:

Prepaid Insurance	
June 1	600

During June, the Prepaid Insurance account shows this beginning balance, as shown in Exhibit 4.4. At June 30, Prepaid Insurance must be adjusted. Insurance expense is one month of the prepayment ($600 × 1/6 = $100). The adjusting entry transfers $100 from Prepaid Insurance to Insurance Expense as shown:

June 30	Insurance Expense ($600 × 1/6)	100	
	Prepaid Insurance		100
	To record insurance expense.		

After posting, Prepaid Insurance and Insurance Expense appear as shown:

Prepaid Insurance			
June 1	600	June 30	100
Bal.	500		

Insurance Expense	
June 30	100
Bal.	100

As a result of the adjustment, Prepaid Insurance starts July with a $500 balance.

¶405.02   ACCRUED EXPENSE

An accrued expense is an expense for which cash is yet to be paid.

The second category of adjusting journal entries relates to accrued expenses. An **accrued expense** is an expense for which cash is yet to be paid. For example, each day that an employee works, the firm owes a day's wages. Thus, on a daily basis, a firm accrues wages expense. However, firms usually only pay wages once or twice per month. Rather than recording wages expense on a daily basis, the accountant waits until the end of the period. Journal entries for accrued wages are shown below. Another example of an accrued expense is the interest expense that accrues on a note payable.

¶405.02.01   Wages Expense

JK Productions pays wages to employees on the 15th day and the last day of each month. The payment on the 15th is for the first half of the month and the payment on the last day is for the second half. However, if the last day falls on the weekend, JK Productions waits until the following Monday to prepare paychecks. During June, JK Productions paid its employees for the first half of the month. The journal was as follows:

June 15	Wages Expense	2,000	
	Cash		2,000
	To pay wages.		

After posting, the Wages Expense account in the general ledger is as shown:

Wages Expense	
June 15	2,000

Accrued wages for the second half of June are recorded on June 30, which is a Saturday. JK Productions waits until the following Monday, July 2, to disburse paychecks. There is no outlay of cash on June 30; thus, instead of crediting cash as before, Wages Payable is credited as shown:

June 30	Wages Expense	2,000	
	Wages Payable		2,000
	To accrue wages expense.		

After posting to the general ledger, the Wages Expense and Wages Payable accounts are as follows:

Wages Expense	
June 15	2,000
June 30	2,000
Bal.	4,000

Wages Payable		
	June 30	2,000
	Bal.	2,000

As a result of the adjustment on June 30, Wages Expense shows a full months' wages and Wages Payable shows the amount owed. All adjustments for an accrued but not yet paid expense include an increase (debit) to an expense account and an increase (credit) to a liability account. Wages Payable is a liability account that represents payments owed to employees. When paychecks are disbursed on July 2, the journal entry is:

July 2	Wages Payable	2,000	
	Cash		2,000
	To record payment of wages.		

¶405.02.02   Income Tax

Benjamin Franklin said that two things are certain, death and taxes. Individuals and corporations must pay income tax. An accrual for income tax expense and the corresponding income tax payable is one more adjustment that a business firm must make. JK Productions pays its taxes once per year, but the company accrues its income tax expense at the end of each month. JK Productions estimates its income tax for June to be $760. The entry is as follows:

June 30	Income Tax Expense	760	
	Income Tax Payable		760
	To accrue income tax expense.		

After posting, the general ledger accounts would appear as shown:

Income Tax Expense	
June 30	760
Bal.	760

Income Tax Payable		
	June 30	760
	Bal.	760

¶405.03   DEFERRED (UNEARNED) REVENUE

Another category of adjusting journal entries concerns deferred revenues. Deferred means delayed. As the name suggests, **deferred revenue** results when cash is collected before the revenue is earned. In other words, the actual earning of the revenue is delayed until the firm provides the service. This creates a liability called unearned revenue. Once the service is provided, the firm records the revenue and removes the liability.

Imagine that *Sports Illustrated* magazine sells annual subscriptions of its magazine at a discounted rate for customers who pay for the entire year in advance. When the company records the receipt of the order and the cash received, the revenue has not really been earned because each month's issue has not been shipped. The company does not want to misrepresent the revenue as earned all in one month, so the total amount is debited to Cash and credited to Unearned Subscription Fees. The Unearned Subscription Fees account is a liability, and represents products owed to customers. As each month's issue is shipped, one month's subscription is earned; thus, Unearned Subscription Fees is debited and Subscription Fees Earned is credited.

Suppose that on June 20, a sports team pays JK Productions in advance to videotape three games. Each game will be recorded separately. Every member of the team wants copies of all three videos. The total fee equals $6,000. The team pays $6,000 in advance to JK Productions. The videos of the first game are to be delivered on June 30, with the second and third game videos to be delivered July 10 and July 20, respectively. JK Productions records the receipt of cash and the liability as follows:

Deferred (unearned) revenue is a liability account that represents services owed to a customer.

June 20	Cash	6,000	
	Unearned Videography Fees		6,000
	Received cash in advance for videography fees.		

Unearned Videography Fees is a liability because JK Productions is obligated to provide videography services for the customer. The June 30 trial balance (Exhibit 4.4) shows Unearned Videography Fees with a credit balance of $6,000. On June 30, when the videos of the first game are delivered, JK Productions earns one-third of the $6,000 (i.e., $2,000). Consequently, the firm records the following adjusting entry:

June 30	Unearned Videography Fees ($6,000 × 1/3)	2,000	
	Videography Fees Revenue		2,000
	To record unearned videography fees that has been earned.		

After posting the adjustment, Unearned Videography fees is reduced to $4,000 and Videography Fees Revenue is increased by $2,000, as shown:

Unearned Videography Fees			
June 30	2,000	June 20	6,000
		Bal.	4,000

Videography Fees Revenue			
			13,000
		June 30	2,000
		Bal.	15,000

All unearned (deferred) revenues are accounted for in this manner. Remember, unearned revenue is not revenue, but a liability.

¶405.04   ACCRUED REVENUE

Accrued revenue is earned but not yet received.

The last category of adjusting journal entries is accrued revenue. An **accrued revenue** is a revenue that has been earned but cash payment is yet to be collected. For an employee, a paycheck is payment for accrued revenue, as he or she is being compensated for time already worked.

As another example of accrued revenue, suppose a customer of JK Productions requests videography services at two awards ceremonies. The first ceremony is on June 15 and the second is on July 15. The total fee is $800 and is due on July 15. Consequently, at the end of June, JK Productions has earned half of the fee, $400, even though they have not yet received any cash. On June 30, JK Productions makes the adjusting journal entry to record accrued videography fees revenue:

June 30	Accounts Receivable ($800 × 1/2)	400	
	Videography Fees Revenue		400
	To accrue videography fees revenue.		

As shown on JK Productions' trial balance back in Exhibit 4.4, Accounts Receivable has an unadjusted balance of $4,000 and Videography Fees Revenue has an unadjusted balance of $13,000. The June 30 adjusting entry for accrued videography fees revenue results in the following general ledger account balances:

Accounts Receivable

	4,000		
June 30	400		
Bal.	4,400		

Videography Fees Revenue

			13,000
		June 30	2,000
		June 30	400
		Bal.	15,400

Accounting for accrued revenues always includes a debit to a receivable account and a credit to a revenue account. The debit to the receivable, which is an asset, increases the account. The credit to Videography Fees Revenue, which is a revenue account, increases the account.

¶405.05 RECAP OF ADJUSTING JOURNAL ENTRIES

One reason for making adjusting journal entries is to properly measure business financial performance on the income statement. Recording revenues when earned and expenses when incurred help accomplish this financial measurement. Each adjusting entry affects either a revenue or an expense account.

A second purpose of adjusting entries is to properly show business financial position on the balance sheet. Exhibit 4.5 lists the four categories of adjusting entries. Each adjusting entry affects at least one balance sheet account and one income statement account. This is because each adjusting entry affects either an asset or a liability (contained in the balance sheet), while also affecting either an expense or revenue (contained in the income statement).

Exhibit 4.5 CATEGORIES OF ADJUSTING JOURNAL ENTRIES

		Income Statement	
		Expense	*Revenue*
Balance Sheet	Asset	**DEFERRED EXPENSE:** Prepaid expenses are apportioned between two or more periods. Debit: Expense Credit: Asset	**ACCRUED REVENUE:** Make entry for revenue earned but not yet received. Debit: Asset (receivable) Credit: Revenue
	Liability	**ACCRUED REVENUE:** Make entry for expense incurred but not yet paid for. Debit: Expense Credit: Liability	**DEFERRED EXPENSE:** Unearned revenues are apportioned between two or more periods. (Customer prepaid) Debit: Liability (unearned revenue) Credit: Revenue

Exhibit 4.6 lists the adjusting journal entries previously described for JK Productions. Part I lists the transaction data for each adjustment. Part II provides the adjusting entries and Part III shows the general ledger accounts after posting the adjusting entries.

In your personal finances, have you ever accrued an expense?

Exhibit 4.6 ADJUSTING ENTRIES FOR JK PRODUCTIONS

Part I: Adjustment Transaction Data

(a)	Used $700 of supplies.
(b)	Prepaid insurance expired, $100.
(d)	Accrued wages, $2,000.
(d)	Accrued income tax, $760.
(e)	Amount of unearned videography fees that has been earned, $2,000.
(f)	Accrued videography fees revenue, $400.

Part II: Adjusting Journal Entries:

(a)	Supplies Expense	700	
	Supplies		700
	To record supplies used.		
(b)	Insurance Expense	100	
	Prepaid Insurance		100
	To record insurance expense.		
(c)	Wages Expense	2,000	
	Wages Payable		2,000
	To accrue wages expense.		
(d)	Income Tax Expense	760	
	Income Tax Payable		760
	To accrue income tax expense.		
(e)	Unearned Videography Fees	2,000	
	Videography Fees Revenue		2,000
	To record unearned videography fees that has been earned.		
(f)	Accounts Receivable	400	
	Videography Fees Revenue		400
	To accrue videography fees revenue.		

Part III: General Ledger Accounts

ASSETS

Cash					Land	
Bal.	40,900			Bal.	40,000	

Accounts Receivable					Building	
	4,000			Bal.	30,000	
(g)	400					
Bal.	4,400					

Supplies		
	1,000	700
Bal.	300	

Prepaid Insurance		
	600	100
Bal.	500	

Exhibit 4.6 ADJUSTING ENTRIES FOR JK PRODUCTIONS (CONTINUED)

LIABILITIES

Accounts Payable		
	Bal.	700

Unearned Videography Fees			
(f)	2,000		6,000
		Bal.	4,000

Wages Payable		
		0
(d)		2,000
	Bal.	2,000

Income Tax Payable		
		0
(e)		760
	Bal.	760

Part III: General Ledger Accounts

STOCKHOLDERS' EQUITY

Common Stock		
	Bal.	100,000

Retained Earnings		
	Bal.	0

Dividends		
Bal.	1,000	

REVENUES AND EXPENSES

Videography Fees Revenue		
		13,000
(f)		2,000
(g)		400
	Bal.	15,400

Insurance Expense		
	0	
(b)	100	
Bal.	100	

Wage Expense		
	2,000	
(d)	2,000	
Bal.	4,000	

Supplies Expense		
	0	
(a)	700	
Bal.	700	

Advertising Expense		
Bal.	200	

Income Tax Expense		
	0	
(e)	760	
Bal.	760	

¶406

Preparing the Adjusted Trial Balance

LEARNING OBJECTIVE 6: Prepare an adjusted trial balance.

The adjusting process began with the unadjusted trial balance (Exhibit 4.4). After the adjusting entries are journalized and posted, the general ledger accounts are as shown in Exhibit 4.6, Part III.

An effective way to prepare the adjusted trial balance is to create a worksheet, as shown in Exhibit 4.7. On the left side, all account titles are listed. The next column shows the unadjusted trial balance amounts, which is labeled simply "trial balance." Next are the adjustments. The last column shows the adjusted trial balance amounts. The amounts in this column are used to prepare the adjusted trial balance. This adjusted trial balance is then used to generate the financial statements.

Exhibit 4.7, page 1 of 2 JK PRODUCTIONS
Worksheet to Prepare Adjusted Trial Balance June 30, 20Y1

	Trial Balance		Adjustments				Adjusted Trial Balance	
	Dr.	Cr.		Dr.		Cr.	Dr.	Cr.
Cash	$40,900		f	$400			$40,900	
Accounts Receivable	4,000				a	$700	4,400	
Supplies	1,000				b	100	300	
Prepaid Insurance	600						500	
Land	40,000						40,000	
Building	30,000						30,000	
Accounts Payable		$700						$700
Unearned VideographyFees		6,000	e	2,000				4,000
Wages Payable		0			c	2,000		2,000
Income Tax Payable		0			d	760		760
Common Stock		100,000						100,000
Retained Earnings		0						0
Dividends	1,000						1,000	
Videography Fees Revenue		13,000			e	2,000		15,400
					f	400		
Wage Expense	2,000		c	2,000			4,000	
Advertising Expense	200						200	
Supplies Expense	0		a	700			700	
Insurance Expense	0		b	100			100	
Income Tax Expense	0		d	760			760	
Total	$119,700	$119,700		$5,960		$5,960	$122,860	$122,860

Exhibit 4.7, page 2 of 2 JK PRODUCTIONS
Adjusted Trial Balance June 30, 20Y1

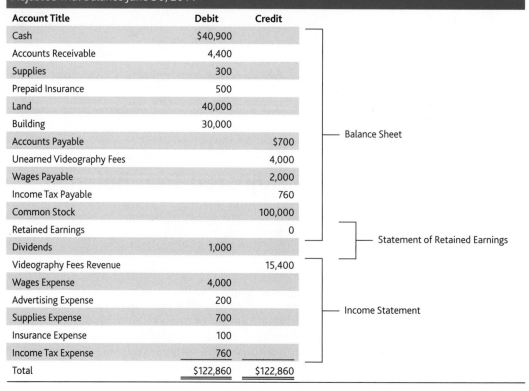

Account Title	Debit	Credit	
Cash	$40,900		
Accounts Receivable	4,400		
Supplies	300		
Prepaid Insurance	500		
Land	40,000		
Building	30,000		
Accounts Payable		$700	Balance Sheet
Unearned Videography Fees		4,000	
Wages Payable		2,000	
Income Tax Payable		760	
Common Stock		100,000	
Retained Earnings		0	Statement of Retained Earnings
Dividends	1,000		
Videography Fees Revenue		15,400	
Wages Expense	4,000		
Advertising Expense	200		Income Statement
Supplies Expense	700		
Insurance Expense	100		
Income Tax Expense	760		
Total	$122,860	$122,860	

Adjusted trial balance worksheets can be efficiently prepared using spreadsheet software such as Microsoft Excel. Instead of manually adding up columns and rows, a formula is entered into the spreadsheet which automatically makes those calculations.

FOCUS ON TECHNOLOGY

Using Microsoft Excel: Preparing Adjusted Trial Balance Worksheet

Using Excel, we will recreate Exhibit 4.8, a worksheet for an adjusted trial balance. If you need further instruction at any point, refer to the Excel information in the Appendix in Chapter 2.

1. File Identification Area: In an Excel worksheet, create a file identification area like the one shown in Exhibit 4.8.
2. Input Area: Create the input area with the account information shown in Exhibit 4.8.
3. Output Area: Enter the accounts names and headings into your output area as shown in Exhibit 4.8. You will insert the lines for the border last. The entire output area will be formula driven. First, use formulas to insert the amounts from the input area into the Trial Balance columns. For instance, the formula for Cash (=D11) should be typed into cell D27.
4. Adjustments: Again, use formulas to insert the adjustments. For instance, the first adjustment is service revenue accrued of $1,000. This affects two accounts. To debit accounts receivable for $1,000, type: =K12 into cell G28. To credit service fees revenue for $1,000, type: =K12 into cell I36. Insert the remaining two adjustments.
5. Adjusted Trial Balance: This section contains formulas that add and/or subtract the values from the trial balance and adjustments.

    The formula for the asset accounts (cash, accounts receivable, supplies), dividends, and the expense accounts (wages expense, supplies expense) is: Trial Balance amount + Adjustment Debit – Adjustment Credit. For example, the formula for the adjusted accounts receivable is =D28+G28-I28.

    The formula for the liability accounts (accounts payable, wages payable), retained earnings, and the revenue account for service fees is: Trial Balance value – Adjustment Debit + Adjustment Credit. For example, the formula for the adjusted wages payable in cell K31 is =E31-G31+I31.
6. Total: To sum each of the columns, use the autosum icon. Rather than using autosum, you can type in the appropriate formula. The formula to sum the first column of the trial balance (cell D40) is: =sum(D27:D38).
7. Cell Border: To create the table lines, highlight the entire area you want boxed in and format them with a border.

Exhibit 4.8 WORKSHEET TO PREPARE ADJUSTED TRIAL BALANCE

	A	B	C	D	E	F	G	H	I	J	K
1	**IDENTIFICATION AREA:**										
2	File name: Adjusted Trial Balance Worksheet										
3	Designer: B. Quick										
4	File created:										
5	Input Required			Cash, accounts receivable, supplies, accounts payable, wages payable,							
6				common stock, retained earnings, dividends,							
7				wages expense, supplies expense							
8	Output Required:			Adjusted trial balance worksheet							
9											
10	**INPUT AREA:**										
11	Cash			60,000			Adjustment Data:				
12	Accounts Receivable			10,000			a. Service fees revenue accrued				1,000
13	Supplies			2,000			b. Supplies used				500
14	Accounts Payable			4,000			c. Wages accrued				2,000
15	Wages Payable			0							
16	Common Stock			65,000							
17	Retained Earnings			10,000							
18	Dividends			1,000							
19	Service Fees Revenue			10,000							
20	Wages Expense			16,000							
21	Supplies Expense			0							
22											
23	**OUTPUT AREA:**									Adjusted	
24				Trial Balance			Adjustments			Trial Balance	
25				Dr.	Cr.		Dr.		Cr.	Dr.	Cr.
26	Cash			$60,000						$60,000	
27	Accounts Receivable			**10,000**		a	$1,000			11,000	
28	Supplies			2,000				b	$500	1,500	
29	Accounts Payable				$4,000			c	2,000		$4,000
30	Wages Payable				0						2,000
31	Common Stock				65,000						65,000
32	Retained Earnings				10,000						10,000
33	Dividends			1,000						1,000	
34	Service Fees Revenue				10,000			a	1,000		11,000
35	Wages Expense			16,000		c	2,000			18,000	
36	Supplies Expense			0		b	500			500	
37											
38	TOTAL			$89,000	$89,000		$3,500		$3,500	$92,000	$92,000

¶407

Preparing Closing Journal Entries

LEARNING OBJECTIVE 7: Close the books.

Closing the books entails setting revenue and expense accounts back to zero using closing entries in preparation for the next accounting period.

Closing entries transfer the balances from the revenue, expense, and dividends accounts into the Retained Earnings account.

Temporary account balances are closed to retained earnings at the end of the accounting period.

Permanent accounts are not closed; their balances are carried forward to the next period.

At the end of June, JK Productions presents its profit, or loss, on the income statement and its financial position on the balance sheet. The company expects to continue in business next month, and for countless months to come. The revenue and expense accounts show the amounts for the month of June. At the end of the accounting period, the revenue and expense accounts must be set to zero. This is referred to as "closing the books." **Closing the books** prepares the accounts for recording transactions in the next accounting period.

Closing entries transfer the balances from revenue, expense, and dividends accounts to the Retained Earnings account; thus, revenue, expense, and dividends accounts start the next period with zero balances. As a result, the Retained Earnings account is adjusted to its proper balance. The closing entries are analogous to re-setting the scoreboard at the end of a football game. No points are on the scoreboard at the start of the next game. No money is in revenue, expense, or dividends accounts at the start of an accounting period.

Since revenue, expense, and dividends accounts are closed at the end of each period and start each period with a zero balance, these accounts are called "**temporary accounts**." On the other hand, assets, liabilities, and stockholders' equity accounts are called "**permanent accounts**." Permanent accounts are not closed; their balances are carried over to the next accounting period.

Temporary accounts, except for dividends, are used to calculate net income. Permanent accounts do not affect net income. The ending balance in a permanent account, also called a "balance sheet account," becomes the beginning balance in the subsequent period.

To close the books of a corporation, take the following steps. Each step is illustrated using the closing journal entries for JK Productions.

a. Debit each revenue account for the same amount as its credit balance. Credit the Retained Earnings account for the total of all revenues. As a result, the sum total of revenues is transferred to Retained Earnings. JK Productions has one revenue account.

June 30	Videography Fees Revenue	15,400	
	Retained Earnings		15,400
	To close the revenue account.		

b. Credit each expense account for the same amount as its debit balance. Debit the Retained Earnings account for the total of all expenses. As a result, the sum total of expenses is transferred to Retained Earnings.

June 30	Retained Earnings	5,760	
	Wages Expense		4,000
	Advertising Expense		200
	Supplies Expense		700
	Insurance Expense		100
	Income Tax Expense		760
	To close the expense accounts.		

c. Credit the Dividends account for the same amount as its debit balance. While Dividends is not an expense account and does not affect net income, Dividends has the same effect on Retained Earnings as expenses.

June 30	Retained Earnings	1,000	
	Dividends		1,000
	To close the dividends account.		

¶407

After the journal entries are posted, the accounts will be as shown in Exhibit 4.9.

Exhibit 4.9 POSTING CLOSING ENTRIES

	Wages Expense		
	4,000	Clo.	4,000
Bal.	0		

	Advertising Expense		
	200	Clo.	200
Bal.	0		

	Supplies Expense		
	700	Clo.	700
Bal.	0		

	Insurance Expense		
	100	Clo.	100
Bal.	0		

	Income Tax Expense		
	760	Clo.	760
Bal.	0		

	Videography Fees Revenue		
Clo.	15,400		15,400
		Bal.	0

a

b

	Retained Earnings		
Clo.	5,760		0
Clo.	1,000	Clo.	15,400
		Bal.	8,640

c

	Dividends		
	1,000	Clo.	1,000
Bal.	0		

After the closing entries are made, a final trial balance, called the "post-closing trial balance" is prepared. The post-closing trial balance for JK Productions is shown in Exhibit 4.10. Only balance sheet accounts have balances, as the income statement accounts and Dividends account are now closed and have zero balances.

Is there anything that you "close" in preparation for a new semester?

Exhibit 4.10 JK PRODUCTIONS
Post-Closing Trial Balance June 30, 20Y1

Account Title	Debit	Credit
Cash	$40,900	
Accounts Receivable	4,400	
Supplies	300	
Prepaid Insurance	500	
Land	40,000	
Building	30,000	
Accounts Payable		$700
Unearned Videography Fees		4,000
Wages Payable		2,000
Income Tax Payable		760
Common Stock		100,000
Retained Earnings		8,640
Total	$116,100	$116,100

Part II: Financial Reporting and Ethics

¶408

Preparing the Financial Statements

> **LEARNING OBJECTIVE 8:** Prepare the financial statements from the adjusted trial balance on the work sheet.

The financial statements include the income statement, statement of retained earnings, balance sheet, and statement of cash flows. Information from the adjusted trial balance is sufficient to prepare all the financial statements except the statement of cash flows.

¶408.01   INCOME STATEMENT

How do the owners know if their firm is profitable? The income statement shows the profit of the firm. In accounting, net income is the amount by which revenues exceed expenses. Net income, also called "net earnings" or "profit," has a very precise meaning to accountants and to users of financial statements:

Revenues – Expenses = Net Income (Net Loss)

If expenses are more than revenues, a **net loss** occurs.

The income statement displays the firm's revenue accounts and expense accounts. The June income statement for JK Productions is shown at the top of Exhibit 4.11.

Exhibit 4.11 FINANCIAL STATEMENTS OF JK PRODUCTIONS

JK Productions
Income Statement for Month Ended June 30, 20Y1

Revenue		
Videography Fees Revenue		$15,400
Expenses		
Wages Expense	$4,000	
Advertising Expense	200	
Supplies Expense	700	
Insurance Expense	100	$5,000
Income Before Tax		10,400
Income Tax Expense		760
Net Income		$9,640

JK Productions
Statement of Retained Earnings for Month Ended June 30, 20Y1

Retained Earnings, June 1, 20Y1	$0
Add: Net Income	9,640
Subtotal	$9,640
Less: Dividends	1,000
Retained Earnings, June 30, 20Y1	$8,640

JK Productions
Balance Sheet June 30, 20Y1

ASSETS		LIABILITIES	
Cash	$40,900	Accounts Payable	$700
Accounts Receivable	4,400	Unearned Videography Fees	4,000
Supplies	300	Wages Payable	2,000
Prepaid Insurance	500	Income Tax Payable	760
Land	40,000	Total Liabilities	$7,460
Building	30,000		
		STOCKHOLDERS' EQUITY	
		Common Stock	$100,000
		Retained Earnings	8,640
		Total Stockholders' Equity	108,640
		Total Liabilities and	
Total Assets	$116,100	and Stockholder's Equity	$116,100

Net income is a firm's profit.

¶408.02 STATEMENT OF RETAINED EARNINGS

The statement of retained earnings shows the change in retained earnings. Net income is added to the beginning balance of retained earnings and then dividends are subtracted. The June statement of retained earnings for JK Productions is shown in the middle of Exhibit 4.11.

¶408.03 BALANCE SHEET

How would you benefit from preparing an income statement for your personal finances?

The balance sheet shows the assets, liabilities, and stockholders' equity accounts. Recall the accounting equation: Assets = Liabilities + Stockholders' Equity. Note that the retained earnings amount reflects the balance after the changes reported on the statement of retained earnings. The June balance sheet for JK Productions is shown at the bottom of Exhibit 4.11.

¶409 Financial Statement Format

> **LEARNING OBJECTIVE 9:** Be able to use either of the two formats for the income statement and for the balance sheet.

Business firms have some flexibility in how the financial statements are arranged. The income statement and balance sheet can be prepared in two basic formats.

¶409.01 INCOME STATEMENT FORMAT

A single-step income statement involves only one step in computing net income; that step is the subtraction of expenses from revenues.

A multi-step income statement includes several subtotals to accentuate important relationships among revenues and expenses.

A **single-step income statement** shows all revenues under a heading such as "Revenues" or "Revenues and Gains." Expenses are shown together under a heading such as "Expenses" or "Expenses and Losses." Single-step means there is only one step to compute net income; that step is the subtraction of expenses from revenues.

A **multi-step income statement** includes several subtotals to accentuate important relationships among revenues and expenses. A multi-step income statement typically shows gross profit, operating income, and earnings before tax. Exhibit 4.12 presents the multi-step income statement for Marvel Enterprises, Inc. The single-step income statement is shown for comparison, and is adapted from the multi-step income statement.

Exhibit 4.12 MULTI-STEP VERSUS SINGLE-STEP INCOME STATEMENTS

Marvel Enterprises, Inc.
Consolidated Statement of Operations (Adapted as Multi-Step)
For Year Ended December 31, 20Y1

	($ Thousands)
Net Sales	$351,798
Cost of Sales and Operating Expenses	241,036
Operating Income	110,762
Other Income and Gains	1,798
Income Before Tax	112,560
Income Tax Expense	(39,071)
Other expense	(14,785)
Net Income	$58,704

Marvel Enterprises, Inc.
Consolidated Statement of Operations (Adapted as Single-Step)
For Year Ended December 31, 20Y1

	($ Thousands)
Revenues:	
Net Sales	$351,798
Other Income and Gains	1,798
Total Revenues	$353,596
Expenses:	
Cost of Sales and Operating Expenses	$241,036
Income Tax Expense	39,071
Other Expense	14,785
Total Expenses	294,892
Net Income	$58,704

A balance sheet in account format has assets on the left with liabilities and stockholders' equity on the right.

BALANCE SHEET FORMAT

The balance sheet can be arranged with the assets shown on the left and liabilities and stockholders' equity shown on the right. This arrangement is called the "**account format**," and is presented in Exhibit 4.13.

Exhibit 4.13 JK PRODUCTIONS BALANCE SHEET (ACCOUNT FORMAT) JUNE 30, 20Y1

ASSETS		LIABILITIES	
Cash	$40,900	Accounts Payable	$700
Accounts Receivable	4,400	Unearned Videography Fees	4,000
Supplies	300	Wages Payable	2,000
Prepaid Insurance	500	Income Tax Payable	760
Land	40,000	Total Liabilities	$7,460
Building	30,000		
		STOCKHOLDERS EQUITY	
		Common Stock	$100,000
		Retained Earnings	8,640
		Total Stockholders Equity	108,640
Total Assets	$116,100	Total Liabilities and Stockholders Equity	$116,100

The majority of large corporations use the **report format**. The report format presents the assets at the top, while liabilities and stockholders' equity follow underneath. The JK Productions balance sheet in report format is shown in Exhibit 4.14.

Exhibit 4.14 JK PRODUCTIONS BALANCE SHEET (REPORT FORMAT) JUNE 30, 20Y1

ASSETS	
Current Assets	
Cash	$40,900
Accounts Receivable	4,400
Supplies	300
Prepaid Insurance	500
Long-Term Assets	
Land	40,000
Building	30,000
Total Assets	$116,100
LIABILITIES AND STOCKHOLDERS EQUITY	
Liabilities	
Accounts Payable	$700
Unearned Videography Fees	4,000
Wages Payable	2,000
Income Tax Payable	760
Total Liabilities	$7,460
Stockholders Equity	
Common Stock	$100,000
Retained Earnings	8,640
Total Stockholders Equity	108,640
Total Liabilities and Stockholders Equity	$116,100

The balance sheet in report format displays assets at the top with liabilities and stockholders' equity accounts underneath.

¶410

Ethical Issues Pertaining to Accrual Accounting

LEARNING OBJECTIVE 10: Understand the ethical issues associated with accrual accounting.

Auditors provide assurance that publicly-traded companies follow GAAP in preparing their financial statements, including the proper accruals of revenues and expenses. At the beginning of the twenty-first century, in the aftermath of questionable accounting practices and major corporate failures, many Americans became concerned about the quality of auditing among U.S. corporations. In response, Congress passed the **Sarbanes-Oxley Act** (SOX). Key provisions of SOX include:

- Establishing a Public Company Accounting Oversight Board (Board) consisting of five full-time members to set "auditing, quality control, ethics, independence and other standards relating to the preparation of audit reports;"
- Limiting the types of consulting services audit firms can provide for their public company audit clients;
- Requiring retention of audit work papers necessary to support the audit report for seven years;
- Requiring auditors to report on internal control, perform tests of compliance with SEC rules and regulations, perform concurring partner reviews, and rotate lead and concurring partners at least every five years; and
- Prohibiting audit firms from auditing public companies whose CEO, CFO, controller, or equivalents worked for the audit firm during the preceding year.

Accrual accounting provides a clear picture of profit or loss resulting from business operations. Cash basis accounting does not provide a complete picture of profitability because expenses incurred and revenues earned have not been attributed to the period. However, the accrual method may lead to ethical dilemmas for a company's management.

Suppose that on December 1, 20Y1, U-Pak-It pays $12,000 for six months of property insurance that goes into effect immediately. U-Pak-It should report $2,000 (1/6) as Insurance Expense on December 31. However, if 20Y1 is a banner year for profits and net income is higher than expected, top management may be tempted to expense the full $12,000 in 20Y1, rather than apportioning $10,000 of the amount to 20Y2. Of course, this accounting treatment makes 20Y1's net income appear lower than it should, and 20Y2's appear higher. If all the expense gets reported eventually, why would management want to shift expenses from one period to another? The reason is that for corporations, whose stock is publicly traded, a smooth upward trend in net income is very desirable. A company that can be relied upon to consistently increase profit every year will usually have a higher stock price than a firm whose profits go up and down from year to year. Furthermore, top managers often own many shares of stock in the firm where they work. If the stock increases in value, the managers receive direct personal benefit.

To "smooth income" or "manage earnings" by using unethical accounting practices is unacceptable. Shifting expenses from one period to another violates GAAP (i.e., the expense recognition principle). Perhaps in the short run, a company can escape detection and get away with this type of fraud. Ultimately, however, such schemes are exposed. The external or internal auditors may discover the fraud. As a result, the managers involved lose their good reputations and often receive stiff fines or prison sentences. The Sarbanes-Oxley Act of 2002 established a new board to strengthen the audit process. The Act also increased prison sentences for fraud.

The media naturally highlights companies that are in financial and legal trouble. When Enron collapsed due to mismanagement and questionable accounting practices, the company was featured in daily news reports. This can cause the public to think that unethical business practices are more common than they really are. The truth is that the vast majority of business firms conduct business in a fair and ethical manner.

? *What motivated the government to intervene and pass the Sarbanes-Oxley Act?*

¶410

FOCUS ON ETHICS

Ethics and Social Responsibility at JC Penney

James Cash Penney operated under the policy "do unto others as you would have others do unto you" and appropriately named his first store the Golden Rule. When Mr. Penney founded his store in 1902, many courtesies that today's customers expect from a retail store such as money-back returns, standardized pricing, and customer service were not commonly offered. His store helped change the way retailers do business. Mr. Penney is quoted as saying, "Let all of us, who are in business, keep the well-being of our country in mind. No man can contribute to his country better things than the fruits of industry, individual integrity, enthusiasm for America and American institutions." In keeping with this motto, the JC Penney Company is committed to investing in community programs like JCPenney Afterschool Fund, a charitable organization that provides children with high-quality after-school programs. The company also supports community health and welfare issues primarily through support of local United Ways nationwide. In addition, JC Penney recognizes the volunteer work of its employees in the community through an annual award.

¶411

Concluding Remarks

You have progressed further down the road in your knowledge of accounting. Now you know about the adjustments that accounts undergo before being included in the financial statements. You know about the trial balance and closing entries. We discussed JC Penney's business cycle. The business cycle involves cash, and whenever cash is around, a few people may be tempted to take some. You know the saying – money is the root of all kinds of evil. This leads into the next chapter, which includes steps to safeguard a company's cash.

¶412

Chapter Review

LEARNING OBJECTIVE 1

Describe how the measurement of profitability and the assessment of financial position is valuable to people within and outside the firm.

Company management measures profitability and financial strength to determine if business operations are meeting company goals. Nothing reveals the successful teamwork of the functional areas more than a healthy profit. For a profit-oriented company, profit is the end result of a successful business cycle. In addition to management, a host of external users are interested in the financial viability of business firms. Investors are keenly interested in whether the company is profitable, and thus, generating a return on their investment. Investors, suppliers, lenders, and other external users must have financial reports to evaluate a firm's profitability and financial strength.

LEARNING OBJECTIVE 2

Describe the activities that comprise the business cycle.

The business cycle is the process of converting cash into goods and services for sale and then selling these goods and services in order to convert resources back into cash. The idea is to take in more cash from selling goods and services than to disburse cash to pay for materials, labor, and overhead. The business cycle can be broken down into four basic operating cycles: (1) expenditure cycle, (2) conversion cycle, (3) revenue (marketing) cycle, and (4) financial cycle.

Successful business operations depend on skilled people in the functional areas such as marketing, purchasing, production, finance, human resources, information management, and accounting. Frequently, people working in different functional areas are called to work together in teams to solve business problems and make plans for future operations. For example, marketing provides sales forecasts to production, so that the appropriate number of products can be produced. Using the sales forecasts and estimated production costs, accountants prepare budgets based on anticipated revenues and costs.

LEARNING OBJECTIVE 3

Explain the key steps in the accounting process.

The accounting process involves the steps in which accountants assimilate financial data for the purpose of producing the firm's financial statements. The accounting process starts with recording transactions and produces the financial statements. The periodicity concept requires that accounting information regarding a firm's business cycle be reported in regular intervals. The basic accounting period is one year. A fiscal year can be any 12-month time period. The fiscal year for most business firms is the calendar year from January 1 to December 31. The expense recognition principle simply states that expenses must be recorded in the accounting period in which they were used to generate revenue.

LEARNING OBJECTIVE 4

Implement accrual basis accounting.

Accrue means "to come into existence." Revenues and expenses often come into existence, even when cash has not changed hands. Accrual accounting shows revenues when earned, even if cash is not received. Accrual accounting shows expenses when incurred, even if cash is not disbursed.

LEARNING OBJECTIVE 5

Make the four basic types of adjusting journal entries.

There are four basic categories of adjustments: (1) deferred expense – a prepaid expense, (2) accrued expense – an expense incurred but not yet paid for, (3) deferred revenue – unearned revenue, and (4) accrued revenue – revenue earned but not yet received. Each adjusting entry affects at least one balance sheet account and one income statement account. This is because each adjusting entry affects either an asset or a liability (contained in the balance sheet), while also affecting either an expense or revenue (contained in the income statement).

¶412

LEARNING OBJECTIVE 6

Prepare an adjusted trial balance.

To prepare the adjusted trial balance, you start with account balances from the unadjusted trial balance, post the adjusting entries, and then prepare the adjusted trial balance.

LEARNING OBJECTIVE 7

Close the books.

Closing the books prepares the accounts for recording transactions in the next accounting period. Closing entries transfer the balances in revenue, expense, and dividends accounts to the Retained Earnings account; thus, revenue, expense, and dividends accounts start the next period with zero balances.

LEARNING OBJECTIVE 8

Prepare the financial statements from an adjusted trial balance.

The financial statements include the income statement, statement of retained earnings, balance sheet, and statement of cash flows. Information from the adjusted trial balance is sufficient to prepare all but the statement of cash flows.

LEARNING OBJECTIVE 9

Be able to use either of the two formats for the income statement and for the balance sheet.

A company has some flexibility in how the financial statements are arranged. There are two basic formats each for the income statement and balance sheet. The income statement can be either single-step or multi-step. The balance sheet can be either account format or report format.

LEARNING OBJECTIVE 10

Understand the ethical issues associated with accrual accounting.

Accrual accounting may cause ethical dilemmas for a company's management. Management may be tempted to "smooth income" or "manage earnings" by using unethical accounting practices. Such behavior spells disaster for the firm and its management.

¶413   Glossary

Account format (for a balance sheet)

A balance sheet with an account format is arranged with the assets shown on the left, and liabilities and stockholders' equity shown on the right.

Accounting process

The accounting process involves the steps in which accountants assimilate financial data for the purpose of producing the firm's financial statements.

Accrual basis accounting

The accrual basis of accounting records the financial effects of transaction in the periods in which those transactions occur rather than only in the periods in which cash is received or paid by the company.

Accruals

Accruals are adjustments made to accounts when the firm incurs an expense before paying cash, or earns revenue before receiving cash payment.

Accrued expense

An accrued expense is an expense for which cash is yet to be paid.

Accrued revenue

An accrued revenue is a revenue that has been earned but cash is yet to be collected.

Business cycle

The business cycle is the process of converting cash into goods and services for sale and then selling these goods and services in order to convert resources back into cash.

Cash basis accounting

The cash basis of accounting records revenues only if cash is received and expenses only if cash is disbursed.

Closing the books

Closing the books prepares the accounts for recording transactions in the next accounting period by setting the account balances to zero.

Closing entries

Closing entries transfer the balances in revenue, expense, and dividends accounts to the Retained Earnings account.

Conversion cycle

The conversion cycle involves the transformation of a firm's resources into products or services that are then sold to customers.

Deferrals

Deferrals are adjustments made to accounts when the firm either receives or pays cash in advance.

Deferred expense

A deferred expense, also called "prepaid expense," is a prepayment for an item, such as rent or supplies, which will become an expense in the future.

Deferred revenue

Deferred revenue, also called "unearned revenue," occurs when a firm collects cash for a service or product that it has not yet provided.

Expenditure cycle

This cycle includes purchasing of goods and services, plus payroll processing.

Financial cycle

This cycle concerns financing and investing activities, as well as financial reporting.

Interim period

An interim period is an accounting period that is less than a year.

Multi-step income statement

A multi-step income statement includes several subtotals to accentuate important relationships among revenues and expenses.

Net income

Net income is the amount by which revenues exceed expenses. Net income is also referred to as "net earnings or profit."

Net loss

Net loss occurs when a business firm's expenses are more than its revenues.

Periodicity concept

The periodicity concept requires that accounting information be reported in regular intervals.

Permanent accounts

The asset, liability, and stockholders' equity accounts are called "permanent" (or "real") accounts because the balances in these accounts at the end of one accounting period appear in the balance sheet and are carried forward to the subsequent period.

Report format (for a balance sheet)

A balance sheet in report format presents the assets at the top, with liabilities and stockholders' equity shown underneath.

Revenue cycle

Revenue cycle, also called the "marketing cycle," encompasses the marketing-related activities of the firm, such as sales order processing, shipping, and accounts receivable.

Single-step income statement

A single-step income statement involves only one step in computing net income; that step is the subtraction of expenses from revenues.

Temporary accounts

The revenue, expense, and dividends accounts are often referred to as "temporary" (or "nominal") accounts because they ultimately result in or represent changes in Retained Earnings that occur during an accounting period. All of the temporary accounts are closed to Retained Earnings at the end of the accounting period.

¶414

Appendix: Computerized Processing of Accounting Information

With the possible exception of Johann Gutenberg's movable type printing press (and printing of the famed Gutenberg Bible) in 1455, no single invention has changed the course of history more than the computer. Computerized processing of accounting information facilitates financial recording and analysis. Computations such as determining balances can be done automatically. Instead of storing information on paper documents, information is stored on an electronic device such as magnetic tape or magnetic disk. Electronic storage enables faster access, processing, and report preparation. Furthermore, and most important to accounting, computer processing results in greater accuracy than manual processing, assuming that the programming is reliable.

In a manual system, the general journal is used to update the general ledger. In computer environments, transaction files are used to update master files. Thus, for computer processing, the general journal is called the "**general journal transaction file**" and the general ledger is called the "**general ledger master file.**" The flowchart in Exhibit 4.A illustrates what happens in a computerized accounting system or activity.

Exhibit 4.A Flowchart of Computerized Accounting Processing

FLOWCHART

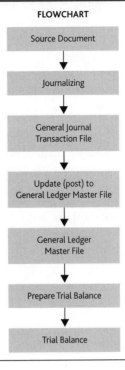

Source Document

↓

Journalizing

↓

General Journal Transaction File

↓

Update (post) to General Ledger Master File

↓

General Ledger Master File

↓

Prepare Trial Balance

↓

Trial Balance

Has the computer enhanced your ability to keep track of your personal finances?

As shown in Exhibit 4.A, the accounting process starts with source documents (such as a sales invoice) that provide the basis for journal entries, which are subsequently posted to general ledger accounts. Keep in mind, that the steps in accounting processing are essentially the same whether they are done manually or electronically.

The accumulation, storage, and processing of vast amounts of financial data once required armies of "number-crunchers." Now the number-crunching is turned over to computers. Accountants are able to focus on other roles in the firm, such as financial analysis, operational auditing, internal control evaluation, and managerial planning. Accountants prepare a wide variety of financial information and recommendations. With the increased availability and sharing of information comes the social and ethical responsibility to ensure that the information is accurate and complete. Ensuring accuracy and completeness of financial information is a key responsibility of accountants.

¶414

¶415   Chapter Assignments

QUESTIONS

1. **[Obj. 1]** What types of transactions do accountants track and report? How does this reporting help management?

2. **[Obj. 1]** Why are lenders and suppliers interested in a company's financial position before conducting business with them?

3. **[Obj. 2]** Why is profit a key goal of a business? List some ways a firm can help prevent employees from trying to achieve this goal through unethical business practices.

4. **[Obj. 2]** What is the accounting definition of net income?

5. **[Obj. 2]** Describe the business cycle.

6. **[Obj. 3]** What is the periodicity concept?

7. **[Obj. 3]** Describe the revenue and expense recognition principles.

8. **[Obj. 4]** Compared to the cash basis, how does accrual basis accounting provide a more complete and accurate picture of business financial activity?

9. **[Obj. 4]** When is revenue earned?

10. **[Obj. 5]** What are the four basic categories of adjustments?

11. **[Obj. 5]** Define the following:
    a. deferred (prepaid) expense
    b. accrued expense
    c. accrued revenue
    d. deferred (unearned) revenue

12. **[Obj. 5]** What two things did Benjamin Franklin say are certain?

13. **[Obj. 5]** How can spreadsheet software assist with the adjusting process?

14. **[Obj. 7]** What does "closing the books" mean?

15. **[Obj. 7]** Describe closing entries.

16. **[Obj. 7]** What are temporary accounts and why are they called temporary?

17. **[Obj. 7]** What are permanent accounts and why are they called permanent?

18. **[Obj. 9]** What are the two income statement formats?

19. **[Obj. 9]** What are the two balance sheet formats?

20. **[Obj. 10]** Why would top managers at a business firm be tempted to "smooth income" or "manage earnings" through unethical accounting practices?

21. **[Appendix]** In computer environments, what is the relationship between transaction files and master files? How does this apply to the general journal and general ledger?

22. **[Appendix]** Why are flowcharts useful for describing accounting systems or activities?

SHORT EXERCISES – SET A

Building Accounting Skills

1. **[Obj. 5]** Journal Entry to Record Supplies Used: Suppose $680 of supplies were on hand at the beginning of August. On August 15, an additional $725 of supplies was purchased. Only $200 of supplies was on hand at the end of August. What adjusting journal entry should be made on August 31?

2. **[Obj. 5]** Using T Accounts: Using T accounts, record the beginning balances and transactions for the Supplies and Supplies Expense accounts from Exercise A1. (**Note:** An example can be found in the discussion of supplies under Deferred Expense.)

3. **[Obj. 5]** Journal Entry for Prepaid Rent: On Sept. 1 you move into a new apartment; rent is $600 a month. The landlord requires you to pay two months' rent in advance. As the renter, record the prepaid rent as a journal entry in your general journal.

4. **[Obj. 5]** Journal Entries for Unearned Fees: Suppose that on March 1, 20Y1 IBM Corporation was paid $24,000 in advance for computer services that were to be provided over the next two years.
    a. What journal entry would be made on March 1 for the computer services fees paid in advance?
    b. Assuming adjusting entries are made at year-end, what entry would be made on December 31?

5. **[Obj. 5]** Recording Adjusting Entry and T Accounts: On September 1, your company rents new office space that requires two months rent in advance. Rent per month is $600. The journal entry to record payment of the prepaid rent is as follows.

Sep 1	Prepaid Rent	1,200	
	Cash		1,200

At the end of September, half of the prepaid expense is used and has become an expense.
    a. Show the adjusting journal entry to Rent Expense and Prepaid Rent for Sept. 30.
    b   What type of adjustment is this?
    c. Show the T accounts for Prepaid Rent and Rent Expense.

6. **[Obj. 5]** Recording Adjusting Entry and T Accounts: On April 1 your company buys supplies for $500 and made this entry:

Apr. 1	Supplies	500	
	Cash		500

The amount of supplies used during April, $400 worth, is the supplies expense.
    a. Show the adjusting entry to Supplies Expense and Supplies for April 30.
    b. What type of adjustment is this?
    c. Show the T accounts for Supplies Expense and Supplies.

7. **[Obj. 5]** Recording Adjusting Entry and T Accounts: On January 1 your company pays $3,000 for insurance; this is six months of insurance in advance. The journal entry is as follows.

Jan. 1	Prepaid Insurance	3,000	
	Cash		3,000

    a. Make the adjusting entry to Prepaid Insurance on Jan. 31.
    b. What type of adjustment is this?
    c. Show the T accounts for Prepaid Insurance and Insurance Expense.

8. **[Obj. 5]** Recording Adjusting Entry and T Accounts: Your company estimates its income tax for May to be $10,000.
    a. Make the appropriate adjusting entry to Income Tax Expense and Income Tax Payable for May 31.
    b. What type of adjustment is this?
    c. Show the T accounts for Income Tax Expense and Income Tax Payable.

9. **[Obj. 5]** Recording Adjusting Entry and T Accounts: Domino's Pizza is supplying the pizzas for a graduation bash. The person throwing the party pays $250 in advance. Domino's records the following journal entry.

May 5	Cash	250	
	Unearned Pizza Revenue		250

Domino's delivers the pizzas to the party on May 13.

a. Make the adjusting entry on May 13.
b. What type of adjustment is this?
c. Show the T accounts for Unearned Pizza Revenue and Pizza Revenue.

10. **[Obj. 5]** Adjusting Entry for Accounts Receivable: The New York Times has a customer who paid in advance $10,000 for advertising on June 1 for ads to be run in the month of June. The Times' journal entry for June 1 was:

June 1	Cash	10,000	
	Unearned Advertising Revenue		10,000

Make the Times' adjusting entry on June 30. What type of adjustment is this?

11. **[Obj. 7]** Journal Entry to Close Revenue Account: Assume your company has $10,000 in Fees Revenue at the end of the accounting period. What journal entry is required to close the revenue account?

SHORT EXERCISES – SET B

Building Accounting Skills

1. **[Obj. 5]** Journal Entry to Record Supplies Used: Suppose $200 of supplies were on hand at the beginning of August. Supplies purchased during August amounted to $550. Only $100 of supplies was on hand at the end of August. What adjusting journal entry should be made on August 31?

2. **[Obj. 5]** Using T Accounts: Using T accounts, record the beginning balances and transactions for the Supplies and Supplies Expense accounts from Exercise B1. (**Note:** An example can be found in the discussion of supplies under Deferred Expense.)

3. **[Obj. 5]** Journal Entry for Prepaid Rent: On Sept. 1 you move into a new apartment; rent is $1,000 a month. The landlord requires you to pay two months' rent in advance. As the renter, record the prepaid rent as a journal entry in your general journal.

4. **[Obj. 5]** Journal Entries for Unearned Fees: Suppose that on March 1, 20Y1 Microsoft Corporation was paid $48,000 in advance for computer services that were to be provided over the next two years.

a. What journal entry would be made on March 1 for the computer services fees paid in advance?
b. Assuming adjusting entries are made at year-end, what entry would be made on December 31?

5. **[Obj. 5]** Recording Adjusting Entry and T Accounts: On September 1, your company rents new office space that requires two months rent in advance. Rent per month is $1200. The journal entry to record payment of the prepaid rent is as follows.

Sept. 1	Prepaid Rent	2,400	
	Cash		2,400

At the end of September, half of the prepaid expense is used and has become an expense.

a. Show the adjusting journal entry to Rent Expense and Prepaid Rent for Sep. 30.
b. What type of adjustment is this?
c. Show the T accounts for Prepaid Rent and Rent Expense.

6. **[Obj. 5]** Recording Adjusting Entry and T Accounts: On April 1 your company buys supplies for $1,000 and made this entry:

Apr. 1	Supplies	1,000	
	Cash		1,000

The amount of supplies used during April, $400 worth, is the supplies expense.
   a. Show the adjusting entry to Supplies Expense and Supplies for April 30.
   b. What type of adjustment is this?
   c. Show the T accounts for Supplies Expense and Supplies.

7. **[Obj. 5]** Recording Adjusting Entry and T Accounts: On January 1 your company pays $6,000 for insurance; this is six months of insurance in advance. The journal entry is as follows.

Jan. 1	Prepaid Insurance	6,000	
	Cash		6,000

   a. Make the adjusting entry to Prepaid Insurance on Jan. 31.
   b. What type of adjustment is this?
   c. Show the T accounts for Prepaid Insurance and Insurance Expense.

8. **[Obj. 5]** Recording Adjusting Entry and T Accounts: Your company estimates its income tax for May to be $5,000.
   a. Make the appropriate adjusting entry to Income Tax Expense and Income Tax Payable for May 31.
   b. What type of adjustment is this?
   c. Show the T accounts for Income Tax Expense and Income Tax Payable.

9. **[Obj. 5]** Adjusting Entry for Revenue: Pizza Hut is supplying the pizzas for a graduation bash. The person throwing the party pays $125 in advance. Pizza Hut's records the following journal entry.

May 5	Cash	125	
	Unearned Pizza Revenue		125

Pizza Hut delivers the pizzas to the party on May 13.
   a. Make the adjusting entry on May 13.
   b. What type of adjustment is this?
   c. Show the T accounts for Unearned Pizza Revenue and Pizza Revenue.

10. **[Obj. 5]** Adjusting Entry for Accounts Receivable: The Shreveport Times has a customer who paid $5,000 in advance for advertising on March 1 for ads to be run in the month of March. The Times' journal entry for March 1 was:

March 1	Cash	5,000	
	Unearned Advertising Revenue		5,000

Make the Times' adjusting entry on March 31. What type of adjustment is this?

11. **[Obj. 7]** Journal Entry to Close Revenue Account: Assume your company has $25,000 in Fees Revenue at the end of the accounting period. What journal entry is required to close the revenue account?

PROBLEMS – SET A

Applying Accounting Knowledge

1. **[Obj. 5]** Using T Accounts: The accounting records of Pier Two Exports include the following unadjusted balances at March 31: Accounts Receivable $2,000; Supplies $3,200; Wages Payable $1,000; Unearned Service Revenue $600; Service Revenue $7,500; Wages Expense $4,000; Supplies Expense $0. Pier Two Exports accumulated the following data to make the March 31 adjusting entries:
   a. Wages owed to employees: $3,000
   b. Supplies on hand: $1,600
   c. Service revenue accrued: $2,100
   d. Unearned service revenue that has been earned: $400

   Required: Set up T accounts for all the above, with their beginning balances. Next, post the adjustments directly in the accounts, keying each adjustment amount by letter. Show the adjusted balance for each account. No journal entries are required.

2. **[Obj. 5]** Recording Adjusting Entries: Suppose IBM faced the following situations:
   a. Employee wages owed for three days of a five-day workweek; weekly payroll is $10,000.
   b. Income before income tax is $50,000. The income tax rate is 40 percent.
   c. Prepaid insurance, beginning, $800. Payments for insurance during the period, $1,000. Prepaid insurance, ending $1,200.
   d. Unearned service fees that were earned during the period, $7,700.
   e. Supplies on hand at the beginning of the period, $3,300. Supplies on hand at the end of the period, $2,000.

   Required: Make the adjusting journal entry for each situation at Dec. 31.

3. **[Obj. 5]** Recording Adjusting Entries: Suppose Mercury Shoe Company faced the following situations at the end of June:
   a. Supplies at the beginning of the month: $1,000. Supplies purchased during the month: $1,200. Supplies on hand at the end of the month: $900
   b. Prepaid insurance expired: $200
   c. Accrued wages: $2,350
   d. Accrued income tax: $1,800
   e. Accrued service fees revenue: $330
   f. Amount of unearned service fees that has been earned: $1,400

   Required: Make the adjusting journal entry for each situation on June 30, 20Y1.

4. **[Obj. 5]** Recording Adjusting Entries: Suppose Corinthian Consulting Company faced the following situations at the end of October 20Y1.
   a. Supplies used: $200
   b. Prepaid Insurance at the beginning of the month: $800. Prepaid Insurance purchased during the month: $200. Prepaid Insurance that has not expired at the end of the month: $500
   c. Accrued wages: $1,100
   d. Accrued income tax: $840
   e. Accrued service fees revenue: $920
   f. Amount of unearned service fees that has been earned: $620

   Required: Make the adjusting journal entry for each situation.

5. **[Obj. 7 & 8]** Preparing Closing Entries: The adjusted trial balance for JC Penney is shown below.

   Required:
   a. Prepare closing entries.
   b. What is the amount of net income?

JC Penney
Adjusted Trial Balance January 25, 20Y1

	($ Millions)	
Account Title	**Debit**	**Credit**
Cash	$2,474	
Accounts Receivable	705	
Inventory	4,945	
Prepaid Expenses	229	
Property & Equipment, Net	4,901	
Other Long-Term Assets, Net	4,613	
Accounts Payable		$3,791
Other Current Liabilities		368
Long Term Liabilities		5,947
Income Tax Payable		1,391
Common Stock		3,553
Retained Earnings		2,573
Dividends	161	
Sales Revenue		32,347
Cost of Sales	22,573	
Selling, General & Admin. Expense	8,667	
Internet Expense	388	
Other Expenses	101	
Income Tax Expense	213	
Total	$49,970	$49,970

6. **[Obj. 7 & 8]** Preparing Closing Entries: The adjusted trial balance for Joe's Auto Body Shop is shown below.

Required:
a. Prepare closing entries.
b. What is the amount of net income?

Joe's Auto Body Shop
Adjusted Trial Balance November 30, 20Y1

Account Title	Debit	Credit
Cash	$6,240	
Accounts Receivable	24,550	
Supplies	8,300	
Prepaid Insurance	1,050	
Land	57,800	
Accounts Payable		5,600
Unearned Service Fees		2,400
Wages Payable		1,560
Income Tax Payable		525
Common Stock		10,000
Additional Paid-In Capital		30,000
Retained Earnings		24,145
Dividends	1,200	
Service Fees Revenue		30,420
Wage Expense	2,320	
Utility Expense	150	
Supplies Expense	2,400	
Insurance Expense	275	
Income Tax Expense	365	
Total	$115,750	$115,750

7. **[Obj. 6]** Preparing Adjusted Trial Balance Worksheet: Required: Using the following adjustments from Problem A3 regarding Mercury Shoe Company, complete the worksheet started below.
   a. Supplies at the beginning of the month: $1,000. Supplies purchased during the month: $1,200. Supplies on hand at the end of the month: $900
   b. Prepaid insurance expired: $200
   c. Accrued wages: $2,350
   d. Accrued income tax: $1,800
   e. Accrued service fees revenue: $330
   f. Amount of unearned service fees that has been earned: $1,400

Mercury Shoe Company
Worksheet to Prepare Adjusted Trial Balance June 30, 20Y1

	Trial Balance		Adjustments		Adjusted Trial Balance	
	Dr.	Cr.	Dr.	Cr.	Dr.	Cr.
Cash	$41,300					
Accounts Receivable	3,000					
Supplies	2,200					
Prepaid Insurance	600					
Land	40,000					
Equipment	30,000					
Accounts Payable		$1,300				
Unearned Service Fees		6,000				
Wages Payable		0				
Income Tax Payable		0				
Common Stock		100,000				
Retained Earnings		0				
Dividends	1,000					
Service Fees Revenue		13,000				
Wage Expense	2,000					
Fuel Expense	200					
Supplies Expense	0					
Insurance Expense	0					
Income Tax Expense	0					
Total	$120,300	$120,300	0	0	0	0

8. **[Obj. 6]** Preparing Adjusted Trial Balance Worksheet: Required: Using the following adjustments from Problem A4 regarding Corinthian Consulting Company, complete the worksheet below.
    a. Supplies used: $200
    b. Prepaid Insurance at the beginning of the month: $800. Prepaid Insurance purchased during the month: $200. Prepaid Insurance that has not expired at the end of the month: $500
    c. Accrued wages: $1,100
    d. Accrued income tax: $840
    e. Accrued service fees revenue: $920
    f. Amount of unearned service fees that has been earned: $620

Corinthian Consulting Company
Worksheet to Prepare Adjusted Trial Balance October 31, 20Y1

	Trial Balance		Adjustments		Adjusted Trial Balance	
	Dr.	Cr.	Dr.	Cr.	Dr.	Cr.
Cash	$12,450					
Accounts Receivable	2,420					
Supplies	600					
Prepaid Insurance	1,000					
Land	30,500					
Equipment	28,800					
Accounts Payable		$2,420				
Unearned Service Fees		3,260				
Wages Payable		0				
Income Tax Payable		0				
Common Stock		66,000				
Retained Earnings		0				
Dividends	800					
Service Fees Revenue		6,830				
Wage Expense	1,440					
Fuel Expense	500					
Supplies Expense	0					
Insurance Expense	0					
Income Tax Expense	0					
Total	$78,510	$78,510	0	0	0	0

9. **[Obj. 8]** Financial Reporting with and without the Cash Basis of Accounting: At the start of 20Y1, General Auto Company had $10,000 in cash. During the year, the company made sales of $88,800 (assume all on account) and collected cash of $62,600 from customers. Cost of sales was $40,000, which was paid in cash. All other expenses totaled $30,000, of which the company has paid $25,000 and still owes $5,000.

Required:
a. Based on the above information, compute the net income or net loss for General Auto Company.
b. Based on the above information, what items would be reported on the balance sheet?
c. Assume that General Auto uses the cash basis of accounting. What would be the net income or net loss?
d. Assuming the cash basis of accounting, what items would be shown on the balance sheet?
e. Evaluate: How much profit is General Auto making as a percentage of sales? Besides increasing sales, how might profit be increased?

10. **[Obj. 8]** Preparing Financial Statements: The adjusted trial balance of JC Penney (adapted) is shown below.

JC Penny
Adjusted Trial Balance January 25, 20Y1

	($ Millions)	
Account Title	**Debit**	**Credit**
Cash	$2,474	
Accounts Receivable	705	
Inventory	4,945	
Prepaid Expenses	229	
Property & Equipment, Net	4,901	
Other Long-Term Assets, Net	4,613	
Accounts Payable		$3,791
Other Current Liabilities		368
Long Term Liabilities		5,947
Income Tax Payable		1,391
Common Stock		3,553
Retained Earnings		2,573
Dividends	161	
Sales Revenue		32,347
Cost of Sales	22,573	
Selling, General & Admin. Expense	8,667	
Internet Expense	388	
Other Expenses	101	
Income Tax Expense	213	
Total	$49,970	$49,970

JC Penney's fiscal year ends on the last Saturday in January.

Required:
a. Prepare Penney's income statement.
b. Prepare Penney's statement of retained earnings for year ended Jan. 25, 20Y1.
c. Prepare Penney's balance sheet on January 25, 20Y1.
d. Draw arrows linking the three statements. (Refer to Exhibit 4.11.)
e. Evaluate: How would you assess Penney's financial situation?

11. **[Obj. 8]** Preparing Financial Statements: The adjusted trial balance for Breathtaking Beauty Salon, Inc. follows.

Breathtaking Beauty Salon, Inc.
Adjusted Trial Balance November 30, 20Y1

Account Title	Debit	Credit
Cash	$450	
Accounts Receivable	6,790	
Supplies	4,560	
Prepaid Expenses	345	
Land	72,000	
Building	54,800	
Accounts Payable		$29,510
Unearned Service Fees		800
Wages Payable		890
Income Tax Payable		660
Common Stock		75,000
Retained Earnings		22,820
Dividends	600	
Service Fees Revenue		12,695
Wages Expense	640	
Fuel Expense	300	
Supplies Expense	770	
Insurance Expense	300	
Income Tax Expense	820	
Total	$142,375	$142,375

Required:
a. Prepare the Salon's income statement
b. Prepare the Salon's statement of retained earnings for the month ended November 30, 20Y1.
c. Prepare the Salon's balance sheet for November 30, 20Y1.
d. Draw the arrows linking the three statements. (Refer to Exhibit 4.11.)
e. Evaluate: How would you assess the Salon's financial situation?

12. **[Obj. 8]** Preparing Financial Statements: Assume the account balances provided in Problem A11, except change the adjusted trial balance amounts to:

Cash	$1,240
Wages Expense	$5,990
Supplies	$6,454
Income Tax Expense	$3,041
Service Fees Revenue	$22,950

Required:
a. Prepare income statement.
b. Prepare statement of retained earnings for the month ended November 30, 20Y1.
c. Prepare balance sheet for November 30, 20Y1.
d. Draw the arrows linking the three statements. (Refer to Exhibit 4.11.)
e. Evaluate: How would you assess the company's financial situation?

PROBLEMS – SET B

Applying Accounting Knowledge

1. **[Obj. 5]** Using T Accounts: The accounting records of The Pet Shop include the following unadjusted balances at March 31: Accounts Receivable $1,000; Supplies $1,600; Wages Payable $500; Unearned Service Revenue $300; Service Revenue $3,750; Wages Expense $2,000; Supplies Expense $0. The Pet Shop accumulated the following data to make the March 31 adjusting entries:
   a. Wages owed to employees, $1,500
   b. Supplies on hand, $800
   c. Service revenue accrued, $1,050
   d. Unearned service revenue that has been earned, $200

   Required: Set up T accounts for all of the above, with their beginning balances. Next, post the adjustments directly in the accounts, keying each adjustment amount by letter. Show the adjusted balance for each account. No journal entries are required.

2. **[Obj. 5]** Preparing Adjusting Entries: Suppose the local Cinemark Cinema faced the following situations:
   a. Employee wages owed for three days of a five-day workweek; weekly payroll is $5,000.
   b. Income before income tax is $25,000. The income tax rate is 40 percent.
   c. Prepaid insurance, beginning, $400. Payments for insurance during the period, $500. Prepaid insurance, ending $600.
   d. Unearned service fees that were earned during the period, $3,850.
   e. Supplies on hand at the beginning of the period, $1,650. Supplies on hand at the end of the period, $1,000.

   Required: Make the adjusting journal entry for each situation at Dec. 31.

3. **[Obj. 5]** Preparing Adjusting Entries: Suppose Copy Corner faced the following situations at the end of June:
   a. Supplies on hand at the beginning of the month, $1,000. Supplies purchased during the month, $1,200. Supplies on hand at the end of the month, $1,800.
   b. Prepaid insurance expired, $400.
   c. Accrued wages, $4,700.
   d. Accrued income tax, $3,600.
   e. Accrued service fees revenue, $660.
   f. Amount of unearned service fees that has been earned, $2,800.

   Required: Make the adjusting journal entry for each situation on June 30, 20Y1.

4. **[Obj. 5]** Preparing Adjusting Entries: Suppose Albertson's Grocery faced the following situations at the end of October 20Y1.
   a. Supplies used, $400.
   b. Prepaid Insurance at the beginning of the month, $800. Prepaid Insurance purchased during the month, $200. Prepaid Insurance that has not expired at the end of the month, $500.
   c. Accrued wages, $2,200
   d. Accrued income tax, $1,680.
   e. Accrued service fees revenue, $1,840.
   f. Amount of unearned service fees that has been earned, $1,240.

   Required: Make the adjusting journal entry for each situation.

5. **[Obj. 7 & 8]** Preparing Closing Entries: The adjusted trial balance for Saks Avenue follows:

Required:
a. Prepare closing entries.
b. What is the amount of net income?

Saks Avenue
Adjusted Trial Balance January 25, 20Y1

Account Title	($ Millions) Debit	Credit
Cash	$4,948	
Accounts Receivable	1,410	
Inventory	9,890	
Prepaid Expenses	458	
Property & Equipment, Net	9,802	
Other Long-Term Assets, Net	9,226	
Accounts Payable		$7,582
Other Current Liabilities		736
Long Term Liabilities		11,894
Income Tax Payable		2,782
Common Stock		7,106
Retained Earnings		5,146
Dividends	322	
Sales Revenue		64,694
Cost of Sales	45,146	
Selling, General & Admin. Expense	17,334	
Interest Expense	776	
Other Expenses	202	
Income Tax Expense	426	
Total	$99,940	$99,940

6. **[Obj. 7 & 8]** Preparing Closing Entries: The adjusted trial balance for Morgan Accounting Firm is shown below.

Required:
a. Prepare closing entries.
b. What is the amount of net income?

Morgan Accounting Firm
Adjusted Trial Balance November 30, 20Y1

Account Title	Debit	Credit
Cash	$12,480	
Accounts Receivable	49,100	
Supplies	16,600	
Prepaid Insurance	2,100	
Land	115,600	
Accounts Payable		11,200
Unearned Service Fees		4,800
Wages Payable		3,120
Income Tax Payable		1,050
Common Stock		20,000
Additional Paid-In Capital		60,000
Retained Earnings		48,290
Dividends	2,400	
Service Fees Revenue		60,840
Wages Expense	4,640	
Utility Expense	300	
Supplies Expense	4,800	
Insurance Expense	550	
Income Tax Expense	730	
Total	$231,500	$231,500

7. **[Obj. 6]** Preparing Adjusted Trial Balance Worksheet: Required: Using the following adjustments from Problem B3 regarding Copy Corner for the month of June, complete the worksheet started below.

    a. Supplies on hand at the beginning of the month, $1,000. Supplies purchased during the month, $1,200. Supplies on hand at the end of the month, $1,800.
    b. Prepaid insurance expired, $400.
    c. Accrued wages, $4,700.
    d. Accrued income tax, $3,600.
    e. Accrued service fees revenue, $660.
    f. Amount of unearned service fees that has been earned, $2,800.

Copy Corner
Worksheet to Prepare Adjusted Trial Balance June 30, 20Y1

	Trial Balance		Adjustments		Adjusted Trial Balance	
	Dr.	Cr.	Dr.	Cr.	Dr.	Cr.
Cash	$41,300					
Accounts Receivable	3,000					
Supplies	2,200					
Prepaid Insurance	600					
Land	40,000					
Equipment	30,000					
Accounts Payable		$1,300				
Unearned Service Fees		6,000				
Wages Payable		0				
Income Tax Payable		0				
Common Stock		100,000				
Retained Earnings		0				
Dividends	1,000					
Service Fees Revenue		13,000				
Wage Expense	2,000					
Fuel Expense	200					
Supplies Expense	0					
Insurance Expense	0					
Income Tax Expense	0					
Total	$120,300	$120,300	0	0	0	0

8. **[Obj. 6]** Preparing Adjusted Trial Balance Worksheet: Required: Using the following adjustments from Problem B4 regarding Albertson's Grocery at the end of October 20Y1, complete the worksheet below.
   a. Supplies used: $400.
   b. Prepaid Insurance at the beginning of the month: $800. Prepaid Insurance purchased during the month: $200. Prepaid Insurance that has not expired at the end of the month: $500.
   c. Accrued wages: $2,200
   d. Accrued income tax: $1,680.
   e. Accrued service fees revenue: $1,840.
   f. Amount of unearned service fees that has been earned: $1,240.

Albertson's Grocery
Worksheet to Prepare Adjusted Trial Balance October 31, 20Y1

	Trial Balance		Adjustments		Adjusted Trial Balance	
	Dr.	Cr.	Dr.	Cr.	Dr.	Cr.
Cash	$12,450					
Accounts Receivable	2,420					
Supplies	600					
Prepaid Insurance	1,000					
Land	30,500					
Equipment	28,800					
Accounts Payable		$2,420				
Unearned Service Fees		3,260				
Wages Payable		0				
Income Tax Payable		0				
Common Stock		66,000				
Retained Earnings		0				
Dividends	800					
Service Fees Revenue		6,830				
Wage Expense	1,440					
Fuel Expense	500					
Supplies Expense	0					
Insurance Expense	0					
Income Tax Expense	0					
Total	$78,510	$78,510	0	0	0	0

9. **[Obj. 8]** Financial Reporting with and without the Cash Basis of Accounting: At the start of 20Y1, Good Used Cars had $20,000 in cash. During the year, the company made sales of $177,600 (assume all on account) and collected cash of $125,200 from customers. Cost of sales was $80,000, which was paid in cash. All other expenses totaled $60,000, of which the company has paid $50,000 and still owes $10,000.

Required:
   a. Based on the above information, compute the net income or net loss for Good Used Cars.
   b. Based on the above information, what items would be reported on the balance sheet?
   c. Assume that Good Used Cars uses the cash basis of accounting. What would be the net income or net loss?
   d. Assuming the cash basis, what items would be shown on the balance sheet?
   e. Evaluate: Is Good Used Cars making an adequate profit relative to its sales? Besides increasing sales, how might profit be increased?

10. **[Obj. 8]** Preparing Financial Statements: The adjusted trial balance of Saks Avenue follows. Saks' fiscal year ends on the last Saturday in January.

Saks Avenue
Adjusted Trial Balance January 25, 20Y1

Account Title	($ Millions) Debit	Credit
Cash	$4,948	
Accounts Receivable	1,410	
Inventory	9,890	
Prepaid Expenses	458	
Property & Equipment, Net	9,802	
Other Long-Term Assets, Net	9,226	
Accounts Payable		$7,582
Other Current Liabilities		736
Long Term Liabilities		11,894
Income Tax Payable		2,782
Common Stock		7,106
Retained Earnings		5,146
Dividends	322	
Sales Revenue		64,694
Cost of Sales	45,146	
Selling, General & Admin. Expense	17,334	
Interest Expense	776	
Other Expenses	202	
Income Tax Expense	426	
Total	$99,940	$99,940

Required:

a. Prepare Saks' income statement.

b. Prepare Saks' statement of retained earnings for the year ended January 25, 20Y1.

c. Prepare Saks' balance sheet on January 25, 20Y1.

d. Draw arrows linking the three statements. (Refer to Exhibit 4.11.)

e. Evaluate: How would you assess Saks' financial situation?

11. **[Obj. 8]** Preparing Financial Statements: The adjusted trial balance for Sharp Nails follows.

Sharp Nails Adjusted Trial Balance November 30, 20Y1		
Account Title	**Debit**	**Credit**
Cash	$225	
Accounts Receivable	3,395	
Supplies	2,280	
Prepaid Expenses	172	
Land	36,000	
Building	27,400	
Accounts Payable		$14,755
Unearned Service Fees		400
Wages Payable		445
Income Tax Payable		330
Common Stock		37,500
Retained Earnings		11,410
Dividends	300	
Service Fees Revenue		6,347
Wages Expense	320	
Fuel Expense	150	
Supplies Expense	385	
Insurance Expense	150	
Income Tax Expense	410	
Total	$71,187	$71,187

Required:
a. Prepare the income statement for Sharp Nails.
b. Prepare Sharp Nails' statement of retained earnings for the month ended November 30, 20Y1.
c. Prepare Sharp Nails' balance sheet for November 30, 20Y1.
d. Draw the arrows linking the three statements. (Refer to Exhibit 4.11.)
e. Evaluate: How would you assess the financial situation of Sharp Nails?

12. **[Obj. 8]** Preparing Financial Statements: Same as Problem B11 regarding Sharp Nails, except change the adjusted trial balance amounts to:

Cash	$620
Wages Expense	$2,995
Supplies	$3,227
Income Tax Expense	$1,521
Service Fees Revenue	$11,475

Required:
a. Prepare income statement
b. Prepare statement of retained earnings for the month ended November 30, 20Y1.
c. Prepare balance sheet for November 30, 20Y1.
d. Draw the arrows linking the three statements. (Refer to Exhibit 4.11.)
e. Evaluate: How would you assess the company's financial situation?

CROSS-FUNCTIONAL PERSPECTIVES

Discussion Questions

1. **[Obj. 2]** List the four basic operating cycles within the business cycle. Briefly describe their functions.

2. **[Obj. 2]** In accounting terms, describe the marketing/revenue cycle and how it interacts with the accounting department.

3. **[Obj. 2]** Explain how the expenditure cycle interacts with the accounting department.

4. **[Obj. 2]** Describe accounting's connection with the conversion cycle, also referred to as the "production cycle."

5. **[Obj. 2]** How is accounting dependent upon the financial cycle?

6. **[Obj. 2]** People working in different functional areas of a firm work together to solve business problems and make plans for future operations. Give an example of this.

Cross-Functional Case:
Implementing Company Strategies

JC Penney's primary objective for its department store and catalog business is to re-establish and solidify the customer franchise, and strengthen customer confidence that JC Penney consistently offers fashionable, quality merchandise at value prices. The company hopes to improve department stores to competitive levels of profitability. To achieve this objective, the company wants to implement the following five strategies:
1. Have and maintain a competitive expense structure.
2. Attract and retain experienced and professional workforce.
3. Provide competitive, fashionable merchandise assortments.
4. Have a compelling and appealing marketing program.
5. Present vibrant and energized store environments.

Required: What can each of the following departments do to implement JC Penney's five strategies?
a. Accounting
b. Finance
c. Human resources (personnel)
d. Purchasing
e. Marketing

EXCEL ASSIGNMENTS

1. **[Obj. 8 & 9]** Preparing Multi-Step Income Statement: Intel Corporation is the world's largest semiconductor chipmaker. Major products include microprocessors, boards, flash memory, and Ethernet connectivity products. Shown below are account balances at fiscal year end December 28, 20Y1. The input area on your worksheet should include the account balances. The output area should include the income statement. The output area should be formula-driven, based on amounts in the input area.

	($ Millions)
Net Revenue	$26,764
Cost of Sales	13,446
Research and Development Expense	4,034
Marketing and Administrative Expense	4,334
Other Expenses	746
Income Tax Expense	1,087

Required: Prepare a multi-step income statement for Intel using the above information and Excel. Print your worksheet

2. **[Obj. 8 & 9]** Preparing Single-Step Income Statement: Use the information from the previous assignment to prepare a single-step income statement. The output area should be formula-driven, based on amounts in the input area.

   Required: Prepare a single-step income statement for Intel using Excel. Print your worksheet.

3. **[Obj. 6]** Preparing Adjusted Trial Balance Worksheet: Use Excel to create a worksheet similar to the one shown in Exhibit 4.8. List all accounts on the left, then set up columns for the trial balance, adjustments, and adjusted trial balance. Prepare your worksheet in good form, with an identification area, input area, and output area. The input area should include the trial balance (unadjusted) account balances and the adjustment data shown below. The output area should include the actual adjusted trial balance worksheet. The worksheet should be totally formula-driven, based on amounts shown in the input area.

   Required: Prepare an adjusted trial balance worksheet for Express Delivery Company using Excel. Print your worksheet.

Trial Balance (unadjusted) Account Balances	
Cash	37,277
Accounts Receivable	2,343
Supplies	2,440
Prepaid Insurance	490
Land	92,160
Accounts Payable	2,200
Unearned Delivery Fees	11,400
Wages Payable	3,400
Income Tax Payable	4,460
Common Stock	20,000
Additional Paid-In Capital	30,000
Retained Earnings	26,400
Dividends	4,000
Delivery Fees Revenue	53,800
Wages Expense	12,400
Fuel Expense	550
Supplies Expense	0
Insurance Expense	0
Income Tax Expense	0

Adjustments:	
a. Supplies used	1,220
b. Prepaid insurance expired	245
c. Accrued wages	4,200
d. Accrued income tax	1,450
e. Accrued delivery fees revenue	4,840

4. **[Obj. 6]** Preparing Adjusted Trial Balance: Continue from Excel assignment 3.

   Required: Add the adjusted trial balance to your output area, based on amounts in the worksheet. Print your worksheet.

5. **[Obj. 8]** Preparing Financial Statements: Continue from Excel assignment 4.

   Required: Based on the amounts in the adjusted trial balance, add the following to your output area: (a) income statement, (b) statement of retained earnings, and (c) balance sheet. Print your worksheet.

6. **[Obj. 6]** Preparing Adjusted Trial Balance Worksheet: Same as Excel assignment 3, except change the adjustment data to the following adjustments:
   a. Supplies used $644
   b. Prepaid insurance expired $154
   c. Accrued wages $3,530
   d. Accrued income tax $842
   e. Accrued delivery fees revenue $8,900

   Required: Prepare an adjusted trial balance worksheet using Excel. Print your worksheet.

7. **[Obj. 6]** Preparing Adjusted Trial Balance: Continue from Excel Assignment 6.

   Required: Prepare an adjusted trial balance using Excel, based on amounts in the worksheet. Print your worksheet.

8. **[Obj. 8]** Preparing Financial Statements: The adjusted trial balance for Joe's Auto Body Shop is shown below. On your worksheet, put the adjusted trial balance in the input area. The output area should include the income statement, statement of retained earnings, and balance sheet. (See Exhibit 4.8 for example). All amounts in the output area should be formula-driven, based on amounts in the input area.

Required: Prepare the income statement, statement of retained earnings, and balance sheet for Joe's Auto Body Shop using Excel. Print your worksheet.

Joe's Auto Body Shop Adjusted Trial Balance November 30, 20Y1		
Account Title	**Debit**	**Credit**
Cash	$6,240	
Accounts Receivable	24,550	
Supplies	8,300	
Prepaid Insurance	1,050	
Land	24,500	
Building	44,400	
Accumulated Depreciation — Building		$11,100
Accounts Payable		5,600
Unearned Service Fees		2,400
Wages Payable		1,560
Income Tax Payable		525
Common Stock		10,000
Additional Paid-In Capital		30,000
Retained Earnings		24,775
Dividends	1,200	
Service Fees Revenue		30,420
Wage Expense	2,320	
Utility Expense	150	
Supplies Expense	2,400	
Insurance Expense	275	
Depreciation Expense — Building	630	
Income Tax Expense	365	
Total	$116,380	$116,380

9. **[Obj. 8]** Preparing Financial Statements: Same as Excel assignment 8, except change the adjusted trial balance amounts as shown: Cash $2,440, Supplies $11,560, Wages Payable $2,475, and Income Tax Expense $1,820.

Required: Prepare the income statement, statement of retained earnings, and balance sheet for Joe's Auto Body Shop using Excel. Print your worksheet.

WEB ASSIGNMENTS

1. **[Obj. 2]** Use a Web search tool (e.g., Google) and find information on "earnings management." Prepare a one-page report. Use at least two Web sources. Cite your sources, including their Web addresses, in your report.

2. **[Obj. 2]** Use a Web search tool (e.g., Google) and find information about the business cycle of the firm. You should note that there are many articles about the business cycle of the national economy; this is different from the business cycle of the firm. Prepare a one-page report. Use at least two Web sources. Cite your sources, including their Web addresses, in your report.

3. **[Obj. 2]** In 20Y1, Nokia had net sales of EUR 29.5 billion (euro currency). It reported an operating profit of EUR 5 billion. Convert Nokia's net sales and operating profit to current year U.S. dollars. Do a search on Google to find a website that converts foreign currency.

4. **[Obj. 8]** Go to the New York Stock Exchange website and look up the description of General Electric Company (GE). Go to the website for GE or do a search on Google to find the current year's financial statements for GE. Prepare a short report on General Electric Company. Include the following information:
   a. The company's description from the NYSE
   b. The fiscal year end date
   c. The income statement format (single-step or multi-step)
   d. The amount of net income
   e. The balance sheet format (account format or report format)
   f. Total assets

5. **[Obj. 8]** Go to the New York Stock Exchange website and look up the description for a company of your choosing. Go to that company's website or do a search on Google to find the current year's financial statements of that company. Prepare a short report on the company including the following information:
   a. The company's description from the NYSE.
   b. The fiscal year end date.
   c. The income statement format (single-step or multi-step).
   d. The amount of net income.
   e. The balance sheet format (account format or report format).
   f. Total assets.

6. **[Obj. 10]** Go to the website for JC Penney or do a search on Google to find the history of James Cash Penney; describe his "golden rule" and how it affected the way he conducted business.

7. **[Obj. 10]** According to the Sarbanes-Oxley Act, what services are unlawful for a public accounting firm to provide to a current audit client? To find the answer, go to the website for the American Institute of Certified Public Accountants (AICPA) and look under Section 201: **Services Outside The Scope Of Practice Of Auditors; Prohibited Activities**, or do a search on Google.

8. **[Obj. 10]** Suppose an accountant quits working for an accounting firm and less than a year later becomes the CEO of ACME Manufacturing Company. As the new CEO, he wants to hire his old accounting firm to perform the audit for Acme. Is there a conflict of interest? To find the answer, go to the website for the American Institute of Certified Public Accountants (AICPA) and look under Section 206 of the Sarbanes-Oxley Act: Conflicts of Interest, or do a search on Google.

9. **[All Obj.]** Go to the website for JC Penney or do a search on Google to find an accounting related news item from the past year, such as JC Penney reporting on its sales and earnings. Give a one-paragraph summary of the news item.

10. **[Global]** One of the necessities in accounting for multi-national companies is converting foreign currency. Do a search on Google for a website that converts foreign currency; find the value of one U.S. dollar in British pounds, Hong Kong dollars, and Mexican pesos.

¶416   Test Prepper

Use this sample test to gauge your comprehension of the chapter material.

True/False Questions

___ 1. The accounting process starts with the trial balance and finishes with recording transactions.

___ 2. The periodicity concept requires that accounting information regarding a firm's business cycle be reported in regular intervals.

___ 3. A fiscal year always starts in January and ends in December.

___ 4. The cash basis of accounting applies the expense recognition principle.

___ 5. Accrual accounting is more complete, and therefore, more accurate than cash basis accounting.

___ 6. Accounts are adjusted at the end of an accounting period to ensure that all previously unrecorded revenues and expenses are recorded in the period in which earned or incurred.

___ 7. Accruals are adjustments made to accounts when the firm either receives or pays cash in advance.

___ 8. Deferred revenue results when cash is collected before the revenue is earned.

___ 9. A closing entry for the expense accounts includes a credit to Retained Earnings.

___ 10. Closing entries include the transfer of balances from revenue, expense, and dividends accounts to the Retained Earnings account.

Multiple-Choice Questions

___ 1. Which of the following statements is not true regarding net income?
   a. Net income is shown on the income statement.
   b. If expenses increase, net income decreases.
   c. Net income is synonymous with revenues.
   d. Net income is also called "net earnings."
   e. Net income is also called "net profit."

___ 2. Which of the following is not an operating cycle within the business cycle?
   a. marketing/revenue cycle
   b. expenditure cycle
   c. conversion cycle
   d. financial cycle
   e. recycling cycle

___ 3. Which of the following states that expenses must be recorded in the accounting period in which they were used to generate revenue?
   a. economic entity concept
   b. expense recognition principle
   c. periodicity concept
   d. cost principle
   e. monetary unit concept

___ 4. Which of the following is not true about accrual accounting?
   a. Accrual accounting is less accurate than cash basis accounting.
   b. Revenues are recorded when they are earned, even if cash is not received.
   c. Expenses are recorded when they are incurred, even if cash is not disbursed.
   d. Accrual accounting is more complete than cash basis accounting.
   e. Accrual accounting applies the expense recognition principle.

___ 5. A prepayment for an item that will become an expense in the future is:
   a. a deferred revenue
   b. an accrued revenue
   c. an accrued expense
   d. a deferred expense
   e. an accrued equity

___ 6. An example of an accrued expense is:
   a. prepaid insurance
   b. prepaid supplies
   c. wages expense
   d. prepaid rent
   e. all of the above

___ 7. A revenue that has been earned, but cash payment is yet to be collected, is:
   a. a deferred revenue
   b. an accrued revenue
   c. an accrued expense
   d. a deferred expense
   e. a deferred liability

___ 8. A prepayment for an item that will become an expense in the future is:
   a. a deferred revenue
   b. an accrued revenue
   c. an accrued expense
   d. a deferred expense
   e. a deferred liability

___ 9. Setting the revenue and expense accounts to zero at the end of the accounting period is referred to as:
   a. reformatting the books
   b. opening the books
   c. closing the books
   d. restarting the books
   e. accrual basis accounting

___ 10. Which of the following is not a provision of the Sarbanes-Oxley Act (SOX)?
   a. Requiring retention of audit work papers necessary to support the audit report for 15 years.
   b. Establishing a Public Company Accounting Oversight Board.
   c. Limiting the types of consulting services audit firms can provide for their public company audit clients.
   d. Prohibiting audit firms from auditing public companies whose CEO, CFO, Controller, or equivalents worked for the audit firm during the preceding year.
   e. Requiring auditors to report on internal control.

Chapter

5

Cash, Internal Controls, and Ethics

LEARNING OBJECTIVES

After studying Chapter 5, you should be able to do the following:

1. Describe how accounting issues concerning cash and internal control affect people within and outside the firm.
2. Describe the importance of cash in company operations.
3. Discuss internal controls over cash, prepare a cash budget, and reconcile a bank statement.
4. Identify the function of each of the components of internal control structure.
5. Explain the purpose of an audit and the need for audits in financial reporting.
6. Relate how business firms facilitate ethical decision-making.

CHAPTER CONTENTS

Cash, Internal Controls, and Ethics

FOCUS ON BUSINESS

Standards of Business Conduct at ExxonMobil Corporation

What if a house painter does impeccable work, but often overbills his customers for the hours he works. This painter won't be in business very long. ExxonMobil believes the way the company conducts business is as important as the results obtained. For nearly forty years, ExxonMobil has promoted business ethics and integrity through its 12-page booklet entitled, *Standards of Business Conduct*. Some of the topics included in this booklet are: ethics, antitrust, conflicts of interest, environment, product safety, and alcohol and drug use.

In 1999, Exxon and Mobil merged to form the ExxonMobil Corporation, a multinational giant in almost every aspect of the energy and petrochemical business. With oil and gas explorations on six of seven continents, the company is the largest non-government gas marketer and reserves holder. Fuels are marketed under the Exxon, Mobil, and Esso brands.

ExxonMobil believes that a well-founded reputation for scrupulous dealing is a priceless company asset. Accountants also believe that an untarnished reputation is invaluable. ExxonMobil, as well as people in general, rely on the accuracy and honesty of financial statements prepared by accountants. Accountants apply various standards and controls, as described in this chapter, to ensure accurate and complete financial reporting.

Source: *ExxonMobil.com*

¶501 Applications to People Within and Outside the Firm

LEARNING OBJECTIVE 1: Describe how accounting issues concerning cash and internal control affect people within and outside the firm.

The management of cash is one of the most critical tasks faced by a business. Poor cash management is one of the primary reasons that businesses fail, since cash is essential for operations. Both internal and external users are concerned with the protection and proper use of cash resources.

¶501.01 INTERNAL USERS

All departments within a firm need cash to pay employees and to purchase the items necessary to carry out company operations. At ExxonMobil, cash is needed to pay for oil and gas explorations. The purchase of drilling and refining equipment requires cash. Like any other company, the marketing department at ExxonMobil needs cash for advertising and marketing research. Every employee, in every department, should be wary of careless use of company resources, including cash.

To safeguard cash and the other assets of an organization, an internal control structure must be put in place. An internal control structure helps safeguard the assets of a business and helps ensure the reliability of accounting records. One part of the internal control structure concerns information and communication within the company's accounting system. If the accounting information is not reliable, how can marketing determine which products are selling well and which are not? How can production determine the costs of manufacturing various products? The internal control structure will be discussed in more detail later in the chapter.

¶501.02 EXTERNAL USERS

People external to ExxonMobil rely on the financial information provided to them. If internal controls are weak, there is a higher probability that errors and intentional misrepresentations will occur in the financial statements. How can investors trust that profits are accurately stated on financial reports, if the accounting information is unreliable? How can lenders determine whether ExxonMobil has the ability to pay back a loan, if the accounting information in unreliable? A solid system of internal controls thus provides greater trust by external users that a company's reports can be relied upon.

¶502

Cash and Cash Equivalents

 Everyone relates to the need for cash. Do you use controls to ensure that you have cash when needed or to safeguard your cash from theft?

Liquidity refers to how readily an asset can be converted to cash.

A cash equivalent is a short-term, highly liquid investment that will convert to cash in less than 90 days.

> **LEARNING OBJECTIVE 2:** Describe the importance of cash in company operations.

Cash is generally not a company's largest asset, but it is always a critically important one. Cash is necessary to carry on business operations. Without cash, a company cannot function, at least not for long. This is why one of the four financial statements—the statement of cash flows—focuses solely on cash.

Cash includes the coins and currency on hand, deposits in company bank accounts, and checks and money orders made out to the company. Cash is the first asset listed on the balance sheet. Assets are customarily listed in order of **liquidity**, that is, how readily an asset can be converted to cash. By definition, cash is the most liquid of all assets.

Some corporations, such as Procter and Gamble, list cash and cash equivalents together as the first item on the balance sheet. In the notes that accompanied its financial statements, **cash equivalents** were defined as highly liquid investments with maturities of three months or less. Examples of liquid investments are short-term bank certificates of deposit and short-term government securities. Since these investments are converted to cash in such a short time, they can be regarded as cash. By making these investments with idle cash, Procter and Gamble is able to generate additional income.

¶503

Internal Control Over Cash

Using the definition of cash equivalents above, how much cash do you have?

> **LEARNING OBJECTIVE 3:** Discuss internal controls over cash, prepare a cash budget, and reconcile a bank statement.

Cash is more vulnerable to theft than other assets. Since cash can be hidden from view, a thief can carry away cash much easier than inventory or equipment. Further, cash is subject to electronic theft and computer crime. A person with access to computer-based bank accounts can move cash with the push of a button. Thus, internal controls are critical for cash.

The concept of internal control has ancient origins. For example, a biblical report describes the use of dual custody of assets by the Apostle Paul. His reason for using internal controls was summed up with this statement: "We want to avoid any criticism of the way we administer this liberal gift. For we are taking pains to do what is right, not only in the eyes of the Lord but also in the eyes of men."[1] Paul recognized that internal controls prevent dishonest persons from doing wrong, but just as importantly prevent honest persons from being the subject of suspicion and false accusation.

In the past, most businesses were owned and operated by one person. Under this form of business, the control structure was very simple. The owner-operator maintained firsthand knowledge of all aspects of the business. In other words, he or she kept an eye on things so that nothing was stolen or lost. Today the dominant form of business is the corporation in which the owners, that is, the stockholders, rely on business managers to operate the firm. Business managers rely on the accounting information system to supply them with the financial information they need to make effective decisions. To ensure the accuracy and reliability of this information, a system of internal controls is established.

Inadequate internal controls can foster an environment in which employees and officers of a company are tempted to engage in questionable activities and accounting practices. Assuming that officers and employees are honest, strong controls should be provided to guard them from suspicion and false accusations. As for dishonest employees, strong controls will hopefully either prevent or reveal wrongdoing.

¶503.01   PREVENTIVE AND FEEDBACK CONTROLS

Two categories of internal controls are preventive and feedback.

In general, the internal controls of a company can be categorized as one of the following:

- **Preventive controls** help deter errors (unintentional misrepresentations) and irregularities (intentional misrepresentations) from occurring.
- **Feedback controls** identify errors and irregularities after they occur so that corrective action may be taken.

Both categories of accounting controls are essential in a company's control structure.

The separation of duties involves assigning the tasks related to a particular transaction among two or more employees.

An example of a preventive control is segregation of related organizational functions, also called the "**separation of duties**." This control involves assigning the tasks related to a particular transaction among two or more employees. In particular, the physical custody of an asset should be kept separate from the record keeping function. For example, the person who is responsible for writing checks for disbursements at ExxonMobil should not be assigned the task of reconciling the bank account. Other preventive controls include:

- Hiring competent and ethical employees
- Written policies and procedures
- Physical security of firm assets
- Appropriate management supervision
- Adequate documents and records

The second category of internal controls, feedback controls, are effective only if they include the following characteristics: (1) benefits exceed costs of operating the controls; (2) deviations from the benchmark (e.g., budget or standards) are reported on a timely basis; (3) relevant and understandable information is provided; and (4) the manager takes action in a timely manner. Feedback controls include cash management controls; these involve procedures and techniques that help ensure cash is accounted for and spent on items approved by management. Practical examples of cash management or feedback controls include:

- Cash budget
- Bank checking account
- Bank reconciliation

¶503.02   CASH BUDGET

The cash budget is used to project financing needs and to provide internal controls over cash inflows and outflows.

The **cash budget** acts as a management tool and enables the company to project financing needs. It also provides internal control over cash inflows and outflows. As shown in Exhibit 5.1, the cash budget starts with the beginning cash balance, adds expected cash receipts (inflows), and subtracts expected cash disbursements (outflows). The result is the expected cash available. In its budget, the company has established the amount of cash it wants to have on hand at the end of the period; this is called the "budgeted cash balance." If the budgeted cash balance is more than the cash available, then financing is needed to make up the difference. In the case of Exhibit 5.1, financing is needed for $85 million. If the cash available had exceeded the budgeted cash balance, then no new financing would be needed.

Exhibit 5.1 CASH BUDGET
Argonaut Shipping Company Cash Budget For Year Ended December 31, 20Y1

	($ Millions)	
Cash balance, Jan. 1, 20Y1		$162
Estimated cash receipts		
Collections from customers	$12,748	
Sales of assets	160	12,908
		13,070
Estimated cash disbursements		
Payment of operating expenses	8,760	
Purchase of equipment	3,700	
Payment of debt	330	
Dividends	240	13,030
Cash available before financing		40
Budgeted cash balance, December 31, 20Y1		125
New financing needed		$85

¶503.03   BANK CHECKING ACCOUNT

Under a lockbox system, firms arrange for customers to send cash payments to an address that is effectively a bank account.

A very basic internal control over cash is setting up a bank checking account. By keeping cash in the bank account, the company relies on the bank to safeguard the cash. Banks prepare detailed statements listing the cash transactions of their depositors.

A business should deposit all cash receipts in its bank account. Cash receipts come from three basic sources: over-the-counter, in the mail, and electronic funds transfer (EFT). Employees receive over-the-counter cash receipts at the business location. Typically, cash registers are used to maintain control over these cash receipts. Only authorized cashiers can open the registers. The registers generate a record of sales transactions and cash received. At the end of the day, a manager can verify that the record matches the amount in the register.

Cash received by mail in the form of checks should be carefully controlled and accounted for by personnel in the mailroom. Procedures should be established to ensure that money received from customers or other sources is accumulated and sent to the treasurer for deposit. Some businesses arrange for customers to send cash payments to an address that is effectively a bank account. This arrangement is referred to as a "**lockbox system.**" The lockbox system avoids the handling of cash by company personnel.

Electronic funds transfer is an arrangement whereby cash is transferred from one company's bank account to another company's bank account. For example, a company like McDonald's or Target can use EFT to pay suppliers for purchases. As a result, these companies will not have to write as many checks.

A business should make payments by writing a check on its bank account, instead of using cash on hand. By making deposits to and payments from the bank account, all cash transactions are documented by the bank. This helps ensure that all cash transactions of the business firm are recorded and properly accounted for in the firm's accounting records. The one exception is for very small payments, in which case, cash payment can be made from a petty cash fund, which is described later in this chapter.

A remittance advice is a document that specifies the purpose of the check.

To pay money out of the bank checking account, the depositor prepares a check. The **check** is a legal document that directs the bank to pay a specific cash amount to a designated person or company. Some companies prepare a remittance advice that corresponds to each check written. A **remittance advice** is a document that specifies the purpose of the check, such as paying for advertising. The remittance advice is sometimes attached to the check itself.

¶503.04 BANK RECONCILIATION

The bank reconciliation is a very important internal control over cash because it provides feedback on whether the transactions affecting cash have been recorded properly. The purpose of a bank reconciliation is to resolve differences between the cash balance on the bank statement and the cash balance on the accounting records (books). An example of a bank statement is shown in Exhibit 5.2. The company's record of cash transactions must be reconciled to the bank's record of cash transactions shown on the bank statement. If errors have been made by the firm on the books or by the bank on the bank statement, they can be identified and corrected.

Exhibit 5.2 BANK STATEMENT FOR JK PRODUCTIONS

Metropolitan National Bank
1601 South Avenue
Memphis, TN 55555

ACCOUNT STATEMENT

Customer Account:

JK Productions Company

1121 Sweetbriar — Checking Account Summary

Memphis, TN 55555 — As of 09/30/Y1

Beginning Balance	Total Deposits	Total Withdrawals	Ending Balance
$22,043	$1,322	$8,745	$14,620

DEPOSITS		DATE	AMOUNT
Deposit		09/06	$1,322

WITHDRAWALS

Checks:

Number	Date	Amount
57324	09/04	$4,850
57325	09/08	$2,250
57327	09/12	$558
57328	09/23	$900

Other withdrawals:

Item	Date	Amount
Service Charge	09/05	$15
Check Order	09/07	$28
NSF	09/18	$144

The Cash account at JK Productions shows the deposits made and the payments disbursed.

Account: CASH					
Date		Item	Debit	Credit	Balance
20Y1					
Sep.	1	Balance			22,043
	2	Check # 57324		4,850	17,193
	5	Cash receipt	1,322		18,515
	6	Check # 57325		2,250	16,265
	8	Check # 57326		784	15,481
	10	Check # 57327		568	14,913
	21	Check # 57328		900	14,013
	25	Check # 57329		1,222	12,791
	30	Cash receipt	9,455		22,246

The debit entries, on September 5 and 30, indicate receipts of cash. The credit entries on September 2, 6, 8, 10, 21, and 25 indicate disbursements of cash. The journal entries for cash receipts involve a debit to the cash account and a credit to some other account. The journal entries for check disbursements involve a credit to the cash account and a debit to some other account. The journal entries have all been recorded on the dates shown, and cash has been increased (debited) or decreased (credited) accordingly.

What happens when a check amount on the books does not match up with the bank statement? Either the company or the bank has made an error. Let's consider the check written on September 10 for $568. In examining the bank statement and cancelled check, it is determined that the check was actually written for $558; there is a difference of $10. Thus, the Cash account in the books is in error and must be corrected. Any differences between the bank statement and the books must be reconciled, including errors such as this. Errors can go both ways, but are less likely to be on the part of the bank. A journal entry must be made to correct the balance in the Cash account and the balance in the Supplies account.

A bank reconciliation consists of two parts, as shown in Exhibit 5.3. The first part starts with the cash balance stated by the bank. Next, cash transactions recorded on the company books, but not shown on the bank statement, are added to or subtracted from the bank balance. Two such items shown in Exhibit 5.3 are deposits in transit and outstanding checks. After adding and subtracting these items, the result is the adjusted, or true, cash balance.

Exhibit 5.3 BANK RECONCILIATION
JK Productions Bank Reconciliation September 30, 20Y1

Bank:	Balance, September 30			$14,620
	Add: Deposits in transit			9,455
	Less: Outstanding checks	No. 57326	$(784)	
		No. 57329	(1,222)	(2,006)
				$22,069
Books:	Balance, September 30			$22,246
	Add: Correction of book error Check No. 57327, for $558, erroneously recorded for $568, for purchase of supplies		$10	
	Less: NSF check from customer		(144)	
	Cost of checks		(28)	
	Bank Service charge		(15)	(177)
	Adjusted cash balance			$22,069

Deposits in transit are cash deposits that were made after the bank prepared the bank statement. Deposits in transit have already been recorded on the books and must be added to the bank balance.

Outstanding checks are checks that have been recorded on the company books, but have not cleared the bank. Thus, they are not shown on the bank statement. Outstanding checks must be subtracted from the bank balance.

The second part of the bank reconciliation begins with the book balance for cash, which is the balance in the cash account of the company accounting records. Next, add or subtract items that are shown on the bank statement but are not recorded on the books. Also, if errors have occurred, such as incorrectly recording a check amount, then adjustments must be made for these.

In Exhibit 5.3, the first item under the book balance is an addition of $10 for incorrectly recording a check. The bank correctly deducted $558, the amount of the check, from the bank account. However, the check had been recorded by the company accountant as $568, this is $10 too much.

The next item under the book balance in Exhibit 5.3 is a non-sufficient funds (NSF) check of $144. This is a check received from a customer that "bounced" after it was deposited. "Bounced" means that the customer's check did not clear due to lack of cash in the customer's checking account. Originally, both the bank and the company added the $144 check to the company's cash balance as part of a deposit. When the bank discovered that the funds to cover the check were not in the customer's account, it deducted the amount from the company's cash balance. The company learns of this event when it receives the bank statement showing an NSF notation. The other two items affecting the book balance of cash include a $28 charge for the cost of checks purchased and a bank service charge of $15. Both of these items must be deducted from the book balance.

After adding and subtracting items from the book balance, the result is the adjusted, or true, cash balance. All adjustments made to the book balance will require journal entries, for the purpose of updating the company's cash account records. Journal entries to be made are as follows:

Sept. 30	Cash	10	
	Supplies		10
	To correct error in recording check ($558 check was recorded as $568).		
Sept. 30	Accounts Receivable	144	
	Cash		144
	To record NSF check from customer.		
Sept. 30	Checks Expense	28	
	Cash		28
	To record purchase of checks.		
Sept. 30	Bank Service Charge Expense	15	
	Cash		15
	To record bank service charge.		

FOCUS ON TECHNOLOGY

Using Microsoft Excel: Preparing a Bank Reconciliation

Using Excel, we will recreate the bank reconciliation in Exhibit 5.3.

1. File Identification Area: In an Excel worksheet, set up a file identification area. Remember to include name, filename, date created, input required, and output required. For input required, you may simply put "amounts from bank statement and books." Output required is bank reconciliation.

2. Input Area: Your input area should contain the following. (Be sure to put each amount in a cell by itself so that the cell address can be used in formulas within the output area.)

Balance per bank, Sep 30		$14,620
Deposits in transit		9,455
Outstanding checks:	No. 57326	784
	No. 57330	1,222
Balance per books, Sep 30		22,246
Error correction		10
Non-sufficient funds check from customer		144
Cost of ordering checks		28
Bank service charge		15

3. Output Area: Your output area should resemble Exhibit 5.3. Use formulas to compute the adjusted cash balances.

¶503.05 PETTY CASH FUND

Business firms often find it helpful to keep small amounts of cash on hand to pay for small expenditures, such as document delivery, stamps, or minor office items needed right away. This small amount of cash on hand is customarily referred to as the "**petty cash fund**." A designated amount is assigned to petty cash and the amount is constantly maintained. Assume the petty cash fund is established at $200. The journal entry to record setting up petty cash would be as follows:

April 1	Petty Cash	200	
	Cash		200
	To set up petty cash fund.		

Before the entry to establish Petty Cash, the Cash account had a balance of $10,000. After posting the entry, the Petty Cash account (fund) and the Cash account in the general ledger appear as follows:

Petty Cash   **Account No. 176**

				Balance	
Date		Debit	Credit	Debit	Credit
April	1	200		200	

Cash   **Account No. 101**

				Balance	
Date		Debit	Credit	Debit	Credit
March	31	10,000		10,000	
April	1		200		9,800

A petty cash custodian keeps track of the money in the fund. Each time a payment is made, the custodian lists the expenditures, as shown below.

List of Petty Cash Expenditures:	
Overnight mail delivery fee	$21.50
Stamps	37.00
Coffee	15.50
Total	$74.00

The cash in the petty cash fund and total amount on the list of petty cash expenditures should always add up to the designated amount, in this case, $200. This is an internal control feature. Thus, if the total expenditures are $74, there should be $126 remaining in the petty cash fund. When it is time to replenish the petty cash fund, cash is taken from the Cash account and given to the petty cash custodian. At that time, the amount needed to replenish the petty cash fund is charged to Miscellaneous Expense. Assume the company decides to replenish the petty cash fund on May 1. A check for $74 is prepared and the cash is placed in the petty cash fund. The entry is recorded as follows:

May 1	Miscellaneous Expense	74	
	Cash		74
	To replenish the petty cash fund.		

¶503.06   CASH DISBURSEMENTS PROCESS

Writing checks to make payments provides for better control over cash. In addition, many business firms require the preparation of a voucher before cash is disbursed. The **voucher** is a document that authorizes preparation of a check. Exhibit 5.4 shows the order in which documents are prepared leading up to check preparation. The voucher is the final document in a voucher package that is sent to the treasurer, the company officer typically assigned the task of preparing checks for disbursement.

Exhibit 5.4 DOCUMENT FLOW LEADING TO CHECK PREPARATION

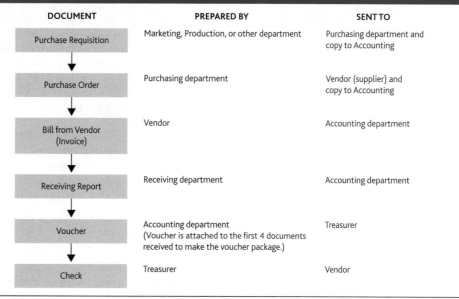

DOCUMENT	PREPARED BY	SENT TO
Purchase Requisition	Marketing, Production, or other department	Purchasing department and copy to Accounting
Purchase Order	Purchasing department	Vendor (supplier) and copy to Accounting
Bill from Vendor (Invoice)	Vendor	Accounting department
Receiving Report	Receiving department	Accounting department
Voucher	Accounting department (Voucher is attached to the first 4 documents received to make the voucher package.)	Treasurer
Check	Treasurer	Vendor

? *Why would it be beneficial for you to reconcile your bank statement?*

When the treasurer receives the voucher package, the documents are reviewed for consistency. For example, the items shown on the purchase order should match those received on the receiving report. The check is prepared and all the documents are stamped "paid." This ensures that all bills are paid just once, and only when all supporting documents are present.

¶504

Components of Internal Control Structure

LEARNING OBJECTIVE 4: Identify the function of each of the components of an internal control structure.

An internal control structure helps safeguard assets and ensure the reliability of accounting records.

The preventive and feedback controls established by a company are components of its overall internal control structure. Two goals of a firm's **internal control structure** are to (1) safeguard assets, and (2) ensure the reliability of accounting records. Many factors affect a firm's internal control structure. Components of the internal control structure include the following:

- The control environment
- Risk assessment
- Information and communication
- Control activities
- Monitoring

¶504.01

The control environment sets the parameters in which business transactions are recorded.

THE CONTROL ENVIRONMENT

The **control environment** of a company sets the parameters in which business transactions are recorded. The control environment is determined by management's overall attitude, awareness, and actions. The control environment consists of several elements including: (1) management's integrity and ethics, (2) management's philosophy and operating style, (3) the organizational structure, (4) an effective audit committee, (5) established methods of assigning authority and responsibility, and (6) personnel policies and procedures. All departments within a company work together to achieve a control environment in which assets are safeguarded and transactions are handled appropriately.

¶504.02   RISK ASSESSMENT

Risk assessment defines areas where risk is great in regard to loss of assets or errors occurring in the accounting records.

Risk assessment is the second component in the internal control structure. **Risk assessment** is the process of defining areas where risk of loss of assets or errors in the accounting records are great, so that appropriate internal controls can be established. For example, a retail business like Target faces the risks that employees or customers will steal merchandise. The company must assess how and when these risks take place so that corrective measures can be taken.

¶504.03   INFORMATION AND COMMUNICATION

An accounting system is comprised of the methods used to record, classify, summarize, and report the entity's transactions.

The third component of a firm's internal control structure concerns information and communication within the firm's accounting system. A firm's **accounting system** is comprised of the methods used to record, classify, summarize, and report the entity's transactions. For example, the accounting system at JC Penney records and classifies the company's sales transactions derived from department store sales and from online catalog sales. All these sales transactions are ultimately summarized and reported on the company's income statement.

¶504.04   CONTROL ACTIVITIES

Control activities are the policies and procedures that ensure the implementation of company directives.

The fourth component of a firm's internal control structure is the existence of effective control activities. **Control activities** are the policies and procedures established by management to ensure that company plans and directives are implemented. Control activities provide reasonable assurance that specific firm objectives will be achieved.

As an example, the control activities used by a movie theater are shown in Exhibit 5.5

Exhibit 5.5 CONTROL STRUCTURE OF A MOVIE THEATER

Policy/Procedure	Category of Control Procedure	Benefits
1. The use of pre-numbered tickets required for patron admittance.	Proper recording. Independent checks on performance.	Enables an independent count of patrons. Determines the total cash that should be collected.
2. Separation of duties between employee collecting cash (selling ticket to patron) and employee authorizing admission.	Separation of duties. Authorization of transactions. Access to assets.	Prevents one individual from receiving cash and authorizing admission.
3. Use of different tickets (colors, types) for different admission prices.	Independent checks on performance.	Enables a reconciliation of persons admitted (ticket stubs) with cash collected.
4. Employee authorizing admission should retain a portion of each ticket.	Independent checks on performance. Proper recording.	Enables an independent count of the number of patrons.
5. Cash register should have "locked-in" totals.	Access to assets. Independent checks on performance.	Enables reconciliation of items sold by the cashier to cash collected. Discourages theft.
6. Before each cashier leaves, the cash on hand should be reconciled to cash register tape totals or ticket stubs.	Independent checks on performance.	Enables cash overages and shortages to be identified with a particular cashier.
7. Cash receipts should be deposited intact on a daily basis.	Access to assets.	Minimizes the chances of embezzlement, robbery, etc. Improves cash management.

If the internal control activities used by the movie theater are working as intended, then management can do the following:

1. Reconcile cash receipts from movie tickets sales to the
   ■ cash register totals,
   ■ tickets sold by cashier (determined through pre-numbered tickets), and
   ■ tickets collected by person monitoring admission.
2. Compare the bank deposit slip to the entry in the cash receipts journal and trace to the posting in the general ledger account for cash.

 JK Productions uses the following control activities to help safeguard the handling of cash in its business: cash is deposited nightly, excess cash is periodically removed from the registers, and personnel do not go to the bank alone or at the same time every day.

¶504.05   MONITORING

Monitoring is the evaluation on a regular basis of the quality of internal control.

Monitoring is the fifth component of a firm's internal control structure. Monitoring is the evaluation on a regular basis of the quality of internal control. This includes periodic review of company compliance with management's policies and procedures. Many companies have an internal audit department to assist with the monitoring process.

¶505   Auditing the Financial Statements

Have you noticed any internal controls in the places where you do business?

LEARNING OBJECTIVE 5: Explain the purpose of an audit and the need for audits in financial reporting.

An audit is an examination of financial statements by an independent, professional accountant to verify that the statements are presented fairly and prepared according to GAAP.

As the corporate form of business developed, the owners (stockholders) were often no longer physically present at the firm. Consequently, the owners (stockholders) rely on the work of managers to ensure that the corporation is operating properly and to provide accurate financial reports on those operations. To help ensure that corporate financial reports are reliable, the owners (stockholders) often depend on the work of auditors, who are hired to examine those reports.

An **audit** is an independent examination of a company's financial statements by a professional accountant to determine that the statements have been presented fairly and prepared using generally accepted accounting principles (GAAP). A key concern for a firm's management is the reliability and integrity of the reports produced by the accounting system. In the case of a publicly-traded company, users of its annual financial statements (such as investors) need some form of assurance that the statements do not contain material misstatements, either intentional or unintentional. An independent external auditor provides this assurance. Even though auditors offer important assurances, ultimate responsibility for the fairness of the financial statements rests with management.

The two major categories of auditing are external auditing and internal auditing. External audits are primarily, but not exclusively, for use by external parties such as investors, lenders, and government agencies. Internal audits are customarily intended for use within the firm, by management only.

¶505.01   EXTERNAL AUDITING

A CPA performs an external audit to determine whether a firm's financial statements are in conformity with GAAP.

A CPA is licensed by the state to provide high quality professional accounting services.

An external audit is an audit conducted by an independent accountant and is the most well-known type of audit. The term "external" means that the auditor does not work for the company being audited. An external auditor performs an **external audit** to determine whether a company's financial statements are in conformity with GAAP. External auditors are Certified Public Accountants (CPAs) who work for CPA firms or operate their own practices. A **Certified Public Accountant (CPA)** is a person licensed by the state to provide high-quality professional services, such as auditing, tax, and consulting. CPA firms are hired by business firms to audit their financial statements. For example, the Coca-Cola Company hired the public accounting firm, Ernst & Young, to audit its financial statements.

External audits are required of publicly-traded companies. An independent CPA must conduct the external audit. The external auditor must maintain his or her independence by having no material financial interest or stake in the outcome of the audit. In conducting an external or financial statement audit of a publicly-traded company, CPAs must comply with Generally Accepted Auditing Standards (GAAS) issued by the Public Company Accounting Oversight Board (PCAOB).

Based on the audit evidence obtained regarding adherence to established accounting standards, the auditor formulates an audit opinion that is then communicated to interested parties. In financial statement audits, this communication occurs in the form of an audit report that accompanies the annual report of the financial statements of a company. Exhibit 5.6 shows the audit report for McDonald's Corporation. Additionally, the auditor also issues a separate, more detailed report internally to the audited firm.

Exhibit 5.6 AUDIT REPORT FOR MCDONALD'S CORPORATION

Report of Independent Registered Public Accounting Firm

The Board of Directors and Shareholders of McDonald's Corporation

We have audited the accompanying consolidated balance sheets of McDonald's Corporation as of December 31, 2011 and 2010, and the related consolidated statements of income, shareholders' equity, and cash flows for each of the three years in the period ended December 31, 2011. These financial statements are the responsibility of the Company's management. Our responsibility is to express an opinion on these financial statements based on our audits.

We conducted our audits in accordance with the standards of the Public Company Accounting Oversight Board (United States). Those standards require that we plan and perform the audit to obtain reasonable assurance about whether the financial statements are free of material misstatement. An audit includes examining, on a test basis, evidence supporting the amounts and disclosures in the financial statements. An audit also includes assessing the accounting principles used and significant estimates made by management, as well as evaluating the overall financial statement presentation. We believe that our audits provide a reasonable basis for our opinion.

In our opinion, the financial statements referred to above present fairly, in all material respects, the consolidated financial position of McDonald's Corporation at December 31, 2011 and 2010, and the consolidated results of its operations and its cash flows for each of the three years in the period ended December 31, 2011, in conformity with U.S. generally accepted accounting principles.

We also have audited, in accordance with the standards of the Public Company Accounting Oversight Board (United States), McDonald's Corporation's internal control over financial reporting as of December 31, 2011, based on criteria established in Internal Control-Integrated Framework issued by the Committee of Sponsoring Organizations of the Treadway Commission, and our report dated February 24, 2012, expressed an unqualified opinion thereon.

ERNST & YOUNG LLP
Chicago, Illinois
February 24, 2012

Source: *SEC.gov*

¶505.02

An internal audit, also referred to as a "management" or "operational audit," evaluates the economy and efficiency with which company resources are utilized and whether goals have been attained.

INTERNAL AUDITING

Accountants who work for the company can perform an internal audit. Many companies establish an internal audit department for this purpose. An **internal audit** is concerned with evaluating the economy and efficiency with which scarce resources are utilized, and whether company goals and objectives have been attained. Internal auditors often review all aspects of a company to determine whether any improvements can be made in departmental operations. For example, Samsung, the cell phone manufacturer, has accountants who work solely for that company. Some of these accountants work in Samsung's internal audit department. Samsung's internal auditors may perform an internal audit to examine the quantity and cost of cell phones being produced by Samsung's manufacturing plants. The auditors can then compare these figures to the company's budget and operating goals. An internal audit is often referred to as a **"management audit"** or **"operational audit."**

FOCUS ON GLOBAL TRADE

Complications of a Multinational Audit

Issues that can complicate the audit of a multinational company include:

- **Local laws.** The laws of the country in which a firm is based may differ from the laws of a host country where the firm is operating. For example, laws may differ on environmental standards, employee rights, or what constitutes a bribe.
- **Local business practices.** Certain business practices can make it very difficult to substantiate a transaction with source documents. This is especially true in countries where cash is the preferred mode of payment.
- **Language barrier.** Critical details can get lost in translation.
- **Foreign currency.** The auditor must be knowledgeable about transfer requirements and currency restrictions.

¶505.03   ACCOUNTING CAREERS

Accounting is a field of great diversity and opportunity. There are basically three fields of work for accountants: (1) in public accounting at a CPA firm, such as Deloitte & Touche or Grant Thornton; (2) in industry at a company, such as Microsoft or ExxonMobil; and (3) in a government entity or not-for-profit organization, such as the Internal Revenue Service or the Salvation Army.

Accountants perform a variety of tasks, such as preparing financial statements, recording business transactions, analyzing costs and efficiency gains from new technologies, developing strategies for mergers and acquisitions, creating and using information systems to track financial performance, and developing tax strategies. Recognizing the importance of these processes reinforces why the American Institute of Certified Public Accountants (AICPA) maintains an ethics code for accountants to follow.

Accountants work with people and information pertaining to all areas of the firm, from marketing to finance, from human resources to production. Basically, accountants learn how the business functions; they see the big picture. Because accountants must understand all aspects of a business, this helps them to be more effective in leadership positions in the company. A high proportion of CEOs and company presidents have an accounting background. Accounting jobs are expected to increase in future years. The increased demand for accountants is partly due to the increasing complexity of corporate transactions and to the growth in the government sector. The boxed insert on careers in accounting provides more detail regarding the three fields of work for accountants.

FOCUS ON ACCOUNTING

CAREER OPPORTUNITIES IN ACCOUNTING

Public Accounting

Public accounting firms offer three types of services to their clients: (1) auditing and other assurance services, (2) tax planning and compliance services, and (3) management consulting services. Public accountants are called external or independent accountants because they are not employees of the business firm but rather independent contractors hired to provide specialized services.

Private Industry

Accountants who work for firms in private industry are called management accountants, though their actual job titles may vary. Private industry companies like General Motors hire accountants such as Senior Financial Analysts, Accounts Payable Supervisors, and Cost Accountants. From rock bands to Microsoft, Wal-Mart to MGM Studios, all businesses require the knowledge and skills of the professional accountant.

Government and Nonprofit Organizations

In the federal government, accounting graduates work in a number of places such as the Internal Revenue Service (IRS), the Comptroller General's Office, the Central Intelligence Agency (CIA), or the Federal Bureau of Investigation (FBI). Accounting professionals develop operating strategies and implement organizational missions within state and city governments. In nonprofit organizations, such as the Red Cross and the March of Dimes, accountants perform duties such as tracking and reporting contributions and expenditures.

If you are an auditor, why is independence so important?

¶506   Making Ethical Decisions

LEARNING OBJECTIVE 6: Relate how firms facilitate ethical decision-making.

If people fail to live up to ethical ideals, detailed rules and monitoring adherence to those rules are often necessary. Many companies choose to provide employees with a variety of practical approaches for making ethical decisions, such as company guidelines and ethics codes.

¶506.01   RULES, POLICIES, AND GUIDELINES

Legal rules are a starting point for making an ethical choice. For example, you can apply existing copyright protection laws to determine whether permission or payment is necessary to use a software product for a specific application.

A second approach to resolving an ethical question is to apply the formal policies of your company or of an appropriate professional organization. For example, the Code of Ethics and Professional Conduct of the Association for Computing Machinery includes provisions for respecting the privacy of others and honoring confidentiality. While members of the association could ignore this code on a legal basis, they might use the provisions to help determine ethical courses of action.

A third approach to making an ethical choice is to use an informal guideline such as your moral intuition. What would your mother or father say if you acted in that way? How would you feel if you saw your situation described in the newspaper? Does the situation "smell bad"? Would you use your behavior as a marketing tool?

Two other guidelines, which could be used in making a decision, are the principle of consistency and the principle of respect. To apply the principle of consistency, you assume that everyone who faces a similar decision makes the same choice as you. For example, if you believe that copying software rather than purchasing it is ethical, examine the implication of every consumer copying the software.

The Golden Rule: "Do unto others as you would have them do unto you."

To apply the principle of respect, you make the choice that treats people with the greatest respect. This implies that you act towards others in the same way that you hope they would act towards you. This principle is referred to as the "Golden Rule": "*Do unto others as you would have them do unto you.*" This was the guiding principle followed by Mr. J.C. Penney when starting his company.

¶506.02   CORPORATE ETHICS CODES

Many firms have adopted a corporate ethics code. In ExxonMobil's Standards of Business Conduct, company guidelines state, "No one in the ExxonMobil organization has the authority to make exceptions to these policies [on business conduct]. Regardless of how much difficulty we encounter or pressures we face in performing our jobs, no situation can justify their willful violation." Business people need formal standards on which to base decisions regarding ethical issues such as information security, personal privacy, use of company resources, care for the environment, and professional behavior. Further steps taken by ExxonMobil to ensure integrity are listed in Exhibit 5.7.

Exhibit 5.7 STEPS TO ENSURE INTEGRITY AT EXXONMOBIL

- A substantial majority of the Board of Directors are non-employees.
- The Board Audit Committee is empowered to investigate any matters brought to its attention and has 100% non-employee membership.
- An independent internal audit staff assesses compliance with policies and procedures, and evaluates control effectiveness in about 300 audits conducted annually around all business units.
- Steps are taken to assure the independence of both internal and external auditors.
- Employees regularly review and discuss expectations and are encouraged to raise questions or concerns.
- Violations are promptly reviewed, communicated upward, and acted upon.

Adherence to absolute standards does not mean all decisions are obvious or easy. Ethical dilemmas will still occur. Ethical dilemmas occur in all functional areas of the firm, including accounting, finance, human resources, marketing, and production. Everyone occasionally faces decisions and situations requiring ethical judgment.

Ethical use of information systems, especially on the Web, has become a major concern for business managers and information system professionals. Businesses routinely limit or monitor their employees' use of the Web to protect themselves from lawsuits for sexual harassment and to counter the loss of productivity associated with surfing the Web.

Guarding personal privacy is a major business issue since computer information systems are capable of maintaining large amounts of data about individuals without their knowledge. People often face ethical dilemmas regarding the use of that information. For example, what should you do if, after promising your employees that the data on their computers is private, you learn that one employee has stolen company information? What if you learn that one employee has plans to harm another? Should you examine their data files?

¶506.03

Integrity is knowing what's right and having the courage to do it.

PERSONAL INTEGRITY

Personal integrity can be defined as knowing what's right and having the courage to do it. Society expects companies and professionals to operate with integrity and according to ethical standards. Corporate and professional ethics provide guidance to businesspersons in carrying out business operations. Professional organizations, such as the American Institute of CPAs, maintain ethics codes for their members. At one time, there was not much interest in individual ethics. Personal integrity was a matter of individual conscience and personal values. This is no longer the case.

Personal integrity is directly linked to corporate accountability. The former CEO of PricewaterhouseCoopers, Sam DiPiazza, put it this way: "Worldwide, corporate integrity is subject to investor doubt, employee anxiety, and new legislation and regulation. It has become dramatically clear that the foundation of corporate integrity is personal integrity. News reports have repeatedly shown us that individual failures of integrity can be the source of vast corporate deceptions."[2] Mr. DiPiazza believes that too many companies overly emphasize performance without emphasizing the integrity with which high performance is achieved.

Taking the right course of action is very important, as many people may be affected by your decision. Ethical decision-making requires consideration of the following important questions. Does the action cause unnecessary social harm or fail to serve the public interest? Does the action violate any basic human rights? Does the action abridge any commonly-accepted duties? Additional questions to consider in ethical decision-making are shown in Exhibit 5.8.

Exhibit 5.8 QUESTIONS TO CONSIDER FOR ETHICAL DECISION MAKING

- Are there legal concerns?
- Is it right?
- Does it comply with company values?
- Does it comply with the principles of your profession (for accountants, GAAP)?
- Would you be embarrassed by your decision if others knew about it?
- Who else is affected by this event? (others in the company, customers, etc.)
- Are you willing to take sole responsibility for this decision?
- Is there another course of action that does not create an ethical dilemma?
- How will it look in the newspaper?
- Do you think a reasonable person would agree with your decision? (Ask an appropriate person.)

In the complicated world of business, discerning the right course of action is not always easy. Business firms can help their employees make ethical decisions by providing guidelines, some general and some specific to their line of business. There are some values that are universally accepted as good practices in business or life in general. Michael Josephson, in Chapter 1 of *Ethical Issues in the Practice of Accounting*, lists "Ten Universal Values" as: honesty, integrity, promise keeping, fidelity, fairness, caring, respect for others, responsible citizenship, pursuit of excellence, and accountability.[3] In every society and culture around the world, people who demonstrate these values are admired and respected. These values are essential for productively carrying out business and social activities. Depending on whether people have or lack personal integrity will determine the progress or decline of the firms in which they work and the society in which they live.

¶506.04

"Honor is better than honors."

HOW DO YOU MEASURE PERSONAL SUCCESS?

Ethical values provide the foundation on which a civilized society exists. Without the foundation, civilization collapses. On a personal level, everyone must answer the following question: What is my highest aspiration? The answer might be wealth, fame, knowledge, popularity, or integrity. Be on guard: If integrity is secondary to any of the alternatives, it will be sacrificed in situations in which a choice must be made. Such situations will inevitably occur in every person's life.

Many people think of fame and fortune when they measure success. However, at some point in life, most people come to realize that inner peace and soul-deep satisfaction come not from fame and fortune, but from living a life based on integrity and noble character. President Lincoln put it this way: "Honor is better than honors."[4] At a Congressional Hearing concerning business and accounting ethics, Truett Cathy, founder of Chick-Fil-A, quoted Proverbs 22:1: "A good name is more desirable than great riches; to be esteemed is better than silver or gold."[5] According to President Lincoln and Mr. Cathy, personal success is achieved by living an honorable life.

Maintaining high ethical standards in accounting and business can be difficult. People will undoubtedly ask, "If everyone else is cheating, then how can an ethical person possibly succeed?" This is the wrong question. The real question is, how does one measure success? Exhibit 5.9 provides a poignant essay on the foolishness of measuring success by the accumulation of wealth or power.

Exhibit 5.9 HOW DO YOU MEASURE SUCCESS?

In 1923, a very important meeting was held at the Edgewater Beach Hotel in Chicago. Attending this meeting were nine of the richest men in the world: (1) Charles Schwab, President of the world's largest independent steel company; (2) Samuel Insull, President of the world's largest utility company; (3) Howard Hopson, President of the largest gas firm; (4) Arthur Cutten, the greatest wheat speculator; (5) Richard Whitney, President of the New York Stock Exchange; (6) Albert Fall, member of the President's Cabinet; (7) Leon Frazier, President of the Bank of International Settlements; (8) Jessie Livermore, the greatest speculator in the Stock Market; and (9) Ivar Kreuger, head of the company with the most widely distributed securities in the world.

Twenty-five years later, (1) Charles Schwab had died in bankruptcy, having lived on borrowed money for five years before his death; (2) Samuel Insull had died virtually penniless after spending some time as a fugitive from justice; (3) Howard Hopson was insane; (4) Arthur Cutten died overseas, broke; (5) Richard Whitney had spent time in Sing-Sing; (6) Albert Fall had been pardoned from prison so he could die at home; and the other three men [(7) Leon Fraizer, (8) Jessie Livermore, and (9) Ivar Kreuger] each died by suicide.

Measured by wealth and power these men achieved success, at least temporarily. Making a lot of money may be an acceptable goal, but money most assuredly does not guarantee a truly successful life.

Many people consider fame and fortune when they measure success. In reality, a quality life is measured by strength of character and personal integrity, not by fame and fortune. In his testimony at the congressional hearing on accounting and business ethics , Truett Cathy, founder of Chik-Fil-A, quoted Solomon: "A good name is more desirable than great riches; to be esteemed is better than silver or gold." Perhaps the most important question about your life is: How do you measure success?

Source: K. T. Smith and L. M. Smith, Business and Accounting Ethics, Website: *http://goo.gl/ThAor*, May 25, 2012.

The success of a business is dependent upon each individual doing his or her part.

 How do you measure success for yourself?

The world is made up of individuals like you. Never underestimate the power of one person or one vote. In 1645, one vote gave Oliver Cromwell control of England. In 1845, one vote brought the state of Texas into the United States. In 1923, Adolph Hitler gained control of the Nazi Party by one vote. In 1941, one vote preserved the Selective Service System just 12 weeks before Pearl Harbor was attacked. The success of a nation, a profession, a business, is dependent upon each individual doing his or her part. Whether you do your part depends on your personal integrity.

¶507

Concluding Remarks

In this chapter, you learned how important cash is to a business and how to use various internal controls for safeguarding that cash. Effective internal controls also help ensure the reliability of a company's accounting records. Accurate and reliable financial reporting depends on the technical competence and ethical character of the people involved. Personal integrity is promoted by companies such as ExxonMobil and organizations such as the American Institute of Certified Public Accountants (AICPA).

An audit provides assurance that financial statements are prepared according to generally accepted accounting principles. Users of financial statements need some form of assurance that these documents do not contain material misstatements, either intentional or unintentional. Reliability and accuracy are imperative in reporting the accounts that will be featured in the next chapter – accounts receivable and notes receivable.

¶508

Chapter Review

LEARNING OBJECTIVE 1

Describe how accounting issues concerning cash and internal control affect people within and outside the firm.

All departments within a firm depend on cash being available to pay employees and to purchase the items necessary to carry out company operations. To safeguard cash and the other assets of an organization, an internal control structure must be put into place. People external to the business firm rely on the financial information provided to them. If internal controls are weak, there is a higher probability that errors and intentional misrepresentations will occur in the financial statements.

LEARNING OBJECTIVE 2

Describe the importance of cash in company operations.

Every business needs cash to carry on business operations. Without cash, a company cannot function, at least not for long. This is why one of the four financial statements, the statement of cash flows, focuses solely on cash.

LEARNING OBJECTIVE 3

Discuss internal controls over cash, prepare a cash budget, and reconcile a bank statement.

Business managers rely on the accounting information system to supply them with the financial information they need to make effective decisions. To ensure the accuracy and reliability of this information, a system of internal controls is established. In general, the internal controls of a company can be categorized as preventive controls and feedback controls. Preventive controls prevent errors (unintentional misrepresentations) and irregularities (intentional misrepresentations) from occurring. Feedback controls identify errors and irregularities after they occur so that corrective action may be taken.

Since cash is more vulnerable to theft than other assets, internal controls over cash are vital. One form of control, the cash budget, provides internal control over cash inflows and outflows and enables the company to project financing needs. A second very basic form of control over cash is the bank checking account. A third important internal control over cash is the bank reconciliation because it provides feedback on whether the transactions affecting cash have been recorded properly.

LEARNING OBJECTIVE 4

Identify the function of each of the components of internal control structure.

Two goals of a firm's control structure are to safeguard assets and to ensure the reliability of accounting records. Components of the internal control structure include the control environment, risk assessment, information and communication, control activities, and monitoring.

LEARNING OBJECTIVE 5

Explain the purpose of an audit and the need for audits in financial reporting.

An audit is an appraisal of evidence by an independent third party, according to established criteria. A key concern for a firm's management is the reliability and integrity of the reports produced by the accounting system. In the case of a publicly-traded company, users of the firm's annual financial statements (such as investors) need some form of assurance that these documents do not contain material misstatements, either intentional or unintentional. An independent external auditor provides this assurance. In business, the most well-known type of audit is the external audit of a firm's financial statements.

LEARNING OBJECTIVE 6

Relate how business firms facilitate ethical decision-making.

Ethical guidelines in accounting and business provide guidance to businesspersons to act in a way that facilitates, and indeed encourages, public confidence in their products and services. Confidence in business managers, accountants, and the stock market is created and sustained only by ethical leadership from the business community, accounting profession, and government.

Endnotes

1. Second Epistle to the Corinthians, *The Holy Bible, New International Version*, Grand Rapids, Michigan: Zondervan, 1996, 979.
2. Sam DiPiazza, CEO of PriceswaterhouseCoopers, "It's All Down to Personal Values," http:www. pwcglobal.com, May 13, 2003.
3. M. Josephson, Chapter 1 in W. Steve Albrecht, ed., *Ethical Issues in the Practice of Accounting*, Cincinnati, South-Western Publishing Co., 1992.
4. Lincoln. A., Ethics Quotes, University Ethics Office, University of Illinois, Website: http://www. ethics.uillinois.edu/resources/quotes.cfm, January 12, 2012.
5. T. Cathy, Testimony to the U.S. House of Representatives Subcommittee on Commerce, Trade, and Consumer Protection: Hearing on Oath Taking, Truth Telling, and Remedies in the Business World, July 26, 2002.

¶509

Glossary

Accounting system

A firm's accounting system is comprised of the methods used to record, classify, summarize, and report the entity's transactions.

Audit

An audit is an independent examination of a company's financial statements by a professional accountant to determine that the statements have been presented fairly and prepared using generally accepted accounting principles.

Cash budget

The cash budget is a feedback control that is used to project financing needs and to provide internal controls over cash inflows and outflows.

Cash equivalent

A cash equivalent is a short-term, highly liquid investment, including money market accounts, commercial paper, and U.S. Treasury bills, that will convert to cash in less than 90 days.

Certified Public Accountant (CPA)

A CPA is licensed by the state to provide high quality professional services, such as auditing, tax, and consulting.

Check

The check is a legal document that directs the bank to pay a specific cash amount to the designated person or company.

Control activities

Control activities are the policies and procedures established by management to ensure that company plans and directives are implemented.

Control environment

The control environment sets the parameters in which business transactions are recorded.

External audit

An external audit (also called financial statement audit) is an audit conducted by an independent Certified Public Accountant (CPA).

Feedback controls

A feedback control identifies errors and irregularities after they occur so that corrective action may be taken.

Internal audit

An internal audit determines whether the operations of the firm are achieving the firm's goals and objectives. Internal audits include management audits, internal control audits, and compliance audits.

Internal control structure

Two goals of a firm's internal control structure are to (1) safeguard assets and (2) ensure the reliability of accounting records. Components of the internal control structure include: the control environment, risk assessment, information and communication, control activities, and monitoring.

Lockbox system

A lockbox system is an arrangement whereby business firms arrange for customers to send cash payments to an address that is effectively a bank account.

Liquidity

Liquidity refers to how readily an asset can be converted to cash.

Management audit

A type of internal audit, the management audit (also called operational audit), is concerned with evaluating the economy and efficiency with which scarce resources are utilized, and whether goals and objectives have been attained.

Monitoring

With regard to internal control, monitoring is the evaluation on a regular basis of the quality of internal control.

Operational audit

A type of internal audit, the operational audit (also called management audit), is concerned with evaluating the economy and efficiency with which scarce resources are utilized, and whether goals and objectives have been attained.

Petty cash fund

The petty cash fund is a small amount of cash kept on hand by a firm in order to pay for minor expenditures.

Preventive controls

A preventive control prevents errors (unintentional misrepresentations) and irregularities (intentional misrepresentations) from occurring.

Remittance advice

A remittance advice is a document that specifies the purpose of the check, such as paying for advertising.

Risk assessment

Risk assessment is the process of defining areas where risk of loss of assets or errors in the accounting records are great, so that appropriate internal controls can be established.

Separation of duties

The separation of duties involves assigning the tasks related to a particular transaction among two or more employees.

Voucher

The voucher is a document that authorizes preparation of a check.

¶510

Appendix: E-Business and E-Risk

Technology has had a profound effect on accounting and business. Electronic business, or **e-business**—the exchange of goods or services using an electronic infrastructure—began with the early computers of the 1950s. However, not until development of the World Wide Web in the 1990s did e-business really take off. A brief history of the Web and e-commerce is shown in Exhibit 5.A

Exhibit 5.A INFORMATION TECHNOLOGY: HISTORICAL TIMELINE PERTAINING TO THE WEB AND E-COMMERCE	
1946	The first electronic computer, ENIAC, is constructed at the University of Pennsylvania.
1958	To counter Soviet technological advances, the U.S. forms the Advanced Research Projects Agency (ARPA), with the Department of Defense, to develop U.S. prominence in science and technology applicable to the military.
1969	ARPANET, the forerunner of the Internet, established with four nodes: UCLA, Stanford, UC-Santa Barbara, and University of Utah.
1970	First applications of electronic data interchange (EDI).
1984	Science fiction author William Gibson coins the term "cyberspace" in his novel, Neuromancer. Internet host computers exceed 1,000.
1991	Tim Berners-Lee, working at CERN in Geneva, develops a hypertext system to provide efficient information access. He posts the first computer code of the World Wide Web in a relatively innocuous newsgroup, "alt.hypertext." Later, people refer to the Internet itself as the Web.
1994	Pizza Hut sells pizza on its website. First Virtual, the first cyberbank, opens.
1995	*The Bottom Line is Betrayal* authored by K.T. Smith, D.L. Crumbley, and L.M. Smith: the first business educational novel focused on international trade, global marketing, and emerging technologies.
1997	Inception of business-to-business (B2B) e-commerce. US Postal Service issues electronic postal stamps.
1999	Melissa computer virus is propagated via email attachments.
2011	All U.S. publicly traded companies must use eXtensible Business Reporting Language (XBRL) for financial reporting.
2012	Internet host computers (i.e., computers with a registered IP address) exceed 200 million. Users in over 180 countries are connected.

E-business is simply business; it's the way business is done in the twenty-first century. The Internet and e-business activities shape characteristics of the "e-conomy" as a global, digital, high velocity market economy. Globalization means re-shaping existing markets and exploring new ones as the marketplace becomes more dynamic, reflecting real-time supply and demand changes. E-business is Internet-based; the World Wide Web is widely used for both business-to-business (B2B) transactions and business-to-consumer (B2C) transactions. The B2B market is from five to seven times larger than B2C. The B2B market is predicted to reach $5.7 trillion in the early 21st century. The B2C market is growing as fast but is characterized by a much smaller average transaction size.

Since technology plays a key role in all aspects of business today, we use computer networks to transmit accounting and other information around the firm. Many businesses maintain websites to conduct e-commerce with customers, as well as to provide information to interested parties around the world. Technology facilitates these business activities, but there are some downsides. Business managers must beware of potential problems associated with e-commerce. People must take precautions against computer crime, malicious hackers, and computer viruses.

E-risk is the potential for financial and technological problems resulting from doing business on the Internet (e-business). Changes in economic, industrial, and regulatory conditions mean new challenges. Troublemakers are out there in cyberspace seeking systems to misuse. Just for the fun of it, there are people who try to hack into a firm's computer system. Once access to the system is achieved, intruders can potentially cause major problems by deleting or changing data.

Instead of hacking into systems, some people create havoc by writing computer programs that replicate themselves and sometimes carry out malicious programming instructions such as erasing files. Such programs are generally referred to as computer viruses. Computer viruses infiltrate information systems. Accounting systems that are not secured against viruses threaten a company's survivability and profitability of e-business operations. In June 2005, a hacker accessed credit card files in the CardSystems Inc.'s database. The company processes credit card transactions for small to mid-sized businesses. The hacker compromised the security of over 40 million cards issued by MasterCard, Visa USA Inc., American Express Co., and Discover. Because of the security breach, several banks were negatively affected, such as J.P. Morgan Chase & Co. and Washington Mutual Inc.

Victims of cyber crime include Internet media companies like Yahoo.com and credit card processors like CardSystem Inc. In February 2000, Yahoo.com was one of many Internet sites affected by a group of cyber-terrorists who hacked into the site and made alterations to program coding. The problem was so severe that Yahoo.com was forced to shut down in order to repair the damage and stop the unauthorized activity. As a result of the site closing, program changes were made to help prevent future break-ins.

Risks related to e-business on the Web include the following:

- The changing e-business environment alters risks, so old solutions may no longer work.
- International business activity expands the scale and scope of risks.
- Computing power, connectivity, and speed can spread viruses, facilitate system compromise, and compound errors in seconds, potentially affecting interconnected parties.
- Hackers never stop devising new techniques; thus, new tools mean new vulnerabilities.
- Digitization creates unique problems for digital information and transactions.

Since the Internet was not designed for business, it was not designed to control and manage business risks. In the beginning, the Internet was restricted to researchers for shared computing and communication. This changed with the introduction of the user-friendly, graphical World Wide Web in the early 1990s. E-business includes market research, knowledge management, product selection, production, ordering, payment, and delivery. Conducting financial and other transactions over the Web is ever expanding in our global economy. Along with this expansion comes the need for protection against and management of e-risks.

APPENDIX GLOSSARY

E-business

E-business is exchanging goods or services using an electronic infrastructure.

E-risk

E-risk is the potential for financial and technological problems resulting from doing business on the Internet (e-business).

¶510

¶511   # Chapter Assignments

QUESTIONS

1. **[Obj. 1]** What is an internal control structure?

2. **[Obj. 1]** Why are people external to a firm interested in that firm's internal control structure?

3. **[Obj. 2]** What assets are included in the term "cash"?

4. **[Obj. 2]** What is liquidity?

5. **[Obj. 3]** Internal controls help prevent dishonest persons from doing wrong. In your opinion, how do controls help honest persons?

6. **[Obj. 3]** Distinguish between preventive controls and feedback controls.

7. **[Obj. 3]** What is the function of a cash budget?

8. **[Obj. 3]** How does a bank reconciliation establish control over cash?

9. **[Obj. 3]** Assume that your bank statement shows a non-sufficient funds (NSF) check of $200 from one of your customers. Where would this be shown on the bank reconciliation?

10. **[Obj. 4]** What are the components of the internal control structure?

11. **[Obj. 4]** What is the purpose of risk assessment?

12. **[Obj. 4]** What is a firm's accounting system comprised of?

13. **[Obj. 4]** What are control activities?

14. **[Obj. 4]** Define monitoring.

15. **[Obj. 5]** What is an audit?

16. **[Obj. 5]** In business, what is the most well known type of audit? Why is this audit important?

17. **[Obj. 5]** What is the difference between an internal audit and an external audit?

18. **[Obj. 5]** Describe the external audit, the role of auditor independence, and the rules by which external audits are done.

19. **[Obj. 5]** What are the three fields of work for accountants?

20. **[Obj. 6]** What is the purpose of ethics in accounting and business?

21. **[Obj. 6]** Laws and regulations are helpful. However, they cannot sustain public confidence in business, accounting, or the stock market. What is required to sustain confidence?

22. **[Obj. 6]** What are the universal values identified by Michael Josephson?

23. **[Obj. 6]** What are some questions to consider in ethical decision-making?

SHORT EXERCISES – SET A

Building Accounting Skills

1. **[Obj. 3]** Feedback Controls: Describe the characteristics of effective feedback controls and give some examples.

2. **[Obj. 3]** Preventive Controls: Describe the characteristics of effective preventive controls and give some examples.

3. **[Obj. 3]** Journal Entry for NSF Check: Assume that your bank statement shows a non-sufficient funds (NSF) check of $100 from one of your customers. What journal entry should be recorded for the NSF check?

4. **[Obj. 3]** Internal Controls: Internal controls help safeguard company assets and ensure the reliability of the accounting records. Describe how internal controls help protect employees.

5. **[Obj. 3]** Preventive and Feedback Controls: Assume that you're the owner of a roller skating rink. Describe the preventive and feedback controls you might use.

6. **[Obj. 3]** Journal Entry to Create Petty Cash Fund: Assume your company has decided it needs a petty cash fund. What is the journal entry to set up a petty cash fund of $300?

7. **[Obj. 3]** Journal Entry to Replenish Petty Cash Fund: You have been told to replenish the company's petty cash fund. $100 has been spent on miscellaneous expenses. You write a check for $100 made out to cash, and the cash is placed in the petty cash fund. Prepare the journal entry for this transaction.

8. **[Obj. 3]** Journal Entry to Replenish Petty Cash Fund: You are the petty cash custodian at work. It's time to replenish the petty cash fund. The following expenditures have been made using petty cash: $39 for postage, $54 for an ink cartridge, and $30 for envelopes. Prepare the journal entry to replenish the petty cash fund.

9. **[Obj. 4]** Internal Control Structure: Name the two components of the internal control structure that you think are the most important and explain why.

SHORT EXERCISES – SET B

Building Accounting Skills

1. **[Obj. 3]** Journal Entry for NSF Check: Assume that your bank statement shows a non-sufficient funds (NSF) check of $75 from one of your customers. What journal entry should be recorded for the NSF check?

2. **[Obj. 3]** Internal Controls: What is the purpose of internal controls for company assets, accounting records, and employees?

3. **[Obj. 3]** Feedback Controls: Describe how feedback controls contribute to internal control.

4. **[Obj. 3]** Preventive Controls: Describe how preventive controls contribute to internal control.

5. **[Obj. 3]** Preventive and Feedback Controls: Assume that you're the owner of an indoor go-cart track. Describe the preventive and feedback controls you might use.

6. **[Obj. 3]** Journal Entry to Create Petty Cash Fund: Assume your company has decided it needs a petty cash fund. What is the journal entry to set up the petty cash fund of $400?

7. **[Obj. 3]** Journal Entry to Replenish Petty Cash Fund: You have been told to replenish the company's petty cash fund. $200 has been spent on miscellaneous expenses. You write a check for $200 made out to cash, and the cash is placed in the petty cash fund. Prepare the journal entry for this transaction.

8. **[Obj. 3]** Journal Entry to Replenish Petty Cash Fund: You are the petty cash custodian at work. It's time to replenish the petty cash fund. The following expenditures have been made using petty cash: $8 for light bulbs, $32 for coffee and doughnuts, and $3 for napkins. Prepare the journal entry to replenish the petty cash fund.

9. **[Obj. 4]** Internal Control Structure: Summarize the five components of the internal control structure.

PROBLEMS – SET A

Applying Accounting Knowledge

1. **[Obj. 3]** Bank Reconciliation: Southwest Moving Company received its bank statement for the month ended November 30, 20Y1. Information from the bank statement and from the company's books is as follows:

Balance per bank, Nov. 30		$969
Deposits in transit		234
Outstanding checks:	No. 1941	54
	No. 1945	356
Balance per books, Nov. 30		952
Non-sufficient funds check from customer		124
Cost of ordering checks		10
Bank service charge		25

Required: Prepare the bank reconciliation for Southwest Moving Company.

2. **[Obj. 3]** Cash Budget: The following information is for Read-a-lot Books, Inc. The amounts are in thousands of dollars.

Cash balance, Jan. 1, 20Y1	$10
Budgeted cash balance, Dec. 31, 20Y1	30
Collections from customers	420
Sale of assets	20
Payments of operating expenses	399
Purchase of equipment	12
Payment of debt	24
Dividends	8

Required:
a. Prepare a cash budget for Read-a-lot Books, Inc. for the year ended December 31, 20Y1. Refer to Exhibit 5.1 for help in setting up the cash budget.
b. Evaluate: What is Read-a-lot's financial situation in regard to cash receipts and disbursements? Does the company need additional financing?

3. **[Obj. 3]** Cash Budget: Hercules Moving Corporation has provided the following amounts in thousands of dollars:

Cash balance, Jan. 1, 20Y1	$790
Budgeted cash balance, Dec. 31, 20Y1	500
Collections from customers	4,440
Sale of assets	225
Payments of operating expenses	4,230
Purchase of equipment	348
Payment of debt	190
Dividends	224

Required:
a. Prepare a cash budget for the year ended December 31, 20Y1. Refer to Exhibit 5.1 for help in setting up the cash budget.
b. Evaluate: What is Hercules' financial situation in regard to cash receipts and disbursements? Does the company need additional financing?

4. **[Obj. 3]** Bank Reconciliation and Journal Entries: Express Travel Company received its bank statement for the month ended October 31, 20Y1. Information from the bank statement and from the company's books is as follows:

Balance per bank, Oct. 31		$4,327
Deposits in transit		678
Outstanding checks:	No. 1776	89
	No. 1812	56
Balance per books, Oct. 31		4,891
Non-sufficient funds check from customer		23
Cost of ordering checks		12
Bank service charge		5

Also, a check for $389 worth of supplies was erroneously recorded in the company books as $398.

Required:
a. Prepare the bank reconciliation.
b. Prepare journal entries resulting from the reconciliation.

5. **[Obj. 3]** Bank Reconciliation and Journal Entries: Lube Stop received its bank statement for the month ended July 31, 20Y1. Information from the bank statement and from the company's books is as follows:

Balance per bank, July. 31		$15,530
Outstanding checks:	No. 240	25
	No. 245	130
	No. 246	60
Balance per books, July 31		15,367
Non-sufficient funds check from customer		50

Also, a check for $259 for utilities was erroneously recorded in the company books as $257.

Required:
a. Prepare the bank reconciliation.
b. Prepare journal entries resulting from the reconciliation.

6. **[Obj. 3]** Bank Reconciliation and Journal Entries: Atlantic Construction Company received its bank statement for the month ended March 31, 20Y1. Information from the bank statement and from the company's books is as follows:

Balance per bank, March 31		$52,458
Deposits in transit		18,420
Outstanding checks:	No. 1066	17,796
Balance per books, March 31		48,903
Bank service charge		15

Also, a check for $260 worth of supplies was erroneously recorded in the company books as $206.

Required:
a. Prepare the bank reconciliation.
b. Prepare journal entries resulting from the reconciliation.

7. **[Obj. 3]** Bank Reconciliation and Journal Entries: Atlantic Construction Company received its bank statement for the month ended April 30, 20Y1. Information from the bank statement and from the company's books is as follows:

Balance per bank, April 30		$39,467
Deposits in transit		12,440
Outstanding checks:	No. 1066	17,796
	No. 1122	9,834
Balance per books, April 30		27,772
Non-sufficient funds check from customer		5,250
Cost of ordering checks		30

Required:
a. Prepare the bank reconciliation for Atlantic Construction Co.
b. Prepare journal entries resulting from the reconciliation.

8. **[Obj. 4]** Control Procedures: Go to a movie theater and observe its internal control procedures regarding tickets. Keep in mind the first four control procedures shown in Exhibit 5.5: pre-numbered tickets, segregation of duties, different tickets, and keeping a portion of the ticket.

Required:
a. Explain what control procedures the theater is using.
b. Evaluate: Do you think the controls are adequate to safeguard company assets and ensure the reliability of the accounting records? Would you change anything?

9. **[Obj. 6]** Ethics: Professor Plum is preparing a final exam to be given to his financial accounting class. He is having trouble finishing the last part of the exam and decides he needs some refreshment. He leaves the test and answer key in plain view on his desk while he goes to the departmental office for a cup of coffee. Professor Plum does not close his office door as he plans to be gone no more than a couple of minutes. Almost immediately after leaving the office, one of his students, Taylor White, walks up to the office door. Taylor is seeking advice on how to prepare for the final exam. Glancing into the office, Taylor notices that Professor Plum is not present. Taylor cannot help but see the test and answer key on Professor Plum's desk. At that same moment, Professor Plum returns to find Taylor standing at the office door, looking toward the test.

Required:
a. If you were Taylor, what would you do?
b. If you were Professor Plum, what would you think about Taylor?
c. How could this problem have been prevented?

PROBLEMS – SET B

Applying Accounting Knowledge

1. **[Obj. 3]** Bank Reconciliation: Hot Dogs 'R' Us received its bank statement for the month ended November 30, 20Y1. Information from the bank statement and from the company's books is as follows:

Balance per bank, Nov. 30		$850
Deposits in transit		135
Outstanding checks:	No. 1941	150
	No. 1945	180
Balance per books, Nov. 30		832
Non-sufficient funds check from customer		137
Cost of ordering checks		15
Bank service charge		25

Required: Prepare the bank reconciliation for Hot Dogs 'R' Us.

2. **[Obj. 3]** Cash Budget: The following information is for Hollywood Video Rentals, Inc. The amounts are in thousands of dollars.

Cash balance, Jan. 1, 20Y1	$20
Budgeted cash balance, Dec. 31, 20Y1	60
Collections from customers	840
Sale of assets	40
Payments of operating expenses	798
Purchase of equipment	24
Payment of debt	48
Dividends	16

Required:
a. Prepare a cash budget for Hollywood Video Rentals, Inc. for the year ended December 31, 20Y1.
b. Evaluate: What is Hollywood's financial situation in regard to cash receipts and disbursements? Does the company need additional financing?

3. **[Obj. 3]** Cash Budget: Roadrunner Moving Corporation provides the following amounts in thousands of dollars:

Cash balance, Jan. 1, 20Y1	$395
Budgeted cash balance, Dec. 31, 20Y1	250
Collections from customers	2,220
Sale of assets	112
Payments of operating expenses	2,115
Purchase of equipment	174
Payment of debt	95
Dividends	112

Required:
a. Prepare a cash budget for the year ended December 31, 20Y1.
b. Evaluate: What is Roadrunner's financial situation in regard to cash receipts and disbursements? Does the company need additional financing?

4. **[Obj. 3]** Bank Reconciliation and Journal Entries: International Travel Company received its bank statement for the month ended October 31, 20Y1. Information from the bank statement and from the company's books is as follows:

Balance per bank, Oct. 31		$21,500
Deposits in transit		1,356
Outstanding checks:	No. 2318	1,105
	No. 2320	63
Balance per books, Oct. 31		21,661

Also, a check for $314 for utilities was erroneously recorded as $341.

Required:
a. Prepare the bank reconciliation.
b. Prepare journal entries resulting from the reconciliation.

5. **[Obj. 3]** Bank Reconciliation and Journal Entries: International Travel Company received its bank statement for the month ended May, 20Y1. Information from the bank statement and from the company's books is as follows:

Balance per bank, May 31		$8,082
Outstanding checks:	No. 1776	178
	No. 1812	112
Balance per books, May 31		7,782
Non-sufficient funds check from customer		55
Cost of ordering checks		14
Bank service charge		20

Also, a check for $314 worth of supplies was erroneously recorded as $413.

Required:
a. Prepare the bank reconciliation.
b. Prepare journal entries resulting from the reconciliation.

6. **[Obj. 3]** Bank Reconciliation and Journal Entries: Collegiate Bookstore received its bank statement for the month ended March 31, 20Y1. Information from the bank statement and from the company's books is as follows:

Balance per bank, March 31		$50,458
Deposits in transit		18,420
Outstanding checks:	No. 1066	17,796
	No. 1070	9,834
	No. 1075	350
Balance per books, March 31		42,173
Non-sufficient funds check from customer		1,250
Bank service charge		25

Required:
a. Prepare the bank reconciliation.
b. Prepare journal entries resulting from the reconciliation.

7. **[Obj. 3]** Bank Reconciliation and Journal Entries: Collegiate Bookstore received its bank statement for the month ended June 30, 20Y1. Information from the bank statement and from the company's books is as follows:

Balance per bank, June 30		$37,467
Deposits in transit		10,440
Outstanding checks:	No. 366	17,796
	No. 368	9,834
Balance per books, June 30		20,647
Non-sufficient funds check from customer		320
Cost of ordering checks		30

Also, a check for $240 worth of supplies was erroneously recorded as $220.

Required:
a. Prepare the bank reconciliation for Collegiate Bookstore.
b. Prepare journal entries resulting from the reconciliation.

8. **[Obj. 4]** Control Procedures: Go to your local Walmart or a similar store and observe its internal control procedures regarding product returns. Some of the control procedures shown in Exhibit 5.5 will be applicable.

Required:
a. Explain the control procedures used by the store.
b. Evaluate: Do you think the controls are adequate to safeguard company assets and ensure the reliability of the accounting records? Would you change anything?

9. **[Obj. 6]** Ethics: Refer to the essay in Exhibit 5.9, "How do you measure success?"

Required: Describe another example in which fame and fortune did not equate to true success. How do you measure success?

CROSS-FUNCTIONAL PERSPECTIVES

Discussion Questions

1. **[Obj. 3]** What are some examples of preventive controls that engage all departments within a firm?

2. **[Obj. 3]** Besides the accountant, who else in the firm provides input or is interested in the cash budget?

3. **[Obj. 4]** How do the employees of a firm work together to create a viable control environment?

4. **[Obj. 4]** Select three of the seven categories of control activities and explain which departments within a firm could be involved in that activity.

Cross-Functional Case: Accounting and Marketing Face an Ethical Dilemma

Acme Appliance Company is finishing up business in the last week of December 20Y1. Business was similar to last year, about $100 million in sales. This was disappointing to the company, which had hoped to increase sales by 10 percent. At a departmental meeting, a salesperson pointed out that Latehurst Corporation, a prominent customer, historically places an extremely large order in December but had not done so this year.

The marketing manager, Ed Edgekins, makes a sales call to Mr. Latehurst, CEO of Latehurst Corporation. Mr. Latehurst explains that his firm recently moved operations to a new and larger facility. The transition led to a delay in placing the order. Mr. Latehurst said his order of $10,045,050 would definitely go out on January 2, the first working day in 20Y2. Ed is happy to learn that Latehurst Corporation will be placing a hefty order. In fact, this means that in a practical sense, Acme Appliance Company did achieve its goal of increasing sales by 10 percent. However, technically, the sale will not be recorded until 20Y2. This is frustrating to Ed. He wants to achieve the company goal, but he also wants to do what's right. He wonders if there is a way to record the transaction in 20Y1.

Ed meets with the chief accountant of Acme Appliance, Sally Goodright, to discuss the situation. Explaining the verbal commitment for an upcoming order from Mr. Latehurst, Ed asks,

"Can we record the sale this year?" He emphasizes that the order would significantly improve this year's company profits and, thus, please top management and company stockholders. Ed cajoles, "Who knows? We might even get a bonus."

Sally admits, "I understand the practical reasons for recording the sale this year, but I can't record a transaction without a sales invoice to support it."

Ed blurts out, "Is that all that's holding this up?!" Ed knows that a sales invoice is not prepared until the purchase order is received and the items are shipped to the customer. Yet, given his conversation with Mr. Latehurst, he practically has the purchase order. The meeting ends with Ed and Sally concurring that they need to give the matter more thought.

What Sally knows and Ed does not, is that top management of Acme Appliance previously authorized her to allocate 5 percent of any increase over last year's sales among departmental managers as a Christmas bonus. The bonus would be about $25,000 to Sally. This would be especially helpful to Sally, as she had incurred twice that much in medical bills taking care of a family member. On a personal level, she hopes that Ed can come up with a sales invoice. Turning to her computer, she starts to write an email to Ed, then stops to reconsider the situation.

Required: Answer the following questions:
a. What does generally accepted accounting principles (GAAP) say about recording the sale?
b. Why are source documents important?
c. What would you do if you were the accounting manager? On what are you basing your decision? What are the possible consequences?
d. What would you do if you were the marketing manager? On what are you basing your decision? What are the possible consequences?

EXCEL ASSIGNMENTS

1. **[Obj. 3]** Cash Budget: The following information is for Argonaut Shipping Company:

	($ Millions)
Cash balance, Jan. 1, 20Y1	$200
Budgeted cash balance, Dec. 31, 20Y1	250
Collections from customers	8,920
Sale of assets	500
Payments of operating expenses	7,820
Purchase of equipment	1,250
Payment of debt	220
Dividends	100

Required: Prepare a cash budget for Argonaut Shipping Company for year ended Dec. 31, 20Y1 using Excel. Print your worksheet.

2. **[Obj. 3]** Cash Budget: Same as Excel assignment 1, except change the budgeted cash balance, December 31 to $300 million.

Required: Prepare a cash budget for Argonaut Shipping Company for year ended December 31, 20Y1 using Excel. Print your worksheet.

3. **[Obj. 3]** Cash Budget: The following information is for Acme Appliance Company:

	($ Thousands)
Cash balance, Jan. 1, 20Y1	$480
Budgeted cash balance, Dec. 31, 20Y1	750
Collections from customers	98,400
Sale of assets	640
Payments of operating expenses	86,000
Purchase of equipment	10,800
Payment of debt	400
Dividends	2,480

Required: Prepare a cash budget for Acme Appliance Company for year ended December 31, 20Y1 using Excel. Print your worksheet.

4. **[Obj. 3]** Cash Budget: Same as Excel assignment 3, except change the cash balance, January 1 from $480 thousand to $680 thousand.

   Required: Prepare a cash budget for Acme Appliance Company for year ended December 31, 20Y1 using Excel. Print your worksheet.

5. **[Obj. 3]** Bank Reconciliation: Southwest Manufacturing Company received its bank statement for the month ended June 30, 20Y1. Information from the bank statement and from the company's books is as follows.

Balance per bank, June 30		$22,368
Deposits in transit		3,425
Outstanding checks:	No. 2478	105
	No. 2533	2,456
Balance per books, June 30		24,103
Non-sufficient funds check from customer		789
Cost of ordering checks		52
Bank service charge		30

   Required: Using Excel, prepare the bank reconciliation and print your worksheet.

6. **[Obj. 3]** Bank Reconciliation: Same as Excel assignment 5, except change the following: Balance per Bank is $357,782; Deposits in transit $38,200; Balance per Books is $399,600; and NSF check is $6,097.

   Required: Using Excel, prepare the bank reconciliation and print your worksheet.

7. **[Obj. 3]** Bank Reconciliation and Journal Entries: Dakota Drilling Company received its bank statement for the month ended August 31, 20Y1. Information from the bank statement and from the company's books is as follows:

Balance per bank, Aug. 31		$2,459
Deposits in transit		244
Outstanding checks:	No. 378	98
	No. 399	236
Balance per books, Aug. 31		2,750
Non-sufficient funds check from customer		228
Cost of ordering checks		18
Bank service charge		35

   Also, a check for $6,840 worth of supplies was erroneously recorded as $6,740.

   Requirements:
   a. Prepare the bank reconciliation using Excel. Print your worksheet.
   b. Using Excel, prepare journal entries resulting from the reconciliation. Print your worksheet.

8. **[Obj. 3]** Bank Reconciliation and Journal Entries: Same as Excel assignment 7, except change the following: Balance per bank is $12,953; Deposits in transit $820; Balance per books is $13,750; and NSF check is $158.

   Requirements:
   a. Prepare the bank reconciliation using Excel. Print your worksheet.
   b. Using Excel, prepare journal entries resulting from the reconciliation. Print your worksheet.

WEB ASSIGNMENTS

1. **[Obj. 4]** Search the Web for facts on information security. Prepare a one-page report. Use at least three Web sources. Cite your sources, including Web addresses, in your report.

2. **[Obj. 5]** Go to the website for the American Institute of CPAs and prepare a brief report on the requirements to become a Certified Public Accountant.

3. **[Obj. 5]** Go to the website for Marvel Enterprises or do a search on Google to find the auditor's report on Marvel's most recent financial statements. Who was the auditor? Were the financial statements presented fairly according to GAAP?

4. **[Obj. 5]** Can the Securities Exchange Commission (SEC) and/or the Public Company Accounting Oversight Board order a special inspection of any registered public accounting firm at any time? To find the answer, go to the website for the American Institute of Certified Public Accountants (AICPA) and look under Section 104 of the Sarbanes-Oxley Act: **Inspections of Registered Public Accounting Firms**, or do a search on Google.

5. **[Obj. 5]** Can the coordinating partner of an audit team stay on the team indefinitely? To find the answer, go to the website for the American Institute of Certified Public Accountants (AICPA) and look under Section 203 of the Sarbanes-Oxley Act: **Audit Partner Rotation**, or do a search on Google.

6. **[Obj. 6]** One of the prominent accounting firms is Ernst and Young. Go to its website, or do a search on Google, and list and explain the company's six core values.

7. **[Obj. 6]** Search the Web regarding accounting ethics. Prepare a one-page report. Cite at least three sources.

8. **[Obj. 6]** Search the Web for information on "The Witch of Wall Street." Prepare a one-page report. Cite your source.

¶512

Test Prepper

Use this sample test to gauge your comprehension of the chapter material.

True/False Questions

___ 1. Preventive controls identify errors and irregularities after they occur so that corrective action may be taken.

___ 2. The cash budget is an internal control device because it provides feedback concerning cash inflows and outflows.

___ 3. The purpose of a cash budget is to resolve differences between the cash balance on the bank statement and the cash balance on the accounting records.

___ 4. Writing checks to make payments provides for better control over cash.

___ 5. A non-sufficient funds check was received in the amount of $50. The resulting journal entry will increase (debit) accounts receivable for $50.

___ 6. Risk assessment is the process of defining areas where risk of loss of assets or errors in the accounting records are great, so that appropriate internal controls can be established.

___ 7. An external audit is an examination of a company's financial statement by a company manager to determine that the statement has been presented fairly and prepared using GAAP.

___ 8. External audits are required of publicly-traded companies.

___ 9. An internal audit can be designed to evaluate internal controls.

___ 10. The American Institute of Certified Public Accountants maintains an ethical code for accountants to follow.

Multiple-Choice Questions

__ 1. Which of the following is not considered to be cash?
   a. currency on hand
   b. deposits in company bank accounts
   c. savings bonds in company name
   d. checks made out to the company
   e. money orders made out to the company

__ 2. The journal entry to set up the petty cash fund includes a debit to
   a. petty cash expense
   b. miscellaneous expense
   c. petty cash
   d. cash
   e. petty cash payable

__ 3. A document that specifies the purpose of the check is a
   a. lockbox
   b. memo
   c. checking account
   d. remittance advice
   e. bank reconciliation

__ 4. Regarding a bank reconciliation, which of the following statements is not true of outstanding checks?
   a. They have been recorded on the company books.
   b. They have not cleared the bank yet.
   c. They are not shown on the bank statement.
   d. They are shown on the bank statement.
   e. They should be subtracted from the bank balance.

__ 5. A document that authorizes preparation of a check is a
   a. voucher
   b. petty cash fund
   c. remittance advice
   d. bank statement
   e. memo

__ 6. Which of the following refers to a short-term, highly liquid investment that will convert to cash in less than 90 days?
   a. cash equivalent
   b. remittance advice
   c. lockbox
   d. petty cash fund
   e. voucher

__ 7. What is the component of internal control structure that involves evaluating the quality of internal control?
   a. communicating
   b. stocking
   c. risk enhancement
   d. monitoring
   e. control activation

__ 8. Which type of audit is concerned with evaluating the economy and efficiency with which scarce resources are utilized, and whether goals and objectives have been attained?
   a. external audit
   b. resource audit
   c. industry audit
   d. management audit
   e. major audit

__ 9. Which of the following is not true regarding an internal audit?
   a. Helps determine whether the operations of the firm are achieving the firm's goals.
   b. Helps evaluate the efficiency with which the company is utilizing its scarce resources.
   c. Helps management determine whether any improvements can be made in departmental operations.
   d. Can be performed by an accountant who works for the company being audited.
   e. Must be performed by a CPA.

__ 10. Accountants who work for industry firms are called
   a. external accountants
   b. independent accountants
   c. management accountants
   d. external auditors
   e. independent auditors

Chapter

6

Accounts Receivable and Notes Receivable

LEARNING OBJECTIVES

After studying Chapter 6, you should be able to do the following:

1. Describe how the proper accounting for accounts and notes receivable is important to people within and outside the firm.
2. Define accounts receivable and notes receivable.
3. Perform the accounting process for accounts receivable and explain related management issues.
4. Illustrate how to account for uncollectible accounts receivable.
5. Explain the features of notes receivable, including interest calculations and journal entries.
6. Describe methods a firm might use to accelerate cash inflows.
7. Perform analytic review using three key financial ratios: current ratio, acid-test ratio, and average collection period.

CHAPTER CONTENTS

Accounts Receivable and Notes Receivable

FOCUS ON BUSINESS

Intel Corporation's Accounts Receivable

If you own a computer or cell phone, you are very likely in possession of an Intel product. As a manufacturing company, Intel is the world's largest semiconductor chip maker for the computing and communications industries. Intel's products include microprocessors, application processors used in cellular handsets and handheld computing devices, networking and communications products such as Ethernet connectivity products, optical and network processing components, and embedded control chips. Founded in 1968, Intel currently has over 78,000 employees in 60 countries around the world, from Argentina to Vietnam.

Some of Intel's customers buy on account, that is, the customer promises to pay for the products at a future date. These financial claims against customers are represented in accounts receivable. Intel reported $3,978 million in accounts receivable one year. Yet, some customers will never pay their bill, and these amounts will become uncollectible accounts. How does Intel know how much of its accounts receivable will become uncollectible? At the end of the year, Intel estimated the amount of its uncollectible accounts. According to the expense recognition principle, bad debt expenses must be reported in the period in which the sales were originally made. Accounting practices provide two ways of estimating this expense; both will be covered in this chapter. By the way, Intel estimated its uncollectible accounts to equal $64 million.

Source: *Intel.com*

¶601 Applications to People Within and Outside the Firm

LEARNING OBJECTIVE 1: Describe how the proper accounting for accounts receivable and notes receivable is important to people within and outside the firm.

If you have ever wanted an item such as a new mountain bike, but did not have the cash to purchase it, you can appreciate that a certain business might allow you to buy the bike on account. For example, if Mountain Adventure Shop extends credit to you for the purchase, the business expects you to pay the amount at a predetermined time in the future. Mountain Adventure Shop would record an account receivable that reflects the amount you owe. As much as you welcome the convenience of this arrangement, you probably also understand how important it is that the transaction be recorded accurately.

¶601.01 INTERNAL USERS

Within a business, various managers use the information recorded in accounts receivable and notes receivable. For example, the marketing department at Intel uses receivable records to answer questions such as: Who are our major customers? Which customers pay their accounts on time? What is our average collection period? Using data from the accounts receivable records, marketing managers might target promotions toward certain customers or provide incentives to customers who lag in payment of their accounts. Similarly, the collections department at Intel must track accounts that have become uncollectible so that the accounting records can be updated to reflect the decreased value of the company's accounts receivable.

¶601.02 EXTERNAL USERS

Are you currently making monthly payments toward the purchase of an item?

Customers may be users of accounts and notes receivable. If you have an account with Intel, you expect your account to be kept up-to-date and accurate by Intel's accountants. Other external parties like investors and lending institutions rely on the accurate reflection of receivables in a company's financial reports. In certain industries, accounts receivable and notes receivable comprise a large portion of a company's assets and thus contribute to a positive impression of the financial health of a business. If these assets are overstated or understated, the financial condition of the company is distorted.

¶602

Accounts receivable represents a financial claim against customers.

Types of Receivables

Accounts receivable represents a financial claim against customers.

? *Have you borrowed money from a bank in order to pay for your education? If so, the bank has a notes receivable with your name on it.*

LEARNING OBJECTIVE 2: Define accounts receivable and notes receivable.

A **receivable** is a financial claim against an individual or business, usually resulting from the sale of goods or services or by lending money. Accounts receivable and notes receivable are the most prevalent categories of receivables. **Accounts receivable** represent a firm's financial claims against customers. Accounts receivable are obtained by selling products or services on credit. Sometimes, accounts receivable are called "trade receivables" because they result from the trade or business in which the company is engaged. **Notes receivable** result from contractual agreements in which one party borrows money from another.

¶603

Accounts Receivable

A notes receivable represents the money one party has borrowed from another.

LEARNING OBJECTIVE 3: Perform the accounting process for accounts receivable and explain related management issues.

Liquidity refers to how rapidly an item can be converted to cash.

Accounts receivable is the third most liquid asset, after cash and short-term investments. As you recall, liquidity refers to how rapidly an item can be converted to cash. Liquidity is important because a company must have sufficient cash to pay bills as they become due.

Accounts receivable is a current asset. Current assets are those that will be used up, sold, or converted to cash within the year. When a firm extends credit to customers, payment is typically due in 30 to 60 days. All other assets are designated as long-term assets. Examples of long-term assets include land, buildings, and equipment.

¶603.01

WHY SELL ON CREDIT?

People involved in business transactions must be comfortable in extending a certain degree of trust to those with whom they are doing business.

Many companies in the United States extend credit to their customers. In effect, they trust their customers to be ethical and pay at a future date. By offering credit options, businesses can often capture sales from customers who might not have cash immediately available for desired purchases. For our economy to function and expand, people involved in business transactions must be comfortable in extending a certain degree of trust to those with whom they are doing business.

If a customer does not pay the amount due, an uncollectible account expense, or bad debt expense, results. Some people purposely do not pay their financial commitments, thus breaking the law. Others may experience extenuating circumstances resulting in financial ruin or bankruptcy. The degree of bad debt experience is different among companies. At Intel, bad debts are only about 0.21 percent of net sales. Other companies have bad debts of 1 to 2 percent of net sales. At the other extreme, retailers such as Walmart do not sell on credit. Only cash and credit cards are accepted for payment, which do not result in bad debt expense. Selling on credit does not refer to accepting credit card purchases, because the credit card company assumes the risk of nonpayment. Selling on credit refers to the business itself extending credit and providing products or services before payment.

Since bad debts decrease a company's profits, you may wonder why a company would continue to extend credit to its customers. As long as the bad debt expense is less than the profits generated from credit sales, the company benefits from selling on credit. Accounting for bad debts is described later in this chapter.

¶603.02

JOURNALIZING AND POSTING

The accounts receivable subsidiary ledger contains all the names and transactions for every customer who purchases items on account.

When customers purchase items on account from a business, an account receivable is established for each customer. As you recall, an account receivable is money owed to the company by an individual customer, resulting from sales made on account, that is, on credit.

When a sale on account is made, the debit is posted to the Accounts Receivable account and the credit is made to Sales. Thus the journal entry is in balance within the general ledger. In addition, a debit to the customer's account in the accounts receivable subsidiary ledger must be made to update that customer's individual account. The **accounts receivable subsidiary ledger** is a ledger that contains all the individual names and transactions for every customer who purchases items on account. In computer environments, the

A control account shows the total balance of all accounts in its corresponding subsidiary ledger.

accounts receivable subsidiary ledger is called the "accounts receivable master file," just as the general ledger is called the "general ledger master file." The Accounts Receivable account in the general ledger is called a "**control account**;" it shows the total balance of all accounts in its corresponding subsidiary ledger.

To illustrate the recording of an account receivable transaction, assume a credit sale of $100 is made to Jean Deaux on May 4. The journal entry is recorded in the general journal as follows:

May 4	Account Receivable – J. Deaux	100	
	Sales		100
	To record credit sale.		

In the general ledger, the entry is posted to the Accounts Receivable control account and the Sales account. In addition, the debit is posted to Jean Deaux's subsidiary account in the accounts receivable subsidiary ledger, as shown below:

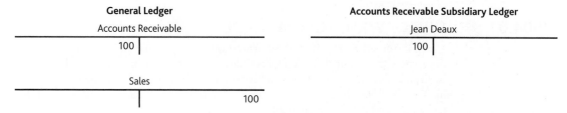

The balance of the Accounts Receivable control account in the general ledger is always equal to the total of all account balances in the accounts receivable subsidiary ledger. For example, assume three more credit sales are made as follows: $200 to Millard Fillmore; $750 to James Garfield; and $400 to Rutherford Hayes. After posting, the balances in the Accounts Receivable control account and subsidiary accounts are as follows:

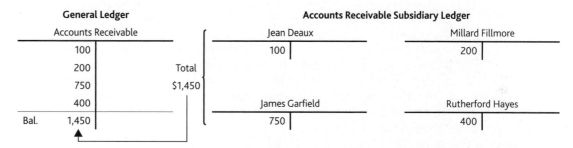

Assume that on May 14 Jean Deaux sends in payment of $50 on his account. The journal entry is recorded as follows:

May 14	Cash	50	
	Account Receivable – J. Deaux		50
	To record payment on account.		

After posting, the general ledger and subsidiary accounts would appear as follows.

General Ledger

Cash

	2,950	
	50	
Bal.	3,000	

Accounts Receivable

	1,450	**50**	
Bal.	1,400		

Accounts Receivable Subsidiary Ledger

Jean Deaux

	100	**50**	
Bal.	50		

Millard Filmore

200	

James Garfield

750	

Rutherford Hayes

400	

? As a customer, are businesses trusting you to some degree? Is trust involved when customers purchase items on the Internet or by using a personal check?

¶603.02

After payment from Jean Deaux, the balance in the Accounts Receivable control account is $1,400. Note that this is the same amount as the total of all account balances in the accounts receivable subsidiary ledger: 50 + 200 + 750 + 400 = $1,400.

¶604   Uncollectible Accounts Receivable

LEARNING OBJECTIVE 4: Illustrate how to account for uncollectible accounts receivable.

Uncollectible accounts receivable are typically referred to as "bad debts." Bad debt expense is an operating expense like wages and insurance. Bad debt expense is a normal business expense that should be anticipated by a company that sells goods or services on a credit basis. Companies can account for bad debts in two ways: the direct write-off method or the allowance method.

¶604.01   DIRECT WRITE-OFF METHOD

Under the **direct write-off method** of accounting for uncollectible accounts receivable, the business identifies a specific account that is uncollectible and writes it off by removing the amount from the customer's account receivable (a credit) and debiting Bad Debt Expense. Assume that a sale to Garth Vader is made in 20Y1 for $500. In 20Y2, his account is determined to be uncollectible. The following entry is made to record the bad debt expense in 20Y2:

August 1	Bad Debt Expense	500	
	Accounts Receivable – G. Vader		500
	To write off uncollectible account by direct write-off method.		

The direct write-off method is a less-than-ideal approach because it is not consistent with generally accepted accounting principles. First, the expense recognition principle is violated. If the sale to Garth Vader is made in 20Y1 but his account receivable is written off in 20Y2, then revenues are recorded in one year and corresponding expenses are recorded in the following year. As a result, net income is overstated in 20Y1 and understated in 20Y2. In contrast, the allowance method, which is described in the next section, records the bad debt expense in the same period in which the corresponding sales revenue is recorded.

Another deficiency of the direct write-off method is that Accounts Receivable is shown at its full amount on the balance sheet; it is not adjusted to account for any estimated bad debts, as is done under the allowance method.

¶604.02   ALLOWANCE METHOD

The allowance method is preferred over the direct write-off method because it follows the revenue and expense recognition principles and shows the net realizable value of accounts receivable.

The **allowance method** of accounting for uncollectible accounts writes off an estimated amount in the period in which the related sales take place. Later, when a specific account receivable is determined to be uncollectible, that customer's account balance is reduced to zero.

The allowance method follows the revenue and expense recognition principles in that revenues earned during the period are matched with the expenses incurred to generate that revenue. In other words, the expense recognition principle requires that bad debt expense be recorded in the same period that the related sales revenue is recorded.

¶604.02.01   Allowance for Doubtful Accounts

The allowance method writes off an estimated amount in the period in which the related sales take place.

Accounting for bad debts under the allowance method is accomplished by recording a debit to Bad Debt Expense and a credit to Allowance for Doubtful Accounts for the estimated uncollectible amount. The Allowance for Doubtful Accounts represents the amount of accounts receivable that are expected to be uncollectible. Allowance for Doubtful Accounts, also called "allowance for uncollectible accounts," is a contra-asset to the Accounts Receivable account. When a credit sale is made, the company assumes that the customer will eventually pay off his or her account receivable balance. Exactly which customers will fail to pay is unknown, of course.

The Allowance for Doubtful Accounts represents the amount of accounts receivable that are expected to be uncollectible.

Under the aging of accounts receivable approach, each account receivable is evaluated based on how long it has been outstanding.

To illustrate, assume Mountain Adventure Shop has a balance of $95,000 in Accounts Receivable on December 31, 20Y1. Based on past experience, the shop knows that all customers will not pay what they owe. The manager estimates that 5 percent of accounts due will not be collected and makes this journal entry at the end of the year:

Dec. 31	Bad Debt Expense	4,750	
	Allowance for Doubtful Accounts		4,750
	To record bad debt expense ($95,000 × .05).		

This entry matches the income earned during 20Y1 with the estimated bad debts associated with those sales.

While businesses use a variety of ways to estimate bad debts, two popular approaches to estimating bad debts are the aging of accounts receivable approach and the percentage of sales approach. The goal of each approach is to predict the amount of accounts receivable that will be written off as uncollectible.

¶604.02.02   Estimating Bad Debts Using Aging of Accounts Receivable

The **aging of accounts receivable** is a balance-sheet approach for estimating bad debts, in that it utilizes accounts from the balance sheet. Under this approach, each account receivable is evaluated based on how long it has been outstanding. Using past company experience, the probability that the account is uncollectible is assessed. Accounting software packages often provide automatic aging analyses.

To illustrate aging of accounts receivable, assume that Blue Bell Ice Cream Company's accounts are as follows before year-end adjusting entries:

Accounts Receivable		Allowance for Doubtful Accounts	
104,000			2,000

As shown, Blue Bell has $104,000 of Accounts Receivable and $2,000 in the Allowance for Doubtful Accounts on December 31, 20Y1. Before year-end adjustments are made, an aging analysis, shown in Exhibit 6.1, estimates that the company will not collect $11,058 of its accounts receivable.

Exhibit 6.1 BLUE BELL ICE CREAM AGING OF ACCOUNTS RECEIVABLE					
			Age of Account		
Customer	**1-30 Days**	**31-60 Days**	**61-90 Days**	**Over 90 Days**	**Total Balance**
Albertson's	$8,200				$8,200
HEB Grocery		$6,300			$6,300
Kroger			$4,500		$4,500
Food for Less			$2,500		$2,500
Garth Vader				$500	$500
Other Accounts	$28,480	$22,200	$20,800	$10,520	$82,000
Total	$36,680	$28,500	$27,800	$11,020	$104,000
Estimated Percentage Uncollectible	5%	10%	15%	20%	
Estimated Amount Uncollectible	$1,834	$2,850	$4,170	$2,204	$11,058

For year-end adjustments, the balance in Allowance for Doubtful Accounts must be increased to the estimated amount of $11,058. Remember that the Allowance for Doubtful Accounts already has a balance of $2,000. The adjusting entry is made at the end of the period, as shown:

Dec. 31	Bad Debt Expense	9,058	
	Allowance for Doubtful Accounts		9,058
	To record bad debt expense and adjust allowance account to $11,058 ($9,058 + $2000).		

The general ledger includes the following balances at year-end.

Accounts Receivable		Allowance for Doubtful Accounts	
104,000			2,000
		Adj.	9,058
		Bal.	11,058

The net realizable value of accounts receivable is the amount that the company expects to collect from customers.

The difference between the gross amount of accounts receivable and the allowance for doubtful accounts is referred to as the "**net realizable value of accounts receivable**." Thus, the balance sheet shows Blue Bell's net realizable value of accounts receivable to be $92,942 ($104,000 – $11,058). This is the amount that Blue Bell expects to collect from customers.

¶604.02.03 Estimating Bad Debts Using Percentage of Sales

The percentage of sales approach estimates bad debt expense as a percentage of sales.

The percentage-of-sales approach is the second popular approach to estimating bad debts. Using **percentage of sales**, the amount of uncollectible accounts receivable (bad debts) is computed as a percentage of sales. This is an income statement approach because it starts with the sales amount from the income statement.

Let's re-estimate Blue Bell's bad debts using the percentage-of-sales method. Once again we'll look at the account balances for Blue Bell Ice Cream Company, prior to end-of-period adjusting entries:

Accounts Receivable		Allowance for Doubtful Accounts	
104,000			2,000

Blue Bell's customers owe $104,000 to the company with a balance of $2,000 in Allowance for Doubtful Accounts. The credit department predicts additional bad debt expense of 2 percent of total sales. Total sales were $750,000; 2 percent of that equals $15,000. Under the percentage of sales method, the allowance account is increased by the full amount of the additional bad debt estimate. The journal entry to record bad debt expense is shown below:

Dec. 31	Bad Debt Expense ($750,000 × .02)	15,000	
	Allowance for Doubtful Accounts		15,000
	To record bad debt expense and increase the allowance account by $15,000.		

This adjusting entry records estimated bad debt expense for the year and updates the allowance account. After adjustment, the general ledger accounts are shown as follows:

Accounts Receivable		Allowance for Doubtful Accounts	
104,000			2,000
		Adj.	15,000
		Bal.	17,000

Blue Bell's customers still owe $104,000, but the company does not expect to collect $17,000 of this amount. The balance sheet will show the net realizable value of accounts receivable, $87,000 ($104,000 – $17,000), the amount Blue Bell actually expects to collect.

¶604.02.04 Writing off a Specific Account

As the collections department of a company attempts to collect amounts due from customers, it becomes clear over time that certain accounts are uncollectible. When using the allowance method, the entry to write off a specific account involves a debit to Allowance for Doubtful Accounts and a credit to Accounts Receivable. A credit is also made to the customer's account within the accounts receivable subsidiary ledger.

For example, assume that Green's Grocer owes Blue Bell Ice Cream $4,000 at October 30. After eight months of attempted collections, Blue Bell determines that the customer cannot pay on the account. The following entry is recorded:

June 30	Allowance for Doubtful Accounts	4,000	
	Accounts Receivable – Green's Grocer		4,000
	To write off Green's Grocer account receivable.		

Through this entry, the account for Green's Grocer has been reduced to zero and the allowance for doubtful accounts no longer shows the account as doubtful, but removes it entirely from Accounts Receivable.

¶604.03   ETHICAL ISSUES REGARDING ACCOUNTING FOR UNCOLLECTIBLE ACCOUNTS

When using the allowance method of accounting for uncollectible accounts, both the aging approach and the percentage-of-sales approach involve using estimates and management's professional judgment. To accomplish profit goals or to keep stock prices stable, some managers may use estimates to manipulate earnings. When examining estimates made for accounting purposes, the ethical motivations behind changes of estimates should be considered. As an illustration, suppose Tex Tools Company has the following experience with uncollectible accounts over the past three years:

Year	Sales	Amount Uncollectible	% Uncollectible
1	700,000	7,000	1%
2	800,000	16,000	2%
3	900,000	27,000	3%

Sales for the fourth year are $1,000,000. How much should the company record as uncollectible, or bad debt expense, for the fourth year? Based on existing bad economic conditions and loose internal credit policies, the accounting department projects uncollectible accounts will be at least 4 percent of sales, continuing a steady upward trend in the percentage uncollectible. Thus, the accounting department recommends the following entry:

Year 4			
Dec. 31	Bad Debt Expense	40,000	
	Allowance for Doubtful Accounts		40,000
	To record bad debt expense ($1,000,000 × .04).		

As with any company, the stock price of Tex Tools is greatly affected by its profitability. Bad debt expense of $40,000 is an operating expense that reduces net income by $40,000. Assume that the $40,000 of bad debt expense results in a net income of $180,000. Wall Street analysts previously forecasted that the company would have a net income of $200,000.

Management fears that missing the forecast by $20,000 (10 percent) will drastically hurt the company's stock price. To prevent this outcome, management prepares another analysis to support a lower estimated uncollectible rate. The following chart reflects management's rationale for using a 2 percent uncollectible rate, instead of 4 percent:

Year	Sales	Amount Uncollectible	% Uncollectible
1	$700,000	$7,000	1%
2	$800,000	$16,000	2%
3	$900,000	$27,000	3%
	Average % uncollectible		**2%**

Have you ever written off a bad debt?

Using this analysis, management insists that since sales in Year 4 are $1,000,000, then bad debt expense should be $20,000 ($1,000,000 × .02). Instead of the earlier recommendation, the company would record the following journal entry:

Year 4			
Dec. 31	Bad Debt Expense	20,000	
	Allowance for Doubtful Accounts		20,000
	To record bad debt expense ($1,000,000 × .02).		

By making bad debt expense $20,000 instead of $40,000, the company meets Wall Street's earnings forecast for the company. Wall Street analysts commend the company for meeting its earnings forecast. Consequently, the price of the company stock goes up.

Based on the illustration above, you can see how the estimate of bad debt expense might be manipulated to achieve a higher profit. In this illustration, a higher estimate of bad debt expense will result in a lower stock price. However, this is a short-term problem. In the long run, if the company is successful, the stock price will recover. On the other hand, a lower estimate of bad debt expense, that ultimately falls short of actual bad debts, results in future negative repercussions. The additional bad debt expense will be mismatched on future financial statements, causing future net income to be understated. If financial information is intentionally misrepresented, management may face civil and criminal penalties.

¶605 Notes Receivable

LEARNING OBJECTIVE 5: Explain the features of notes receivable, including interest calculations and journal entries.

A promissory note is a written promise to pay a definite sum at a definite future time.

Along with accounts receivable on a company's balance sheet, you will also often find notes receivable. As you recall, notes receivable result from contractual agreements in which one party borrows money from another. The most common type of note receivable results from a **promissory note** ("promise to pay"). A typical promissory note is shown in Exhibit 6.2.

Exhibit 6.2 PROMISSORY NOTE

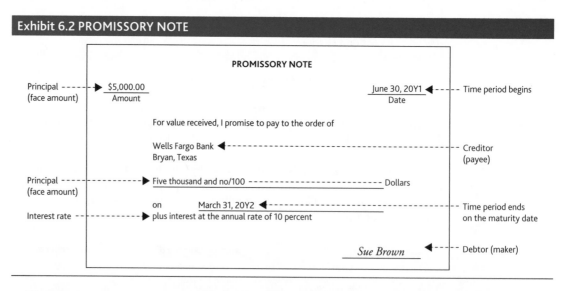

The creditor loans the money and the debtor borrows the money.

The parties to a promissory note include the **creditor**, who loans the money, and the **debtor**, who borrows the money. From the creditor's perspective, the promissory note is a note receivable. To the debtor, the promissory note is a note payable.

The principal is the amount of money loaned and the maturity date marks the end of the loan.

The interest rate is expressed as a yearly percentage rate unless stated otherwise.

The **principal** is the amount loaned by a creditor and borrowed by the debtor. Exhibit 6.2 presents a note for which the time period or term of the note begins on June 30, 20Y1 and ends nine months later on March 31, 20Y2. Thus, on March 31, 20Y2, Sue Brown (the debtor or maker) promises to pay Wells Fargo Bank (the creditor or payee) the principal of $5,000 plus 10 percent interest for the year. The end of the loan's time period is called the "**maturity date**." The interest rate is always expressed for an annual period (i.e., the annual percentage rate) unless specifically stated otherwise. To the creditor, **interest** is the compensation for the risk of lending money. The interest is revenue to the creditor, Wells Fargo Bank, and an expense to the debtor, Sue Brown.

When Sue Brown signs the promissory note, she receives $5,000 from Wells Fargo Bank. The bank records the following journal entry:

20Y1			
June 30	Note Receivable – Sue Brown	5,000	
	Cash		5,000
	To record note receivable.		

Wells Fargo Bank earns interest revenue during July to December. On December 31, the bank records accrued interest revenue for six months as shown:

Dec. 31	Interest Receivable ($5,000 × .10 × 6/12)	250	
	Interest Revenue		250
	To record interest revenue accrued.		

On the maturity date, March 31, the bank has accrued interest revenue from January 1 to March 31, three months at an annual percentage rate of 10 percent. The calculation for interest revenue is as shown:

Principal × Interest rate × Time period = Amount of interest
$5,000 × .10 × 3/12 = $125

Sue Brown pays the note on March 31, 20Y2; thus, the bank collects the principal and the accumulated interest. Wells Fargo Bank makes the following entry:

20Y2			
Mar. 31	Cash	5,375	
	Note Receivable – Sue Brown		5,000
	Interest Receivable		250
	Interest Revenue ($5,000 × .10 × 3/12)		125
	To record collection of note.		

A business might choose to sell goods and services on notes receivable instead of selling on accounts receivable. Accounts receivable are typically due in 30 to 60 days. A note receivable might be used for longer payment terms. For example, suppose Acme Motor Company sells $10,000 of motors to General Electric. Acme receives a 120-day promissory note at 12 percent annual interest. The entry to record the sale and note receivable is as shown:

? Do you know anyone who signed a promissory note to obtain funds to pay for college expenses?

Aug. 1	Notes Receivable – GE	10,000	
	Sales Revenue		10,000
	To record sale by accepting note for payment.		

Entries to record the resulting interest revenue and collection follow the same format previously described under the section on promissory notes.

Sometimes companies replace a customer's account receivable with a note receivable when the account receivable is past due. In this case, the company credits the account receivable and debits the note receivable. Suppose Acme Motor Company accepts a note receivable from customer Bill Jones in place of his past-due account receivable. The entry is as shown:

Mar. 1	Note Receivable	600	
	Account Receivable – B. Jones		600
	To accept note receivable in place of past-due account receivable.		

Entries to record interest revenue and collection of the note follow the same format previously described.

¶606 Managing Receivables and Cash

LEARNING OBJECTIVE 6: Describe methods a firm might use to accelerate cash inflows.

There are times when companies need to accelerate their cash inflows. One way this can be accomplished is to accept customer payments on credit cards. Receipt of cash when credit cards are used is faster than if those sales were made on account. Most retail businesses allow customers to make purchases using credit cards like American Express, Discover, or VISA. Suppose Marvel Enterprises sells $2,000 of merchandise to a customer who charges the amount on her Discover card. Marvel makes the following entry:

Dec. 10	Cash	1,960	
	Financing Expense	40	
	Sales Revenue		2,000
	To record credit card sale.		

Marvel deposits the Discover card slip in the bank and thereupon receives a discounted amount ($1,960) of the total sale of $2,000. Discover collects 2 percent, which is $40 ($2,000 × .02 = $40). For Marvel, the $40 financing charge is an operating expense. Providing customers with the convenience of using credit cards often increases sales, but those sales come with financing charges, which reduce the amount of cash collected.

A factor is a firm that buys the accounts receivable of another company.

Another way that a company might accelerate its cash inflows is to sell its accounts receivable to another business firm. The firm that buys the accounts receivable is called a "**factor**." The factor pays the company an immediate amount, less a financing expense, for the receivables, then the factor attempts to collect the receivables itself. Suppose Intel Corporation sells $200,000 of its accounts receivable to a factor for $190,000. The factor earns $10,000, assuming that the customer pays the full $200,000. Intel benefits from the arrangement because it has immediate access to $190,000 of cash. Intel records the factoring of its accounts receivable as shown:

Aug. 1	Cash	190,000	
	Financing Expense	10,000	
	Accounts Receivable		200,000
	To record sale of accounts receivable.		

Another way a company might seek to improve cash flow management is by examining its credit policies. Normally, businesses perform credit checks on customers prior to extending them credit. The goal of approving customers, so that they can buy on credit, is to facilitate sales to those customers who can reasonably be expected to make payment in a timely manner. Credit approval is a part of customer order processing, as shown in Exhibit 6.3.

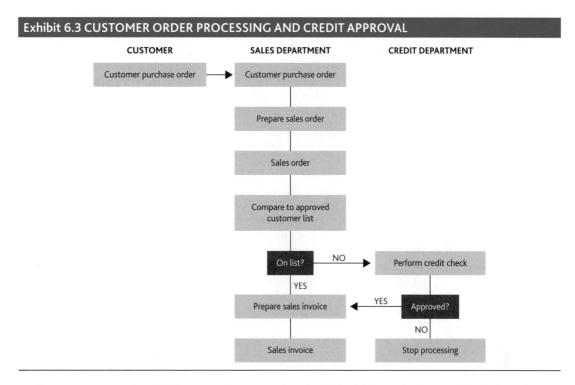

Exhibit 6.3 CUSTOMER ORDER PROCESSING AND CREDIT APPROVAL

Customer approval establishes control over credit sales. If bad debt expense is too high, then the customer credit approval process can be tightened.

¶607 Analyzing Liquidity and Receivables

LEARNING OBJECTIVE 7: Perform analytic review using three key financial ratios: current ratio, acid-test ratio, and average collection period.

Both management and external users of financial statements, especially investors and creditors, want to know how well a company is doing. Financial statement information is the starting point. Basic questions, such as the following, can be answered by simply reading the financial statements:

(1) How much profit did the company make?
(2) What are the total assets?
(3) What was the net cash flow?

Analytic review is an evaluation of a company's financial health, based on ratios of its financial statement items.

The next step, after reading the basic information, is to perform an analytic review of the financial statement data. **Analytic review** is an evaluation of a company's financial health, based on ratios of financial statement items, and comparing those ratios to ratios in prior time periods and to industry averages.

A ratio by itself is not very meaningful. To be of real value, a ratio must be compared to past years' ratios and to industry averages. This enables you to answer two important questions: (1) What is the trend? (2) How does the company compare to other companies in the same industry?

Three financial ratios can be particularly helpful in evaluating receivables:

- Current ratio
- Acid-test ratio
- Average collection period

Each of these ratios provides insight into the financial strength of a company. They indicate how rapidly a company can acquire and pay cash.

¶607.01

The current ratio measures how well the company is able to meet short-term financial obligations.

CURRENT RATIO

The **current ratio** measures how well the company is able to meet short-term financial obligations. The current ratio is referred to as a "liquidity ratio" because it concerns the ability to convert assets to cash in order to pay bills. To compute the current ratio, divide current assets by current liabilities. Current liabilities are those debts that are payable within one year.

Intel Corporation's current ratio is computed as follows ($ millions):

$$\text{Current Ratio} = \frac{\text{Current Assets}}{\text{Current Liabilities}} = \frac{21,194}{9,234} = 2.29$$

This ratio indicates that current assets are 2.29 times as much as current liabilities. In other words, Intel has $2.29 in current assets available to pay each $1 of current liabilities. If the current ratio increases from year to year, this is usually regarded as a positive trend. Generally speaking, a higher current ratio is better than a lower current ratio. If the industry average is 2.25, then Intel's ratio of 2.29 compares favorably to other firms.

Without knowing either the company's current ratio from past years or the industry average, it would be difficult to say whether a ratio is good or bad. In the case of a new, small business like JK Productions, computing its current ratio at the end of its first month of operations will provide a comparison for future current ratio computations. Current assets for JK Productions include cash, accounts receivable, supplies, and prepaid insurance equaling $46,100. Current liabilities include accounts payable, unearned videography fees, wages payable, and income tax payable totaling $7,460. Thus, JK Productions' current ratio is 6.18 ($46,100 / $7,460). This ratio indicates that current assets are 6.18 times as much as current liabilities.

¶607.02

The acid-test ratio is a more rigorous measure of liquidity than the current ratio.

ACID-TEST RATIO

Like the current ratio, the acid-test ratio measures how well the company is able to meet short-term financial obligations. However, the **acid-test ratio** is a more rigorous measure of liquidity than the current ratio because only the most liquid of the current assets are included in its computation. The numerator is comprised of cash, short-term investments, and accounts receivable; the denominator is current liabilities. The acid-test ratio excludes less liquid current assets such as inventory from the calculation. A company with a lot of slow-moving inventory may have an excellent current ratio but still be unable to acquire the cash needed to pay bills.

Intel's acid-test ratio, also called the "quick ratio," is shown below ($ millions):

$$\text{Acid-Test Ratio} = \frac{\text{Cash + S-T Investments + A/R}}{\text{Current Liabilities}} = \frac{7,324 + 5,448 + 3,914}{9,234} = 1.8$$

As a more rigorous measure of liquidity, Intel's acid-test ratio is 1.8. As you will recall, Intel's current ratio is 2.29. The ratio of 1.8 indicates that Intel has $1.80 of quick assets available to pay each $1 of current liabilities. In other words, quick assets are 1.8 times as much as current liabilities. As a general rule, an acid-test ratio higher than one is considered good. However, as previously stated, to truly evaluate whether a ratio is good or bad, the ratio must be compared to past years' ratios and to industry averages.

¶607.03

AVERAGE COLLECTION PERIOD

$$\text{One Day's Sales} = \text{Net Sales} / 365 = 38,826 / 365 = 106$$

$$\text{Avg. Collection Period*} = \frac{\text{Average A/R}}{\text{One Day's Sales}} = \frac{(\text{Beg. A/R} + \text{Ending A/R}) / 2}{106}$$

$$= \frac{(2,999 + 3,914) / 2}{106} = 32.6 \text{ Days}$$

The average collection period shows how quickly receivables are collected.

The average collection period is another helpful measurement when evaluating a company's receivables. The **average collection period**, also referred to as "**days' sales in receivables**," shows how quickly a company collects its receivables. Once a business makes a credit sale, the next step is collecting the cash payment from the customer. The shorter the collection period, the more cash is on hand to pay bills. To calculate the average collection period, the first step is to calculate one day's sales. The second step is to divide average receivables by one day's sales. The computation of Intel's average collection period is shown below ($ millions):

As shown, Intel's average collection period is 32.6 days. Compared to other firms, this is a very good ratio. The average collection period is affected by the credit terms of the company. If sales are made on credit terms of "net 30," then receivables should be collected in about 30 days.

Ensuring that the firm has an adequate supply of cash for operations is a key task of the company's finance department. Consequently, financial mangers keep a close eye on the average collection period. If the average collection is too high, the company may need to find other sources of financing, such as factoring receivables or borrowing money from a bank. In addition to the finance department, managers in the marketing and credit departments are concerned about the average collection period. If the ratio is too high, customer approval and credit policies may need examination and revision.

Which financial ratio would Best Buy find most helpful in analyzing its receivables?

FOCUS ON TECHNOLOGY

Using Microsoft Excel: Calculating Current Ratio, Acid-Test Ratio, and Average Collection Period

Using Excel, we will calculate three financial ratios (current ratio, acid-test ratio, and average collection period) with the information from Intel's financial statements. If you need further instruction at any point, refer to the Excel information from the Appendix in Chapter 2.

1. File Identification Area: In an Excel worksheet, set up a file identification area. For input required, you may simply put "amounts from financial statements." Output required is current ratio, acid-test ratio, and average collection period.

2. Input Area: Your input area should contain the following data from Intel's financial statements. (Be sure to put each amount in a cell by itself so that the cell address can be used in formulas within the output area.)

	($ Millions)
Current Assets	18,925
Current Liabilities	6,595
Cash	7,404
Short-Term Investments	3,382
Accounts Receivable, Jan. 1	2,607
Accounts Receivable, Dec. 28	2,574
Net Sales	26,764

3. Output Area: Use the following formulas to the financial ratios. The division symbol in Excel is the backslash (/).

Current Ratio = Current assets / Current liabilities

Acid-Test Ratio = (Cash + Short-term investments + A/R) / Current liabilities

Average Collection Period = Average accounts receivable / One day's sales

---

¶608

Concluding Remarks

As we dig deeper into the operations of a company, we learned in this chapter the relevance of accounts and notes receivable. We went "behind the scenes" of a credit purchase and learned that not everyone pays their bills. We learned how companies like Intel estimate and record uncollectible accounts. Since accounts and notes receivable are sources of cash, it is important to stay abreast of a company's receivables. Financial ratios can measure how quickly a company's receivables are being collected and how easily a company can meet its short-term financial obligations. Cash must be coming into the company in order to replenish inventory and maintain operations. The cost of inventory is a major expense for a retailer. Accounting for inventory will be the focus of the next chapter.

¶609 Chapter Review

LEARNING OBJECTIVE 1

Describe how the proper accounting for accounts and notes receivable is important to people within and outside the firm.

Accounts and notes receivable are readily available sources of cash in most companies. Everyone within a company has a stake in accurate accounting for cash and other current assets. Marketing, in particular, relies on accurate and complete accounting records of customers' accounts receivable.

Outside the firm, customers and vendors are interested in the accurate accounting for their accounts. In addition, investors depend on accountants to accurately report the amount of accounts receivable; for example, investors expect the amount shown on the balance sheet for accounts receivable to be collectible.

LEARNING OBJECTIVE 2

Define accounts receivable and notes receivable.

A receivable is a financial claim against an individual or business. Accounts receivable and notes receivable are the most prevalent categories of receivables. Accounts receivable represent a firm's financial claims against customers and are obtained by selling products or services on credit. Notes receivable result from contractual agreements in which one party borrows money from another.

LEARNING OBJECTIVE 3

Perform the accounting process for accounts receivable and explain related management issues.

Accounts receivable is the third most liquid asset, after cash and short-term investments. Accounts receivable are financial claims against customers and are obtained by selling products or services on credit. Sometimes, accounts receivable are called "trade receivables" because they result from the trade or business in which the company is engaged.

LEARNING OBJECTIVE 4

Illustrate how to account for uncollectible accounts receivable.

When a company sells products or services on credit, not all customers will pay off their accounts receivable. These uncollectible accounts are called "bad debts." The allowance method and the direct write-off method are two methods of accounting for uncollectible accounts receivable. The allowance method writes off an estimated amount in the period in which the related sales take place. This method is preferred because it follows the expense recognition principle and shows the net realizable value of accounts receivable. The Allowance for Doubtful Accounts represents the amount of accounts receivable that are expected to be uncollectible.

Under the direct write-off method, a specific uncollectible account receivable is credited to reduce the account balance to zero, and the corresponding debit is made to Bad Debt Expense.

Two popular approaches for estimating bad debts include the aging of accounts receivable and the percentage of sales methods. Under the aging of accounts receivable approach, each account receivable is evaluated based on how long it has been outstanding. Under the percentage-of-sales approach, the amount of uncollectible accounts receivable is computed as a percentage of sales.

LEARNING OBJECTIVE 5

Explain the features of notes receivable, including interest calculations and journal entries.

Notes receivable result from contractual agreements in which one party borrows money from another. The most common type of note receivable results from a promissory note ("promise to pay"). The parties to a promissory note are referred to as the "creditor," who loans the money, and the "debtor," who borrows the money. To the creditor, the promissory note is a note receivable. To the debtor, the promissory note is a note payable.

LEARNING OBJECTIVE 6

Describe methods a firm might use to accelerate cash inflows.

Companies sometimes need to accelerate cash inflows. One way this can be accomplished is by accepting customer payments on credit cards. Providing customers with the convenience of using credit cards often increases sales, but those sales come with financing charges, which reduce the amount of cash collected.

Another method used to accelerate cash inflows is to factor accounts receivable. The company has immediate access to cash paid by the factor, but a financing charge is applied. Cash flows may also be managed by examining a firm's credit policies. A company may be able to accelerate cash inflows by having more stringent credit terms and application processes.

LEARNING OBJECTIVE 7

Perform analytic review using three key financial ratios: current ratio, acid-test ratio, and average collection period.

Analytic review is an evaluation of a company's financial health, based on ratios of financial statement items, and comparing those ratios to ratios in prior time periods and to industry averages. Three financial ratios can be particularly helpful in evaluating receivables: (1) current ratio, which is a measure of liquidity; (2) acid-test ratio, which is a rigorous measure of liquidity that includes only the most liquid of the current assets; and (3) average collection period, which shows how quickly receivables are collected.

¶610

Glossary

Accounts receivable

Accounts receivable represents a financial claim against customers.

Account receivable

An account receivable is money owed to the company by an individual customer, resulting from sales made on account, or on credit.

Accounts receivable subsidiary ledger

The accounts receivable subsidiary ledger is a ledger that contains all the individual names and transactions for every customer who purchases items on account. The total of this ledger should equal the balance in the Accounts Receivable control account.

Acid-test ratio

The acid-test ratio, also called the "quick ratio," is a rigorous measure of liquidity that includes only the most liquid of the current assets. The formula is as follows: (cash + short-term investments + accounts receivable) / current liabilities.

Aging of accounts receivable

The aging of accounts receivable method is a balance-sheet approach for estimating bad debts or the amount of uncollectible accounts receivable.

Allowance for doubtful accounts

The Allowance for Doubtful Accounts represents the amount of accounts receivable that are expected to be uncollectible.

Allowance method

The allowance method is a method of accounting for uncollectible accounts by writing off an estimated amount of bad debts in the period in which the related sales take place.

Analytic review

Analytic review is an evaluation of a company's financial health, based on ratios of financial statement items, and a comparison of those ratios to prior time periods and industry averages.

Average collection period

The average collection period shows how quickly receivables are collected.

Control account

A general ledger control account shows the total balance of all accounts in its corresponding subsidiary ledger.

Creditor

A creditor is the party who loans money.

Current ratio

The current ratio is a measure of liquidity. The current ratio equals current assets divided by current liabilities.

Debtor

A debtor is the party who borrows money.

Direct write-off method

The direct write-off method is an approach for accounting for bad debts, which is contrary to the expense recognition principle. Under this method, the uncollectible account receivable is credited to reduce the account balance to zero, and the corresponding debit is made to Bad Debt Expense.

Factor

A factor is a firm that buys the accounts receivable of another company.

Interest

To the creditor, interest is the compensation for the risk of lending money.

Maturity date

The end of a loan's time period is called the "maturity date."

Net realizable value of accounts receivable

The net realizable value of accounts receivable is the amount of accounts receivable that is expected to be collected from customers; the amount is the difference between the gross amount of accounts receivable and the allowance for doubtful accounts.

Notes receivable

Notes receivable result from contractual agreements in which one party borrows money from another.

Percentage of sales

The percentage of sales method for estimating bad debt expense is an income statement approach that computes the amount of bad debts as a percentage of sales.

Principal

The principal is the amount loaned by a creditor and borrowed by a debtor.

Promissory note

A promissory note is a written promise to pay a definite sum at a definite future time.

Receivable

A receivable is a financial claim against an individual or business firm, usually resulting from the sale of goods and services and by lending money.

Appendix: Short-Term Investments (Marketable Securities)

A company expects to sell short-term investments within one year.

Short-term investments, also referred to as marketable securities, are investments that a company expects to sell within one year. Short-term investments are listed after cash on the balance sheet of a typical company. There are three types of short-term investments:

- Trading investments
- Held-to-maturity investments whose maturity occurs within one year
- Available-for-sale investments

The majority of firms invest their extra cash in their own operations. However, some firms make substantial investments in marketable securities.

In 20Y1, Intel placed $5,448 million in short-term investments. This is shown in the current assets section of Intel's Balance Sheet in Exhibit 6.A.

Exhibit 6.A CURRENT ASSETS OF INTEL CORPORATION DECEMBER 31, 20Y1	
Current Assets:	($ Millions)
Cash	$7,324
Short-term investments	5,448
Accounts receivable	3,914
Total inventories	3,126
Other current assets	1,382
Total current assets	$21,194

TRADING INVESTMENTS

A company plans to sell a trading investment within a few months or less.

A **trading investment** is one that the company plans to sell within a few months or less. The goal of acquiring a trading investment is to sell it for more than its cost. A trading investment is typically the stock of another company. Suppose that on December 10, 20Y2, Intel Corporation acquires 1,000 shares of General Motors for $50 per share and 1,000 shares of Microsoft at $25 per share. The journal entry by Intel is as follows:

Dec. 10	Short-Term Investment		75,000	
	Cash			75,000
	Purchase of 1,000 shares of GM at $50 each and 1,000 shares of Microsoft at $25 each.			

Assume that on December 25 Intel receives a cash dividend of $2,000 from General Motors. The entry to record receipt of the dividend is shown below:

Dec. 25	Cash		2,000	
	Dividend Revenue			2,000
	To record cash dividend received.			

Intel's fiscal year ends on the last Saturday in December. Assume that the last Saturday of December in 20Y2 is December 29. On that day, Intel prepares its financial statements. On the balance sheet, trading investments are shown at fair market value. Assume that General Motors stock is trading for $46 per share and Microsoft is trading for $26 per share. The trading portfolio is now valued at $72,000 as shown below:

Investment	Cost	Market Value
General Motors (1,000 shares)	$50,000	$46,000
Microsoft (1,000 shares)	25,000	26,000
Total	$75,000	$72,000

Intel must adjust the the value of its trading investments as shown:

Dec. 29	Unrealized Loss on Investments	3,000	
	Allowance to Adjust Short-Term Investments to Market		3,000
	To record unrealized loss on trading portfolio and adjust trading investments to market value.		

The unrealized loss of $3,000 on the investment is shown on the income statement. This loss is "unrealized" because the investment has not been sold yet. The balance sheet shows the short-term investments of $75,000 along with the allowance to adjust short-term investments of $3,000. The allowance reduces the trading investments to their market value of $72,000. This allowance account is a contra-asset. Financial statement presentation is shown in Exhibit 6.B.

Exhibit 6.B REPORTING SHORT-TERM INVESTMENTS ON THE BALANCE SHEET AND INCOME STATEMENT IN 20Y3

Balance Sheet		Income Statement	
Current Assets:		Other Revenue and Gains (Losses):	
Short-term investments	$75,000	Dividend revenue	$2,000
Less: Allowance to adjust short-term investments to market	(3,000)	Unrealized loss on investments	(3,000)
Short-term investments (market)	$72,000		

Suppose the price of General Motors stock goes up to $55 the following year and Intel sells all 1,000 shares on March 26. The journal entry is as shown:

Mar. 26	Cash	55,000	
	Short-Term Investments		50,000
	Realized Gain on Investments		5,000
	To record sale of 1,000 shares of GM at $55 per share; cost of $50 per share.		

At the end of the fiscal year, December 28, 20Y3, the trading portfolio consists of just the Microsoft stock, which is now valued at $28 per share:

Investment	Cost	Market Value
Microsoft (1,000 shares)	$25,000	$28,000

Consequently, the allowance to adjust short-term investments to market should be adjusted to have a *debit* balance of $3,000. Recall that the allowance account started the year with a *credit* balance of $3,000. Thus, the adjusting entry is as follows:

Dec. 28	Allowance to Adjust Short-Term Investments to Market	6,000	
	Unrealized Gain on Investments		6,000
	To record unrealized gain on trading portfolio and adjust trading investments to market value.		

Exhibit 6.C shows the financial statement presentation at year-end for 20Y3. The income statement includes both a realized gain and an unrealized gain of $5,000 and $6,000, respectively.

Exhibit 6.C REPORTING SHORT-TERM INVESTMENTS ON THE BALANCE SHEET AND INCOME STATEMENT IN 20Y3

Balance Sheet		Income Statement	
Current Assets:		Other Revenue and Gains (Losses):	
Short-term investments	$25,000	Realized gain on investment	$5,000
Plus: Allowance to adjust short-term investments to market	3,000	Unrealized gain on investments	(6,000)
Short-term investments (market)	$28,000		

¶611.02

Held-to-maturity investments include bonds and notes, which a company plans to hold until maturity.

HELD-TO-MATURITY INVESTMENTS

A second type of short-term investments or marketable securities is held-to-maturity investments. **Held-to-maturity investments** include bonds and notes, which a company buys and plans to hold until maturity. To qualify as short-term, maturity must occur within one year. Assume Intel purchases $6,000 of New York City municipal bonds that mature in 90 days. The purchase of these securities is recorded as shown:

Dec. 1	Short-Term Investments	6,000	
	Cash		6,000
	Purchase of NYC municipal bonds.		

On December 31, the New York City municipal bonds have accrued interest of $50. The adjusting entry for the accrued interest revenue is as shown:

Dec. 31	Short-Term Investments	50	
	Interest Revenue		50
	To record accrued interest revenue on NYC municipal bonds.		

¶611.03

Available-for-sale-securities are short-term investments in debt or equity securities that do not fit the criteria for other types of investments.

AVAILABLE-FOR-SALE SECURITIES

A third type of short-term investments is available-for-sale securities. **Available-for-sale-securities** are investments in debt or equity securities that do not fit the criteria for trading investments or held-to-maturity investments. They are classified as short-term or long-term depending on how long the company plans to hold the investment. Debt securities are bonds and notes. Equity securities are stocks. Available-for-sale securities are accounted for the same as trading investments, except that unrealized gains or losses are not reported on the income statement. Unrealized gains or losses from available-for-sale securities are shown in the stockholders' equity section of the balance sheet.

APPENDIX GLOSSARY

If you were making a short-term investment for your firm, what type of short-term investment would you choose?

Available-for-sale-securities

Available-for-sale-securities are investments in debt or equity securities that do not fit the criteria for the other two types of short-term investment: trading investments or held-to-maturity investments.

Held-to-maturity investments

Held-to-maturity investments include bonds and notes that the company plans to hold until maturity.

Trading investment

A trading investment is a short-term investment that the company plans to sell within a few months or less.

Short-term investments

Short-term investments, also referred to as marketable securities, are investments that a company expects to sell within one year.

¶612   # Chapter Assignments

QUESTIONS

1. **[Obj. 1]** How can inaccurate reporting of accounts receivable and notes receivable present a distorted view of a company's financial condition?

2. **[Obj. 1]** In what way can receivable records be helpful to the marketing department of a company?

3. **[Obj. 2]** What is a receivable?

4. **[Obj. 2]** List and define the two most prevalent categories of receivables.

5. **[Obj. 3]** What is liquidity and why is it important?

6. **[Obj. 3]** Since bad debt expense results from credit sales, why do companies sell on credit? Why does a company that sells on credit depend on customers being ethical?

7. **[Obj. 4]** What is the allowance for doubtful accounts?

8. **[Obj. 4]** What is aging of accounts receivable?

9. **[Obj. 4]** Define the net realizable value of accounts receivable.

10. **[Obj. 4]** Identify two deficiencies of the direct write-off method of accounting for bad debts.

11. **[Obj. 4]** Is the direct write-off method ever acceptable under GAAP?

12. **LO 4** How does a company benefit from meeting earnings forecasts of Wall Street analysts?

13. **[Obj. 5]** Who are the parties to a note receivable?

14. **[Obj. 5]** On a promissory note, or notes receivable, what does the principal and the maturity date represent?

15. **[Obj. 7]** What is analytic review?

16. **[Obj. 7]** What three financial ratios are helpful in evaluating receivables?

17. **[Obj. 7]** To be of real value, financial ratios must be compared to what?

18. **[Appendix]** Define short-term investment and list three types.

SHORT EXERCISES – SET A

Building Accounting Skills

1. **[Obj. 4]** Journal Entry to Write off Uncollectible Account: Suppose that a customer, Eve Adams, declares bankruptcy. Her account receivable of $700 is deemed uncollectible on March 26. If the company uses the allowance method what journal entry is made?

2. **[Obj. 4]** Journal Entry to Write off Uncollectible Account: Same as previous question, but the company uses the direct write-off method.

3. **[Obj. 4]** Adjusting Entries to Record Bad Debt Expense: ABM Computer Corporation had sales of $724,000 for its fiscal year ending on December 31, 20Y1. ABM is preparing to make its year-end adjusting entry to record bad debt expense for 20Y1. In prior years, bad debts have been 2 percent of sales. The current balance of Accounts Receivable is $152,600 and Allowance for Doubtful Accounts has a credit balance of $480. Based on an aging of accounts receivable analysis, $13,600 of accounts receivable is estimated to be uncollectible. Make the year-end adjusting entry to record bad debt expense assuming the following:
   a. ABM uses the aging analysis method to estimate bad debt expense.
   b. Make the year-end adjusting entry to record bad debt expense assuming ABM uses the percentage of sales method to estimate bad debt expense.

4. **[Obj. 4]** Adjusting Entries to Record Bad Debt Expense: Deep South Drilling Company earned sales revenue of $6,290,000 for its fiscal year ending on December 31, 20Y1. Deep South is preparing to make its year-end adjusting entry to record bad debt expense for 20Y1. In prior years, bad debts have been 4 percent of sales. The current balance of Accounts Receivable is $946,000 and Allowance for Doubtful Accounts has a credit balance of $29,700. Based on an aging of accounts receivable analysis, $225,000 of accounts receivable is estimated to be uncollectible. Make the year-end adjusting entry to record bad debt expense assuming the following:
   a. Deep South Drilling uses the aging of accounts receivable method to estimate bad debt expense.
   b. Deep South Drilling uses the percentage-of-sales method to estimate bad debt expense.

5. **LO 4:** Journal Entry to Write off an Account Receivable: Turtle Bay Chip Company, on March 31, deemed the following account receivable to be uncollectible: Abram Electronics $625. What journal entry should be made to write off this account, assuming the following details:
   a. Turtle Bay uses the percentage-of-sales method to account for bad debts.
   b. Turtle Bay uses the aging of accounts receivable method to account for bad debts.
   c. Turtle Bay uses the direct write-off method to account for bad debts.

6. **[Obj. 5]** Journal Entries for Promissory Note: Suppose that on March 31, Intel Corporation accepts a promissory note in payment for a sale of $20,000 of processing chips to a customer, ABM Computer Corporation. The note matures in three months on July 1. The interest rate is 6 percent.
   a. What journal entry is made on March 31?
   b. Assuming all interest revenue is accrued on the maturity date, what entry is made on July 1?

7. **[Obj. 5]** Journal Entries for Promissory Note: Suppose that Marvel Enterprises signs a promissory note and receives $120,000 in cash from Wells Fargo Bank. The note is dated July 31 and matures in six months on February 1. The interest rate is 5 percent.
   a. What journal entry does the bank make on July 31?
   b. Assuming that the bank accrues interest revenue on December 31, what adjusting entry is made on December 31?
   c. Marvel pays the note's maturity value to the bank on February 1. What entry is made on February 1?

8. **[Obj. 5]** Journal Entries for Promissory Note: Suppose that Jacob Johnson signs a promissory note and receives $24,000 in cash from First National Bank. The note is dated April 1 and matures on July 1 of the same year. The interest rate is 8 percent.
   a. What journal entry does the bank make on April 1?
   b. Johnson pays the note's maturity value to the bank on July 1. What entry is made on July 1?

9. **[Obj. 5]** Computing Interest: Suppose a $10,000 promissory note has an interest rate of 8 percent and a term of six months. What is the total amount of interest the note will earn?

10. **[Obj. 6]** Journal Entry for Credit Card Sale: On June 4, Argonaut Shipping Company makes a credit card sale of $12,000. The credit card company receives 3 percent in finance charges. What journal entry does Argonaut record?

11. **LO 6:** Journal Entry for Credit Card Sales: General Tire Company wants to accelerate cash inflows. One way to speed up cash receipts is to accept customer payments on credit. Make the journal entry for the following:

> On April 7, General Tire Company makes $50,000 of credit card sales that incurred a 2 percent finance charge.

SHORT EXERCISES – SET B

Building Accounting Skills

1. **[Obj. 4]** Journal Entry to Write off Uncollectible Account: Suppose that a customer declares bankruptcy. The customer's account receivable of $500 is deemed uncollectible on March 26. If the company uses the allowance method what journal entry is made?

2. **[Obj. 4]** Journal Entry to Write off Uncollectible Account: Same as previous question, but the company uses the direct write-off method.

3. **[Obj. 4]** Adjusting Entries to Record Bad Debt Expense: Pear Computer Corporation had sales of $362,000 for its fiscal year ending on December 31, 20Y1. Pear is preparing to make its year-end adjusting entry to record bad debt expense for 20Y1. In prior years, bad debts have been 2 percent of sales. The current balance of Accounts Receivable is $76,300 and of Allowance for Doubtful Accounts has a credit balance of $240. Based on an aging of accounts receivable analysis, $6,800 of accounts receivable is estimated to be uncollectible. Make the year-end adjusting entry to record bad debt expense assuming the following:
   a. Pear uses the aging analysis method to estimate bad debt expense.
   b. Pear uses the percentage of sales method to estimate bad debt expense.

4. **[Obj. 4]** Adjusting Entries to Record Bad Debt Expense: Texas Oil Company earned sales revenue of $12,580,000 for its fiscal year ending on December 31, 20Y1. Texas Oil is preparing to make its year-end adjusting entry to record bad debt expense for 20Y1. In prior years, bad debts have been 4 percent of sales. The current balance of Accounts Receivable is $1,892,000 and Allowance for Doubtful Accounts has a credit balance of $59,400. Based on an aging of accounts receivable analysis, $450,000 of accounts receivable is estimated to be uncollectible. Make the year-end adjusting entry to record bad debt expense assuming the following:
   a. Texas Oil uses the aging of account receivable method to estimate bad debt expense.
   b. Texas Oil uses the percentage of sales method to estimate bad debt expense.

5. **[Obj. 4]** Journal Entry To Write off an Account Receivable: Crispy Chip Company, on March 31, deemed the following account receivable to be uncollectible: Corner Store $325. What journal entry should be made to write off this account, assuming the following details:
   a. Crispy Chip uses the percentage-of-sales method to account for bad debts.
   b. Crispy Chip uses the aging of accounts receivable method to account for bad debts.
   c. Crispy Chip uses the direct write-off method to account for bad debts.

6. **[Obj. 5]** Journal Entries for Promissory Note: Suppose that on March 31, Intel Corporation accepts a promissory note in payment for a sale of $10,000 of processing chips to a customer, Pear Computer Corporation. The note matures in three months on July 1. The interest rate is 8 percent.
   a. What journal entry is made on March 31?
   b. Assuming all interest revenue is accrued on the maturity date, what entry is made on July 1?

7. **[Obj. 5]** Journal Entries for Promissory Note: Suppose that Mars Candy, Inc. signs a promissory note and receives $240,000 in cash from Wells Fargo Bank. The note is dated July 31 and matures in six months on February 1. The interest rate is 5 percent.
   a. What journal entry does the bank make on July 31?
   b. Assuming that the bank accrues interest revenue on December 31, what adjusting entry is made on December 31?
   c. Mars pays the note's maturity value to the bank on February 1. What entry is made on February 1?

8. **[Obj. 5]** Journal Entries for Promissory Note: Suppose that Will Barefoot signs a promissory note and receives $12,000 in cash from American Bank. The note is dated January 1 and matures on April 1 of the same year. The interest rate is 7 percent.
   a. What journal entry does the bank make on January 1?
   b. Will Barefoot pays the note's maturity value to the bank on April 1. What entry is made on April 1?

9. **[Obj. 5]** Computing Interest: Suppose a $20,000 promissory note has an interest rate of 7 percent and a term of six months. What is the total amount of interest the note will earn?

10. **[Obj. 6]** Journal Entry for Credit Card Sale: On May 13, your company makes a credit card sale of $6,000. The credit card company receives 3 percent in finance charges. What journal entry do you record?

11. **[Obj. 6]** Journal Entry for Credit Card Sales: Burger Barn wants to accelerate cash inflows. One way to speed up cash receipts is to accept customer payments on credit cards. Make the journal entry for the following:

    On April 7, Burger Barn makes $25,000 of credit card sales that incurred a 2 percent finance charge.

PROBLEMS – SET A

Applying Accounting Knowledge

1. **[Obj. 3]** Recording and Posting Journal Entries for Accounts Receivable: Argonaut Shipping maintains an accounts receivable subsidiary ledger. The following transactions occurred during March:

   March 2   Marvel Enterprises purchased $850 of services on account.
   March 5   Intel purchased $550 of services on account.
   March 10   JC Penney purchased $1,250 of services on account.
   March 15   Marvel Enterprises purchased $250 of services on account.
   March 16   JC Penney made payment of $350 on account.
   March 20   Royal Dutch Shell purchased $750 of services on account.

   Required:
   a.   Make journal entries for all transactions.
   b.   Post journal entries to the general ledger and to the accounts receivable subsidiary ledger, starting with account balances shown below.

General Ledger		Accounts Receivable Subsidiary Ledger			
Cash		**JC Penney**		**Marvel**	
1,050		650			
Bal. 1,050		Bal. 650			
Accounts Receivable		**Intel**		**Shell**	
650					
Bal. 650					
Sales					
	1,700				
	Bal. 1,700				

2. **[Obj. 3]** Recording and Posting Journal Entries for Accounts Receivable: Starbucks maintains an accounts receivable subsidiary ledger. The following transactions occurred during June:

June 2   Secretary Temps purchased $425 of products on account.
June 5   Ambulance Chasers purchased $275 of products on account.
June 10   Bank One purchased $625 of products on account.
June 15   Secretary Temps purchased $125 of products on account.
June 16   Bank One made payment of $175 on account.
June 20   Century 21 purchased $375 of products on account.

Required:
a.   Make journal entries for all transactions.
b.   Post journal entries to the general ledger and to the accounts receivable subsidiary ledger, starting with account balances shown below.

General Ledger		Accounts Receivable Subsidiary Ledger		

Cash		Bank One		Secretary Temps
525		325		
525		325		

Accounts Receivable		Ambulance Chasers		Century 21
325				
325				

Sales	
	850
	850

3. **[Obj. 3]** Recording and Posting Journal Entries for Accounts Receivable: Copy Corner maintains an accounts receivable subsidiary ledger. The following transactions occurred during May:

May 2   Customer #1 purchased $200 of merchandise on account.
May 5   Customer #2 purchased $125 of merchandise on account.
May 10   Customer #3 purchased $300 of merchandise on account.
May 15   Customer #1 purchased $50 of merchandise on account.
May 16   Customer #3 made payment of $75 on account.
May 20   Customer #4 purchased $175 of merchandise on account.

Required:
a.   Make journal entries for all transactions.
b.   Post journal entries to the general ledger and to the accounts receivable subsidiary ledger, starting with account balances shown below.

General Ledger		Accounts Receivable Subsidiary Ledger		

Cash		Customer #1		Customer #2
250				
250				

Accounts Receivable		Customer #3		Customer #4
150		150		
150		150		

Sales	
	400
	400

4. **LO 3** Recording and Posting Journal Entries for Accounts Receivable: Ion Electronics, Inc. maintains an accounts receivable subsidiary ledger. The following transactions occurred during July:

July 2   Jim Larson purchased $400 of merchandise on account.
July 5   Ed Kinnibrew purchased $250 of merchandise on account.
July 10   Abe Jones purchased $600 of merchandise on account.
July 15   Jim Larson purchased $100 of merchandise on account.
July 16   Abe Jones made payment of $150 on account.
July 20   Roger Moses purchased $350 of merchandise on account.

Required:

a. Make journal entries for all transactions.
b. Post journal entries to the general ledger and to the accounts receivable subsidiary ledger, starting with account balances shown below.

General Ledger

Cash

	500	
Bal.	500	

Accounts Receivable

	300	
Bal.	300	

Sales

		800
	Bal.	800

Accounts Receivable Subsidiary Ledger

Abe Jones

	300	
Bal.	300	

Ed Kinnibrew

Jim Larson

Roger Moses

5. **[Obj. 6]** Flowcharting Customer Payments Processing: Argonaut Shipping Company receives customer payments in the mailroom. The amount of each payment is keyed into a customer payment transaction file. The customer payment transaction file is input into a program that updates the accounts receivable (A/R) subsidiary ledger (master file). The program also prints an accounts receivable report that shows the account balance of each individual A/R subsidiary account and the total for all accounts, which is the balance of the A/R control account in the general ledger. Customer payments are forwarded to the treasurer for deposit in the company's bank account.

Required: Fill in the flowchart of customer payment processing with the appropriate descriptions.

Description:
a. Customer Payment $ (use twice).
b. Update A/R Subsidiary Ledger (Master File) and Print A/R Report.
c. A/R Report.
d. To Treasurer.
e. Key in Payment Amount.
f. A/R Subsidiary Ledger (Master File).

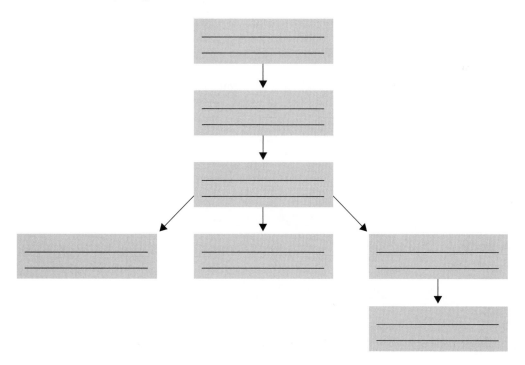

6. **[Obj. 4]** Analyzing Aging of Accounts Receivable: Below is information regarding accounts receivable on December 31.

	Age of Account			
Customer	1-30 Days	31-60 Days	61-90 Days	Over 90 Days
Hershey Company	$821			
Nestle Corporation		$678		
Crane Labs			$925	
Swan Real Estate Company			$657	
Dove Candy Factory				$1,242
Other Accounts	$18,256	$4,620	$1,990	$827
Percentage Uncollectible:	2%	4%	7%	11%

Required:

a. Prepare an aging of accounts receivable analysis using the age-of-account information. Show the amounts uncollectible by age of account and the total estimated amount uncollectible.

b. Assuming that the allowance for doubtful accounts has a current credit balance of $150, make the journal entry to adjust the allowance account and to record bad debt expense.

c. Evaluate: Do you think the percentages of uncollectible accounts are high or low? Assume the industry average for the total estimate of uncollectible accounts is 3%.

7. **[Obj. 4]** Analyzing Aging of Accounts Receivable: Same as Problem A6, except the percentages uncollectible have been changed. Below is information regarding accounts receivable on December 31.

	Age of Account			
Customer	1-30 Days	31-60 Days	61-90 Days	Over 90 Days
Hershey Company	$821			
Nestle Corporation		$678		
Crane Labs			$925	
Swan Real Estate Company			$657	
Dove Candy Factory				$1,242
Other Accounts	$18,256	$4,620	$1,990	$827
Percentage Uncollectible:	3%	5%	9%	12%

Required:

a. Prepare an aging of accounts receivable analysis using the age-of-account   information. Show the amounts uncollectible by age of account and the total estimated amount uncollectible.

b. Assuming that the allowance for doubtful accounts has a current credit balance of $150, make the journal entry to adjust the allowance account and to record bad debt expense.

c. Evaluate: Do you think the percentages of uncollectible accounts are high or low? Assume the industry average for the total estimate of uncollectible accounts is 3.5%.

8. **[Obj. 7]** Computing Financial Ratios: The following information is from Crane Construction's financial statements.

Current Assets	$56,440
Current Liabilities	18,990
Cash	5,600
Short-Term Investments	16,200
Accounts Receivable, Jan. 1	25,667
Accounts Receivable, Dec. 31	19,843
Net Sales	258,360

Required:
a. Calculate the current ratio, acid-test ratio, and average collection period.
b. Evaluate: Is Crane Construction able to meet its short-term financial obligations?

9. **[Obj. 7]** Computing Financial Ratios: The following information is from Jiffy Lube's financial statements.

Current Assets	$66,440
Current Liabilities	28,990
Cash	15,600
Short-Term Investments	26,200
Accounts Receivable, Jan. 1	35,667
Accounts Receivable, Dec. 31	29,843
Net Sales	268,360

Required:
a. Calculate three financial ratios: current ratio, acid-test ratio, and average collection period.
b. Evaluate: Is Jiffy Lube able to meet its short-term financial obligations?

10. **[Obj. 7]** Computing Financial Ratios: The following information is from Tuxedo Rental's financial statements.

Current Assets	$23,000
Current Liabilities	5,000
Cash	7,000
Short-Term Investments	1,000
Accounts Receivable, Jan. 1	8,000
Accounts Receivable, Dec. 31	5,000
Net Sales	79,000

Required:
a. Calculate three financial ratios: current ratio, acid-test ratio, and average collection period.
b. Evaluate: Is Tuxedo Rental able to meet its short-term financial obligations?

11. **[Obj. 7]** Computing Financial Ratios: The following information is from Flowershop's financial statements.

Current Assets	$22,460
Current Liabilities	4,980
Cash	6,202
Short-Term Investments	820
Accounts Receivable, Jan. 1	7,831
Accounts Receivable, Dec. 31	4,540
Net Sales	78,920

Required:
a. Calculate the current ratio, acid-test ratio, and average collection period.
b. Evaluate: Is the Flowershop able to meet its short-term financial obligations?

12. **[Appendix]** Recording Journal Entries for Investments: Suppose Goodyear Tire Company decides to use some of its idle cash and invest in Dell Computer Corporation and AOL Time Warner. Goodyear plans to sell both investments within two months; thus, both short-term investments meet the criteria for classification as trading investments.

    Required: Make journal entries for the following:
    a. On Nov. 10, 20Y1, Goodyear acquires 2,000 shares of Dell at $20 per share and 1,000 shares of AOL Time Warner at $15 per share.
    b. On Nov. 25, 20Y1, Goodyear receives a cash dividend of $500 from Dell.
    c. On December 31, 20Y1, Goodyear's fiscal year-end, Dell stock is trading for $17 per share and AOL Time Warner is trading for $16 per share.
    d. On Feb. 28, 20Y2, Goodyear sells all 2,000 shares of Dell for $22 per share.
    e. On Dec. 31, 20Y2, Goodyear's trading portfolio consists of only the 1,000 shares of AOL Time Warner, which are trading for $18 per share.

13. **[Appendix]** Balance Sheet and Income Statement: Suppose Goodyear Tire Company has the following trading portfolio of short-term investments, which are categorized as trading investments, on December 31. Both stocks were purchased earlier in the year. The Allowance to Adjust Short-Term Investments to Market started the year with a zero balance. During the year Ford paid a cash dividend of $5,000.

Trading Portfolio:		
Investment	Cost	Market Value
IBM (2,000 shares)	$150,000	$136,000
Ford (10,000 shares)	100,000	105,000
Total	$250,000	$241,000

    Required: Show how the investments affect the balance sheet and income statement?

14. **[Appendix]** Balance Sheet and Income Statement: Suppose Goodyear Tire Company has the following trading portfolio of two short-term investments, which are categorized as trading investments, on December 31. Both stocks were purchased earlier in the year. In addition to these two stocks, Goodyear bought 1,000 shares of Disney for $20 per share and sold them for $24 per share. The Allowance to Adjust Short-Term Investments to Market started the year with a $9,000 credit balance.

Trading Portfolio:		
Investment	Cost	Market Value
Motorola (20,000 shares)	$200,000	$196,000
GM (10,000 shares)	350,000	360,000
Total	$550,000	$556,000

    Required: Show how the investments affect the balance sheet and income statement?

15. **[Appendix]** Recording Journal Entries for Bonds: Held-to-maturity investments are a category of short-term investments that consists of bonds and notes, which the company plans to hold until maturity. Assume that on November 1, 20Y1, J.C. Penney purchases $10,000 of City of Houston municipal bonds that mature in four months on February 29, 20Y2 and pay 6 percent interest.

    Required: Make journal entries for the following:
    a. Purchase of the bonds on November 1, 20Y1.
    b. Accrual of interest revenue on December 31, 20Y1.
    c. Accrual of interest revenue on February 29, 20Y2.
    d. Receipt of maturity value of the bonds on February 29, 20Y2.

16. **[Appendix]** Balance Sheet and Income Statement: Held-to-maturity investments are a category of short-term investments that consists of bonds and notes, which the company plans to hold until maturity. Assume that on October 1, 20Y1, JC Penney purchases $20,000 of City of San Antonio municipal bonds that mature in four months on January 31, 20Y2 and pay 6 percent interest.

    Required: How does this investment affect the 20Y1 balance sheet and income statement?

PROBLEMS – SET B

Applying Accounting Knowledge

1. **[Obj. 3]** Recording and Posting Journal Entries for Accounts Receivable: American Accountants maintains an accounts receivable subsidiary ledger. The following transactions occurred during March:

    March 2   Marvel Enterprises purchased $1,700 of services on account.
    March 5   Intel purchased $1,100 of services on account.
    March 10   JC Penney purchased $2,500 of services on account.
    March 15   Marvel Enterprises purchased $500 of services on account.
    March 16   JC Penney made payment of $700 on account.
    March 20   Royal Dutch Shell purchased $1,500 of services on account.

    Required:
    a. Make journal entries for all transactions.
    b. Post journal entries to the general ledger and to the accounts receivable subsidiary ledger, starting with account balances shown below.

General Ledger				Accounts Receivable Subsidiary Ledger			

Cash	
2,100	
2,100	

JC Penney	
1,300	
1,300	

Marvel	

Accounts Receivable	
1,300	
1,300	

Intel	

Shell	

Sales	
	3,400
	3,400

2. **[Obj. 3]** Recording and Posting Journal Entries for Accounts Receivable: Daily Donuts maintains an accounts receivable subsidiary ledger. The following transactions occurred during June:

    June 2   Secretary Temps purchased $400 of products on account.
    June 5   Ambulance Chasers purchased $200 of products on account.
    June 10   Bank One purchased $600 of products on account.
    June 15   Secretary Temps purchased $100 of products on account.
    June 16   Bank One made payment of $100 on account.
    June 20   Century 21 purchased $300 of products on account.

    Required:
    a. Make journal entries for all transactions.
    b. Post journal entries to the general ledger and to the accounts receivable subsidiary ledger, starting with account balances shown below.

General Ledger		Accounts Receivable Subsidiary Ledger	

    Cash

500	
500	

    Bank One

300	
300	

    Secretary Temps

    Accounts Receivable

300	
300	

    Ambulance Chasers

    Century 21

    Sales

	800
	800

3. **[Obj. 3]** Recording and Posting Journal Entries for Accounts Receivable: Office Max maintains an accounts receivable subsidiary ledger. The following transactions occurred during July:

    July 2   Customer #1 purchased $300 of merchandise on account.
    July 5   Customer #2 purchased $225 of merchandise on account.
    July 10   Customer #3 purchased $400 of merchandise on account.
    July 15   Customer #1 purchased $150 of merchandise on account.
    July 16   Customer #3 made payment of $175 on account.
    July 20   Customer #4 purchased $275 of merchandise on account.

    Required:
    a. Make journal entries for all transactions.
    b. Post journal entries to the general ledger and to the accounts receivable subsidiary ledger, starting with account balances shown below.

General Ledger		Accounts Receivable Subsidiary Ledger	

    Cash

350	
350	

    Customer #1

    Customer #2

    Accounts Receivable

250	
250	

    Customer #3

250	
250	

    Customer #4

    Sales

	600
	600

4. **[Obj. 3]** Recording and Posting Journal Entries for Accounts Receivable: Eon Electronics, Inc. maintains an accounts receivable subsidiary ledger. The following transactions occurred during July:

July 2   Jim Larson purchased $800 of merchandise on account.
July 5   Ed Kinnibrew purchased $500 of merchandise on account.
July 10   Abe Jones purchased $1,200 of merchandise on account.
July 15   Jim Larson purchased $200 of merchandise on account.
July 16   Abe Jones made payment of $300 on account.
July 20   Roger Moses purchased $700 of merchandise on account.

Required:

a. Make journal entries for all transactions.
b. Post journal entries to the general ledger and to the accounts receivable subsidiary ledger, starting with account balances shown below.

General Ledger

Cash
| 1,000 | |
| 1,000 | |

Accounts Receivable
| 600 | |
| 600 | |

Sales
| | 1,600 |
| Bal. | 1,600 |

Accounts Receivable Subsidiary Ledger

Abe Jones
| 600 | |
| 600 | |

Ed Kinnibrew
| | |

Jim Larson
| | |

Roger Moses
| | |

5. **[Obj. 4]** Analyzing Aging of Accounts Receivable: Below is information regarding accounts receivable on December 31.

Customer	Age of Account			
	1-30 Days	31-60 Days	61-90 Days	Over 90 Days
Hershey Company	$821			
Nestle Corporation		$678		
Crane Labs			$925	
Swan Real Estate Company			$657	
Dove Candy Factory				$1,242
Other Accounts	$18,256	$4,620	$1,990	$827
Percentage Uncollectible:	4%	6%	10%	13%

Required:

a. Prepare an aging of accounts receivable analysis using the age-of-account information. Show the amounts uncollectible by age of account and the total estimated amount uncollectible.
b. Assuming that the allowance for doubtful accounts has a current credit balance of $300, make the journal entry to adjust the allowance account and to record bad debt expense.
c. Evaluate: Do you think the percentages of uncollectible accounts are high or low? Assume the industry average for the total estimate of uncollectible accounts is 5%.

6. **[Obj. 4]** Analyzing Aging of Accounts Receivable: Same as Problem B5, except the percentages uncollectible have been changed. Below is information regarding accounts receivable on December 31.

Age of Account	1-30 Days	31-60 Days	61-90 Days	Over 90 Days
Percentage Uncollectible:	1%	2%	6%	10%
Individual Accounts Receivable:				
Hershey Company	$821			
Nestle Corporation		$678		
Crane Labs			$925	
Swan Real Estate Company			$657	
Dove Candy Factory				$1,242
Other Accounts	$18,256	$4,620	$1,990	$827

Required:

a. Prepare an aging of accounts receivable analysis using the age-of-account information. Show the amounts uncollectible by age of account and the total estimated amount uncollectible.

b. Assuming that the allowance for doubtful accounts has a current credit balance of $300, make the journal entry to adjust the allowance account and to record bad debt expense.

c. Evaluate: Do you think the percentages of uncollectible accounts are high or low? Assume the industry average for the total estimate of uncollectible accounts is 2%.

7. **[Obj. 7]** Computing Financial Ratios: The following information is from the financial statements for Sports Gear, Inc.

Current Assets	$76,440
Current Liabilities	38,990
Cash	5,600
Short-Term Investments	16,200
Accounts Receivable, Jan. 1	25,667
Accounts Receivable, Dec. 31	19,843
Net Sales	220,360

Required:

a. Calculate the current ratio, acid-test ratio, and average collection period.

b. Evaluate: Is Sports Gear able to meet its short-term financial obligations?

8. **[Obj. 7]** Computing Financial Ratios: The following information is from the financial statements for the Music Store:

Current Assets	$77,000
Current Liabilities	39,000
Cash	6,000
Short-Term Investments	17,000
Accounts Receivable, Jan. 1	26,000
Accounts Receivable, Dec. 31	20,000
Net Sales	221,000

Required:

a. Calculate three financial ratios: current ratio, acid-test ratio, and average collection period.

b. Evaluate: Is the Music Store able to meet its short-term financial obligations?

9. **[Obj. 7]** Computing Financial Ratios: Computing Financial Ratios: The following information is from the financial statements of MovieBuster.

Current Assets	$33,000
Current Liabilities	10,000
Cash	7,000
Short-Term Investments	1,000
Accounts Receivable, Jan. 1	8,000
Accounts Receivable, Dec. 31	5,000
Net Sales	69,000

Required:

a. Calculate three financial ratios: current ratio, acid-test ratio, and average collection period.
b. Evaluate: Is the MovieBuster able to meet its short-term financial obligations?

10. **[Obj. 7]** Computing Financial Ratios: The following information is from the financial statements of Sky Diving, Inc.

Current Assets	$32,460
Current Liabilities	9,980
Cash	6,202
Short-Term Investments	820
Accounts Receivable, Jan. 1	7,831
Accounts Receivable, Dec. 31	4,540
Net Sales	68,920

Required:

a. Calculate the current ratio, acid-test ratio, and average collection period.
b. Evaluate: Is Sky Diving, Inc. able to meet its short-term financial obligations?

11. **[Appendix]** Recording Journal Entries for Investments: Suppose your company decides to use some of its idle cash and invest in Dell Computer Corporation and AOL Time Warner. You plan to sell both investments within two months; thus, both short-term investments meet the criteria for classification as trading investments.

Required: Make journal entries for the following:

a. On Nov. 10, 20Y1, you acquire 1,000 shares of Dell at $20 per share and 500 shares of AOL Time Warner at $15 per share.
b. On Nov. 25, 20Y1, you receive a cash dividend of $200 from Dell.
c. On December 31, 20Y1, your fiscal year-end, Dell stock is trading for $17 per share and AOL Time Warner is trading for $16 per share.
d. On Feb. 28, 20Y2, you sell all 1,000 shares of Dell for $22 per share.
e. On Dec. 31, 20Y2, your trading portfolio consists of only the 500 shares of AOL Time Warner, which are trading for $18 per share.

12. **[Appendix]** Balance Sheet and Income Statement: Suppose Procter & Gamble has the following trading portfolio of short-term investments, which are categorized as trading investments, on December 31. Both stocks were purchased earlier in the year. The Allowance to Adjust Short-Term Investments to Market started the year with a zero balance. During the year Ford paid a cash dividend of $5,000.

Trading Portfolio:		
Investment	Cost	Market Value
IBM (4,000 shares)	$300,000	$272,000
Ford (20,000 shares)	200,000	210,000
Total	$500,000	$482,000

Required: Show how the investments affect the balance sheet and income statement?

13. **[Appendix]** Balance Sheet and Income Statement: Suppose Procter and Gamble has the following trading portfolio of two short-term investments, which are categorized as trading investments, on December 31. Both stocks were purchased earlier in the year. In addition to these two stocks, Procter and Gamble bought 2,000 shares of Disney for $20 per share and sold them for $24 per share. The Allowance to Adjust Short-Term Investments to Market started the year with a $9,000 credit balance.

Trading Portfolio:		
Investment	**Cost**	**Market Value**
Motorola (10,000 shares)	$100,000	$98,000
GM (5,000 shares)	175,000	180,000
Total	$275,000	$278,000

Required: How would the investments affect the balance sheet and income statement?

14. **[Appendix]** Recording Journal Entries for Bonds: Held-to-maturity investments are a category of short-term investments that consists of bonds and notes, which the company plans to hold until maturity. Assume that on November 1, 20Y1, Sears purchases $20,000 of City of Dallas municipal bonds that mature in four months on February 29, 20Y2 and pay 6 percent interest.

Required: Make journal entries for the following:
a. Purchase of the bonds on November 1, 20Y1.
b. Accrual of interest revenue on December 31, 20Y1.
c. Accrual of interest revenue on February 29, 20Y2.
d. Receipt of maturity value of the bonds on February 29, 20Y2.

15. **[Appendix]** Balance Sheet and Income Statement: Held-to-maturity investments are a category of short-term investments that consists of bonds and notes, which the company plans to hold until maturity. Assume that on October 1, 20Y1, Sears purchases $40,000 of City of Chicago municipal bonds that mature in four months on January 31, 20Y2 and pay 6 percent interest.

Required: How would this investment affect the 20Y1 balance sheet and income statement?

CROSS-FUNCTIONAL PERSPECTIVES

Discussion Questions

1. **[Obj. 3]** What are current assets? Give an example of a current asset and explain which department would be reporting it.

2. **[Obj. 4]** Besides accounting, which departments are especially interested in the aging of an accounts receivable report?

3. **[Obj. 7]** Besides accounting, which departments are especially interested in the company's acid-test ratio and why?

4. **[Obj. 7]** Besides accounting, which departments are especially interested in the company's average collection period and why?

Cross-functional Case: Should the Company Go Wireless?

Cranium Books is deciding whether to purchase PCs with Intel Centrino mobile technology for its entire sales force. Cranium Books is a small publishing company that sells educational materials to the home school market. The company has a sales force of 10 people who cover the entire United States. The sales people do a great deal of traveling, which imposes plenty of downtime at airports and hotels. Wanting to make this downtime productive, the president of Cranium Books thinks that PCs equipped with Intel's Centrino integrated wireless capability will provide the sales people with new ways to stay productive during their traveling. Since wireless LAN hotspots have become prevalent in public places, the president believes that wireless PCs could increase the productivity of each salesperson by 11 hours per week.

The president has called a meeting with the company's advisors from accounting, finance, human resources, and sales. Purchasing 10 new PCs at $2,000 each is a large investment for Cranium Books. The president wants to consider the cost and ramifications of this decision from all viewpoints.

Required: From the perspective of each of the following business managers, list what they might consider to be the pros and cons of purchasing a new wireless PC for each of the sales people.
a. Accounting
b. Finance
c. Human resources
d. Sales

EXCEL ASSIGNMENTS

1. **[Obj. 4]** Accounts Receivable Subsidiary Ledger: Suppose you recently started work at Argonaut Shipping Company. Your supervisor has asked for the account balances of each customer's account receivable at the end of May. In the input area of your worksheet, show the customer's name, beginning balance, credit purchases, and payments. The output area must include the customer's name, beginning balance, credit purchases, payments, and ending balance. In addition, include totals for all financial columns. Use the following information:

Accounts Receivable Subsidiary Ledger (Master File)			
Customer Name	Beginning Balance	Credit Purchases	Payments
JC Penney	$3,640	$1,741	$4,181
Sears	8,450	15,226	13,676
Stein Mart	1,826	1,368	1,994
Target	5,224	1,295	4,619
Toys 'R' Us	6,975	11,110	7,585
Walmart	12,920	2,860	15,580

Required: Create an Excel worksheet that shows account balances of each customer's account receivable at the end of May. Print your worksheet.

2. **[Obj. 4]** Accounts Receivable Subsidiary Ledger: Suppose you recently started work at Armstrong Tire Company. Your supervisor has asked for the account balances of each customer's account receivable at the end of December. In the input area of your worksheet, show the customer's name, beginning balance, credit purchases, and payments. The output area must include the customer's name, beginning balance, credit purchases, payments, and ending balance. In addition, include totals for all financial columns. Use the following information:

Accounts Receivable Subsidiary Ledger (Master File)			
Customer Name	Beginning Balance	Credit Purchases	Payments
Daimler Chrysler	$92,341	$5,609	$85,400
Ford Motor Company	28,225	24,556	44,200
General Motors	62,992	12,360	71,200
Honda	15,555	5,400	19,800
Rolls Royce	24,000	6,080	25,440
Toyota	18,000	12,222	19,300

Required: Create an Excel worksheet that shows account balances of each customer's account receivable at the end of December. Print your worksheet.

3. **[Obj. 4]** Aging of Accounts Receivable Analysis: Include the information below in the input area of your worksheet. The output area should show the amounts uncollectible by age of account and the total estimated amount uncollectible.

Age of Account	1-30 Days	31-60 Days	61-90 Days	Over 90 Days
Percentage Uncollectible:	2%	5%	8%	12%
Individual Accounts Receivable:				
ABC Motors	$970			
Blockbuster		$412		
Blockbuster			$534	
Signature Lawn Service			$406	
Mars Construction Corporation				$820
Other Accounts	$14,248	$4,420	$2,780	$2,280

Required: Prepare an aging of accounts receivable analysis using Excel. Print your worksheet.

4. **[Obj. 4]** Aging of Accounts Receivable Analysis: Same as Excel assignment 3, except change the percentages uncollectible as follows:

Age of Account	1-30 Days	31-60 Days	61-90 Days	Over 90 Days
Percentage Uncollectible:	3%	6%	9%	14%

Required: Prepare an aging of accounts receivable analysis using Excel. Print your worksheet.

5. **[Obj. 4]** Aging of Accounts Receivable Analysis: Include the information below in the input area of your worksheet. The output area should show the amounts uncollectible by age of account and the total estimated amount uncollectible.

Age of Account	1-30 Days	31-60 Days	61-90 Days	Over 90 Days
Percentage Uncollectible:	1%	2%	5%	8%
Individual Accounts Receivable:				
Dell Computer	$358			
Kraft Foods		$999		
Kraft Foods			$188	
Artesian Water			$212	
Endor Machinery Company				$924
Other Accounts	$14,680	$6,420	$4,568	$1,725

Required: Prepare an aging of accounts receivable analysis using Excel. Print your worksheet.

6. **[Obj. 4]** Aging of Accounts Receivable Analysis: Same as Excel assignment 5, except change the percentages uncollectible as follows:

Age of Account	1-30 Days	31-60 Days	61-90 Days	Over 90 Days
Percentage Uncollectible:	2%	4%	9%	11%

Required: Prepare an aging of accounts receivable analysis using Excel. Print your worksheet.

7. **[Obj. 5]** Calculating Maturity Value: Using the information below regarding five notes receivable, calculate the maturity values. Set up an Excel worksheet that shows the principal, interest, and time period in the input area. The output area must show principal, interest, time period, amount of interest, and maturity value. Print your worksheet.

	Note Receivable				
	a	b	c	d	e
Principal	2,000	5,000	10,000	12,000	100,000
Interest rate	4%	5%	7%	12%	8%
Time period (months)	3	6	4	12	18

Required: Create an Excel worksheet that shows principal, interest, time period, amount of interest, and calculates maturity value. Print your worksheet.

8. **[Obj. 5]** Calculating Maturity Value: Using the information below regarding five notes receivable, calculate the maturity values. Set up an Excel worksheet that shows the principal, interest, and time period in the input area. The output area must show principal interest, time period, amount of interest, and maturity value.

	Note Receivable				
	a	b	c	d	e
Principal	1,000	8,000	5,000	10,000	120,000
Interest rate	3%	6%	14%	10%	5%
Time period (months)	2	4	12	6	36

Required: Create an Excel worksheet that shows principal, interest, time period, amount of interest, and calculates maturity value. Print your worksheet.

9. **[Obj. 7]** Computing Financial Ratios: Using the information below from Intel's financial statements, calculate three financial ratios: current ratio, acid-test ratio, and average collection period. Set up your worksheet with financial statement data in the input area and ratios in the output area.

	($ Millions)
Current Assets	$18,925
Current Liabilities	6,595
Cash	7,404
Short-Term Investments	3,382
Accounts Receivable, Jan. 1	2,607
Accounts Receivable, Dec. 28	2,574
Net Sales	26,764

Required: Create an Excel worksheet that calculates current ratio, acid-test ratio, and average collection period for Intel. Print your worksheet.

10. **[Obj. 7]** Computing Financial Ratios: Using the information below from TJH Company's financial statements, calculate three financial ratios: current ratio, acid-test ratio, and average collection period. Set up your worksheet with financial statement data in the input area and ratios in the output area.

	($ Thousands)
Current Assets	$26,890
Current Liabilities	3,421
Cash	2,555
Short-Term Investments	7,245
Accounts Receivable, Jan. 1	8,950
Accounts Receivable, Dec. 31	9,964
Net Sales	54,778

Required: Create an Excel worksheet that calculates current ratio, acid-test ratio, and average collection period for the TJH Company. Print your worksheet.

WEB ASSIGNMENTS

1. **[Obj. 5]** Search the Web for information on the topic of bad debts in the retail industry. Prepare a one-page report. Cite at least three sources.

2. **[Obj. 7]** Select any company and find its financial statements on the Web (e.g., on the company's website, the New York Stock Exchange website, or do a search on Google). Using the pertinent information from the financial statements, calculate the current ratio, acid-test ratio, and average collection period.

3. **[Career]** Go to the website for Intel. What accounting jobs are currently available within the company?

4. **[Ethics]** Go to the website for Intel or do a search on Google to find Intel's rules on Corporate Governance and Social Responsibility. Describe the rules that pertain specifically to accounting? (**Hint:** Look under Ethics and Compliance regarding public communications and filings.)

5. **[All Obj.]** Go to the website for Intel or do a search on Google to find an accounting related news item from the past year pertaining to Intel. Give a one- paragraph summary of it.

¶613

Test Prepper

Use this sample test to gauge your comprehension of the chapter material.

True/False Questions

___ 1. Accounts receivable, notes receivable, and short-term investments are usually readily available sources of cash.

___ 2. Liquidity refers to how rapidly an item can be converted to stock.

___ 3. The Allowance for Doubtful Accounts represents the amount of accounts receivable that are expected to be uncollectible.

___ 4. Accounting for bad debts is accomplished by a debit to Aging of Accounts Receivable and a credit to Bad Debt Expense.

___ 5. The direct write-off method of accounting for uncollectible accounts writes off an estimated amount in the period in which the related sale takes place.

___ 6. On a promissory note, the principal is the amount borrowed by a creditor and loaned by the debtor.

___ 7. Notes receivable result from contractual agreements in which one party borrows money from another.

___ 8. The average collection period shows how quickly a company is collecting its receivables.

___ 9. The current ratio is a more rigorous test than acid-test ratio in measuring how well a company is able to meet short-term financial obligations.

___ 10. Accounts receivable represent a firm's financial claims against its suppliers.

Multiple-Choice Questions

___ 1. Which of the following is not true regarding accounts receivable?
   a. Represents a financial claim against customers.
   b. Are obtained by selling products on credit.
   c. Sometimes called trade receivables.
   d. Refers to how rapidly an item can be converted to cash.
   e. Can be obtained by selling services on credit.

___ 2. A general ledger _____ shows the total balance of all accounts in its corresponding subsidiary ledger.
   a. control account
   b. customer's account
   c. liquidity account
   d. receivable account
   e. debit account

___ 3. Which of the following is true regarding accounts receivable that become uncollectible?
   a. Referred to as bad debts.
   b. Categorized as an operating expense like wages and insurance.
   c. Recorded in the period in which the sale was originally made.
   d. Is a normal business expense for a company that sells goods on a credit basis.
   e. All of the above are true.

___ 4. When predicting the amount of accounts receivable that will be written off as uncollectible, which approach evaluates each account receivable based on how long it has been outstanding?
   a. percentage-of-sales
   b. aging of accounts receivable
   c. net realizable value of accounts
   d. control method
   e. direct write-off method

___ 5. Which of the following result from contractual agreements in which one party borrows money from another?
   a. short-term investments
   b. accounts receivable
   c. notes receivable
   d. marketable liabilities
   e. deferred chargebacks

___ 6. On a note receivable, the _____ is the amount loaned by a creditor and borrowed by the debtor.
   a. prepaid liability
   b. interest
   c. debtor's due
   d. creditor
   e. principal

___ 7. On a note receivable, the interest rate is always expressed for a(n) _____ unless specifically stated otherwise.
   a. annual period
   b. 4-month period
   c. billing statement
   d. 6-month period
   e. 1-month period

___ 8. Which of the following is not true regarding an analytic review?
   a. It is an evaluation of a company's financial health.
   b. It is based on ratios of financial statement items.
   c. The current ratio is not helpful in evaluative receivables.
   d. A ratio by itself is not very meaningful.
   e. The acid-test ratio is helpful in evaluating receivables.

___ 9. Which of the following approaches to estimating bad debt expense computes the amount of uncollectible accounts receivable as a percentage of sales?
   a. percentage-of-sales
   b. aging of accounts receivable
   c. net realizable value of accounts
   d. control method
   e. direct write-off method

___ 10. Which of the following is a ledger that contains all the individual names and transactions for every customer who purchases items on account.
   a. aging of accounts receivable ledger
   b. accounts receivable subsidiary ledger
   c. credit account ledger
   d. direct write-off ledger
   e. notes receivable ledger

Chapter

7

Accounting for the Merchandising Firm

LEARNING OBJECTIVES

After studying Chapter 7, you should be able to do the following:

1. Describe why people within and outside a merchandising firm are interested in cost of goods sold and inventory amounts.
2. Define inventory.
3. Explain how inventory and cost of goods sold affect income.
4. Describe how managers use different inventory costing methods to achieve profit, tax, and cash flow goals.
5. Contrast the periodic and perpetual systems of accounting for inventory.
6. Describe various analysis tools and inventory types that can be used to better track and manage inventory.
7. Explain the link between inventory and the accounting neutrality, lower of cost or market, full disclosure, materiality, and comparability.
8. Identify international accounting issues that managers must consider regarding inventory.

CHAPTER CONTENTS

Accounting for the Merchandising Firm

FOCUS ON BUSINESS

Walmart: An Abundance of Merchandise

Can you imagine the massive quantities of merchandise that flow in and out of Walmart stores every day? In the fiscal year ending January 31, 20Y1, the company paid approximately $240.4 billion for merchandise that it resold to customers. This amount is called cost of goods sold. The company is constantly involved in purchasing products from suppliers and manufacturers. Some items may have been purchased early in the fiscal year, while others were purchased more recently. How does the accountant assign a cost of sales to products as they are sold to customers? What value is assigned to the products on the shelf at the end of the year? These questions are answered through inventory costing.

On a typical day, Walmart has $25 billion in merchandise on its shelves and in its warehouses. With this much money involved, you can understand why the company is concerned with efficient inventory systems. The retailing giant spearheaded the launch of an inventory management system that uses radio frequency identification (RFID) technology. With chips attached to products and scanners in warehouses, tracking of inventory is streamlined and costs over the long-term are decreased.

As you will learn in this chapter, there are various ways to account for and manage inventory systems. Each has a different effect on cost of good sold, ending inventory valuation, and net income.

Source: *www.walmartstores.com*

¶701

Applications to People Within and Outside the Firm

LEARNING OBJECTIVE 1: Describe why people within and outside a merchandising firm are interested in cost of goods sold and inventory amounts.

A retailer is a merchandising firm.

Some people say that the day after Thanksgiving, commonly called "Black Friday," is the busiest shopping day of the year. One year, Walmart earned $1.52 billion in sales on Black Friday. Did Walmart make a profit that day? To answer that question, we must determine what the costs of goods sold were on that day. As you learned in Chapter 1, cost of goods sold is the cost of the inventory that a company sells to its customers. A **merchandising firm**, also called a "retailer," earns income by buying products (merchandise) at wholesale prices and selling them at higher, retail prices.

¶701.01

INTERNAL USERS

Accounting for cost of goods sold and inventory is relevant to several people within a merchandising firm. In the marketing department at Walmart, buyers use inventory records to know which products are selling, which need restocking, and which products should be discontinued due to low sales. A history of product costs helps the buyer identify the most economic suppliers. Walmart managers also use cost of goods data to determine the appropriate selling price for a product. Salespeople may use cost figures to know how low a price can be reduced and still make a profit.

Because the cost of goods sold is a major expense for all merchandising firms, top management stays keenly attentive to its fluctuations. To maintain profits, management must keep a constant check on costs. When cost of goods increases, action must be taken to either increase store prices, reduce inventory costs by switching suppliers or selecting lower cost products, cut costs elsewhere (such as personnel), or raise revenue through increased sales.

¶701.02 EXTERNAL USERS

In a typical merchandising firm, who are the people interested in inventory?

The cost of goods sold has a significant effect on gross profit and net income. These amounts are listed on the income statement for Walmart, as they are for all companies. External investors and lenders are interested in costs of goods sold and net income since those amounts influence the firm's profitability and financial strength.

In this chapter, you will learn how to account for inventory and cost of goods sold. This information enables businesses to effectively control costs and thereby increase profitability.

¶702 What Is Inventory?

LEARNING OBJECTIVE 2: Define inventory.

For a merchandising firm, inventory is all the merchandise that is available for sale to customers.

For a merchandising firm, **inventory** includes all goods or products that are available for sale to customers. Merchandise inventory, often referred to simply as "inventory," includes items such as clothing at JC Penney, books at Barnes and Noble, and movies at Blockbuster Video. Since the cost of inventory is a merchandising firm's biggest expense, keeping track of inventory is critical to successful business operations. For example, Exhibit 7.1 shows the vast inventory carried by Walmart, the world's largest retailer. For the two years shown, Walmart's inventory accounts for 83 to 85% of total current assets.

Exhibit 7.1 WALMART CORPORATION
Partial Balance Sheet (Adapted) January 31, 20Y2 and 20Y1

Current Assets:	20Y2 ($ Millions)	%	20Y1 ($ Millions)	%
Cash	$6,414	15%	$5,488	14%
Receivables	2,662	6%	1,715	4%
Inventories	32,191	73%	29,762	77%
Prepaid expenses & other	2,557	6%	1,889	5%
Total current Assets	$43,824	100%	$38,854	100%

Service companies generally have no inventory, since they sell services, not products. Some service companies may carry small inventories of merchandise that support the services they provide. An example of this is the videography company we've used in previous chapters, JK Productions. Even though JK Productions is largely a service business, it also sells safety- and sports-related videos, which are kept in inventory.

In contrast, the inventories of a manufacturing firm take three different forms: Finished Goods Inventory, Work-in-Process Inventory, and Raw Materials Inventory. Besides finished goods that are available for sale to customers, inventory also includes partially-completed goods and raw materials that are to be used in the production process. The three firm types and their respective inventories are shown in Exhibit 7.2.

Exhibit 7.2 TYPES OF BUSINESS FIRMS AND INVENTORY	
Types of Business Firms	**Types of Inventory**
Merchandiser (Retailer)	Merchandise inventory
Service Firm	No inventory
Manufacturer (Production firm)	Raw materials inventory Work-in-process inventory Finished goods inventory

Ending inventory is the merchandise on hand at the end of an accounting period.

Although there are many similarities in the accounting for all types of inventory, this chapter will focus on the accounting treatment of inventory at merchandising firms. In these businesses, once an item is sold, it is removed from the inventory list and its cost is added to the cost of goods sold. Accounting for the quantity of items listed in inventory is essentially a straightforward process of ascertaining how many units are on hand. Merchandise on hand at the end of an accounting period is called "**ending inventory.**" Commonly, the inventory on hand is physically counted at year-end to ensure the accuracy of the accounting records and to obtain the ending inventory, which is listed on the balance sheet under current assets.

Suppose Home Depot buys 10 riding lawnmowers for resale at $800 each. Home Depot marks them up by $200, and sells seven of the mowers for $1,000 each. The company's balance sheet reports three mowers still in inventory, while the income statement reports the cost of the seven mowers sold, as shown below:

If you owned a jewelry store, describe the types of inventory you would likely maintain and track.

Balance Sheet (partial)		Income Statement (partial)	
Current Assets:		Sales Revenue:	
Cash	$XXX	(7 mowers @ $1,000)	$7,000
Accounts Receivable	XXX	Cost of Goods Sold:	
Inventory		(7 mowers @ $800)	5,600
(3 mowers @ $800)	2,400	Gross Profit	$1,400
Prepaid Expenses	XXX		

¶703   Cost of Goods Sold

LEARNING OBJECTIVE 3: Explain how inventory and cost of goods sold affect income.

As you recall, the cost of inventory that a company sells to its customers is called the cost of goods sold (also referred to as cost of sales). For a merchandiser, the cost of goods sold comprises the company's largest expense.

¶703.01   COMPUTING COST OF GOODS SOLD

Determining the cost per unit of inventory is not as straightforward as determining the quantity. This is because inventory may be purchased at different prices throughout the year. Consequently, accountants must determine which unit costs are assigned to cost of goods sold on the income statement, and which unit costs are assigned to ending inventory on the balance sheet.

The computation of cost of goods sold involves three specific amounts:

- The cost of inventory on hand at the start of the period (beginning inventory)
- The cost of purchases of inventory made throughout the period
- The cost of inventory on hand at the end of the period (ending inventory)

More than one accounting method is available for determining the cost of goods sold on the income statement and the ending inventory on the balance sheet. Before looking at the different inventory costing methods, let's examine a basic computation of cost of goods sold. Assume the company, In the Dog House, sells only doghouses. The company's beginning inventory consists of three doghouses costing $100 each. The company purchases twenty more doghouses during the accounting period for $100 each. Thus, the company has 23 doghouses available for sale, with a total cost of $2,300 (23 × $100). At the end of the accounting period, the five doghouses left unsold make up the ending inventory value of $500 (5 × $100). Subtracting the ending inventory from cost of goods available results in a cost of goods sold of $1,800 ($2,300 – $500). This example is illustrated below in Exhibit 7.3.

Exhibit 7.3 BASIC COMPUTATION OF COST OF GOODS SOLD IN THE DOG HOUSE

Cost of Goods Sold:	
Beginning Inventory (3 units at $100 each)	$300
+ Purchases (20 units at $100)	2,000
= Cost of Goods Available for Sale (23 units at $100 each)	$2,300
– Ending Inventory (5 units at $100)	(500)
= Cost of Goods Sold (18 units at $100)	$1,800

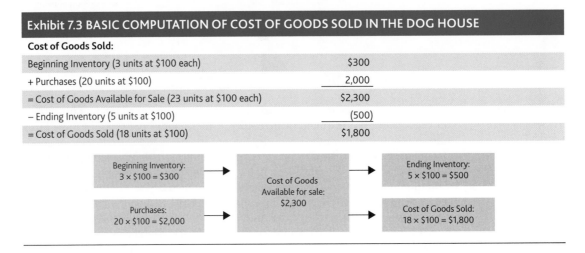

¶703.02   COST OF GOODS SOLD ON THE INCOME STATEMENT

Gross profit = Net sales – Cost of goods sold

Exhibit 7.4 takes a closer look at the 20Y2 income statement for Walmart, which shows that cost of goods sold was over $240 billion. As you can see, cost of goods sold is subtracted from net sales to compute **gross profit**. Thus, gross profit, also referred to as "**gross margin**," is simply the difference between net sales and cost of goods sold. Operating expenses are subtracted from gross profit to compute operating income. Operating expenses include such items as advertising and salaries. Finally, non-operating expenses are subtracted from operating income to calculate net income. Non-operating expenses consist of accounts like interest expense and income tax expense. As shown in the bottom line of Exhibit 7.4, managing and controlling costs for its huge amount of inventory helped earn Walmart a net income of over $11 billion in 20Y2.

? As a percentage of sales, do you think cost of goods sold might be higher at Walmart or at Macy's Department Store? Why?

Exhibit 7.4 WALMART CORPORATION
Income Statement (Adapted) Years Ended January 31, 20Y2 and 20Y1

	20Y2 ($ Millions)	20Y1 ($ Millions)
Net Sales	$312,427	$285,222
Other income, net	3,227	2,910
Cost of Goods Sold	(240,391)	(219,793)
Gross Profit	$75,263	$68,339
Operating Expenses	(56,733)	(51,248)
Operating Income	$18,530	$17,091
Non-Operating Expenses	(7,299)	(6,824)
Net Income	$11,231	$10,267

¶704 Inventory Costing Methods

> **LEARNING OBJECTIVE 4:** Describe how managers use different inventory costing methods to achieve profit, tax, and cash flow goals.

The cost of an item in inventory can vary depending on when and where it was purchased. For example, assume American Eagle buys a large quantity of jeans at a certain price in March. A couple of months later, the company buys more jeans, but at a higher cost because the supplier has increased the price. For the next jean purchase in October, American Eagle switches to a new supplier and obtains a price that is lower than the first purchase. Thus, jeans are listed in inventory at three different costs. At the end of the accounting period, how does the accountant determine the cost of jeans that have sold and the cost of jeans that are left in inventory?

Four different inventory costing methods are available for determining the cost of ending inventory and the cost of goods sold. The business manager must select which accounting method to use; all methods are approved under generally accepted accounting principles (GAAP), although each has its own inherent advantages and disadvantages. When the unit costs of inventory vary, each inventory costing method results in different amounts for cost of goods sold and ending inventory. Remember, cost of goods sold is shown on the income statement, while ending inventory is shown on the balance sheet. These amounts will affect net income, tax expense, and cash flow. The four inventory costing methods are as follows:

- Specific Identification Method
- First-In, First-Out (FIFO) Method
- Last-In, First-Out (LIFO) Method
- Weighted Average Method

¶704.01

The specific identification method keeps track of the cost of individual inventory items.

SPECIFIC IDENTIFICATION METHOD

The **specific identification method,** also known as the "specific unit cost method," requires a company to keep track of the cost of individual inventory items. In other words, inventory is valued according to the specific cost of each inventory unit. For example, assume that a Circuit City store has three Sony computers for sale. Circuit City purchased one low-end model for $500. The other two computers, which were loaded with higher processing speed, more software, and more memory, were purchased for $1,000 each. If the store sells the two more expensive models, the cost of goods sold is $2,000 ($1,000 × 2). The low-end model is the only unit left in inventory; thus, ending inventory is $500.

The specific identification method is usually used for inventory items that have unique characteristics, such as high quality artwork, automobiles, jewelry, and real estate. The method is too costly to perform for inventory units that have common characteristics, such as barrels of oil, pounds of nails, reams of printer paper, or jeans.

The other three inventory costing methods, FIFO, LIFO, and weighted average, are conceptually different from the specific identification method. FIFO, LIFO, and weighted average assume flows of units into and out of inventory. These three methods are not concerned with the unit cost of a specific inventory item.

To illustrate these three methods, consider the following situation involving one type inventory item at Walmart. Suppose that one Walmart store starts the year with 20 Hewlett-Packard inkjet printer cartridges that cost $15 each, as shown in Exhibit 7.5. Later in the year, Walmart purchases 20 inkjet cartridges for $22 each and then an additional 20 inkjet cartridges for $35 each. During the year, Walmart sells a total of 45 inkjet cartridges. What cost should be assigned to the 45 cartridges sold and the cost of the remaining 15 cartridges in ending inventory? The answer will vary depending on which inventory costing method is used. In the following paragraphs, we will make the computations using the FIFO, LIFO, and weighted average methods.

Exhibit 7.5 INVENTORY EXAMPLE USING INK JET CARTRIDGES

Beginning Inventory (20 units @ $15 each)		$300
Purchases:		
No. 1 (20 units @ $22 each)	$440	
No. 2 (20 units @ $35 each)	700	
Total Purchases		1,140
Cost of Goods Available for sale (60 units)		$1,440
Ending Inventory (15 units)		?
Cost of Goods Sold (45 units)		$?

¶704.02

FIRST-IN, FIRST-OUT (FIFO) METHOD

Using the **first-in, first-out (FIFO) method**, the cost of the *first* inventory unit is assumed to be the *first* cost transferred out to cost of goods sold. Thus, the cost of the units remaining in ending inventory is based on the cost of the last units purchased. Under FIFO, cost flow follows product flow.

FIRST-IN, FIRST-OUT (FIFO)

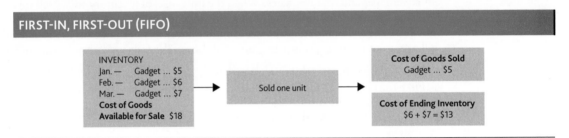

Let's refer to our Walmart scenario and calculate cost of goods sold and ending inventory value under FIFO (Exhibit 7.6). Recall that we must be able to account for a total of 60 available cartridges – 45 that were sold and 15 that remain in ending inventory. The Exhibit 7.6 computation begins with the cost of goods available for sale (or $1,440), which was calculated in Exhibit 7.5. [Note that this amount will be the same under any cost assignment method.] Next, ending inventory under FIFO is composed of the *last* fifteen cartridges purchased at $35 each for a total of $525. The first 45 cartridges acquired, either from beginning inventory or the earliest purchases, are recorded at their respective costs and make up the cost of goods sold. Finally, the difference between cost of goods available for sale and ending inventory results in a cost of goods sold of $915 based on FIFO.

Exhibit 7.6 COST OF GOODS SOLD AND ENDING INVENTORY UNDER FIFO

FIFO Method	
Cost of Goods Available for Sale (60 units)	$1,440
Ending Inventory (last 15 units available):	
15 units from Purchase No. 2, $15 each	(525)
Cost of Goods Sold (first 45 units available)*	$915
*Cost of Goods Sold:	
20 units from beginning inventory, $15 each	$300
20 units from Purchase No. 1, $22 each	440
5 units from Purchase No. 2, $35 each	175
	$915

¶704.03 LAST-IN, FIRST-OUT (LIFO) METHOD

The **last-in, first-out (LIFO) method** is based on the assumption that the costs of the *last* items purchased should be assigned to the *first* items sold. Therefore, the cost of the units remaining in ending inventory is comprised of the cost of the oldest units, which include beginning inventory and the earliest purchases. The cost of goods sold is made up of the most recent purchases.

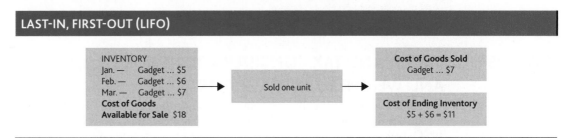

For our Walmart example, Exhibit 7.7 shows that ending inventory consists of fifteen cartridges from beginning inventory, costing $15 each. Thus, the value of ending inventory is $225 (15 × $15), which is less than the value under the FIFO method. When the ending inventory is subtracted from cost of goods available, the result equals a cost of goods sold of $1,215 (based on costs of the most recently acquired 45 units).

Exhibit 7.7 COST OF GOODS SOLD AND ENDING INVENTORY UNDER LIFO

LIFO Method	
Cost of Goods Available for Sale (60 units)	$1,440
Ending Inventory (first 15 units available):	
15 units from beginning inventory, $15 each	(225)
Cost of Goods Sold (last 45 units available)*	$1,215
*Cost of Goods Sold:	
20 units from Purchase No. 2, $35 each	$700
20 units from Purchase No. 1, $22 each	440
5 units from beginning inventory, $15 each	75
	$1,215

¶704.04 WEIGHTED AVERAGE METHOD

The **weighted average method**, also referred to as the "average cost method," is based on the weighted average cost of inventory during the period. Calculation of the weighted average cost is as shown below:

$$\text{Weighted average cost per unit} = \frac{\text{Cost of goods available}}{\text{Number of units available}}$$

$$\text{Weighted average cost of ending inventory} = \text{Number of units on hand at end of period} \times \text{Weighted average cost per unit}$$

As shown in Exhibit 7.8, the weighted average cost of inventory available for sale is $24 per unit ($1,440 / 60 units). Ending inventory is $360 ($24 × 15 units) and cost of goods sold is $1,080 ($24 × 45 units).

A store such as Walmart might use the weighted average inventory costing method for products that have very little fluctuation in price or if management thinks the price fluctuations will not make a material difference in the store's accounting records.

Weighted average cost of ending inventory = Weighted average cost per unit × Number of units.

Exhibit 7.8 COST OF GOODS SOLD AND ENDING INVENTORY UNDER WEIGHTED AVERAGE

Weighted Average Method	
Cost of Goods Available for Sale	
(see Part A, $1,440/60 units = $24 average cost each)	$1,440
Ending Inventory (15 units @ $24 each)	(360)
Cost of Goods Sold (45 units @ $24 each)	$1,080

¶704.05 PROFIT AND TAX CONSIDERATIONS FOR FIFO, LIFO, AND WEIGHTED AVERAGE COST

In our Walmart example, the per-unit cost of inventory ranged from $15 to $22 to as high as $35. As we have seen, when the cost of inventory is changing, the various inventory costing methods (FIFO, LIFO, weighted average) result in different cost of goods sold and ending inventory amounts. Exhibit 7.9 summarizes the impact of the different inventory methods on ending inventory, cost of goods sold, and gross profit.

Exhibit 7.9 IMPACT OF INVENTORY METHODS ON GROSS PROFIT

	FIFO		LIFO		Weighted Average	
Net Sales		$2,000		$2,000		$2,000
Cost of Goods Sold:						
Goods available for sale	$1,440		$1,440		$1,440	
Ending Inventory	(525)		(225)		(360)	
Cost of Goods Sold		(915)		(1,215)		(1,080)
Gross Profit		$1,085		$785		$920

If inventory costs increase during a period, FIFO results in the greatest ending inventory amounts because the most recent higher costs are included. Thus, in the Walmart example, the most recent purchase of more expensive inkjet cartridges is left in inventory, while the initial lower-costing cartridges are assigned to cost of goods sold. The outcome is a lower cost of goods sold under FIFO than when using the other methods of inventory costing. As you can see from Exhibit 7.9, subtracting this lower cost of goods sold from net sales also results in a higher gross profit.

In this same situation of rising inventory costs, the value of LIFO ending inventory is lowest because it includes the initial or earliest costs, which are less costly than recent purchases. The recent, more expensive cartridges, under this flow assumption, are included in costs of goods sold. As a consequence, LIFO results in the lowest ending inventory, the highest cost of goods sold, and comparably less gross profit.

Since the weighted average method is based on the weighted average cost of inventory during the period, it produces values between the FIFO and LIFO amounts. As shown in Exhibit 7.9, the weighted average value for cost of goods sold is less than FIFO but greater than LIFO. As a result, the weighted average value for gross profit is also between the other two inventory costing methods.

In periods where inventory costs are going down, FIFO results in a higher cost of goods sold because it contains the earlier, higher cost units. LIFO, on the other hand, results in a lower cost of goods sold under these conditions because it contains the recent, lower cost units.

Since the method of inventory costing affects gross profit, it also affects net income. For a merchandising firm, net income is the amount left after deducting operating expenses from gross profit. The method producing the highest gross profit will naturally also produce the highest net income.

To illustrate the impact of inventory cost methods on net income, let's build on the information in Exhibit 7.9. Assume the store's operating expenses are $700 and the income tax rate is 40 percent of income before tax. As shown in Exhibit 7.10, during a period of rising inventory costs, net income is highest under the FIFO inventory method, which has the highest gross profit. LIFO results in the lowest net income due to a lower gross profit.

	FIFO	LIFO	Weighted Average
Exhibit 7.10 IMPACT OF INVENTORY METHODS ON NET INCOME			
Gross Profit	$1,085	$785	$920
Operating Expenses	700	700	700
Income Before Tax	$385	$85	$220
Income Tax Expense (.40)	154	34	88
Net Income	$231	$51	$132

As you can see from Exhibit 7.10, taxes are also directly affected by the inventory costing method. In our Walmart example, the lowest tax expense is achieved through LIFO, which has the lowest gross profit. During periods of rising prices, LIFO results in the lowest taxable income and consequently the lowest income tax expense

As a company selects an inventory method, it must prioritize the need to show a higher profit or to reduce income tax payments. Since LIFO reduces income tax expense, LIFO is a popular inventory method. About one-third of all business firms employ the LIFO method. However, since a company's earnings ultimately affect stock prices, most managers and stockholders prefer a higher net income. During a period of rising prices, FIFO results in the highest net income. This may explain why FIFO remains the most popular inventory method, used by 44 percent of all firms as shown in Exhibit 7.11.

Exhibit 7.11 PERCENTAGE OF COMPANIES USING VARIOUS INVENTORY METHODS

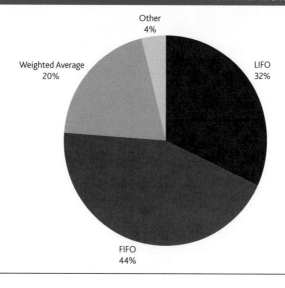

Other
4%

Weighted Average
20%

LIFO
32%

FIFO
44%

Let's consider why a company like JK Productions might choose a particular method of inventory costing to fulfill its income goals and address tax implications. JK Productions sells videos that help improve athletic performance, such as batting tips. It buys the instructional videos in the wholesale market and then sells them to its customers at a small profit. Kay, as accountant and co-founder of the firm, determined that the best cost of inventory approach for JK Productions is LIFO, because it results in the lowest taxable income, and thus, the lowest income tax expense.

FOCUS ON TECHNOLOGY

Using Microsoft Excel: Preparing a Chart

Using Excel, we will recreate the chart in Exhibit 7.11, which compares cost of goods sold using the FIFO, LIFO, and weighted average methods. The amounts for cost of goods sold under each method are obtained from Exhibit 7.9.

	FIFO	LIFO	Weighted Average
Cost of Goods Sold	915	1,215	1,080

1. Enter the necessary data onto your Excel worksheet in the following format:
2. Highlight the data range that contains the information to be charted (i.e. the cells containing all the titles and amounts you just entered). The titles are being included so that Chart Wizard can use them in the chart legend.
3. Click on the Chart Wizard icon (picture of blue, yellow, and red columns). Chart Wizard will immediately launch into a four-step process to create your chart.
4. In step one, you select a specific chart type. Select the first option – column chart. There are several sub-types of column charts; we will use the first option, which is already highlighted. You only need to click on "Next" to go to the next step.
5. In step two, Chart Wizard is simply confirming the data range that you previously highlighted. There is a display showing what your chart currently looks like. Click "Next."
6. Several chart-enhancing options are made available here. These options can also be accessed after the chart is completed by right clicking on the chart. Further enhancements are not needed for this example, so click "Next."
7. Click "Finish" and the chart will appear on your worksheet. Like any other object, clicking on the chart or items within the chart will enable you to move or enlarge it.

¶704.06   INCOME STATEMENT VS. BALANCE SHEET

A primary goal of accounting is to provide information to help people make effective decisions. In the case of business managers, this information helps them run the company in a more profitable manner. For investors, accounting information helps make informed investment decisions for higher returns. The financial statements, including the measurement of cost of goods sold and inventory, are designed to provide an understanding of the company's financial situation.

In the case of inventory costing, more than one accounting method is permissible. The differences between inventory methods result in a trade-off between the income statement and balance sheet, at least in terms of how well the actual financial situation is shown. Before a company chooses its inventory valuation method, much consideration is given to the impact of that decision.

LIFO leads to the most realistic income statement because it uses the most recent inventory costs in computing cost of goods sold. This method gives a better picture of what it would actually cost to replace the inventory that was sold. Thus, a better matching of revenues and expenses is achieved. While the income statement is presented in a better light by using LIFO, it also results in the assignment of older, less current costs of inventory on the balance sheet. This means that when using LIFO during periods of rising prices, the inventory amount on the balance sheet presents a total that is considerably less than what it would cost to replace those items at current costs.

In contrast, FIFO results in a better balance sheet presentation but a worse income statement presentation. FIFO puts the more current inventory costs on the balance sheet, while assigning the older, and more out-of-date inventory costs to cost of goods sold on the income statement.

Another issue associated with inventory costing method is the impact on taxes. During periods of rising prices, LIFO results in the lowest income tax expense. This is because LIFO puts the higher inventory costs in cost of goods sold, which thereby reduces taxable income.

In summary, LIFO provides a more realistic income statement presentation and FIFO yields a more objective balance sheet presentation. Assuming prices are rising, LIFO results in lower tax liability. The weighted average method results in amounts that fall somewhere between FIFO and LIFO outcomes.

¶704.07 ETHICS AND INVENTORY MANAGEMENT

A guiding principle for managers is that accounting methods should be used to provide a clear picture of a company's financial situation.

According to GAAP, there are different ways to compute the cost of inventory. Which inventory costing method do you think is the most logical?

FOCUS ON ETHICS

Social Responsibility and the Corporation

Managing a corporation means more than making a profit. Many companies consider social responsibility to be a high priority as well. At Walmart, when thousands of its employees were called as national reservists to active duty in Iraq, the company made a decision to help the financial condition of those employees. By law, the employer is required to save the reservist's job, but is not required to pay the employee while on leave. While the reservist receives military pay, the military salary is usually lower than that of the civilian job. This causes a financial hardship for those called to duty. Walmart alleviated that financial burden for its employees by committing to make up the difference in salary if their military pay was less than their regular wages.

Source: *www.walmartstores.com*

Under LIFO, the most recently-purchased inventory becomes part of cost of goods sold. As a result, business managers may be tempted to use LIFO to manipulate net income. When prices are rising, managers who want to reduce company net income in order to lower tax expense can purchase large quantities of high-priced inventory near year-end. If managers want a higher net income, they can postpone inventory purchases until the next year.

LIFO liquidation occurs when LIFO is used and inventory on hand declines below the quantity of the prior period.

Postponing major inventory purchases causes inventory on hand to significantly decline. When LIFO is used and inventory on hand declines below the quantity of the prior period, this event is referred to as "**LIFO liquidation**." Generally, managers prefer to avoid LIFO liquidation, since it results in higher income taxes based on the higher net income. However, managers may be under pressure to show a higher net income, which usually results in a higher company stock price.

The choice of a certain inventory costing method should be made to provide a clear financial picture of a company's situation. Managers must carefully consider their motivations behind choices of and changes to accounting methods.

¶705 Periodic vs. Perpetual Systems

> **LEARNING OBJECTIVE 5:** Contrast the periodic and perpetual systems of accounting for inventory.

With a periodic inventory system, inventory is accounted for at the end of the period.

Two different types of systems can be used to track inventories: the periodic system or perpetual system. When a company waits until the end of the period to ascertain the amount of ending inventory, this is known as the "**periodic inventory system**." For example, because JK Productions has a small quantity of inventory items, the units on hand are counted at the end of the year to determine their cost.

With a perpetual inventory system, inventory is accounted for continuously.

Some companies prefer to keep count of inventory in a continuous fashion; this is known as a "**perpetual inventory system**." When a unit is sold in a perpetual inventory system, the inventory records are immediately updated. The company continuously knows how much inventory is on hand. For example, at many department stores, when a sale is made, the cash register records the amount of the sale and what was sold and updates inventory as each transaction occurs. At any given time, a manager can check to see how much of an inventory item is available.

¶705.01 RECORDING TRANSACTIONS UNDER THE PERIODIC INVENTORY SYSTEM

Journal entries for inventory transactions will vary depending on whether the perpetual or periodic system is used. In the periodic system, cost of goods sold is not determined until the end of the period, following the physical count of inventory. To illustrate, suppose we use an account called "Purchases" to accumulate the costs of merchandise purchased during the period. At the end of the period, the amount of cost of goods sold is attained by (a) transferring the cost of beginning inventory to Cost of Goods Sold, (b) setting up ending inventory based on the physical count, and (c) transferring the cost of Purchases to Cost of Goods Sold. The corresponding journal entries are shown in Exhibit 7.12.

Exhibit 7.12 JOURNAL ENTRIES UNDER A PERIODIC INVENTORY SYSTEM

1. *Purchase 20 units at $100 each on account:*

Purchases	2,000	
Accounts Payable		2,000

2. *Sell 18 units at $150 each on account:*

Accounts Receivable	2,700	
Sales Revenue		2,700

3. *Adjusting entries at end of period to update inventory and record cost of goods sold.*

  (a) *Transfer cost of beginning inventory to Cost of Goods Sold:*

Cost of Goods Sold	300	
Inventory (beginning: 3 units @ $100)		300

  (b) *Set up ending inventory based on physical count:*

Inventory (ending: 5 units @ $100)	500	
Cost of Goods Sold		500

  (c) *Transfer cost of Purchases to Cost of Goods Sold:*

Cost of Goods Sold	2,000	
Purchases		2,000

T-Accounts

Inventory			Cost of Goods Sold			Purchases		
Beg.	300	300		300	500	Beg.	2,000	2,000
	500			2,000				
Bal.	500		Bal.	1,800		Bal.	0	

¶705.02 RECORDING TRANSACTIONS UNDER THE PERPETUAL INVENTORY SYSTEM

With the perpetual system, a journal entry is made to the Cost of Goods Sold account every time a sales transaction occurs. Exhibit 7.13 presents the journal entries under the perpetual inventory system. When units are purchased, a journal entry increases the Inventory account by that amount. For the sales transaction, two entries are made. The first records the increase to Accounts Receivable and the increase to Sales Revenue. The second records the increase to Cost of Goods Sold and the decrease to Inventory. Notice that the resulting balances for the Inventory and Cost of Goods Sold accounts are the same as under the periodic system, when using FIFO.

Exhibit 7.13 JOURNAL ENTRIES UNDER A PERPETUAL INVENTORY SYSTEM

1. *Purchase on account of 20 units at $100 each.*

Inventory	2,000	
Accounts Payable		2,000

2. *Sale of 18 units on account, sale price of $150 each and cost of $100 each.*

  (a)

Accounts Receivable	2,700	
Sales Revenue		2,700

  (b)

Cost of Goods Sold	1,800	
Inventory		1,800

T-Accounts

Inventory			Cost of Goods Sold	
Beg.	300	1,800	1,800	
	2,000			
Bal.	500		Bal. 1,800	

¶705.03   TERMS OF SALE AND PRODUCT RETURNS

When a company sells its products, the seller and buyer agree to terms of the sale such as when payment is to be made and who pays delivery or freight costs. All departments within a company work together to get the product to the customer, thus all departments are affected by the terms of the sale. Terms of sale vary among industries and are usually shown on the sales invoice. For example, payment might be expected in 30 or 60 days. The invoice would be printed with terms "n/30" or "n/60" and read as "net 30" or "net 60." This means that payment is due in either 30 or 60 days from the date on the invoice.

¶705.03.01   Sales Discounts

Some companies provide a sales discount to encourage early payment from customers. By receiving payment earlier, the company making the sale improves its liquidity, that is, accounts receivable are more quickly converted to cash. A common sales discount is "2/10, n/30." This means that the customer can receive a 2 percent discount by paying within 10 days, or can wait 30 days and pay the full amount.

¶705.03.02   Freight Costs

FOB shipping point indicates that the buyer pays for delivery of the merchandise.

Either the buyer or seller can pay the delivery or freight costs. The buyer records shipping costs in the Freight-In account. The Freight-Out account is used by the seller to record shipping costs. Freight-In means that it is the cost of shipping goods "in" from suppliers. Freight-Out means that it is the cost of shipping goods "out" to customers. Thus the "In" or "Out" distinguishes the two types of freight costs, from the buyer or seller's perspective.

FOB destination indicates that the seller pays for delivery of the merchandise.

The terms of sale indicate who pays the transportation costs. **FOB shipping point** indicates the seller puts the product "free on board" at the point of origin. The title (or ownership) transfers to the buyer at the point of origin. In the case of FOB shipping point, the seller does not pay any transportation costs and the buyer pays for delivery of the merchandise. Conversely, **FOB destination** indicates that the seller pays for delivery of the merchandise to its destination. In this case, title stays with the seller during shipping.

¶705.03.03   Purchases Returns and Allowances

A purchase return is a reduction in the cost of purchases, which occurs when the buyer returns products to the seller.

If a buyer is dissatisfied with the products purchased, the buyer can usually return the products to the seller. The buyer records this as a **purchase return**, which results in a decrease in the cost of purchases. Sometimes a buyer is awarded a deduction in the amount owed, known as a **"purchase allowance."** Under the periodic inventory system, the Purchases Returns and Allowances account is credited for these types of transactions.

¶705.03.04   Net Purchases

A purchase allowance is a reduction in the cost of purchases, which occurs when the seller grants the buyer a deduction from the amount owed.

For simplicity, this book will generally refer to net purchases as purchases. Likewise, this book typically refers to net sales as sales. The accounts used to compute net purchases are summarized below.

	Purchases
–	Purchase discounts
–	Purchase returns and allowances
+	Freight-in
	Net purchases

The amounts affecting net sales are summarized below. Unlike Freight-In, which affects the computation of net purchases, Freight-Out does not affect the calculation of net sales. Freight-Out would be shown with other selling expenses on the income statement.

¶705.03.05

If a buyer returns products, the seller records this as a sales return.

A sales allowance is a deduction given by the seller to the buyer on the amount owed.

Sales Returns and Allowances

If a buyer returns products to the seller, the seller records this as a **sales return.** Another reduction to sales revenue is a **sales allowance**, which is a deduction awarded by the seller to the buyer on the amount owed. The Sales Returns and Allowances account is a contra-revenue account and is deducted from Sales on the income statement. The accounts used to compute net sales are summarized below.

	Sales revenue
−	Sales discounts
−	Sales returns and allowances
	Net sales

¶706

Consider a store in which you often shop. Does that company appear to be using a periodic or perpetual inventory system?

Evaluating Inventory

LEARNING OBJECTIVE 6: Describe various analysis tools and inventory types that can be used to better track and manage inventory.

Inventory is critical to company operations. Managing it successfully is a key to profitability and is significant in terms of quantity, cost, and its effect on a company's financial ratios.

¶706.01

THE AMOUNT OF INVENTORY TO PURCHASE

To meet the demands of customers, business managers must decide how much inventory to buy. Suppose you are the purchasing manager for Target and are planning a purchase of Compaq personal computers for sale in your electronics department. You have decided on several different models of Compaq computers. Next, you must decide how many computers to purchase. If you fail to buy enough computers to meet demand, your customers will turn to your competitors to make their purchases. If you buy more computers than you can sell, you stand to lose money since technology products become outdated quickly. Despite the large size of a Target store, space cannot be provided for items that are not selling. A good manager tries to make every foot of shelf and floor space as profitable as possible.

To determine the quantity of inventory to buy, the manager requires three amounts:

1. **An estimated or budgeted amount for cost of goods sold.** The budgeted cost of goods sold is based on an estimate of sales for next period (also called the "sales forecast"). The marketing department usually prepares the sales forecast, based on marketing research and prior sales. From this sales forecast, the cost of those sales, that is, the cost of goods sold can be budgeted for the next period.
2. **An estimated or budgeted amount for ending inventory.** This is the amount of inventory you predict will be needed to start the next period. A store would be unwise to sell its entire inventory during one period due to the risk of not having merchandise on hand to sell to customers at the start of the next period.
3. **The actual amount of beginning inventory.** This is the inventory currently on hand.

How these amounts are used to calculate purchases is shown below:

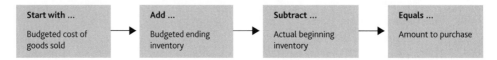

Start with ...	Add ...	Subtract ...	Equals ...
Budgeted cost of goods sold	Budgeted ending inventory	Actual beginning inventory	Amount to purchase

Using dollar estimates, the formula to determine purchases is as follows:

	Cost of goods sold, budgeted for next period	$20,000
+	Ending inventory, budgeted for next period	1,000
=	Cost of goods available for sale, per budget	$21,000
−	Beginning inventory, end of prior period	2,000
=	Purchases (how much inventory to buy)	$19,000

Of course, if the budgeted cost of goods sold and budgeted ending inventory are not good estimates, then the formula will fail to calculate the appropriate amount of inventory to buy. Accounting decisions are not always obvious and straightforward, but instead rely on estimates and calculations.

Since inventory is a major item affecting the balance sheet and income statement of most companies, business managers make good faith efforts to successfully manage inventory. An effective tool that helps all departmental managers keep track of inventory and spot potential problems is financial ratio analysis.

¶706.02 FINANCIAL RATIOS

A financial ratio shows the proportionate value of a financial statement item relative to other items.

Financial ratios show the proportionate values of financial statement items relative to other items. A financial ratio is a calculation, usually derived by dividing one financial statement item by one or more other financial statements items. The resulting ratio, or percentage, provides the reader some important information about an aspect of the company's financial situation.

¶706.02.01 Inventory Turnover Ratio

Businesses must sell their inventory to generate a profit. If inventory sits in the store or the warehouse, the company makes no money. In fact, a company incurs substantial expenses to maintain a store or to rent warehouse space. Consequently, when inventory is not moving (selling), a company is in a lose-lose situation.

Inventory turnover is a measure of how fast inventory is selling.

The ratio, **inventory turnover**, is a measure of how fast inventory is selling. Inventory turnover is the ratio of cost of goods sold to average inventory as follows:

Inventory turnover = Cost of goods sold / Average inventory

Average inventory can be calculated by taking the beginning inventory of the period, adding the ending inventory, and dividing by two.

Suppose Circuit City starts the year with $10 million in inventory, ends the year with $12 million in inventory, and reports $94 million in cost of goods sold. Inventory turnover is calculated as follows ($ in millions):

Inventory turnover = $94 / (($10 + $12) / 2) = 8.5 times per year (every 43 days)

In other words, Circuit City sells the entire inventory it has on hand every 43 days or 8.5 times during the year.

A review of the inventory turnover ratio can help managers more effectively run the company. For example, if the inventory turnover was 8.5 last period and 6.0 in the current period, managers would be concerned why inventory was not selling as fast. This could be a serious problem, especially since high-tech products can quickly become obsolete. Some products that don't sell in the current period may have to be substantially marked-down in price in order to sell in the next period. This would hurt profitability. On the other hand, inventory turnover that is high is not always a good thing; it could signal that inventory levels are insufficient to meet demand.

¶706.02.02 Gross Profit Margin

The gross profit margin indicates the business firm's capacity to sell its inventory at a profit.

Gross profit margin, also called "**gross profit percentage**," indicates the firm's capacity to sell its inventory at a profit. Gross profit margin is the ratio of gross profit to net sales revenue. You will recall that gross profit is the difference between net sales revenue and cost of goods sold. The gross profit margin for Walmart is calculated as follows (amounts in billions):

$$\text{Gross profit margin} = \text{Gross profit / Net sales revenue}$$

$$= \$53 / \$244$$

$$= 21.7\%$$

In the case of Walmart above, every dollar in sales results in a gross profit of 21.7 cents. In other words, 21.7% of net sales revenue is gross profit, from which selling and administrative expenses are subtracted to arrive at net income. The gross profit margin is closely monitored by business managers and by investors. A decline in gross profit margin from one period to the next would cause serious concern to managers and investors. Often, a small drop in gross profit margin is connected to a large drop in net income.

Additional tools that help managers keep track of inventory and spot potential problems include the use of the just-in-time inventory system and the gross profit method for estimating inventory.

¶706.03   JUST-IN-TIME INVENTORY

The just-in-time inventory system purchases inventory just as the company needs it.

The **just-in-time inventory** system purchases inventory just as the company needs it. This system enables a company to minimize costs associated with keeping inventory on hand. For retailers, when inventory does not arrive in time, then the company will disappoint its customers and lose revenues. Consequently, for a just-in-time system to work, there must be close coordination between a company and its suppliers. Walmart has such a relationship with its suppliers. Due to Walmart's importance to its suppliers and its policy of treating suppliers like partners, Walmart can obtain low ordering costs even with small and frequent orders. This reduces the amount of inventory Walmart must accumulate. Walmart's efficient supply chain is a key factor in sustaining its low-price leadership among retailers,

¶706.04   ESTIMATING INVENTORY USING THE GROSS PROFIT METHOD

The gross profit method is an effective approach to estimate the cost of ending inventory.

Occasionally, a company must estimate the amount of its inventory. Suppose a natural disaster, such as a flood or fire, destroys the inventory. So that an insurance claim can be filed for losses, an estimate of the amount of inventory lost is required. The **gross profit method**, also called the "**gross margin method**," is an effective approach to estimate the cost of ending inventory. To estimate ending inventory using the gross profit method, a company needs to know the following:

- Beginning inventory
- Purchases
- Net sales
- Gross profit margin*

  * *The gross profit method is based on the assumption that the company's gross profit margin remains relatively stable from year to year.*

Suppose part of Walmart's inventory is lost in a fire. To obtain reimbursement from the insurance company, Walmart must estimate its ending inventory. The accounting records show beginning inventory, net purchases, and net sales through the date of the fire. Gross profit is estimated by multiplying Walmart's gross profit margin of 21.7 percent (given earlier) by net sales revenue. The computations for estimating inventory using the gross profit method are shown below.

Beginning Inventory		$50,000
Purchases		430,000
Cost of Goods Available for Sale		$480,000
Cost of Goods Sold:		
Net Sales Revenue	$500,000	
Less Estimated Gross Profit (.217)	108,500	
Estimated Cost of Goods Sold		391,500
Estimated Ending Inventory		$88,500

If you were selling hand-made pottery, how would you determine whether your inventory is selling at a profit?

As you can see, cost of goods sold is subtracted from goods available to estimate ending inventory. Walmart would claim an ending inventory of $88,500 when filing with the insurance company.

The gross profit method is useful for other purposes as well. As a part of normal operations, inventory is counted at the end of the period. To help ensure the accuracy of the count, the gross profit method can be used as a double-check on the accuracy of the count. If the amount derived from the gross profit method is significantly different from the count, managers should check for errors in the count.

¶707 Application of Accounting Concepts

> **LEARNING OBJECTIVE 7:** Explain the link between inventory and the accounting neutrality, lower of cost or market, full disclosure, materiality, and comparability.

Accounting for business transactions, including inventory transactions, must follow generally accepted accounting principles. For many types of transactions, very specific rules must be followed. In other cases, only broad concepts are available. Five broad concepts that pertain to inventory include the following: neutrality, lower of cost or market, full disclosure, materiality, and comparability.

¶707.01 NEUTRALITY

It is important for companies to fairly represent financial data using the best information available. This means companies cannot overstate assets or income in order to make their financial statements look better. The concept of **neutrality** requires companies to remain unbiased when making decisions related to presenting financial data. Neutrality is a component of relevance and faithful representation discussed in Chapter 1, which requires accounting data to be fairly presented. In other words, if there are two possible alternatives of accounting for an item, companies should be very careful to remain unbiased in selecting the best option. The company should choose the option that best represents its financial position to investors. Some companies may be tempted to select the alternative that makes their financial statements look better, but this would be damaging to investors.

If there are alternatives to accounting for an item, companies should be very careful to remain unbiased in selecting the best alternative.

For example, suppose Ford Motor Company paid $400,000 for inventory that has become obsolete. The current value of the inventory is most likely only equal to $100,000. In order to faithfully represent its financial position, Ford must record a $300,000 loss and write down the value of inventory to $100,000. On the other hand, suppose Ford paid $200,000 for inventory that now has a market value of $250,000. Accounting standards require that Ford leave the inventory at its cost of $200,000; Ford is not permitted to write up the value to $250,000. This prevents the company from reporting the inventory at an artificially high value.

¶707.02 LOWER OF COST OR MARKET

Lower of cost or market mandates that inventory be shown at the lower of its cost or its market value.

The accounting concept of "**lower of cost or market**" mandates that inventory be shown on the financial statements at the lower of either its historical cost or its market value. You will recall that historical cost includes the price paid plus any expenditure necessary to prepare the asset for use. Market value typically refers to replacement cost, in other words, the cost of replacing the inventory at current prices.

When the replacement cost (market value) of inventory drops below its historical cost, the firm is required to decrease value of inventory to its market value. Consequently, the balance sheet shows inventory at its lower of cost or market (LCM) value.

How is inventory decreased in value to lower of cost or market? Suppose JC Penney paid $50,000 for its ending inventory of October 31, but on December 31 the replacement cost of the same items is $42,000. Penney's balance sheet on December 31 must show inventory at the LCM value of $42,000. Exhibit 7.14 shows the impact of LCM on the income statement and the balance sheet.

Exhibit 7.14 IMPACT OF LOWER-OF-COST-OR-MARKET (LCM)

JC Penney Company Income Statement (Partial) For Year Ended December 31, 20Y1

Sales Revenue		$180,000
Cost of Goods Sold:		
Beginning Inventory (LCM = Cost)	$45,000	
Purchases	100,000	
Cost of Goods Available for Sale	$145,000	
Ending Inventory:		
Cost = $50,000; Market value = $42,000; LCM =	(42,000)	
Cost of Goods Sold		103,000
Gross Profit		$77,000

JC Penney Company Balance Sheet (Partial) December 31, 20Y1

Current Assets:		
Cash		$XXX
Accounts Receivable		XXX
Inventory, at LCM (Cost = $50,000, Market = $42,000		42,000
Prepaid Expenses		XXX
Total Current Assets		$X,XXX

Businesses can choose from several inventory costing methods such as LIFO, FIFO, weighted average, or specific identification. No matter which inventory costing method is used, the firm must apply LCM to that method. LCM is a requirement of GAAP.

¶707.03   FULL DISCLOSURE PRINCIPLE

The full disclosure principle requires that financial reports include sufficient information for readers to make informed decisions.

The **full disclosure principle** requires that a firm's financial reports include sufficient information for readers to make informed decisions. GAAP requires disclosure of relevant, reliable, and comparable financial information. With regard to inventory, the firm must report which inventory costing method is used. As you recall, the choice of accounting method for inventory can cause substantial differences in net income. For example, an investor may be choosing between two companies, one using FIFO and another using LIFO. The LIFO company shows a lower net income, but only because it uses the LIFO method. If the investor doesn't know this, he or she might invest in the wrong company. Exhibit 7.15 shows a note to the financial statements regarding inventory from JC Penney's annual report.

Exhibit 7.15 EXCERPT OF NOTE REGARDING MERCHANDISE INVENTORIES FROM J.C. PENNEY'S FINANCIAL STATEMENTS

Merchandise Inventories

Inventories for Department Stores and Catalog are valued primarily at the lower of cost (using the last-in, first-out or "LIFO" method) or market, determined by the retail method for department stores and average cost for catalog.

¶707.04   MATERIALITY IN ACCOUNTING

Materiality in accounting requires that a firm rigidly adheres to GAAP only for items that are significant or material to the firm.

The concept of **materiality in accounting** requires that a business rigidly adheres to GAAP only for items that are significant or material to the firm. For accounting purposes, the term "material" means that if the information were known, then it would change the decision of the reader, such as an investor or a lender. If an item is immaterial, then accountants do not have to meticulously follow GAAP. As a result, accountants can spend less time accounting for items that are immaterial and thereby reduce the cost of accounting.

One common application of the concept of materiality occurs when an accountant is trying to determine whether an asset should be capitalized as an asset and depreciated, or written off as an expense of doing business. Depreciation is the process of allocating an asset's cost to expense over the asset's estimated useful life. For example, a stapler that costs five dollars may be used on average for five years. Technically, according to GAAP, the stapler should be set up as an asset that incurs depreciation expense. However, because of the small and immaterial amount involved, the business will simply charge the entire $5 cost of the stapler to office supplies expense in the year the stapler is purchased, and will not record depreciation expense over the five-year useful life.

¶707.05

Comparability generally requires that an accounting procedure not be changed from one fiscal period to another.

COMPARABILITY

Comparability requires that companies apply the same accounting procedures and methods from one time period to the next. However, this does not preclude a business firm from ever changing how it accounts for an item. If a company can justify a reason for an accounting change, the company must disclose that the change was made. For example, a company might change from the FIFO inventory method to the LIFO method, with the justification that LIFO better reflects current expenses.

If a change from FIFO to LIFO is made, a company would disclose it on the financial statements. The note to the financial statements would indicate that the change from FIFO to LIFO has been made, why it was made, and how much it affected net income.

¶708

[?] Does the full disclosure principle play a role in your personal finances?

International Issues

LEARNING OBJECTIVE 8: Identify international accounting issues that managers must consider regarding inventory.

In Chapter 1 we discussed some of the general differences between US GAAP and IFRS. One specific difference relates to inventory. In the United States, companies may use FIFO, LIFO, or weighted average method of inventory costing. In countries where IFRS has been adopted, LIFO is not acceptable. Nearly every nation allows FIFO and the weighted average method.

Additionally, in some cases the market value used for lower of cost or market under IFRS will differ from the value used under U.S. GAAP. Both standards do require companies to record inventory on the balance sheet at the lower of cost or market, but the actual value used could be different under the two sets of standards.

[?] For the average investor who wants to invest in an internationally diversified portfolio of stocks, what is the benefit of having all companies in the world use International Financial Reporting Standards?

FOCUS ON GLOBAL TRADE

Walmart's International Suppliers

Walmart has more than 3,200 facilities in the United States and more than 1,100 in Mexico, Japan, Puerto Rico, Canada, Argentina, Brazil, China, Korea, Germany and the United Kingdom. How does Walmart effectively acquire inventory for this widespread array of stores? Walmart imports direct merchandise from over 64 countries. The company's list of suppliers is lengthy and growing. Besides requiring a particular quality of merchandise, Walmart calls for conformity by its suppliers to certain ethical standards and business practices as set forth in its company policy. For example, employees of suppliers must meet the age requirements, receive minimum wage and overtime compensation, and be granted at least one day off per week.

Source: *www.walmartstores.com*

¶709

Concluding Remarks

This chapter opened with the question of how the accountants at Walmart determine the cost of goods sold and the cost of inventory left on the shelves, since the cost of an item can vary depending on when it was purchased. This led to a discussion of inventory costing methods, with each method resulting in different amounts for cost of goods sold and ending inventory. Besides determining the cost of inventory, you learned about other aspects of inventory that are important to the merchandising firm, such as evaluating how much inventory to purchase. Now that you know how to account for inventory items, it's time to look at the larger assets owned by a company, such as buildings and equipment. This is the topic of the next chapter.

¶710

Chapter Review

LEARNING OBJECTIVE 1

Describe why people within and outside a merchandising firm are interested in cost of goods sold and inventory amounts.

Accounting for cost of goods sold and inventory is relevant to many people within a merchandising firm. In the marketing department, buyers use inventory records to know which products are selling, which need restocking, and which products should be discontinued due to low sales. Since the cost of goods sold is the major expense of the merchandising firm, top management is keenly attentive to its fluctuations. To maintain profits, management must keep a constant check on costs. Because the valuation of inventory and the cost of goods sold affects net income, investors and lenders are also interested in the these costs.

LEARNING OBJECTIVE 2

Define inventory.

Inventory includes all of the goods or products that are available for sale to customers. Merchandise inventory, referred to simply as inventory, includes items such as clothing at JC Penney, books at Barnes and Noble, and movies at Blockbuster. Since the cost of inventory is a merchandising firm's biggest expense, keeping track of inventory is critical to successful business operations.

LEARNING OBJECTIVE 3

Explain how inventory and cost of goods sold affect income.

The cost of the inventory that a company sells to its customers is called cost of goods sold. Cost of goods sold = Beginning inventory + Purchases − Ending inventory. In calculating net income on the income statement, cost of goods sold is subtracted from sales revenue. For merchandising firms, cost of goods sold is usually the biggest expense on the income statement.

Determining the cost per unit of inventory is not as straightforward as determining the quantity. This is because inventory may be purchased at different prices throughout the year. Consequently, accountants must determine which unit costs are assigned to cost of goods sold on the income statement and which unit costs are assigned to ending inventory on the balance sheet.

LEARNING OBJECTIVE 4

Describe how managers use different inventory costing methods to achieve profit, tax, and cash flow goals.

More than one accounting method is available for determining the cost of goods sold on the income statement and the ending inventory on the balance sheet. The four inventory costing methods are: Specific Identification Method; First-In, First-Out (FIFO) Method; Last-In, First-Out (LIFO) Method; and Weighted Average Method.

The specific identification method requires a company to keep track of the cost of individual inventory items. Under the LIFO (last-in, first-out) method, the last costs into inventory are the first costs out to costs of goods sold. Under FIFO (first-in, first-out), the first costs into inventory are the first costs out to cost of goods sold. The weighted average method is based on the weighted average cost of all inventory units available for sale during the period.

LEARNING OBJECTIVE 5

Contrast the periodic and perpetual systems of accounting for inventory.

When a company waits until the end of the period to ascertain the amount of ending inventory, this is known as the "periodic inventory system." Some companies prefer to keep count of inventory in a continuous fashion; this is known as a "perpetual inventory system." When a unit is sold in a perpetual inventory system, the inventory records are immediately updated. Using either inventory system, financial ratio analysis is an effective tool that helps managers keep track of inventory and spot potential problems.

LEARNING OBJECTIVE 6

Describe various analysis tools and inventory types that can be used to better track and manage inventory.

Managers use a variety of tools and techniques to evaluate inventory. To compute the amount of inventory to purchase, use the following formula: (Budgeted cost of goods sold + Ending inventory) – Beginning inventory. To measure how fast inventory is selling, the inventory turnover rate is measured. Gross profit margin helps management indicate the business firm's capacity to sell its inventory at a profit. The just-in-time inventory system purchases inventory just as the company needs it, thus enabling a company to minimize costs associated with keeping inventory on hand.

LEARNING OBJECTIVE 7

Explain the link between inventory and the accounting concepts of neutrality, lower of cost or market, full disclosure, materiality, and comparability.

Accounting for business transactions, including inventory transactions, must follow generally accepted accounting principles. Five *concepts* that pertain to inventory include: neutrality, lower of cost or market, full disclosure, materiality, and comparability. Neutrality requires financial data to be free from bias. Specifically, if a company is presented with two accounting alternatives it should pick the alternative that most fairly represents its financial position. The temptation for some companies is to select the alternative that makes its financial statements look the most favorable, but this would be inappropriate because of neutrality and faithful representation. The accounting concept of lower of cost or market mandates that inventory be shown on the financial statements at the lower of its historical cost or its market value. The full disclosure principle requires that a business firm's financial reports include sufficient information for readers to make informed decisions about the firm. The concept of materiality requires that a business firm rigidly adhere to GAAP only for items that are significant to the firm, but may deviate from GAAP for insignificant items. The characteristic of comparability requires that companies apply the same accounting procedures and methods from one time period to the next.

LEARNING OBJECTIVE 8

Identify international accounting issues that managers must consider regarding inventory.

In the United States, companies may use FIFO, LIFO, or weighted average method of inventory costing. In countries where IFRS has been adopted, however, LIFO is not acceptable. Nearly every nation allows FIFO and the weighted average method. This is one specific difference between IFRS and U.S. GAAP.

¶711

Glossary

Comparability

Comparability is a qualitative characteristic which states that financial statements are better when companies apply the same accounting procedures and methods from one time period to the next.

Ending inventory

Ending inventory is the merchandise on hand at the end of an accounting period.

Financial ratio

A financial ratio shows the proportionate value of a financial statement item relative to other items.

First-in, first-out (FIFO) method

Using the first-in, first-out (FIFO) inventory costing method, the cost of the *first* inventory unit is assumed to be the *first* cost transferred out to cost of goods sold.

FOB destination

FOB destination indicates that the seller pays for delivery of the merchandise to its destination.

FOB shipping point

FOB shipping point indicates the seller puts the product "free on board" at the point of origin; the seller does not pay any transportation costs. The buyer pays for delivery of the merchandise.

Full disclosure principle

The full disclosure principle requires that a business firm's financial reports include sufficient information for readers to make informed decisions about the firm.

Gross margin

Gross margin, also called "gross profit," is the amount by which sales revenue exceeds cost of goods.

Gross margin method

The gross margin method, also called the "gross profit method," is an effective approach to estimate the cost of ending inventory.

Gross profit

Gross profit, also called "gross margin," is the amount by which sales revenue exceeds cost of goods.

Gross profit margin

Gross profit margin, also called "gross profit percentage," is the ratio of gross profit to net sales revenue.

Gross profit method

The gross profit method, also called the "gross margin method," is an effective approach to estimate the cost of ending inventory. Estimated ending inventory = (beginning inventory + purchases) – (net sales revenue – estimated gross profit).

Gross profit percentage

Gross profit percentage, also called "gross profit margin," is the ratio of gross profit to net sales revenue.

Inventory

Merchandise inventory includes all of the assets held for sale to customers in the continuing operations of the business.

Inventory turnover

Inventory turnover is the ratio of cost of goods sold to average inventory; it is a measure of how fast inventory is selling.

Just-in-time inventory

The just-in-time inventory system purchases inventory just as the company or consumer needs it. This system can reduce costs associated with inventory.

Last-in, first-out (LIFO) method

Using the last-in, first-out (LIFO) inventory costing method, the cost of the *last* inventory unit is assumed to be the *first* cost transferred out to cost of goods sold.

LIFO liquidation

LIFO liquidation occurs when LIFO is used and inventory on hand declines below the quantity of the prior period.

Lower of cost or market

The accounting concept of lower of cost or market mandates that inventory be shown on the financial statements at the lower of its historical cost or its market value.

Materiality in accounting

The concept of materiality in accounting requires that a business firm rigidly adheres to GAAP only for items that are significant to the firm, but may deviate from GAAP for insignificant items.

Neutrality

Neutrality requires companies to remain unbiased when making decisions related to presenting financial data. Neutrality is a component of faithful representation.

Periodic inventory system

A company uses the periodic inventory system when it waits until the end of the period to ascertain the amount of ending inventory by multiplying the quantity of units by their cost per unit.

Perpetual inventory system

A company uses the perpetual inventory system when it keeps count of inventory in a continuous fashion. When a unit is sold, the inventory records are immediately updated.

Purchase allowance

A purchase allowance is a reduction in the cost of purchases, which occurs when the seller grants the buyer a deduction from the amount owed.

Purchase return

A purchase return is a reduction in the cost of purchases, which occurs when the buyer returns products to the seller.

Sales allowance

A sales allowance is a deduction awarded by the seller to the buyer on the amount owed.

Sales return

If a buyer returns products to the seller, the seller records this as a sales return.

Specific identification method

The specific identification method is a type of inventory costing in which inventory is valued according to the specific cost that can be identified for each inventory unit.

Weighted average method

Using the weighted average inventory costing method, inventory value is based on the weighted average cost of all inventory units available for sale during the period.

Chapter Assignments

QUESTIONS

1. **[Obj. 1]** What is the function of a merchandising firm?

2. **[Obj. 2]** What is inventory?

3. **[Obj. 2]** Describe the difference between inventory at a manufacturing firm and inventory at a retail firm, also called a "merchandising firm."

4. **[Obj. 3]** What three specific amounts are used to calculate cost of goods sold?

5. **[Obj. 3]** Describe how cost of goods sold, operating expenses, and non-operating expenses are used to calculate net income.

6. **[Obj. 4]** What are the four inventory costing methods? Briefly describe how the specific identification method differs from the other three methods.

7. **[Obj. 4]** Explain how the FIFO inventory method works.

8. **[Obj. 4]** Explain how the LIFO inventory method works.

9. **[Obj. 4]** Explain how the weighted average inventory method works.

10. **[Obj. 4]** Which inventory method provides a more realistic income statement presentation? Which inventory method gives a better balance sheet presentation?

11. **[Obj. 4]** In deciding which method to use for accounting for inventory, what is the guiding ethical principle that managers should follow?

12. **[Obj. 4]** How can the inventory method be used to lower taxes?

13. **[Obj. 4]** What is LIFO liquidation? How does LIFO liquidation affect taxes?

14. **[Obj. 4]** Why should managers keep track of inventory?

15. **[Obj. 4]** Describe the three types of business firms and corresponding types of inventory.

16. **[Obj. 5]** Contrast the periodic and perpetual inventory systems.

17. **[Obj. 5]** Describe a type of firm in which the periodic inventory system might be preferred.

18. **[Obj. 5]** Describe a type of firm in which the perpetual inventory system might be preferred.

19. **[Obj. 6]** What are two tools managers can use to keep track of inventory?

20. **[Obj. 6]** What is just-in-time inventory? What are the benefits and potential hazards?

21. **[Obj. 6]** What information is needed to estimate ending inventory using the gross profit method?

22. **[Obj. 6]** What is the inventory turnover ratio?

23. **[Obj. 6]** What is a gross profit margin?

24. **[Obj. 7]** Describe the following five accounting concepts:
    a. Neutrality
    b. Lower of cost or market
    c. Full disclosure
    d. Materiality
    e. Comparability

25. **[Obj. 8]** Compare the U.S. GAAP and IFRS with regard to use of FIFO, LIFO, and weighted average methods of accounting for inventory.

26. **[Obj. 8]** Do international accounting standards have similarities to U.S. inventory accounting methods, regarding lower of cost or market?

SHORT EXERCISES – SET A

Building Accounting Skills

1. **[Obj. 3]** Computing Purchases Amount. Assume that cost of goods sold is $12,000, beginning inventory is $3,000, and ending inventory is $2,700. Compute the amount of purchases.

2. **[Obj. 3]** Computing Purchases Amount. Assume that cost of goods sold is $45,000, beginning inventory is $10,000, and ending inventory is $5,000. Compute the amount of purchases.

3. **[Obj. 3]** Accounting for Sales on Income Statement: Suppose JC Penney buys 10 men's suits for $100 each. The balance sheet shows 2 suits left in inventory and the income statement shows 8 suits were sold at $200 each. How would the sale of the suits be accounted for on the income statement? Prepare a partial income statement showing this. (**Hint:** Your income statement should include sales revenue, cost of goods sold, and gross profit.)

4. **[Obj. 3]** Calculating Cost of Goods Sold: Given the following information, calculate cost of goods sold.

Beginning inventory (4 units @ $100 each)	$400
Ending inventory (6 units @ $100 each)	600
Purchases (30 units @ $100 each)	3,000

5. **[Obj. 3]** Calculating Cost of Goods Sold: Same as previous problem, except change ending inventory from 6 units to 5 units; and change purchases from 30 units to 25 units.

6. **[Obj. 5]** Journal Entries with Perpetual Inventory System: Make journal entries for the following transactions using the perpetual inventory system.
   a. Purchase 30 units of inventory at $50 each.
   b. Sale of 10 units, sale price of $80 each and cost of $50 each.

7. **[Obj. 5]** Journal Entries with Periodic Inventory System: Make journal entries for the following transactions using the periodic system.
   a. Purchase 20 units of inventory at $200 each.
   b. Sale of 12 units at $300 each.

8. **[Obj. 5]** Perpetual Inventory System: What two accounts are affected by a purchase of inventory using the perpetual system?

9. **[Obj. 6]** Inventory Formula: What is the formula for determining how much inventory to purchase?

10. **[Obj. 6]** Calculating Gross Profit Margin: Suppose Kroger has a gross profit of $12 million and net sales revenue of $240 million. What is Kroger's gross profit margin?

SHORT EXERCISES – SET B

Building Accounting Skills

1. **[Obj. 3]** Computing Purchases Amount. Assume that cost of goods sold is $17,000, beginning inventory is $5,000, and ending inventory is $4,200. Compute the amount of purchases.

2. **[Obj. 3]** Computing Purchases Amount. Assume that cost of goods sold is $50,000, beginning inventory is $9,000, and ending inventory is $5,000. Compute the amount of purchases.

3. **[Obj. 3]** Accounting for Sales on Income Statement: Suppose Gatsby Tuxedos buys 10 tuxedos for $200 each. The balance sheet shows 2 tuxedos left in inventory and the income statement shows 8 tuxedos were sold at $400 each. How would the sale of the suits be accounted for on the income statement? Prepare a partial income statement showing this. (**Hint:** Your income statement should include sales revenue, cost of goods sold, and gross profit.)

4. **[Obj. 3]** Calculating Cost of Goods Sold: Given the following information, calculate cost of goods sold.

Beginning inventory (4 units @ $50 each)	$200
Ending inventory (6 units @ $50 each)	300
Purchases (30 units @ $50 each)	1,500

5. **[Obj. 3]** Calculating Cost of Goods Sold: Same as previous problem, except change ending inventory from 6 units to 5 units; and change purchases from 30 units to 25 units.

6. **[Obj. 5]** Journal Entries with Perpetual Inventory System: Make journal entries for the following transactions using the perpetual inventory system.
   a. Purchase 30 units of inventory at $100 each.
   b. Sale of 10 units, sale price of $160 each and cost of $100 each.

7. **[Obj. 5]** Journal Entries with Periodic Inventory System: Make journal entries for the following transactions using the periodic system.
   a. Purchase 200 units of inventory at $5 each.
   b. Sale of 120 units at $8 each.

8. **[Obj. 5]** Periodic Inventory System: What two accounts are affected by a purchase of inventory using the periodic system?

9. **[Obj. 6]** Calculating Gross Profit Margin: Suppose Albertson's Grocery has a gross profit of $16 million and net sales revenue of $640 million. What is Albertson's gross profit margin?

PROBLEMS – SET A

Applying Accounting Knowledge

1. **[Obj. 3]** Preparing an Income Statement: Suppose Hasbro Company has the following income statement amounts for the year ended December 31, 20Y1.

	($ Millions)
Net sales	$345
Cost of goods sold	206
Operating expenses	57
Non-operating expenses	12

Required:
a. Prepare an income statement in good form.
b. Evaluate: Would you characterize Hasbro's financial performance as favorable or unfavorable?

2. **[Obj. 3]** Preparing an Income Statement: Suppose Home Depot has the following income statement amounts for the year ended December 31, 20Y1.

	($ Millions)
Net sales	$2,440
Cost of goods sold	1,720
Operating expenses	330
Non-operating expenses	115

Required:
a. Prepare an income statement in good form.
b. Evaluate: Suppose that Home Depot's competitor, Lowe's, reported its cost of goods sold at 60% of sales. How does cost of goods at Home Depot compare to cost of goods at Lowe's? What are the potential benefits and pitfalls if a company reduces its cost of goods sold?

3. **[Obj. 3 & 4]** Comparing Different Inventory Methods: Suppose Lowe's Corporation has the following inventory and purchase information.

Beginning inventory (20 units @ $15 each)	$300
Purchases:	
No. 1 (20 units @ $32 each)	640
No. 2 (20 units @ $40 each)	800
Ending inventory of 15 units.	

Required:
a. Compute cost of goods available for sale.
b. Compute cost of goods sold under FIFO, LIFO, and weighted average.
c. Evaluate: Assuming inventory costs are rising, which inventory costing method do you recommend using and why?

4. **[Obj. 3 & 4]** Comparing Different Inventory Methods: Same as previous problem, except ending inventory has been changed. Suppose Lowe's Corporation has the following inventory and purchase information.

Beginning inventory (20 units @ $15 each)	$300
Purchases:	
No. 1 (20 units @ $32 each)	640
No. 2 (20 units @ $40 each)	800
Ending inventory of 10 units.	

Required:
a. Compute cost of goods available for sale.
b. Compute cost of goods sold under FIFO, LIFO, and weighted average.
c. Evaluate: Assuming inventory costs are rising, which inventory costing method do you recommend using and why?

5. **[Obj. 6]** Calculating Inventory Turnover Ratio: The following is inventory information for two separate companies.

	Express Manufacturing Co. ($ Millions)	Major Builders, Inc. ($ Millions)
Beginning inventory	$75	$15
Ending inventory	25	45
Cost of goods sold	500	900

Required:
a. Calculate the inventory turnover ratio for each company.
b. Evaluate: Which company turns its inventory over faster? What are the ramifications of this?

6. **[Obj. 6]** Calculating Inventory Turnover Ratio: The following is inventory information for two separate companies.

	Sofa Haven ($ Millions)	Mattresses & More ($ Millions)
Beginning inventory	$21	$37
Ending inventory	19	43
Cost of goods sold	400	600

Required:
a. Calculate the inventory turnover ratio for each company.
b. Evaluate: Which company turns its inventory over faster? What are the ramifications of this?

7. **[Obj. 6]** Estimating Ending Inventory: Suppose a flood completely destroyed the ending inventory at Tri-State Supply Company. The company needs to estimate the amount of inventory destroyed in order to file an insurance claim.

Beginning inventory	$77,000
Purchases	656,000
Net sales revenue	824,000
Estimated gross profit	181,000

Required: Use the gross profit method to estimate Tri-State's ending inventory.

8. **[Obj. 6]** Estimating Ending Inventory: Same as previous problem except change purchases and estimated gross profit have been changed. Suppose a flood completely destroyed the ending inventory at Tri-State Supply Company. The company needs to estimate the amount of inventory destroyed in order to file an insurance claim.

Beginning inventory	$77,000
Purchases	696,000
Net sales revenue	824,000
Estimated gross profit	161,000

Required: Use the gross profit method to estimate Tri-State's ending inventory.

9. **[Obj. 3 & 7]** Preparing Partial Income Statement: The following information is for Dilles Department Store, from the year ended December 31, 20Y1.

	($ Thousands)
Sales revenue	$360,000
Beginning inventory	94,000
Purchases	212,000
Ending inventory	124,000

Required:
a. Prepare a partial income statement for Dilles Department Store, starting with sales revenue and ending with gross profit.
b. Evaluate: Suppose that Dilles' competitor, Macy's, reported its cost of goods sold at 50% of sales. How does cost of goods sold at Dilles compare to cost of goods sold at Macy's? What are the potential benefits and pitfalls if a company reduces its cost of goods sold?

10. **[Obj. 3 & 7]** Preparing Partial Income Statement: The following information is for Dilles Department Store, from the year ended December 31, 20Y2.

	($ Thousands)
Sales revenue	$415,000
Beginning inventory	94,000
Purchases	312,000
Ending inventory	124,000

Required:
a. Prepare a partial income statement for Dilles Department Store, starting with sales revenue and ending with gross profit.
b. Evaluate: Dilles' cost of goods increased from last year. Suppose that Dilles' competitor, Macy's, reported its cost of goods sold at 50% of sales. How does cost of goods sold at Dilles compare to cost of goods sold at Macy's? What actions might management take in order to offset the increase in the cost of goods sold?

PROBLEMS – SET B

Applying Accounting Knowledge

1. **[Obj. 3]** Preparing an Income Statement: Suppose Mattel, Inc. has the following income statement amounts for the year ended December 31, 20Y1.

	($ Millions)
Net sales	$690
Cost of goods sold	412
Operating expenses	114
Non-operating expenses	24

Required:
a. Prepare an income statement in good form.
b. Evaluate: Would you characterize Mattel's financial performance as favorable or unfavorable?

2. **[Obj. 3]** Preparing an Income Statement: Suppose Target has the following income statement amounts for the year ended December 31, 20Y1.

	($ Millions)
Net sales	$4,880
Cost of goods sold	3,440
Operating expenses	660
Non-operating expenses	230

Required:
a. Prepare an income statement in good form.
b. Evaluate: Suppose that Target's competitor, K-Mart, reported its cost of goods sold at 61% of sales. How does cost of goods sold at Target compare to cost of goods sold at K-Mart? What are the potential benefits and pitfalls if a company reduces its cost of goods sold?

3. **[Obj. 3 & 4]** Comparing Different Inventory Methods: Suppose Walmart Corporation has the following inventory and purchase information.

Beginning inventory (200 units @ $15 each)	$3,000
Purchases:	
No. 1 (200 units @ $32 each)	6,400
No. 2 (200 units @ $40 each)	8,000
Ending inventory of 150 units.	

Required:
a. Compute cost of goods available for sale.
b. Compute cost of goods sold under FIFO, LIFO, and weighted average.
c. Evaluate: Assuming inventory costs are rising, which inventory costing method do you recommend using and why?

4. **[Obj. 3 & 4]** Comparing Different Inventory Methods: Same as previous problem regarding Walmart, except ending inventory has been changed. Suppose Walmart Corporation has the following inventory and purchase information.

Beginning inventory (200 units @ $15 each)	$3,000
Purchases:	
No. 1 (200 units @ $32 each)	6,400
No. 2 (200 units @ $40 each)	8,000
Ending inventory of 100 units.	

Required:
a. Compute cost of goods available for sale.
b. Compute cost of goods sold under FIFO, LIFO, and weighted average.
c. Evaluate: Assuming inventory costs are rising, which inventory costing method do you recommend using and why?

5. **[Obj. 6]** Calculating Inventory Turnover Ratio: The following is inventory information for two separate companies.

	Dollar King ($ Thousands)	Big Buck ($ Thousands)
Beginning inventory	$35	$18
Ending inventory	15	22
Cost of goods sold	250	400

Required:

a. Calculate the inventory turnover ratio for each company.

b. Evaluate: Which company turns its inventory over faster? What are the ramifications of this?

6. **[Obj. 6]** Calculating Inventory Turnover Ratio: The following is inventory information for two separate companies.

	Game Stop ($ Millions)	Bath & Body ($ Millions)
Beginning inventory	$42	$74
Ending inventory	38	86
Cost of goods sold	800	400

Required:

a. Calculate the inventory turnover ratio for each company.

b. Evaluate: Which company turns its inventory over faster? What are the ramifications of this?

7. **[Obj. 6]** Estimating Ending Inventory: Suppose a flood completely destroyed the ending inventory of your company. You need to estimate the amount of inventory destroyed in order to file an insurance claim.

Beginning inventory	$38,500
Purchases	328,000
Net sales revenue	412,000
Estimated gross profit	90,500

Required: Use the gross profit method to estimate Tri-State's ending inventory.

8. **[Obj. 6]** Estimating Ending Inventory: Same as previous problem except purchases and estimated gross profit have been changed. Suppose a flood completely destroyed the ending inventory of your company. You need to estimate the amount of inventory destroyed in order to file an insurance claim.

Beginning inventory	$38,500
Purchases	348,000
Net sales revenue	412,000
Estimated gross profit	80,500

Required: Use the gross profit method to estimate Tri-State's ending inventory.

9. **[Obj. 3 & 7]** Preparing Partial Income Statement: The following information is for Macy's Department Store, from the year ended December 31, 20Y1.

	($ Thousands)
Sales revenue	$720,000
Beginning inventory	188,000
Purchases	424,000
Ending inventory	248,000

Required:

a. Prepare a partial income statement for Macy's Department Store, starting with sales revenue and ending with gross profit.

b. Evaluate: Suppose that Macy's competitor, Neiman Marcus, reported its cost of goods sold at 50% of sales. How does cost of goods sold at Macy's compare to cost of goods sold at Neiman Marcus? What are the potential benefits and pitfalls if a company reduces its cost of goods sold?

10. **[Obj. 3 & 7]** Preparing Partial Income Statement: The following information is for Macy's Department Store, from the year ended December 31, 20Y2.

	($ Thousands)
Sales revenue	$830,000
Beginning inventory	188,000
Purchases	624,000
Ending inventory	248,000

Required:

a. Prepare a partial income statement for Macy's Department Store, starting with sales revenue and ending with gross profit.

b. Evaluate: Macy's cost of goods increased from last year. Suppose that Macy's competitor, Neiman Marcus, reported its cost of goods sold at 50% of sales. How does cost of goods sold at Macy's compare to cost of goods sold at Neiman Marcus? What actions might management take in order to offset the increase in the cost of goods sold?

CROSS-FUNCTIONAL PERSPECTIVES

Discussion Questions

1. **[Obj. 3]** Give examples of how information regarding cost of goods sold and inventory may be used by managers in the marketing department of a merchandising firm.

2. **[Obj. 3]** Why is top management in a merchandising firm attentive to fluctuations in cost of goods sold? What actions might be taken in order to offset an increase in the cost of goods sold?

3. **[Obj. 4]** FIFO is used by 44 percent of business firms. Explain why stockholders may have an influence on a company's choice to use FIFO rather than LIFO or weighted average.

4. **[Obj. 6]** Besides accountants, who within a firm is interested in the inventory turnover ratio?

5. **[Obj. 6]** Besides accountants, who within a firm is interested in the gross profit margin and why?

Cross-Functional Case: Inventory Costing Quandary

Walmart divides its many outlets into three operating segments: Walmart Stores, Sam's Club, and International. The Walmart Stores and Sam's Club segments include domestic units only. These segments use different inventory costing methods to suit their particular needs. The needs of the segments may differ for reasons such as the economic environment, higher turnover of inventory, or stocking more products with low profit margins, such as food items.

The method of inventory costing affects the value of ending inventory, cost of goods sold, gross profit, and net income. People representing various functions of the firm have diverse goals regarding these financial figures. A primary goal of accounting is to supply financial statements that provide an accurate understanding of the company's financial situation and help people make effective decisions. LIFO leads to the most realistic income statement. LIFO uses recent inventory costs in computing cost of goods sold, thus it gives a better picture of what it would actually cost to replace the inventory that was sold. However, FIFO leads to the most realistic balance sheet because it puts recent inventory costs under ending inventory, providing a better picture of what's in stock.

One dilemma for management in selecting an inventory method is determining a priority between reducing income tax payments or showing a higher profit. During a time of rising prices, LIFO produces lower income tax payments and FIFO produces higher profit. The weighted average method results in amounts between FIFO and LIFO

Of course, stockholders prefer to maximize net income because stock prices will usually increase. During a period of rising prices, FIFO results in the highest net income. The choice of inventory costing method requires a consideration of the trade-offs and goals at hand.

Required: For the Walmart Stores segment only, choose a method of inventory costing: LIFO, FIFO, or weighted average. From the perspective of each of the following, state the pros and cons of the method you choose.
a. Stockholder
b. Owner
c. Top management
d. Accountant

EXCEL ASSIGNMENTS

1. **[Obj. 3]** Calculating Cost of Goods Sold: The input area of your worksheet should include beginning inventory, purchases, and ending inventory. The output area should include beginning inventory, purchases, cost of goods available for sale, ending inventory, and cost of goods sold. Set up the worksheet so that the amounts in the output area are automatically derived from amounts in the input area.

   Use the following information:

Beginning inventory	$500
Ending inventory	200
Purchases	2,700

   Required: Create an Excel spreadsheet to calculate cost of goods sold. Print your worksheet.

2. **[Obj. 3]** Calculating Cost of Goods Sold: Same as previous assignment except use the following information:

Beginning inventory	$2,200
Ending inventory	6,400
Purchases	33,100

   Required: Create an Excel spreadsheet to calculate cost of goods sold. Print your worksheet.

3. **[Obj. 3]** Preparing an Income Statement: In the input area of your worksheet, include the four items listed below. The output area should contain: net sales, cost of goods sold, gross profit, operating expenses, operating income, non-operating expenses, and net income. The output area should be formula-driven based on values in the input area. Suppose Motorola Corporation has the following income statement amounts for the year ended January 31, 20Y1:

	($ millions)
Net sales	$892
Cost of goods sold	578
Operating expenses	194
Non-operating expenses	39

Required: Prepare an income statement for Motorola using Excel. Print your worksheet.

4. **[Obj. 3]** Preparing an Income Statement: Same as previous assignment, except use the following amounts:

	($ millions)
Net sales	$297
Cost of goods sold	159
Operating expenses	72
Non-operating expenses	32

Required: Prepare an income statement for Motorola using Excel. Print your worksheet.

5. **[Obj. 3 & 4]** Computing Cost of Goods Sold Using Different Inventory Methods: Design an Excel worksheet to carry out Problem 3 in Set A (from the previous section entitled "Problems"). In the input area of your worksheet, include: beginning inventory, purchases, ending inventory using FIFO, ending inventory using LIFO, and ending inventory using weighted average.

Beginning inventory (20 units @ $15 each)	$300
Purchases:	
No. 1 (20 units @ $32 each)	640
No. 2 (20 units @ $40 each)	800
Ending inventory of 15 units.	

Required:
a. Compute cost of goods available for sale.
b. Compute cost of goods sold under FIFO, LIFO, and weighted average. Print your worksheet.

6. **[Obj. 3 & 4]** Computing Cost of Goods Sold Using Different Inventory Methods: Design an Excel worksheet to carry out Problem 4 in Set A (from the previous section entitled "Problems"). In the input area of your worksheet, include: beginning inventory, purchases, ending inventory using FIFO, ending inventory using LIFO, and ending inventory using weighted average.

Beginning inventory (20 units @ $15 each)	$300
Purchases:	
No. 1 (20 units @ $32 each)	640
No. 2 (20 units @ $40 each)	800
Ending inventory of 10 units.	

Required:
a. Compute cost of goods available for sale.
b. Compute cost of goods sold under FIFO, LIFO, and weighted average. Print your worksheet.

7. **[Obj. 6]** Estimating Ending Inventory: Suppose a fire completely destroyed the ending inventory at AAA Manufacturing Company. The company needs to estimate the amount of inventory destroyed to file an insurance claim. Use the information below in the input area of your worksheet and include the following in the output area: Beginning Inventory, Purchases, Cost of Goods Available for Sale, Net Sales Revenue, Estimated Gross Profit, Estimated Cost of Goods Sold, and Estimated Ending Inventory.

	($ Thousands)
Beginning Inventory	$56,200
Purchases	123,700
Net Sales Revenue	278,440
Estimated Gross Profit	136,000

Required: Prepare an Excel worksheet to estimate ending inventory for AAA Manufacturing Company. Print your worksheet.

8. **[Obj. 6]** Estimating Ending Inventory: Same as previous Excel assignment except change purchases to $140 million and estimated gross profit to $156 million.

   Required: Prepare an Excel worksheet to estimate ending inventory for AAA Manufacturing Company. Print your worksheet.

9. **[Obj. 3 & 7]** Preparing Partial Income Statement: In preparing Kroger's income statement, the input area of your worksheet should include the four items listed below. The output area should include a partial income statement in good form, starting with sales revenue and ending with gross profit. The following information is for Kroger's Grocery Store from the year ended December 31, 20Y1.

	($ Thousands)
Sales Revenue	$169,900
Beginning Inventory	18,500
Purchases	124,300
Ending Inventory	31,000

   Required: Prepare a partial income statement for Kroger's Grocery Store, starting with sales revenue and ending with gross profit. Print your worksheet.

10. **[Obj. 3 & 7]** Preparing Partial Income Statement: Same as previous Excel assignment except change sales revenue to $527 million and purchases to $375 million.

    Required: Prepare a partial income statement for Kruger's Grocery Store, starting with sales revenue and ending with gross profit. Print your worksheet.

WEB ASSIGNMENTS

1. **[Obj. 3]** Go to the website of a major retail corporation such as JC Penney, and determine the proportion of cost of goods sold to sales. For example, JC Penney's cost of goods sold was 69 percent of sales ($22,573,000,000 / $32,347,000,000) at the time of this writing.

2. **[Obj. 4]** Go to the website of a major retail corporation such as JC Penney, and determine what accounting method is used for inventory. **Hint:** Look in the notes to the financial statements.

3. **[All Obj.]** Go to the website for Walmart or do a search on Google to find an accounting related news item pertaining to Walmart. Give a one- paragraph summary of it.

4. **[Career]** Go to the website for Walmart. What accounting jobs are currently available within the company?

5. **[Ethics]** The principles and practices used by Sam Walton are still being used in Walmart stores today. Go to the website for Walmart or do a search on Google for Sam Walton's, "Three Basic Beliefs;" briefly describe them.

¶713

Test Prepper

Use this sample test to gauge your comprehension of the chapter material.

True/False Questions

__ 1. The cost of the inventory that a company sells to its customers is called "cost of goods sold."

__ 2. Net profit is the difference between net sales and cost of goods sold.

__ 3. Customers determine which unit costs are assigned to cost of goods sold and which unit costs are assigned to ending inventory.

__ 4. When the cost of inventory is changing, the various inventory costing methods can result in different cost of goods sold and ending inventory amounts.

__ 5. With LIFO, the cost of the units remaining in ending inventory is based on the cost of the last units purchased.

__ 6. When a unit is sold in a periodic inventory system, the inventory records are immediately updated.

__ 7. Gross profit margin is the ratio of gross profit to net sales revenue.

__ 8. The accounting concept of lower of cost or market mandates that inventory be shown on the financial statements at the higher of its historical cost or its market value.

__ 9. Comparability requires that companies apply the same accounting procedures and methods from one time period to the next.

__ 10. Nearly every nation allows FIFO and the weighted average method.

Multiple-Choice Questions

__ 1. If Dell Computer Company starts the year with $20 million of inventory, ends the year with $10 million of inventory, and has $450 million of cost of goods sold, what is Dell's inventory turnover ratio?
a. 10
b. 20
c. 22.5
d. 30
e. 45

__ 2. Which inventory costing method uses the cost of the first inventory unit as the first cost to be transferred out to cost of goods sold?
a. specific identification method
b. first-in, first-out (FIFO) method
c. last-in, first-out (LIFO) method
d. weighted average method
e. random access method

__ 3. During periods of rising inventory costs, which inventory costing method results in the highest gross profit, thus making net income higher?
a. specific identification method
b. first-in, first-out (FIFO) method
c. last-in, first-out (LIFO) method
d. weighted average method
e. random access method

__ 4. During periods of rising inventory costs, which inventory costing method results in the lowest gross profit, thus making net income lower?
a. specific identification method
b. first-in, first-out (FIFO) method
c. last-in, first-out (LIFO) method
d. weighted average method
e. perpetual inventory method

__ 5. Which inventory system waits until the end of the period to ascertain the amount of ending inventory?
   a. periodic inventory system
   b. perpetual inventory system
   c. ending inventory system
   d. random access inventory system
   e. exit inventory system

__ 6. Which of the following is a measure of how fast inventory is selling?
   a. gross profit percentage
   b. gross profit margin
   c. just-in-time inventory
   d. inventory turnover ratio
   e. sales turnover ratio

__ 7. Which of the following statements is not true regarding neutrality?
   a. Requires that financial statements report amounts that fairly represent the company's financial position.
   b. Companies should be careful not to overstate assets.
   c. Companies should be careful not to understate liabilities.
   d. Assets and income are less likely to be overstated.
   e. Assets and income are more likely to be overstated.

__ 8. _____ typically refers to the cost of replacing the inventory at current prices.
   a. Market value
   b. Historical cost
   c. Neutrality
   d. Original cost
   e. Didactic inflation

__ 9. Which of the following concepts require that a business firm rigidly adheres to GAAP only for items that are significant to the firm?
   a. full disclosure principle
   b. neutrality
   c. materiality in accounting
   d. comparability
   e. concept of significance

__ 10. Which of the following concepts require that a business firm's financial reports include sufficient information for readers to make informed decisions about the firm?
   a. full disclosure principle
   b. neutrality
   c. materiality in accounting
   d. comparability
   e. concept of significance

8

Plant Assets, Intangibles, and Long-Term Investments

LEARNING OBJECTIVES

After studying Chapter 8, you should be able to do the following:

1. Describe the importance of long-term assets to people within and outside a business.
2. Report how different departments contribute to asset acquisition decisions.
3. Calculate the cost of a plant asset such as land, building, or equipment.
4. Describe how assets are depreciated using various depreciation methods.
5. Describe and record the disposal of plant assets.
6. Identify accounting issues pertaining to natural resources and depletion.
7. Identify types of intangible assets and account for amortization expense.
8. Describe the characteristics of long-term investments.

CHAPTER CONTENTS

FOCUS ON BUSINESS

Carmike Cinema: The Ultimate Movie-Going Experience

Stadium seating, high-backed chairs, wall-to-wall screens, and digital sound — the ultimate movie-going experience! Movie theaters across the country have undergone renovations so that they can provide a state-of-the-art experience to their customers. Carmike Cinema, Inc. is no exception. As one of the premier motion picture exhibitors in the United States, many of its 300+ theaters have undergone reconstruction.

When converting a theater to stadium style seating, what happens to the old seats? If Carmike sold the old seats, would they incur a gain or a loss on the sale? What is the book value for a theater seat? Now that the theater is enhanced with state-of-the-art features, how has the cost of the building changed? Accountants must deal with these issues. Thankfully, there are generally accepted accounting principles to help determine the cost of company assets. This chapter will delve into accounting for assets such as buildings and equipment.

Source: *Carmike.com*

¶801

Applications to People Within and Outside the Firm

A long-term asset is beneficial to a company for more than one year and is not intended for resale to customers.

LEARNING OBJECTIVE 1: Describe the importance of long-term assets to people within and outside a business.

Businesses have two basic types of assets: current assets and long-term assets. As you recall, current assets are those that will be used up, sold, or converted to cash within the year (or the normal operating cycle, if longer than one year). A **long-term asset** is beneficial to the operations of a firm for more than one year and is not intended for resale to customers. Consequently, business managers must be very careful to make good decisions regarding the amount and timing of purchases of long-term assets. Long-term assets include plant assets, intangibles, and long-term investments. Each of these will be discussed in this chapter.

¶801.01   INTERNAL USERS

To be able to produce automobiles, General Motors needs long-term assets such as manufacturing plants and robotic equipment. These assets are very expensive and, once acquired, are difficult to resell. Making correct decisions regarding the acquisition of long-term assets is a cross-functional process that involves several departments within the company. First, the marketing manager forecasts future sales based on marketing research. Next, the production department determines how much plant and equipment is necessary to produce the quantity of automobiles that marketing believes can be sold. Hiring plans for assembly line workers are formulated in the human resources department. Accountants keep track of the costs and expenses associated with long-term assets. Thus, all activities within a firm are connected in some way to long-term assets.

¶801.02   EXTERNAL USERS

Which of your possessions would be considered a long-term asset: car, computer, cell phone, or umbrella?

Just as internal managers make decisions regarding long-term assets, external users rely on the financial statements affected by these decisions. Investors are interested in a firm's plant assets, intangibles, and long-term investments, since these assets can be beneficial or detrimental to the future earnings of the company. A company improves its financial situation if it purchases the appropriate amount of plant assets and makes wise long-term investments. However, a company may experience financial difficulties due to poor long-term investment decisions or improper decisions regarding the purchase of plant assets. For example, Carmike Cinema once experienced financial difficulties when it borrowed money to build numerous theaters during a short period of time. The company was carrying too much debt due to its large investment in plant assets (i.e., buildings). Investors lost confidence in Carmike's ability to pay off its debt and make a profit; thus, Carmike's stock price dropped dramatically. Investors, as well as other people outside the firm, are keenly interested in long-term assets when judging the financial viability of a company.

¶802 Cross-Functional Issues Regarding Asset Purchases

LEARNING OBJECTIVE 2: Report how different departments contribute to asset acquisition decisions.

When a company embarks upon the process of determining which plant assets are necessary to carry out company operations, the decision involves cross-functional participation. Various departments within the company contribute information such as current and future needs of the company, existing capabilities and resources, options and cost estimates for the asset, and market demand.

Suppose Carmike Cinema is considering the purchase of new registers to process ticket and concession sales. Accounting information will help Carmike's managers decide how much money is available for purchasing new registers. Once available funds are known, the managers of the theater operations will select the appropriate style of registers. Managers can review past maintenance expenses on registers of the same type. If the accounting records indicate that a certain type of register requires frequent repairs, than another, more reliable register may be selected.

Since computerized registers capture all point-of-sale information relating to ticket and concession sales, they provide valuable information to many departments within Carmike. For example, people in charge of inventory, purchasing, and sales processing depend on the data generated by the registers. Thus, managers within these departments will have input on the capabilities they require from the new registers to be purchased.

In a past experience as a member of a team, what is a decision made by the team that you might have made differently if you had been working by yourself?

FOCUS ON TECHNOLOGY

Information Technology Helps Carmike

Carmike Cinemas' operating expenses are the lowest in the industry thanks to the company's information technology systems, I.Q. 2000 and I.Q. Zero. Designed by Carmike, these systems capture all point of sale information relating to ticket and concession sales, plus process payroll information. The information is instantly transmitted to corporate headquarters, which enables executive management to coordinate the administrative functions, maximize efficiency, and control costs. With the aid of these systems, cinema managers spend less time "number-crunching" and more time managing day-to-day operations.

Source: *Carmike.com*

¶803 Cost of Plant Assets

LEARNING OBJECTIVE 3: Calculate the cost of a plant asset such as land, building, or equipment.

Plant assets are used in the operations of the company and have a useful life exceeding one year.

Plant assets are tangible long-term assets that have a useful life exceeding one year and are used in the operations of the company. Plant assets, also called "fixed assets," are tangible, which means they have a physical existence. Examples of plant assets are land, buildings and equipment, and natural resources.

Exhibit 8.1 shows several types of plant assets and the related expenses of depreciation and depletion. **Depreciation** is the process of allocating a long-term tangible asset's cost to expense over the asset's estimated useful life. **Useful life** is the length of time a long-term asset can be expected to perform its function.

Depreciation is the process of allocating a long-term tangible asset's cost to expense over the asset's estimated useful life.

Useful life is the length of time a long-term asset can be expected to perform its function.

Depletion is the part of the cost of a natural resource that is used up in a period.

Depletion is the part of the cost of a natural resource that is used up in a period.

Exhibit 8.1 TYPES OF PLANT ASSETS AND RELATED EXPENSES

Plant Asset (Balance Sheet)		Related Expense (Income Statement)
Land		No depreciation expense
Building Equipment Furniture & Fixtures		Depreciation
Timber Copper ore Petroleum (oil & gas)		Depletion

As you can see, land is not expensed like the other plant assets. The cost of plant assets such as buildings and equipment are gradually allocated to depreciation expense over their useful lives. Land is never depreciated, as its usefulness does not diminish. In the case of natural resources, such as timber or petroleum reserves, their costs are also expensed, but the expense is called "depletion." Depreciation and depletion are described in more detail later in the chapter.

¶803.01

Market value is the current worth of an asset, which is the price it can be sold for.

HISTORICAL COST VS. MARKET VALUE

When a company purchases a plant asset, what cost is recorded in the accounting records? Accounting principles require that tangible plant assets, like equipment, be shown at historical cost, not market value. The historical cost of an asset includes the price paid plus any expenditure necessary to prepare the asset for use. **Market value** is the current worth of an asset, in other words, the price it can be sold for. The historical cost of an asset is known, while the market value is typically very difficult to precisely determine. If equipment, such as a security camera, is purchased for $2,000, then we say that the historical cost, or simply the cost, of the equipment is $2,000. Suppose we could sell the equipment for $3,000. The market value of the equipment is $3,000. What should the balance sheet show for the cost of the camera: $2,000 or $3,000? The balance sheet shows the camera's historical cost of $2,000, not its market value of $3,000.

One reason market value is often difficult to determine is because equipment that is very valuable and useful for one company may have little or no value for another company. For example, Intel Corporation makes computer chips. Suppose Intel wished to sell some chip-making equipment that cost $100,000. Who would buy it? Motorola also makes chips, but Motorola may not need more equipment. Furthermore, the Intel chip-making equipment may not be compatible with Motorola's assembly line. The bottom line is that Intel's chip-making equipment may be well worth $100,000 if the company wants to produce computer chips, but it may not be able to sell that equipment to anyone else.

The historical cost of an asset includes the price paid for the asset as well as any additional expenditure necessary to get the asset ready for use. For example, the cost of the chip-making equipment at Intel might be as follows:

Price	$89,200
Taxes	8,100
Delivery and setup	2,700
Cost of equipment	$100,000

The asset account is debited for the complete cost of $100,000, which includes the price paid, taxes, and delivery and setup fees.

¶803.02

THE COST OF LAND

The cost of land is the total of its purchase price and any related expenditures necessary to acquire the land and make the land ready for use. Related expenditures might include real estate agent commissions, lawyers' fees, survey fees, accrued taxes that the buyer pays, costs of clearing the land, grading, or removing unwanted buildings. Depreciation is not charged to land because land has an unlimited useful life.

Land improvements such as driveways, sprinkler systems, and fences should not be included in the cost of land. These items have a limited life of their own and are depreciated. Land Improvements is a separate account from Land.

Suppose Carmike Cinemas, Inc. purchases land on which the company plans to build a 24-screen movie theater complex. Carmike pays $500,000 for the land. The company pays cash of $50,000 and borrows $450,000 on a note payable from Wells Fargo Bank. Carmike also pays cash of $15,000 in real estate commissions, $2,000 in survey fees, $6,000 for clearing and grading the land, and lawyers' fees of $3,000. Carmike pays $120,000 in cash for construction of a driveway and parking lot. What amount should Carmike record as the cost of the land? The cost of the land includes the following:

Purchase price	$500,000
Related costs:	
Real estate commission	15,000
Survey fees	2,000
Clearing and grading	6,000
Lawyers' fees	3,000
Cost of land	$526,000

The land account would be debited for the total cost of $526,000, which includes the purchase price and other expenditures necessary to get the land ready for use. The cost of the driveway and parking lot is not included in the cost of land, but would be recorded separately in a Land Improvements account. Journal entries for the above two transactions would be recorded as follows:

Land	526,000	
Notes Payable		450,000
Cash		76,000
Purchase land.		
Land Improvements	120,000	
Cash		120,000
Pay for driveway and parking lot.		

The Land and Land Improvements accounts would be shown under Assets on the balance sheet. The Notes Payable account would be shown under Liabilities on the balance sheet.

¶803.03   THE COST OF BUILDINGS

When a building is acquired, the cost of the building includes its purchase price and any other expenditure necessary to prepare the building for its intended use. Examples of other expenditures that may be added to the cost of the building include real estate commissions, taxes paid, and necessary repairs.

The balance sheet for JK Productions shows the cost of its office building as $30,000. Before moving into the building, the roof had to be repaired. The $30,000 amount includes taxes and roof repairs, which were paid to make the building ready for use.

If a company constructs its own building, then the cost of the building includes all the expenditures associated with construction and making the building ready for use. Costs assigned to a building under construction include expenditures such as building permits, materials, labor, architectural fees, interest on construction loans, and legal fees.

¶803.04   THE COST OF EQUIPMENT

The cost of equipment includes the price paid for the equipment plus any expenditure necessary to get the equipment ready for use. Examples of such expenditures include shipping fees, insurance during transit, sales and other taxes paid, installation costs, and test runs. Equipment is depreciated over its useful life. Once equipment is set up and placed in operation, expenditures for maintenance, taxes, and insurance are expensed.

¶803.05 LUMP-SUM PURCHASES

Occasionally, a company will purchase several assets all together for one lump-sum price. Assume Ford Motor Company purchases land and a building for a lump-sum price of $540,000. Ford must assign a separate cost to the land and building. How much of the price should be allocated to the land and how much to the building?

The proportional value approach is the most widely-used method of allocating a lump-sum price among the individual assets. Exhibit 8.2 shows example calculations using the proportional value approach. In this example, the appraised value of the land is $120,000 and the building is appraised at $480,000. Using the proportional values to determine the individual costs to be allocated, results in the land being assigned a cost of $108,000 and the building a cost of $432,000.

Exhibit 8.2 ALLOCATION OF LUMP-SUM PURCHASE PRICE USING THE PROPORTIONAL VALUE APPROACH

Asset	Appraised Value	Proportion of Appraised Value		
Land	$120,000	120,000 / 600,000	=	20%
Building	480,000	480,000 / 600,000	=	80%
	$600,000	100%		
Asset	Total Cost	Proportion of Appraised Value		Assigned Cost
Land	540,000 ×	20%	=	$108,000
Building	540,000 ×	80%	=	432,000
				$540,000

Assuming Ford pays cash, the journal entry to record the purchase of the land and building is as follows:

Land	108,000	
Building	432,000	
Cash		540,000
Purchase land and building.		

¶803.06 CAPITAL EXPENDITURE VS. REVENUE EXPENDITURE

A capital expenditure is a purchase of plant assets that benefits future accounting periods.

When a company buys plant assets, such as equipment, which will be used for several years, this is called a "capital expenditure." A **capital expenditure** is a purchase that benefits future accounting periods. For example, when JK Productions purchases computer equipment that it expects to use for several years, the purchase is a capital expenditure. The purchase of $10,000 of computer equipment is recorded as follows:

Feb. 1	Computer Equipment	10,000	
	Cash		10,000
	Purchase computer equipment.		

When a purchase is treated as a capital expenditure, the expenditure is "capitalized," meaning that an asset is recorded. At the time of the purchase, the cost of the equipment does not affect net income on the income statement. On the purchase date, only balance sheet accounts are affected, in this case, the assets Computer Equipment and Cash. Later, when the Computer Equipment is depreciated, depreciation expense will reduce net income on the income statement. Depreciation will be discussed later.

A **revenue expenditure** is an expenditure that involves maintaining, repairing, and operating plant assets. For example, when a company's copy machine is repaired, this is a revenue expenditure. The payment of the bill would be recorded as follows:

Feb. 2	Maintenance Expense	40	
	Cash		40
	Payment for repair to copier.		

A revenue expenditure involves maintaining, repairing, and operating plant assets.

When an expenditure is treated as a revenue expenditure, then the expenditure is "expensed." The payment of $40 for maintenance expense affects net income. Maintenance expense, along with other expenses, is subtracted from revenues on the income statement. When revenues are greater than expenses, the company has a net profit, also called "net income." If expenses exceed revenues, the company has a net loss.

When the copy machine was acquired, the purchase price was recorded as a capital expenditure and listed as an asset on the balance sheet. The copier benefits future accounting periods. Once equipment is placed in operation, expenditures for maintenance, taxes, and insurance are expensed, not capitalized. The income statement shows revenue expenditures necessary for keeping the copier and other plant assets operating (like those expenses of purchasing ink cartridges and making repairs).

¶803.07   ETHICS AND CAPITAL EXPENDITURES

Because the classification of capital expenditures and revenue expenditure require a degree of judgment by managers, various ethical dilemmas may emerge. Suppose you are a top manager for Southwest Manufacturing Company. Your company's stock price is down. The company's net income has been below investor expectations for the past two years. As a result, many investors have lost confidence in the company's ability to make a solid profit. You have seen the income statement that is about to be released to the public. The net income is short of expectations, by a very narrow margin of 1 percent. The pre-release income statement is shown in Exhibit 8.3.

Exhibit 8.3 SOUTHWEST MANUFACTURING COMPANY	
Pre-Release Income Statement For Year Ended 12/31/08	
Sales Revenue	$10,000,000
Cost of Goods Sold	5,000,000
Gross Profit	5,000,000
Expenses*	4,010,000
Net Income	$990,000
Net Income Predicted by Wall Street Analysts: $ 1,000,000.	

* Expenses include repairs to equipment of $10,000.
Note: The company has 1,000,000 shares of stock outstanding. Net income is $990,000 or 99 cents per share. Wall Street analysts had predicted net income would be $1 per share. The company will fall short of expectations by just one cent per share.

After carefully reviewing all the items on the income statement, you determine that if the recent repairs to company equipment had been capitalized instead of expensed, net income would be increased by 1 percent. The repairs would be added to assets and not subtracted from revenues, thus increasing overall net income. This increased net income is just enough to meet expectations, which would cause investors to perceive that the company is back on track. The impact of achieving profit expectations would likely have a dramatic impact on the stock price.

You might be tempted to capitalize the expenditure and thereby improve the company's profit. You might try to rationalize this incorrect accounting procedure in two ways: (1) it would help the stockholders, as the stock price would improve, and (2) the amount of money involved is very small, only 1 percent of net income. However, to manipulate the earnings, by using erroneous accounting, is misleading and a criminal offense.

¶804   Depreciating Plant Assets

> **LEARNING OBJECTIVE 4:** Describe how assets are depreciated using various depreciation methods.

Since a plant asset, other than land, will eventually wear out, the cost of the plant asset is allocated to an expense account over the asset's useful life. As already stated, depreciation is the process of allocating a long-term tangible asset's cost to expense over the asset's useful life. In other words, the cost of the long-term

Depreciation is the allocation of an asset's cost to expense over its useful life.

asset is systematically written off over the asset's estimated useful life and allocated to the current period as an expense. As a result, the expense of an asset follows the revenue it produces. For example, equipment that is purchased one year may be used for the next 10 years to produce revenues. At the end of 10 years, the equipment may be worn out and no longer useful for anything. Logically, the cost of the equipment should be allocated to expense over the same time period that the equipment is used in operations. This is exactly what GAAP requires by way of depreciation expense.

The estimated salvage value is the anticipated cash value of an asset at the end of its useful life.

Assume that on January 1, 20Y1, Sears purchases a new delivery truck for $80,000. The truck will be used to ship goods from its warehouses to retail stores. The truck is expected to be used for 5 years, run about 30,000 miles per year, and then be sold to a used auto wholesaler for $5,000. The estimated **salvage value**, also called "**residual value**," is the anticipated cash value of an asset at the end of its useful life. For the truck, the salvage value is its wholesale price of $5,000. Exhibit 8.4 summarizes the amount to be depreciated for the Sears truck.

Exhibit 8.4 DETERMINING DEPRECIABLE COST

1. Cost	$80,000	
2. Salvage value	5,000	
3. Depreciable cost	$75,000	
Estimated useful life:	5 years	
	Estimated total lifetime mileage is 150,000 miles	

Depreciable cost is the cost of an asset less its salvage value.

The cost of the asset, less its salvage value, is its **depreciable cost**. This is the amount that will be depreciated by the end of the asset's useful life. Thus, when we say depreciation is the allocation of an asset's cost to expense over its useful life, we mean the asset's depreciable cost, not its acquisition cost.

What causes an asset to depreciate, that is, decline in usefulness? There are two basic causes of depreciation:

■ **Physical deterioration** is the normal wear and tear that gradually breaks down a physical asset until it is no longer functional. Keeping an asset repaired and well maintained can maximize its useful life, but eventually the asset must be discarded.

■ **Obsolescence** is the process in which an asset becomes inefficient or out-of-date in doing its job. For example, a computer purchased four years ago may still work as well today as when purchased; however, a new computer may be needed to take advantage of new technologies or simply to do tasks more quickly. Thus, the old computer, though still functional, has become obsolete.

From an accounting standpoint, there is no need to distinguish why an asset has a limited life, whether it is due to physical deterioration or obsolescence. The important thing is that the asset's depreciable cost is allocated to expense over its useful life as the asset generates revenue.

You should be clear that depreciation is not about setting aside money to replace an asset, but is simply allocating the asset's cost to expense. A company may set aside money for future asset purchases, but this is a separate matter from depreciation. Furthermore, depreciation has nothing to do with the asset's market value. A company records depreciation based on depreciable cost and useful life, not based on changes in market value. In fact, a company would need to depreciate an asset even if the market value of the asset has increased. This frequently happens with buildings, since the market value of real estate often appreciates.

¶804.01   METHODS OF DEPRECIATION

A company must choose the most appropriate depreciation method from a number of acceptable methods. The three most commonly used depreciation methods are as follows:

■ Straight-line method
■ Units-of-production method
■ Double-declining-balance method

Straight-line method

The straight-line method allocates an equal amount of depreciation expense to each year of the asset's useful life.

The **straight-line depreciation method** allocates an equal amount of depreciation expense to each year of the asset's useful life. The formula for straight-line depreciation is as follows:

$$\text{Straight-line depreciation per year} = \frac{\text{Cost} - \text{Salvage value}}{\text{Useful life, in years}}$$

Using the information about the truck in Exhibit 8.4, straight-line depreciation is calculated as:

$$\text{Straight-line depreciation per year} = \frac{\$80{,}000 \ (\text{cost}) - \$5{,}000 \ (\text{salvage value})}{5 \ (\text{useful life in years})}$$

$$= \$15{,}000$$

The journal entry to record depreciation expense is as follows:

20Y1			
Dec. 31	Depreciation Expense, Truck	15,000	
	Accumulated Depreciation, Truck		15,000
	To record depreciation on truck.		

The entry to record depreciation has an impact on assets via the Accumulated Depreciation account and on expenses via the Depreciation Expense account. Depreciation Expense is part of a company's expenses and is shown on the income statement. Accumulated Depreciation is shown on the balance sheet in the asset section. The entry to record depreciation affects the accounting equation as follows:

Assets	=	Liabilities	+	Stockholders' Equity	–	Expenses
– 15,000	=	0	+		–	15,000
(Accum. Dep.)						(Dep. Expense)

On the balance sheet, accumulated depreciation for the truck is shown in the asset section, next to the Truck account. With a credit balance, Accumulated Depreciation reduces the value of the truck account, which has a debit balance. Accumulated Depreciation is referred to as a "contra-asset" because it reduces the value of a related asset account. This may seem confusing at first, that is, an asset account with a credit balance. However, it allows the asset, in this case the truck, to be shown at its original cost. Thus, a person can examine the accounting records to determine the original cost of an asset and how much has been depreciated.

The book value of an asset is the cost minus its accumulated depreciation.

Exhibit 8.5 shows the cost and accumulated depreciation of the truck for all five years of its useful life. The difference between cost and accumulated depreciation is referred to as the asset's "**book value**" or "**carrying value**." When the asset is fully depreciated, the book value is equal to its salvage value.

Exhibit 8.5 SCHEDULE OF DEPRECIATION EXPENSE USING STRAIGHT-LINE METHOD

	Cost	Annual Depreciation Expense	Accumulated Depreciation	Book Value
Jan 1, 20Y1	$80,000			$80,000
Dec 31, 20Y1	80,000	$15,000	$15,000	65,000
Dec 31, 20Y2	80,000	15,000	30,000	50,000
Dec 31, 20Y3	80,000	15,000	45,000	35,000
Dec 31, 20Y4	80,000	15,000	60,000	20,000
Dec 31, 20Y5	80,000	15,000	75,000	5,000

Note: Depreciable cost = $80,000 cost – $5,000 salvage value = $75,000

JK Productions uses the straight-line method to depreciate its computer equipment that costs $10,000. The equipment is expected to have a useful life of five years with no salvage value. At the end of five years, the equipment will be out-dated. The annual depreciation is $2,000 ($10,000 / 5 years).

FOCUS ON TECHNOLOGY

Using Microsoft Excel: Calculating Straight-Line Depreciation

Using Excel, we will recreate the straight-line depreciation schedule in Exhibit 8.5. We will be calculating depreciation for a truck purchased for $80,000, has a salvage value of $5,000, and estimated to have a useful life of 5 years.

1. **File Identification Area:** In an Excel worksheet, set up a file identification area. Include name, filename, date created, input required (i.e., the above information on the truck), and output required (i.e., straight-line depreciation schedule).
2. **Input Area:** Type in the following.

	A	B	C	D
13				
14	INPUT AREA:			
15	Cost of truck			80,000
16	Salvage value of truck			5,000
17	Truck's useful life in years			5

3. **Output Area:** Set up the headings for your depreciation schedule to resemble Exhibit 8.5. Type the dates in the left column. Type in these formulas under the following headings:

- **Cost:** =$D$15

   Note: The dollar signs are inserted so that you can copy the formula into the remaining cells without causing the cell address to change. This is called "absolute addressing."

- **Annual Depreciation Expense:** =($D$15 – $D$16) / $D$17

- The first entry is on Dec. 31, 20Y1.

- **Accumulated Depreciation:** write a formula adding last year's accumulated depreciation with the current year's depreciation expense. The first entry is on Dec. 31, 20Y1.

   Note: Do not use dollar signs in this formula so that you can copy it into other cells. Without dollar signs, Excel will automatically change cell addresses to correspond to the row in which the formula is copied. This is called "relative addressing."

- **Book Value:** Write a formula subtracting accumulated depreciation from cost. You can copy this formula (without dollar signs) into the remaining cells.

¶804.01.02 Units-of-Production Method

The units-of-production depreciation method allocates depreciation expense according to the units of output or service provided by the asset.

The **units-of-production depreciation method** allocates depreciation expense proportionately according to the units of output or service provided by the asset. In the case of the truck, the units of output are miles driven. The truck is estimated to have a useful life of 150,000 miles. The truck's depreciable cost of $75,000 is divided by 150,000 miles. Thus, $.50 of depreciation expense is allocated to the truck for each mile driven. The formula for units-of-production depreciation is as follows:

$$\text{Units-of-production depreciation per unit of output} = \frac{\text{Cost – Salvage value}}{\text{Useful life in units of production}}$$

$$= (\$80,000 – \$5,000) / 150,000 \text{ miles}$$

$$= \$.50 \text{ per mile}$$

Exhibit 8.6 shows the depreciation schedule for the truck using the units-of-production method. The "number of units" is the number of miles the truck was driven each year.

Exhibit 8.6 SCHEDULE OF DEPRECIATION EXPENSE USING UNITS-OF-PRODUCTION METHOD

	Cost	Depreciation Per Unit of Production*	Number of Units	Depreciation Expense	Accumulated Depreciation	Book Value
Jan 1, 20Y1	$80,000					$80,000
Dec 31, 20Y1	80,000	$0.50	25,000	$12,500	$12,500	67,500
Dec 31, 20Y2	80,000	0.50	35,000	17,500	30,000	50,000
Dec 31, 20Y3	80,000	0.50	30,000	15,000	45,000	35,000
Dec 31, 20Y4	80,000	0.50	40,000	20,000	65,000	15,000
Dec 31, 20Y5	80,000	0.50	20,000	10,000	75,000	5,000

* **Note:** Depreciation expense per unit of production equals $0.50 per mile ($80,000 – $5,000) / 150,000 miles). Depreciation cost is $75,000 ($80,000 cost – $5,000 salvage value).

The units-of-production method resembles the straight-line method in that they both start with the same depreciable cost amount of $75,000. They differ in that the depreciation expense under the units-of-production method varies from year to year depending on the units produced. However, at the end of the asset's useful life, both methods result in the same total accumulated depreciation of $75,000. Also under both methods, the asset's useful life ends with a book value that equals the salvage value of $5,000.

¶804.01.03   Double-Declining-Balance Method

The double-declining-balance method calculates annual depreciation by multiplying the asset's declining book value by a fixed percentage rate.

The **double-declining-balance method** calculates annual depreciation by multiplying the asset's declining book value by a fixed percentage rate. The formula for the double-declining-balance depreciation rate is as follows:

Double-declining-balance annual depreciation rate   =   (1 / useful life in years) × 2

Exhibit 8.7 shows the depreciation schedule for the truck using the double-declining-balance method. The depreciation rate shown in Exhibit 8.7 is calculated as follows: (1/5) × 2 = 40%. The useful life of the truck is five years. For each year except the final year, the book value is multiplied by the double-declining-balance rate (40 percent) to calculate the depreciation expense for the year. The depreciation expense in the final year is the amount necessary to reduce the asset's book value to its salvage value, in this case, $5,000. When an asset is fully depreciated to its salvage value, no more depreciation expense is taken, but the asset remains on the books until it is removed from service.

Exhibit 8.7 SCHEDULE OF DEPRECIATION EXPENSE USING DOUBLE-DECLINING-BALANCE METHOD

	Cost	DDB Rate	Annual Depreciation Expense	Accumulated Depreciation	Book Value
Jan 1, 20Y1	$80,000				$80,000
Dec 31, 20Y1	80,000	0.40	$32,000	$32,000	48,000
Dec 31, 20Y2	80,000	0.40	19,200	51,200	28,800
Dec 31, 20Y3	80,000	0.40	11,520	62,720	17,280
Dec 31, 20Y4	80,000	0.40	6,912	69,632	10.368
Dec 31, 20Y5	80,000		5,368*	75,000	5,000

* **Note:** The final year's depreciation is the amount necessary to reduce the book value to the salvage value. Except for the final year, Annual Depreciation Expense is calculated by multiplying the DDB rate by the declining Book Value, starting with the initial book value of $80,000.

The double-declining-balance rate is twice the straight-line rate. Unlike the straight-line and units-of-production methods, the double-declining-balance method ignores salvage value in calculating depreciation expense, except in the last year of an asset's useful life. Also unlike the other two methods, the double-declining-balance method starts with the initial book value of the asset, which is also the original cost of the asset. Using double-declining balance, the asset's depreciation expense is much higher in the early years of the asset's useful life than under the other methods.

Accelerated depreciation methods charge higher amounts to depreciation expense in early years.

Depreciation methods that charge higher amounts to depreciation expense in early years are referred to as "**accelerated depreciation methods**." The double-declining-balance method is an accelerated depreciation method.

¶804.02 DEPRECIATION FOR A PARTIAL YEAR

If a company buys a plant asset midway through a year, then depreciation expense must be computed for the partial year. Suppose Carmike Cinemas, Inc. purchases a building for $400,000 on October 1, 20Y1. The building's estimated useful life is 25 years, and its estimated salvage value is $25,000. Carmike's fiscal year end is December 31. How much should Carmike record for depreciation expense at the end of the year? Two steps are followed in computing a partial year's depreciation:

1. Calculate a full year's depreciation.
2. Multiply the full year's depreciation by the proportion of the year in which the company owned the asset.

The calculation of depreciation expense for the Carmike Cinema building is shown below. Carmike uses straight-line depreciation.

Full year = ($400,000 – $25,000) / 25 years = $15,000

Partial year = $15,000 × 3/12 = $3,750

The journal entry on December 31 would be recorded as follows:

Dec. 31	Depreciation Expense, Building	3,750	
	Accumulated Depreciation, Building		3,750
	To record 3 months' depreciation.		

Since companies purchase plant assets as they are needed for operations, the purchase dates do not necessarily occur at the beginning of the year or the month. Typically, an asset purchased before the 15th of the month will get a full month's depreciation. If the asset is purchased after the 15th, the asset would be charged no depreciation for that month.

¶804.03   CHANGE IN ACCOUNTING ESTIMATE

A change in accounting estimate is a revision to an accounting estimate such as an asset's estimated useful life.

When a plant asset is purchased, company managers must estimate how long the asset will be used. The estimated useful life, along with estimated salvage value, is used to calculate depreciation. Later, after the asset has been used in operations, managers sometimes realize that the estimate of useful life must be revised. Such a revision is called a "**change in accounting estimate.**"

Assume FedEx paid $20,000 for a forklift and initially estimated the useful life at five years with no salvage value. The company used the forklift for three years. Using straight-line depreciation, annual depreciation expense is $4,000 ($20,000 / 5 years). At the end of three years, accumulated depreciation is $12,000 and the asset's book value is $8,000 ($20,000 – $12,000). According to the original estimate, the forklift should have two more years of useful life; however, management determines that the forklift has four more years of useful life. Consequently, depreciation expense for the remaining four years is calculated as follows:

Remaining depreciable book value / Estimated useful life remaining = New annual depreciation

$$\$8,000 \: / \: 4 \text{ years} \quad = \quad \$2,000$$

The entry to record depreciation starting in Year 4 is as follows:

What is a legitimate reason for changing an accounting estimate?

Dec. 31	Depreciation Expense, Forklift	2,000	
	Accumulated Depreciation, Forklift		2,000
	To record depreciation after new useful life estimate.		

¶804.04   EXTRAORDINARY REPAIRS

An extraordinary repair extends the remaining useful life of an asset.

Ordinary repairs are often necessary to keep an asset in operating condition. If the company truck gets a flat tire, it must be repaired. If a window breaks on the building, a new window must be installed. These types of repairs have no effect on the operation of the asset or its original estimated useful life. Sometimes, however, a special type of repair, called an "**extraordinary repair,**" actually extends the remaining useful life of an asset.

Assume that one of Pizza Hut's trucks, which carry supplies from its warehouse to restaurants, originally costs $40,000. The truck has an estimated useful life of four years, and an estimated salvage value of $8,000. The truck has been depreciated using the straight-line method for three years. Depreciation expense recorded for each of the first three years was $8,000 ($40,000 – $8,000) / 4). At the end of the third year, on December 28, the truck is given a major overhaul for $10,000. As a result, the useful life of the truck is extended two years beyond the original estimate. The extraordinary repair decreases accumulated depreciation on the truck by the amount of the repair. The entry to record this extraordinary repair is as follows:

Dec. 28	Accumulated Depreciation, Truck	10,000	
	Cash		10,000
	To record extraordinary repair.		

As a result of the extraordinary repair, the annual depreciation expense must be recalculated. The calculation is shown in Exhibit 8.8.

Exhibit 8.8 IMPACT OF EXTRAORDINARY REPAIR ON DEPRECIATION

Before Extraordinary Repair:

Cost	$40,000
Accumulated Depreciation	24,000 *
Book Value	$16,000

*((40,000 – 8,000) / 4) × 3 years = 24,000

After Extraordinary Repairs:

Cost	$40,000
Accumulated Depreciation	14,000 **
Book Value	$26,000
Less Salvage Value	8,000
Depreciable Cost Remaining	$18,000
Divided by new remaining useful life	3 years
New Annual Depreciation Expense	$6,000

**24,000 – 10,000 repair = 14,000

The original cost of the truck remains the same. However, following the extraordinary repair, the truck's book value (cost – accumulated depreciation) is increased from $16,000 ($40,000 – $24,000) to $26,000 ($40,000 – $14,000). The depreciable cost remaining on the truck is $18,000 ($26,000 – $8,000 salvage value). The remaining years of useful life for the truck has been extended from one to three. Thus, depreciation expense for the next three years would be recorded as follows:

Dec. 31	Depreciation Expense, Truck	6,000	
	Accumulated Depreciation, Truck		6,000
	To record annual depreciation.		

¶804.05   TAX CONSIDERATIONS REGARDING DEPRECIATION

An important issue related to depreciation is income tax consequences. Depreciation is often calculated differently for tax purposes. This is because tax laws are based on political considerations, which are not necessarily the same as financial reporting considerations. For example, the government may want to encourage investment in equipment that reduces pollution.

The tax law may permit depreciation over three years, even though the pollution-reducing equipment is expected to actually last six years. For accounting purposes, the equipment would be depreciated over its useful life of six years. Compared to the income statement, depreciation expense on the tax return is higher. As a result, taxable income is less than accounting net income. In effect, the company legitimately has two sets of books for depreciation, one for the tax return and another for the financial statements. The ability to depreciate the asset more quickly for tax purposes gives the company an incentive to purchase the pollution-reducing equipment.

¶804.06   ETHICS AND DEPRECIATION

The ability to make a change in an accounting estimate may lead to an ethical dilemma. By changing an accounting estimate, the estimated useful life of a plant asset is usually increased. This results in lower annual depreciation expense. By lowering depreciation expense, net income and stockholders' equity are both increased. Suppose FedEx is having a lackluster year and net income is well below investor expectations. Naturally, FedEx managers will look for ways to improve earnings.

Failing to meet earnings expectations will negatively affect a company's stock price. People that own stock in the company, which typically include company managers, naturally prefer that the stock price go up, not down. Managers may be tempted to make a change in the accounting estimate of the useful lives of depreciable assets for the purpose of improving financial performance.

If you were a manager at FedEx and you could improve net income by revising the estimated useful lives of plant assets, would you? If doing so would lead to a significant increase in your bonus income and a possible promotion at work, would you make the change in accounting estimate? Two things should be considered in resolving this ethical dilemma.

First, changes in an accounting estimate that are not based on a realistic expectation of a longer useful life, may lead to loss of your job and possible criminal charges.

Second, investors may see through this attempt to manipulate earnings. According to GAAP, the change in accounting estimate and its effect on net income must be disclosed in a company's annual report. Investors may realize that net income was increased only as a result of the accounting change, not actual improvements in operations. Thus, stock price will not go up. In fact, the stock price may decline, as investors may regard the change as an attempt to fool them. Consequently, they may have less trust in the company.

FOCUS ON BUSINESS

Disclosure at Carmike

Why would a business manager be tempted to manipulate numbers on the financial statements and thereby mislead the owners of the company?

Carmike Cinemas, Inc. is committed to full, fair, accurate, and timely disclosure in its accounting reports. This includes public communications and reports submitted to the SEC. To back up this commitment, Carmike does the following:

- Implements disclosure controls and procedures.
- Requires the maintenance of accurate and complete records.
- Prohibits false or misleading entries on its books.
- Requires the complete documentation and recording of transactions in the company's accounting records.

Source: *www.Carmike.com*

¶805

Disposal of Depreciable Plant Assets

LEARNING OBJECTIVE 5: Describe and record the disposal of plant assets.

Plant assets are disposed of when they are worn out, obsolete, or are no longer useful. A company can dispose of an asset by selling it, exchanging it, or simply discarding it. Exhibit 8.9 shows the various methods for disposing of an asset.

Exhibit 8.9 METHODS OF DISPOSAL OF PLANT ASSET

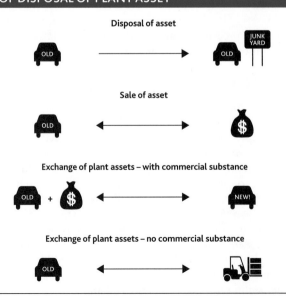

Determining when an asset should be disposed of is typically a cross-functional decision. In order to make a wise decision, input is needed from multiple company departments. The current status of an asset and its impact on operations, options for disposing of the asset, and cost estimates for replacing the asset are required. Consider the following illustration of a plant asset disposal decision. The shipping department may put in a request to exchange the current delivery truck for a new one because the old truck breaks down frequently. The marketing department also wants a new delivery truck because deliveries aren't being made on time due to truck breakdowns, thus causing customer relations nightmares. On the other hand, the finance department may recommend postponing the new truck purchase due to lack of currently available funds.

Suppose ExxonMobil disposes of equipment that cost $100,000. The asset was estimated to have a 10-year useful life and zero salvage value. Using the straight-line method, depreciation expense was recorded at $10,000 per year. At the end of 10 years, the general ledger shows the following balances in the related asset accounts:

Equipment		Accum. Depreciation, Equipment	
100,000			100,000

Once an asset is fully depreciated (book value equals salvage value) and the asset continues to be used in operations, the asset is kept on the books but no additional depreciation expense is recorded. In the example of the ExxonMobil equipment, if the equipment is used for an 11th year, no depreciation expense would be recorded. The asset's cost and accumulated depreciation would remain on the books, and be included on the balance sheet.

¶805.01   DISPOSAL OF A FULLY-DEPRECIATED ASSET

Suppose the ExxonMobil equipment whose book value is zero is discarded on December 31. The entry to record the disposal is as follows:

Dec. 31	Accumulated Depreciation, Equipment	100,000	
	Equipment		100,000
	To record disposal of fully-depreciated equipment.		

As a result of this entry, the general ledger balances would now be zero as follows:

	Equipment				Accum. Depreciation, Equipment		
Beg.	100,000	Dec. 31	100,000	Dec. 31	100,000	Beg.	100,000
Bal.	-0-					Bal.	-0-

As shown above, when ExxonMobil disposes of equipment, the company eliminates both the asset's cost ($100,000) and the asset's accumulated depreciation ($100,000) from the general ledger, also called the "books." There is no gain or loss from disposing of this equipment.

¶805.02   DISPOSAL OF A PARTIALLY-DEPRECIATED ASSET

When an asset is discarded before it is fully depreciated, then the company incurs a loss from the disposal. Suppose that on April 30, Coca-Cola Company discards bottling equipment that cost $30,000 and which has accumulated depreciation of $28,000. Thus, the book value is $2,000. Discarding this equipment results in a loss, recorded as shown:

Apr. 30	Accumulated Depreciation, Bottling Equip.	28,000	
	Loss on Disposal of Bottling Equip.	2,000	
	Bottling Equipment		30,000
	To record disposal of bottling equipment.		

Coca-Cola Company disposed of an asset with a $2,000 book value and received nothing. Consequently, the company incurs a $2,000 loss, which decreases net income. The loss is included as Other Income (Expense) on the income statement. Losses reduce net income just as expenses do. Gains increase net income just as revenues do.

¶805.03   SALE OF A PLANT ASSET

Instead of simply discarding a plant asset, a company may sell the asset. Suppose Royal Dutch Shell acquired an oil rig for a cost of $800,000 on January 1, 20Y1. The rig's estimated useful life is 6 years and its estimated salvage value is $80,000. Assuming Royal Dutch uses straight-line depreciation, the yearly depreciation expense for the oilrig is $120,000 (($800,000 − $80,000) / 6 years).

After just 4 1/2 years, Royal Dutch determines the rig is obsolete and sells it to a salvage company for $200,000 on June 30, 20Y5. Before recording the sale, Royal Dutch must record a partial-year's depreciation expense for January through June 20Y5, as shown:

20Y5			
June 30	Depreciation Expense, Oil Rig	60,000	
	Accumulated Depreciation, Oil Rig		60,000
	To record partial-year's depreciation. ((800,000 − 80,000) / 6) × 6/12 = 60,000)		

The general ledger balances for the Oil Rig account and Accumulated Depreciation, Oil Rig account are now as follows.

Oil Rig		
Jan. 1, 20Y5	800,000	

Accumulated Depreciation, Oil Rig		
	Dec. 31, 20Y1	120,000
	Dec. 31, 20Y2	120,000
	Dec. 31, 20Y4	120,000
	Dec. 31, 20Y4	120,000
	June 31, 20Y5	60,000
	Balance	540,000

The oil rig's book value is $260,000 ($800,000 − $540,000). Since the sale price of the asset ($200,000) is less than the book value, the company must record a loss on the sale as follows:

20Y5			
June 30	Cash	200,000	
	Accumulated Depreciation, Oil Rig	540,000	
	Loss on Sale of Oil Rig	60,000	
	Oil Rig		800,000
	To record loss on sale of oil rig.		

If Royal Dutch had sold the oil rig for $300,000 instead of $200,000, the company would have reported a gain of $40,000 (sale price of $300,000 − book value of $260,000). In this case, the entry would be recorded as follows:

20Y5			
June 30	Cash	300,000	
	Accumulated Depreciation, Oil Rig	540,000	
	Oil Rig		800,000
	Gain on Sale of Oil Rig		40,000
	To record gain on sale of oil rig.		

¶805.04   EXCHANGES OF PLANT ASSETS

Sometimes a company will trade in an old asset on the purchase of a new asset. When a trade is made, the value of the asset(s) given up will always equal the value of the asset(s) received. Otherwise, one of the parties involved would not agree to the trade. If the values of the plant assets being exchanged are different, one of the parties will have to pay the difference with cash.

Commercial substance means the transaction will change the economic position of the companies involved.

For example, let's assume you have an old computer. It works, but you want to upgrade. Dell agrees to allow you to trade in the old computer in exchange for a new computer. Along with the old computer, Dell will require you to give them enough cash to make up the difference in the value of the two computers.

Most of the time, when two parties exchange plant assets they record the difference in the fair market value of the asset given up and its book value as a gain or a loss. This is the same as when you sell a plant asset for cash discussed in the previous section. This is true if the exchange has commercial substance. **Commercial substance** means the transaction will change the economic position of the companies involved. In some cases, if the transaction lacks commercial substance, the standards may prevent a party from recording a gain.

¶805.04.01   Exchanges with Commercial Substance

A gain on the exchange of plant assets occurs when the fair value of the asset given up exceeds the book value, just like in a sale of plant assets. As long as the exchange has commercial substance, an exchange transaction is recorded very similar to a sales transaction. For example, suppose that on March 1, FedEx trades in an old delivery truck on the purchase of a new delivery truck. The exchange will change the economic position of both companies. The old truck cost $20,000 and has accumulated depreciation of $18,000; thus, the book value of the truck is $2,000. However, the market value of the old truck is $5,000. If FedEx trades the old truck and also pays $22,000 cash for the new truck, then the value of the new truck must be $27,000 ($5,000 market value of old truck plus $22,000 cash paid). Since the market value of the old truck was higher than the book value, a $3,000 gain must be recorded ($5,000 market value minus $2,000 book value). The transaction is recorded as follows:

Mar. 1	Truck (new)	27,000	
	Accumulated Depreciation, Truck (old)	18,000	
	Truck (old)		20,000
	Cash		22,000
	Gain		3,000
	To record exchange of plant assets – with commercial substance		

It is important to remember the fair value of the asset(s) given up must equal the fair value of the asset(s) received. A company may not always know the market value of both assets. As long as the market value of one plant asset is known, the market value of the other plant asset can be found. In the example above we found the market value of the new truck by adding the cash paid to the market value of the old truck ($5,000 plus $22,000). If we had known the market value of the new truck instead, we could have solved for the market value of the old truck. This would be done by subtracting the amount of cash paid from the market value of the new truck ($27,000 market value of new truck minus $22,000 cash paid).

¶805.04.02   Exchanges Lacking Commercial Substance

If an exchange lacks commercial substance and results in a gain, one party is effectively treated as a buyer while the other is treated as a seller, even though they are trading plant assets. The party paying cash is treated like a buyer, while the party receiving cash is treated like a seller. In the sale of a plant asset, the seller would receive cash and record a gain, but the buyer would never record a gain for a purchase.

In an exchange that lacks commercial substance and results in a gain, the party paying cash ("buyer") is not allowed to record a gain at the time of the trade. The buyer must defer the gain until the asset is sold. This is done by reducing the value of the asset being received by the amount of the gain. If the transaction results in a loss, the loss will be booked immediately by either party regardless of commercial substance.

Let's take the same example as above, but assume the transaction lacks commercial substance. All of the information would be the same as the example above, but the transaction would not change the companies' economic position. The entry would be recorded as follows:

Mar. 1	Truck (new)		~~27,000~~ 24,000	
	Accumulated Depreciation, Truck (old)		18,000	
	Truck (old)			20,000
	Cash			22,000
	~~Gain~~			~~3,000~~
	To record exchange of plant assets — no commercial substance.			

The gain above was crossed out to show that no gain can be recognized. To balance the entry and defer the gain, the value of the new truck must be reduced by the amount of the gain.

The party receiving cash is treated as the "seller" and may be able to record part of the gain based on the scenarios below.

1) If the cash received is greater than or equal to 25% of the transaction, then the entire gain can be recognized.
2) If cash received is less than 25% of the transaction, then only that percentage of the gain can be recognized. The gain recognized would be calculated as follows:

$$\frac{\text{Cash Received}}{\text{Cash Received + Fair Value of the Asset Received}} \times \text{ Total Gain } = \text{ Gain Recognized}$$

To illustrate, assume that FedEx trades forklift A, originally purchased for $10,000, for forklift B. Forklift A has accumulated depreciation of $8,000. The market value of forklift A is $5,000. In exchange, FedEx receives forklift B and $1,000 cash. Forklift B typically sells for $4,000. The transaction will not impact the economic position of FedEx. We must first determine the total gain on the exchange. Additionally, since FedEx is receiving cash in this scenario, we must determine the portion of the gain FedEx can recognize as follows:

Calculate gain on transaction:

Fair value of forklift A		$5,000
Book value of forklift A		2,000
Total gain	=	$3,000

Calculate cash as a percentage of the total transaction:

$$\frac{\$1,000 \text{ (cash)}}{\$1,000 \text{ (cash)} + \$4,000 \text{ (forklift B)}} = 20\%$$

Since 20% is less than 25%, FedEx can only recognize 20% of the total gain. If cash had been greater than or equal to 25% of the total transaction then FedEx could have recognized the entire gain.

Calculate the gain to be recognized and the gain to be deferred:

Gain recognized = 20%*3,000 = 600

Gain deferred = 3,000 – 600 = 2,400

The gain deferred must reduce the amount recorded for forklift B, thus, it will not be recorded at its market value. Instead it will be recorded at $1,600 ($4,000 market value minus $2,400 gain deferred).

Mar. 1	Forklift B	~~1,600~~	
	Cash	1,000	
	Accumulated Depreciation, Forklift A	8,000	
	Forklift A		10,000
	~~Gain~~		~~600~~

¶805.04.03 Recap of Exchanges

When an exchange has commercial substance both parties record a gain or loss based on the difference in the fair value and book value of the asset given up.

When an exchange lacks commercial substance, the party paying cash must defer the entire gain. When an exchange lacks commercial substance, the party receiving cash will record the entire gain if cash is greater than or equal to 25% of the transaction. If cash is less than 25% of the transaction, the party receiving cash can only recognize that percentage of the gain and must defer the rest. If a loss is incurred on a transaction it must be recognized immediately, regardless of commercial substance.

Accounting for exchanges of assets is summarized in Exhibit 8.10.

Have you ever disposed of an asset by selling it or exchanging it?

Exhibit 8.10 ACCOUNTING FOR EXCHANGES OF PLANT ASSETS

		Lacks Commercial Substance		
	With Commercial Substance	**Cash Paid**	**Cash Received ≥ 25%**	**Cash Received < 25%**
Gain Recognized	Yes	No	Yes	Partial gain
Loss Recognized	Yes	Yes	Yes	Yes

¶806 Natural Resources and Depletion

LEARNING OBJECTIVE 6: Identify accounting issues pertaining to natural resources and depletion.

Natural resources are products of nature, such as timber, iron ore, coal, and petroleum reserves.

For many companies, natural resources are a major part of total assets. **Natural resources** are products of nature, such as timber, iron ore, coal, and petroleum reserves. Natural resources are different from other plant assets, which are manufactured by human effort. However, human effort in the form of cutting, mining, smelting, and drilling are necessary to transform natural resources into usable raw materials, such as lumber, iron, and oil.

When natural resources are acquired, they are recorded at their purchase price. In the same way that other plant assets are expensed through depreciation, natural resources are expensed through depletion.

Depletion expense is recorded much like units-of-production depreciation. Assume that International Paper Corporation on April 1, 20Y1, buys rights to cut the timber on 1,000 acres of land for $1,000,000. The entry to record the purchase is as follows:

April 1	Timber Reserves	1,000,000	
	Cash		1,000,000
	To record purchase of timber reserves.		

Depletion expense is calculated as $1,000 per acre cut ($1,000,000 / 1,000 acres). Assuming 200 acres are cut at the end of 20Y1 and all the timber was used, depletion expense is recorded as follows:

Dec. 31	Depletion Expense, Timber Reserves	200,000	
	Accumulated Depletion, Timber Reserves		200,000
	To record depletion of timber: 200 acres @ $1,000 per acre cut.		

You may have depleted part of your supply of bottled water this month.

The balance sheet shows timber under plant assets as follows:

Timber Reserves	$1,000,000
Less Accumulation Depletion	200,000
Net Timber Reserves	$800,000

¶807   Intangible Assets and Amortization

LEARNING OBJECTIVE 7: Identify types of intangible assets and account for amortization expense.

Intangible assets have no physical existence but represent a right to current and future benefits.

Intangible assets are long-term assets that have no physical existence but represent a right to current and future benefits. Examples of intangible assets include leases on land, oil rights, patents, trademarks, goodwill, licenses, or copyrights. Exhibit 8.11 shows how to account for some of the most common types of intangibles.

Exhibit 8.11 ACCOUNTING FOR INTANGIBLE ASSETS

Intangible asset	How to account for the asset
Copyright	
Provides exclusive rights to publish and sell books, musical compositions, or other literary works for the lifetime of the author plus 50 years. Copyrights include computer software. Copyrights are granted by the federal government.	Record a copyright at its purchase price and then amortize over its useful life. Typically, a copyright is amortized over a useful life of 2 to 4 years.
Patent	
Provides exclusive rights to produce and sell a specific product or process. Patents are granted by the federal government and last for 17 years.	Record a patent at its purchase price plus any litigation costs necessary to defend the patent. A patent is amortized over its useful life, which is 17 years or less.
Trademark	
Provides unique identification to a company product or service. Trademarks and brand names are registered.	A trademark is recorded at its purchase price and amortized over its useful life. If the trademark is expected to benefit operations indefinitely, then it should not be amortized.
Franchise or License	
Grants exclusive rights to market a product or service in a specific location, or to use a special process or formula. A company or a government agency can grant a franchise or license.	Record a franchise or license at its purchase price. The franchise or license may have an indefinite useful life, and thus is not amortized. Otherwise, it is amortized over its useful life.
Goodwill	
Designates the amount by which the purchase cost for a business exceeds the fair market value of its net assets (assets minus liabilities).	Record goodwill at its purchase price. Goodwill is not amortized but rather is tested at least annually for impairment. If impaired, the carrying value is adjusted downward.

Amortization is the process of expensing the cost of an intangible asset over its useful life.

Goodwill designates the amount by which the price paid for a company exceeds the fair market value of its net assets.

Intangible assets are recorded at their acquisition cost. In most cases, an intangible's cost is then allocated to expense in the same manner that plant assets are depreciated and natural resources are depleted. The process of expensing the cost of an intangible asset over its useful life is called "**amortization.**" Intangible assets that are *not* amortized are goodwill and other intangibles that do not have a finite useful life. **Goodwill** relates to the good relationship of a business with its customers, a reputation for good service or quality goods, or excellent management. Goodwill designates the amount by which the price paid for a company exceeds the fair market value of its net assets. It is important to note that goodwill is only recorded when there is an exchange transaction that involves the purchase of an entire business.

Amortization expense is usually calculated using a straight-line approach. Intangible assets typically have no salvage value. Amortization expense is generally charged directly against the intangible asset and not added to an accumulated amortization account.

Suppose that on January 1, CCH publishing company buys the copyright to a book written by a popular author. CCH pays the author $240,000. Legally, the copyright grants an exclusive right to use the material for the author's life plus 50 years. In the case of the book, CCH estimates the useful life to be only 4 years (the amount of time the book is expected to generate sales). The entries to record the purchase of the copyright and the first year's amortization are as follows:

Jan. 1	Copyright	240,000	
	Cash		240,000
	To purchase copyright.		
Dec. 31	Amortization Expense, Copyright	60,000	
	Copyright		60,000
	To amortize cost of copyright: $240,000 / 4 years = $60,000 per year.		

At the end of the first year, the balance sheet of CCH shows the copyright with a balance of $180,000 ($240,000 – $60,000). After 2 years, the balance is $120,000; after 3 years, $60,000; and after 4 years, zero.

As another example, suppose that on July 1, Boeing Corporation purchases a patent for a new type of aircraft engine. Boeing pays the inventor $1,700,000 for the patent. Legally, a patent provides exclusive rights to produce and sell a specific product or process, usually for 20 years. However, Boeing expects the patent to be useful for only 10 years, after which the engine design will be obsolete. The entries to record the purchase of the patent on July 1 and a half-year's depreciation on December 31 are as follows:

July 1	Patent	1,700,000	
	Cash		1,700,000
	To purchase patent.		
Dec. 31	Amortization Expense , Patent	85,000	
	Patent		85,000
	To amortize cost of patent for one-half year: $1,700,000 / 10 = $170,000 per year × 6/12 = $85,000.		

Some people think that research and development costs should be included with intangible assets. **Research and development (R&D) costs** are expenditures for studying and creating new products or processes. In many companies, research and development costs are regarded as the most important asset, intangible or otherwise. This is especially true for companies in industries such as computers, aerospace, and pharmaceuticals. However, according to GAAP, R&D expenditures are not classified as assets. R&D expenditures are recorded as an expense in the period in which the expenditures are made.

¶808 Long-Term Investments

LEARNING OBJECTIVE 8: Describe the characteristics of long-term investments.

The final type of long-term asset presented in this chapter is long-term investments. If an investment does not meet the two criteria for a short-term investment, then it is classified as a long-term investment. The two criteria for labeling an investment short-term are: (1) the investment must be liquid, that is, easily converted to cash; and (2) management must plan to sell the investment within the coming year. Thus, a **long-term investment** is an investment expected to be held for longer than one year or is not liquid.

There are two basic types of long-term investments: equity securities and debt instruments. Investments in **equity securities** are investments in the stock of other companies. Investments in **debt instruments** are investments in bonds or notes issued by other companies. Debt instruments generally represent an obligation by the issuer to pay interest for a specified time period and then to return the principal amount of the bond or note.

On the balance sheet, assets are usually listed in order of liquidity, with the more liquid being listed first. Exhibit 8.12 shows the location of long-term investments in the asset section of a typical balance sheet.

? *Suppose you invent a capsule that will turn a gallon of water into gasoline. What intangible asset do you need in order to protect your invention?*

R&D costs are expenditures for studying and creating new products or processes.

A long-term investment is either expected to be held for longer than one year or is not liquid.

There are two basic types of long-term investments: equity securities and debt instruments.

Equity securities are corporate stocks.

Debt instruments are bonds and notes.

? What companies would you consider to be good long-term investments? Why?

Exhibit 8.12 PLACEMENT OF INVESTMENTS ON THE BALANCE SHEET	
Current Assets	($ Thousands)
Cash	$4,000
Short-Term Investments	2,000
Accounts Receivable	10,000
Inventory	6,000
Total Current Assets	$22,000
Long-Term Assets	
Long-Term Investments	$3,000
Land	8,000
Building & Equipment	12,000
Intangible Assets	2,000
Total Long-Term Assets	$25,000

FOCUS ON ETHICS

Insider Information and Trading

In 2003, Martha Stewart was investigated for participating in illegal insider trading. The case involved stock that she sold after receiving a tip from her former broker. During the investigation, she lied to investigators. Martha wasn't found guilty of insider trading, but she did go to jail for obstructing the investigation.

Under Carmike Cinemas' company guidelines, employees are instructed not to use confidential information obtained from Carmike in order to speculate in securities, commodities, real estate or business ventures. They also must not pass on such information to others. "Carmike Cinemas prohibits the misuse of *material* non-public information in securities trading." Information is material if a reasonable investor would consider it important in deciding whether to buy, sell or hold securities. Material information, if known to the public, could be expected to substantially affect the market price of a security.

Source: *www.Carmike.com*

¶809

Concluding Remarks

Some interesting questions where posed at the beginning of this chapter concerning Carmike Cinema renovating many of its theaters. If Carmike sells its old theater seats, whether or not Carmike incurs a gain or loss on the sale depends on the book value of the seats and the amount for which they are sold. The book value of the seats is the difference between the cost and accumulated depreciation of the seats. Most likely, the seats are already fully depreciated and thus, the book value is equal to the salvage value. The salvage value of the seats was determined when they were first purchased.

Another question posed concerned the effect of the renovation on the cost of the building. A renovation, if it extends a building's useful life, qualifies as an extraordinary repair. Accounting for an extraordinary repair does not change the cost of an asset. However, the amount spent on the extraordinary repair decreases accumulated depreciation and thereby increases the building's book value.

Carmike borrowed money to finance renovations. This increased Carmike's liabilities. In the next chapter, you will learn how to account for liabilities. We will also discuss different ways for acquiring the funds needed to finance company operations.

¶810 Chapter Review

LEARNING OBJECTIVE 1

Describe the importance of long-term assets to people within and outside a business.

There are two basic types of assets: current assets and long-term assets. Long-term assets include plant assets, intangibles, and long-term investments. All activities within a firm are connected in some way to long-term assets. Accountants keep track of the costs and expenses associated with long-term assets. People outside of the firm take into consideration long-term assets when judging the financial viability of a company.

LEARNING OBJECTIVE 2

Report how different departments contribute to asset acquisition decisions.

Long-term assets affect the operations of a business firm for a number of years. The decision as to which assets are needed is a cross-functional decision. Input is needed from several departments in the company. Current and future needs of the company, existing capabilities and resources, options and cost estimates for the asset, and market demand are important factors. When a company makes a decision to purchase a plant asset, accounting can determine the annual depreciation expense, based on the asset's cost, salvage value, and estimated useful life. The annual depreciation expense is an important consideration in making a plant asset purchase decision, but it is certainly not the only one. Naturally, a company must purchase the appropriate plant assets necessary to carry out company operations.

LEARNING OBJECTIVE 3

Calculate the cost of a plant asset such as land, building, or equipment.

The cost of an asset includes the price paid for the asset as well as any additional expenditure necessary to get the asset ready for use. The cost of plant assets such as buildings and equipment are gradually allocated to depreciation expense over their useful lives. Land is never depreciated, as its usefulness does not diminish. In the case of natural resources, such as timber or petroleum reserves, their cost is also expensed, but the expense is called "depletion" instead of depreciation.

LEARNING OBJECTIVE 4

Describe how assets are depreciated using various depreciation methods.

The cost of the asset, less its salvage value, is its depreciable cost, or amount to be depreciated. Thus, when we say depreciation is the allocation of an asset's cost to expense over its useful life, we mean the asset's depreciable cost, not its acquisition cost.

A company must choose the most appropriate depreciation method from a number of acceptable methods. The three most commonly used depreciation methods are straight-line, units of production, and double-declining-balance.

LEARNING OBJECTIVE 5

Describe and record the disposal of plant assets.

Plant assets are disposed of when they are worn out, obsolete, or for some other reason no longer useful. A company can dispose of an asset by selling it, exchanging it, or simply discarding it. Determining when an asset should be disposed of is typically a cross-functional decision. In order to make a wise decision, input is needed from multiple company departments, such as the current status of the asset and its impact on operations, options for disposing of the asset, and cost estimates for replacing the asset.

LEARNING OBJECTIVE 6

Identify accounting issues pertaining to natural resources and depletion.

Natural resources are a major part of the total assets of many companies. Natural resources are products of nature, such as timber, iron ore, coal, and petroleum reserves. When natural resources are acquired, they are recorded at their purchase price. In the same way that other plant assets are expensed through depreciation, natural resources are expensed through depletion.

LEARNING OBJECTIVE 7

Identify intangible assets and account for amortization expense.

Intangible assets are long-term assets that have no physical existence but represent a right to current and future benefits. Examples of intangible assets include leases on land, oil rights, patents, or copyrights. Intangible assets are recorded at their acquisition cost. In most cases, an intangible's cost is then allocated to expense in the same manner that plant assets are depreciated and natural resources are depleted. The process of expensing the cost of an intangible asset over its useful life is called "amortization."

LEARNING OBJECTIVE 8

Describe the characteristics of long-term investments.

Long-term investments are investments the company expects to hold for longer than one year or that are not liquid. The two basic types of long-term investments are equity securities and debt instruments. Investments in equity securities are investments in stock of other companies. Stock represents ownership of a corporation. Investments in debt instruments are investments in bonds or notes issued by other companies. Debt instruments generally represent an obligation by the issuer to pay interest for a specified time period and then to return the principal amount of the bond or note.

¶811

Glossary

Accelerated depreciation methods

Accelerated depreciation methods charge higher amounts to depreciation expense in the early years of an asset's useful life. The double-declining-balance method is an example of an accelerated depreciation method.

Amortization

The process of expensing the cost of an intangible asset over its useful life is called "amortization."

Book value

For plant assets, book value is the difference between its cost and accumulated depreciation. This may also be referred to as "carrying value."

Capital expenditure

A capital expenditure is a purchase that benefits future accounting periods.

Carrying value

For plant assets, carrying value is the difference between its cost and accumulated depreciation. The carrying value is the book value.

Change in accounting estimate

A change in accounting estimate is a revision to an accounting estimate, such as an asset's estimated useful life.

Commercial substance

Commercial substance means a transaction will change the economic position of the companies involved.

Copyright

A copyright provides exclusive rights to publish and sell books, musical compositions, or other literary works for the lifetime of the author plus 50 years. Copyrights include computer software. The federal government grants copyrights.

Debt instruments

Debt instruments are bonds and notes. Debt instruments generally represent an obligation by the issuer to pay interest for a specified time period and then to return the principal amount of the bond or note.

Depletion

The part of the cost of a natural resource that is used up in a period is called "depletion."

Depreciable cost

The cost of the asset, less its salvage value, is its depreciable cost. This is the total amount that will be depreciated by the end of the asset's useful life.

Depreciation

Depreciation is the process of allocating a long-term tangible asset's cost to expense over the asset's estimated useful life.

Double-declining-balance depreciation method

The double-declining balance method calculates annual depreciation by multiplying the asset's declining book value by a fixed percentage, which is twice the straight-line rate.

Equity securities

Equity securities are corporate stocks. Stock represents ownership of a corporation.

Extraordinary repair

An extraordinary repair extends the remaining useful life of an asset. An extraordinary repair is recorded with a debit to Accumulated Depreciation and a credit to the Asset account.

Franchise

A franchise grants exclusive rights to market a product or service in a specific location, or to use a special process or formula. A company or a government agency can grant a franchise.

Goodwill

Goodwill may refer to the excess of the cost of a group of assets, usually a business, over the fair market value of the net assets, if they were purchased individually. Goodwill may also refer to a good relationship of a business with its customers.

Intangible assets

Intangible assets have no physical existence but represent a right to current and future benefits.

Land improvements

Land improvements have a limited life and are depreciated. Examples of land improvements include driveways, sprinkler systems, and fences.

License

A license grants exclusive rights to market a product or service in a specific location, or to use a special process or formula. A company or a government agency can grant a license.

Long-term asset

A long-term asset is beneficial to the operations of a firm for more than one year and is not intended for resale to customers.

Long-term investment

A long-term investment is an investment expected to be held for longer than one year or is not liquid.

Market value

Market value is the current worth of an asset; in other words, it is the price that the asset can be sold for.

Natural resources

Natural resources are a product of nature, such as timber, iron ore, coal, and petroleum reserves.

Obsolescence

Obsolescence is the process in which an asset becomes inefficient or out-of-date in doing its job.

Patent

A patent provides exclusive rights to produce and sell a specific product or process. Patents are granted by the federal government and last for 17 years.

Physical deterioration

Physical deterioration is the normal wear and tear that gradually breaks down a physical asset until it is no longer functional.

Plant assets

Plant assets, also called "fixed assets," are tangible assets that have a useful life exceeding one year and are used in the operations of the company.

Research and development (R&D) costs

Research and development costs are expenditures for studying and creating new products or processes.

Residual value

The estimated residual value is the anticipated cash value of an asset at the end of its useful life. This is also referred to as "salvage value."

Revenue expenditure

A revenue expenditure is an expenditure that involves maintaining, repairing, and operating plant assets.

Salvage value

The estimated salvage value is the anticipated cash value of an asset at the end of its useful life. This is also referred to as "residual value."

Straight-line depreciation method

The straight-line depreciation method allocates an equal amount of depreciation expense to each year of the asset's useful life.

Trademark

A trademark provides unique identification to a company product or service. Trademarks are registered.

Units-of-production depreciation method

The units-of-production depreciation method allocates depreciation expense proportionately according to the units of output or service provided by the asset.

Useful life

Useful life is the length of time a long-term asset can be expected to perform its function.

¶812   Appendix: Accounting for Long-Term Investments

Long-term investments include investments in equity securities (stocks of other companies) and investments in debt instruments (bonds or notes issued by other companies). This appendix describes how to account for long-term investments in equity securities and for long-term investments in debt securities.

¶812.01   LONG-TERM INVESTMENTS IN EQUITY SECURITIES

Long-term investments in stock, also called "equity securities," may be accounted for using one of three methods. The method used depends on the percentage of stock owned. The three accounting methods are as follows:

- Market value method
- Equity method
- Consolidated subsidiary method

¶812.01.01   Market Value Method

20% *The market value method is used when the investor owns less than 20% of a company's stock and is considered non-influential and non-controlling.*

The **market value method** can be used only when the investment is non-influential and non-controlling ownership of less than 20 percent of a company's voting stock. The market value method applies to available-for-sale investments in stock that the company anticipates selling at its market value. For example, if Walmart buys Disney stock, Walmart must buy less than 20 percent of Disney's stock, and plan to sell the stock for its market value in the future.

Under the market value method, a long-term investment in stock is reported at its current market value on the day of purchase. Suppose that on April 1, Walmart buys 10,000 shares of Disney common stock at $30 per share, the current market price. Walmart expects to keep the investment for more than one year, and then sell it for its market value. The transaction is recorded as shown:

April 1	Long-Term Investment	300,000	
	Cash		300,000
	To record investment, $30 × 10,000 shares.		

Suppose Disney pays a $0.12 dividend per share on October 1. Walmart records the collection of the dividend as shown:

Oct. 1	Cash	1,200	
	Dividend Revenue		1,200
	To record dividend received, $0.12 × 10,000 shares.		

On the balance sheet, the long-term investment in Disney stock must be shown at market value. Assume that Disney stock on December 31 is trading for $31 per share; $1 more than its purchase price. Thus, Walmart records the following entry to increase the investment to its market value:

Dec. 31	Allowance to Adjust Investment to Market	10,000	
	Unrealized Gain on Investment		10,000
	To adjust investment to market value (10,000 × $1).		

The account, Allowance to Adjust Investment to Market, is an asset account that corresponds to the Long-Term Investment Account. The allowance adjusts the Long-Term Investment to its market value. The investment's cost, $300,000, is increased by the Allowance of $10,000, resulting in a carrying value of $310,000.

The investment and Allowance accounts have the following balances on December 31:

Long-Term Investment	Allowance to Adjust Investment to Market
300,000	10,000

If the market price per share had been $29 instead of $31, then the Allowance account would have a $10,000 credit balance, instead of a debit balance. In that case, the market value of the investment would be $290,000.

Exhibit 8.A shows how the Long-Term Investment and the Unrealized Gain on Investment is reported on Walmart's financial statements when the Disney stock price is $31. The Long-Term Investment is shown on the balance sheet at its carrying value (cost + allowance).

Exhibit 8.A FINANCIAL STATEMENT PRESENTATION OF LONG-TERM INVESTMENTS AND UNREALIZED GAIN

INCOME STATEMENT		
Revenues		$200,000
Expenses, including income tax		150,000
Net Income		$50,000
Other Comprehensive Income:		
Unrealized Gain on Investment	**$10,000**	
Less Income Tax (40%)	**(4,000)**	**6,000**
Comprehensive Income		$56,000
BALANCE SHEET		
Assets:		
Total Current Assets		$XXX
Long-Term Investments at market value (300,000 + 10,000)		**310,000**
Land		XXX
Building & Equipment (net)		XXX
Stockholders' Equity:		
Common Stock		$120,000
Retained Earnings		240,000
Accumulated Other Comprehensive Income: Unrealized Gain on Investments (net of tax)		**6,000**
Total Stockholders' Equity		$366,000

The unrealized gain is shown on the income statement and on the balance sheet. First, the unrealized gain is shown on the income statement as part of Other Comprehensive Income, which is shown in a separate section below net income. Next, the amount is reflected on the balance sheet as part of Accumulated Other Comprehensive Income, which is a separate section of stockholders' equity.

At some point, the company sells its long-term investment in available-for-sale investments. This results in a realized gain or loss on the investment. Suppose that on November 2, Walmart sells its investment in Disney stock for $32 per share. The transaction is recorded as shown:

Nov. 2	Cash	320,000	
	Long-Term Investment (cost)		300,000
	Gain on Sale of Investment		20,000
	To record sale of long-term investment.		

At the year-end, Walmart must update the two accounts: Allowance to Adjust Investment to Market and Unrealized Gain on Investment.

¶812.01.02   Equity Method

20% to 50%

The equity method is used when an investor owns 20 to 50 percent of a company's stock and thus, can influence company decisions.

The second method to account for long-term investments in stock is the equity method. The **equity method** to account for investments is used when the investor owns 20 to 50 percent of a company's stock. The equity method is used because it reflects the investor's potential to significantly affect a company's decisions through its ownership of 20 to 50 percent of the stock. A significant investor can influence decisions such as company policies, personnel selections, and research and development.

When an investment is purchased under the equity method, it is recorded at cost. Suppose Ford Motor Company purchases 8,000 shares of Southwest Brake Company at $100 per share. The 8,000 shares account for 40 percent of Southwest Brake Company's common stock. The transaction is recorded as shown:

Mar. 15	Long-Term Investment	800,000	
	Cash		800,000
	To record equity-method investment.		

Ford, the investor, now owns 40 percent of Southwest Brake Company, the investee. Consequently, Ford applies this percentage of ownership, 40 percent to record its part of the investee's dividends and net income. Assuming Southwest Brake pays a total cash dividend of $100,000, Ford receives 40 percent of this dividend. Ford records the dividend as follows:

Nov. 1	Cash ($100,000 × .40)	40,000	
	Long-Term Investment		40,000
	To record cash dividend from equity-method investments.		

The dividend increases the investor's (Ford's) cash; thus, Cash is increased (debited). However, payment of a dividend is considered to be a reduction or payback of the investee's (Southwest Brake) Long-Term Investment account, which is decreased (or credited).

Assume that Southwest Brake reports net income of $250,000. Ford records 40 percent of this net income as follows:

Dec. 31	Long-Term Investment	100,000	
	Equity-Method Investment Revenue		100,000
	To record investment revenue under equity method (40% × $250,000).		

Under the equity method of accounting, net income of the investee increases the investor's Long-Term Investments; a loss decreases Long-Term Investments. When using the equity method, Ford discloses its Long-Term Investments in the general ledger and on the financial statements as shown in Exhibit 8.B.

Exhibit 8.B ACCOUNTING FOR LONG-TERM INVESTMENT USING THE EQUITY METHOD

Long-Term Investments

Mar. 15	800,000	Nov. 1	40,000
Dec. 31	100,000		
Dec. 31 Bal.	860,000		

BALANCE SHEET (Partial)

Assets:	
Total Current Assets	$XXX
Long-Term Investments, at equity	**860,000**
Building & Equipment (net)	XXX

INCOME STATEMENT (Partial)

Operating Income	$XXX
Other Revenues and Expenses:	
Equity-Method Investment Revenue	**100,000**
Net Income	$XXX

When an equity-method long-term investment is sold, the gain or loss is calculated as the difference between the sales proceeds and the carrying value, which is the book value of the investment. Assume that Ford sells its 40 percent of the Southwest Brake Company stock for $900,000. Ford incurs a gain from the sale. The sale would be recorded as shown:

Jan. 21	Cash	900,000	
	Long-Term Investment		860,000
	Gain on Sale of Investment		40,000
	To record sale of investment.		

¶812.01.03   Consolidated Subsidiary Method

Many large corporations own a majority interest, also called "controlling interest," in other corporations. A **majority (controlling) interest** is ownership of more than 50 percent of an investee corporation's voting stock. In this case, the consolidated subsidiary method is used to account for the long-term investment in stock. When an investor company owns more than 50 percent of the investee company's stock, the investor company is called the "**parent company**" and the investee company is called the "**subsidiary company**."

The consolidated subsidiary method of accounting for a long-term investment is typically referred to as "consolidation accounting." **Consolidation accounting** is the combining of the financial statements of all companies that are controlled by one parent corporation. As a result, the parent corporation prepares a single set of consolidated financial statements that carry the name of the parent corporation. **Consolidated financial statements** are financial statements of the parent corporation combined with its majority-owned subsidiaries.

By combining the parent and its subsidiary corporation financial statements into one overall set of statements, the parent and its subsidiaries appear as a single corporation. For example, General Electric (GE) owns 80 percent of NBC Universal. Thus, the financial statements for GE and NBC are prepared into a single set of consolidated statements under the GE name. The consolidated financial statements provide a better understanding of the total financial situation than by reports of the parent and subsidiaries separately. When combining a parent and subsidiary corporation, the resulting consolidated financial statements show the total asset, liability, and equity amounts controlled by the parent.

Why should one company purchase another company? By acquiring control of another company, the investor can take full advantage of another company's operations. When Disney acquired ABC, Disney could promote its products and services on a major television network. The decision by Disney to acquire ABC was a cross-functional decision. For example, the marketing department used the acquisition of ABC to more effectively promote Disney products. Vital to making the acquisition happen, the finance department had to structure the $5.2 billion purchase.

When one company purchases another, the parent company typically pays more for the subsidiary company than the market value of the subsidiary's net assets. The amount exceeding market value is called "goodwill." Disney reports goodwill on its balance sheet, resulting from its purchase of subsidiary companies such as ABC.

If a parent company owns less than 100 percent of a subsidiary, then the parent must disclose the amount of a subsidiary's stock held by stockholders besides the parent. This amount is called "**minority interest**." Minority interest is shown in the liability section of the parent company's consolidated balance sheet.

¶812.02   LONG-TERM INVESTMENT IN DEBT INSTRUMENTS

Long-term investments may also take the form of debt instruments, also called "debt securities." Debt instruments are bonds and notes. When an investor purchases bonds and notes, with the intention to hold them until maturity, these are classified as **held-to-maturity investments**. Held-to-maturity investments are usually long-term investments.

Suppose General Electric Corporation purchases $100,000 of 6% GM bonds at a price of 98.2 on March 1, 20Y1. General Electric plans to hold the bonds for 36 months until they mature on March 1, 20Y4. Interest dates are March 1 and September 1. General Electric must amortize the bonds' carrying value from their cost of $98,200 up to $100,000 over their term to maturity. The investment in bonds is recorded as follows:

20Y1			
Mar. 1	Long-Term Investment in Bonds	98,200	
	Cash		98,200
	To record bond investment ($100,000 × .982)		

On September 1, the receipt of the interest payment and the straight-line amortization of the bond discount are recorded as follows:

Sep. 1	Cash	3,000	
	Interest Revenue		3,000
	To record semi-annual interest on bonds ($100,000 × .06 × 6/12).		
Sep. 1	Long-Term Investment in Bonds	300	
	Interest Revenue		300
	To record amortization of bond discount, using straight-line method (($100,000 – $98,200) / 36 × 6).		

At the fiscal year-end, the investor must make two adjusting entries. The first is for the accrued interest revenue and the second is to amortize the discount. The adjusting entries are as follows:

20Y1			
Dec. 31	Interest Receivable	2,000	
	Interest Revenue		2,000
	To record accrued interest revenue ($100,000 × .06 × 4/12).		
Dec. 31	Long-Term Investment in Bonds	200	
	Interest Revenue		200
	To record amortization of bond discount using straight-line method (($100,000 – $98,000) / 36 × 4).		

A bond may be purchased at a price higher than its face value. This is called a "premium" and it must be amortized, just as a discount must be amortized.

APPENDIX GLOSSARY

Consolidated financial statements

Consolidated financial statements are financial statements of the parent corporation combined with its majority-owned subsidiaries.

Consolidation accounting

Consolidation accounting is the combining of the financial statements of all companies that are controlled by one parent corporation.

Equity method

The equity method to account for investments is used when the investor owns 20 to 50 percent of a company's stock.

Held-to-maturity investments

Held-to-maturity investments include bonds and notes, which an investor intends to hold until maturity. They are usually long-term investments.

Majority (controlling) interest

A majority (controlling) interest is ownership of more than 50 percent of a corporation's voting stock.

Market value method

The market value method is used to account for long-term investments when the investment is non-influential and non-controlling ownership of less than 20 percent of a company's voting stock.

Minority interest

Minority interest is the amount of a subsidiary's stock held by stockholders other than the parent company.

Parent company

A parent company is a company that owns more than 50 percent of the stock of another company, known as a "subsidiary company."

Subsidiary company

A company is a subsidiary company when another company owns more than 50 percent of its stock. The company owning the subsidiary is called the "parent company."

¶813   # Chapter Assignments

QUESTIONS

1. **[Obj. 1]** Describe long-term assets.

2. **[Obj. 1]** Why are investors interested in a firm's long-term assets?

3. **[Obj. 2]** Who decides which assets to purchase? How does the accountant contribute to this decision?

4. **[Obj. 3]** Define plant assets and give examples.

5. **[Obj. 3]** On the balance sheet, should plant assets be shown at their cost or market value? Why? Could an ethical dilemma result from using market value?

6. **[Obj. 3]** Why are land improvements (e.g. driveways and fences) shown in a separate account from land?

7. **[Obj. 3]** When equipment is purchased, how is the cost of the equipment determined? How might the accountant depend on information from other departments within the firm in order to determine the cost of the equipment?

8. **[Obj. 3]** Distinguish between capital expenditures and revenue expenditures.

9. **[Obj. 3]** What sort of ethical dilemma might occur regarding whether to expense or capitalize repairs to equipment?

10. **[Obj. 4]** Why are plant assets depreciated?

11. **[Obj. 4]** What is the difference between depreciable cost and acquisition cost?

12. **[Obj. 4]** What are the two basic causes of depreciation? What effect does information technology have?

13. **[Obj. 4]** Describe the three most commonly used depreciation methods.

14. **[Obj. 4]** What is a change in useful life and how does it affect depreciation?

15. **[Obj. 4]** What is an extraordinary repair?

16. **[Obj. 4]** Why is depreciation sometimes calculated differently for tax purposes than for financial reporting purposes? Does this pose an ethical dilemma?

17. **[Obj. 5]** Why and how are plant assets disposed of? In your opinion, how does the global market affect plant disposal?

18. **[Obj. 5]** When is the disposal of a plant asset a cross-functional decision, involving more than accountants?

19. **[Obj. 5]** What is an exchange of a plant asset? What accounting issues are involved in an exchange?

20. **[Obj. 6]** What are natural resources and how are they different from other assets?

21 . **[Obj. 6]** What is depletion?

22. **[Obj. 7]** Describe intangible assets and the process of amortization.

23. **[Obj. 7]** Describe research and development (R&D) costs. Why do some people argue that R&D costs should be capitalized and not expensed?

24. **[Obj. 8]** What is a long-term investment?

SHORT EXERCISES – SET A

Building Accounting Skills

1 . **[Obj. 3]** Recording an Asset Acquisition: Suppose that on March 1, Sears purchases land on which the company plans to build a retail store. Sears pays $200,000 for the land. The company pays cash of $20,000 and borrows $180,000 on a note payable from Wells Fargo Bank. Sears also pays cash of $12,000 in real estate commissions, $1,000 in survey fees, $10,000 for clearing and grading the land, and lawyers' fees of $2,000. Sears pays $150,000 in cash for construction of a driveway and parking lot. What amount should Sears record as the cost of the land? Prepare each of the following:
   a. A schedule tabulating the cost of the land.
   b. The journal entry to record the land purchase.
   c. The journal entry to record land improvements.

2. **[Obj. 3]** Recording an Asset Acquisition: Suppose that on February 14, Royal Dutch Shell purchases equipment for $50,000. Shell pays cash of $15,000 and borrows $35,000 on a note payable from Wells Fargo Bank. Shell also pays cash of $800 for shipping fees, $50 for insurance during transit, $2,000 in installation costs, and $400 for test runs. What amount should Shell record as the cost of the equipment? Prepare each of the following:
   a. A schedule tabulating the cost of the equipment.
   b. The journal entry to record the equipment purchase.

3. **[Obj. 3]** Recoding a Lump-Sum Purchase: Suppose that on September 1, 20Y1, Apple Computer Company purchases land and a building for a lump-sum price of $820,000. Apple must assign a separate cost to the land and building. How much of the price should be allocated to the land and how much to the building? The appraised value of the land is $180,000 and the appraised value of the building is $720,000. Prepare each of the following:
   a. Allocation schedule of lump-sum purchase price to the individual assets.
   b. The journal entry to record the lump-sum purchase.

4. **[Obj. 4]** Calculating Depreciation: Suppose that on January 1, 20Y1, Hewlett Packard Corporation purchases equipment that costs $10,000, has a useful life of 4 years, and a salvage value of $2,000. The equipment is expected to produce 5,000 isolinear chips over its lifetime. In the first year, the equipment produced 1,500 isolinear chips. Calculate the first year's depreciation using straight-line, units-of-production, and double-declining balance method. Show your calculations.

5. **[Obj. 4]** Recording Depreciation for a Partial Year: Suppose Home Depot Corporation purchases a building for $250,000 on April 1, 20Y1. The building's estimated useful life is 20 years, and its estimated salvage value is $10,000. The company fiscal year end is December 31.
   a. How much should Home Depot record for depreciation expense at the end of the year?
   b. Make the journal entry to record depreciation expense at the year-end.

6. **[Obj. 4]** Changing Accounting Estimates: Assume Sears paid $5,000 for photo-imaging equipment and initially estimated the useful life at five years with no salvage value. The company used the equipment for three years. Using straight-line depreciation, annual depreciation expense is $1,000 ($5,000 / 5 years). According to the original estimate, the equipment should have 2 more years of useful life; however, management determines that the equipment has four more years of useful life.
   a. Calculate depreciation expense for the fourth year after the change in accounting estimate.
   b. Make the journal entry to record depreciation expense at the year-end.

7. **[Obj. 4]** Recording Extraordinary Repairs: Assume that one of Coca-Cola Corporation's delivery trucks, which carries beverages from a bottling plant to warehouses, originally costs $50,000. The truck has an estimated useful life of 4 years and no salvage value. The truck has been depreciated using the straight-line method for 2 years. At the end of the second year, on December 31, the truck is given a major overhaul for $5,000. As a result, the useful life of the truck is extended one year beyond the original estimate.

   a. What entry would be made to record the extraordinary repair at the end of the second year?

   b. As a result of the extraordinary repair, the annual depreciation expense must be recalculated. What is the new amount of annual straight-line depreciation expense to be recorded in years three to five? Show your calculation.

   c. Make the journal entry to record depreciation at the end of the third year.

8. **[Obj. 5]** Disposing of a Plant Asset: Suppose that on June 1, General Electric Corporation discards manufacturing equipment that cost $80,000 and which has accumulated depreciation of $75,000. Make the journal entry to record the disposal.

9. **[Obj. 6]** Recording Purchase and Depletion of Natural Resources: Suppose that on July 1, Georgia Pacific Corporation purchases rights to cut the timber on 2,000 acres of land for $4,000,000. On December 31, a total of 200 acres have been cut and all the timber was used.

   a. Make the journal entry to record the purchase.

   b. Make the journal entry to record depletion at the end of the year.

10. **[Obj. 7]** Recording Purchase and Amortization of an Intangible Asset: Suppose that on January 1, CCH publishing company buys the copyright to a book written by a popular author. CCH pays the author $50,000. Legally, the copyright grants an exclusive right to use the material for the author's life plus 50 years. However, CCH estimates the useful life to be only 2 years (the amount of time the book will generate sales).

    a. Make the journal entry to record the purchase.

    b. Make the journal entry to record amortization at the end of the year.

11. **[Appendix]** Recording Purchase of a Long-Term Investment: Suppose that on July 1, Coca-Cola Corporation buys 10,000 shares of JC Penney common stock at $40 per share, the current market price. Coca-Cola expects to keep the investment for more than one year, and then sell it for its market value. Assume JC Penney pays a $0.15 dividend per share on November 15. Assume that JC Penney stock on December 31 is trading for $41 per share.

    a. Make the journal entry to record the purchase.

    b. Make the journal entry to record the dividend received

    c. Make the journal entry to adjust the investment to market.

12. **[Appendix]** Recording Long-Term Investments: Suppose Home Depot Corporation purchases $100,000 of 6% Target Corporation bonds at a price of 101.8 on March 1, 20Y1. Home Depot plans to hold the bonds for 36 months until they mature on March 1, 20Y4. Interest dates are March 1 and September 1. Home Depot must amortize the bonds' carrying value from their cost of $101,800 down to $100,000 over their term to maturity.

    a. How should the investment be recorded on March 1, 20Y1?

    b. What journal entry would be made to record the receipt of the interest payment on September 1?

    c. Assuming straight-line amortization is used, what is the journal entry to record the amortization of the bond premium on September 1?

    d. Make the two adjusting entries necessary on December 31 to record accrued interest revenue and to record amortization of the premium.

SHORT EXERCISES – SET B

Building Accounting Skills

1. **[Obj. 3]** Recording an Asset Acquisition: Suppose that on June 20, Microsoft Corporation purchases land on which the company plans to build an office building. Microsoft pays $700,000 for the land. The company pays cash of $140,000 and borrows $560,000 on a note payable from CitiBank. Microsoft also pays cash of $21,000 in real estate commissions, $3,000 in survey fees, $22,000 for clearing and grading the land, and lawyers' fees of $4,000. Microsoft pays $300,000 in cash for construction of a driveway and parking lot. What amount should Microsoft record as the cost of the land? Prepare each of the following:
   a. A schedule tabulating the cost of the land.
   b. The journal entry to record the land purchase.
   c. The journal entry to record land improvements.

2. **[Obj. 3]** Recording an Asset Acquisition: Suppose that on April 1, Ford Motor Company purchases equipment for $300,000. Ford pays cash of $100,000 and borrows $200,000 on a note payable from J.P. Morgan Bank. Ford also pays cash of $2,200 for shipping fees, $500 for insurance during transit, $5,000 in installation costs, and $7,200 for test runs. What amount should Ford record as the cost of the equipment? Prepare each of the following:
   a. A schedule tabulating the cost of the equipment.
   b. The journal entry to record the equipment purchase.

3. **[Obj. 3]** Recording a Lump-Sum Purchase: Suppose that on November 5, 20Y1, Midas Corporation purchases land, building, and equipment for a lump-sum price of $780,000. Midas must assign a separate cost to the land, building, and equipment. How much of the price should be allocated to the land, how much to the building, and how much to the equipment? The appraised value of the land is $150,000, appraised value of the building is $600,000, and appraised value of the equipment is $250,000. Prepare each of the following:
   a. Allocation schedule of lump-sum purchase price to the individual assets.
   b. The journal entry to record the lump-sum purchase.

4. **[Obj. 4]** Calculating Depreciation: Suppose that on January 1, 20Y1, Apple Computers purchases equipment that costs $19,000, has a useful life of 4 years, and a salvage value of $3,000. The equipment is expected to produce 5,000 isolinear chips over its useful life. The first year, the equipment produced 1,500 chips. Calculate the first year's depreciation using straight-line, units-of-production, and double-declining balance method. Show your calculations.

5. **[Obj. 4]** Recording Depreciation for a Partial Year: Suppose Nestle Corporation purchases equipment for $50,000 on October 1, 20Y1. The equipment's estimated useful life is 10 years, and its estimated salvage value is $2,000. The company fiscal year end is December 31.
   a. How much should Nestle record for depreciation expense at the end of the year?
   b. Make the journal entry to record depreciation expense at the year-end.

6. **[Obj. 4]** Changing Accounting Estimates: Assume Caterpillar Company paid $100,000 for track-making equipment and initially estimated the useful life at 8 years with no salvage value. The company used the equipment for 6 years and recorded depreciation using the straight-line method. According to the original estimate, the equipment should have 2 more years of useful life; however, management determines that the equipment has 5 more years of useful life.
    a. Calculate depreciation expense for Year 7 after the change in accounting estimate.
    b. Make the journal entry to record depreciation expense at the year-end.

7. **[Obj. 4]** Recording Extraordinary Repairs: Assume that a shoe-making machine at Nike Corporation originally costs $75,000. The machine has an estimated useful life of 5 years and no salvage value. The truck has been depreciated using the straight-line method for 3 years. Depreciation expense recorded for each of the first three years was $15,000 ($75,000 / 5). At the end of the third year, on December 31, the machine is given a major overhaul for $10,000. As a result, the useful life of the machine is extended three years beyond the original estimate, to a total of eight years.
    a. What entry would be made to record the extraordinary repair at the end of the third year?
    b. As a result of the extraordinary repair, the annual depreciation expense must be recalculated. What is the new amount of annual straight-line depreciation expense to be recorded in years four to eight? Show your calculation.
    c. Make the journal entry to record depreciation at the end of the fourth year.

8. **[Obj. 5]** Disposing of a Plant Asset: Suppose that on November 1, Procter & Gamble Corporation discards equipment that cost $5,000 and which has accumulated depreciation of $5,000. Make the journal entry to record the disposal.

9. **[Obj. 6]** Recording Natural Resources and Depletion: Suppose that on February 1, ExxonMobil Corporation purchases rights to explore for and produce oil on 10,000 square miles of land and ocean for $10,000,000. Oil reserves are estimated at 100 million barrels. On December 31, a total of 2 million barrels have been produced.
    a. Make the journal entry to record the purchase.
    b. Make the journal entry to record depletion at the end of the year.

10. **[Obj. 7]** Recording Intangible Assets and Amortization: Suppose that on January 1, Sony Corporation buys the copyright to a song written by a popular musician. Sony pays the author $45,000. Legally, the copyright grants an exclusive right to use the material for the author's life plus 50 years. However, Sony estimates the useful life to be only 3 years (the amount of time the song will generate sales).
    a. Make the journal entry to record the purchase.
    b. Make the journal entry to record amortization at the end of the year.

11. **[Appendix]** Recording Long-Term Investments Using the Equity Method: Suppose Dell Computer Company purchases 4,000 shares of Acme PC Company at $100 per share on January 15 as a long-term investment. The 4,000 shares account for 30 percent of Acme PC Company's common stock. Dell, the investor, now owns 30 percent of Acme PC Company, the investee. Consequently, Dell applies this percentage of ownership, 30 percent to record its part of the investee's dividends and net income. On October 1, Acme pays a total cash dividend of $100,000. On December 31, Acme reports net income of $300,000.
    a. How does Dell record the purchase transaction on January 15?
    b. How would Dell record receipt of the cash dividend on October 1?
    c. How would Dell record its share of Acme's net income?

12. **[Appendix]** Recording Long-Term Investments in Debt Instruments: Suppose Kroger Corporation purchases $200,000 of 6% IBM bonds at a price of 96.4 on March 1, 20Y1. Kroger plans to hold the bonds for 36 months until maturity on March 1, 20Y4. Interest dates are March 1 and September 1. Kroger must amortize the bonds' carrying value from their cost of $192,800 up to $200,000 over their term to maturity.
    a. How should the investment be recorded on March 1, 20Y1?
    b. What journal entry would be made to record the receipt of the interest payment on September 1?
    c. Assuming straight-line amortization is used, what is the journal entry to record the amortization of the bond discount on September 1?
    d. Make the two adjusting entries necessary on December 31 to record accrued interest revenue and to record amortization of the discount.

PROBLEMS – SET A

Applying Accounting Knowledge

1. **[Obj. 4]** Calculating Depreciation: Suppose that on January 1, 20Y1, General Motors purchased equipment that costs $40,000, has a useful life of 5 years, and a salvage value of $5,000.

    Required:
    a. Calculate the annual depreciation expense using the straight-line method. Prepare a schedule of depreciation expense for all five years of the equipment's useful life — showing cost, annual depreciation expense, accumulated depreciation, and book value at the end of each year.
    b. Evaluate: How does the schedule of depreciation expense for this equipment help managers evaluate the contribution of the equipment to company operations?
    c. Evaluate: In addition to depreciation, what other expenses associated with the equipment should managers consider in evaluating the equipment's operating costs?

2. **[Obj. 4]** Calculating Depreciation: Same as problem A1, except the cost and salvage value have been changed. Suppose that on January 1, 20Y1 General Motors purchased equipment that costs $50,000, has a useful life of 5 years, and a salvage value of $10,000.

    Required:
    a. Calculate the annual depreciation expense using the straight-line method. Prepare a schedule of depreciation expense for all five years of the equipment's useful life — showing cost, annual depreciation expense, accumulated depreciation, and book value at the end of each year.
    b. Evaluate: How does the schedule of depreciation expense for this equipment help managers evaluate the contribution of the equipment to company operations?
    c. Evaluate: In addition to depreciation, what other expenses associated with the equipment should managers consider in evaluating the equipment's operating costs?

3. **[Obj. 4]** Calculating Depreciation: On January 1, 20Y1, Junior's Tire Factory purchased a machine for $160,000. The machine is expected to produce 300,000 tires over its useful life and then have a salvage value of $10,000. Tire production each year is as follows:

Year	Tires Produced
20Y1	50,000
20Y2	70,000
20Y3	60,000
20Y4	80,000
20Y5	40,000

Required:

a. Prepare a schedule of depreciation expense using the units-of-production method. Include the following items in the schedule:
   - Cost
   - Depreciation per Unit
   - Number of Units
   - Annual Depreciation Expense
   - Accumulated Depreciation
   - Book Value

b. Evaluate: Why is the units-of-production method an appropriate method for depreciating this machine?

4. **[Obj. 4]** Calculating Depreciation: Same as problem A3, except the cost and salvage value have been changed. On January 1, 20Y1, Junior's Tire Factory purchased a machine for $124,000. The machine is expected to produce 300,000 tires over its useful life and then have a salvage value of $4,000. Tire production each year is as follows:

Year	Tires Produced
20Y1	50,000
20Y2	70,000
20Y3	60,000
20Y4	80,000
20Y5	40,000

Required:

a. Prepare a schedule of depreciation expense using the units-of-production method. Include the following items in the schedule:
   - Cost
   - Depreciation per Unit
   - Number of Units
   - Annual Depreciation Expense
   - Accumulated Depreciation
   - Book Value

b. Evaluate: Why is the units-of-production method an appropriate method for depreciating this machine?

5. **[Obj. 4]** Calculating Depreciation: Suppose that on January 1, 20Y1, FedEx purchased a delivery truck for $75,000. The truck has an estimated useful life of 5 years and an estimated salvage value of $5,000.

Required:

a. Prepare a schedule of depreciation expense using the double-declining balance method for all five years — showing cost, annual depreciation expense, accumulated depreciation, and book value at the end of each year.

b. Evaluate: In addition to depreciation, what other expenses associated with the equipment should managers consider in evaluating the equipment's operating costs?

6. **[Obj. 4]** Calculating Depreciation: Same as problem A5, except the cost and estimated salvage value have been changed. Suppose that on January 1, 20Y1, FedEx purchased a delivery truck for $57,000. The truck has an estimated useful life of 5 years and an estimated salvage value of $7,000.

Required:
a. Prepare a schedule of depreciation expense using the double-declining balance method for all five years — showing cost, annual depreciation expense, accumulated depreciation, and book value at the end of each year.
b. Evaluate: In addition to depreciation, what other expenses associated with the equipment should managers consider in evaluating the equipment's operating costs?

7. **[Obj. 5]** Recording the Sale of a Plant Asset: Suppose Armstrong Tire Company acquired a tire-making machine for a cost of $300,000 on January 1, 20Y1. The machine's estimated useful life is 7 years and its estimated salvage value is $20,000. Armstrong uses straight-line depreciation; thus, the yearly depreciation expense for the machine is $40,000 ((300,000 − 20,000) / 7). After just 4 1/2 years, Armstrong determines the machine is obsolete and sells it to a salvage company for $100,000 on June 30, 20Y5. Before recording the sale, Armstrong must record a partial-year's depreciation expense for January through June 20Y5.

Required:
a. How much accumulated depreciation has been recorded for the machine's first four years, 20Y1 to 20Y4?
b. Prepare the journal entry to record the partial year's depreciation for 20Y5.
c. Prepare the journal entry to record the sale.

8. **[Obj. 5]** Recording the Sale of a Plant Asset: Same as problem A7, but the sale price has been changed. Suppose Armstrong Tire Company acquired a tire-making machine for a cost of $300,000 on January 1, 20Y1. The machine's estimated useful life is 7 years and its estimated salvage value is $20,000. Armstrong uses straight-line depreciation. After just 4 1/2 years, Armstrong determines the machine is obsolete and sells it to a salvage company for $150,000 on June 30, 20Y5. Before recording the sale, Armstrong must record a partial-year's depreciation expense for January through June 20Y5.

Required:
a. How much accumulated depreciation has been recorded for the machine's first four years, 20Y1 to 20Y4?
b. Prepare the journal entry to record the partial year's depreciation for 20Y5.
c. Prepare the journal entry to record the sale.

9. **[Obj. 5]** Recording the Exchange of Plant Assets – Commercial Substance: Suppose that on January 2, Starbucks Corporation trades in old coffee-making equipment on the purchase of cookie-making equipment. The old equipment cost $12,000 and has accumulated depreciation of $10,000. Assume the transaction has commercial substance. Starbucks trades in the old equipment and also pays $12,000 cash for the new equipment. If there is no trade-in, then the cash price for the new equipment is $15,000.

Required:
a. How are gains and losses accounted for in an exchange of plant assets when the transaction has commercial substance?
b. What is the cost assigned to the new equipment?
c. What must the current value of the old equipment be?
d. What is the total gain/loss on the exchange?
e. Make the journal entry to record the exchange.

10. **[Obj. 5]** Recording the Exchange of Similar Assets—Commercial Substance: Same as problem A9, but the cash price for the new equipment has been changed. Suppose that on January 2, Starbucks Corporation trades in old coffee-making equipment on the purchase of cookie-making equipment. The old equipment cost $12,000 and has accumulated depreciation of $10,000. Assume the transaction has commercial substance. Starbucks trades in the old equipment and also pays $12,000 cash for the new equipment. If there is no trade-in, then the cash price for the new equipment is $13,000.

    Required:
    a. How are gains and losses accounted for in an exchange of plant assets when the transaction has commercial substance?
    b. What is the cost assigned to the new equipment?
    c. What must the current value of the old equipment be?
    d. What is the total gain/loss on the exchange?
    e. Make the journal entry to record the exchange.

11. **[Obj. 5]** Recording the Exchange of Plant Assets—Lacks Commercial Substance: Suppose that on January 2, Midas Brake Company trades in old diagnostic equipment on the purchase of new diagnostic equipment. The old equipment cost $6,000 and has accumulated depreciation of $4,000. Assume the transaction lacks commercial substance. Midas trades in the old equipment and also pays $7,000 cash for the new equipment. The old equipment would sell for $3,000, if there were no trade-in. The fair market value of the new equipment is unknown.

    Required:
    a. How are gains and losses accounted for in an exchange of plant assets when the transaction lacks commercial substance?
    b. What is the fair market value of the new equipment?
    c. What is the total gain/loss on the exchange?
    d. Make the journal entry to record the exchange.

12. **[Obj. 5]** Recording the Exchange of Plant Assets—Lacks Commercial Substance: Same as problem A11, but the cash price of the new equipment is different. Suppose that on April 1, Midas Brake Company trades in old diagnostic equipment on the purchase of new diagnostic equipment. The old equipment cost $10,000 and has accumulated depreciation of $4,000. Assume the transaction lacks commercial substance. Midas trades in the old equipment and received the new equipment and $1,000 in cash. The old equipment would sell for $8,000, if there were no trade-in. The fair market value of the new equipment is unknown.

    Required:
    a. How are gains and losses accounted for in an exchange of plant assets when the transaction lacks commercial substance?
    b. What is the fair market value of the new equipment?
    c. What is the total gain/loss on the exchange?
    d. Make the journal entry to record the exchange.

PROBLEMS – SET B

Applying Accounting Knowledge

1. **[Obj. 4]** Calculating Depreciation: Suppose that on January 1, 20Y1, the Veterinary Clinic purchased equipment that costs $60,000, has a useful life of 5 years, and a salvage value of $5,000.

   Required:
   a. Calculate the annual depreciation expense using the straight-line method. Prepare a schedule of depreciation expense for all five years of the equipment's useful life — showing cost, annual depreciation expense, accumulated depreciation, and book value at the end of each year.
   b. Evaluate: How does the schedule of depreciation expense for this equipment help the owner evaluate the contribution of the equipment to business operations?
   c. Evaluate: In addition to depreciation, what other expenses associated with the equipment should the owner consider in evaluating the equipment's operating costs?

2. **[Obj. 4]** Calculating Depreciation: Same as problem B1, except the cost and salvage value have been changed. Suppose that on January 1, 20Y1, the Veterinary Clinic purchased equipment that costs $70,000, has a useful life of 5 years, and a salvage value of $10,000.

   Required:
   a. Calculate the annual depreciation expense using the straight-line method. Prepare a schedule of depreciation expense for all five years of the equipment's useful life — showing cost, annual depreciation expense, accumulated depreciation, and book value at the end of each year.
   b. Evaluate — How does the schedule of depreciation expense for this equipment help the owner evaluate the contribution of the equipment to company operations?
   c. Evaluate — In addition to depreciation, what other expenses associated with the equipment should be considered in evaluating the equipment's operating costs?

3. **[Obj. 4]** Calculating Depreciation: On January 1, 20Y1, Firestone Tire Factory purchased a machine for $190,000. The machine is expected to produce 300,000 tires over its useful life and then have a salvage value of $10,000. Tire production each year is as follows:

Year	Tires Produced
20Y1	50,000
20Y2	70,000
20Y3	60,000
20Y4	80,000
20Y5	40,000

   Required:
   a. Prepare a schedule of depreciation expense using the units-of-production method. Include the following items in the schedule: Cost, Depreciation per Unit, Number of Units, Annual Depreciation Expense, Accumulated Depreciation, and Book Value
   b. Evaluate — Why is the units-of-production method an appropriate method for depreciating this machine?

4. **[Obj. 4]** Calculating Depreciation: Same as Problem B3, except the cost and salvage value have been changed. On January 1, 20Y1, Firestone Tire Factory purchased a machine for $270,000. The machine is expected to produce 300,000 tires over its useful life and then have a salvage value of $15,000. Tire production each year is as follows:

Year	Tires Produced
20Y1	50,000
20Y2	70,000
20Y3	60,000
20Y4	80,000
20Y5	40,000

Required:
a. Prepare a schedule of depreciation expense using the units-of-production method. Include the following items in the schedule: Cost, Depreciation per Unit, Number of Units, Annual Depreciation Expense, Accumulated Depreciation, and Book Value
b. Evaluate: Why is the units-of-production method an appropriate method for depreciating this machine?

5. **[Obj. 4]** Calculating Depreciation: Suppose that on January 1, 20Y1, UPS purchased a delivery truck for $68,000. The truck has an estimated useful life of 5 years and an estimated salvage value of $5,000. Prepare a schedule of depreciation expense using the double-declining balance method.

Required:
a. Prepare a schedule of depreciation expense using the double-declining balance method for all five years — showing cost, annual depreciation expense, accumulated depreciation, and book value at the end of each year.
b. Evaluate: In addition to depreciation, what other expenses associated with the equipment should managers consider in evaluating the equipment's operating costs?

6. **[Obj. 4]** Calculating Depreciation: Same as problem B5, except the cost and estimated salvage value have been changed. Suppose that on January 1, 20Y1, UPS purchased a delivery truck for $86,000. The truck has an estimated useful life of 5 years and an estimated salvage value of $7,000.

Required:
a. Prepare a schedule of depreciation expense using the double-declining balance method for all five years, showing cost, annual depreciation expense, accumulated depreciation, and book value at the end of each year.
b. Evaluate: In addition to depreciation, what other expenses associated with the equipment should managers consider in evaluating the equipment's operating costs?

7. **[Obj. 5]** Recording the Sale of a Plant Asset: Suppose the Authentic Tortilla Company acquired a tortilla-making machine for a cost of $160,000 on January 1, 20Y1. The machine's estimated useful life is 7 years and its estimated salvage value is $20,000. Armstrong uses straight-line depreciation; thus, the yearly depreciation expense for the machine is $20,000 ((160,000 – 20,000) / 7). After just 4 1/2 years, Armstrong determines the machine is obsolete and sells it to a salvage company for $50,000 on June 30, 20Y5. Before recording the sale, the company must record a partial-year's depreciation expense for January through June 20Y5.

Required:
a. How much accumulated depreciation has been recorded for the machine's first four years, 20Y1 to 20Y4?
b. Prepare the journal entry to record the partial year's depreciation for 20Y5.
c. Prepare the journal entry to record the sale.

8. **[Obj. 5]** Recording the Sale of a Plant Asset: Same as problem B7, but the sale price has been changed. Suppose the Authentic Tortilla Company acquired a tortilla-making machine for $160,000 on January 1, 20Y1. The machine's estimated useful life is 7 years and its estimated salvage value is $20,000. Armstrong uses straight-line depreciation. After just 4 1/2 years, Armstrong determines the machine is obsolete and sells it to a salvage company for $75,000 on June 30, 20Y5. Before recording the sale, the company must record a partial-year's depreciation expense for January through June 20Y5.

Required:
a. How much accumulated depreciation has been recorded for the machine's first four years, 20Y1 to 20Y4?
b. Prepare the journal entry to record the partial year's depreciation for 20Y5.
c. Prepare the journal entry to record the sale.

9. **[Obj. 5]** Recording the Exchange of Plant Assets — Commercial Substance: Suppose that on January 2, the Great American Cookie Company trades in old coffee-making equipment on the purchase of cookie-making equipment. The old equipment cost $24,000 and has accumulated depreciation of $20,000. Assume the transaction has commercial substance. The company trades in the old equipment and also pays $24,000 cash for the new equipment. If there is no trade-in, then the cash price for the new equipment is $30,000.

Required:
a. How are gains and losses accounted for in an exchange of plant assets when the transaction has commercial substance?
b. What is the cost assigned to the new equipment?
c. What must the current value of the old equipment be?
d. What is the total gain/loss on the exchange?
e. Make the journal entry to record the exchange.

10. **[Obj. 5]** Recording the Exchange of Similar Assets — Commercial Substance: Same as problem B9, but the cash price has been changed. Suppose that on January 2, the Great American Cookie Company trades in old coffee-making equipment on the purchase of cookie-making equipment. The old equipment cost $24,000 and has accumulated depreciation of $20,000. Assume the transaction has commercial substance. The company trades in the old equipment and also pays $24,000 cash for the new equipment. If there is no trade-in, then the cash price for the new equipment is $26,000.

Required:
a. How are gains and losses accounted for in an exchange of plant assets when the transaction has commercial substance?
b. What is the cost assigned to the new equipment?
c. What must the current value of the old equipment be?
d. What is the total gain/loss on the exchange?
e. Make the journal entry to record the exchange.

11. **[Obj. 5]** Recording the Exchange of Plant Assets – Lacks Commercial Substance: Suppose that on January 2, Coca-Cola Bottling Company trades in old equipment on the purchase of new equipment. The old equipment cost $12,000 and has accumulated depreciation of $8,000. Assume the transaction lacks commercial substance. The company trades in the old equipment and also pays $14,000 cash for the new equipment. The old equipment would sell for $6,000, if there were no trade-in. The fair market value of the new equipment is unknown.

Required:
a. How are gains and losses accounted for in an exchange of plant assets when the transaction lacks commercial substance?
b. What is the fair market value of the new equipment?
c. What is the total gain/loss on the exchange?
d. Make the journal entry to record the exchange.

12. **[Obj. 5]** Recording the Exchange of Plant Assets – Lacks Commercial Substance: Suppose that on April 1, Coca-Cola Bottling Company trades in old equipment on the purchase of new equipment. The old equipment cost $15,000 and has accumulated depreciation of $10,000. Assume that the transaction lacks commercial substance. The company trades in the old equipment received the new equipment and $2,000 in cash. The old equipment would sell for $9,000, if there were no trade-in. The fair market value of the new equipment is unknown.

Required:
a. How are gains and losses accounted for in an exchange of plant assets when the transaction lacks commercial substance?
b. What is the fair market value of the new equipment?
c. What is the total gain/loss on the exchange?
d. Make the journal entry to record the exchange.

CROSS-FUNCTIONAL PERSPECTIVES

Discussion Questions

1. **[Obj. 2]** Why does the decision to acquire assets often involve input from multiple departments within a company?

2. **[Obj. 5]** Why does the decision to dispose of an asset often involve input from multiple departments within a company?

3. **[Obj. 7]** In what way is a company's research and development team dependent upon other departments within the company?

4. **Appendix:** How does the acquisition of another company affect the departments within the parent company?

Cross-functional Case: Can Carmike Make a Profit in Your Town?

Carmike Cinema, Inc. is deciding whether to build a new movie theater in the city in which your college is located. You are part of a team whose task is to determine the feasibility of opening a new Carmike theater in your town. Your team will research the cost of building a theater, analyze the market's supply and demand for theaters, and make a recommendation to build or not to build. This will be a preliminary feasibility study. If there is already a Carmike theater in your town, then the company is considering building a second theater. The team's tasks are discussed in the following paragraphs according to operating functions.

Marketing. The main task is to determine if there is enough demand in the area to support another theater. In other words, are there enough moviegoers? Here are ideas to help gauge demand: Are the current theaters doing a good business? Are the parking lots full? Question a theater employee regarding attendance. Find out the population of your town and the surrounding areas from which people may travel to attend the theater. Divide the population by the number of theaters in town to determine the population share for each theater.

After gauging demand, determine how many screens the new theater should have. For simplification, assume that each theater screen will accommodate 200 people. Marketing must also recommend what ticket prices to charge.

Accounting. Provide a projected income statement. This includes projected revenues, expenses, and net income. Revenues consist of ticket sales and concession sales. Assume the national average for yearly ticket revenue is $125,000 per theater screen. Additional revenue comes from concession sales. Assume that concession revenue is 25 percent of ticket revenue.

Expenses include fixed and variable expenses. Assume that fixed expenses are $90,000 per screen per year. Variable expense is 15 percent of ticket revenue.

Finance. The main task is to explore financing options for construction of the theater. Assume that Carmike must borrow the money to build. Estimated construction cost is $200,000 per screen. Assume that Carmike can either take out a 15-year loan at 6 percent interest or a 30-year loan at 7 percent interest. Which do you recommend?

Personnel. Determine the number of employees needed to operate the new theater. Can these positions be filled from the local area?

Required:

a. Make your recommendation of whether or not a new theater should be built in your town. What are the reasons behind your recommendation?

b. How many screens should the theater hold? What are the ticket prices?

c. Show potential profitability through a projected income statement.

d. How much financing is needed to build the theater and what type of financing should Carmike use? Why?

e. How many employees will be needed to operate the new theater?

EXCEL ASSIGNMENTS

1. **[Obj. 3]** Lump-Sum Purchases: Suppose that on September 1, 20Y1, Maytag Appliance Company purchases land and a building for a lump-sum price of $400,000. The company must assign a separate cost to the land and building. How much of the price should be allocated to the land and how much to the building? The appraised value of the land is $150,000 and the appraised value of the building is $350,000.

Required:

a. Prepare an Excel worksheet that shows the allocation schedule of lump-sum purchase price to the individual assets. The input area should include the lump-sum cost and the appraised values of the individual assets.

b. Prepare the journal entry to record the lump-sum purchase.

2. **[Obj. 3]** Lump-Sum Purchases: Suppose that on March 5, 20Y1, B&O Railroad Company purchases land, building, and equipment for a lump-sum price of $780,000. The company must assign a separate cost to each asset. How much of the price should be allocated to the land, to the building, and to the equipment? The appraised value of the land is $250,000, of the building is $400,000, and of the equipment is $350,000.

Required:

a. Prepare an Excel worksheet that shows the allocation schedule of lump-sum purchase price to the individual assets. The input area should include the lump-sum cost and the appraised values of the individual assets.

b. Prepare the journal entry to record the lump-sum purchase.

3. **[Obj. 4]** Straight-Line Depreciation: Suppose that on January 1, 20Y1, Kaybee Toy Company purchases equipment that costs $60,000, has a useful life of 5 years, and a salvage value of $5,000.

    Required:
    a. Prepare an Excel worksheet that shows the schedule of depreciation expense for all five years of the equipment's useful life – showing cost, annual depreciation expense, accumulated depreciation, and book value at the end of each year.
    b. How does the schedule of depreciation expense for this equipment help managers evaluate the contribution of the equipment to company operations?

4. **[Obj. 4]** Straight-Line Depreciation: Repeat the same requirements as those listed in Excel-3, except change the cost of the equipment from $60,000 to $70,000, and change the salvage value from $5,000 to $10,000.

5. **[Obj. 4]** Units-of-Production Depreciation: On January 1, 20Y1, Winchester Company purchased a machine for $200,000. The machine is expected to produce 300,000 locks over its useful life and then have a salvage value of $20,000. Lock production each year is as follows:

Year	Locks Produced
20Y1	50,000
20Y2	70,000
20Y3	60,000
20Y4	80,000
20Y5	40,000

Required:
a. Prepare a worksheet that shows the schedule of depreciation expense using the units-of-production method. The input area should include the cost, salvage value, and useful life in units of production. The output area should include the calculation of the depreciable cost per unit and the schedule of depreciation expense. The schedule should include the following items:
    ■ Cost
    ■ Depreciation per Unit
    ■ Number of Units
    ■ Annual Depreciation ExpenseAccumulated Depreciation
    ■ Book Value
b. Why is the units-of-production method an appropriate method for depreciating this machine?

6. **[Obj. 4]** Units-of-Production Depreciation: Repeat the same requirements as those listed in Excel-5, except change the cost from $200,000 to $250,000, and change salvage value from $20,000 to $10,000.

7. **[Obj. 4]** Double-Declining-Balance Depreciation: Suppose that on January 1, 20Y1, Coca-Cola Company purchases a delivery truck for $85,000. The truck has an estimated useful life of 5 years and an estimated salvage value of $10,000.

Required:
a. Using the double-declining balance method, prepare a schedule of depreciation expense for all five years – showing cost, annual depreciation expense, accumulated depreciation, and book value at the end of each year.
b. In addition to depreciation, what other expenses associated with the equipment should managers consider in evaluating the equipment's operating costs?

8. **[Obj. 4]** Double-Declining-Balance Depreciation: Repeat the same requirements as those listed in Excel-7, except change the cost from $85,000 to $68,000, and change the estimated salvage value from $10,000 to $6,000.

WEB ASSIGNMENTS

1. **[Obj. 3]** Select any company and find its financial statements on the Web (e.g. on the company's website, the New York Stock Exchange website, or a search on Google). Using the information from the financial statements, list the company's long-term assets. What is the ratio of the company's long-term assets to total assets? What is your interpretation of this ratio?

2. **[Obj. 5]** In 2000, Carmike Cinemas filed for Chapter 11 of the Bankruptcy Code. Yet, today the company is thriving and growing. Go to the website for Carmike Cinemas or do a search on Google in order to discover what happened to financially turn the company around.

3. **[Obj. 7]** Go to the Financial Accounting and Standards Board (FASB) website and prepare a summary of FASB Statement No. 142, *Goodwill and Other Intangible Assets.*

4. **[Ethics]** Go to the website for Carmike Cinemas. What mandates do you find given to the company's financial officers regarding accurate and complete financial records?

5. **[All Obj.]** Go to the website for Carmike Cinemas or do a search on Google for an accounting-related news item regarding Carmike. Give a one-paragraph summary.

¶814   Test Prepper

Use this sample test to gauge your comprehension of the chapter material.

True/False Questions

___ 1. The cost of an asset includes the price paid for the asset as well as any expenses necessary to get the asset ready for use.

___ 2. Land is never depreciated, as its usefulness does not diminish.

___ 3. A capital expenditure is an expenditure that involves maintaining, repairing, and operating plant assets.

___ 4. Depreciation is the allocation of an asset's cost to expense over its useful life.

___ 5. The difference between the cost of an asset and its accumulated depreciation is always its salvage value.

___ 6. Once an accounting estimate is determined, any change to the estimate is considered unethical.

___ 7. Once an asset is fully depreciated and the asset continues to be used in operations, the asset is kept on the books, but no additional depreciation expense is recorded.

___ 8. The part of the cost of a natural resource that is used up in a period is charged to amortization expense.

___ 9. Intangible assets are long-term assets that have no physical existence, but represent a right to current and future benefits.

___ 10. Investments in debt instruments are investments in stock of other companies.

Multiple-Choice Questions

___ 1. Which is not true regarding a revenue expenditure?
   a. Involves the operation of plant assets.
   b. Involves the maintenance of plant assets.
   c. Involves the repair of plant assets.
   d. Involves the purchase of plant assets.
   e. Revenue expenditures are expensed.

___ 2. Which of the following does not describe a plant asset?
   a. It has a physical existence.
   b. It is used in the operations of the company.
   c. It is tangible.
   d. It is intangible.
   e. It has a useful life exceeding one year.

___ 3. A building's historical cost is $100,000. When the accumulated depreciation was $50,000, the building was sold for $60,000. The journal entry to record the sale will include a:
   a. debit to Building for $100,000.
   b. credit to Building for $50,000.
   c. debit to Accumulated Depreciation for $100,000.
   d. credit to Accumulated Depreciation for $50,000.
   e. credit to Gain on Sale for $10,000.

___ 4. Which of the following items is not included in the cost of a piece of land?
   a. Addition of a driveway
   b. Real estate commissions
   c. Lawyers' fees
   d. Costs of clearing the land
   e. Accrued taxes that the buyer pays

__ 5. Suppose Microsoft Corporation purchases equipment for $50,000. The salvage value is $10,000 and the useful life is estimated to be 5 years. If straight-line depreciation is used, how much is the annual depreciation expense?
  a. $2,000
  b. $5,000
  c. $8,000
  d. $10,000
  e. $20,000

__ 6. Suppose General Electric Corporation purchases a delivery truck for $90,000. The truck is estimated to have a useful life of 100,000 miles. The salvage value is estimated to be $10,000. What is the units-of-production depreciation per unit of output?
  a. $.10 per unit
  b. $.50 per unit
  c. $.80 per unit
  d. $.90 per unit
  e. $1.00 per unit

__ 7. Which of the following allocates an equal amount of depreciation expense to each year of the asset's useful life?
  a. units-of-production depreciation method
  b. straight-line depreciation method
  c. double-declining-balance method
  d. accelerated depreciation method
  e. formula one depreciation method

__ 8. Which of the following calculates annual depreciation by multiplying the asset's declining book value by a fixed percentage rate?
  a. units-of-production depreciation method
  b. straight-line depreciation method
  c. double-declining-balance method
  d. accelerated depreciation method
  e. formula one depreciation method

__ 9. When dissimilar assets are exchanged, which of the following is not true?
  a. Gains are recognized for financial reporting purposes.
  b. Losses are recognized for financial reporting purposes.
  c. Gains are recognized for tax purposes.
  d. Losses are recognized for tax purposes.
  e. Losses are not recognized for tax purposes.

__ 10. Suppose IBM Corporation disposes of manufacturing equipment that cost $90,000 and receives nothing on the disposal. The equipment has accumulated depreciation of $76,000. The salvage value had previously been estimated to be $10,000. What is the gain or loss on disposal?
  a. Gain of $14,000
  b. Gain of $4,000
  c. Loss of $4,000
  d. Loss of $10,000
  e. Loss of $14,000

Chapter

Liabilities

LEARNING OBJECTIVES

After studying Chapter 9, you should be able to do the following:

1. Describe the importance of liabilities to people within and outside the business.
2. Account for current liabilities.
3. Describe long-term liabilities.
4. Identify the effects of issuing bonds versus stock.
5. Explain how and why the level of a company's debt is evaluated.
6. Distinguish types of leases and account for lease liabilities.
7. Describe the impact of pensions and post-retirement benefits on financial reporting.

CHAPTER CONTENTS

Liabilities

FOCUS ON BUSINESS

Product Recall by Proctor & Gamble

In a rare cleaning frenzy, you are vacuuming with the new Swifter Sweep+Vac distributed by Proctor & Gamble. Passing by the TV, you are distracted by "The Price is Right" and leave the Sweep+Vac running. Soon, you smell smoke coming from the vacuum cleaner. The rotor has locked causing heat to build up and produce smoke. What should you do? (a) panic and call the fire department; (b) vow never to vacuum again; or (c) return the vacuum and get your money back.

Within three months of introducing the battery-operated Sweep+Vac, Proctor & Gamble received 14 complaints of overheating. The vacuum cleaner was sold in the United States, Canada, and Puerto Rico. The company decided to voluntarily recall the vacuum and discontinue all sales. Even though the cost of recalling the product resulted in a liability and impacted the financial condition of the company, Procter & Gamble opted to protect the safety of its customers.

There are many types of liabilities, especially for a company as large and diverse as Proctor & Gamble. The company has been in business for over 165 years and markets nearly 300 brands in over 160 countries. Some of the brands you may recognize include Crest, Charmin, Pringles, Bounty, Folgers, Clairol, and Tide. Through this chapter, you will learn the ins and outs of accounting for liabilities.

Source: *www.pg.com*

¶901 Applications to People Within and Outside the Firm

LEARNING OBJECTIVE 1: Describe the importance of liabilities to people within and outside the business.

As you recall, liabilities are the debts or economic obligations of a firm. These debts are owed by the business and are payable to persons or other firms. Incurring debt, that is, borrowing money, is one way that a business can acquire the funds needed to finance company operations. The liability section is the second of three main sections on the balance sheet.

¶901.01 INTERNAL USERS

Within a firm, business managers must decide whether to pay for items with cash on hand or to purchase items using debt financing. While managers may prefer to borrow and conserve cash on hand, there is a limit to how much suppliers and lending institutions will allow a company to borrow. With this in mind, financial managers within a company must factor in existing debt, interest charges, and repayment terms when considering incurring more debt.

For a manufacturing firm such as the Proctor & Gamble Company (P&G), raw materials are needed for the production of goods. P&G can purchase raw materials using the company's cash on hand or, alternatively, purchase raw materials on credit from a supplier. The latter kind of purchase results in a liability to the supplier through an account payable. Similarly, if P&G decides to purchase new manufacturing equipment, the company might use cash on hand to pay for the equipment or instead might finance the purchase with a loan from a bank. When a loan is used the transaction involves a note payable to the bank.

¶901.02   EXTERNAL USERS

Outside the firm, investors, lenders, and suppliers pay close attention to a company's liabilities. While many companies use debt to finance some operations, too much debt increases the risk that the company will be unable to repay the loans. This increased risk raises a red flag for financial analysts and stockholders. If Proctor & Gamble takes on additional debt, the stockholders may worry that the company will fail to make a reasonable profit. For a smaller company, stockholders may worry that the company will go out of business entirely. If a company cannot meet its financial obligations, it will encounter difficulty in securing future loans or purchasing materials on credit.

¶902   Current Liabilities

LEARNING OBJECTIVE 2: Account for current liabilities.

It is dishonest to intentionally give an erroneous estimate.

Liabilities are classified into two major categories: current liabilities and long-term liabilities. Current liabilities are those that are due within one year or less. Examples of current liabilities include accounts payable, short-term payables, the current portions of long-term notes payable, accrued expenses, payroll payable, unearned revenue, and warranty payable.

Most current liabilities are recorded at definitely determinable amounts. For example, if Proctor & Gamble purchases $1,000 of raw materials from a supplier on credit, then Proctor & Gamble owes a definite amount of $1,000 to the supplier. At a future time, Proctor & Gamble must pay the supplier the $1,000 owed.

Some current liabilities are not definitely determinable amounts, but exist as estimated amounts. For example, if Hewlett Packard sells computers with 90-day warranties, then the company must repair or replace computers that break down during the warranty period. Hewlett Packard must estimate the liability for the warranty payable on the computers it expects to repair or replace during the warranty period. Since the exact amount of the warranty payable cannot be determined, Hewlett Packard's balance sheet would show the estimated liability amount.

In the case of estimated liabilities, a company may be tempted to underestimate the amount to improve the appearance of the company's financial position. However, failure to show the best estimate would be unethical and possibly fraudulent. In addition, the real liability will eventually have to be paid and questions may arise regarding the original estimate. The loss of trust in a company's financial reports can lead to declining stock price. In addition, the company's reputation and credit rating could be seriously damaged.

The following types of current liabilities will be discussed in the sections below:

- accounts payable
- short-term notes payable
- current portions of long-term notes payable
- accrued liabilities
- payroll liabilities
- deferred (unearned) revenue
- warranty payable
- income taxes payable

¶902.01   ACCOUNTS PAYABLE

Accounts payable represent amounts owed to suppliers for credit purchases of goods and services. Accounts payable are sometimes referred to as "trade accounts payable," because they result from purchases of goods and services necessary to carry on the trade or business operations of the company.

In many cases, a company will use computer software to keep track of inventory quantities. In this way, when inventory quantities drop to a certain point, an order is automatically placed to replenish the inventory. When the items are received, the Inventory and the Accounts Payable accounts are increased. Suppose Sears purchases $2,000 worth of CD players on account from Sony Corporation on August 1. Sears records the purchase as follows:

Aug. 1	Inventory	2,000	
	Accounts Payable		2,000
	To record purchase of inventory on account.		

¶902.02 SHORT-TERM NOTES PAYABLE

Another type of current liability is a short-term note payable. Businesses routinely borrow money or purchase assets using short-term notes payable. Notes payable are represented by legal documents called "promissory notes," which indicate the principal amount borrowed, interest rate, and time period of the loan.

Suppose JK Productions is selling so many copies of its videos that it needs to purchase a DVD recorder which makes multiple DVD copies. JK decides it would be cost-effective to take on the liability of a short-term note payable to acquire cash for the purchase. So JK Productions borrows $3,000 with a promissory note to First American Bank on February 1. The principal amount of $3,000 is to be repaid in six months with 6 percent interest. The interest rate stated on a note is the annual interest rate; thus, the total interest to be paid in six months is $90 ($3,000 × .06 × 6/12). JK Productions records issuance of the note and subsequent payment as follows:

Feb. 1	Cash	3,000	
	Note Payable		3,000
	To record issuance of 6-month 6% promissory note.		
Aug. 1	Note Payable	3,000	
	Interest Expense	90	
	Cash		3,090
	To record payment of note.		

¶902.03 CURRENT PORTIONS OF LONG-TERM NOTES PAYABLE

If a company incurs debt payable more than one year in the future, this debt is classified as a long-term liability. However, sometimes part of the long-term debt is payable within the upcoming year and must be classified as a current liability. For example, the current liabilities section of the balance sheet of McDonald's Corporation has an item labeled "current maturities of long-term debt."

¶902.04 ACCRUED LIABILITIES

Another type of current liability is the accrued liability. Accrued liabilities are expenses that have been incurred but not yet paid. This is why accrued liabilities are also called "accrued expenses." Accrued liabilities are usually recorded along with other adjusting entries at the end of an accounting period.

McDonald's Corporation reports several accrued liabilities on its balance sheet, including the following expenses incurred, but not yet paid:

- Accrued interest
- Accrued restructuring and restaurant closing costs
- Accrued payroll and other liabilities
- Income taxes

¶902.05 PAYROLL LIABILITIES

Payroll liabilities are the current liabilities for payroll expenses that have been incurred but not yet paid.

Payroll and corresponding payroll taxes are major expenses for most companies, particularly for service firms such as banks, law firms, and real estate businesses. Employers are responsible for collecting payroll deductions like taxes from employee paychecks. These amounts are classified as liabilities until they are paid over to the appropriate government agencies. In addition, employers incur additional taxes on payroll. **Payroll liabilities** are the current liabilities for payroll expenses that have been incurred but not yet paid.

¶902.05.01   Employee Payroll and Deductions

Payroll, also referred to as "employee compensation," includes wages, salaries, bonuses, and commissions. Wages are paid to employees based on an hourly rate. The number of hours worked is multiplied by the wage rate. Salaries are paid to employees based on a monthly or annual rate. Bonuses are extra compensation above and beyond regular pay. Bonuses are often associated with the attainment of a company profit goal or operating objective. Commissions are often paid to salespersons and typically are based on a percentage of the sales made.

Net pay is your take-home pay.

Gross pay is the total amount of pay earned by an employee. For example, if you make $10 per hour and worked 40 hours in one week, your gross pay would be $400. Employees are often more interested in their net pay. **Net pay**, also called "take-home pay," is the amount left over after withholding all deductions. Deductions withheld from an employee's pay include federal income tax, state income tax, social security tax (also called "FICA tax"—Federal Insurance Contribution Act), Medicare tax, health insurance, and pension contributions. The employer must accurately calculate the employee's gross pay, deductions, and payroll taxes. Since these tax rates change periodically, the employer must be diligent to update its payroll calculations.

Suppose that the January 15 payroll for Southwest Construction Company included the following:

- wages $50,000
- federal income tax withholdings $9,200
- state income tax withholdings $2,200
- social security tax withholdings $3,100
- Medicare tax withholdings $725
- health insurance withholdings $1,300
- pension contributions withholdings $3,000

The journal entry to record the payroll is as follows:

Jan. 15	Wages Expense	50,000	
	Employee Federal Income Tax Payable		9,200
	Employee State Income Tax Payable		2,200
	Social Security Tax Payable		3,100
	Medicare Tax Payable		725
	Health Insurance Payable		1,300
	Pension Contributions Payable		3,000
	Wages Payable		30,475
	To record payroll, withholdings, and net pay.		

As shown, a total of $19,525 in deductions is withheld from employees' gross pay of $50,000, leaving take-home pay of $30,475.

¶902.05.02   Employer's Payroll Taxes

In addition to withholding the appropriate taxes from an employee's paycheck, the law also requires that the employer itself accrue and pay certain payroll taxes. First, the employer must match the amount of FICA paid by its employees. Also, federal unemployment insurance tax (FUTA), state unemployment insurance tax (SUTA), and Medicare tax is paid by the employer to state and federal governments. Some employers voluntarily contribute to the health insurance and pension plans. Exhibit 9.1 breaks down the company's payroll liability into its components.

Exhibit 9.1 COMPONENTS OF A COMPANY'S PAYROLL LIABILITY

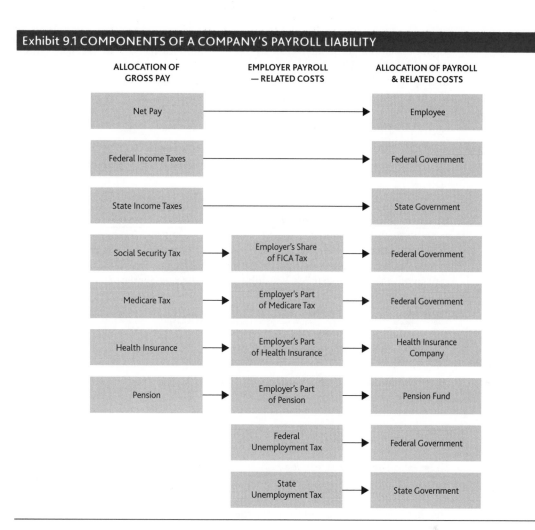

In the example of Southwest Construction Company's payroll, the company now must record its own payroll tax and benefits expenses associated with this period's payroll. Southwest Construction Company must accrue federal and state unemployment tax, Medicare tax, and employer's matching portion of social security tax. In addition, Southwest pays half of the health insurance premium and half of the pension contributions. The entry is as follows:

Jan. 15	Payroll Taxes and Benefits Expense	10,975	
	Social Security Tax Payable		3,100
	Medicare Tax Payable		725
	Federal Unemployment Tax Payable		150
	State Unemployment Tax Payable		2,700
	Health Insurance Payable		1,300
	Pension Contributions Payable		3,000
	To record payroll taxes and related costs.		

When each tax or benefit is paid over to the appropriate government agency or organization, the payable account is debited and Cash is credited.

¶902.06   DEFERRED (UNEARNED) REVENUE

A deferred (unearned) revenue is a current liability until the company delivers the goods or services.

Another type of current liability is a deferred revenue. A **deferred revenue**, also called "unearned revenue," results when a customer pays cash in advance before receiving goods or services. Because there is an obligation to deliver goods or services at a future date, the business must record a liability.

Suppose that on October 1, Flamboyant Sign Company is hired to prepare a sign with the company logo for Wells Fargo Bank. Wells Fargo pays $5,000 for the sign in advance. On October 1, Flamboyant records a liability, Unearned Sign Sales Revenue. Flamboyant Sign Company completes the sign and delivers it to Wells Fargo on October 18. On that same day, Flamboyant removes the liability and records a revenue, Sign Sales Revenue. The two transactions are recorded by Flamboyant as follows:

Oct. 1	Cash	5,000	
	Unearned Sign Sales Revenue		5,000
	To record payment in advance on sign to be delivered to Wells Fargo.		
Oct. 18	Unearned Sign Sales Revenue	5,000	
	Sign Sales Revenue		5,000
	To record revenue earned on sale for which payment was previously received.		

Another example of deferred revenue is when a company collects payment in advance for rent. Suppose Adobe Apartments leases an apartment to Nick Morgan for $800 per month. Nick pays three months' rent in advance on November 1. Adobe records the prepayment as shown:

Nov. 1	Cash	2,400	
	Unearned Rent Revenue		2,400
	To record cash received for three months' rent.		

At the month end on November 30, Adobe Apartments has earned one month's rent revenue and records an adjusting entry as follows:

Nov. 30	Unearned Rent Revenue	800	
	Rent Revenue		800
	To record rent revenue earned.		

The liability, Unearned Rent Revenue, is decreased and the revenue, Rent Revenue, is increased. Over the three-month period, Adobe earns the rent paid in advance and eliminates the liability.

¶902.07   WARRANTY LIABILITIES

Many company products are sold with a guarantee or warranty that states if the product is defective, it will be replaced. The expense of replacing products constitutes a current liability for the company. The matching principal requires that warranty expense be recorded in the same period that the company records sales revenue. Because the company does not know the exact amount of products that will be returned in the future, the company must estimate the warranty expense and corresponding warranty liability based on past experience.

Suppose Epson Corporation provides a 90-day warranty on its printers. The warranty makes Epson printers more appealing to the consumer and, thus, helps increase sales. Based on past experience, the company expects 2 percent of the printers to be returned and replaced under the warranty. The average printer costs $100. Assume that 800 printers are sold in December. The warranty liability, which is an accrued liability, is recorded as follows:

Dec. 31	Warranty Expense		1,600	
	Warranty Liability			1,600
	To record estimated product warranty expense:			
	Quantity of units sold		800	
	Rate of replacement	×	.02	
	Estimated units to be replaced		16	
	Estimated cost per unit	×	$100	
	Est. product warranty liability		$1,600	

When a printer is returned for replacement under warranty, the cost of the printer is charged against Warranty Liability. Assume that on January 10, a customer returns a defective printer. A new printer, costing $100, is given to the customer. The transaction is recorded as follows:

Jan. 10	Warranty Liability	100	
	Inventory		100
	Replace defective product sold under warranty.		

The decision of whether to provide a warranty requires input from multiple departments. Production reports on what types of warranties may be needed for the product and which are feasible for the company to undertake. The marketing department provides information regarding what warranties the competition offers, how consumers view different types of warranties, and to what extent these warranties affect sales. The accounting department estimates the cost of providing a warranty and how it will affect company profits.

¶902.08 INCOME TAXES PAYABLE

Do you have any current liabilities?

The last type of current liability we will discuss is income taxes payable. Like individuals, corporations are taxed on their income. The federal government collects corporate income tax, as do most states and some cities. At the end of the year, the corporation makes an adjusting entry to record its estimated income tax liability. The exact amount of income tax liability is usually not known until the following year. The entry to record federal income tax liability is as follows:

Dec. 31	Income Taxes Expense	24,800	
	Income Taxes Payable		24,800
	To record estimated federal income taxes payable.		

FOCUS ON GLOBAL TRADE

Corporate Income Taxes Around the World

How much should a corporation pay in taxes? Most people think that corporations should pay something to support the national government of the countries in which they do business. Clearly, national governments provide or oversee support systems that are essential for business operations, such as roads, railway networks, airports, seaports, and communications systems. National governments also provide a system of laws to regulate commerce and to facilitate economic growth.

Corporate income tax rates vary around the world. The highest corporate income tax rates are found in Bolivia and Taiwan; both have a 50 percent tax rate. At the other end of the spectrum, the corporate income tax rate is zero in the Bahamas, Cayman Islands, and Liberia. Countries with little or no income tax are referred to as tax havens. These countries hope to attract businesses with their favorable tax structure. Naturally, tax haven countries still need to collect taxes to pay for government services. Instead of income taxes, these national governments rely on other taxes such as property taxes, payroll taxes, and sales taxes.

Below is a list of recent corporate income tax rates in various countries. Many countries, such as the U.S., have a progressive tax structure. This means that the tax rate is less on the lower levels of income and more on higher levels of income. The tax rates shown are the highest tax rates, but usually not all the corporate income is subject to this high rate.

Country	Highest corporate income tax rate	Country	Highest corporate income tax rate
Argentina	35	Liberia	0
Australia	36	Mexico	35
Bahamas	0	Morocco	35
Bolivia	50	Netherlands	35
Brazil	25	Nigeria	30
Cayman Islands	0	Peru	30
Canada	38	Philippines	33
Chile	35	Poland	34
China	30.9	Russia	43
France	36.6	South Africa	35
Germany	42.2	Spain	35
Hungary	18	Sweden	28
India	35	Taiwan	50
Indonesia	30	Uganda	30
Israel	36	Ukraine	30
Jamaica	33.3	United Kingdom	31
Japan	34.5	U.S.A.	39
Kazakhstan	30	Uzbekistan	33
Kenya	32.5	Vietnam	32
Korea, Republic of	28		

Source: *Worldbank.org*

¶903   Long-Term Liabilities

LEARNING OBJECTIVE 3: Describe long-term liabilities.

The second major category of liabilities on a firm's balance sheet is long-term liabilities, also called "non-current liabilities" or "long-term debt." Long-term liabilities are the financial obligations of the firm that are due more than one year in the future. Like current liabilities, long-term liabilities can either be an explicit amount or an estimated amount. Long-term liabilities are often very large financial commitments that require years of future cash outlays.

¶903.01   BONDS PAYABLE

A bond represents debt owed by the issuer to the bondholder.

A **bond** is a type of long-term liability that represents debt owed by the issuer to the bondholder. A bond is essentially a loan taken out by the issuer. You are probably familiar with the United States Savings Bond, in which a person gives money to the United States government in return for a bond. At a future time, the government returns the amount invested plus interest to the bondholder.

An underwriter buys and resells bonds.

When a company issues bonds, the bonds are usually first purchased by an underwriter, such as Merrill Lynch. An **underwriter** buys bonds from the issuing company and then resells them to others. Bond issuers are debtors; bondholders are creditors. The **bond principal** is the amount to be received on the maturity date. The principal is the sum of money owed on the bond, on which interest is charged. The principal is also referred to as the bond's "**face value**," "**maturity value**," "denomination," or "**par value**." The bond issuer promises to repay the bond's principal at a future maturity date, and to pay interest at a specified rate at future designated times.

The bond principal, also called "face value," is the amount to be received on the maturity date.

A bond certificate states the issuing corporation, principal amount, annual interest rate, interest payment dates, and maturity date.

When a bond is purchased, the bondholder usually receives a bond certificate, shown in Exhibit 9.2. The **bond certificate** is a legal document showing the name of the issuing corporation, the principal amount, the annual interest rate, interest payment dates (usually twice per year), and the maturity date. The principal amount is usually stated in $1,000 increments.

Exhibit 9.2 BOND CERTIFICATE

Source: *oldstocks.com*

Investors buy and sell bonds in bond markets, just as stocks are bought and sold in stock markets. The world's largest bond market is the New York Exchange. Thousands of bonds are bought and sold here. When a bond is sold, the bond's price is stated as a percentage of its principal, or face value. For example, if a bond sells for 105, that means a $1,000 bond sold for $1,050 ($1,000 × 1.05). The amount that a bond sells for above its face value is called a "premium," in this case, $50.

If a bond sells for less than its principal or face value, the amount below face value is called a "discount." If a bond sells at 100, the bond is said to have sold at par or face value. Rarely does a bond sell for exactly its face value.

¶903.02

Secured bonds provide a guarantee of repayment, while unsecured bonds do not.

The bond issue is the number of bonds issued.

TYPES OF BONDS

Bonds may be secured or unsecured. **Secured bonds** provide a guarantee of repayment by pledging specified corporate assets. **Unsecured bonds**, also called "**debentures**," are backed only by the good faith of the borrower, that is, the issuer. Therefore, unsecured bonds are a riskier investment for bondholders. The term **bond issue** specifies the total number of bonds issued, such as one hundred $1,000 bonds. A supplementary agreement, the **bond indenture**, specifies the restrictions, rights, and privileges associated with the bonds.

¶903.03

The bond indenture is a supplementary agreement listing the restrictions, rights, and privileges of the bonds.

Present value is the monetary worth today of an amount to be received at a future time.

PRESENT VALUE OF MONEY

Money received today is worth more than the same amount of money received a year from now. If you receive the money now, you can invest it and thus, have more money in the future. Investors refer to this concept as the "time value of money," which simply means that money earns income over time. **Present value** (PV) is the monetary worth today of an amount to be received at a future time.

Suppose you were a contestant on a game show. You win the big prize: $100,000 paid to you five years from now. However, you also have the option to immediately receive the present value of the money. Being a college student who needs money for tuition and food, you would like to receive the money now, but you're wondering just how much that would be.

To determine the present value of money to be received in the future, you need to know three things: the future amount, the time period, and the interest rate per period. Interest is the cost of using money, which is interest expense to the borrower and interest revenue to the lender. The time period is the number of periods in which interest is allocated. For example, if interest is allocated annually for five years, then there are five periods. If interest is allocated quarterly for five years, then there are 20 periods.

Let's compute the present value of $100,000 in the game show example: There are five periods (five years) and the interest rate is 6% per year. Exhibit 9.3 shows the present values of $1 for various time periods and interest rates. According to the exhibit, you find that the present value of $1 at five periods in the future at an interest rate of 6% is $0.747. Multiply this amount times the $100,000 (.747 × $100,000) and the present value of your winnings is $74,700. This means that receiving $74,700 today is equal in value to receiving $100,000 five periods from now, assuming an interest rate of 6% per period.

Exhibit 9.3 PRESENT VALUE OF $1

Periods	4%	5%	6%	7%	8%
1	0.962	0.952	0.943	0.935	0.926
2	0.925	0.907	0.890	0.873	0.857
3	0.889	0.864	0.840	0.816	0.794
4	0.855	0.823	0.792	0.763	0.735
5	0.822	0.784	0.747	0.713	0.681
6	0.790	0.746	0.705	0.666	0.630
7	0.760	0.711	0.665	0.623	0.583
8	0.731	0.677	0.627	0.582	0.540
9	0.703	0.645	0.592	0.544	0.500
10	0.676	0.614	0.558	0.508	0.463
11	0.650	0.585	0.527	0.475	0.429
12	0.625	0.557	0.497	0.444	0.397

An annuity pays a fixed amount of money at the end of each period for a specified number of periods.

Instead of a single future payment of $100,000, suppose the game show host awards you $100,000 to be paid out over the next five years at $20,000 a year. In other words, you would receive an annuity of $20,000 for five years. An **annuity** pays a fixed amount of money at the end of each period for a specified number of periods. Again, you have the option of receiving the present value of the annuity. Since you need the money now, you decide to take the present value. Let's do the computations and find out how much you will receive.

Exhibit 9.4 shows the present value of *annuity* of $1. According to the exhibit, the present value of annuity of $1 for five periods at an interest rate of 6% is $4.212. Multiple 4.212 times $20,000 and the present value of your annuity is $84,240. In other words, receiving $84,240 today is equal in value to receiving $20,000 at the end of the next five periods, assuming an interest rate of 6% per period.

Exhibit 9.4 PRESENT VALUE OF ANNUITY OF $1

Periods	4%	5%	6%	7%	8%
1	0.962	0.952	0.943	0.935	0.926
2	1.886	1.859	1.833	1.808	1.783
3	2.775	2.723	2.673	2.624	2.577
4	3.630	3.546	3.465	3.387	3.312
5	4.452	4.329	4.212	4.100	3.993
6	5.242	5.076	4.917	4.767	4.623
7	6.002	5.786	5.582	5.389	5.206
8	6.733	6.463	6.210	5.971	5.747
9	7.435	7.108	6.802	6.515	6.247
10	8.111	7.722	7.360	7.024	6.710
11	8.760	8.306	7.887	7.499	7.139
12	9.385	8.863	8.384	7.943	7.536

¶903.04 BOND PRICING AND PRESENT VALUE

Market price, or market value, is the price a bond sells for.

Because bonds involve the receipt of money in the present and the payment of money in the future, you can see how the time value of money relates to bonds. The price that a bond sells for is referred to as its **"market price"** or **"market value."** The bond's market price is the combined present value of two items:

1. The present value of the bond's face value or principal amount to be received on the maturity date.
2. The present value of the bond's cash interest payments, which are paid periodically at designated future dates, usually twice per year.

For example, the market price of a $1,000 bond might be $1,030, which is 103 percent of its principal or face value. Let's examine how that market price is derived:

PV of principal (face value)	$635
PV of cash interest payments	395
Bond market price	$1,030
Bond principal	1,000
Bond premium	$30

The calculations of the present value (PV) of the principal and cash interest payments shown above will be described in the sections that follow. For now, let's just concentrate on whether the bond is selling at a premium or a discount. If the combined present values of the bond's principal and cash interest payments is more than the bond's principal, then the bond sells at a premium. In this case, the bond's market price is $1,030, resulting in a bond premium of $30. However, if the combined present values of the bond's principal and cash interest payments is less than the bond's principal, then the bond sells at a discount. For example, the bond's market price might be only $980, resulting in a bond discount of $20.

¶903.05 — INTEREST RATE ON BONDS

Stated interest rate is the rate stated on the bond certificate. Market interest rate is the rate demanded by the market.

The interest rate on a bond is stated on the bond certificate, along with the dates that the cash interest payments are made. The **stated interest rate**, also called "face interest rate," sets the amount of cash interest to be paid to the bondholder.

Suppose that on February 1, Walt Disney Company issues $100,000 in bonds with a stated interest rate of 6%, payable semiannually. As a result, Disney pays $6,000 of interest annually on the bonds ($100,000 × .06); $3,000 on each semiannual payment date.

Whether a bond issues at a premium or a discount is determined by the relationship between the bond's stated interest rate and the market interest rate. The **market interest rate**, also called "effective interest rate," is the interest rate demanded by investors for the loan of their money. In other words, the market interest rate is the rate that bonds of similar risk are currently paying in the market. Companies that issue bonds usually try to match the bond's stated interest rate to the market interest rate. This is very difficult to do because the market interest rate fluctuates by the minute.

Exhibit 9.5 shows how the Disney bond issue with 6% stated interest rate is affected by the market interest rate. If the market rate is 6%, then the bonds are issued at face value, also called "principal" or "maturity value." In other words, the bonds are sold for their face value. When the stated interest rate does not match the market rate, people pay more (premium) or less (discount) for the bonds, thus causing the cash interest payments relative to the amount actually paid for the bonds to be the market interest rate. For example, if the market rate is 7%, then the bonds are issued at a discount. A discount means that people are paying less than the bond's face value. If the market interest rate is 5%, then the bonds are issued at a premium. People are willing to pay more than the face value of the bonds.

Exhibit 9.5 DETERMINING BOND ISSUE PRICE		
Stated Interest Rate	Market Interest Rate	Issue Price
6%	6%	Face Value: $100,000 bonds issued for $100,000
6%	7%	Discount: $100,000 bonds sell for less than $100,000
6%	5%	Premium: $100,000 bonds sell for more than $100,000

Bond amortization reduces the bond's discount or premium to zero over the term of the bond.

Bond amortization is the process of reducing the bond's discount or premium to zero, over the term of the bond. Amortizing a bond discount or premium results in interest expense being higher or lower, respectively, than the bond's stated interest rate.

¶903.06 — ISSUING BONDS AT PAR

Suppose Disney issues $100,000 in 6% bonds that mature in four years. Assume these bonds are issued at par on January 1, 20Y1. The bonds have semiannual interest payment dates of January 1 and July 1. The bond issue transaction is recorded as follows:

20Y1			
Jan. 1	Cash	100,000	
	Bonds Payable		100,000
	To issue 6%, 4-year bonds at par.		

Disney records the receipt of $100,000 in cash on the day the bonds are issued. The investors who purchased the bonds may later sell the bonds in the bond markets. The bonds may be bought and sold by investors many times before their maturity date. The buy-and-sell transactions between investors have no effect on Disney.

Disney records the first interest payment on July 1 as follows:

20Y1			
July 1	Interest Expense	3,000	
	Cash		3,000
	To record bond interest payment ($100,000 × .06 × 6/12).		

On December 31, Disney accrues interest expense and interest payable for the six months from July to December. (The interest payment date is January 1.) The accrued interest is recorded as follows:

20Y1			
Dec. 31	Interest Expense	3,000	
	Interest Payable		3,000
	To record accrued bond interest ($100,000 × .06 × 6/12).		

The bonds mature four years from the January 1, 20Y1 issue date. Disney pays off the bonds in 20Y5 and makes the following entry:

20Y5			
Jan. 1	Bonds Payable	100,000	
	Cash		100,000
	To pay off bonds at maturity.		

¶903.07 ISSUING BONDS AT A DISCOUNT

Companies sometimes issue bonds at a discount due to economic conditions and business events. Suppose that on January 1, 20Y1, Proctor & Gamble (P&G) issues $100,000 of its 7%, 3-year bonds, when the market interest rate is 8%. The interest payment dates are January 1 and July 1. Because the market interest rate is above the bond interest rate, the market price of the bonds falls below the face value of the bonds. Exhibit 9.6 shows the calculation of the market price, which is the present value of the bonds' face value to be received at maturity, combined with the present value of the bonds' cash interest payments.

Exhibit 9.6 DETERMINING MARKET PRICE OF BONDS

Proctor & Gamble issues $100,000 of 7%, 3-year bonds. The market interest rate is 8%. The market price of the bonds is their present value. The present value (PV) of the bonds is the sum of the PV of the principal and the PV of the cash interest payments. The following items must be identified in order to calculate present value.

1. Identify the number of time periods: 6 periods (3 years with 2 interest payments per year).
2. Identify the market interest rate: 8%. Since there are two payments per year, use one-half the annual rate for the calculation, that is 4%.
3. Identify the cash interest payment for the bonds: Principal of $100,000 times the stated interest rate per period of 3.5% (an annual interest rate of 7% with two interest payments per year) equals $3,500.

Calculation:

PV of Principal	
Principal × PV of single amount	
$100,000 × .790* (6 periods at 4%) =	$79,000
PV of cash interest payments	
Cash interest payment × PV of annuity	
($100,000 × .035) × PV of annuity	
$3,500 × 5.242** (6 periods at 4%) =	18,347
	$97,347 present value of bonds

* from PV of $1 Table (Exhibit 9.3)

** from PV Annuity of $1 Table (Exhibit 9.4)

Investors are willing to pay a market price of $97,347 for the Proctor & Gamble bonds. P&G receives cash of $97,347 and records the sale or issuance of the bonds as follows:

20Y1			
Jan. 1	Cash	97,347	
	Discount on Bonds Payable	2,653	
	Bonds Payable		100,000
	To issue 7%, 3-year bonds at a discount.		

On January 1, P&G shows the Bonds Payable and the Discount on Bonds Payable in the liability section of its balance sheet as follows:

Long-Term Liabilities:	
Bonds Payable	$100,000
Less Discount on Bonds Payable	(2,653)
	$97,347

Discount on Bonds Payable is a contra-liability account, which is subtracted from the Bonds Payable account. The result is the carrying value, or present value, of the bonds.

¶903.08   AMORTIZING A BOND DISCOUNT

Each year, Proctor & Gamble makes total cash interest payments of $7,000 ($100,000 × .07) on the bonds it issued on January 1, 20Y1. This is not the total interest expense. The total interest expense is the sum of all the cash interest payments plus the discount, as shown:

Interest payments ($100,000 × .07 × 3 years)	$21,000
Discount on bonds payable	2,653
Total interest expense	$23,653

Total interest expense includes the $21,000 in cash payments plus the $2,653 discount. In this manner, the discount causes the interest paid on the bond to be equal to the market interest rate, not the bond stated interest rate. Thus, the market interest rate becomes the actual interest expense of the bond.

If a bond is issued at a discount, then the interest expense is always more than the cash interest payment. To calculate the actual interest expense, the company must amortize the discount. If you recall from the last chapter, amortization is the process of expensing the cost of an intangible asset over its useful life. Exhibit 9.7 shows an amortization schedule using the effective interest method (remember that effective interest rate is another name for market interest rate).

On January 1, 20Y1, the bond carrying value is $97,347 and the bond discount balance is $2,653. On each interest payment date, the cash interest payment is a constant $3,500. The interest expense is the market interest rate multiplied by the bond carrying value. The difference between the interest payment and the interest expense is how much the bond discount is amortized.

The Discount on Bonds Payable will be amortized, that is, reduced to zero, over the life of the bonds. The Discount on Bonds Payable is amortized by subtracting it from the bond discount value and adding it to the bond carrying value. As a result, on January 1, 20Y4 (the maturity date), the bond discount is reduced to zero, and the bond carrying value has been increased to $100,000 (the face of the bond).

Exhibit 9.7 AMORTIZATION OF BOND DISCOUNT
Using the Effective Interest Method

Issue Date:	Jan. 1, 20Y1
Maturity Date:	Jan. 1, 20Y4
Maturity Value:	100,000
Issue Price:	97,347
Bond Stated Interest Rate:	7.00%
Bond Stated Interest Rate — Semiannual:	3.50%
Market Interest Rate on Issue Date:	8.00%
Market Interest Rate on Issue Date — Semiannual:	4.00%

A	B	C	D	E	F
Interest Payment	Interest Payment (3.5% of Principle)	Interest Expense (4% of Carrying Value)	Discount Amortization (C – B)	Bond Discount Balance	Bond Carrying Value
Jan. 1, 20Y1				$2,653	$97,347
July 1	$3,500	$3,894	$394	2,259	97,741
Jan. 1, 20Y2	3,500	3,910	410	1,849	98,151
July 1	3,500	3,926	426	1,423	98,577
Jan. 1, 20Y3	3,500	3,943	443	980	99,020
July 1	3,500	3,961	461	520	99,480
Jan. 1, 20Y4	3,500	4,020*	520	(0)	100,000

* Adjusted for rounding effect.

Now, as we turn our attention to recording the transactions related to the interest payments on the January 1, 20Y1 bonds, we see that P & G makes its first $3,500 semiannual interest payment on July 1. P&G's interest expense is more than $3,500. Using amounts from Exhibit 9.7, the journal entry to record the interest expense and the cash interest payment is shown below.

20Y1			
July 1	Interest Expense	3,894	
	Discount on Bonds Payable		394
	Cash		3,500
	To pay bond interest and amortize bond discount.		

The entry on July 1 amortizes the Discount on Bonds Payable. The amortization process achieves two goals. First, the amortization adjusts the bond carrying value toward its maturity value. Second, the amortization apportions the discount to interest expense.

On December 31, 20Y1, P&G accrues interest (not paid until January 1, 20Y2) and amortizes the bond discount for July to December. Using the amounts from Exhibit 9.7, the journal entry is as follows:

20Y1			
Dec. 31	Interest Expense	3,910	
	Discount on Bonds Payable		410
	Interest Payable		3,500
	To accrue bond interest and amortize bond discount.		

On December 31, 20Y1, P&G includes the bond interest expense on its income statement. P&G shows the Interest Payable, Bonds Payable, and the Discount on Bonds Payable in the liability section of its balance sheet as follows.

INCOME STATEMENT FOR 20Y1		
Interest Expense (3,894 + 3,910)		$7,804
BALANCE SHEET AT DECEMBER 31, 20Y1		
Current Liabilities:		
Interest Payable		$3,500
Long-Term Liabilities:		
Bonds Payable	$100,000	
Less Discount on Bonds Payable	(1,849)	$98,151

On January 1, 20Y4, the bonds mature. The bond discount is now amortized to zero and the bonds' carrying value is $100,000. P&G retires the bonds by paying $100,000 to the bondholders:

20Y4			
Jan. 1	Bonds Payable	100,000	
	Cash		100,000
	To retire bonds.		

¶903.09   ISSUING BONDS AT A PREMIUM

Let's consider a situation in which bonds are issued at a premium. Suppose that on January 1, 20Y1, Proctor & Gamble issues $100,000 of 4-year, 9% bonds, when the market interest rate is 8%. The interest payment dates are January 1 and July 1. Since the market interest rate is below the bond's stated interest rate, the market price of the bonds rises above the maturity value of the bonds. The procedure to calculate bond's market price was previously shown in Exhibit 9.6. In this case, assume that the bond's market price is $103,400. Thus, the bond premium is $3,400.

Investors are willing to pay $103,400 for P&G bonds with a maturity value of only $100,000 because the bonds make cash interest payments of 9%, which is more than the market interest rate of 8%.

From the P&G perspective, the company sells the bonds for $103,400. P&G receives cash of $103,400 on January 1, 20Y1. The journal entry for January 1 is recorded as follows:

20Y1			
Jan. 1	Cash	103,400	
	Bonds Payable		100,000
	Premium on Bonds Payable		3,400
	To issue 9%, 4-year bonds at a premium.		

¶903.10   AMORTIZING A BOND PREMIUM

On July 1, 20Y1, P&G makes its first interest payment and begins amortization of the bond premium. Exhibit 9.8 shows how the bond premium is amortized, using the effective interest method.

Exhibit 9.8 AMORTIZATION OF BOND PREMIUM
Using the Effective Interest Method

Issue Date:	Jan. 1, 20Y1
Maturity Date:	Jan. 1, 20Y4
Maturity Value:	100,000
Issue Price:	103,400
Bond Stated Interest Rate:	9.00%
Bond Stated Interest Rate — Semiannual:	4.50%
Market Interest Rate on Issue Date:	8.00%
Market Interest Rate on Issue Date — Semiannual:	4.00%

A	B	C	D	E	F
Interest Payment Date	**Interest Payment (4.5% of Principle)**	**Interest Expense (4% of Carrying Value)**	**Premium Amortization (B – C)**	**Bond Premium Balance**	**Bond Carrying Value**
Jan. 1, 20Y1				$3,400	$103,400
July 1	$4,500	$4,136	$364	3,036	103,036
Jan. 1, 20Y2	4,500	4,121	379	2,657	102,657
July 1	4,500	4,106	394	2,264	102,264
Jan. 1, 20Y3	4,500	4,091	409	1,854	101,854
July 1	4,500	4,074	426	1,428	101,428
Jan. 1, 20Y4	4,500	4,057	443	986	100,986
July 1	4,500	4,039	461	525	100,525
Jan. 1, 20Y5	4,500	3,975*	525	0	100,000

* Adjusted for rounding effect.

20Y1			
July 1	Interest Expense	4,136	
	Premium on Bonds Payable	364	
	Cash		4,500
	To pay bond interest and amortize bond premium.		

On December 31, P&G records the accrued interest on the bonds as follows:

20Y1			
Dec. 31	Interest Expense	4,121	
	Premium on Bonds Payable	379	
	Interest Payable		4,500
	To accrue bond interest and amortize bond premium.		

At the end of 20Y1, P&G's income statement includes the bond interest expense. P&G's balance sheet shows the Interest Payable, Bonds Payable, and Premium on Bonds Payable as follows:

INCOME STATEMENT FOR 20Y1		
Interest Expense (4,136 + 4,121)		$8,257
BALANCE SHEET AT DECEMBER 31, 20Y1		
Current Liabilities:		
Interest Payable		$4,500
Long-Term Liabilities		
Bonds Payable	$100,000	
Plus Premium on Bonds Payable	2,657	$102,657

The premium on bonds payable is added to the maturity value of the bonds to calculate the bonds' carrying value, which at December 31, 20Y1, is $102,657. Over the life of the bond, the premium is incrementally reduced to zero, so that the bonds' carrying value will equal the bonds' maturity value on the maturity date. The amortization of the premium reduces the interest expense.

¶903.11   STRAIGHT-LINE METHOD OF BOND AMORTIZATION

Using the effective interest amortization method, the bond's actual interest expense is precisely computed. Bond interest expense can be approximated using the simpler straight-line amortization method. The straight-line method cannot be used to make the accounting entries if it causes material differences from the effective interest method. Using the straight-line method, the bond discount or premium is allocated into equal periodic amounts over the bond's term. As a result, the interest expense is the same in each interest period.

Let's use the straight-line method for the Proctor & Gamble bonds previously shown in Exhibit 9.8. The bond premium of $3,400 would be allocated among the eight payment periods. Thus, the bond premium would be amortized $425 ($3,400 / 8) each period. The amortization schedule, using the straight-line method, is shown in Exhibit 9.9.

Exhibit 9.9 AMORTIZATION OF BOND PREMIUM
Using the Straight-Line Interest Method

Issue Date:	Jan. 1, 20Y1
Maturity Date:	Jan. 1, 20Y4
Maturity Value:	100,000
Issue Price:	103,400
Bond Stated Interest Rate:	9.00%
Bond Stated Interest Rate — Semiannual:	4.50%
Market Interest Rate on Issue Date:	8.00%
Market Interest Rate on Issue Date — Semiannual:	4.00%

A	B	C	D	E	F
Interest Payment Date	Interest Payment (4.5% of Principle)	Interest Expense (B – D)	Premium Amortization (3,400 / 8)	Bond Premium Balance	Bond Carrying Value
Jan. 1, 20Y1				$3,400	$103,400
July 1	$4,500	$4,075	$425	2,975	102,975
Jan. 1, 20Y2	4,500	4,075	425	2,550	102,550
July 1	4,500	4,075	425	2,125	102,125
Jan. 1, 20Y3	4,500	4,075	425	1,700	101,700
July 1	4,500	4,075	425	1,275	101,275
Jan. 1, 20Y4	4,500	4,075	425	850	100,850
July 1	4,500	4,075	425	425	100,425
Jan. 1, 20Y5	4,500	4,075	425	0	100,000

What do you see as the benefits of owning bonds, as opposed to other types of investments?

Proctor & Gamble's entry to record the interest and amortization of the bond premium under the straight-line method would be as follows:

20Y1			
July 1	Interest Expense	4,075	
	Premium on Bonds Payable	425	
	Cash		4,500
	To pay bond interest and amortize bond premium.		

¶904

Raising Capital: Stocks vs. Bonds

LEARNING OBJECTIVE 4: Identify the effects of issuing bonds versus stocks.

Earlier, this chapter described how bonds payable are used to borrow money for company operations. Another way to obtain capital is by issuing stock. Management must evaluate which method is the optimum way for a company to obtain capital: (1) borrow the money by issuing bonds payable, or (2) raise the money by issuing stock. Each approach offers certain advantages:

Leveraging is the use of borrowed funds to increase earnings for the business owners.

- Issuing bonds payable does not affect stockholders' equity. Current stockholders retain the same share of ownership. Earnings per share go up, assuming earnings on debt exceed interest expense. This situation is referred to as "**leveraging**." Leveraging is also referred to as "trading on equity."
- Issuing stock does not increase liabilities or interest expense; thus, this approach is less risky than issuing bonds payable.

Earnings per share is the company's net income per share.

How will the decision to issue bonds payable or stock affect a company's earnings per share? **Earnings per share (EPS)** is a key financial ratio investors use to evaluate a company's performance, and is computed by dividing the company's net income, less preferred dividends, by the number of shares of common stock. Since EPS is a sign of a company's health in the form of net income per share, managers must carefully evaluate any decision that directly affects net income and shares of stock.

Suppose Baggins Pipe Company is planning to build a new plant. One million dollars in cash is needed. Should Baggins borrow the money with bonds or issue stock? Baggins has net income of $600,000 and 200,000 shares of common stock outstanding. Company management is evaluating two financing plans. The first is to issue $1 million of 8% corporate bonds payable. The second is to issue 100,000 share of common stock for $1 million. Management anticipates that the new plant, acquired with the cash, will generate income of $400,000 before interest and taxes. The tax rate is 40 percent.

Exhibit 9.10 shows that Baggins Pipe Company is projected to have higher EPS by issuing bonds instead of issuing stock. This occurs because the company earns more on the investment ($192,000) than the interest it pays on the bonds ($80,000).

Exhibit 9.10 IMPACT OF ISSUING STOCK vs. BONDS ON EARNINGS PER SHARE		
	Plan 1: Stock Issue Issue 100,000 Shares of Common Stock for $1 million	**Plan 2: Bond Issue** Issue Bonds Payable of $1 million at 8%
Earnings (Net Income) before Expansion		$600,000	$600,000
Expected Plant Earnings Before Interest & Tax	$400,000	$4000,000
Less Interest Expense	0	80,000
Expected Plant Earnings Before Tax	$400,000	$320,000
Less Income Tax	160,000	128,000
Expected Plant Earnings	240,000	192,000
Total Company Earnings	$840,000	$792,000
Earnings Per Share (EPS) after Expansion		
Plan 1 (300,000 common stock shares)	$2.80	
Plan 2 (200,000 common stock shares)		$3.96

Note: The tax rate is 40 percent.

As noted, borrowing leads to a higher earnings per share for Baggins Pipe Company. However, borrowing is riskier than issuing stock. When a company borrows money, it must pay the interest expense regardless of how well the company is doing. On the other hand, if the company issues stock, the dividend can be reduced or eliminated in a bad year.

FOCUS ON TECHNOLOGY

Using Microsoft Excel: Comparing Stock vs. Bonds

Using Excel, we will recreate Exhibit 9.10: The Impact of Issuing Stock vs. Bonds on EPS. A company is planning to build a new plant and needs one million dollars in cash to do so. Which results in a higher EPS — borrowing the money with bonds payable or raising the money by issuing stock?

1. File Identification Area: In an Excel worksheet, create a file identification area showing the filename, input required, and other appropriate information. The input required is listed below in the Input Area. The output required is the "Impact of Issuing Stock Versus Bonds on EPS."
2. Input Area: Type in the following.

Earnings (Net Income) before expansion	600,000
Expected plant earnings before interest & tax	400,000
Shares of common stock without stock issue	200,000
Shares of common stock after stock issue, Plan 1	300,000
Bonds payable, Plan 2	1,000,000
Interest rate on bonds, Plan 2	8%
Income tax rate	40%

3. Output Area: Set up your headings to resemble Exhibit 9.10. Insert amounts from the input area. Create formulas where needed. Helpful Hints:

- The interest expense for bonds equals bonds payable times the interest rate. There is no interest expense for the stock issue.
- Income tax equals the tax rate times the expected plant earnings before tax.
- EPS for Plan 1 equals total company earnings divided by the shares of common stock after stock issue. EPS for Plan 2 equals total company earnings divided by the shares of common stock without the stock issue.

? Could you possibly leverage money when buying a car?

¶905

Evaluating the Level of Debt

LEARNING OBJECTIVE 5: Explain how and why the level of a company's debt is evaluated.

Determining when and how much money to borrow is a huge challenge for business managers. As shown above, borrowing can lead to higher earnings per share, although debt does carry certain risks. Accounting information can help top management evaluate how much debt is too much.

Major borrowing is a cross-functional decision that requires information from different departments in the company. For example, the marketing department may project a substantial increase in product demand that warrants an increase in production. However, production can only increase output by building an additional manufacturing plant. This requires obtaining money (capital) to build the plants. The finance department must determine the cost of different financing arrangements. Accounting can calculate and report the estimated impact of the additional sales and higher operating costs on the firm's profits. Ultimately, the company's top management evaluates the information from all departments and makes the final decision.

Business managers and financial analysts use the **times-interest-earned ratio** to assess the company's ability to pay interest expense. This financial ratio, also called the "interest coverage ratio," is calculated by dividing operating income by interest expense. Thus, the ratio shows the number of times that operating income can cover interest expense. The higher the ratio, the easier a company can pay its interest expense. A company with a very low times-interest-earned ratio may have difficulty covering its interest expense. In extreme cases, the ratio may foreshadow potential bankruptcy.

Interpreting what a ratio conveys requires some kind of comparison, such as to other companies in the same industry. Exhibit 9.11 shows the times-interest-earned ratio for two merchandising companies: Stein Mart, Inc. and JC Penney Company, Inc.

Exhibit 9.11 COMPUTING TIMES INTEREST EARNED RATIO

				JC Penney	Stein Mart
Times interest earned ratio	=	Operating Income	=	790,000	7,934
		Interest Expense	=	261,000	1,688
			=	3.0	4.7

Note: Amounts are in thousands of dollars.

JC Penney has a lower times-interest-earned ratio than Stein Mart. JC Penney's income from operations covers its interest expense three times, while Stein Mart's interest coverage ratio is 4.7 times. Stein Mart is less risky on this ratio than JC Penney. Because JC Penney is a much larger and more well established company than Stein Mart, JC Penney can likely manage a lower interest coverage ratio.

¶906 Lease Liabilities

LEARNING OBJECTIVE 6: Distinguish types of leases and account for lease liabilities.

Another type of long-term liability is a lease liability. When a company needs equipment or other operating assets, cash may not be available to make the purchase. In this case, the company may borrow money to purchase the equipment, or it may obtain a short-term or long-term lease to acquire the equipment. A **lease** is an arrangement in which a tenant (lessee) agrees to make rent payments to a property owner (lessor) in return for use of the property. Leases are accounted for differently, depending on whether they are categorized as operating (short-term) leases or capital (long-term) leases.

¶906.01 OPERATING LEASE

An **operating lease** is short-term and cancelable. Once the lease expires, there are no provisions for the lessee to continue using the property in the future. The lessee accounts for an operating lease as follows:

Dec. 31	Rent Expense	2,000	
	Cash		2,000
	To record lease payment.		

The journal entry for the operating lease includes a debit to Rent Expense (or Lease Expense) and a credit to Cash. The lessee's balance sheet does not show the leased asset or a lease liability.

¶906.02 CAPITAL LEASE

Unlike an operating lease, a **capital lease** is long-term and non-cancelable. A capital lease is more like an installment purchase than an actual lease. According to GAAP (Financial Accounting Standards Board Statement No. 13), a capital lease must meet one of the following criteria:

- Title of the leased asset transfers from the lessor to the lessee at the end of the lease term. In other words, the lessee owns the asset when the lease ends.

- The lease agreement includes a bargain purchase option; thus, the lessee is expected to purchase the leased asset.
- The term of the lease is 75% or more of the leased asset's useful economic life.
- Present value of lease payments is 90% or more of the leased asset's market price.

Many companies use capital leases to acquire the assets needed for operations. Capital leases are popular for several reasons. First, capital leases cost less than operating leases. Second, a lease does not require an immediate outlay of cash for a down payment. Third, rent payments are fully deductible for tax purposes.

Suppose that on January 1, 20Y1, JK Productions signs a 5-year lease to obtain a company vehicle that normally retails at $22,000. The lease agreement specifies that JK make annual payments of $5,000 (at the end of each year) for five years, which is the estimated useful life of the vehicle. At the end of the lease term, ownership of the vehicle transfers to JK. According to GAAP, JK's lease should be accounted for as a capital lease, because the initial facts indicate that two criteria are satisfied:

1. ownership transfers, and
2. the 75% test is satisfied (5-year lease/5-year useful life = 100%).

A lease provides the right to use an asset in exchange for periodic rent payments. To record a capital lease, the present value of the lease must be calculated; in this case, the present value of the periodic rent payments. Assuming JK's interest cost is 8 percent, the present value of the lease is $19,965 ($5,000 × 3.993 — Factor for PV Annuity, 5 periods, 8%; Exhibit 9.4). Thus, the capital lease is recorded as follows:

20Y1			
Jan. 1	Vehicle Under Capital Lease	19,965	
	Liability Under Capital Lease		19,965
	To record capital lease of vehicle.		

The balance sheet of JK Productions discloses the capital lease. The Equipment Under Capital Lease is a long-term asset and Liability Under Capital Lease is a long-term liability. In addition, each year JK Productions records depreciation on the capital lease.

¶906.03   DECIDING ON THE TYPE OF LEASE

The decision to acquire assets with an operating lease or capital lease may be a tough choice. Suppose you are the vice-president of finance at McDonald's. The company plans to lease restaurant and warehouse facilities overseas; these assets are valued at $2 billion. The lease can be set up as an operating lease or as a capital lease. What factors would you consider to make this decision?

If McDonald's goal is to lock in a long-term arrangement, then a capital lease may be preferred. In addition, you may be able to negotiate a lower rent payment with a long-term capital lease. On the other hand, the capital lease requires that you capitalize the leased asset and record the lease liability as if you had purchased the asset with long-term debt. The capital lease increases both total assets and total liabilities on the balance sheet. In contrast, the operating lease has no impact on the balance sheet.

Let's consider the cross-functional issues. From the perspective of the vice-president of operations and the restaurant managers, the goal is to acquire the assets needed for doing business, regardless of whether an operating or capital lease is used. However, the vice-present of finance is concerned about which financing arrangement will decrease short-term profitability. A decision may hurt profits in the short-term, but may be beneficial in the long-term. There is sometimes a trade-off between short-term and long-term profitability. This is not an easy decision because estimates must be made on future conditions.

Debt ratio equals total liabilities divided by total assets.

Another consideration in deciding which type of lease to use is the resulting effect on the company's debt ratio. Previously, we used the times-interest-earned ratio to assess the company's ability to pay its interest expense out of operating income. The **debt ratio** helps investors and lenders assess the financial position of a company, specifically, the weight of debt on the company's financial resources. The debt ratio is computed by dividing total liabilities by total assets. If the ratio is judged as being too high, then the company may have to pay a higher interest rate on future borrowings. Exhibit 9.12 shows the impact of using a capital lease on the company's debt ratio.

Have you ever been a party to a lease? Would you categorize it as an operating or capital lease?

Exhibit 9.12 OPERATING LEASE VERSUS CAPITAL LEASE
(Amounts in Millions)

Operating Lease:

$$\text{Debt Ratio} = \frac{\text{Total Liabilities}}{\text{Total Assets}} = \frac{13.5}{25.5} = 52.9\%$$

Capital Lease:

$$\text{Debt Ratio} = \frac{\text{Total Liabilities}}{\text{Total Assets}} = \frac{13.5 + 2}{25.5 + 2} = \frac{15.5}{27.5} = 56.4\%$$

As shown in Exhibit 9.12, the debt ratio is 52.9% using an operating lease and 56.4% using a capital lease. If a debt ratio of 56.4% causes McDonald's to pay a significantly higher interest rate on future borrowings, then you will choose to use an operating lease, rather than a capital lease.

¶907   Pensions and Post-Retirement Benefits

LEARNING OBJECTIVE 7: Describe the impact of pensions and post-retirement benefits on financial reporting.

A pension plan provides compensation to employees after they retire. Post-retirement benefits include other retiree benefits, primarily in the form of health care and life insurance.

Many companies provide pension plans and other post-retirement benefits for their employees. A **pension plan** is an arrangement in which employees receive compensation after they retire. **Post-retirement benefits** include other retiree benefits like health care and life insurance. Typically, employees contribute part of their paycheck to their pension plan, with the company often providing a matching contribution.

Pension contributions accumulate in a pension fund. The company's liability for future pension payments also accumulates. Each year, the company must compare the pension plan assets to the pension plan's accumulated obligations. If the pension plan assets are more than the accumulated obligations, the plan is over-funded. In this case, the plan assets and obligations are reported only in notes to the financial statements. However, if the pension plan obligations exceed the plan assets, then the pension plan is under-funded, and the net liability amount must be reported as a long-term pension liability on the balance sheet.

On its financial statements, Proctor & Gamble disclosed that its pension plan was under-funded as follows:

- Fair value of plan assets of $2.3 billion
- Accumulated pension benefit obligations of $4.6 billion

If you are employed, does your employer offer a pension plan to its employees?

As a result, P&G's balance sheet included a long-term pension liability of $2.3 billion ($4.6 – $2.3). This net pension liability is included with other long-term liabilities.

Pension plans and post-retirement benefits are among the most complex areas of accounting. Determining the accumulated benefit obligations can be particularly challenging, as they are based on assumptions about life expectancies, age of retirees, and anticipated future healthcare costs.

¶908   Concluding Remarks

At this point you know the difference between short and long-term liabilities. You could look at the financial statements of Proctor & Gamble, or any company, and recognize whether the liability is short-term or long-term. You can evaluate the merits of a company raising capital through issuing bonds or stock, and whether it should incur more debt. You can explain the financial reporting issues regarding leases and pension plans. You are becoming a fairly savvy business person. Now you're ready for a glimpse at the high rollers of the market place — corporations. In Chapter 10, we will look at the advantages and disadvantages of being incorporated, including how corporations can raise large amounts of capital more easily than sole proprietorships or partnerships.

Chapter Review

LEARNING OBJECTIVE 1

Describe the importance of liabilities to people within and outside the business.

Liabilities are one of the three main sections on the balance sheet. Liabilities are financial obligations or the debts owed by the business. Incurring debt, that is, borrowing money, is one way that a business can acquire the money it needs to finance company operations. Within a firm, business managers must decide whether to pay for items with cash on hand or to purchase items using debt financing. When liabilities become too large, then the risk increases that the company will be unable to pay them off. If the risk is high, then the company's stock price will fall. Stockholders worry that the company will either fail to make a reasonable profit, or that it will go out of business.

LEARNING OBJECTIVE 2

Account for current liabilities.

Liabilities are classified into two major categories: current liabilities and long-term liabilities. Current liabilities are those that are due within one year or less. Examples of current liabilities include accounts payable, short-term payables, the current portion of long-term notes payable, accrued expenses, payroll payable, unearned revenue, and warranty payable.

LEARNING OBJECTIVE 3

Describe long-term liabilities.

Long-term liabilities are the financial obligations of the firm that are due more than one year in the future. Long-term liabilities are often large financial commitments that require years of future cash outlays. Long-term liabilities include bonds payable, lease liabilities, and pensions and post-retirement benefits.

A bond is a type of security, which represents debt owed by the issuing company to the bondholder. A bond is essentially a loan taken out by the issuer. Investors buy and sell bonds in bond markets, just as stocks are bought and sold in stock markets. The price that a bond sells for is referred to as its "market price" or "market value." When initially issued, the bond's market price is the combined present value of two items: the present value of the bond's principal amount and the present value of the bond's cash interest payments. If the market price is more than the bond's principal, then the bond sells at a premium. If the market price is less than the bond's principal, then the bond sells at a discount.

LEARNING OBJECTIVE 4

Identify the effects of issuing bonds versus stocks.

Management must evaluate which method is the optimum way for a company to obtain capital: (1) borrow the money with bonds payable, or (2) raise the money by issuing stock. Issuing bonds payable does not affect stockholders' equity. Current stockholders retain the same share of ownership. Earnings per share go up, assuming earnings on debt exceeds interest expense. This situation is referred to as "leveraging." Issuing stock does not increase liabilities or interest expense; thus, this approach is less risky than issuing bonds payable.

LEARNING OBJECTIVE 5

Explain how and why the level of a company's debt is evaluated.

Determining when and how much money to borrow is a major concern to business managers. Borrowing can lead to higher earnings per share, but debt carries certain risks. Business managers and financial analysts use a financial ratio, the times-interest-earned ratio, to assess the company's ability to pay interest expense. This ratio is calculated by dividing operating income by interest expense.

LEARNING OBJECTIVE 6

Distinguish types of leases and account for lease liabilities.

A lease is an arrangement in which a tenant (lessee) agrees to make rent payments to a property owner (lessor) in return for use of the property. Leases are accounted for differently, depending on whether they are categorized as operating (short-term) leases or capital (long-term) leases.

LEARNING OBJECTIVE 7

Describe the impact of pensions and post-retirement benefits on financial reporting.

Many companies provide pension plans and other post-retirement benefits for their employees. A pension plan is an arrangement in which employees receive compensation after they retire. Post-retirement benefits include other retiree benefits, primarily health care and life insurance.

¶910

Glossary

Annuity

An annuity pays a fixed amount of money at the end of each period for a specified number of periods.

Bond

A bond is a type of security, which represents debt owed by the issuer to the bondholder.

Bond amortization

Bond amortization is the process of reducing the bond's discount or premium to zero, over the term of the bond. Amortizing a bond discount or premium results in interest expense being higher or lower, respectively, than the bond's stated interest rate.

Bond certificate

The bond certificate is a legal document showing the name of the issuing corporation, the principal amount, the annual interest rate, interest payment dates (usually twice per year), and the maturity date.

Bond face value

A bond's face value, also called the "principal amount," is the amount to be received by the bondholder on the maturity date.

Bond indenture

A bond indenture is a supplementary agreement listing the restrictions, rights, and privileges of the bonds.

Bond issue

A bond issue specifies the total number of bonds issued.

Bond principal

A bond's principal is the amount to be received by the bondholder on the maturity date. This amount is also referred to as the bond's "face value" or "maturity value."

Bond stated interest rate

For bonds, the stated interest rate, also called "face interest rate," sets the amount of cash interest to be paid to the bondholder.

Capital lease

A capital lease is a long-term and non-cancelable liability.

Debentures

Debentures are unsecured bonds that are backed only by the good faith of the borrower.

Debt ratio

Debt ratio is total liabilities divided by total assets.

Deferred revenue

A deferred revenue, also called "unearned revenue," results when a customer pays cash in advance before receiving the goods or services.

Earnings per share (EPS)

EPS is calculated by dividing the firm's net income, less preferred dividends, by common shares outstanding. EPS shows the firm's earnings per share of common stock.

Face value of a bond

A bond's face value, also called a bond's "principal" or "maturity value," is the amount to be received by the bondholder on the maturity date.

Lease

A lease is an arrangement in which a tenant (lessee) agrees to make rent payments to a property owner (lessor) in return for use of the property.

Leveraging

Leveraging, also referred to as "trading on equity," occurs when earnings on borrowed money exceeds the related interest expense, resulting in higher earnings for the business owners.

Market interest rate

The market interest rate, also called "effective interest rate," is the rate of interest paid in the market on bonds of similar risk.

Market price of a bond

Market price, also referred to as "market value," is the selling price of a bond.

Market value of a bond

Market value, also referred to as "market price," is the selling price of a bond.

Maturity value of a bond

A maturity value is the amount to be received by the bondholder on the maturity date. This amount is also referred to as the bond's "principal" or "face value."

Net pay

Net pay, also called "take-home pay," is the amount left over after withholding all deductions.

Operating lease

An operating lease is a short-term and cancelable lease.

Par value of a bond

Par value is the sum of money owed on a bond. The par value is also referred to as the bond's "face value," "maturity value," or "denomination."

Payroll liabilities

Payroll liabilities are liabilities for payroll expenses that have been incurred but not yet paid.

Pension plan

A pension plan is an arrangement in which employees receive compensation after they retire.

Post-retirement benefits

Post-retirement benefits include retiree benefits, primarily in the form of health care and life insurance.

Present value

Present value is the monetary worth today of an amount to be received at a future time.

Secured bonds

Secured bonds provide a guarantee of repayment by pledging specified corporate assets.

Times-interest-earned ratio

The times-interest-earned ratio, also called "interest coverage ratio," assesses the company's ability to pay interest expense. It is calculated by dividing operating income by interest expense.

Underwriter

An underwriter buys bonds from the issuing company and then resells them to others.

Unsecured bonds

Unsecured bonds, also called "debentures," are backed only by the good faith of the borrower.

¶911   # Chapter Assignments

QUESTIONS

1. **[Obj. 1]** Describe liabilities.

2. **[Obj. 1]** Within the firm, what decision must business managers make regarding paying for items?

3. **[Obj. 1]** What risk results from a large amount of liabilities?

4. **[Obj. 2 & 3]** Distinguish between the two major categories of liabilities.

5. **[Obj. 2]** Describe liabilities that are not a definitely determinable amount.

6. **[Obj. 2]** List several types of current liabilities.

7. **[Obj. 2]** Define the following:
   a. accrued liabilities
   b. deferred revenues

8. **[Obj. 2]** Suppose that on December 31 Pizza Hut Corporation estimates its federal income tax liability as $144,000. What journal entry should Pizza Hut record?

9. **[Obj. 3]** List examples of long-term liabilities.

10. **[Obj. 3]** Define the following:
    a. bond
    b. underwriter
    c. bond principal
    d. bond certificate

11. **[Obj. 3]** Distinguish between secured bonds and unsecured bonds.

12. **[Obj. 3]** What is the time value of money and how does it relate to present value?

13. **[Obj. 3]** What determines if a bond sells at a premium or a discount?

14. **[Obj. 3]** Assume General Motors issues $200,000 of 6%, 4-year bonds on January 1. Interest is to be paid semiannually. The bonds' market value is $192,000. What is the journal entry on January 1 to record the bond issue?

15. **[Obj. 3]** Assume General Motors issues $150,000 of 6%, 3-year bonds on January 1. Interest is to be paid semiannually. The bonds' market value is $153,000. What is the journal entry on January 1 to record the bond issue?

16. **[Obj. 3]** On Jan. 1, 20Y5, Pony Express Corporation retires bonds that have a carrying value of $200,000. The bonds were originally issued at a discount on Jan. 1, 20Y1 but the discount is now fully amortized. What is the journal entry to record the retirement of these bonds?

17. **[Obj. 4]** Describe the concept of leveraging.

18. **[Obj. 4]** Contrast the advantages of issuing bonds versus issuing stock to raise cash.

19. **[Obj. 4]** What is earnings per share?

20. **[Obj. 5]** In evaluating a company's level of debt, business managers and financial analysts use the times-interest-earned ratio. How is this ratio calculated?

21. **[Obj. 6]** What is a lease and why are leases accounted for in different ways?

22. **[Obj. 6]** Suppose Pacific Timber Company agrees to an operating lease. The first payment of $5,000 is made on December 31. What journal entry is recorded?

23. **[Obj. 6]** A capital lease is long-term and non-cancelable. A capital lease must meet one of four criteria. What are the four criteria?

24. **[Obj. 6]** What is the debt ratio and how is it used to evaluate a company's financial position?

25. **[Obj. 7]** What is a pension plan?

26. **[Obj. 7]** How is a pension plan accounted for? What does over-funded and under-funded mean?

SHORT EXERCISES — SET A

Building Accounting Skills

1. **[Obj. 2]** Recording Payroll Liabilities: Suppose that the March 15 payroll for Neon Light Company included the following: wages $60,000, federal income tax withholdings $8,400, state income tax withholdings $3,200, social security tax withholdings $4,650, Medicare tax withholdings $1,100, health insurance withholdings $1,600, and pension contributions withholdings $4,000. What is the journal entry to record the payroll, withholdings, and net pay?

2. **[Obj. 2]** Recording Payroll Liabilities: In addition to recording the payroll, withholding, and net pay above, Neon Light Company must also record employer taxes and other benefits associated with payroll. Neon must pay the employer portion of Social Security and Medicare. Neon also pays federal and state unemployment tax, $200 and $3,100, respectively. In addition, Neon pays half of the health insurance premium and half of the pension contributions. What is the journal entry to record payroll taxes and benefits expense?

3. **[Obj. 2]** Recording Deferred Revenues: Suppose that on February 1, Mammoth Paint Corporation is hired to paint some vehicles for Dynamic Taxi Company. On that same day, Dynamic pays for the paint job in advance, $10,000. Mammoth completes the paint job for Dynamic on February 14.
   a. Record the entry by Mammoth for receipt of the advance payment on Feb. 1.
   b. Record the entry by Mammoth at the completion of the paint job on Feb. 14.

4. **[Obj. 2]** Recording Warranty Liabilities: Suppose Green Tractor Company provides a 120-day warranty on its tractors. The warranty makes Green tractors more appealing to the consumer and, thus, helps increase sales. Based on past experience, 3 percent of the tractors will probably be returned and replaced under the warranty. The average tractor costs $10,000. Assume that 100 tractors are sold in July. Make the entry to record the warranty liability on July 31 and show calculations for the warranty liability.

5. **[Obj. 3]** Recording Bond Transactions: Suppose Superior Drug Company has $100,000 in 5% bonds that mature in five years. Assume these bonds are issued at par on January 1, 20Y1. The bonds have semiannual interest payment dates of January 1 and July 1.
   a. Record the bond issue on January 1, 20Y1.
   b. Record the first interest payment on July 1, 20Y1.
   c. Record the accrued interest on December 31, 20Y1.
   d. Record the paying off of the bonds on the maturity date of January 1, 20Y6.

6. **[Obj. 3]** Computing Present Values: Use the present value tables in Exhibit 9.3 and 9.4 to calculate the market value of General Dynamics Company bonds. The company issues $100,000 of 7%, 5-year bonds on January 1, 20Y1. Interest is paid semiannually. On January 1, 20Y1, the market interest rate is 8%.
   a. Will the market value of the bonds be above or below the maturity value of $100,000?
   b. Determine the present value (market price) of the bonds and show your calculations.

7. **[Obj. 3]** Computing Present Values: Use the present value tables in Exhibit 9.3 and 9.4 to calculate the market value of Continental Cell Phone Company bonds. The company issues $200,000 of 9%, 4-year bonds on January 1, 20Y1. Interest is paid semiannually. On the bond issue date, the market interest rate is 8%.
   a. Will the market value of the bonds be above or below the maturity value of $200,000?
   b. Determine the present value (market price) of the bonds and show your calculations.

8. **[Obj. 3]** Recording Bonds Issued at a Discount: Suppose Toy Warehouse, Inc. issues $100,000 of 5%, 3-year bonds on January 1, 20Y1. Interest is to be paid semiannually. On the issue date, the bonds' market value is $94,000.
   a. What journal entry is made to record the bond issue on January 1, 20Y1?
   b. How would the Bonds Payable and Discount on Bonds Payable be shown in the liability section of the balance sheet on January 1, 20Y1?
   c. What is the total interest expense over the 3-year term of the bonds?

9. **[Obj. 3]** Recording Bonds Issued at a Premium: Suppose Toy Warehouse, Inc. issues $100,000 of 8%, 4-year bonds on January 1, 20Y1. Interest is to be paid semiannually. On the issue date, the bonds' market value is $104,000.
   a. What journal entry is made to record the bond issue on January 1, 20Y1?
   b. How would the Bonds Payable and Premium on Bonds Payable be shown in the liability section of the balance sheet on January 1, 20Y1?
   c. What is the total interest expense over the 4-year term of the bonds?

10. **[Obj. 6]** Recording a Capital Lease: Suppose that on January 1, 20Y1, Rocky Mountain Moving Company signs a lease to obtain a moving van. The lease agreement specifies that Rocky make annual payments of $20,000 for six years, which is the estimated useful life of the vehicle. At the end of the lease term, ownership of the vehicle transfers to Rocky.
    a. Assuming Rocky's annual interest cost is 7 percent, what is the present value of the lease?
    b. What entry is made to record the lease agreement on January 1, 20Y1?

SHORT EXERCISES — SET B

Building Accounting Skills

1. **[Obj. 2]** Recording Payroll Liabilities: Suppose the June 15 payroll for Comics Company included the following: wages $30,000, federal income tax withholdings $4,200, state income tax withholdings $1,600, social security tax withholdings $2,325, Medicare tax withholdings $550, health insurance withholdings $800, and pension contributions withholdings $2,000. What is the journal entry to record the payroll, withholdings, and net pay?

2. **[Obj. 2]** Recording Payroll Liabilities: In addition to recording the payroll, withholding, and net pay above, Comics Company must also record employer taxes and other benefits associated with payroll. Comics must pay the employer portion of social security and Medicare. Comics also pays federal and state unemployment tax, $100 and $1,550, respectively. In addition, Comics pays half of the health insurance premium and half of the pension contributions. What is the journal entry to record payroll taxes and benefits expense?

3. **[Obj. 2]** Recording Deferred Revenues: Suppose that on March 1, Tubs & Beyond is hired to provide and install bathtubs for House Builders, Inc. On that same day, House Builders pays for the job in advance, $5,000. Tubs & Beyond completes the job on March 14.
    a. Record the entry by Tubs & Beyond for receipt of the advance payment on March 1.
    b. Record the entry by Tubs & Beyond at the completion of the job on March 14.

4. **[Obj. 2]** Recording Warranty Liabilities: Suppose Aloha Waterbeds provides a 120-day warranty on its waterbeds. The warranty makes Aloha more appealing to the consumer and, thus, helps to increase sales. Based on past experience, 3 percent of the waterbeds will probably be returned and replaced under the warranty. The average waterbed costs $1,000. Assume that 100 waterbeds are sold in April. Make the entry to record the warranty liability on April 30; show calculations for the warranty liability.

5. **[Obj. 3]** Recording Bond Transactions: Suppose Starbucks has $200,000 in 5% bonds that mature in five years. Assume these bonds are issued at par on January 1, 20Y1. The bonds have semiannual interest payment dates of January 1 and July 1.
    a. Record the bond issue on January 1, 20Y1.
    b. Record the first interest payment on July 1, 20Y1.
    c. Record the accrued interest on December 31, 20Y1.
    d. Record the paying off of the bonds on the maturity date of January 1, 20Y6.

6. **[Obj. 3]** Calculating Present Values: Use the present value tables in Exhibits 9.3 and 9.4 to calculate the market value of Mustang Motor Company bonds. The company issues $100,000 of 9%, 5-year bonds on January 1, 20Y1. Interest is to be paid semiannually. On the issue date, the market interest rate is 10%.
    a. Will the market value of the bonds be above or below the maturity value of $100,000?
    b. Determine the present value (market price) of the bonds and show your calculations.

7. **[Obj. 3]** Calculating Present Values: Use the present value tables in Exhibits 9.3 and 9.4 to calculate the market value of Super Shoe Company bonds. The company issues $100,000 of 9%, 6-year bonds on January 1, 20Y1. Interest is to be paid semiannually. On the issue date, the market interest rate is 8%.
    a. Will the market value of the bonds be above or below the maturity value of $100,000?
    b. Determine the present value (market price) of the bonds and show your calculations.

8. **[Obj. 3]** Recording Bonds Issued at a Discount: Suppose Superior Shoe Company issues $100,000 of 6%, 3-year bonds on January 1, 20Y1. Interest is to be paid semiannually. On the issue date, the bonds' market value is $97,000.
    a. What journal entry is made to record the bond issue on January 1, 20Y1?
    b. How would the Bonds Payable and Discount on Bonds Payable be shown in the liability section of the balance sheet on January 1, 20Y1?
    c. What is the total interest expense over the 3-year term of the bonds?

9. **[Obj. 3]** Recording Bonds Issued at a Premium: Suppose Joe's Sports Store issues $100,000 of 7%, 4-year bonds on January 1, 20Y1. Interest is to be paid semiannually. On the issue date, the bonds' market value is $106,000.
    a. What journal entry is made to record the bond issue on January 1, 20Y1?
    b. How would the Bonds Payable and Premium on Bonds Payable be shown in the liability section of the balance sheet on January 1, 20Y1?
    c. What is the total interest expense over the 4-year term of the bonds?

10. **[Obj. 6]** Recording a Capital Lease: Suppose that on January 1, 20Y1, Big Town Recording Company signs a lease to obtain recording equipment. The lease agreement specifies that Big Town make annual payments of $10,000 for 10 years, which is the estimated useful life of the equipment. At the end of the lease term, ownership of the equipment transfers to Big Town.
    a. Assuming Big Town's annual interest cost is 6 percent, what is the present value of the lease?
    b. What entry is made to record the lease agreement on January 1, 20Y1?

PROBLEMS — SET A

Applying Accounting Knowledge

1. **[Obj. 3]** Amortizing a Bond Discount Using the Effective Interest Method: If a bond is issued at a discount, then the interest expense is always more than the cash interest payment. Assume that on January 1, 20Y1, Metro Electric Company issues $100,000 of 9%, 3-year bonds when the market rate is 10%. Interest payments are made semiannually. On January 1, 20Y1, the bond carrying value is $97,442 and the discount is $2,558. The Discount on Bonds Payable will be amortized, that is, reduced to zero over the life of the bonds.

    Required:
    a. Prepare an amortization table using the effective interest method showing the following column headings:

A	B	C	D	E	F
Interest Payment Date	Interest Payment (4.5% of Principle)	Interest Expense (5% of Carrying Value)	Discount Amortization (C – B)	Bond Discount Balance	Bond Carrying Value

    b. Evaluate: What are the benefits and risks to the company of borrowing money with bonds payable?

2. **[Obj. 3]** Amortizing Bond Discount Using Straight-Line Interest Method: Same as problem A1 but use the straight-line interest method. Assume that on January 1, 20Y1, Metro Electric Company issues $100,000 of 9%, 3-year bonds when the market rate is 10%. Interest payments are made semiannually. On January 1, 20Y1, the bond carrying value is $97,442 and the discount is $2,558. The discount on bonds payable will be amortized, that is, reduced to zero over the life of the bonds.

    Required:
    a. Prepare an amortization table using the straight-line interest method showing the following column headings:

A	B	C	D	E	F
Interest Payment Date	Interest Payment (4.5% of Principle)	Interest Expense (B + D)	Discount Amortization (2,558/6)	Bond Discount Balance	Bond Carrying Value

    b. Evaluate: What are the benefits and risks to the company of borrowing money with bonds payable?

3. **[Obj. 3]** Amortizing a Bond Premium Using the Effective Interest Method: If a bond is issued at a premium, then the interest expense is always less than the cash interest payment. Assume that on January 1, 20Y1, Metro Electric Company issues $100,000 of 9%, 3-year bonds when the market rate is 8%. Interest payments are made semiannually. On January 1, 20Y1, the bond carrying value is $102,589 and the premium is $2,589. The premium on bonds payable will be amortized, that is, reduced to zero over the life of the bonds.

Required:
a. Prepare an amortization table showing the following column headings:

A	B	C	D	E	F
Interest Payment Date	Interest Payment (4.5% of Principle)	Interest Expense (4% of Carrying Value)	Premium Amortization (B – C)	Bond Premium Balance	Bond Carrying Value

b. Evaluate: What are the benefits and risks to the company of borrowing money with bonds payable?

4. **[Obj. 3]** Amortizing a Bond Premium Using the Straight-Line Interest Method: If a bond is issued at a premium, then the interest expense is always less than the cash interest payment. Assume that on January 1, 20Y1, Metro Electric Company issues $100,000 of 10%, 4-year bonds when the market rate is 8%. Interest payments are made semiannually. On January 1, 20Y1, the bond carrying value is $106,800 and the premium is $6,800. The premium on bonds payable will be amortized, that is, reduced to zero over the life of the bonds.

Required:
a. Prepare an amortization table using the straight-line method showing the following column headings:

A	B	C	D	E	F
Interest Payment Date	Interest Payment (5% of Principle)	Interest Expense (B – D)	Premium Amortization	Bond Premium Balance	Bond Carrying Value

b. Evaluate: What are the benefits and risks to the company of borrowing money with bonds payable?

5. **[Obj. 3]** Recording Bonds Payable Issued at a Discount: On January 1, 20Y1 Carson Packaging Company issues $100,000 of 6%, 4-year bonds, with a discount of $1,600. On the maturity date, January 1, 20Y5, the discount is reduced to zero and the bond carrying value is $100,000, the maturity value. On July 1, 20Y1, Carson makes its first $3,000 semiannual interest payment and also records the discount amortization of $200. On December 31, 20Y1, Carson accrues its second $3,000 semiannual interest liability along with its discount amortization of $200.

Required:
a. Record the bond issue on January 1, 20Y1.
b. Record the first interest payment on July 1, 20Y1.
c. Record the accrued interest on December 31, 20Y1.
d. Record the paying off of the bonds on the maturity date of January 1, 20Y5.
e. Evaluate: Do you think it was a good business decision for Carson Packaging to issue the bonds?

6. **[Obj. 3]** Recording Bonds Payable Issued at a Premium: On January 1, 20Y1 Carson Packaging Company issues $100,000 of 6%, 4-year bonds, with a premium of $2,400. On the maturity date, January 1, 20Y5, the premium is reduced to zero and the bond carrying value is $100,000, the maturity value. On July 1, 20Y1, Carson makes its first $3,000 semiannual interest payment. Carson accrues interest expense on that date of $2,700 and also records the premium amortization of $300. On December 31, 20Y1, Carson accrues its second $3,000 semiannual interest liability along with its premium amortization of $300.

Required:
a. Record the bond issue on January 1, 20Y1.
b. Record the first interest payment on July 1, 20Y1.
c. Record the accrued interest on December 31, 20Y1.
d. Record the paying off of the bonds on the maturity date of January 1, 20Y5.
e. Evaluate: Do you think it was a good business decision for Carson Packaging to issue the bonds?

7. **[Obj. 5]** Comparing Equity Versus Debt Financing: Suppose Southwest Lumber Company is planning to build a new sawmill. Three million dollars in cash is needed. Should Southwest borrow the money with bonds payable or raise the money by issuing stock? Southwest currently has net income of $250,000 and 200,000 shares of common stock outstanding. Company management is evaluating two financing plans for the new sawmill project. The first is to issue 100,000 shares of common stock for $3 million. The second is to issue $3 million of 4% corporate bonds payable. Management anticipates that the new sawmill, acquired with the cash, will generate income of $400,000 before interest and taxes. Southwest's income tax rate is 40%.

Required:
a. Prepare an analysis showing a comparison of the EPS resulting from issuing bonds versus issuing stock.
b. Evaluate: Which option is a better business decision? Why?

8. **[Obj. 5]** Compare Times-Interest-Earned Ratios: Compute the times interest earned ratio for Southwest Moving Company and Fast Shipping Corporation. Operating income and interest expense for Southwest are $280,000 and $75,000, respectively. Operating income and interest expense for Fast are $975,000 and $350,000, respectively.

Required:
a. Prepare calculations of the times-interest-earned ratio for the two companies.
b. Evaluate: Interpret the results of your calculations.

9. **[Obj. 6]** Compare a Capital Lease to an Operating Lease: A company's decision to acquire assets with an operating lease or capital lease often requires careful consideration. Suppose you are the vice-president of finance at Fuji Photo Company. The company has total assets of $5.1 billion and total liabilities of $2.2 billion. The company is planning to lease a manufacturing plant overseas; these assets are valued at $800 million. The company is concerned about the impact of the lease on its debt ratio. The lease can be set up as an operating lease or as a capital lease.

Required:
a. Calculate the impact on the company's debt ratio using an operating lease and using a capital lease (show work).
b. Evaluate: How does the choice of lease type potentially affect the company?

PROBLEMS — SET B

Applying Accounting Knowledge

1. **[Obj. 3]** Amortizing a Bond Discount Using the Effective Interest Method: If a bond is issued at a discount, then the interest expense is always more than the cash interest payment. To calculate the effective (actual) interest expense, the company must amortize the discount. Assume that on January 1, 20Y1, Eye Shades Company issues $100,000 of 8%, 3-year bonds when the market rate is 10%. Interest payments are made semiannually. On January 1, 20Y1 the bond carrying value is $94,904 and the discount is $5,096. The Discount on Bonds Payable will be amortized, that is, reduced to zero over the life of the bonds.

Required:

a. Prepare an amortization table showing the following column headings:

A	B	C	D	E	F
Interest Payment Date	Interest Payment (4% of Principle)	Interest Expense (5% of Carrying Value)	Discount Amortization (C – B)	Bond Discount Balance	Bond Carrying Value

b. Evaluate: What are the benefits and risks to the company of borrowing money with bonds payable?

2. **[Obj. 3]** Amortizing a Bond Discount Using the Straight-Line Method: Same as Problem B1 but use the straight-line interest method. If a bond is issued at a discount, then the interest expense is always more than the cash interest payment. To calculate the effective (actual) interest expense, the company must amortize the discount. Assume that on January 1, 20Y1, Eye Shades Company issues $100,000 of 8%, 3-year bonds when the market rate is 10%. Interest payments are made semiannually. On January 1, 20Y1 the bond carrying value is $94,904 and the discount is $5,096. The Discount on Bonds Payable will be amortized, that is, reduced to zero over the life of the bonds.

Required:

a. Prepare an amortization table using the straight-line interest method showing the following column headings:

A	B	C	D	E	F
Interest Payment Date	Interest Payment (4% of Principle)	Interest Expense (B + D)	Discount Amortization (5,096/6)	Bond Discount Balance	Bond Carrying Value

b. Evaluate: What are the benefits and risks to the company of borrowing money with bonds payable?

3. **[Obj. 3]** Amortizing a Bond Premium: If a bond is issued at a premium, then the interest expense is always less than the cash interest payment. To calculate the effective (actual) interest expense, the company must amortize the premium. Assume that on January 1, 20Y1, Eye Shades Company issues $100,000 of 10%, 3-year bonds when the market rate is 8%. Interest payments are made semiannually. On January 1, 20Y1 the bond carrying value is $105,210 and the premium is $5,210. The Premium on Bonds Payable will be amortized, that is, reduced to zero over the life of the bonds.

   Required:
   a. Prepare an amortization table showing the following column headings:

A	B	C	D	E	F
Interest Payment Date	Interest Payment (5% of Principle)	Interest Expense (4% of Carrying Value)	Premium Amortization (B – C)	Bond Premium Balance	Bond Carrying Value

   b. Evaluate: What are the benefits and risks to the company of borrowing money with bonds payable?

4. **[Obj. 3]** Amortizing a Bond Premium Using the Straight-Line Interest Method: If a bond is issued at a premium, then the interest expense is always less than the cash interest payment. Assume that on January 1, 20Y1, Eye Shades Company issues $100,000 of 9%, 5-year bonds when the market rate is 8%. Interest payments are made semiannually. On January 1, 20Y1, the bond carrying value is $104,100 and the premium is $4,100. The Premium on Bonds Payable will be amortized, that is, reduced to zero over the life of the bonds.

   Required:
   a. Prepare an amortization table using the straight-line method showing the following column headings:

A	B	C	D	E	F
Interest Payment Date	Interest Payment (4.5% of Principle)	Interest Expense (B – D)	Premium Amortization	Bond Premium Balance	Bond Carrying Value

   b. Evaluate: What are the benefits and risks to the company of borrowing money with bonds payable?

5. **[Obj. 3]** Recording Bonds Payable Issued at a Discount: On January 1, 20Y1, Electronic Arts issues $200,000 of 6%, 4-year bonds, with a discount of $3,200. On the maturity date, January 1, 20Y5, the discount is reduced to zero and the bond carrying value is $200,000, the maturity value. On July 1, 20Y1, Electronic Arts makes its first $6,000 semiannual interest payment and also records the discount amortization of $400. Electronic Arts accrues interest expense on that date of $6,400. On December 31, 20Y1, Electronic Arts accrues its second $6,000 semiannual interest liability along with its discount amortization of $400.

   Required:
   a. Record the bond issue on January 1, 20Y1.
   b. Record the first interest payment on July 1, 20Y1.
   c. Record the accrued interest on December 31, 20Y1.
   d. Record the paying off of the bonds on the maturity date of January 1, 20Y5.
   e. Evaluate: Do you think it was a good business decision for Electronic Arts to issue the bonds?

6. **[Obj. 3]** Recording Bonds Payable Issued at a Premium: On January 1, 20Y1, Electronic Arts issues $200,000 of 6%, 4-year bonds, with a premium of $4,800. On the maturity date, January 1, 20Y5, the premium is reduced to zero and the bond carrying value is $200,000, the maturity value. On July 1, 20Y1, Electronic Arts makes its first $6,000 semiannual interest payment and also records the premium amortization of $600. Electronic Arts accrues interest expense on that date of $5,400. On December 31, 20Y1, Electronic Arts accrues its second $6,000 semiannual interest liability along with its premium amortization of $600.

    Required:
    a. Record the bond issue on January 1, 20Y1.
    b. Record the first interest payment on July 1, 20Y1.
    c. Record the accrued interest on December 31, 20Y1.
    d. Record the paying off of the bonds on the maturity date of January 1, 20Y5.
    e. Evaluate: Do you think it was a good business decision for Electronic Arts to issue the bonds?

7. **[Obj. 5]** Comparing Equity Versus Debt Financing: Suppose Boudreaux Fishing Company is planning to build a new dock. Two million dollars in cash is needed. Should Boudreaux borrow the money with bonds payable or raise the money by issuing stock? Boudreaux currently has net income of $500,000 and 200,000 shares of common stock outstanding. Company management is evaluating two financing plans. The first is to issue 100,000 shares of common stock for $2 million. The second is to issue $2 million of 5% corporate bonds payable. Management anticipates that the new dock, acquired with the cash, will generate income of $600,000 before interest and taxes. Boudreaux's income tax rate is 40%.

    Required:
    a. Prepare an analysis showing a comparison of the EPS resulting from issuing stock versus issuing bonds.
    b. Evaluate: Which option is a better business decision? Why?

8. **[Obj. 5]** Comparing Times-Interest-Earned Ratios: Compute the times-interest-earned ratio for Bevo Moving Company and Reveille Movers. Operating income and interest expense for Bovine are $324,000 and $90,000, respectively. Operating income and interest expense for Reveille are $180,000 and $25,000, respectively.

    Required:
    a. Prepare calculations of the times-interest-earned ratio for the two companies.
    b. Evaluate: Interpret the results of your calculations.

9. **[Obj. 6]** Compare a Capital Lease to an Operating Lease: A company's decision to acquire assets with an operating lease or capital lease often requires careful consideration. Suppose you are the vice-president of finance at Mountain Bicycle Company. The company has total assets of $840 million and total liabilities of $190 million. The company is planning to lease a manufacturing plant; these assets are valued at $120 million. The company is concerned about the impact of the lease on its debt ratio. The lease can be set up as an operating lease or as a capital lease.

    Required:
    a. Calculate the impact on the company's debt ratio using an operating lease and using a capital lease (show work).
    b. Evaluate: How does the choice of lease type potentially affect the company?

CROSS-FUNCTIONAL PERSPECTIVES

Discussion Questions

1. **[Obj. 2]** Assume you are a manager for Nokia. The company is introducing a new cell phone into the market and you are responsible for deciding the type of warranty that will accompany the phone. In order to make an effective decision, what kinds of information do you need from other departments within the company?

2. **[Obj. 5]** Why does the decision to borrow a large sum of money require input from multiple departments within a company?

3. **[Obj. 6]** In deciding whether to acquire assets with an operating lease or a capital lease, what are some of the trade-offs between the two options and what departments are interested in the decision?

Cross-Functional Case: Computers vs. People

Due to advances in computer technology and software, computers now perform functions that once required a person. Examples include self-checkout counters, ATMs, digitalized phone operators, on-line travel arrangements, and self-serve gas pumps. Computers have taken over accounting jobs related to crunching numbers and processing information. Many large businesses have increased productivity by using computers instead of people, especially office workers such as clerks and secretaries. When productivity increases, there is economic growth. In the past, this has led to an increase in jobs and wages. For example, the cell phone industry and Web business have created a myriad of new jobs.

Suppose Proctor & Gamble is considering borrowing a large sum of money in order to install an advanced computer system at the corporate headquarters. This system will increase productivity and decrease salary expense (10 percent of the clerical jobs will be eliminated).

Required: As the managing partner at corporate headquarters, what information do you need from the following areas in order to make a cost-effective decision?
a.   Accounting
b.   Finance
c.   Information technology
d.   Human resources

EXCEL ASSIGNMENTS

1. **[Obj. 3]** Calculating Present Value: Use the present value tables in Exhibits 9.3 and 9.4 to calculate the market value of Adventure Travel Company bonds. The company issues $100,000 of 8%, 4-year bonds on January 1, 20Y1. Interest is to be paid semiannually. On the issue date, the market interest rate is 10%.

    Required:
    a.   Will the market value of the bonds be above or below the maturity value of $100,000?
    b.   Prepare an Excel worksheet that calculates the market value of the bonds.
    c.   Prepare the journal entry to record the bond issue.

2. **[Obj. 3]** Calculating Present Value: Use the present value tables in Exhibits 9.3 and 9.4 to calculate the market value of Adventure Travel Company bonds. The company issues $100,000 of 10%, 4-year bonds on January 1, 20Y1. Interest is to be paid semiannually. On that date, the market interest rate is 8%.

    Required:
    a. Will the market value of the bonds be above or below the maturity value of $100,000?
    b. Prepare an Excel worksheet that calculates the market value of the bonds.
    c. Prepare the journal entry to record the bond issue.

3. **[Obj. 3]** Amortizing Bond Discount: If a bond is issued at a discount, then the interest expense is always more than the cash interest payment. To calculate the effective (actual) interest expense, the company must amortize the discount. Assume that on January 1, 20Y1, Baggins Bag Company issues $100,000 of 9%, 4-year bonds when the market rate is 10%. Interest payments are made semiannually. On January 1, 20Y1, the bond carrying value is $96,784 and the discount is $3,216. The Discount on Bonds Payable will be amortized, that is, reduced to zero over the life of the bonds.

    Required:

A	B	C	D	E	F
Interest Payment Date	Interest Payment (4.5% of Principle)	Interest Expense (5% of Carrying Value)	Discount Amortization (C – B)	Bond Discount Balance	Bond Carrying Value

    a. Prepare an Excel worksheet of the amortization table showing the following column headings.
    b. Prepare the journal entries to record the bond issue and the first interest payment.

4. **[Obj. 3]** Amortizing a Bond Premium: If a bond is issued at a premium, then the interest expense is always less than the cash interest payment. To calculate the effective (actual) interest expense, the company must amortize the premium. Assume that on January 1, 20Y1, Baggins Bag Company issues $100,000 of 10%, 5-year bonds when the market rate is 8%. Interest payments are made semiannually. On January 1, 20Y1 the bond carrying value is $108,155 and the premium is $8,155. The Premium on Bonds Payable will be amortized, that is, reduced to zero over the life of the bonds.

    Required:
    a. Prepare an Excel worksheet of the amortization table showing the following column headings.

A	B	C	D	E	F
Interest Payment Date	Interest Payment (5% of Principle)	Interest Expense (4% of Carrying Value)	Premium Amortization (B – C)	Bond Premium Balance	Bond Carrying Value

    b. Prepare the journal entry to record the bond issue and the first interest payment.

5. **[Obj. 4]** Comparing Equity Versus Debt Financing: Suppose Texas Hat Corporation is planning to build a new factory. Two million dollars in cash is needed. Should the company borrow the money with bonds payable or raise the money by issuing stock? The company currently has net income of $350,000 and 200,000 shares of common stock outstanding. Company management is evaluating two financing plans for the new factory project. The first is to issue 100,000 shares of common stock for $2 million. The second is to issue $2 million of 6% corporate bonds payable. Management anticipates that the new factory, acquired with the cash, will generate income of $400,000 before interest and taxes. The company's income tax rate is 40%.

    Required:
    a. Prepare a worksheet that compares the company's EPS resulting from issuing stock versus issuing bonds.
    b. Explain your results.

6. **[Obj. 4]** Comparing Equity Versus Debt Financing: Suppose Superior Oil Corporation is planning to build a new refinery. Ten million dollars in cash is needed. Should the company borrow the money with bonds payable or raise the money by issuing stock? The company currently has net income of $500,000 and 200,000 shares of common stock outstanding. Company management is evaluating two financing plans for the new factory project. The first is to issue 100,000 shares of common stock for $10 million. The second is to issue $10 million of 8% corporate bonds payable. Management anticipates that the new refinery, acquired with the cash, will generate income of $3 million before interest and taxes. The company's income tax rate is 40%.

Required:
a. Prepare a worksheet that compares the company's EPS resulting from issuing stock versus issuing bonds.
b. Explain your results.

7. **[Obj. 5]** Computing the Times-Interest-Earned Ratio: Prepare calculations of the times-interest-earned ratio for two manufacturing companies: Zanzibar Company and Xerxes Corporation. Operating income and interest expense for Zanzibar are $82,000 and $22,000, respectively. Operating income and interest expense for Xerxes are $558,000 and $25,000, respectively.

Required:
a. Prepare an Excel worksheet that shows calculations of the time-interest-earned ratio for the two companies.
b. Interpret results.

WEB ASSIGNMENTS

1. **[Obj. 2]** Visit the website for the Internal Revenue Service and list the employment taxes that must be paid by a small business owner.

2. **[Obj. 2]** Search the Web for information on progressive and regressive taxation. Prepare a one-page report outlining the differences. Cite at least three sources.

3. **[Obj. 2]** Select any company and find its financial statements on the Web (e.g., at the company's website, the New York Stock Exchange website, or a search on Google). Using the information from the financial statements, identify the company's tax expense and tax liability. A company's earnings left over after paying corporate income tax are taxed yet again when those earnings are distributed to stockholders in the form of dividends. The stockholders must pay personal income tax on their dividend income. This is sometimes referred to as "double-taxation." Do you think corporate earnings should be taxed twice, once at the corporate level and again at the stockholder level?

4. **[Career]** Go to the website for Proctor & Gamble. What accounting jobs are currently available within the company?

5. **[Ethics]** Go to the website for Proctor & Gamble or do a search on Google to find Proctor & Gamble's "Purpose, Values, and Principles." Describe how the company regards integrity. How does this relate to reporting liabilities on the financial statements?

6. **[All Obj.]** Go to the website for Proctor & Gamble or do a search on Google to find an accounting-related news item from the past year pertaining to Proctor & Gamble. Give a one-paragraph summary of the news item.

¶912 Test Prepper

Use this sample test to gauge your comprehension of the chapter material.

True/False Questions

___ 1. Current liabilities are those that are due within two years or less.

___ 2. Accounts payable is a long-term liability.

___ 3. Present value is the monetary worth today of an amount to be received at a future time.

___ 4. Amortization of the bond discount is the difference between the interest expense and the cash interest payment.

___ 5. Amortization of a bond premium increases interest expense.

___ 6. Leveraging is referred to as "trading on debt."

___ 7. Operating leases and capital leases are accounted for in the same manner.

___ 8. If the assets in a pension plan are more than its accumulated obligations, the plan is called "over-funded."

___ 9. An operating lease is long-term and non-cancelable.

___ 10. Post-retirement benefits include other retiree benefits like health care and life insurance.

Multiple-Choice Questions

___ 1. What do you call the amount owed to suppliers for credit purchases of goods and services?
   a. accounts payable
   b. short-term note payable
   c. current part of long-term notes payable
   d. accrued liabilities
   e. deferred revenue

___ 2. Which of the following is usually not a current liability?
   a. payroll liability
   b. bonds payable
   c. short-term notes payable
   d. income taxes payable
   e. accounts payable

___ 3. Who buys bonds from the issuing company and then resells them to others?
   a. underwriter
   b. bond manager
   c. holding company
   d. insurance agent
   e. bond principal

___ 4. The _____ rate is also called the effective interest rate.
   a. equity
   b. discount
   c. market
   d. face
   e. premium

___ 5. Which of the following is not true regarding earnings per share (EPS)?
   a. EPS is a financial ratio used by investors to evaluate a company's performance.
   b. EPS is computed by dividing the company's net income by the number of shares of common stock.
   c. EPS is the company's gross revenue per share of stock.
   d. EPS is a sign of a company's health.
   e. EPS is the company's net income per share of stock.

___ 6. Which financial ratio is used to assess the company's ability to pay interest expense?
   a. inventory turnover ratio
   b. gross profit percentage
   c. current ratio
   d. acid-test ratio
   e. times-interest-earned ratio

___ 7. Which of the following is a short-term and cancelable lease?
   a. capital lease
   b. current lease
   c. company lease
   d. operating lease
   e. standard lease

___ 8. Which financial ratio helps investors assess the weight of debt on the company's financial resources?
   a. debt ratio
   b. gross profit percentage
   c. current ratio
   d. acid-test ratio
   e. times-interest-earned ratio

___ 9. Which of the following is an arrangement in which employees receive compensation after they retire.
   a. Post-retirement benefits
   b. Pension plan
   c. Mutual fund
   d. Net pay
   e. Retirement party

___ 10. _____ provide a guarantee of repayment by pledging specified corporate assets.
   a. Loan paybacks
   b. Bond equities
   c. Bond assets
   d. Unsecured bonds
   e. Secured bonds

Chapter

10

Accounting for the Corporation

LEARNING OBJECTIVES

After studying Chapter 10, you should be able to do the following:

1. Describe the importance of corporate financial reporting to people within and outside the business.
2. Explain the advantages and disadvantages of the corporate form of business.
3. Discuss the issuance of common stock and cash dividends.
4. Describe the characteristics of preferred stock, account for its issuance, and record dividends for preferred stock.
5. Describe the impact of stock dividends and stock splits.
6. Describe stock option plans.
7. Explain why companies purchase and retire treasury stock, and how to account for treasury stock transactions.

CHAPTER CONTENTS

Accounting for the Corporation

Focus on Business — Is Disney Larger Than Life?

¶1001   Applications to People Within and Outside the Firm

¶1002   Characteristics of the Corporate Form of Business

Focus on Ethics — Disney's Code of Business Conduct and Ethics

¶1003   Common Stock

¶1004   Preferred Stock

¶1005   Stock Dividends and Stock Splits

Focus on Corporations — History of Disney's Stock Splits

¶1006   Stock Option

¶1007   Treasury Stock

Focus on Technology — Using Microsoft Excel: Computing the Effect of Treasury Stock Purchase on Stockholders' Equity

¶1008   Concluding Remarks

¶1009   Chapter Review

¶1010   Glossary

¶1011   Chapter Assignments

¶1012   Test Prepper

FOCUS ON BUSINESS

Is Disney Larger Than Life?

The Walt Disney Company is a mammoth corporation divided into four major business segments: Studio Entertainment, Parks and Resorts, Consumer Products, and Media Networks. Each segment consists of individual businesses that collaborate to achieve company goals. The company's primary financial goals are to maximize earnings and cash flow, and to allocate capital profitability toward growth initiatives that will drive long-term shareholder value. Who makes the decisions that will achieve these goals?

Stockholders own The Walt Disney Company. These stockholders gather to elect a board of directors for one-year terms. The board makes company policy and appoints management to oversee business operations. The annual meetings of Disney stockholders are available live via audio Web cast from its website.

The responsibilities of Disney's board of directors include: oversight of internal control, preparation and presentation of financial reports, and compliance with applicable laws, regulations and company policies. The board depends on Disney's Audit Committee to help fulfill these duties. In this chapter, you'll learn more about accounting for the financial matters of the corporation.

Source: *Disney.com*

¶1001 Applications to People Within and Outside the Firm

LEARNING OBJECTIVE 1: Describe the importance of corporate financial reporting to people within and outside the business.

There are more than nine million corporations operating in the United States today. About 15,000 of these are publicly traded on the stock market. Since this form of business accounts for over $17 trillion in annual revenue, the methods that corporations use to report their financial performance and condition is critical.

¶1001.01 INTERNAL USERS

While accounting is a major task for all types of firms, accounting for a large corporation is an especially complex endeavor. Can you imagine the amount and diversity of financial transactions in which Disney is involved? The challenge of tracking Disney's large numbers of transactions, sometimes in different currencies, requires the effective use of technology and integrated accounting and information systems. Within the Disney corporation, managers rely on financial reports to help them make decisions about when to issue stock, when and how dividends should be declared, and other equity-related issues. Managers of a publicly-traded corporation, such as Disney, must ensure that it meets the reporting requirements of the Securities and Exchange Commission (SEC). This federal agency holds a corporation accountable for its business practices, financial reporting, and explaining the financial condition of the company.

¶1001.02 EXTERNAL USERS

Stockholders of corporations do not have first-hand access to the details of the company's operations and, therefore, depend on the financial reports generated by the corporation's accountants. Potential investors, analysts, and government agencies also rely on a company's financial statements to make investment decisions and forecasts, and to administer appropriate taxation or regulation. In the U.S., and most countries, national governments set up laws and regulations to ensure that corporations provide appropriate reports to their stockholders. In the U.S., a long history of corporate regulation was updated with the passage of

As a consumer in a department store or a restaurant, can you tell whether it operates as a corporation or other form of business?

the Sarbanes-Oxley Act in 2002. This legislation holds top executives more accountable for the effectiveness of company operations and the financial reporting process.

"We have established governance as a high priority at Disney for one simple reason — it's the right thing to do. By investing in Disney, shareholders are placing their trust in the board to help shape the overall course of the company's business and to hold management accountable for its performance. In the end, governance is all about creating an environment that promotes informed, objective decision-making in the interests of all shareholders."

— George Mitchell, Chairman of the Board

¶1002 Characteristics of the Corporate Form of Business

LEARNING OBJECTIVE 2: Explain the advantages and disadvantages of the corporate form of business.

If you have shopped for school supplies at Target, eaten lunch at Chili's, or ordered books from Amazon.com, you have conducted business with a corporation. In regard to total assets and output of goods and services, corporations lead the U.S. economy and significantly affect our daily lives. The following discussion outlines reasons why businesses often choose the corporate form of organization.

¶1002.01 ADVANTAGES

As you learned in Chapter 1, a corporation is a form of business in which ownership is represented by shares of stock. Thus, the owners are called "shareholders" or "stockholders." Have you ever wondered why a business chooses to incorporate? The ability to raise capital, the corporation's separate legal identity, the limited liability of stockholders, the ease of ownership transfer, and the separation of management and ownership are advantages that belong to the corporation.

¶1002.01.01 Ease of Raising Capital

Corporations can raise large amounts of capital more easily than sole proprietorships or partnerships. This is because shares of ownership are available to a large number of potential investors who may purchase as many or few shares as they choose. Consequently, many people may own one corporation.

¶1002.01.02 Unique Legal Entity

A corporation is a unique legal entity. It is separate from its owners (stockholders). In many respects, a corporation has legal rights just like a person. A corporation can purchase, own, and sell property. Corporations can make legal contracts, sue, and can be sued. For example, Disney makes legal contracts with companies like Coca-Cola, in which such contracts may provide for an exclusive sales feature of selling only Dasani bottle water at Disney's U.S. Parks and Resorts. While these contracts are enforceable between Disney and Coca-Cola, they do not involve the stockholders.

¶1002.01.03 Limited Liability

Stockholders have limited liability; they are not responsible for the liabilities of the corporation.

The corporation, not its stockholders, is responsible for its liabilities. If the corporation fails to pay back its debts, the stockholders are not held responsible. In other words, stockholders have **limited liability**. Limited liability means that stockholders have no personal liability for corporate liabilities. If a corporation goes out of business for failure to pay back its loans, the corporate stock becomes worthless. In this case, stockholders lose their investment, but their personal assets cannot be pursued to satisfy the debts of the corporation. Owners of sole proprietorships and partnerships are usually personally liable for the firm's liabilities.

¶1002.01.04 Ease of Ownership Transfer

A corporation can exist forever, even though its ownership may change. Stockholders of major corporations buy and sell ownership through corporate stock on a daily basis. Of course, this is different from sole proprietorships and partnerships, which usually cease to exist when their ownership changes.

¶1002.01.05 Separation of Management and Ownership

As you know, a corporation is owned by its stockholders. Yet, for obvious reasons a large group of stockholders is not able to lead and direct the day-to-day operations and decisions of the business. Therefore, persons who are best qualified to manage and lead the corporation are hired. Ownership and management are separate functions.

¶1002.02 DISADVANTAGES

Many businesses are interested in the benefits provided under the corporate form of business. On the other hand, some businesses are deterred from incorporation because of disadvantages such as increased regulation and tax consequences.

¶1002.02.01 Regulation

Section 404 of the Sarbanes-Oxley Act requires that corporate management prepare an internal control report on an annual basis.

The government, especially the national government, carefully regulates corporations. For example, national legislation requires that U.S. publicly-traded corporations have their financial statements audited annually by a CPA firm. One purpose of these audits is to help reassure stockholders that they can rely on these statements for investment decisions. The audited financial statements are then filed with the Securities and Exchange Commission (SEC). In addition, **Section 404 of the Sarbanes-Oxley Act** of 2002 requires that each year corporate management prepare an internal control report.

The internal control report must include a statement of management's responsibility for establishing and maintaining an adequate internal control structure and procedures for financial reporting. Internal control over financial reporting is defined as a process that provides reasonable assurance regarding the reliability of financial reporting and the compliance of financial statements with GAAP for external purposes. In addition, Section 404 directs the SEC to require that a publicly-traded corporation disclose whether it has adopted a code of ethics for its senior financial officers and the contents of that code.

In addition to domestic regulation, corporations must also adhere to laws that apply to international commerce. The U.S. Congress passed the Foreign Corrupt Practices Act (FCPA) in 1977. The FCPA prohibits any U.S. public company, including any officer, director, or employee, from bribing a foreign official with a gift or payment in an effort to obtain business for the company. Penalties for conviction of such acts include fines and imprisonment.

In addition to the prohibition against bribery, the FCPA requires public companies to devise and maintain a system of internal accounting control. This system of internal control must provide reasonable assurance that transactions are executed in accordance with management's authorization, that transactions are properly recorded, and that access to assets is permitted only by management's authorization. These objectives were originally taken from Statements on Auditing Standards No. 1 (SAS No. 1), Section 320.28, and were incorporated into Section 13(b) of the Securities Exchange Act of 1934. Consequently, the management and employees of a public company may be civilly and criminally liable under the federal securities laws for failing to maintain a sufficient internal control structure.

¶1002.02.02 Taxation

Corporations incur double taxation; earnings are taxed at the corporate level and at the individual level when dividends are dispersed.

Corporations must pay federal and state income taxes on their earnings, just as individuals do. When stockholders receive cash dividends from a corporation, the stockholders pay personal income tax on the dividends. This is referred to as **"double taxation."** In other words, corporate earnings are taxed first at the corporate level and then they are taxed a second time at the individual level when dividends are distributed to stockholders. Sole proprietorships and partnerships do not incur double taxation, as their earnings are directly assigned to individuals, who then pay personal income tax on the earnings.

In addition to income tax, corporations pay a franchise tax to the state in which they are incorporated. The franchise tax is necessary to keep the corporate charter in effect, and thereby allow the corporation to continue operations.

FOCUS ON ETHICS

Disney's Code of Business Conduct and Ethics

The Walt Disney Company is committed to conducting business in accordance with the highest standards of business ethics and complying with applicable laws, rules and regulations. In furtherance of this commitment, the Board of Directors promotes ethical behavior, and has adopted this Code of Business Conduct and Ethics for Directors.

Every Director must:

- Represent the interests of the shareholders of The Walt Disney Company.
- Exhibit high standards of integrity, commitment and independence of thought and judgment.
- Dedicate sufficient time, energy and attention to ensure the diligent performance of his or her duties.

¶1002.03

CREATION AND MANAGEMENT OF A CORPORATION

To create a corporation in the U.S., its organizers must acquire a charter from a state. The charter authorizes the issuance of a designated number of shares of stock. Organizers of the corporation, also referred to as "incorporators," sign the charter, file documents with the Secretary of the State, and establish a set of bylaws to govern the corporation. Once this is done, the corporation begins to exist and the stockholders of the corporation elect the board of directors. This board then establishes the policies of the corporation and elects a chairperson and officers.

The **chief executive officer (CEO)** is customarily the individual of highest authority and responsibility in a corporation. For many corporations, the CEO is the chairperson of the board of directors. Other corporations prefer to have a different person serving in these two roles. In addition to the CEO, the board elects a president, also called the **chief operating officer (COO)**. The president is responsible for daily operations.

Corporations usually have several vice presidents who are responsible for major activities such as marketing, production, human resources, and finance. Typically, the vice president of finance, also called the **chief financial officer (CFO)**, has two subordinates: the treasurer and the controller, who is the chief accountant. This organizational structure provides segregation of duties, with the treasurer handling the cash and the controller keeping the financial records. Exhibit 10.1 shows the organizational structure of typical corporation. The duties and titles of corporate officers varies among corporations, so the officers shown in Exhibit 10.1 are not found in every corporation.

The chief executive officer (CEO) is the highest-ranking officer of the corporation.

The chief operating officer (COO) manages the corporation's day-to-day activities.

The chief financial officer (CFO) is the vice president of finance.

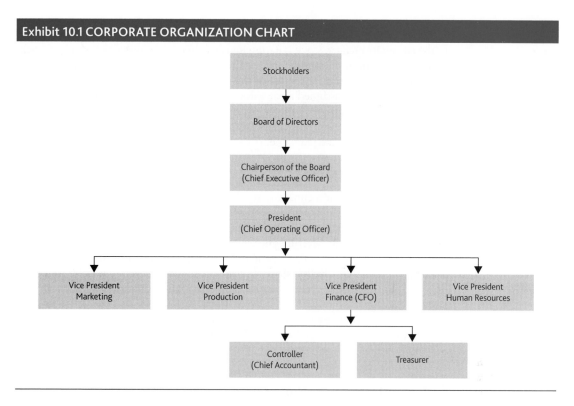

Exhibit 10.1 CORPORATE ORGANIZATION CHART

Stockholders

Board of Directors

Chairperson of the Board
(Chief Executive Officer)

President
(Chief Operating Officer)

Vice President
Marketing

Vice President
Production

Vice President
Finance (CFO)

Vice President
Human Resources

Controller
(Chief Accountant)

Treasurer

¶1003 Common Stock

> **LEARNING OBJECTIVE 3:** Discuss the issuance of common stock and cash dividends.

Common stock is the basic type of stock and carries voting rights for the stockholder.

Preferred stock usually has no voting rights.

Corporations can issue two types of stock: common stock and preferred stock. Not all corporations issue preferred stock, but all corporations issue common stock. **Common stock** is the basic type of stock and carries voting rights for the stockholder. When the word "stock" is used, it is assumed to be "common stock," unless another type of stock is specifically named. **Preferred stock** has preference over common stock in terms of dividends and distribution of assets; however, preferred stock usually has no voting rights. First, we will discuss the particulars of common stock.

¶1003.01 RIGHTS OF COMMON STOCKHOLDERS

Unless there is a specific agreement to the contrary, common stockholders have four basic rights:

1. Vote — Stockholders get one vote for each share of stock. They vote on the board of directors and on other matters that are presented to the stockholders.
2. Receive dividends — Dividends are distributed proportionately to the number of shares of ownership.
3. Liquidation allocation — If the corporation goes out of business, that is, liquidated, stockholders are entitled to a proportionate share of any assets left over after the corporation pays off its debts.
4. Preemption — **Preemption** is the stockholder's right to maintain a proportionate share of ownership in the corporation. For example, assume that you own 10% of Acme Corporation stock and Acme issues 10,000 new shares of stock. Acme must give you the opportunity to purchase 10% (1,000) of the new shares. Shareholders of large corporations oftentimes relinquish preemption rights.

Preemption is the stockholder's right to maintain a proportionate share of ownership in the corporation.

¶1003.02   PAR VALUE

In the corporate charter, stock is designated as either par value stock or no-par stock. A stock's **par value** is an arbitrary amount determined by the incorporators and assigned to each share of a company's stock to represent the minimum legal value of the stock. You may recall when Jay and Kay formed their corporation, they arbitrarily assigned a par value of $1 to JK Productions' stock.

Most companies assign par value to their stock. For those companies that issue no-par stock, there is not a par value. However, no-par stock often is assigned a stated value. Stated value no-par stock is much like par value stock. Like par value, the stated value is an arbitrary amount assigned by the company.

¶1003.03   ISSUING COMMON STOCK

A very effective way for a company to obtain massive amounts of money is to issue stock. When a corporation is formed, the incorporators authorize the number of shares that can be issued. The corporation can sell the stock directly to stockholders or arrange for an underwriter to do so. Underwriters include brokerage firms such as Merrill Lynch.

A corporation may choose to issue only part of its authorized shares. Suppose Acme Auto Company is authorized to issue 100,000 shares but the company issues only 60,000 shares. Thus, 40,000 shares are unissued. In this case, the company is said to have 100,000 shares authorized, and 60,000 shares issued and outstanding.

Sometimes a company will buy back some of its issued stock. Suppose Acme Auto Company purchases 1,000 of its previously issued 60,000 shares. In that case, Acme is said to have 60,000 shares issued but only 59,000 shares outstanding.

¶1003.03.01   Common Stock at Par

Suppose Acme Movie Company needs additional money to expand operations; the company issues (sells) 10,000 shares of $10 par value common stock. If the stock sells for exactly its par value of $10 per share, the entry to record the issuance of 10,000 shares is as follows:

March 2	Cash (10,000 × $10)	100,000	
	Common Stock		100,000
	To issue common stock at par.		

¶1003.03.02   Common Stock Above Par

Stock rarely sells for exactly its par value. Par value is usually set at a very low amount. Consequently, stock usually sells at a price above par. Suppose Acme issues (sells) 10,000 shares of $10 par value common stock. If the stock sells for $12 per share, the entry to record issuance of 10,000 shares is as follows:

April 1	Cash (10,000 × $12)	120,000	
	Common Stock (10,000 × $10)		100,000
	Additional Paid-In Capital – Common (10,000 × $2)		20,000
	To issue common stock above par.		

The common stock is recorded at its par value, $100,000 (10,000 shares × $10 per share). In the above transaction, "Additional Paid-In Capital – Common" is the amount received above par, $20,000 (10,000 shares × $2 per share). Each class of stock should have its own Additional Paid-In Capital account so that managers can identify the amounts paid over par for each class of stock.

The example transactions are for the issuance of new stock from the corporation to stockholders. This is different from the sale of stock from one stockholder to another stockholder. Once stock is initially issued (sold) by the corporation, the stock can then be traded (bought and sold) many times among many different investors. These trades do not affect the accounting records of the corporation. The price paid for stock trades between investors is shown in newspapers such as the Wall Street Journal and on websites such as finance.yahoo.com.

¶1003.03.03 Common Stock Exchanged for Noncash Assets

Sometimes corporations issue stock for assets other than cash, particularly when a corporation is first created. Suppose Disney issues 50,000 shares of $1 par value common stock, which has a market value of $480,000, in exchange for some land and a building, valued at $400,000 and $80,000, respectively. The transaction is recorded as follows:

Aug. 1	Building	80,000	
	Land	400,000	
	Common Stock (50,000 × $1)		50,000
	Additional Paid-In Capital – Common (480,000 – 50,000)		430,000
	To issue $1 par value common stock in exchange for a building and land.		

When a corporation receives noncash assets for stock, the general rule is to record the assets at the fair market value of the stock. If the fair market value of the stock cannot be determined, the fair market value of the assets received can be used.

¶1003.03.04 No-Par Common Stock

When no-par common stock is issued, the full amount received is assigned to the common stock account and there is no additional paid-in capital. For example, in the transaction above, if no-par stock is issued, instead of $1 par value stock, the entry is recorded as follows:

Aug. 1	Building	80,000	
	Land	400,000	
	Common Stock		480,000
	To issue no-par value common stock in exchange for a building and land.		

¶1003.04 CASH DIVIDENDS TO COMMON STOCKHOLDERS

A cash dividend is a distribution of a corporation's earnings to stockholders in the form of cash.

As you know, the key goal of a corporation is to increase the wealth of its owners, that is, the stockholders. When an investor buys stock in a corporation, the investor can benefit financially in two ways: (1) when the price of the stock increases and the investment is more valuable, and (2) when dividends on the stock are paid to stockholders. A **cash dividend** is a distribution of a corporation's earnings to stockholders in the form of cash. The board of directors must decide whether the corporation will pay or not pay a cash dividend.

Corporations are not required to pay dividends. Instead of paying a cash dividend, the board may decide that the stockholders would benefit more if the corporation kept all its retained earnings and reinvested them in company operations. Presumably, this reinvestment may lead to an increase in the corporation's stock price if it causes investors to be optimistic about future improvements for the company.

If the board of directors would like to pay a cash dividend, two things must be present: (1) sufficient retained earnings to declare the dividend, and (2) cash available to pay the dividend. If these conditions exist, the board's declaration establishes a liability for the corporation. In addition, there are three important dates associated with cash dividends:

- **Declaration date** — the date that the board of directors declares its intent to pay a dividend.
- **Date of record** — the date establishing which stockholders will receive the cash dividend. In other words, whoever owns the stock on the date of record will receive the dividend.
- **Payment date** — the date on which the dividend is actually paid.

When the board declares a dividend, the declaration indicates the amount of the dividend, the date of record, and the payment date. The declaration establishes a liability for the corporation.

The number of stockholders in the U.S. is increasing. If you were financially able to purchase stock, which company would you be interested in?

Suppose that on July 1, Disney's board of directors declares a cash dividend of $100,000 to be paid on August 18. The record date is designated as July 20. Thus, anyone owning Disney stock on July 20 will receive the cash on August 18. The journal entries are shown below:

Declaration date, July 1			
July 1	Retained Earnings	100,000	
	Dividends Payable		100,000
	Cash dividend is declared.		
Date of Record, July 20			
	No journal entry		
Payment Date, August 18			
Aug. 18	Dividends Payable	100,000	
	Cash		100,000
	Cash dividend is paid.		

¶1004   Preferred Stock

LEARNING OBJECTIVE 4: Describe the characteristics of preferred stock, account for its issuance, and record dividends for preferred stock.

Preferred stock has preference over common stock in terms of dividends and distribution of assets.

Like common stock, the sale of preferred stock is used to raise money for a corporation. Preferred stock usually has no voting rights, thus allowing corporations to raise capital without diluting common shareholders' control. Preferred stock is stock that has preference over common stock in terms of dividends and the distribution of assets. Preferred stockholders receive dividends before common stockholders and have priority in receiving assets in the event of corporate liquidation. These extra benefits may attract additional investors in the corporation, such as those who are not interested in common stock. As a result, the corporation is able to raise greater amounts of capital.

¶1004.01   ISSUING PREFERRED STOCK

Suppose JC Penney issues 100,000 shares of $5 par value preferred stock. If the preferred stock is sold for $6 per share, the transaction is recorded as follows:

Feb. 1	Cash	600,000	
	Preferred Stock		500,000
	Additional Paid-In Capital – Preferred		100,000
	To issue preferred stock above par:		
	Preferred stock, 100,000 × $5 par value = $500,000;		
	Additional Paid-In Capital – Preferred (100,000 × $1 = $100,000)		

For this preferred stock, assume the company assigns a dividend rate of 4% of the par value. This means that in years for which a dividend is declared, the company plans to pay cash dividends of $0.20 per share ($5 par value × 4%) to the preferred stockholders. This payment takes precedence over any dividend payments to common stockholders.

¶1004.02   CASH DIVIDENDS TO PREFERRED STOCKHOLDERS

As illustrated above, preferred dividends can be designated as a percentage, such as "4% preferred," meaning preferred stockholders receive a dividend that is 4% of the par value. Alternatively, the preferred dividend can be designated as a dollar amount, such as "$0.20 preferred," meaning that preferred shareholders receive a dividend of $0.20 per share, regardless of the par value.

Like common stockholders, preferred stockholders are not guaranteed to receive a dividend. The corporation has to have earnings and the board of directors has to declare the preferred dividend. If the board does not declare a preferred dividend, this is referred to as "passing the dividend." The corporation does not ever have to pay the passed dividends, also called "dividends in arrears," unless the preferred stock is cumulative.

A corporation pays dividends in arrears, plus the current year's dividend, to holders of cumulative preferred stock before paying dividends to common stock shareholders.

Cumulative preferred stock means that shareholders with this type of stock are entitled to receive all dividends in arrears plus the current year's dividend before any dividends are paid to common stock shareholders. Preferred stock is considered cumulative unless it is specifically designated as non-cumulative. Dividends in arrears are not liabilities. Until the board declares the dividend, no liability exists. However, dividends in arrears should be disclosed in the financial statements, typically in a note to the financial statements. The note should indicate that the company must pay dividends in arrears to preferred shareholders prior to paying any dividends to common shareholders.

Let's look at an example for Zany Gadget Corporation, a company whose preferred stock is cumulative. Zany passed (did not pay) the 20Y1, 20Y2, and 20Y3 preferred dividends of $100,000 in each year. In 20Y4, suppose Zany has cash available to pay dividends. If Zany declares a $600,000 dividend in 20Y4, the company must pay the preferred dividends of $100,000 for the three previous years plus the current year, (a total of $400,000), before it can pay common stock dividends. On the declaration date, the entry is recorded as follows:

Would you rather own preferred stock or common stock in a company?

July 1	Retained Earnings	600,000	
	Dividends Payable, Preferred		400,000
	Dividends Payable, Common		200,000
	To declare a cash dividend:		
	Preferred = $100,000 × 4 = $400,000		
	Common = $600,000 – $400,000 = $200,000		

Notice that $400,000 goes to the preferred stockholders to catch up on dividends in arrears plus the current year preferred dividends and the remainder goes to common stockholders.

¶1005 Stock Dividends and Stock Splits

LEARNING OBJECTIVE 5: Describe the impact of stock dividends and stock splits.

Instead of distributing cash to stockholders, corporations may issue additional shares of stock to stockholders. This is done via stock dividends and stock splits. In both cases, the corporation retains its cash for use in business operations, while providing stockholders with additional shares of stock.

¶1005.01 STOCK DIVIDENDS

A stock dividend is a proportional distribution of stock from the corporation to its stockholders.

A **stock dividend** is a proportional distribution of shares of a corporation's stock to its stockholders. A stock dividend affects only stockholders' equity accounts and has no effect on assets or liabilities. Total stockholders' equity is unchanged by a stock dividend. On the dividend declaration date, the amount of the stock dividend is transferred from retained earnings to the contributed capital section (common stock and additional paid-in capital). The amount transferred from Retained Earnings depends on the size of the stock distribution. The following two examples illustrate a distribution of 25% or less and a distribution of more than 25%.

Suppose General Motors declares a 5% stock dividend. At that time, assume that General Motors has 1,000,000 shares of $1 par value common stock outstanding. According to generally accepted accounting principles (GAAP), a stock dividend that is 25% or less of outstanding stock is a "small" dividend. A small stock dividend should be accounted for at the *market value* of the shares issued. The date the stock dividend is disbursed is called the "distribution date." Assume that the stock price on the distribution date is $50 per share. The stock dividend is recorded as follows:

Retained Earnings		2,500,000	
Common Stock			50,000
Additional Paid-In Capital – Common			2,450,000

To distribute a 5% stock dividend.
Retained Earnings = 1,000,000 × .05 × $50 = $2,500,000.
Common Stock = 1,000,000 × .05 × $1 = $50,000.
Additional Paid-In Capital = $2,500,000 – $50,000 = $2,450,000.

A "large" stock dividend is defined as a stock dividend greater than 25% of outstanding stock. For a large stock dividend, GAAP allows the use of *par value* instead of market value to account for the dividend. Suppose Zany Gadget Corporation declares a 50% stock dividend. At that time, Zany has 100,000 shares of $10 par value common stock outstanding. On the distribution date, November 1, the stock price is $30 per share. Since this is a large stock dividend, Zany records the dividend on the distribution date as follows:

Nov. 1	Retained Earnings	500,000	
	Common Stock		500,000
	To distribute a 50% stock dividend (100,000 shares × .50 × $10 par value).		

As shown, Zany records the debit to Retained Earnings at the par value and does not use the market value. As a result, there is *no impact* on Additional Paid-In Capital. The stockholders' equity section of Zany's balance sheet before and after the dividend is shown in Exhibit 10.2.

Exhibit 10.2 STOCKHOLDERS' EQUITY BEFORE AND AFTER LARGE STOCK DIVIDEND	
Zany Stockholders' Equity:	
Before 50% Stock Dividend	
Common stock, $10 par value, 200,000 shares authorized, 100,000 shares issued	$1,000,000
Additional paid-in capital	2,000,000
Retained Earnings	700,000
Total Stockholders' Equity	$3,700,000
After 50% Stock Dividend	
Common stock, $10 par value, 200,000 shares authorized, 150,000 shares issued	$1,500,000
Additional paid-in capital	2,000,000
Retained Earnings	200,000
Total Stockholders' Equity	$3,700,000

The stock dividend allows the corporation to keep cash for operations, while providing some benefit to the stockholders. When a stock dividend is distributed, the market price of the stock should decline in proportion to the increase in the supply of the stock. However, after the initial decline in the stock price, the price may then increase. This is because the lower stock price may be more attractive to a broader range of investors.

¶1005.02   STOCK SPLITS

A stock split lowers the market price of a company's stock by increasing the number of shares outstanding; the lower price attracts investors.

A **stock split** is a method used to lower the market price of a company's stock by increasing the number of shares outstanding. In a 2-for-1 split, two new shares are exchanged for each original share, with the par value of each new share set at one-half the value of the original share. For example, if you owned 200 shares of $10 par Disney stock and a 2-for-1 stock split was declared, you would then own 400 shares of $5 par stock.

Likewise, if the corporation splits its stock 4 for 1, the number of shares outstanding quadruples and each share's par value is decreased by 75%. If the number of shares outstanding after the split should exceed the number of authorized shares, the board of directors must first obtain approval from the state and stockholders to increase the number of authorized shares before declaring the stock split.

When a stock split occurs, the market price of the stock is expected to decrease, just as the market price decreases with a stock dividend. Of course, a stock split results in a more dramatic decrease in the stock price since many more shares of stock are distributed. The lower market price should make the stock attractive to a broader range of investors. The majority of successful corporations like Walmart, Coca-Cola, Intel, and Marvel have split their stocks at one time.

FOCUS ON CORPORATIONS

History of Disney's Stock Splits

Record Date	Payable Date	Amount	Closing, Pre-Split Price
June 19, 1998	July 9, 1998	3 for 1	$111
April 20, 1992	May 15, 1992	4 for 1	$152 7/8
February 10, 1986	March 5, 1986	4 for 1	$142 5/8
December 6, 1972	January 15, 1973	2 for 1	$214 1/2
February 4, 1971	March 1, 1971	2 for 1	$177 3/4
October 26, 1967	November 15, 1967	2 for 1	$105
August 17, 1956	August 20, 1956	2 for 1	Not Available

Source: *Corporate.Disney.go.com.* Accessed on February 9, 2012.

Suppose the market price of Wilco Electronics Company is $100 and that the company wants to decrease the market price to about $25. Thus, Wilco decides to split its common stock 4 for 1. This means that there will be four times as many shares outstanding after the split and the par value per share will be cut by 75%. Prior to the split, Wilco had 10,000 shares of $10 par value common stock issued and outstanding. Exhibit 10.3 shows Wilco's stockholders' equity before and after the 4-for-1 stock split.

For a graduation present, would you rather receive stock in a company that pays dividends or a company that is rumored to soon have a stock split?

Exhibit 10.3 STOCKHOLDERS' EQUITY BEFORE AND AFTER THE 4-FOR-1 STOCK SPLIT

Wilco Stockholders' Equity:	
Before 4-for-1 Stock Split	
Common stock, $10 par value, 50,000 shares authorized, 10,000 shares outstanding	$100,000
Additional paid-in capital	800,000
Retained Earnings	400,000
Total Stockholders' Equity	$1,300,000
After 4-for-1 Stock Split	
Common stock, $2.50 par value, 200,000 shares authorized, 40,000 shares outstanding	$100,000
Additional paid-in capital	800,000
Retained Earnings	400,000
Total Stockholders' Equity	$1,300,000

As shown, Wilco's total stockholders' equity is unchanged after the 4-for-1 stock split. In fact, the amounts in each account are unchanged. Common stock was $100,000 before the split and $100,000 after the split. The difference is that the number of shares outstanding increased from 10,000 to 40,000 and the par value decreased from $10 per share to $2.50 per share. The number of shares authorized also quadrupled from 50,000 to 200,000.

¶1006   Stock Option

LEARNING OBJECTIVE 6: Describe stock option plans.

Under a stock option plan, employees can purchase their company's stock.

Almost every publicly-traded corporation, also called a "public company," encourages its employees to own the stock of their employers. A **stock option plan** is an arrangement by which employees can purchase their company's stock. The stock option plan can be available to all employees or limited to management-level employees.

For stock option plans that are available to all employees, the stock is usually sold for its market price on the date of purchase. For example, suppose that Disney employees purchase 10,000 shares of its $.01 par value stock when the market price is $25 per share. The entry to record the transaction is as follows:

Feb. 14	Cash	250,000	
	Common Stock		100
	Additional Paid-In Capital – Common		249,900
	To issue 10,000 shares of $.01 par value common stock via employee stock option plan.		

For stock option plans that are limited to management-level employees, the plan often provides the managers the option to buy the stock for a fixed price during a designated time period. Consequently, if the stock price rises above that fixed price, the managers will receive a financial benefit, the difference between the market price and the fixed price. This financial benefit is effectively extra compensation based on the increase in the stock price. Consequently, managers are spurred to give their best work so that the company is more successful, and presumably the stock price increases.

Suppose that on April 1, the top management personnel at Disney are given the option to purchase 100,000 shares of $.01 par value common stock at $30 per share for up to one year into the future. On April 1 the market price is $26 per share, so no one exercises the option immediately. Naturally, the managers are waiting and hoping for the stock price to rise above $30 so that they can exercise their options. However, even on April 1 when the exercise price of $30 is above the market price of $26, the stock options have a small fair market value. According to GAAP, specifically SFAS 123(R): Share-Based Payment, employee stock options are expensed at their fair value at the time they are awarded to employees.

Would owning stock of your employer cause you to work harder?

¶1007   Treasury Stock

> **LEARNING OBJECTIVE 7:** Explain why companies purchase and retire treasury stock, and how to account for treasury stock transactions.

Treasury stock is a corporation's own stock, which was issued and later reacquired.

Treasury stock is a corporation's own stock, which was issued and later reacquired. A corporation can purchase shares of its stock just like other investors can. There are several reasons why a corporation may choose to buy back its stock:

- The corporation hopes to later sell the stock at a higher price, and thereby increase cash.
- The corporation is trying to increase its market stock price.
- The shares are needed for distribution to employees under the company stock option plan.
- The corporation is trying to prevent a hostile takeover by another entity.

¶1007.01   PURCHASING TREASURY STOCK

When a company buys its own stock, both the assets and equity of the corporation are decreased. Suppose New England Pharmaceutical Company currently has 20,000 shares of $1 par value common stock issued and outstanding. Additional paid-in capital is $400,000 and retained earnings total $120,000. On June 4, 20Y1, the company buys back 2,000 shares of its stock when the market price is $45 per share. The transaction is recorded as follows:

20Y1			
June 4	Treasury Stock	90,000	
	Cash		90,000
	Purchase 2,000 shares of company stock at $45 per share.		

The stockholders' equity section of the company's balance sheet before and after the purchase of treasury stock is shown in Exhibit 10.4. Note that the treasury stock reduces the company's stockholders' equity by the cost of the treasury stock. Thus, the treasury stock is a contra-stockholders' equity account, whose normal balance is a debit. Other stockholders' equity accounts normally have credit balances.

Exhibit 10.4 EFFECT OF PURCHASE OF TREASURY STOCK ON STOCKHOLDERS' EQUITY	
Before Purchase of Treasury Stock:	
Common stock, $1 par value	$20,000
Additional paid-in capital	400,000
Retained earnings	120,000
Total stockholders' equity	$540,000
After Purchase of Treasury Stock:	
Common stock, $1 par value	$20,000
Additional paid-in capital	400,000
Retained earnings	120,000
Less: Treasury stock	(90,000)
Total stockholders' equity	$450,000

FOCUS ON TECHNOLOGY

Using Microsoft Excel: Computing the Effect of Treasury Stock Purchase on Stockholders' Equity

Using Excel, we will compute a company's total stockholders' equity after it has purchased treasury stock. (This calculation is made in Exhibit 10.4.)

1. File Identification Area: In an Excel worksheet, create a file identification area showing the filename, input required, and other appropriate information. The input required is listed below in the Input Area. The output required is total stockholders' equity.
2. Input Area: Type in the following:

Common stock, $1 par value	$100,000
Additional paid-in capital	$2,000,000
Retained earnings	$600,000
Number of shares of stock purchased	10,000
Market price of a share of stock	$22

3. Output Area: Set up your headings to resemble the second calculation in Exhibit 10.4. Insert amounts from the input area. Create formulas where needed.

¶1007.02   REISSUING TREASURY STOCK

Treasury stock can be reissued at cost, above cost, or below cost. Suppose that two years after the treasury stock purchase, New England Pharmaceutical needs cash for company operations. On August 1, 20Y3, the company's stock is trading on the market for $60 per share. The company sells 2,000 shares of treasury stock at the market price, thus reissuing the stock above cost. The Treasury Stock account is credited for the amount that New England Pharmaceutical originally paid for it, $45 per share. The transaction is recorded as follows:

20Y3			
Aug. 1	Cash	120,000	
	Treasury Stock		90,000
	Additional Paid-In Capital		30,000
	Sold 2,000 shares of treasury stock at $60 per share, previously purchased at $45 per share.		

As a result of the sale, assets and stockholders' equity increase. As shown in Exhibit 10.5, total stockholders' equity increases by $120,000 due to crediting the Treasury Stock account and increasing Additional Paid-In Capital.

Exhibit 10.5 EFFECT OF SALE OF TREASURY STOCK ON STOCKHOLDERS' EQUITY

Before Sale of Treasury Stock:	
Common stock, $1 par value	$20,000
Additional paid-in capital	400,000
Retained earnings	120,000
Less: Treasury stock	(90,000)
Total stockholders' equity	$450,000
After Sale of Treasury Stock:	
Common stock, $1 par value	$20,000
Additional paid-in capital	430,000
Retained earnings	120,000
Total stockholders' equity	$570,000

¶1007.03   RETIREMENT OF STOCK

After buying back its own stock, a corporation may decide to retire the stock by canceling the stock certificates, which takes them out of circulation. Retirement of stock normally requires approval by the stockholders.

Suppose that New England Pharmaceutical does not sell 2,000 shares of its treasury stock, but instead retires the stock. Assume the stock originally sold for $21 a share. The stock has a par value of $1, so the remaining $20 per share was additional paid-in capital. When the stock was originally issued, Common Stock was credited for $2,000 (2,000 × $1 par) and Additional Paid-In Capital was credited for $40,000 (2,000 × $20). The entry to retire the stock is as follows:

20Y3			
Aug. 1	Common Stock (2,000 × $1)	2,000	
	Additional Paid-In Capital (2,000 × $20)	40,000	
	Retained Earnings ($90,000 – $42,000)	48,000	
	Treasury Stock (2,000 × $45)		90,000
	Retire 2,000 shares, $1 par value, that cost $45 per share, and were originally issued at $21 per share ($20 above par).		

Retained Earnings is debited for the difference between the cost of the treasury stock ($90,000) and original selling price of the stock ($42,000). Exhibit 10.6 shows the effect of the retirement of treasury stock. The net effect includes a decrease in Common Stock from $20,000 to $18,000.

What effect does the retirement of stock have on stockholders' equity?

Exhibit 10.6 EFFECT OF RETIREMENT OF TREASURY STOCK ON STOCKHOLDERS' EQUITY	
Before Retirement of Treasury Stock:	
Common stock, $1 par value	$20,000
Additional paid-in capital	400,000
Retained earnings	120,000
Less: Treasury stock	(90,000)
Total stockholders' equity	$450,000
After Retirement of Treasury Stock:	
Common stock, $1 par value	$18,000
Additional paid-in capital	360,000
Retained earnings	72,000
Total stockholders' equity	$450,000

¶1008

Concluding Remarks

Now you know some of the particulars associated with accounting for a corporation. Accuracy and reliability for a corporation's financial statements are imperative due to the additional government regulations and oversight placed upon corporations. One feature of a corporation, such as Disney, that requires unique accounting attention, is stock. Issuing stock, purchasing, stock, and retiring stock, all involve additional tracking and reporting. Due to the quantity and complexity of corporate business transactions, you can understand why a CPA firm needs to audit the financial statements.

In the next chapter, Chapter 11, we'll delve deeper into two of those financial statements, the income statement and the statement of stockholder's equity. We'll examine how they report on the financial matters of a corporation.

Chapter Review

LEARNING OBJECTIVE 1

Describe the importance of corporate financial reporting to people within and outside the business.

Business managers within a company need accounting information and accurate reporting to make decisions about raising capital, paying dividends, purchasing treasury stock, and other equity related issues. Stockholders of corporations do not have first-hand access to company operations and thus depend on corporate financial reports to make investment decisions. In addition, government agencies require publicly-traded corporations to report on their operations in specific manners to help ensure investors that these financial reports can be trusted.

LEARNING OBJECTIVE 2

Explain the advantages and disadvantages of the corporate form of business.

A corporation is a unique legal entity, which is separate from its owners, that is, the stockholders. The corporation, not its stockholders, is responsible for its liabilities. If the corporation fails to pay back its debts, the stockholders are not held responsible. A corporation can exist forever, even though the owners do not. On a daily basis, stockholders of major corporations buy and sell ownership through corporate stock. The stockholders elect a board of directors which determines the policies of the corporation and appoint its top managers.

Government more carefully regulates corporations than it does sole proprietorships and partnerships. Federal legislation requires that U.S. publicly-traded corporations have their financial statements audited annually by a CPA firm. The Sarbanes-Oxley Act of 2002 requires that corporate management prepare an internal control report each year.

LEARNING OBJECTIVE 3

Discuss the issuance of common stock and cash dividends.

Common stock is the basic type of stock for a corporation and carries voting rights for the stockholder. A very effective way for a company to obtain money is to issue stock. A stock's par value is an arbitrary amount determined by the incorporators. Stock normally sells at a price above par because par value is usually set at a very low amount.

A cash dividend is a distribution of a corporation's earnings to stockholders in the form of cash. There are three important dates associated with cash dividends: declaration date, date of record, and the payment date. Corporations are not required to pay dividends. Instead of paying a cash dividend, the board may decide that the stockholders would benefit more if the corporation kept all its retained earnings and reinvested them in company operations.

LEARNING OBJECTIVE 4

Describe the characteristics of preferred stock, account for its issuance, and record dividends for preferred stock.

Like common stock, corporations sell preferred stock to raise money. Preferred stock is stock that has preference over common stock in terms of dividends and the distribution of assets. Preferred stockholders receive dividends before common stockholders, but usually have no voting rights. Preferred stockholders have priority in receiving assets in the event of corporate liquidation.

LEARNING OBJECTIVE 5

Describe the impact of stock dividends and stock splits.

Instead of distributing a cash dividend to shareholders, corporations may issue additional shares of stock to the stockholders. This is done via stock dividends and stock splits. In both cases, the corporation retains its cash for use in business operations, while providing stockholders with additional shares of stock.

LEARNING OBJECTIVE 6

Describe stock option plans.

Almost all publicly-traded corporations, also called "public companies," encourage their employees to purchase company stock. A stock option plan is an arrangement by which employees can purchase their company's stock. The stock option plan can be available to all employees or limited to management-level employees.

LEARNING OBJECTIVE 7

Explain why companies purchase treasury stock and how to account for treasury stock transactions.

Treasury stock is a corporation's own stock, which was issued and later reacquired. A corporation can purchase shares of its own stock just like other investors. There are several reasons why a corporation may choose to buy its stock. These reasons include: (1) the corporation hopes to later sell the stock at a higher price; (2) the corporation is trying to increase its market stock price; (3) the shares are needed for distribution to employees under the company employee stock purchase plan; and (4) the corporation is trying to prevent a hostile takeover by another entity.

After buying treasury stock, a corporation can retire the stock by canceling the stock certificates, thus taking them out of circulation. Retirement of stock normally requires approval by the stockholders.

¶1010

Glossary

Cash dividend

A cash dividend is a distribution of a corporation's earnings to stockholders in the form of cash.

Chief executive officer (CEO)

The chief executive officer (CEO) is customarily the individual of highest authority and responsibility in a corporation. For many corporations, the CEO is the chairperson of the board of directors.

Chief financial officer (CFO)

The chief financial officer is the vice president of finance of a corporation.

Chief operating officer (COO)

The chief operating officer, also called the "president," is responsible for managing the day-to-day activities of the corporation.

Common stock

Common stock is the basic type of stock and carries voting rights for the stockholder. All corporations issue common stock.

Cumulative preferred stock

Holders of cumulative preferred stock are entitled to receive all dividends in arrears and the current year's dividend prior to paying any dividends to common stock shareholders.

Date of record (dividend)

The date of record establishes which stockholders will receive the dividend. Whoever owns the stock on the date of record will receive the dividend.

Declaration date (dividend)

The declaration date is the date that the board of directors declares its intent to pay a dividend.

Double taxation

Double taxation occurs when corporate earnings are taxed first at the corporate level, and then taxed a second time at the individual stockholder level when dividends are distributed.

Limited liability

Limited liability means that stockholders have no personal liability for corporate liabilities.

Par value (stock)

A stock's par value is an arbitrary amount assigned to each share of a company's stock to represent the minimum legal value of the stock.

Payment date (dividend)

The payment date is the date on which the dividend is actually paid.

Preemption

Preemption is the stockholder's right to maintain a proportionate share of ownership in the corporation.

Preferred stock

Preferred stock is stock that has preference over common stock in terms of dividends and the distribution of assets. It usually has no voting rights.

Section 404 of the Sarbanes-Oxley Act

Section 404 of the Sarbanes-Oxley Act requires corporate management to prepare an internal control report on an annual basis.

Stock dividend

A stock dividend is a proportional distribution of stock from the corporation to its shareholders.

Stock option plan

A stock option plan is an arrangement by which employees can purchase their company's stock.

Stock split

A stock split is a method used to lower the market price of a company's stock by increasing the number of shares outstanding.

Treasury stock

Treasury stock is a corporation's own stock, which was issued and later reacquired.

¶1011 # Chapter Assignments

QUESTIONS

1. **[Obj. 2]** In what ways does a corporation have legal rights just like a person?

2. **[Obj. 2]** Stockholders have limited liability. What does this mean?

3. **[Obj. 2]** State some of the government regulations over U.S. publicly-traded corporations regarding financial statements and internal control.

4. **[Obj. 2]** Do corporations pay federal and state income taxes?

5. **[Obj. 2]** What is double taxation?

6. **[Obj. 3]** What is common stock and which business type issues it?

7. **[Obj. 3]** Identify four basic rights normally given to common stockholders.

8. **[Obj. 3]** How is a stock's par value determined?

9. **[Obj. 3]** Who determines how many shares of a corporation's stock to issue?

10. **[Obj. 3]** Identify two ways that stockholders benefit from owning stock.

11. **[Obj. 3]** Are corporations required to pay cash dividends? Why would a corporation not pay cash dividends to benefit its stockholders?

12. **[Obj. 3]** In order to pay a cash dividend, what two things must a corporation have?

13. **[Obj. 3]** With investors buying and selling stock on a daily basis, what determines who is an eligible stockholder for a cash dividend?

14. **[Obj. 4]** In what ways does preferred stock have preference over common stock?

15. **[Obj. 4]** Are preferred stockholders guaranteed to receive a dividend?

16. **[Obj. 4]** What is cumulative preferred stock?

17. **[Obj. 5]** Describe what happens in a stock split.

18. **[Obj. 6]** What is a stock-option plan?

19. **[Obj. 7]** What is treasury stock and why would a corporation acquire any?

20. **[Obj. 7]** What is it called when a corporation buys treasury stock and then cancels the stock certificates, thus taking them out of circulation?

SHORT EXERCISES – SET A

Building Accounting Skills

1. **[Obj. 1]** Characteristics of the Corporation: Describe how a corporation differs from a sole proprietorship or a partnership.

2. **[Obj. 1]** Publicly-Traded Corporations: Approximately how many corporations exist and how many are publicly traded on the stock market? Describe the government's relationship to publicly-traded corporations.

3. **[Obj. 2]** Corporate Form of Business: Match the following terms to the related concepts:
   __ 1. Transfer of ownership
   __ 2. Separate managers and owners
   __ 3. Unique legal entity
   __ 4. Limited liability
   A. The corporation, not its stockholders, is responsible for its liabilities.
   B. A corporation, in many ways, has legal rights just like a person.
   C. The corporation is owned by its stockholders, which elects a board of directors.
   D. A corporation can exist forever.

4. **[Obj. 2]** Corporate Management: Match the following corporate managers to their descriptions:
    ___ 1. Chief financial officer (CFO)
    ___ 2. Chief operating officer (COO)
    ___ 3. Chief executive officer (CEO)
    ___ 4. Treasurer
    ___ 5. Chief accountant
    A. This person handles cash.
    B. This person has the highest authority and responsibility in a corporation.
    C. This person, also known as the controller, maintains the financial records.
    D. This person, also called the president, is responsible for daily operations.
    E. This person supervises the treasurer and controller.

5. **[Obj. 3]** Issuing Common Stock: Assume that on June 20, Toyota Motor Company decides to raise additional money by selling 50,000 shares of $10 par value common stock. How would this transaction be recorded in each of the two following situations?
    a. The stock sells for exactly its par value of $10 per share.
    b. The stock sells for $15 per share.

6. **[Obj. 3]** Issuing Common Stock for Noncash Assets: Assume that on March 26, John Deer Tractor Company issues 10,000 shares of $1 par value common stock, which has a market value of $300,000, in exchange for some land and equipment, valued at $200,000 and $100,000 respectively. How would this transaction be recorded?

7. **[Obj. 3]** Issuing No-Par Common Stock for Noncash Assets: Assume that on March 26, John Deere Tractor Company issues 10,000 shares of no-par common stock, which has a market value of $300,000, in exchange for some land and equipment, valued at $200,000 and $100,000 respectively. How would this transaction be recorded?

8. **[Obj. 3]** Cash Dividends: Describe the three important dates associated with dividends.

9. **[Obj. 3]** Cash Dividends: Suppose that on September 1, Kellogg Corporation's board of directors declares a cash dividend of $500,000 to be paid on October 31. The record date is designated as October 15. Record the journal entries for each of the three dates:
    a. Declaration date,
    b. Date of record, and
    c. Payment date.

10. **[Obj. 4]** Issuing Preferred Stock: Suppose BMW Corporation issues 5,000 shares of $20 par value preferred stock on April 1. Make the journal entry to record the transaction if the preferred stock sells for $50 per share.

11. **[Obj. 4]** Issuing Preferred Stock: CBS Corporation issues 20,000 shares of $5 par value preferred stock on May 1. Make the journal entry to record the transaction if the preferred stock sells for $40 per share.

12. **[Obj. 5]** Stock Dividends: Suppose Mars Corporation declares a 50% stock dividend. Assume that Mars has 400,000 shares of $10 par value common stock outstanding. On the distribution date, December 1, the stock price is $15 per share. Since this is a large stock dividend, Mars records the dividend at par value, not market. Below is the company's stockholders' equity before the stock dividend. What is the stockholders' equity after the stock dividend?

Mars Stockholders' Equity (Before 50% Stock Dividend)	
Common stock, $10 par value, 700,000 shares authorized, 400,000 shares issued	$4,000,000
Additional paid-in capital	2,000,000
Retained Earnings	3,250,000
Total Stockholders' Equity	$9,250,000

SHORT EXERCISES – SET B

Building Accounting Skills

1. **[Obj. 3]** Rights of Stockholders: List and define the four basic rights of a stockholder.

2. **[Obj. 2]** Characteristics of a Corporation: Match the following terms to the related concepts:
   __ 1.   Separate managers and owners
   __ 2.   Transfer of ownership
   __ 3.   Limited liability
   __ 4.   Unique legal entity
   A.   The corporation, not its stockholders, is responsible for its liabilities.
   B.   A corporation, in many ways, has legal rights just like a person.
   C.   The corporation is owned by its stockholders, which elects a board of directors.
   D.   A corporation can exist forever.

3. **[Obj. 2]** Corporate Management: Match the following corporate managers to their descriptions:
   __ 1.   Chief accountant
   __ 2.   Chief executive officer (CEO)
   __ 3.   Chief financial officer (CFO)
   __ 4.   Chief operating officer (COO)
   __ 5.   Treasurer
   A.   This person handles cash.
   B.   This person has the highest authority and responsibility in a corporation.
   C.   This person, also known as the controller, maintains the financial records.
   D.   This person, also called the president, is responsible for daily operations.
   E.   This person supervises the treasurer and controller.

4. **[Obj. 3]** Issuing Common Stock: Assume that on June 20, Saturn Company decides to raise additional money by selling 100,000 shares of $20 par value common stock. How would this transaction be recorded in each of the two following situations?
   a.   The stock sells for exactly its par value of $20 per share.
   b.   The stock sells for $25 per share.

5. **[Obj. 3]** Issuing Common Stock for Noncash Assets: Assume that on March 26, U-Store-It Company issues 20,000 shares of $1 par value common stock, which has a market value of $150,000, in exchange for some land and equipment, valued at $100,000 and $50,000, respectively. How would this transaction be recorded?

6. **[Obj. 3]** Issuing No-Par Common Stock for Noncash Assets: Assume that on June 10, Green Bay Company issues 10,000 shares of no-par common stock, which has a market value of $90,000, in exchange for some land and equipment, valued at $60,000 and $30,000, respectively. How would this transaction be recorded?

7. **[Obj. 3]** Cash Dividends: Explain the significance of each of these dates: declaration date, date of record, and payment date.

8. **[Obj. 3]** Cash Dividends: Suppose that on January 1, Nabisco Corporation's board of directors declares a cash dividend of $250,000 to be paid on March 31. The record date is designated as March 15. Record the journal entries for the following: a. Declaration date, b. Date of record, and c. Payment date.

9. **[Obj. 4]** Issuing Preferred Stock: Suppose Toyota Corporation issues 10,000 shares of $30 par value preferred stock on April 1. Make the journal entry to record the transaction if the preferred stock sells for $50 per share.

10. **[Obj. 4]** Issuing Preferred Stock: Suppose NBC Corporation issues 40,000 shares of $10 par value preferred stock on May 1. Make the journal entry to record the transaction if the preferred stock sells for $40 per share.

11. **[Obj. 5]** Stock Dividends: Suppose Hershey Corporation declares a 50% stock dividend. Assume that Hershey has 200,000 shares of $5 par value common stock outstanding. On the distribution date, December 1, the stock price is $20 per share. Since this is a large stock dividend, Hershey records the dividend at par value, not market. Below is the company's stockholders' equity before the stock dividend. What is the stockholders' equity after the stock dividend?

Hershey Stockholders' Equity (Before 50% Stock Dividend)	
Common stock, $5 par value, 500,000 shares authorized, 200,000 shares issued	$1,000,000
Additional paid-in capital	3,000,000
Retained Earnings	2,500,000
Total Stockholders' Equity	$6,500,000

PROBLEMS – SET A

Applying Accounting Knowledge

1. **[Obj. 4]** Issuing Preferred Stock: Suppose BMW Corporation issues 10,000 shares of $10 par value preferred stock on June 1.

   Required:
   a. Make the journal entry to record the transaction if the preferred stock sells for: 1) $10 per share, 2) $30 per share, and 3) $60 per share.
   b. Evaluate: What might cause the market price of preferred stock to be higher or lower?

2. **[Obj. 4]** Cash Dividends to Preferred Stock: For cumulative preferred stock, shareholders are entitled to receive all dividends in arrears prior to paying any dividends to common stock shareholders. Preferred stock is considered cumulative unless it is specifically designated as non-cumulative. Suppose Target Corporation has 50,000 shares of 4% preferred stock with a par value of $10. Target passed (did not pay) the dividend in 20Y1, 20Y2, and 20Y3. On August 1, 20Y4, Target declares a dividend of $200,000 for 20Y5. How much of the $200,000 dividend goes to preferred shareholders and how much to common shareholders?

   Required: Make the journal entries for the following two situations:
   a. The preferred stock is cumulative.
   b. The preferred stock is non-cumulative.
   c. Evaluate: Who decides whether a corporation will issue a cash dividend? If you were in charge, would you make your company's preferred stock cumulative or non-cumulative? Why or why not?

3. **[Obj. 5]** Stock Dividends: A small stock dividend is one of 25% or less and is accounted for at market value. A large stock dividend is one greater than 25% and may be accounted for at par value.

   Required: Prepare journal entries for the following two scenarios:
   a. Suppose that Sony Corporation declares a 5% stock dividend. Assume that Sony has 2,000,000 shares of $1 par value common stock outstanding. Assume that the stock price on the distribution date of October 1 is $40 per share. Record the stock dividend.
   b. Suppose Sony Corporation declares a 50% stock dividend. Assume that Sony has 2,000,000 shares of $1 par value common stock outstanding. Assume that the stock price on the distribution date of October 1 is $40 per share. Record the stock dividend using the par value approach.

4. **[Obj. 5]** Stock Splits: Suppose the market price of Zales Jewelry Company is $90 and that the company wants to decrease the market price to about $30. Thus, Zales decides to split its common stock 3 for 1. This means that there will be three times as many shares outstanding after the split and the par value per share will be cut by two-thirds. Prior to the split, Zales had 10,000 shares of $9 par common stock issued and outstanding. Shown below is stockholders' equity section of the company's balance sheet before the 3-for-1 stock split.

Zales Stockholders' Equity (Before 3-for-1 Stock Split)	
Common stock, $9 par value, 10,000 shares outstanding	$90,000
Additional paid-in capital	400,000
Retained Earnings	110,000
Total Stockholders' Equity	$600,000

Required: Prepare the stockholders' equity section of the company's balance sheet after the 3-for-1 stock split.

5. **[Obj. 6]** Stock Options: In cases where stock option plans are available to all employees, the stock is usually sold for its market price on the date of purchase. For example, suppose that on March 15, General Motors employees purchase 10,000 shares of $1 par value stock. How would the transaction be recorded?

Required:
a. Prepare journal entries for each of the following market prices: 1) $20, 2) $30, and 3) $40.
b. Evaluate: What might cause the market price of preferred stock to be higher or lower?

6. **[Obj. 6]** Stock Options: In cases where stock option plans are available to all employees, the stock is usually sold for its market price on the date of purchase. For example, suppose that on June 30 Natchez Steamboat Company employees purchase 10,000 shares of $2 par value stock. How would the transaction be recorded?

Required:
a. Prepare journal entries for each of the following market prices: 1) $10, 2) $15, and 3) $20.
b. Evaluate: What might cause the market price of preferred stock to be higher or lower?

7. **[Obj. 7]** Treasury Stock Purchase: Suppose Sears Corporation currently has 100,000 shares of $1 par value common stock issued and outstanding. Additional paid-in capital is $200,000 and retained earnings totals $320,000. On August 4, the company purchases 1,000 shares of its own stock. How would the transaction be affected by different market prices?

Required:
a. Record the transaction for each market price: 1) $65, 2) $75, and 3) $85.
b. Evaluate: What might cause the market price of preferred stock to be higher or lower?

8. **[Obj. 7]** Treasury Stock Purchase: Suppose Sears Corporation currently has 100,000 shares of $1 par value common stock issued and outstanding. Additional paid-in capital is $200,000 and retained earnings totals $320,000. On August 4, the company purchases 1,000 shares of its own stock. Shown below is the stockholders' equity before the purchase of treasury stock. How would the stockholders' equity be affected if the treasury stock was purchased at different market prices?

Stockholders' Equity Before Purchase of Treasury Stock	
Common stock, $1 par value	$100,000
Additional paid-in capital	200,000
Retained earnings	320,000
Total stockholders' equity	$620,000

Required:
a. Show the components of stockholders' equity, assuming treasury stock was purchased at the following three different market prices: 1) $65, 2) $75, and 3) $85.
b. Evaluate: What might cause the market price of treasury stock to be higher or lower?

9. **[Obj. 7]** Treasury Stock Sale: Suppose that a few years after purchasing treasury stock, Spalding Corporation needs cash for company operations. On June 1, the company stock is trading on the market for $30 per share. The company sells its 1,000 shares of treasury stock at the market price. The Treasury Stock account is credited for the amount that Spalding originally paid for it, $20 per share. Below is the company's stockholders' equity prior to the sale of treasury stock.

Stockholders' Equity Before Sale of Treasury Stock	
Common stock, $1 par value	$100,000
Additional paid-in capital	400,000
Retained earnings	200,000
Less: Treasury stock	(20,000)
Total stockholders' equity	$680,000

Required:
a. Prepare journal entry to record sale of treasury stock.
b. Show the components of stockholders' equity after the sale of treasury stock.
c. Evaluate: Why would a company purchase its own stock?

10. **[Obj. 7]** Retirement of Stock: Suppose that a few years after purchasing 1,000 shares of treasury stock for $20,000, Spalding Corporation decides not to sell the stock but instead retires the stock on November 1. Shown below are the stockholders' equity accounts prior to the retirement of the stock.

Stockholders' Equity Before Sale of Treasury Stock	
Common stock (100,000 shares at $1 par value)	$100,000
Additional paid-in capital (100,000 shares at $4)	400,000
Retained earnings	200,000
Less: Treasury stock (1,000 shares)	(20,000)
Total stockholders' equity	$680,000

Required:
a. Prepare journal entry to record retirement of stock.
b. Show the components of stockholders' equity after the retirement of stock.

PROBLEMS – SET B

Applying Accounting Knowledge

1. **[Obj. 4]** Issuing Preferred Stock: Suppose Toyota Corporation issues 20,000 shares of $10 par value preferred stock on June 1.

    Required:
    a. Make the journal entry to record the transaction if the preferred stock sells for: 1) $10, 2) $30, and 3) $60.
    b. Evaluate: What might cause the market price of preferred stock to be higher or lower?

2. **[Obj. 4]** Cash Dividends to Preferred Stock: For cumulative preferred stock, shareholders are entitled to receive all dividends in arrears prior to paying any dividends to common stock shareholders. Preferred stock is considered cumulative unless it is specifically designated as non-cumulative. Suppose Walmart Corporation has 50,000 shares of 4% preferred stock with a par value of $20. Walmart passed (did not pay) the dividend in 20Y1, 20Y2, and 20Y3. On August 1, 20Y4, Walmart declares a dividend of $300,000 for 2011. How much of the $300,000 dividend goes to preferred shareholders and how much to common shareholders?

    Required: Make the journal entries for the following two situations:
    a. The preferred stock is cumulative.
    b. The preferred stock is non-cumulative.
    c. Evaluate: Who decides whether a corporation will issue a cash dividend? If you were in charge, would you make your company's preferred stock cumulative or non-cumulative? Why or why not?

3. **[Obj. 5]** Stock Dividends: A small stock dividend is one of 25% or less and is accounted for at market value. A large stock dividend is one greater than 25% and may be accounted for at par value.

    Required: Prepare journal entries for the following two scenarios:
    a. Suppose that Dell Corporation declares a 5% stock dividend. Assume that Dell has 1,000,000 shares of $1 par value common stock outstanding. Assume that the stock price on the distribution date of October 1 is $30 per share. Record the stock dividend.
    b. Suppose Dell Corporation declares a 50% stock dividend. Assume that Dell has 1,000,000 shares of $1 par value common stock outstanding. Assume that the stock price on the distribution date of October 1 is $30 per share. Record the stock dividend using the par value approach.

4. **[Obj. 5]** Stock Splits: Suppose the market price of Geico Insurance Company is $90 and that the company wants to decrease the market price to about $30. Thus, Geico decides to split its common stock 3 for 1. This means that there will be three times as many shares outstanding after the split. The par value per share will be cut by two-thirds. Prior to the split, Geico had 20,000 shares of $9 par common stock issued and outstanding. Shown below is stockholders' equity section of the company's balance sheet before the 3-for-1 stock split.

Geico Stockholders' Equity (Before 3-for-1 Stock Split)	
Common stock, $9 par value, 20,000 shares outstanding	$180,000
Additional paid-in capital	800,000
Retained Earnings	220,000
Total stockholders' equity	$1,200,000

    Required: Prepare the stockholders' equity section of the company's balance sheet after the 3-for-1 stock split.

5. **[Obj. 6]** Stock Options: In cases where stock option plans are available to all employees, the stock is usually sold for its market price on the date of purchase. For example, suppose that on March 15, Sony Corporation employees purchase 20,000 shares of $1 par value stock. How would the transaction be recorded?

    Required:
    a. Prepare journal entries for each of the following market prices: 1) $20, 2) $30, and 3) $40.
    b. Evaluate: What might cause the market price of preferred stock to be higher or lower?

6. **[Obj. 6]** Stock Options: In cases where stock option plans are available to all employees, the stock is usually sold for its market price on the date of purchase. For example, suppose that on June 30, Coca-Cola employees purchase 20,000 shares of $2 par value stock. How would the transaction be recorded?

    Required:
    a. Prepare journal entries for each of the following market prices: 1) $10, 2) $15, and 3) $30.
    b. Evaluate: What might cause the market price of preferred stock to be higher or lower?

7. **[Obj. 7]** Treasury Stock Purchase: Suppose Target Corporation currently has 100,000 shares of $1 par value common stock issued and outstanding. Additional paid-in capital is $200,000 and retained earnings totals $320,000. On August 4, the company purchases 2,000 shares of its own stock. How would the transaction be affected by different market prices?

    Required:
    a. Record the transaction for each market price: 1) $65, 2) $75, and 3) $85.
    b. Evaluate: What might cause the market price of preferred stock to be higher or lower?

8. **[Obj. 7]** Treasury Stock Purchase: Suppose Target Corporation currently has 200,000 shares of $1 par value common stock issued and outstanding. Additional paid-in capital is $200,000 and retained earnings totals $320,000. On August 4, the company purchases 2,000 shares of its own stock. Shown below is the stockholders' equity before the purchase of treasury stock. How would the stockholders' equity be affected if the treasury stock was purchased at different market prices?

Stockholders' Equity Before Purchase of Treasury Stock	
Common stock, $1 par value	$200,000
Additional paid-in capital	200,000
Retained earnings	320,000
Total stockholders' equity	$720,000

Required:
a. Show the components of stockholders' equity, assuming treasury stock was purchased at the following three different market prices: 1) $65, 2) $75, and 3) $85.
b. Evaluate: What might cause the market price of treasury stock to be higher or lower?

9. **[Obj. 7]** Treasury Stock Sale: Suppose that a few years after purchasing treasury stock, Olive Garden Corporation needs cash for company operations. On June 1, the company stock is trading on the market for $30 per share. The company sells its 2,000 shares of treasury stock at the market price. The Treasury Stock account is credited for the amount that Olive Garden originally paid for it, $20 per share. Below is the company's stockholders' equity prior to the sale of treasury stock.

Stockholders' Equity Before Sale of Treasury Stock	
Common stock, $1 par value	$200,000
Additional paid-in capital	400,000
Retained earnings	200,000
Less: Treasury stock	(40,000)
Total stockholders' equity	$760,000

Required:
a. Prepare journal entry to record sale of treasury stock.
b. Show the components of stockholders' equity after the sale of treasury stock.
c. Evaluate: Why would a company purchase its own stock?

10. **[Obj. 7]** Retirement of Stock: Suppose that a few years after purchasing 2,000 shares of treasury stock for $40,000, Olive Garden Corporation decides not to sell the stock, but instead retires the stock on November 1. Shown below are the stockholders' equity accounts prior to the retirement of the stock.

Stockholders' Equity Before Sale of Treasury Stock	
Common stock (100,000 shares at $1 par value)	$100,000
Additional paid-in capital (100,000 shares at $4)	400,000
Retained earnings	200,000
Less: Treasury stock (2,000 shares)	(40,000)
Total stockholders' equity	$660,000

Required:
a. Prepare journal entry to record retirement of stock.
b. Show the components of stockholders' equity after the retirement of stock.

CROSS-FUNCTIONAL PERSPECTIVES

Discussion Questions

1. **[Obj. 2]** In a typical corporation, describe the roles of the CEO, COO, vice presidents, CFO, treasurer, and controller.

2. **[Obj. 2]** Why might managers within a corporation be even more dependent upon the accounting department than a manager within a sole proprietorship or partnership?

3. **[Obj. 6]** How might managers from any department benefit from a stock option plan?

Cross-functional Case: Hong Kong Disneyland

In September of 2005, Hong Kong Disneyland opened. In anticipation of a large attendance, Disney began booking hotel reservations seven months prior to the park opening. In February 2005, the Vice President of Marketing and Sales, along with the General Manager of Hotel Operations, launched the Hotel Reservation Hotline with an official ceremony. The following information was publicized at the ceremony:

This first phase of Hong Kong Disneyland includes a theme park, two hotels (2,100 hotel rooms), and an area for retail, dining, and entertainment. The Disneyland-style theme park can accommodate 10 million visitors annually. The Disney hotels are the first premium resorts in Hong Kong designed especially for families. Guests enjoy the "Disney Difference," such as "Mickey wake-up calls," bedtime stories on TV, and a complimentary mini-bar. The rooms at the Victorian-style Hong Kong Disneyland Hotel start at HK$1,600. Rooms at the Tinseltown-inspired Hollywood Hotel start at HK$1,000.

Hong Kong Disneyland created 18,000 new jobs initially. The Hong Kong SAR Government estimates that Phase 1 will generate a present economic value of HK$148 billion (US$19 billion) in benefits to Hong Kong over a 40-year period.

Required:
1. If you were the Vice President of Marketing and Sales at Disney, what additional information would you use to promote Hong Kong Disney? For each detail you publicize, state the source of your information (e.g., Disney's marketing department) and the purpose of providing that information.
2. If you were the president of Disney, what information would you present to the stockholders to assure them that Hong Kong Disney is a good business venture? State which departments you would draw critical information from, and why you chose to communicate that information. You may use the factual information stated above, along with explanatory information you create.

EXCEL ASSIGNMENTS

1. **[Obj. 5]** Stock Dividends: Suppose IBM Corporation declares a 5% stock dividend. At that time, assume that IBM has 2,000,000 shares of $1 par value common stock outstanding. According to generally accepted accounting principles (GAAP), a stock dividend of 25% or less is "small" and should be accounted for at the market value of the shares issued. Assume that the stock price on the distribution date is $10 per share. Shown below is the stockholders' equity section of the company's balance sheet.

IBM Stockholders' Equity:	
Before 5% Stock Dividend	
Common stock, $1 par value, 5,000,000 shares authorized, 2,000,000 shares issued	$2,000,000
Additional paid-in capital	3,000,000
Retained Earnings	2,200,000
Total Stockholders' Equity	$7,200,000

Required:
a. Make the journal entry to record the stock dividend.
b. Prepare a worksheet showing the stockholders' equity section before and after the stock dividend.

2. **[Obj. 5]** Stock Dividends: Suppose IBM Corporation declares a 10% stock dividend. At that time, assume that IBM has 2,000,000 shares of $1 par value common stock outstanding. According to generally accepted accounting principles (GAAP), a stock dividend of 25% or less is "small" and should be accounted for at the market value of the shares issued. Assume that the stock price on the distribution date is $10 per share. Shown below is the stockholders' equity section of the company's balance sheet.

IBM Stockholders' Equity:	
Before 10% Stock Dividend	
Common stock, $1 par value, 5,000,000 shares authorized, 2,000,000 shares issued	$2,000,000
Additional paid-in capital	3,000,000
Retained Earnings	2,200,000
Total Stockholders' Equity	$7,200,000

Required:
a. Make the journal entry to record the stock dividend.
b. Prepare a worksheet showing the stockholders' equity section before and after the stock dividend.

3. **[Obj. 5]** Stock Dividends: Suppose Intel Corporation declares a 60% stock dividend. At that time, assume that Intel has 1,000,000 shares of $1 par value common stock outstanding. According to generally accepted accounting principles (GAAP), a stock dividend greater than 25% is "large" and should be accounted for at the par value of the shares issued. Assume that the stock price on the distribution date is $20 per share. Shown below is the stockholders' equity section of the company's balance sheet.

Intel Stockholders' Equity:	
Before 60% Stock Dividend	
Common stock, $1 par value, 4,000,000 shares authorized, 1,000,000 shares issued	$1,000,000
Additional paid-in capital	2,000,000
Retained Earnings	6,400,000
Total Stockholders' Equity	$9,400,000

Required:
a. Make the journal entry to record the stock dividend.
b. Prepare a worksheet showing the stockholders' equity section before and after the stock dividend.

4. **[Obj. 7]** Treasury Stock Purchase: Suppose Home Depot Company currently has 100,000 shares of $1 par value common stock issued and outstanding. Additional paid-in capital is $200,000 and retained earnings totals $420,000. On March 13, the company purchases 2,000 shares of its own stock when the market price is $20 per share. Shown below is the stockholders' equity section of the company's balance sheet prior to the purchase of the treasury stock.

Before Purchase of Treasury Stock:	
Common stock, $1 par value	$100,000
Additional paid-in capital	200,000
Retained earnings	420,000
Total stockholders' equity	$720,000

Required:
a. Make the journal entry to record the treasury stock purchase.
b. Prepare a worksheet showing the stockholders' equity section before and after the treasury stock purchase.

5. **[Obj. 7]** Treasury Stock Purchase: Suppose Circuit City Corporation currently has 500,000 shares of $1 par value common stock issued and outstanding. Additional paid-in capital is $330,000 and retained earnings totals $40,000. On June 20, the company purchases 5,000 shares of its own stock when the market price is $30 per share. Shown below is the stockholders' equity section of the company's balance sheet prior to the purchase of the treasury stock.

Before Purchase of Treasury Stock:	
Common stock, $1 par value	$500,000
Additional paid-in capital	330,000
Retained earnings	40,000
Total stockholders' equity	$870,000

Required:
a. Make the journal entry to record the treasury stock purchase.
b. Prepare a worksheet showing the stockholders' equity section before and after the treasury stock purchase.

6. **[Obj. 7]** Treasury Stock Sale: Suppose that Target Corporation previously purchased 4,000 shares of treasury stock for $20 per share. Now the company needs cash to pay for operations. On April 1, the company stock is trading on the market for $25 per share. The company sells its 4,000 shares of treasury stock at the market price. Shown below is the stockholders' equity section of the company's balance sheet prior to the sale of the treasury stock.

Before Sale of Treasury Stock:	
Common stock, $1 par value	$300,000
Additional paid-in capital	150,000
Retained earnings	120,000
Treasury stock	(80,000)
Total stockholders' equity	$490,000

Required:
a. Make the journal entry to record the sale of treasury stock sale.
b. Prepare a worksheet showing the stockholders' equity section before and after the sale of treasury stock.

7. **[Obj. 7]** Treasury Stock Sale: Suppose that Aerofit Corporation previously purchased 3,000 shares of treasury stock for $20 per share. Now the company needs cash to pay for operations. On June 1, the company stock is trading on the market for $22 per share. The company sells 2,000 of its 3,000 shares of treasury stock at the market price. Shown below is the stockholders' equity section of the company's balance sheet prior to the sale of the treasury stock.

Before Sale of Treasury Stock:	
Common stock, $1 par value	$500,000
Additional paid-in capital	250,000
Retained earnings	40,000
Treasury stock	(60,000)
Total stockholders' equity	$730,000

Required:
a. Make the journal entry to record the sale of treasury stock sale.
b. Prepare a worksheet showing the stockholders' equity section before and after the sale of treasury stock.

8. **[Obj. 7]** Retirement of Stock: Suppose that Pillsbury Corporation previously purchased 5,000 shares of treasury stock for $50 per share. On October 31, the company retires all 5,000 shares. The shares were originally issued for $11 per share, $10 above par. Shown below is the stockholders' equity section of the company's balance sheet prior to the stock retirement.

Before Retirement of Stock:	
Common stock, $1 par value	$145,000
Additional paid-in capital	1,500,000
Retained earnings	1,300,000
Treasury stock	(250,000)
Total stockholders' equity	$2,695,000

Required:
a. Make the journal entry to record the retirement of stock.
b. Prepare a worksheet showing the stockholders' equity section before and after the retirement of stock.

9. **[Obj. 7]** Retirement of Stock: Suppose that Kellogg Corporation previously purchased 10,000 shares of treasury stock for $30 per share. On February 14, the company retires all 10,000 shares. The shares were originally issued for $21 per share, $20 above par. Shown below is the stockholders' equity section of the company's balance sheet prior to the stock retirement.

Before Retirement of Stock:	
Common stock, $1 par value	$100,000
Additional paid-in capital	2,500,000
Retained earnings	3,200,000
Treasury stock	(300,000)
Total stockholders' equity	$5,500,000

Required:
a. Make the journal entry to record the retirement of stock.
b. Prepare a worksheet showing the stockholders' equity section before and after the retirement of stock.

WEB ASSIGNMENTS

1. **[Obj. 2]** Go to the Disney website and list the proposals accepted and rejected by the shareholders at its most recent annual shareholders' meeting. (**Hint:** look under News Releases.) Or do a search on Google to find the information.

2. **[Obj. 2]** Does the Public Company Accounting Oversight Board have any authority over foreign public accounting firms who audit U.S. companies? To find the answer, go to the website for the American Institute of Certified Public Accountants (AICPA) and look under Section 106 of the Sarbanes-Oxley Act: Foreign Public Accounting Firms, or do a search on Google.

3. **[Obj. 2]** Visit the website for the American Institute of Certified Public Accountants (AICPA) to find a summary of the Sarbanes-Oxley Act. Give a summary of Section 303: Improper Influence on Conduct of Audits. Or do a search on Google to find the information.

4. **[Obj. 3]** Go to the Yahoo! Finance website or do a search on Google to find the current stock price for Disney Corporation. What was its high and low for the past year? **Note:** Disney's stock market symbol is DIS.

¶1012

Test Prepper

Use this sample test to gauge your comprehension of the chapter material.

True/False Questions

___ 1. Limited liability means that stockholders have no personal liability for corporate liabilities.

___ 2. The Sarbanes-Oxley Act of 2002 requires that corporate management prepare an internal control report each year.

___ 3. Corporations pay federal income taxes, not state income taxes.

___ 4. A stock's par value is an arbitrary amount determined by the incorporators and legally assigned to each share of a company's stock.

___ 5. A company's stock usually sells at a price below par.

___ 6. A stock dividend lowers the market price of a company's stock by increasing the number of shares outstanding.

___ 7. A dividend plan is an arrangement in which employees can purchase the stock of their company.

___ 8. In many respects, a corporation has legal rights just like a person.

___ 9. A very effective way for a company to obtain massive amounts of money is to issue stock.

___ 10. Preemption is the stockholder's right to maintain a proportionate share of ownership in the corporation.

Multiple-Choice Questions

___ 1. Which of the following is elected by a corporation's board of directors?
   a. Chief executive officer (CEO)
   b. Chief operating officer (COO)
   c. President of the company
   d. all of the above
   e. none of the above

___ 2. Which of the following is a right of a common stockholder?
   a. Voting privileges
   b. Receive dividends
   c. Liquidation allocation
   d. Preemption
   e. all of the above

___ 3. Suppose Dell Computer Corporation issues 100,000 shares of $2 par value common stock. The stock sells for $10 per share. The entry to record issuance of 100,000 shares includes the following:
   a. Debit to Common Stock for $200,000
   b. Credit to Common Stock for $200,000
   c. Credit to Common Stock for $1,000,000
   d. Debit to Additional Paid-In Capital for $800,000
   e. Credit to Additional Paid-In Capital for $1,000,000

___ 4. Which of the following establishes which stockholder will receive a dividend?
   a. Declaration date
   b. Date of record
   c. Payment date
   d. Ownership title
   e. none of the above

___ 5. Which of the following specifies the date that the board of directors declares its intent to pay a dividend?
   a. Declaration date
   b. Date of record
   c. Payment date
   d. Ownership title
   e. none of the above

___ 6. Suppose General Motors declares a 2% stock dividend. At the time, General Motors has 1,000,000 shares of $1 par value common stock outstanding. The stock's market price on the distribution date is $40 per share. Then entry to record the stock dividend includes the following:
   a. Debit to Common Stock for $20,000
   b. Debit to Additional Paid-In Capital for $780,000
   c. Debit to Retained Earnings for $800,000
   d. Credit to Common Stock for $800,000
   e. Credit to Retained Earnings for $780,000

___ 7. Which of the following is a corporation's own stock, which was issued and later reacquired?
   a. Treasury stock
   b. Retirement stock
   c. Preferred stock
   d. Reacquired stock
   e. all of the above

___ 8. Corporate earnings are taxed at the corporate level and at the individual level when dividends are distributed to stockholders. What is this called?
   a. Double duty
   b. Double taxation
   c. Double trouble
   d. Tax burden
   e. Tax dividend

___ 9. When was the Sarbanes-Oxley Act passed?
   a. 2000
   b. 2001
   c. 2002
   d. 2003
   e. 2004

___ 10. Which of the following is responsible for the daily operations of a corporation?
   a. Chief executive officer (CEO)
   b. Board of directors
   c. Chairman of the board
   d. President
   e. all of the above

Chapter

11

More About the Income Statement and Statement of Stockholders' Equity

LEARNING OBJECTIVES

After studying Chapter 11, you should be able to do the following:

1. Describe the importance of the corporate income statement and statement of stockholders' equity to people within and outside the business firm.
2. Discuss key items shown on the income statement.
3. Prepare the statement of stockholders' equity.
4. Explain management's ethical and legal responsibility for the financial statements of a company.

CHAPTER CONTENTS

More About the Income Statement and Statement of Stockholders' Equity

FOCUS ON BUSINESS

What's All the Yahoo About?

While we know that Yahoo is a leading provider of comprehensive online products and services to consumers worldwide, do you know what Yahoo stands for? The acronym means "Yet Another Hierarchical Officious Oracle." Yahoo was created in 1994 by Stanford Ph.D. students David Filo and Jerry Yang. They started their Web guide as a way to keep track of their favorite links. Before long, hundreds of people were accessing their Web guide. A year later, David and Jerry incorporated the business and acquired funding of nearly $2 million in order to start the first online navigational guide to the Web. They hired a CEO and a COO with business experience. Yahoo has become a worldwide communication, search, and media provider. The company is headquartered in Sunnyvale, California, but provides services to over 50 countries in 25 languages.

Yahoo's income statement in a recent year showed that the company earned over $6.3 billion of revenue. Yahoo's net income exceeded $1.2 million. Investors are interested in these amounts plus the company's earnings per share of stock. Does Yahoo have a good quality of earnings? As for Yahoo's statement of stockholders' equity, it reported retained earnings of over $12.5 billion. Why is retained earnings important to stockholders? In this chapter, we'll explore the answers to these questions by looking in more detail at the elements found on the income statement and statement of stockholders' equity.

Source: Yahoo! Annual Reports, *Yahoo.com*

¶1101 Applications to People Within and Outside the Firm

LEARNING OBJECTIVE 1: Describe the importance of the corporate income statement and statement of stockholders' equity to people within and outside the business firm.

The financial statements of a corporation, which include the balance sheet, income statement, statement of stockholders' equity, and statement of cash flows, are all critically important to the evaluation of a company's financial performance. This chapter will take an in-depth look at two of those financial statements: the income statement and statement of stockholders' equity.

¶1101.01 INTERNAL USERS

Within a company, managers use accounting information to make decisions regarding company operations. Effective management leads to better financial performance. In this way, financial statements are report cards of management's performance. For example, marketing managers at Yahoo are interested in whether sales goals have been met or exceeded. The income statement reports sales revenue that can be compared to the targeted sales goals of the marketing department. Yahoo's top management will want to discuss with the marketing managers why sales strategies worked or did not work.

How Yahoo's operating performance compares with its competitors is of concern both to internal users and external users. For example, a key indicator of efficient company operations is the ratio of cost of goods sold to sales revenue. Amounts for both of these items are shown on the income statement. If Yahoo's cost of goods sold to sales ratio is higher than its competitor Google, it may indicate that Yahoo is spending more than it should to acquire or build products. As a result, Yahoo's managers should seek ways to lower costs. The purchasing department may be able to acquire goods from less expensive suppliers. Production managers may be able to develop more efficient, less costly ways to manufacture products. The income statement thereby provides managers with useful information for evaluating and improving company operations.

¶1101.02

EXTERNAL USERS

Investors use information from Yahoo's financial statements to determine future prospects for obtaining a good return on their investment. In the same way, lenders use Yahoo's financial statements to evaluate future prospects of repayment of loans that have been extended to Yahoo.

The income statement reports the firm's net income, often referred to as the "bottom line." For many people, within the firm and outside the firm, the net income, also called "earnings," is the single most important item reported within the financial statements. Stockholders are interested in the net income shown on a company's income statement because a higher net income is typically associated with higher stock prices. Similarly, a higher reported net income is an indicator to creditors that the reporting company can pay its debts when due.

The statement of stockholders' equity provides information of particular interest to investors. The statement reports on transactions such as issuing stock, cash dividends, and stock dividends. The statement shows the changes in retained earnings from one year to the next. Retained earnings are increased by net income and decreased by dividends. Some investors prefer stocks of companies that pay dividends. Other investors prefer stocks of companies that pay little or no dividends, but instead reinvest the earnings back into the company. Investors prefer to invest in companies whose earnings are increasing from year to year. When earnings are increasing, a company may choose to pay out more dividends or reinvest more into the company.

Regarding the management of your personal finances, do you have a good report card?

FOCUS ON GLOBAL TRADE

Going Yahoo Around the World

In its annual report, Yahoo's CEO states that the company's goal is to be the most essential global Internet service for users and businesses. In an effort to expand its international operations, Yahoo follows the principle of build, buy, or partner with other companies. In Indonesia, Yahoo purchased Koprol, a social networking site popular in the area. This allows Yahoo to expand its presence in the area of social networks as well as global expansion.

Yahoo also announced a partnership with Zynga, an international social gaming company. More than 600 million worldwide users can now access Zynga games through several Yahoo services included Yahoo! Messenger and Yahoo! Games.

The CEO of Yahoo attributes the company's achievements to the relentless focus on users, a higher rate of innovation, and ongoing investment in advanced technologies throughout the world. Such activities require astute leadership, effective planning, competent employees, and, of course, cash to pay company operations. The company's financial statements reveal that Yahoo continues to achieve great financial success on a global scale.

Source: *Yahoo.com*

¶1102

Corporate Income Statement

LEARNING OBJECTIVE 2: Discuss key items shown on the income statement.

The income statement summarizes the revenues earned and the expenses incurred by a business over a period of time. If revenues exceed expenses, then net income, also called "profit" or "earnings," results. However, if expenses exceed revenues, a net loss results. Nothing tells more about a company than its net income. Net income is used in the calculation of many important financial performance measures. A number of financial performance measures are described in Chapter 12: "Financial Statement Analysis."

An evaluation of net income involves not only the dollar amount of earnings, but the quality of earnings as well. **Quality of earnings** is an assessment of what makes up earnings and the likelihood that those earnings will continue in the future. Quality of earnings is associated with the accounting methods and

Quality of earnings is an assessment of what makes up earnings and the likelihood that those earnings will continue.

estimates used by management to measure income. Investors, lenders, and other financial statement users will want to know whether earnings are the result of a company's continuing operations or the result of something else. Depending on what generated the earnings, the company may be a better or worse investment, a relatively safe or risky loan customer.

For example, suppose Superior Electronics Corporation and Discount Electronics Corporation have the same net income. Both companies have increased net income by 10% each year for the past three years. Considering dollar amounts alone, the two companies appear very similar. However, Superior's earnings are the result of its manufacturing operations, while Discount Electronics' earnings resulted from selling off buildings and equipment that it no longer needed. Discount's manufacturing operations are actually in turmoil.

Superior Electronics has higher quality of earnings. The company has attained a steady increase in net income resulting from its manufacturing operations. This indicates that management can effectively run the company. On the other hand, Discount's net income resulted from selling assets, not from its operations. Superior Electronics is, therefore, a more attractive investment than Discount Electronics.

In discussing the items that impact a company's quality of earnings, we will be referring to the example income statement in Exhibit 11.1. The income statement is for Acrobatic Equipment Company, a company that manufactures gymnastic equipment sold to customers in the U.S. and other countries. The income statement starts with sales revenue and ends with net income on the "bottom line." In between, are several key items that will be discussed in the following paragraphs. All of these items should be considered when assessing a company's quality of earnings.

Exhibit 11.1 ACROBATIC EQUIPMENT COMPANY Income Statement For Year Ended December 31, 20Y1	
1 Sales Revenue	$200,000
2 Cost of Goods Sold	120,000
3 Gross Profit	$80,000
4 Operating Expenses	30,000
5 Operating Income	$50,000
6 Income Tax Expense	20,000
7 Income from Continuing Operations	$30,000
8 Discontinued Operations ($20,000 less income tax of $8,000)	12,000
9 Income before Extraordinary Item	42,000
10 Extraordinary Loss from Tsunami ($22,000 less income tax savings of $8,800)	(13,200)
11 Net Income	$28,800
Earnings per share on Common Stock (10,000 shares outstanding):	
12 Income from Continuing Operations	$3.00
13 Income from Discontinued Operations	1.20
14 Income before Extraordinary Item	$4.20
15 Extraordinary Loss	(1.32)
16 Net Income	$2.88

¶1102.01 CONTINUING OPERATIONS

Continuing operations for a company are reflected in its main source of revenue, or its core business line. Note that income from continuing operations comprises lines 1 to 7 in Exhibit 11.1. Normally, the company would be expected to have similar income from continuing operations in subsequent years. Notice that income tax expense amounts to $20,000, which is 40% of Acrobatic's operating income and includes both federal and state income taxes. For most U.S. companies, the combined federal and state income tax rate averages about 40%.

A company will try to increase income from continuing operations by increasing revenues, while reducing expenses where possible. This is a cross-functional effort, involving all departments in the company. For example, the marketing department may boost sales through additional salespeople, increased advertising, or identifying new uses for existing products. The production department may find ways to cut manufacturing costs. Techniques can be identified to make the manufacturing process more efficient and require fewer direct labor hours. In addition, the production department may be able to improve quality control, thus leading to less waste of raw materials and to fewer defective finished products.

The cost of goods for Acrobatic Equipment Company amounts to $120,000, which is 60% of sales revenue. Suppose the industry average is 45%. This means that competing firms are building products at a lower cost relative to sales price. Thus, they could sell their products at a lower price and still make a profit. The managers at Acrobatic would be concerned that competing firms would under-price them and, subsequently, entice customers to buy from them instead of Acrobatic.

This example shows how the income statement helps managers identify potential problems, so that corrective action can be taken. This problem would also be of concern to external persons such as investors and lenders. These external parties would question Acrobatic's ability to compete if the company has to spend so much more money to build its products. Even the ability of the company to survive may be questionable.

¶1102.02   INCOME TAX EXPENSE

Tax law determines tax payable and GAAP determines tax expense.

Federal tax law requires corporations to pay corporate income tax just as individuals must pay personal income tax. In addition to federal taxes, some corporations also pay state income taxes. The combined federal and state income tax rate averages about 40%. Accounting for income tax includes two items:

- A liability for Income Tax Payable on the balance sheet.
- An expense for Income Tax Expense on the income statement.

Income tax payable is usually a different amount from income tax expense. The rules for calculating income tax payable are not the same as the rules for calculating income tax expense. Income tax payable is the amount of income tax owed the government. Income tax expense is the amount calculated based on generally accepted accounting principles (GAAP). For example, Acrobatic Equipment Company must fill out its federal income tax return, based on tax laws passed by Congress, to compute its taxable income and resulting tax payable. The company prepares its income statement based on generally accepted accounting principles (GAAP) to compute its operating income and resulting tax expense. Thus, tax law determines tax payable and GAAP determines tax expense. Exhibit 11.2 illustrates the calculations of income tax per tax law and income tax per GAAP.

Exhibit 11.2 CALCULATING TAX EXPENSE AND TAX PAYABLE

Income Tax Payable	=	Tax Income (from income tax return and based on tax laws)	×	Income tax rate
Income Tax Expense	=	Operating Income Before Tax (from income statement and based on GAAP)	×	Income tax rate

Deferred income tax is the difference between income tax payable and income tax expense.

The difference between income tax payable and income tax expense is called "**deferred income tax.**" An example of an item that might lead to deferred income taxes is the depreciation of corporate assets. Acrobatic Equipment Company uses straight-line depreciation based on GAAP for financial reporting purposes and uses an accelerated depreciation method for tax preparation purposes. Acrobatic's depreciation expense is higher on its tax return than on its financial statements. As a result, Acrobatic's taxable income is less than the amount shown on its income statement (operating income before tax).

Acrobatic's tax return resulted in a tax payable of $17,000. The company's tax expense is $20,000, as determined by GAAP and shown on the income statement. The $3,000 difference was caused by different depreciation methods used for financial reporting and tax reporting. The entry to record the tax expense and tax liability is as follows:

Dec. 31	Income Tax Expense	20,000	
	Income Tax Payable		17,000
	Deferred Income Tax		3,000
	To record income tax.		

The income tax expense is shown on the income statement, while income tax payable and deferred income tax are reported on the balance sheet, as shown in Exhibit 11.3. In this case, deferred income tax has a credit balance and is a liability. In other years, income tax expense may have been less than income tax payable; in this case, deferred income tax would have a debit balance and would be an asset. Deferred income tax is a complex matter that is covered extensively in intermediate accounting courses.

Exhibit 11.3 INCOME TAX ON THE FINANCIAL STATEMENTS	
Income Statement	
Income Before Tax	$70,000
Income Tax Expense	(20,000)
Net Income	$50,000
Balance Sheet	
Current Liabilities:	
Income Tax Payable	$17,000
Long-Term Liabilities:	
Deferred Income Tax	3,000*

*Assumes that the beginning balance of Deferred Income Tax was zero, and that the deferral is long-term in nature.

Because GAAP and tax laws are different in some respects, a company must maintain two sets of accounting records, one based on GAAP, and a second based on tax law. Keeping two sets of records, or "books," may seem peculiar or even unethical to persons who don't understand that there is a difference between GAAP and tax law. Generally, however, small business firms simplify operations by maintaining their accounting records on the same basis as their tax return. This is permissible when there is no material difference in income per GAAP and income per tax law.

¶1102.03   DISCONTINUED OPERATIONS

A discontinued operation is a segment of a business that no longer operates.

A business segment is a division of a company.

A **discontinued operation** is a segment of a business that no longer operates. The majority of large publicly-traded companies are involved in more than one type of business. For example, the Walt Disney Company annual report describes four types of company operations: media networks, parks and resorts, studio entertainment, and consumer products. Each of these separately-reported company divisions is referred to as a "**business segment.**"

Occasionally, a corporation may sell one of its business segments. For example, JC Penney sold its Eckerd Drugstore business. In Penney's annual report, CEO Allen Questrom indicated that the company needed to focus on the department store and catalog/Internet opportunities as the priority to maximize shareholder value. JC Penney's discontinued operations that year, which included Eckerd, resulted in a loss of $1.29 billion.

Referring back to Exhibit 11.1, discontinued operations for Acrobatic Equipment Company resulted in a gain of $12,000 (line 8). The discontinued operations are shown net of tax ($20,000 less income tax of $8,000). If an investor or financial analyst were to estimate Acrobatic Equipment Company's *future* net income, the discontinued operations would be excluded from the calculation. Discontinued operations are just that, discontinued, and thus will cause neither a gain nor loss in the future.

¶1102.04   EXTRAORDINARY ITEMS

Extraordinary items are transactions that are characterized as both unusual and infrequent.

Extraordinary items, also called "extraordinary gains and losses," are events or transactions that are characterized as both unusual and infrequent, such as floods, fires, tornados, and hurricanes. Extraordinary items are shown separately from continuing operations. To qualify as unusual, an extraordinary item should be essentially unrelated to the company's usual business activities. To meet the definition of infrequent, an extraordinary item should not be anticipated to happen again in the foreseeable future.

Extraordinary items are customarily shown net of tax. For example, Acrobatic Equipment Company sustains losses of $22,000 resulting from a tsunami (Exhibit 11.1, line 10). The loss reduces Acrobatic's net income, which in turn reduces the company's income tax. Thus, the tax effect reduces the net amount of the loss. The extraordinary loss and the resulting tax effect could have been shown as follows:

Extraordinary loss from tsunami	$(22,000)
Less income tax saving	8,800
Extraordinary loss from tsunami, net of tax	$(13,200)

¶1102.05   OTHER GAINS AND LOSSES

Sometimes an item does not meet the criteria for unusual and infrequent, but the item is not part of continuing operations either. For example, gains and losses resulting from lawsuits, sales of fixed assets, or company restructurings are not extraordinary. These items would be reported as a separate line item designated "Other Gains and Losses." Other gains and losses are shown on the income statement immediately after Operating Income and before Income Tax Expense. Acrobatic Equipment Company did not have any "other" gains and losses.

¶1102.06   EARNINGS PER SHARE ON COMMON STOCK

$$\text{EPS} = \frac{\text{Net Income} - \text{Preferred Dividends}}{\text{Average Common Shares Outstanding}}$$

Earnings per share is the net income per share of outstanding common stock.

The last section of the income statement shows earnings per share information. The **earnings per share** (EPS) is the net income per share of a corporation's outstanding common stock. EPS is often used to evaluate a company's financial performance. The formula to calculate EPS is as follows:

A corporation shows the major components of its income on the income statement. GAAP requires the income statement to show a separate EPS calculation for the following components:

- Income (or loss) from continuing operations
- Income (or loss) before extraordinary items
- Net income (or net loss)

In addition to these, the income statement can also include the EPS amounts for the following:

- Income (or loss) from discontinued operations
- Extraordinary items (gain or loss)

The last section of Exhibit 11.1 reports the EPS amounts as follows:

Earnings per share on common stock (100,000 shares outstanding):	
Income from Continuing Operations	$3.00
Income from Discontinued Operations	1.20
Income before Extraordinary Item	$4.20
Extraordinary Loss	(1.32)
Net Income	$2.88

If a company has preferred dividends, these must be subtracted in the calculation of EPS. This is because preferred shareholders have the first claim to dividends and EPS is the earnings per share of common stock only. Suppose Acrobatic Equipment Company issued preferred dividends of $5,000. This would change the company's EPS amounts as shown in Exhibit 11.4.

Exhibit 11.4 IMPACT OF PREFERRED DIVIDEND ON EPS		
Earnings per share on Common Stock (10,000 shares outstanding):	No Preferred Dividend (Exhibit 10.1)	With $500 Preferred Dividend
Income from Continuing Operations ($30,000)	$3.00	$2.50*
Income from Discontinued Operations ($12,000)	1.20	1.20
Income before Extraordinary Item	$4.20	$3.70
Extraordinary Loss ($13,200)	(1.32)	(1.32)
Net Income	$2.88	$2.38

* **Note:** The preferred dividend is subtracted: ($30,000 – $5,000) / 10,000 shares.

¶1102.07 CAPITAL STRUCTURE AND EPS

A corporation with a complex capital structure has bonds, preferred stocks, or stock options that can be converted to common stock. A corporation without these convertible securities has a simple capital structure.

The capital structure of a corporation refers to the types of securities (i.e., stocks and bonds) that the company has issued. Preferred stocks and bonds can include a feature allowing them to be converted into common stock. As a result, a company with convertible stocks and bonds could potentially have many more shares of common stock. Another possible increase in common stock results from stock options.

A corporation with bonds, preferred stocks, or stock options that can be converted into common stock, is referred to as having a **complex capital structure**. A corporation without these convertible securities has a **simple capital structure**.

Companies with complex capital structures must show two sets of EPS amounts: basic EPS and diluted (reduced) EPS.

- Basic EPS are calculated using the average common shares outstanding.
- Diluted EPS are calculated using the average common shares outstanding plus any additional shares that would result from convertible securities or stock options, if exercised.

¶1102.08 COMPREHENSIVE INCOME

Comprehensive income is the change in stockholders' equity resulting from all sources other than from the stockholders.

On its income statement, Acrobatic Equipment Company shows a net income of $28,800. Net income increases stockholder's equity. There may be other items, not shown on the income statement, that also increase or decrease stockholders' equity. These additional items do not affect net income but are used to calculate comprehensive income. **Comprehensive income** is the change in stockholders' equity resulting from all sources other than from the stockholders themselves. Exhibit 11.5 shows the calculation of comprehensive income for Acrobatic Equipment Company during 20Y1.

Exhibit 11.5 ACROBATIC EQUIPMENT COMPANY Statement of Comprehensive Income (Partial) For Year Ended December 31, 20Y1			
Net Income			$28,800
Other Comprehensive Income:			
Foreign Currency Translation Adjustment (Gain)	$3,000		
Less Income Tax (40%)	(1,200)	1,800	
Unrealized Loss on Long-Term Investment	(2,000)		
Less Income Tax Saving (40%)	800	(1,200)	600
Comprehensive Income			$29,400

The Statement of Comprehensive Income for Acrobatic includes two items after net income. The first is foreign currency translation adjustment, a gain. The second is unrealized loss on long-term investment. Companies with international business operations typically experience gains and losses due to currency fluctuations. Foreign currency translation is further discussed in Chapter 14. Under the current rate method of foreign currency translation, the translation gain or loss is accumulated on a separate line in the stockholders' equity section of the balance sheet and has no impact on net income in the income statement. In this case, the foreign currency translation adjustment amounted to $1,800, net of tax.

The amount of income tax you, as an individual, owe the government is determined by tax laws; thus, would you label your income tax as "tax payable" or "tax expense?

Unrealized gains and losses on long-term investments were previously discussed in Chapter 8. In the case of Acrobatic Equipment Company, an unrealized loss on long-term investments amounted to $1,200, net of tax. Thus, comprehensive income is reduced by that amount.

A key goal of financial reporting, according to GAAP, is to enable investors, lenders, and other financial statement users to have a clear picture of a company's financial position. By reporting comprehensive income in addition to net income, financial statement users can gain a more complete understanding of the company's situation.

¶1103   Statement of Stockholders' Equity

> **LEARNING OBJECTIVE 3:** Prepare the statement of stockholders' equity.

Statement of Stockholders' Equity

> Reports the changes in all the stockholders' equity accounts.

The statement of stockholders' equity reports the changes in all the accounts shown in the stockholders' equity section of the balance sheet. The first line shows the beginning balance of the account and the last line, the ending balance. Between the first and last line are the results of transactions affecting the stockholders' equity accounts.

The statement of stockholders' equity for Acrobatic is shown in Exhibit 11.6. The columns include all the stockholders' equity accounts, with the last column showing the total stockholders' equity.

Exhibit 11.6 ACROBATIC EQUIPMENT COMPANY
Statement of Stockholders' Equity For Year Ended December 31, 20Y1

	Common Stock, $1 Par Value	Additional Paid-In Capital	Retained Earnings	Treasury Stock	Unrealized Gain (Loss) on Investments	Foreign Currency Translation Adjustment	Total Stockholders' Equity
Balance, Dec. 31, 2007	$50,000	$150,000	$64,000	($4,000)	$5,000	$7,200	$272,200
Issuance of Stock	8,000	48,000					56,000
Net Income			28,800				28,800
Cash Dividends			(6,000)				(6,000)
Stock Dividends	5,000	30,000	(35,000)				0
Treasury Stock Purchase				(2,200)			(2,200)
Unrealized Loss on Long-Term Investments					(1,200)		(1,200)
Foreign Currency Translation Adjustment (Gain)						1,800	1,800
Balance, Dec. 31, 2008	$63,000	$228,000	$51,800	($6,200)	$3,800	$9,000	$349,400

FOCUS ON TECHNOLOGY

Using Microsoft Excel: Utilizing Freeze Panes

Sometimes a worksheet contains so many columns, they extend beyond the screen view. This makes it difficult to know which label corresponds to an amount. The "Freeze Panes" command allows you to freeze the label column while scrolling through the other columns of data. In other words, you create a vertical freeze line where the left side of the line remains stationary, while the cells on the other side of the line can be scrolled.

To practice the "Freeze Panes" option with an Excel worksheet, type in the left column of labels along with the seven column headings from Exhibit 11.6 (Statement of Stockholders' Equity).

To use the "Freeze Panes" option, perform the following steps:

1. Click on the cell where you want the freeze to be. For a vertical freeze, the columns to the left of the cell will be frozen. Click on the first cell of the column (i.e., the heading "Common Stock"). For a horizontal freeze, the rows above the cell will be frozen.
2. Click on "Window" in the menu bar and select the Freeze Panes option. To remove the freeze, click on "Window" and select the Unfreeze Panes option.

¶1103.01

Retained earnings represent stockholders' claims to assets resulting from the company's earnings.

RETAINED EARNINGS

Retained earnings is the part of stockholders' equity that represents stockholders' claims to the assets generated from the company's earnings process. As shown in Exhibit 11.6, the statement of stockholders' equity includes retained earnings along with other stockholders' equity accounts. If a company prepares a statement of stockholders' equity, it takes the place of the statement of retained earnings because the statement of stockholders' equity includes more complete information about retained earnings, stock transactions, and related equity accounts. The statement of stockholders' equity is a more comprehensive alternative to the statement of retained earnings. The statement of stockholders' equity provides information about all the stockholders' equity transactions, including the following:

- Net income
- Issuing stock
- Cash dividends
- Stock dividends
- Treasury stock transactions
- Other comprehensive income

Other comprehensive income includes transactions such as unrealized gains (losses) on long-term investments and foreign currency translation adjustments. From the statement of stockholders' equity, you can review the equity transactions affecting Acrobatic Equipment Company. During this period, the following transactions occurred:

- Issued 8,000 shares of common stock when the stock price was $7 per share;
- Earned net income of $28,800;
- Paid a $6,000 cash dividend;
- Issued a stock dividend of 5,000 shares when the stock price was $7 per share;
- Purchased $2,200 of treasury stock;
- Incurred a $1,200 unrealized loss on long-term investments, net of tax; and
- Accrued a foreign currency translation gain of $1,800, net of tax.

Investors are interested in the statement of stockholders' equity for various reasons. Investors can find the company's earnings on the statement of stockholders' equity. Investors can see that Acrobatic had earnings of $28,800 for the year. The statement of stockholders' equity shows whether a company pays dividends. For investors who prefer stocks of companies that pay dividends, Acrobatic Equipment Company may be a good choice. The company paid a cash dividend and a stock dividend. The cash dividend of $6,000 was about 20% of the company's earnings.

The ending-balance information shown in the statement of stockholders' equity corresponds to the stockholders' equity section of the balance sheet. The stockholders' equity section of Acrobatics' balance sheet is shown in Exhibit 11.7.

Exhibit 11.7 ACROBATIC EQUIPMENT COMPANY Balance Sheet (Partial) December 31, 20Y1		
Total Assets		$476,400
Total Liabilities		127,000
Stockholders' Equity:		
Common Stock, $1 Par Value	63,000	
Additional Paid-In Capital	228,000	
Retained Earnings	51,800	
Treasury Stock	(6,200)	
Accumulated Other Comprehensive Income		
Unrealized Loss on LT Investments	3,800	
Foreign Currency Translation Adjustment	9,000	
Total Stockholders' Equity		349,400
Total Liabilities and Stockholders' Equity		$476,400

? *Do you retain or restrict any of your earnings for a specific purpose? If you do, why do you find this practice helpful?*

¶1103.02   RESTRICTIONS ON RETAINED EARNINGS

Retained earnings are necessary to pay dividends. Sometimes corporations choose to restrict retained earnings. A **restriction on retained earnings** indicates a portion of retained earnings that is unavailable for the payment of dividends.

The most common type of restriction on retained earnings is based on a contractual agreement. For example, when a bank loans money to a company, the bank may specify in the loan contract that a certain portion of the company's retained earnings be set aside for a specific use, such as the repayment of debt.

¶1104   Ethical and Legal Responsibility for the Financial Statements

LEARNING OBJECTIVE 4: Explain management's ethical and legal responsibility for the financial statements of a company.

Top management has an ethical and legal obligation to ensure that a company's financial statements are prepared properly. Stockholders, lenders, creditors, suppliers, customers, employees, and the government all rely on top management to lead a company in a way that is beneficial to everyone. Key to that leadership is accurately reporting the financial condition and results of operations in the company's financial statements. Top management has great power over a company's activities and, with great power, comes great responsibility.

In the U.S., the Sarbanes-Oxley Act of 2002 requires that a company's CEO (chief executive officer) and CFO (chief financial officer) certify the quality of the financial statements. Exhibit 11.8 is an excerpt from the certification of the CEO that was included in Yahoo's annual report.

Exhibit 11.8 MANAGEMENT'S RESPONSIBILITY FOR FINANCIAL STATEMENTS: EXCERPT FROM THE CEO'S CERTIFICATION

The Chief Executive Officer of Yahoo! Inc. certifies that:

1. I have reviewed this annual report on form 10-K of Yahoo! Inc.;

2. Based on my knowledge, this report does not contain any untrue statement of a material fact or omit to state a material fact necessary to make the statements made, in light of the circumstances under which such statements were made, not misleading with respect to the period covered by this report;

3. Based on my knowledge, the financial statements, and other financial information included in this report, fairly present in all material respects the financial condition, results of operations and cash flows of the registrant as of, and for, the periods presented in this annual report.

Excerpt from Certification of CEO Pursuant to Securities Exchange Act Rules 13a-14(a) and 15d-14(a) as Adopted Pursuant to Section 302 of the Sarbanes-Oxley Act of 2002.

Accountants for a company are responsible for preparing the financial statements. Additionally, in most countries, including the U.S., the law requires that external, independent auditors audit a company's financial statements. The company's accountants and the company's auditors must competently do their respective jobs and thereby ensure that the financial statements are reliable. Ultimately, however, the company's top management is responsible for the financial statements because when all is said and done, top management is in charge.

¶1105

? In what ways can you prepare yourself to be an ethical businessperson?

Concluding Remarks

We began the chapter asking if Yahoo had a good quality of earnings. You learned that quality of earnings is an assessment of what makes up earnings and the likelihood that those earnings will continue. Yahoo's quality of earnings is good since its earnings come from continuing operations that will likely carry on into the future. Other income statement items were discussed in the chapter, such as earnings per share (EPS). Yahoo's net income per share of outstanding common stock (i.e., EPS) was $0.91.

The chapter also began with a report of Yahoo's retained earnings and a question of why this is important to stockholders. You learned that retained earnings is reported on the statement of stockholders' equity and represents stockholders' claims to assets resulting from the company's earnings. After examining these two financial statements, we'll use the next chapter to look more closely at another financial statement – the statement of cash flows.

¶1106

Chapter Review

LEARNING OBJECTIVE 1

Describe the importance of the corporate income statement and statement of stockholders' equity to people within and outside the business firm.

Within a company, managers use the financial statements to assess a company's financial performance. Outside the company, investors and lenders use information from a company's financial statements to determine future prospects for obtaining a desired return on their investments or the timely repayment of loans. The income statement reports the firm's net income or earnings. The statement of stockholders' equity enables users to assess what caused the changes in equity.

LEARNING OBJECTIVE 2

Discuss key items shown on the income statement.

The income statement summarizes the revenues earned and the expenses incurred by a business over a period of time. If revenues exceed expenses, then net income, also called "profit," is the result. However, if expenses exceed revenues, then there is a net loss. Quality of earnings is an assessment of what makes up earnings and the likelihood that those earnings will continue in the future. Elements like discontinued operations, extraordinary items, and other gains and losses are items not related to ongoing operations.

LEARNING OBJECTIVE 3

Prepare the statement of stockholders' equity.

The statement of stockholders' equity reports the changes in all of the accounts shown in the stockholders' equity section of the balance sheet. This report includes retained earnings along with other stockholders' equity accounts, such as net income, issuing stock, cash dividends, stock dividends, and treasury stock transactions.

LEARNING OBJECTIVE 4

Explain management's ethical and legal responsibility for the financial statements of a company.

Management has an ethical and legal obligation to ensure that a company's financial statements are prepared properly. Stockholders, lenders, creditors, suppliers, customers, employees, and the government all rely on management to accurately report the financial condition and results of operations in the company's financial statements. In the U.S., the Sarbanes-Oxley Act of 2002 requires that a company's CEO and CFO certify the quality of the financial statements.

¶1107   Glossary

Business segment

A business segment is a division of a company; the financial statements of each business segment are reported separately.

Complex capital structure

A corporation with bonds, preferred stocks, or stock options that are convertible into common stock is referred to as having a "complex capital structure."

Comprehensive income

Comprehensive income is the change in stockholders' equity resulting from all sources other than the stockholders themselves.

Deferred income tax

Deferred income tax is the difference between a company's income tax payable and income tax expense.

Discontinued operation

A discontinued operation is a segment of a business that no longer operates.

Earnings per share

Earnings per share (EPS) is the net income per share of a corporation's outstanding common stock

Extraordinary items

Extraordinary items, also called "extraordinary gains and losses," are events or transactions that are characterized as both unusual and infrequent.

Quality of earnings

Quality of earnings is an assessment of what makes up earnings and the likelihood that those earnings will continue in the future.

Restriction on retained earnings

A restriction on retained earnings indicates that a portion of retained earnings is unavailable for the payment of dividends.

Retained earnings

Retained earnings are the part of stockholders' equity representing stockholders' claims to the assets that resulted from the company's earnings.

Simple capital structure

A corporation without convertible securities (i.e., bonds, preferred stocks, or stock options that are convertible into common stock) is referred to as having a "simple capital structure."

¶1108 Chapter Assignments

QUESTIONS

1. **[Obj. 1]** Why are stockholders interested in a company's "bottom line?"

2. **[Obj. 1]** Why are creditors and lenders interested in a company's "bottom line"?

3. **[Obj. 2]** Define "quality of earnings."

4. **[Obj. 2]** What are the characteristics of an extraordinary transaction?

5. **[Obj. 2]** What two items are included when accounting for income tax?

6. **[Obj. 2]** Why are the amounts for income tax payable and income tax expense usually different?

7. **[Obj. 2]** What is deferred income tax?

8. **[Obj. 2]** What is earnings per share?

9. **[Obj. 2]** What is the difference between a complex and simple capital structure?

10. **[Obj. 2]** What is comprehensive income?

11. **[Obj. 3]** How does a restriction on retained earnings affect the payment of dividends?

12. **[Obj. 3]** Why might a corporation put a restriction on retained earnings?

13. **[Obj. 3]** What information is reported in the statement of stockholders' equity?

14. **[Obj. 3]** How does the statement of stockholders' equity differ from the statement of retained earnings?

15. **[Obj. 4]** Why should top management make sure that the company's financial statements are prepared properly?

16. **[Obj. 4]** What requirement does the Sarbanes-Oxley Act of 2002 mandate for the CEO and CFO of a company regarding the company's financial statements?

SHORT EXERCISES – SET A

Building Accounting Skills

1. **[Obj. 1]** Importance of the Financial Statements: Explain why financial statements act as the report cards for a corporation.

2. **[Obj. 2]** Organizing the Income Statement: The following items can be found on a company's income statement. Identify the correct sequence of items, as they should be shown on the income statement. Begin with sales revenue and end with net income.
   ___ a. Sales revenue
   ___ b. Operating expenses
   ___ c. Income from continuing operations
   ___ d. Cost of goods sold
   ___ e. Net income
   ___ f. Extraordinary loss
   ___ g. Gross profit
   ___ h. Operating income
   ___ i. Income tax expense
   ___ j. Discontinued operations

3. **[Obj. 2]** Preparing the Income Statement: Fill in the missing amounts on the income statement for Tonka Tractor Company shown below. Assume the tax rate is 40%.

TONKA TRACTOR COMPANY Income Statement For Year Ended December 31	
Sales Revenue	$75,000
Cost of Goods Sold	a
Gross Profit	$35,000
Operating Expenses	15,000
Operating Income	b
Income Tax Expense	c
Income from Continuing Operations	$12,000
Discontinued Operations	4,8000
Income before Extraordinary Item	$16,800
Extraordinary Loss from Tornado (net of tax)	(1,800)
Net Income	d

4. **[Obj. 2]** Reporting Extraordinary Loss: Extraordinary items are customarily shown net of tax. Suppose Target Corporation sustained losses of $40,000 resulting from a tornado. The loss reduced Target's net income, which in turn reduces the company's income tax. Thus, the tax effect reduces the net amount of the loss. Assume a tax rate of 40%. How could the following be shown on the income statement: a) Extraordinary loss, b) Income tax saving, and c) Extraordinary loss, net of tax?

5. **[Obj. 2]** Reporting Extraordinary Loss: Extraordinary items are customarily shown net of tax. Suppose The Coffee Shop sustained losses of $100,000 resulting from a hurricane. The loss reduced the company's net income, which in turn reduces the company's income tax. Thus, the tax effect reduces the net amount of the loss. Assume a tax rate of 40%. Show how the following could be shown on the income statement: a) Extraordinary loss, b) Income tax saving, and c) Extraordinary loss, net of tax.

6. **[Obj. 2]** Reporting Extraordinary Loss: Extraordinary items are customarily shown net of tax. Suppose Hobby Lobby sustained losses of $200,000 resulting from a flood. The loss reduced the company's net income, which in turn reduces the company's income tax. Thus, the tax effect reduces the net amount of the loss. Assume a tax rate of 30%. Show how the following could be shown on the income statement: a) Extraordinary loss, b) Income tax saving, and c) Extraordinary loss, net of tax.

7. **[Obj. 2]** Reporting Extraordinary Loss: Extraordinary items are customarily shown net of tax. Suppose PetCo sustained losses of $50,000 resulting from a fire. The loss reduced the company's net income, which in turn reduces the company's income tax. Thus, the tax effect reduces the net amount of the loss. Assume a tax rate of 30%. Show how the following could be shown on the income statement: a) Extraordinary loss, b) Income tax saving, and c) Extraordinary loss, net of tax.

8. **[Obj. 2]** Computing Deferred Income Tax: Assume that the tax rate for Peters Vacuum Cleaner Company is 40%. Taxable income based on tax law is $40,000. Operating income before tax on the income statement and based on GAAP is $60,000. The difference between taxable income per tax laws and operating income before tax per GAAP was caused by different depreciation methods. Make the journal entry on December 31 to record income tax expense, income tax liability, and deferred income tax.

9. **[Obj. 2]** Computing Deferred Income Tax: Assume that the tax rate for Wisconsin Cheese Company is 40%. Taxable income based on tax law is $105,000. Operating income before tax on the income statement and based on GAAP is $130,000. The difference between taxable income per tax laws and operating income before tax per GAAP was caused by different depreciation methods. Make the journal entry on December 31 to record income tax expense, income tax liability, and deferred income tax.

10. **[Obj. 2]** Reporting Other Comprehensive Income: The statement of comprehensive income includes: (1) net income and (2) other comprehensive income items such as foreign currency translation adjustment and unrealized gains on long-term investments. Suppose Midas Muffler Company has net income of $50,000, a foreign currency translation adjustment of $6,000 before tax, and an unrealized gain on long-term investments of $12,000 before tax. Assume that the tax rate is 40%. Prepare the statement of comprehensive income.

11. **[Obj. 2]** Reporting Other Comprehensive Income: The statement of comprehensive income includes: (1) net income and (2) other comprehensive income items such as foreign currency translation adjustment and unrealized gains on long-term investments. Suppose Nebraska Corn Company has net income of $75,000, a foreign currency translation adjustment of $9,000 before tax, and an unrealized gain on long-term investments of $18,000 before tax. Assume that the tax rate is 40%. Prepare the statement of comprehensive income.

12. **[Obj. 3]** Preparing the Statement of Stockholders' Equity: Fill in the missing amounts in the statement of stockholders' equity for Nike Shoe Company.

NIKE SHOE COMPANY
Statement of Stockholders' Equity For Year Ended December 31, 20Y2

	Common Stock, $1 Par Value	Additional Paid-In Capital	Retained Earnings	Treasury Stock	Unrealized Gain (Loss) on Investments	Foreign Currency Translation Adjustment	Total Stockholders' Equity
Balance, Dec. 31, 20Y1	30,000	(b)	30,000	(2,000)	3,000	3,000	164,000
Issuance of Stock	5,000	20,000					25,000
Net Income			12,600				12,600
Cash Dividends			(3,000)				(3,000)
Stock Dividends	(a)	12,000	(15,000)				0
Treasury Stock Purchase				(d)			(1,000)
Unrealized Loss on Long-Term Investments					(1,200)		(1,200)
Foreign Currency Translation Adjustment (Gain)						(f)	900
Balance, Dec. 31, 20Y2	38,000	(c)	24,600	(3,000)	(e)	3,900	(g)

13. **[Obj. 4]** Ethical Issues Regarding Financial Statements: The Sarbanes-Oxley Act of 2002 requires a company's CEO (chief executive officer) and CFO (chief financial officer) to certify the quality of the financial statements. Review the certifications by the CEO in Exhibit 11.8 and consider why they are important.
   a. Summarize three of the certifications made by the CEO.
   b. Evaluate why top management makes these certifications.

SHORT EXERCISES – SET B

Building Accounting Skills

1. **[Obj. 1]** Importance of the Financial Statements: If you were the stockholder of a company, why would the statement of stockholders' equity be of interest to you?

2. **[Obj. 2]** Computing Net Income: The income statement for Buzz Yearbook Company includes the following items: sales revenue of $100,000, cost of goods sold of $60,000, operating expenses of $20,000, income tax expense of $10,000, and extraordinary loss of $5,000. What is the company's net income?

3. **[Obj. 2]** Preparing the Income Statement: Fill in the missing amounts on the income statement for Chaco's Chocolate Company shown below. Assume the tax rate is 50%.

CHACO'S CHOCOLATE COMPANY
Income Statement
For Year Ended December 31

Sales Revenue	$180,000
Cost of Goods Sold	a
Gross Profit	$90,000
Operating Expenses	40,000
Operating Income	b
Income Tax Expense	c
Income from Continuing Operations	$25,000
Discontinued Operations	8,000
Income before Extraordinary Item	$33,000
Extraordinary Loss from Earthquake (net of tax)	(3,000)
Net Income	d

4. **[Obj. 2]** Reporting Extraordinary Loss: Extraordinary items are customarily shown net of tax. Suppose Texas Roadhouse sustained losses of $20,000 resulting from a tornado. The loss reduced Texas Roadhouse's net income, which in turn reduced the company's income tax. Thus, the tax effect reduces the net amount of the loss. Assume a tax rate of 40%. Show how the following line items would be reflected on the income statement: a) Extraordinary loss, b) Income tax saving, and c) Extraordinary loss, net of tax.

5. **[Obj. 2]** Reporting Extraordinary Loss: Extraordinary items are customarily shown net of tax. Suppose the Cajun Company sustained losses of $50,000 resulting from a hurricane. The loss reduced the company's net income, which in turn reduces the company's income tax. Thus, the tax effect reduces the net amount of the loss. Assume a tax rate of 40%. How could the following be shown on the income statement: a) Extraordinary loss, b) Income tax saving, and c) Extraordinary loss, net of tax?

6. **[Obj. 2]** Reporting Extraordinary Loss: Extraordinary items are customarily shown net of tax. Suppose U-Haul sustained losses of $100,000 resulting from a flood. The loss reduced the company's net income, which in turn reduces the company's income tax. Thus, the tax effect reduces the net amount of the loss. Assume a tax rate of 30%. How could the following be shown on the income statement: a) Extraordinary loss, b) Income tax saving, and c) Extraordinary loss, net of tax?

7. **[Obj. 2]** Reporting Extraordinary Loss: Extraordinary items are customarily shown net of tax. Suppose Circuit City sustained losses of $200,000 resulting from a fire. The loss reduced the company's net income, which in turn reduces the company's income tax. Thus, the tax effect reduces the net amount of the loss. Assume a tax rate of 30%. How could the following be shown on the income statement: a) Extraordinary loss, b) Income tax saving, and c) Extraordinary loss, net of tax?

8. **[Obj. 2]** Computing Deferred Income Tax: Assume that the tax rate for Vega Motor Company is 50%. Taxable income based on tax laws is $100,000. Operating income before tax, based on GAAP, is $120,000. The difference between taxable income per tax laws and operating income before tax, per GAAP, was caused by different depreciation methods. Make the journal entry on December 31 to record income tax expense, income tax liability, and deferred income tax.

9. **[Obj. 2]** Computing Deferred Income Tax: Assume that the tax rate for Georgia Peach Company is 50%. Taxable income based on tax laws is $150,000. Operating income before tax, based on GAAP, is $180,000. The difference between taxable income per tax laws and operating income before tax per GAAP was caused by different depreciation methods. Make the journal entry on December 31 to record income tax expense, income tax liability, and deferred income tax.

10. **[Obj. 2]** Reporting Other Comprehensive Income: The statement of comprehensive income includes: (1) net income and (2) other comprehensive income items such as foreign currency translation adjustment and unrealized gains on long-term investments. Suppose Auto Parts, Inc. has net income of $100,000, a foreign currency translation adjustment of $12,000 before tax, and an unrealized gain on long-term investments of $24,000 before tax. Assume that the tax rate is 40%. Prepare the statement of comprehensive income.

11. **[Obj. 2]** Reporting Other Comprehensive Income: The statement of comprehensive income includes: (1) net income and (2) other comprehensive income items such as foreign currency translation adjustment and unrealized gains on long-term investments. Suppose Kentucky Horse, Inc. has net income of $75,000, a foreign currency translation adjustment of $8,000 before tax, and an unrealized gain on long-term investments of $16,000 before tax. Assume that the tax rate is 40%. Prepare the statement of comprehensive income.

12. **[Obj. 3]** Prepare the Statement of Stockholders' Equity: Fill in the missing amounts in the statement of stockholders' equity for Bath & Body Company shown below.

BATH & BODY COMPANY
Statement of Stockholders' Equity For Year Ended December 31, 20Y2

	Common Stock, $1 Par Value	Additional Paid-In Capital	Retained Earnings	Treasury Stock	Unrealized Gain (Loss) on Investments	Foreign Currency Translation Adjustment	Total Stockholders' Equity
Balance, Dec. 31, 20Y1	$40,000	(b)	$40,000	($2,000)	$3,000	$3,000	$234,000
Issuance of Stock	5,000	20,000					25,000
Net Income			12,600				12,600
Cash Dividends			(3,000)				(3,000)
Stock Dividends	(a)	12,000	(15,000)				0
Treasury Stock Purchase				(d)			(1,000)
Unrealized Loss on Long-Term Investments					(1,200)		(1,200)
Foreign Currency Translation Adjustment (Gain)						(f)	1,100
Balance, Dec. 31, 20Y2	$48,000	(c)	$34,600	($3,000)	(e)	$4,100	(g)

13. **[Obj. 4]** Ethical Issues Regarding Financial Statements: The Sarbanes-Oxley Act of 2002 requires a company's CEO and CFO to certify the quality of the financial statements. Review the role of the external auditor, company accountants, and the company's top management. Requirements: a) Summarize the roles of the external auditor, company accountants, and top management, and b) Evaluate the respective responsibility of each party.

PROBLEMS – SET A

Applying Accounting Knowledge

1. **[Obj. 2]** Preparing the Income Statement, Including Earnings Per Share (EPS): Suppose Volkswagen Corporation experienced the following revenues and expenses for the year ended December 31.

	($ Thousands)
Sales Revenue	$90,000
Cost of Goods Sold	$50,000
Operating Expenses	$18,000
Discontinued Operations (pre-tax)	$12,000
Extraordinary Loss (pre-tax)	($10,000)
Income Tax Rate	40.0%
Assume there are 10,000 shares of stock outstanding.	

Required: Prepare the income statement for Volkswagen Corporation, including the earnings per share section.

2. **[Obj. 2]** Calculating Earnings Per Share (EPS): Suppose Apple Corporation experienced the following revenues and expenses for the year ended Dec. 31.

	($ Thousands)
Sales Revenue	$50,000
Cost of Goods Sold	$25,000
Operating Expenses	$12,000
Discontinued Operations (pre-tax)	$8,000
Extraordinary Loss (pre-tax)	($4,000)
Income Tax Rate	40.0%
Assume there are 10,000 shares of stock outstanding.	

Required: Prepare the income statement for Apple Corporation, including the earnings per share section. What is Apple's income from continuing operations? What is the company's earnings per share for this period?

3. **[Obj. 2]** Calculating Earnings Per Share (EPS): Suppose BMW Corporation experienced the following revenues and expenses for the year ended Dec. 31.

	($ Thousands)
Sales Revenue	$420,000
Cost of Goods Sold	$214,000
Operating Expenses	$100,000
Discontinued Operations (pre-tax)	$30,000
Extraordinary Loss (pre-tax)	($20,000)
Income Tax Rate	30%
Number of Shares of Stock Outstanding	1,000

Required:

a. Prepare the company's income statement, including the earnings per share section.
b. What is the company's income from continuing operations?
c. What is the company's earnings per share for this period?
d. Evaluate: Assume sales revenue is $360,000, not $420,000. What is EPS?

4. **[Obj. 2]** Calculating Earnings Per Share (EPS): Suppose New Deal Car Company experienced the following revenues and expenses for the year ended Dec. 31.

	($ Thousands)
Sales Revenue	$630,000
Cost of Goods Sold	$380,000
Operating Expenses	$148,000
Discontinued Operations (pre-tax)	$30,000
Extraordinary Gain (pre-tax)	$15,000
Income Tax Rate	30%
Number of Shares of Stock Outstanding	1,000

Required:

a. Prepare the company's income statement, including the earnings per share section.
b. What is the company's income from continuing operations?
c. What is the company's earnings per share for this period?
d. Evaluate: Assume sales revenue is $550,000, not $630,000. What is EPS?

5. **[Obj. 2]** Calculate Impact of Preferred Dividends on Earnings Per Share (EPS): If a company has preferred dividends, these must be subtracted in the calculation of EPS. This is because preferred shareholders have the first claim to dividends and EPS is the earnings per share of common stock. Given the following financial information, determine the impact of the preferred dividend on EPS, that is, net income per share. [**Hint:** Use the format shown in Exhibit 11.4].

Income from Continuing Operations	$40,000
Income from Discontinued Operations (Net of Tax)	$8,000
Extraordinary Loss (Net of Tax)	$5,000
Number of Shares of Stock Outstanding	10,000
Preferred Dividend	$3,000

Required:

a. Complete the schedule of EPS, showing EPS with no preferred dividend and EPS with the preferred dividend.
b. Evaluate: Assume the preferred dividend is $12,000, not $3,000. Prepare a revised schedule.

6. **[Obj. 2]** Calculate Impact of Preferred Dividends on Earnings Per Share (EPS): If a company has preferred dividends, these must be subtracted in the calculation of EPS. This is because preferred shareholders have the first claim to dividends and EPS is the earnings per share of common stock. Given the following financial information, determine the impact of the preferred dividend on EPS, that is, net income per share. [**Hint:** Use the format shown in Exhibit 11.4].

Income from Continuing Operations	$184,000
Income from Discontinued Operations (Net of Tax)	$36,000
Extraordinary Loss (Net of Tax)	$68,000
Number of Shares of Stock Outstanding	10,000
Preferred Dividend	$40,000

Required:

a. Complete the schedule of EPS, showing EPS with no preferred dividend and EPS with the preferred dividend.
b. Evaluate: Assume the preferred dividend is $80,000, not $40,000. Prepare a revised schedule.

7. **[Obj. 2]** Prepare Statement of Comprehensive Income: Prepare a statement of comprehensive income for Bartles Beverage Company for the year ended December 31. Use the following information:

Net Income	$40,000
Foreign Currency Translation Adjustment (Gain), Pre-Tax	$14,000
Unrealized Loss on Long-Term Investment, Pre-Tax	$10,000
Tax Rate	40%

Required:

a. Prepare the statement of comprehensive income.

b. Evaluate: Assume the unrealized loss on long-term investment is $20,000, not $10,000. Prepare a revised schedule.

8. **[Obj. 2]** Prepare Statement of Comprehensive Income: Comprehensive income is the change in stockholders' equity resulting from all sources other than the stockholders themselves. Prepare a statement of comprehensive income for Landlocked Realty Company for the year ended December 31. Use the following information:

	($ Thousands)
Net Income	$684
Foreign Currency Translation Adjustment (Gain), Pre-Tax	$290
Unrealized Loss on Long-Term Investment, Pre-Tax	$120
Tax Rate	40%

Required:

a. Prepare the statement of comprehensive income.

b. Evaluate: Assume the foreign currency translation adjustment (gain) is $40,000 not $290,000. Prepare a revised schedule.

9. **[Obj. 3]** Preparing the Statement of Stockholders' Equity: Use the following information to prepare the statement of stockholders' equity for Nike Shoe Company: Issued 15,000 shares of common stock when the market price was $5 per share, paid a stock dividend of 10,000 shares when the market price was $5 per share, earned net income of $36,000, paid a $9,000 cash dividend, purchased $3,000 of treasury stock, incurred a $6,000 unrealized loss on long-term investments before tax, and accrued a foreign currency translation gain of $5,000 before tax. Assume that the tax rate is 40%.

Required: Complete the statement of stockholders' equity for Nike Shoe Company for the year ended December 31, 20Y2.

NIKE SHOE COMPANY Statement of Stockholders' Equity For Year Ended December 31, 20Y2							
	Common Stock, $1 Par Value	Additional Paid-In Capital	Retained Earnings	Treasury Stock	Unrealized Gain (Loss) on Investments	Foreign Currency Translation Adjustment	Total Stockholders' Equity
Balance, Dec. 31, 20Y1	$100,000	$300,000	$80,000	($7,000)	$8,000	$10,000	$491,000
Issuance of Stock							
Net Income							
Cash Dividends							
Stock Dividends							
Treasury Stock Purchase							
Unrealized Loss on Long-Term Investments							
Foreign Currency Translation Adjustment (Gain)							
Balance, Dec. 31, 20Y2							

10. **[Obj. 3]** Preparing the Statement of Stockholders' Equity: Use the following information to prepare the statement of stockholders' equity for Cairo Brick Company: Issued 20,000 shares of common stock when the market price was $4 per share, paid a stock dividend of 10,000 shares when the market price was $5 per share, earned net income of $36,000, paid a $24,000 cash dividend, purchased $18,000 of treasury stock, incurred an $8,000 unrealized loss on long-term investments (net of tax), and accrued a foreign currency translation gain of $22,000 (net of tax).

Required: Complete the statement of stockholders' equity for Cairo Brick Company for the year ended December 31, 20Y2.

CAIRO BRICK COMPANY
Statement of Stockholders' Equity For Year Ended December 31, 20Y2

	Common Stock, $1 Par Value	Additional Paid-In Capital	Retained Earnings	Treasury Stock	Unrealized Gain (Loss) on Investments	Foreign Currency Translation Adjustment	Total Stockholders' Equity
Balance, Dec. 31, 20Y1	$90,000	$320,000	$40,000	($2,000)	$5,600	$20,000	$473,600
Issuance of Stock							
Net Income							
Cash Dividends							
Stock Dividends							
Treasury Stock Purchase							
Unrealized Loss on Long-Term Investments							
Foreign Currency Translation Adjustment (Gain)							
Balance, Dec. 31, 20Y2							

PROBLEMS – SET B

Applying Accounting Knowledge

1. **[Obj. 2]** Preparing the Income Statement, Including Earnings Per Share (EPS): Suppose Office Depot experienced the following revenues and expenses for the year ended December 31.

	($ Thousands)
Sales Revenue	$180,000
Cost of Goods Sold	$110,000
Operating Expenses	$36,000
Discontinued Operations (pre-tax)	$24,000
Extraordinary Loss (pre-tax)	$20,000
Income Tax Rate	40.0%
Assume there are 10,000 shares of stock outstanding.	

Required: Prepare the income statement for Office Depot, including the earnings per share section.

2. **[Obj. 2]** Preparing the Income Statement, Including Earnings Per Share (EPS): Suppose The Bike Shop experienced the following revenues and expenses for the year ended December 31.

Sales Revenue	$30,000
Cost of Goods Sold	$10,000
Operating Expenses	$5,000
Discontinued Operations (pre-tax)	$3,000
Extraordinary Loss (pre-tax)	$2,000
Income Tax Rate	40.0%
Assume there are 10,000 shares of stock outstanding.	

Required: Prepare the income statement for The Bike Shop, including the earnings per share section.

3. **[Obj. 2]** Calculating Earnings Per Share (EPS): Suppose Oklahoma Buffalo Wings experienced the following revenues and expenses for the year ended Dec. 31.

Sales Revenue	$530,000
Cost of Goods Sold	$260,000
Operating Expenses	$130,000
Discontinued Operations (pre-tax)	$42,000
Extraordinary Loss (pre-tax)	$27,000
Income Tax Rate	30%
Number of Shares of Stock Outstanding	1,000

Required:

a. Prepare the company's income statement, including the earnings per share section.

b. What is the company's income from continuing operations?

c. What is the company's earnings per share for this period?

d. Evaluate: Assume sales revenue is $430,000, not $530,000. What is EPS?

4. **[Obj. 2]** Calculating Earnings Per Share (EPS): Suppose Kansas Oz Company experienced the following revenues and expenses for the year ended Dec. 31.

Sales Revenue	$350,000
Cost of Goods Sold	$200,000
Operating Expenses	$85,000
Discontinued Operations (pre-tax)	$20,000
Extraordinary Gain (pre-tax)	$12,000
Income Tax Rate	40%
Number of Shares of Stock Outstanding	1,000

Required:

a. Prepare the company's income statement, including the earnings per share section.

b. What is the company's income from continuing operations?

c. What is the company's earnings per share for this period?

d. Evaluate: Assume sales revenue is $450,000, not $350,000. What is EPS?

5. **[Obj. 2]** Calculate Impact of Preferred Dividends on Earnings Per Share (EPS): If a company has preferred dividends, these must be subtracted in the calculation of EPS. This is because preferred shareholders have the first claim to dividends and EPS is the earnings per share of common stock. Given the following financial information, determine the impact of the preferred dividend on EPS, that is, net income per share. [**Hint:** Use the format shown in Exhibit 11.4].

Income from Continuing Operations	$130,000
Income from Discontinued Operations (Net of Tax)	$25,000
Extraordinary Loss (Net of Tax)	$18,000
Number of Shares of Stock Outstanding	10,000
Preferred Dividend	$9,000

Required:

a. Complete the schedule of EPS, showing EPS with no preferred dividend and EPS with the preferred dividend.

b. Evaluate: Assume the preferred dividend is $18,000, not $9,000. Prepare a revised schedule.

6. **[Obj. 2]** Calculate Impact of Preferred Dividends on Earnings Per Share (EPS): If a company has preferred dividends, these must be subtracted in the calculation of EPS. This is because preferred shareholders have the first claim to dividends and EPS is the earnings per share of common stock. Given the following financial information, determine the impact of the preferred dividend on EPS, that is, net income per share. [**Hint:** Use the format shown in Exhibit 11.4].

Income from Continuing Operations	$340,000
Income from Discontinued Operations (Net of Tax)	$68,000
Extraordinary Loss (Net of Tax)	$88,000
Number of Shares of Stock Outstanding	10,000
Preferred Dividend	$75,000

Required:

a. Complete the schedule of EPS, showing EPS with no preferred dividend and EPS with the preferred dividend.

b. Evaluate: Assume the preferred dividend is $100,000, not $75,000. Prepare a revised schedule.

7. **[Obj. 2]** Prepare Statement of Comprehensive Income: Prepare a statement of comprehensive income for Mississippi River Company for the year ended December 31. Use the following information:

Net Income	$110,000
Foreign Currency Translation Adjustment (Gain), Pre-Tax	$45,000
Unrealized Loss on Long-Term Investment, Pre-Tax	$20,000
Tax Rate	40%

Required:
a. Prepare the statement of comprehensive income.
b. Evaluate: Assume the unrealized loss on long-term investment is $30,000, not $20,000. Prepare a revised schedule.

8. **[Obj. 2]** Prepare Statement of Comprehensive Income: Prepare a statement of comprehensive income for Connecticut Yankee Company for the year ended December 31. Use the following information:

	($ Thousands)
Net Income	$320
Foreign Currency Translation Adjustment (Gain), Pre-Tax	$140
Unrealized Loss on Long-Term Investment, Pre-Tax	$55
Tax Rate	40%

Required:
a. Prepare the statement of comprehensive income.
b. Evaluate: Assume the foreign currency translation adjustment (gain) is $90,000 not $140,000. Prepare a revised schedule.

9. **[Obj. 3]** Preparing the Statement of Stockholders' Equity: Use the following information to prepare the statement of stockholders' equity for Ukraine Computer Corporation: Issued 7,000 shares of common stock when the market price was $3 per share, paid a stock dividend of 2,000 shares when the market price was $3 per share, earned net income of $50,000, paid a $10,000 cash dividend, purchased $5,000 of treasury stock, incurred a $12,000 unrealized loss on long-term investments (net of tax), and accrued a foreign currency translation gain of $3,000 (net of tax).

UKRAINE COMPUTER CORPORATION
Statement of Stockholders' Equity For Year Ended December 31, 20Y4

	Common Stock, $1 Par Value	Additional Paid-In Capital	Retained Earnings	Treasury Stock	Unrealized Gain (Loss) on Investments	Foreign Currency Translation Adjustment	Total Stockholders' Equity
Balance, Dec. 31, 20Y3	$60,000	$90,000	$180,000	($10,000)	($12,000)	($30,000)	$278,000
Issuance of Stock							
Net Income							
Cash Dividends							
Stock Dividends							
Treasury Stock Purchase							
Unrealized Loss on Long-Term Investments							
Foreign Currency Translation Adjustment (Gain)							
Balance, Dec. 31, 20Y4							

Required: Complete the statement of stockholders' equity for Ukraine Computer Corporation for the year ended December 31, 20Y4.

10. **[Obj. 3]** Preparing the Statement of Stockholders' Equity: Use the following information to prepare the statement of stockholders' equity for Universal Glue Company: Issued 2,000 shares of common stock when the market price was $5 per share, paid a stock dividend of 4,000 shares when the market price was $5 per share, earned net income of $30,000, paid a $3,000 cash dividend, purchased $2,000 of treasury stock, incurred a $4,500 unrealized loss on long-term investments (net of tax), and accrued a foreign currency translation gain of $2,500 (net of tax).

Required: Complete the statement of stockholders' equity for Ukraine Computer Corporation for the year ended December 31, 20Y2.

UNIVERSAL GLUE COMPANY
Statement of Stockholders' Equity For Year Ended December 31, 20Y2

	Common Stock, $1 Par Value	Additional Paid-In Capital	Retained Earnings	Treasury Stock	Unrealized Gain (Loss) on Investments	Foreign Currency Translation Adjustment	Total Stockholders' Equity
Balance, Dec. 31, 20Y1	$100,000	$80,000	$20,000	($1,000)	$4,000	$2,000	$205,000
Issuance of Stock							
Net Income							
Cash Dividends							
Stock Dividends							
Treasury Stock Purchase							
Unrealized Loss on Long-Term Investments							
Foreign Currency Translation Adjustment (Gain)							
Balance, Dec. 31, 20Y2							

CROSS-FUNCTIONAL PERSPECTIVES

Discussion Questions

1. **[Obj. 2]** Within a firm, who has an impact on the firm's quality of earnings?

2. **[Obj. 2]** Outside the firm, who is interested in the quality of earnings?

3. **[Obj. 2]** List some ways that various departments within a company can help increase income by either increasing revenues or decreasing expenses.

Cross-functional Case: Yahoo Acquisition of Citizen Sports

Suppose you were part of the Yahoo project team when Yahoo acquired Citizen Sports, a company that creates sports applications linked to social media sites. Yahoo hopes the acquisition of Citizen Sports will help it expand the social networking aspects of its business. Yahoo can increase users of the sports applications by promoting the games on its website. Citizen Sports' products include fantasy football and other sports-related games that interact with social networking sites. Yahoo Sports already offers fantasy sports leagues to its users, but will be able to further link those leagues to social networks as a result of the acquisition.

Yahoo hopes the additional services and expansion of existing services will increase the number of Yahoo users. This should also give advertisers additional opportunities to target audiences with specific interests.

Required: Before proceeding with acquiring Citizen Sports, what issues would each of the following departments within Yahoo be concerned with?
a.   Accounting
b.   Finance
c.   Human resources
d.   Marketing

EXCEL ASSIGNMENTS

1.   **[Obj. 2]** Preparing the Income Statement, Including Earnings Per Share (EPS): Suppose AeroMexico Airlines Corporation experienced the following revenues and expenses for the year ended December 31.

	($ Thousands)
Sales Revenue	$140,000
Cost of Goods Sold	$78,000
Operating Expenses	$35,000
Discontinued Operations (pre-tax)	$6,000
Extraordinary Loss (pre-tax)	$20,000
Income Tax Rate	40.0%
Assume there are 10,000 shares of stock outstanding.	

Required:
a.   Prepare a worksheet with the items above in the input area and the income statement, including the earnings per share section, in the output area.
b.   If sales revenue is changed to $200,000 and all other items are unchanged, what is EPS (earnings per share)?

2.   **[Obj. 2]** Preparing the Income Statement, Including Earnings Per Share (EPS): Suppose Motorola Corporation experienced the following revenues and expenses for the year ended December 31.

	($ Thousands)
Sales Revenue	$40,000
Cost of Goods Sold	$10,000
Operating Expenses	$5,000
Discontinued Operations (pre-tax)	$8,000
Extraordinary Loss (pre-tax)	$4,000
Income Tax Rate	40.0%
Assume there are 10,000 shares of stock outstanding.	

Required:
a.   Prepare a worksheet with the items above in the input area and the income statement, including the earnings per share section, in the output area.
b.   If sales revenue is changed to $80,000 and all other items are unchanged, what is EPS (earnings per share)?

3. **[Obj. 2]** Preparing the Income Statement, Including Earnings Per Share (EPS): Suppose Sony Corporation experienced the following revenues and expenses for the year ended December 31.

	($ Thousands)
Sales Revenue	$80,000
Cost of Goods Sold	$20,000
Operating Expenses	$10,000
Discontinued Operations (pre-tax)	$16,000
Extraordinary Loss (pre-tax)	$8,000
Income Tax Rate	40.0%
Assume there are 10,000 shares of stock outstanding.	

Required:

a. Prepare a worksheet with the items above in the input area and the income statement, including the earnings per share section, in the output area.

b. If sales revenue is changed to $160,000 and all other items are unchanged, what is net income per share (i.e., EPS)?

4. **[Obj. 3]** Preparing the Statement of Stockholders' Equity: Use the following information to prepare the statement of stockholders' equity for Black Cat Rocket Company: Issued 5,000 shares of common stock when the market price was $4 per share, paid a stock dividend of 10,000 shares when the market price was $5 per share, earned net income of $22,200, paid a $4,000 cash dividend, purchased $1,000 of treasury stock, incurred a $5,000 unrealized loss on long-term investments before tax, and accrued a foreign currency translation gain of $10,000 before tax. Assume that the tax rate is 40%.

BLACK CAT ROCKET COMPANY
Statement of Stockholders' Equity For Year Ended December 31, 20Y2

	Common Stock, $1 Par Value	Additional Paid-In Capital	Retained Earnings	Treasury Stock	Unrealized Gain (Loss) on Investments	Foreign Currency Translation Adjustment	Total Stockholders' Equity
Balance, Dec. 31, 20Y1	$90,000	$270,000	$120,000	($3,000)	($4,000)	$10,000	$483,000
Issuance of Stock	5,000	15,000					
Net Income							
Cash Dividends							
Stock Dividends	10,000	40,000					
Treasury Stock Purchase							
Unrealized Loss on Long-Term Investments							
Foreign Currency Translation Adjustment (Gain)							
Balance, Dec. 31, 20Y2	$105,000	$325,000					

Required: Prepare a worksheet that shows the statement of stockholders' equity. Shown below is the partially completed statement of stockholders' equity.

5. **[Obj. 3]** Preparing the Statement of Stockholders' Equity: Use the following information to prepare the statement of stockholders' equity for Sam's Sign Company: Issued 3,000 shares of common stock when the market price was $5 per share, paid a stock dividend of 5,000 shares when the market price was $6 per share, earned net income of $10,200, paid a $1,000 cash dividend, purchased $2,000 of treasury stock, incurred a $4,000 unrealized loss on long-term investments before tax, and accrued a foreign currency translation gain of $5,000 before tax. Assume that the tax rate is 40%.

Required: Prepare a worksheet that shows the statement of stockholders' equity. Shown below is the partially-completed statement of stockholders' equity.

SAM'S SIGN COMPANY
Statement of Stockholders' Equity For Year Ended December 31, 20Y2

	Common Stock, $1 Par Value	Additional Paid-In Capital	Retained Earnings	Treasury Stock	Unrealized Gain (Loss) on Investments	Foreign Currency Translation Adjustment	Total Stockholders' Equity
Balance, Dec. 31, 20Y1	$40,000	$80,000	$60,000	($4,000)	$6,000	($2,000)	$180,000
Issuance of Stock	3,000	12,000					
Net Income							
Cash Dividends							
Stock Dividends	5,000	25,000					
Treasury Stock Purchase							
Unrealized Loss on Long-Term Investments							
Foreign Currency Translation Adjustment (Gain)							
Balance, Dec. 31, 20Y2	$48,000	$117,000					

6. **[Obj. 3]** Preparing the Statement of Stockholders' Equity: Use the following information to prepare the statement of stockholders' equity for Surf's Up Company: Issued 2,000 shares of common stock when the market price was $7 per share, paid a stock dividend of 4,000 shares when the market price was $6 per share, earned net income of $23,400, paid a $1,000 cash dividend, purchased $4,000 of treasury stock, incurred an $8,000 unrealized loss on long-term investments before tax, and accrued a foreign currency translation gain of $10,000 before tax. Assume that the tax rate is 40%.

Required: Prepare a worksheet that shows the statement of stockholders' equity. Shown below is the partially completed statement of stockholders' equity.

SURF'S UP COMPANY
Statement of Stockholders' Equity For Year Ended December 31, 20Y2

	Common Stock, $1 Par Value	Additional Paid-In Capital	Retained Earnings	Treasury Stock	Unrealized Gain (Loss) on Investments	Foreign Currency Translation Adjustment	Total Stockholders' Equity
Balance, Dec. 31, 20Y1	$60,000	$120,000	$110,000	($2,000)	$5,000	($4,000)	$289,000
Issuance of Stock	2,000	12,000					
Net Income							
Cash Dividends							
Stock Dividends	4,000	20,000					
Treasury Stock Purchase							
Unrealized Loss on Long-Term Investments							
Foreign Currency Translation Adjustment (Gain)							
Balance, Dec. 31, 20Y2	$66,000	$152,000					

WEB ASSIGNMENTS

1. **[Obj. 2]** Go to Yahoo's website, or do a Web search, in order to find the following figures from Yahoo's most recent income statement: revenue, gross profit, and net income. What was Yahoo's tax expense?

2. **[Obj. 2]** Go to Yahoo's website, or do a Web search, in order to find Yahoo's current earnings per share (EPS).

3. **[Obj. 4]** Go to the website for Yahoo, or do a Web search, and find Yahoo's corporate governance. Look at Yahoo's *Guide to Business Conduct and Ethics* and write a paragraph summarizing what is written about financial reporting at Yahoo.

4. **[Career]** Go to a website that lists careers (e.g., careers.yahoo.com) and find three job openings that are suitable for an accounting graduate. Give a brief job description along with a list of responsibilities and requirements for each job.

¶1109   # Test Prepper

Use this sample test to gauge your comprehension of the chapter material.

True/False Questions

__ 1. Quality of earnings is an assessment of the amount of earnings and how long the company has been profitable.

__ 2. Accounting for income tax includes a liability for Income Tax Payable on the balance sheet and an expense for Income Tax Expense on the income statement.

__ 3. Tax law determines tax expense and GAAP determines tax payable.

__ 4. Earnings per share is the revenue per share of a corporation's outstanding common stock.

__ 5. Comprehensive income is the change in stockholders' equity resulting from all sources other than from the stockholders.

__ 6. The statement of stockholders' equity provides more complete information than the statement of retained earnings.

__ 7. Retained earnings represent managers' claims to assets resulting from the company's earnings.

__ 8. Depreciation expense reduces net income but does not reduce cash; thus, cash flow is not affected by depreciation.

__ 9. The capital structure of a corporation refers to the types of securities (i.e., stocks and bonds) that the company has issued.

__ 10. Simple income is the change in stockholders' equity resulting from all sources other than from the stockholders themselves.

Multiple-Choice Questions

__ 1. Extraordinary items are transactions that are characterized as:
   a. Unusual
   b. Infrequent
   c. Costly
   d. a and b
   e. a and c

__ 2. The difference between the income tax payable and income tax expense is called:
   a. tax refund
   b. deferred income tax
   c. true income tax expense
   d. bottom line tax
   e. none of the above

__ 3. A corporation that has bonds, preferred stocks, or stock options that are convertible to common stock is considered to have what type of capital structure?
   a. Convertible
   b. Retained
   c. Complex
   d. Extraordinary
   e. Simple

__ 4. Which of the following reports the changes in all the accounts shown in the stockholders' equity section of the balance sheet?
   a. Income statement
   b. Statement of stockholders' equity
   c. Statement of cash flows
   d. Balance sheet
   e. All the financial statements

__ 5. Which of the following summarizes the revenues earned and the expenses incurred by a business over a period of time?
   a. Income statement
   b. Statement of stockholders' equity
   c. Statement of cash flows
   d. Balance sheet
   e. All the financial statements

__ 6. What is the term for the difference between income tax payable and income tax expense?
   a. Delayed income tax
   b. Deductible income tax
   c. Deferred income tax
   d. Discretionary income tax
   e. Delightful income tax

___ 7. Which of the following transactions concern debt and stockholders' equity?
a. Operating activities
b. Investing activities
c. Financing activities
d. Banking activities
e. All of the above

___ 8. What is the equation for earnings per share (EPS)?
a. (Net income – Preferred dividends) / Average common shares outstanding
b. Preferred dividends / Common shares outstanding
c. (Net income – Common shares outstanding) / Preferred dividends
d. Net income / Average common shares outstanding
e. (Net income + Preferred dividends) / Average common shares outstanding

___ 9. What is the term for the amount of income tax that a company owes the government?
a. Income tax incurred
b. Income tax expense
c. Income tax payable
d. Detained income tax
e. Unavoidable income tax

___ 10. What indicates that a portion of retained earnings is unavailable for the payment of dividends?
a. Retained earnings hold
b. Restriction on retained earnings
c. Complex capital structure
d. Simple capital structure
e. Comprehensive retained earnings

Chapter

12

The Statement of Cash Flows

LEARNING OBJECTIVES

After studying Chapter 12, you should be able to do the following:

1. Describe the importance of the statement of cash flows to people within and outside the business firm.
2. Explain the components within a statement of cash flows.
3. Prepare a statement of cash flows.
4. Demonstrate how to use the statement of cash flows to analyze a company's financial situation.

CHAPTER CONTENTS

The Statement of Cash Flows

FOCUS ON BUSINESS

Analyzing Cash Flows at Yahoo

The balance sheet for Yahoo! Inc. recently showed an increase in cash, from $1,429 million at the start of the year, to $1,569 million at the end of the year.

What were the sources of cash? The statement of cash flows shows that the $140 million increase in cash came from three major sources, as follows (in $millions):

Net cash flows from operating activities	$1,371
Net cash flows from investing activities	(193)
Net cash flows from financing activities	(1,094)
Minus effect of exchange rate changes	56
	$140

Yahoo's cash flow yield is 1.8 times ($1,371 net cash flows from operating activities divided by $751 net income). Thus, the company is generating a cash flow of about 180% of its net income. A cash flow yield greater than 100% is considered good cash-generating efficiency. This indicates that Yahoo has abundant cash flows in excess of cash needed for operations. In this chapter, you will learn what is involved in operating, investing, and financing activities, along with how these activities generate and spend cash.

Source: Yahoo! Annual Reports, *Yahoo.com*

¶1201 Applications to People Within and Outside the Firm

LEARNING OBJECTIVE 1: Describe the importance of the statement of cash flows to people within and outside the business firm.

The statement of cash flows shows the company's inflows and outflows of cash.

Because cash is often considered to be the lifeblood of a business, understanding the statement of cash flows is important to those inside and outside a business. The **statement of cash flows** shows the company's cash receipts and cash payments, that is, the inflows and outflows of cash. The statement of cash flows enables users, within the firm and outside the firm, to determine what caused the changes in cash. Understanding these changes is crucial for a person to accurately assess a company's financial strength.

¶1201.01 INTERNAL USERS

Within a company, managers use the statement of cash flows to determine sources and uses of cash during a period. By effectively understanding how cash is generated and paid out, management can plan for future cash needs and monitor how cash is used. Analysis of the information from the statement of cash flows helps managers at Yahoo understand how much cash the core operations of the business generate or how effectively the company uses its available cash. This knowledge is useful in budgeting for future operations.

¶1201.02 EXTERNAL USERS

Outside the company, investors use information from the statement of cash flows to determine future prospects for obtaining a desired return on their investment in the company and for identifying risk associated with such investments. Financial statement users often find that cash income is a stronger pre-

Regarding the management of your personal finances, do you have a good report card? How's your cash flow?

dictor of future earnings than net income. The valuable information for investors is summarized in the statement's operating, investing, and financing sections. Analysis of the statement of cash flows can help users outside the firm assess situations in which a company may be drowning in debt or not utilizing its cash effectively. Creditors of Yahoo rely on the statement of cash flows to predict whether Yahoo can pay its debts with regularity, while making good use of company resources.

¶1202   The Importance of Cash Flows

> **LEARNING OBJECTIVE 2:** Explain the components within a statement of cash flows.

As stated, the statement of cash flows shows the company's inflows and outflows of cash. While the balance sheet shows balances of certain accounts from one year to the next, it does not provide details of what caused the changes in account balances. The function of the statement of cash flows is to show what caused the changes in the account balance of cash for a given period.

Effective use of cash requires a cross-functional team effort by all departments within a company. Cash is essential to pay for the resources needed in daily operations. All departments must safeguard and wisely use the company's cash. For example, the marketing department should make efforts to ensure that sales are made only to customers who will ultimately pay off their account balances. The purchasing department, working with the treasurer, should help ensure that cash is paid accurately and on time, and only after purchased items have been received and inspected. Accountants provide the financial information that all departments need to evaluate the use of cash and other company assets.

The statement of cash flows classifies the activities of a business into three types: operating activities, investing activities, and financing activities. Examples of these activities are illustrated in Exhibit 12.1. Information contained in the statement of cash flows is based on the identification of changes in income statement and balance sheet accounts. Before preparing the statement of cash flows, an analysis of change in these account balances is required.

Exhibit 12.1 CASH INFLOWS AND OUTFLOWS FOR OPERATING, INVESTING, AND FINANCING ACTIVITIES

Activities	Cash Inflows	Cash Outflows
Operating	Sale of goods and services to customers	Pay wages
	Receipt of interest or dividends on loans or investments	Purchase inventory
	Sale of trading securities	Pay interest
		Pay taxes
		Purchase trading securities
		Pay expenses
Investing	Sale of property, plant, and equipment and other long-term assets	Purchase property, plant, and equipment and other long-term assets
	Sale of long- or short-term held-to-maturity and available-for-sale securities	Purchase long-term or short-term held-to-maturity and available-for-sale securities
Financing	Sale of preferred or common stock	Reacquire preferred or common stock
	Issuance of debt	Repay debt
		Pay dividends

Statement of Cash Flows

> Opperating Activities
> + Investing Activities
> + Financing Activities
>
> Net Increase (Decrease) in Cash

Preparing a statement of cash flows involves four basic steps:

1. Calculate cash flows from operating activities.
2. Calculate cash flows from investing activities.
3. Calculate cash flows from financing activities.
4. Add the results of the above three steps to obtain net changes in cash for the period.

¶1202.01 OPERATING ACTIVITIES

Operating activities involve the day-to-day transactions of a business.

Of the three activities listed in the statement of cash flows, **operating activities** are most significant because they represent the day-to-day transactions. In daily operations, cash receipts are collected from customers and cash payments are made to suppliers and other external parties. Cash is also disbursed for expenses such as employee wages, rent, and taxes. The day-to-day transactions generate revenues, expenses, gains, and losses in the company's primary line of business. Managing operating cash flows is vital to a company's financial success.

Information contained in the operating section of the statement of cash flows is taken from the income statement and current portion of the balance sheet. The income statement, also called the "statement of operations," reports the impact of operating activities on net income. Balance sheet accounts like current assets and current liabilities are affected by operating activities, not cash. For example, a credit sale to a customer increases sales revenue on the income statement and increases accounts receivable on the balance sheet.

¶1202.02 INVESTING ACTIVITIES

Investing activities involve long-term assets and investments.

Investing activities are transactions that involve the purchase and sale of long-term assets and investments. Purchasing and selling land, equipment, or long-term investments are examples of investing activities. Management strives to invest capital in ways that are productive and will help achieve a firm's objectives.

¶1202.03 FINANCING ACTIVITIES

Financing activities involve debt or stockholders' equity.

There are two major ways a company can finance its operations – issue stock or issue debt. Thus, **financing activities** are transactions involving debt or stockholders' equity. Borrowing from and repaying creditors are financing activities. Obtaining cash from and returning cash to stockholders are financing activities. For example, paying a cash dividend reduces cash and retained earnings. In other words, financing activities involve obtaining resources from owners and providing them with a return on their investments, as well as obtaining resources from creditors and repaying the amount borrowed.

¶1203 Preparing the Statement of Cash Flows

> **LEARNING OBJECTIVE 3:** Prepare a statement of cash flows.

The statement of cash flows can be prepared using either the indirect method or the direct method. Both methods show cash flows from operating activities, investing activities, and financing activities. Both methods must conform to GAAP. However, as shown in Exhibit 12.2, the difference between the two methods is the manner in which cash flows from operating activities are reported:

- **Indirect Method:** Makes adjustments to only selected income statement items – those necessary to convert net income into net cash flows from operating activities.
- **Direct Method:** Makes adjustments to all items on the income statement by converting them from the accrual basis to the cash basis, in order to obtain net cash flows from operating activities.

Exhibit 12.2 COMPARING THE INDIRECT METHOD TO THE DIRECT METHOD:
Preparing the Statement of Cash Flows

Indirect Method		Direct Method	
Net income	$X,XXX	Cash receipts from customers	$X,XXX
Adjustments:		Deductions:	
Depreciation, etc.	X,XXX	Cash payments	X,XXX
Net cash flows from operating activities	$X,XXX	Net cash flows from operating activities	$X,XXX

As you can see in Exhibit 12.2, under the indirect method, depreciation is an adjustment to net income to determine net cash flows. When using the accrual basis of accounting, depreciation creates an expense that reduces net income. However, depreciation expense does not cause an outflow of cash; thus, the amount of depreciation expense must be added back to net income to calculate net cash flows. Under the direct method, cash receipts and cash payments are reported. Thus, under the direct method, there is no adjustment for depreciation expense; it is not shown in the calculation because depreciation is neither a receipt nor payment of cash.

Both methods convert income statement items from the accrual basis to the cash basis and both methods achieve the same result. The indirect method is the more widely-used method. Due to its simpler format, more than 90% of business firms use the indirect method. Preparation of a statement of cash flows, using the indirect method, for BLT Corporation is shown in the next section. Companies prefer the indirect method because it is easier to prepare, and it focuses on the differences between net income and net cash flow from operating activities.

¶1203.01   INDIRECT METHOD FOR PREPARING THE STATEMENT OF CASH FLOWS

As shown in Exhibit 12.3, the indirect method begins with net income and then adjusts the income items that do not impact cash. Items that reduce net income, but do not reduce cash, are positive adjustments. Examples of positive adjustments include depreciation, loss on sale of plant assets, decreases in current assets other than cash, and increases in current liabilities.

Exhibit 12.3 PREPARING THE STATEMENT OF CASH FLOWS USING THE INDIRECT METHOD: ADJUSTMENTS

Cash flows from operating activities:

Net income

Adjustments to reconcile net income to net cash flows provided by operating activities:

+	Depreciation expense
+	Loss on sale of plant assets
−	Gain on sale of plant assets
−	Increases in current assets other than cash
+	Decreases in current assets other than cash
+	Increases in current liabilities
−	Decreases in current liabilities

Net cash flows from operating activities

Cash flows from investing activities:

+	Sales of plant assets (e.g., investments, land, building, and equipment)
−	Purchases of plant assets
+	Collections of long-term receivables
−	Long-term loans to others

Net cash flows from investing activities

Cash flows from financing activities:

+	Issuance of stock
+	Sale of treasure stock
−	Purchase of treasury stock
+	Borrowing (issuing notes or bonds payable)
−	Payment of notes or bonds payable
−	Payment of dividends

Net cash flows from financing activities

Net increase (decrease) in cash during the year

+	Cash at December 31, 20Y1
=	Cash at December 31, 20Y2

Items that increase net income but do not increase cash are negative adjustments. Examples of negative adjustments include a gain on the sale of plant assets, increases in current assets other than cash, and decreases in current liabilities.

Let's examine how to prepare a statement of cash flows for BLT Corporation using the indirect method. To prepare this statement, we will need the following information:

- Comparative balance sheets for 20Y1 and 20Y2 (Exhibit 12.4)
- Income statement for 20Y2 (Exhibit 12.5)
- Transactions affecting non-current accounts

Exhibit 12.4 BLT CORPORATION
Comparative Balance Sheets December 31, 20Y2

	20Y2	20Y1	Change	Increase or (Decrease)
		Assets		
Current Assets:				
Cash	$65,000	$38,000	$27,000	Increase
Accounts Receivable (net)	24,500	25,000	(500)	Decrease
Inventory	66,600	94,000	(27,400)	Decrease
Prepaid Expenses	35,500	32,000	3,500	Increase
Total Current Assets	$191,600	$189,000	$2,600	
Investments Available for Sale	112,200	78,000	34,200	Increase
Plant Assets				
Plant Assets	$320,000	$290,000	$30,000	Increase
Accumulated Depreciation	(96,800)	(78,000)	(18,800)	Increase
Total Plant Assets	223,200	212,000	11,200	
Total Assets	$527,000	$479,000	$48,000	
		Liabilities		
Current Liabilities				
Accounts Payable	$147,000	$117,000	$30,000	Increase
Accrued Liabilities	29,000	9,000	20,000	Increase
Income Tax Payable	27,000	33,000	(6,000)	Decrease
Total Current Liabilities	203,000	$159,000	$44,000	
Long-Term Liabilities				
Notes Payable	170,000	190,000	(20,000)	Decrease
Total Liabilities	$373,000	$349,000	$24,000	
		Stockholder's Equity		
Common Stock, $10 par value	$70,000	$60,000	$10,000	Increase
Additional Paid-In Capital	69,000	59,000	10,000	Increase
Retained Earnings	15,000	11,000	4,000	Increase
Total Stockholder's Equity	154,000	130,000	24,000	
Total Liabilities and Stockholder's Equity	$527,000	$479,000	$48,000	

Exhibit 12.5 BLT CORPORATION
Income Statement For Year Ended December 31, 20Y2

Sale Revenue		$380,000
Cost of Goods Sold		270,000
Gross Profit		$110,000
Operating Expenses (including Depreciation Expense of $45,800)		89,000
Operating Income		$21,000
Other Income (Expenses)		
Interest Income	$8,000	
Loss on Sale of Investments	(14,000)	
Gain on Sale of Plant Assets	7,000	1,000
Income Before Income Taxes		$22,000
Income Tax Expense		8,800
Net Income		$13,200

Other transactions affecting noncurrent accounts in 20Y2:

1. Purchased investments for $104,200
2. Sold investments for $56,000 that cost $70,000
3. Purchased plant assets for $20,000
4. Sold plant assets that cost $30,000, with accumulated depreciation of $27,000, for $10,000
5. Issued $40,000 of notes at face value in a noncash exchange for plant assets
6. Repaid $60,000 of notes at face value at maturity
7. Issued 1,000 shares of $10 par value common stock for $20,000
8. Paid cash dividends of $9,200

¶1203.02   OPERATING ACTIVITIES

Converting BLT's net income to net cash flows from operating activities is shown in Exhibit 12.6. Net income is listed at the top, followed by adjustments that convert the accrual-based net income amount into the net cash flow from operating activities. In effect, the accrual-based income statement is converted into a cash-based income statement. While investors and lenders are interested in a company's accrual-based net income, they also pay close attention to whether a company can produce the cash necessary to carry out company operations. This information is provided in the statement of cash flows.

Exhibit 12.6 BLT CORPORATION
Schedule of Cash Flows from Operating Activities (Using the Indirect Method)
For Year Ended December 31, 20Y2

Cash Flows from Operating Activities		
Net Income		$13,200
Adjustments to Reconcile Net Income to Net Cash Flows from Operating Activities		
Depreciation	$45,800	
Loss on Sale of Investments	14,000	
Gain on Sale of Plant Assets	(7,000)	
Changes in Current Assets and Current Liabilities		
Decrease in Accounts Receivable	500	
Decrease in Inventory	27,400	
Increase in Prepaid Expenses	(3,500)	
Increase in Accounts Payable	30,000	
Increase in Accrued Liabilities	20,000	
Decrease in Income Tax Payable	(6,000)	121,200
Net Cash Flows from Operating Activities		$134,400

¶1203.02.01 Depreciation

Depreciation is one of the common adjustments to net income required when preparing the statement of cash flows. At the end of the year, BLT Corporation recorded depreciation as follows:

Depreciation Expense	45,800	
Accumulated Depreciation		45,800
To record annual depreciation on plant assets.		

Remember that depreciation expense reduces net income but does not reduce cash. Since cash flow is not affected by depreciation, the amount recorded as depreciation expense must be added back to BLT's net income for determining net cash flows. Companies may have other expenditures, such as amortization expense, that reduce net income but do not reduce cash. These other non-cash expenditures would be treated in the same way as depreciation on the statement of cash flows.

¶1203.02.02 Gains and Losses

Like depreciation expense, gains and losses affect net income but do not affect cash flows. Consequently, gains and losses are adjustments to net income to determine net cash flows from operating activities. For example, BLT reported a $14,000 loss on sale of investments. Because a loss reduced net income, this $14,000 is added back to net income to convert net income to net cash flows from operating activities.

BLT reports a $7,000 gain on the sale of plant assets, which increases net income by $7,000 but does not affect cash flows. Thus, the $7,000 gain is deducted from net income to convert net income to net cash flows.

¶1203.02.03 Changes in Current Assets

The next step in preparing the statement of cash flows is to examine any changes that have occurred in the balances of current asset accounts:

- An increase in current assets other than cash has a negative effect on cash flows.
- A decrease in current assets other than cash has a positive effect on cash flows.

For example, accounts receivable started the year with $25,000 and ended the year with $24,500 (Exhibit 12.4). Sales revenue was $380,000 (Exhibit 12.5). This means that while BLT's sales were $380,000, the company actually collected $380,500 in cash, so BLT collected some cash from sales made before the current year. In other words, at the end of the year, accounts receivable will have a net decrease if the cash collected exceeds the total amount of sales. As a result, the amount of the decrease is added to net income to determine the net cash flows.

The same logic that is applied to accounts receivable is applied to other current asset accounts. Since inventory decreased by $27,400, this means that BLT spent $27,400 less in cash for purchases than was included in cost of goods sold on the income statement. Consequently, $27,400 is added to net income to derive net cash flows. Prepaid expenses increased from $32,000 to $35,500. Therefore, the increase of $3,500 in prepaid expenses leads to a negative adjustment to net income.

¶1203.02.04 Changes in Current Liabilities

Next, any changes in the balances of current liability accounts should be examined:

- An increase in current liabilities results in a positive adjustment to net cash flows.
- A decrease in current liabilities results in a negative adjustment.

As you can see, these result in the opposite effects of the changes in current assets. For example, as shown in Exhibit 12.4, BLT had a $30,000 increase in Accounts Payable from 20Y1 to 20Y2. This means that BLT paid $30,000 less to creditors than its purchases (included in cost of goods sold) on the income statement. Consequently, $30,000 is added to net income to determine net cash flows.

For the same reason, the increase of $20,000 in Accrued Liabilities is added to net income. Finally, the decrease of $6,000 in Income Tax Payable is deducted from net income to derive net cash flows from operating activities.

¶1203.02.05 Schedule of Cash Flows from Operating Activities

To recap, Exhibit 12.6 reports that by using the indirect method, BLT's net income of $13,200 is adjusted by $121,200, yielding $134,400 in net cash flows from operating activities. In other words, while BLT's net income is $13,200, the company has actual cash flows from operating activities of $134,400 that can be used to pay off debts, buy assets, or pay dividends.

¶1203.03   INVESTING ACTIVITIES

Investing activities are addressed in the second section of the statement of cash flows. Investing activities concern long-term assets and both short-term and long-term investments. The comparative balance sheets for BLT Corporation, shown in Exhibit 12.4, report two long-term assets: investments available for sale and plant assets, but no short-term investments. First, let's examine investment-related transactions that affect BLT Corporation's cash flows.

¶1203.03.01 Investments

BLT's income statement, shown in Exhibit 12.5, reports two investment-related activities: a $14,000 loss on the sale of investments and a $7,000 gain on the sale of plant assets. In addition, the list at the bottom of the exhibit reports five transactions regarding investing activities in 20Y2. These include:

1. Purchased investments for $104,200
2. Sold investments for $56,000 that cost $70,000
3. Purchased plant assets for $20,000
4. Sold plant assets that cost $30,000 with accumulated depreciation of $27,000, for $10,000
5. Issued $40,000 of notes at face value in a noncash exchange for plant assets

The purchase of investments decreases cash and the sale of investments increases cash. The purchase transaction is recorded as a use of cash:

Investments	104,200	
Cash		104,200
To record purchase of investments.		

The sale of investments is recorded as a source of cash:

Cash	56,000	
Loss on Sale of Investments	14,000	
Investments		70,000
To record sale of investments at a loss.		

The effect of the two transactions is a net increase in the Investments account of $34,200 (+$104,200 – $70,000) and a net decrease in Cash of $48,200 (+$56,000 – $104,200). The $14,000 loss on the sale does not decrease cash and was previously included as a positive adjustment in determining net cash flows from operating activities. Next, we examine the company's activities in regard to its plant assets.

¶1203.03.02 Plant Assets

In Exhibit 12.5, we see that several transactions affected plant assets:

- Purchased plant assets for $20,000
- Sale of plant assets for $10,000
- Exchange of $40,000 note payable for plant assets

The purchase of plant assets for $20,000 decreases cash and the sale of plant assets for $10,000 increases cash. The purchase is recorded as shown:

Plant Assets	20,000	
Cash		20,000
To record purchase of plant assets.		

The sale of plant assets is recorded as shown:

Cash	10,000	
Accumulated Depreciation	27,000	
Gain on Sale of Plant Assets		7,000
Plant Assets		30,000
To record sale of plant assets at a gain of $7,000.		

The third transaction affecting plant assets is the exchange of notes payable for plant assets. The transaction is recorded as shown:

Plant Assets	40,000	
Notes Payable		40,000
To record notes issued at face value in exchange for plant assets.		

Reporting investing and financing activities is one of the purposes of the statement of cash flows. The issue of notes payable for plant assets does not affect cash flows, but does involve investing (purchase of plant assets) and financing (issuing notes payable) activities. As a result, the transaction is reported on a separate schedule or at the bottom of the statement of cash flows, as shown in Exhibit 12.7:

Schedule of Noncash Investing and Financing Transactions	
Issue of Notes for Plant Assets	$40,000

The effect of the three transactions on plant assets is a net increase of $30,000 (+ $20,000 – $30,000 + $40,000). The Accumulated Depreciation account is decreased by $27,000 as a result of the sale of plant assets. Accumulated Depreciation was increased by $45,800 with the annual depreciation adjusting entry. Thus, Accumulated Depreciation has a net increase of $18,800 (– $27,000 + $45,000).

¶1203.04 FINANCING ACTIVITIES

Financing activities are the third and final part of the statement of cash flows. Financing transactions concern short-term and long-term borrowing (debt) and stockholders' equity accounts. The transactions, shown in Exhibit 12.5, that concern BLT's financing activities are as follows:

- Issued $40,000 of notes at face value in a noncash exchange for plant assets
- Repaid $60,000 of notes at face value at maturity
- Issued 1,000 shares of $10 par value common stock for $20,000
- Paid cash dividends of $9,200

¶1203.04.01 Notes Payable

The issuance of notes at face value and repayment of notes at face value cause a net decrease in notes payable of $20,000 (+$40,000 – $60,000). When BLT issues notes for plant assets, there is no effect on cash flows. Thus, this transaction is reported in the Schedule of Noncash Investing and Financing Transactions shown at the bottom of the Statement of Cash Flows (Exhibit 12.7). The pay-off causes a $60,000 decrease in cash and is recorded as shown:

Notes Payable	60,000	
Cash		60,000
To record repayment of notes at face value at maturity.		

¶1203.04.02 Common Stock

The issue of 1,000 shares of $10 par value common stock for $20,000 is recorded as follows:

Cash	20,000	
Common Stock		10,000
Additional Paid-In Capital		10,000
To record issue of 1,000 shares of $10 par value common stock.		

This transaction accounts for the increases in the Common Stock and the Additional Paid-In accounts, as shown on the comparative balance sheets (Exhibit 12.4).

¶1203.04.03 Retained Earnings

Next, let's examine the Retained Earnings account to determine what kind of transactions caused the balance to change. Retained Earnings is increased by net income of $13,200 and decreased by the payment of dividends of $9,200, resulting in a $4,000 net increase. This $4,000 net increase in Retained Earnings is shown in Exhibit 12.4. Note that cash is involved only when the dividends are paid. The declaration of dividends involves no cash flows.

¶1203.05   NET INCREASE (DECREASE) IN CASH

Exhibit 12.7 shows the statement of cash flows using the indirect method. Note that the final three lines of the statement lists the net increase or decrease in cash for the period, along with the balances of cash at the beginning and end of the year. By using these balances, the accountant can be sure that all transactions affecting cash have been reported. At the bottom of the statement, the Schedule of Noncash Investing and Financing Transactions is shown. BLT reports a $27,000 increase in cash, resulting in $65,000 cash at the end of the year.

Exhibit 12.7 BLT CORPORATION
Statement of Cash Flows (Using the Indirect Method) For Year Ended December 31, 20Y2

Cash Flows from Operating Activities		
Net Income		$13,200
Adjustments to Reconcile Net Income to Net Cash Flows from Operating Activities		
Depreciation	$45,800	
Gain on Sale of Plant Assets	(7,000)	
Loss on Sale of Investments	14,000	
Changes in Current Assets and Current Liabilities		
Decrease in Accounts Receivable	500	
Decrease in Inventory	27,400	
Increase in Prepaid Expenses	(3,500)	
Increase in Accounts Payable	30,000	
Increase in Accrued Liabilities	20,000	
Decrease in Income Tax Payable	(6,000)	121,200
Net Cash Flows from Operating Activities		$134,400
Cash Flows from Investing Activities		
Purchase of Investments	$(104,200)	
Sale of Investments	56,000	
Purchase of Plant Assets	(20,000)	
Sale of Plant Assets	10,000	
Net Cash Flows from Investing Activities		(58,200)
Cash Flows from Financing Activities		
Repayment of Notes	$(60,000)	
Issue of Common Stock	20,000	
Dividends Paid	(9,200)	
Net Cash Flows from Financing Activities		(49,200)
Net Increase (Decrease) in Cash		$27,000
Cash at Beginning of Year		38,000
Cash at End of Year		$65,000
Schedule of Noncash Investing and Financing Transactions		
Issue of Notes for Plant Assets		$40,000

People who are interested in BLT Corporation's cash flows include the company management, as well as external users such as investors and lenders. Management needs to know if cash is available to carry on company operations. Investors and lenders will use cash flow information to make better decisions about whether to buy the company's stock or to loan money to the company, respectively. If a company's cash flow situation is not good, unethical managers might be tempted to manipulate transactions for the purpose of making the situation appear better than it really is.

One way that the statement of cash flows can be manipulated, involves current liabilities. For example, under the indirect method, an increase in accounts payable results in an increase in cash flows; the increase is shown in the operating activities section of the statement of cash flows. Thus, by inappropriately delaying payment on accounts payable invoices until after the statement preparation date, the company's cash flow situation will appear better than it would have appeared otherwise. Of course, the delayed payment will decrease cash flows in the following period, so at that point, people will become aware of the cash outflow.

Ethical managers will resist the temptation to manipulate the statement of cash flows to make a company's financial situation appear better than it really is. Truthful and accurate financial reporting is a requirement of GAAP. Misleading financial reporting will destroy a company's reputation, which is essential to carry out business operations in the long run. Further, managers who commit fraudulent financial reporting are subject to criminal penalties.

FOCUS ON ETHICS

Ethical Financial Reporting at Yahoo!

Yahoo's company guide to business conduct and ethics clearly spells out exemplary ethical standards for financial reporting. Here is a quote from former CEO, Terry Semel, that emphasizes the important role that all employees play in producing the company's financial statements: "You must provide information that is accurate, complete, objective, relevant, timely and understandable, act in good faith, responsibly, with due care, competence and diligence without misrepresenting or omitting material facts." Yahoo is committed to doing business ethically, especially in regard to its financial reporting. As the company guide says, "Proper record keeping is essential to enable Yahoo and its officers to comply with their obligations to make full, fair, accurate, timely and understandable disclosure in the company's Securities and Exchange Commission filings and in other public documents."

Source: *Yahoo.com*

¶1203.06   DIRECT METHOD FOR PREPARING THE STATEMENT OF CASH FLOWS

As a student, what financing activities are supporting your operating activities, i.e. attending college?

The other approach to preparing the statement of cash flows is the direct method. The main difference between the indirect and direct methods is how the section on cash flows from operating activities is prepared. Using the direct method, the cash flows from operating activities section shows the actual cash receipts and actual cash payments associated with operating activities. Such cash flows are not derived indirectly using adjustments to net income, as under the indirect method. The appendix to this chapter illustrates the direct method of preparing the statement of cash flows.

¶1204   Making Decisions Based on the Statement of Cash Flows

LEARNING OBJECTIVE 4: Demonstrate how to use the statement of cash flows to analyze a company's financial situation.

Cash plays an important role in the financial success of a company. Investors and lenders need to know if a company will have sufficient cash to meet its obligations and how efficiently a company generates cash. The statement of cash flows is very helpful for evaluating a company's free cash flow and cash-generating capacity.

¶1204.01   FREE CASH FLOW

Free cash flow is the amount of cash remaining after deducting funds needed for planned operations.

Free cash flow is how much cash is left over after subtracting the funds necessary to maintain a company's planned operations. A company must disburse cash to pay for operating activities, make interest payments on debt, pay income tax, issue dividends, and purchase capital assets. Since net cash flows from operating activities includes continuing operations, interest, and income tax, the free cash flow is calculated as follows:

$$\text{Free Cash Flow} = \text{Net Cash Flows from Operating Activites} - \text{Dividends} - \text{Purchase of Plant Assets} + \text{Sale of Plant Assets}$$

The free cash flow for BLT Corporation is calculated as follows:

Free Cash Flow = $134,400 − $9,200 − $20,000 + $10,000

= $115,200

¶1204.02 CASH FLOW YIELD

The cash flow yield measures the company's ability to generate operating cash flows in relation to net income.

? *When you consider your personal finances, how would you measure your free cash flow?*

A good measure of a company's cash-generating capacity is cash flow yield. **Cash flow yield** is the ratio of a company's net cash flows from operating activities to its net income. Cash flow yield indicates how efficiently a company can generate cash from its earnings. Cash flow yield for BLT Corporation is calculated as follows:

$$\text{Cash Flow Yield} = \frac{\text{Net Cash Flows from Operating Activities}}{\text{Net Income}}$$

$$= \frac{\$134,400}{\$13,200}$$

$$= 10.2 \text{ times}$$

FOCUS ON TECHNOLOGY

Using Microsoft Excel: Computing Free Cash Flow and Cash Flow Yield

Using Microsoft Excel, we will compute the free cash flow and cash flow yield of a company.

1. File Identification Area: In an Excel worksheet, create a file identification area showing the filename, input required, and other appropriate information.
2. Input Area: Type in the following:

	A	B	C	C	E
13					
14	INPUT AREA:				
15	Net cash flows from operating activities				120,000
16	Net income				90,000
17	Dividends				2,000
18	Purchase of plant assets				60,000
19	Sale of plant assets				35,000

3. Output Area:

   First type in the heading "Free Cash Flows =". In the cell just to the right of your heading, type in the formula "=E15−E17−E18+E19"

   Second, type in the heading "Cash Flow Yield =". In the cell just to the right of your heading, type in the formula "=E15/E16"

   The results should appear as follows:

   OUTPUT AREA:

   Free Cash Flow   =   93,000

   Cash Flow Yield   =   1.333333

¶1205   # Concluding Remarks

At this time, you know what is involved in the three activities reported on the statement of cash flows. Operating activities involve the day-to-day transactions. Investing activities are transactions dealing with long-term assets and investments. Financing activities involve debt or stockholders' equity. Now let's journey into the next chapter where you will learn how to analyze a company's statement of cash flows and other financial statements in order to identify significant trends or relationships among the items contained within them.

¶1206

Chapter Review

LEARNING OBJECTIVE 1

Describe the importance of the statement of cash flows to people within and outside the business firm.

The statement of cash flows shows the company's cash receipts and cash payments, that is, the inflows and outflows of cash. The statement of cash flows enables users, within the firm and outside the firm, to determine what caused the changes in cash. Understanding these changes is crucial for a person to accurately assess a company's financial strength. By effectively understanding how cash is generated and paid out, management can plan for future cash needs and monitor how cash is used. Creditors and investors rely on the statement of cash flows to predict whether a company can pay its debts and dividends with regularity, while making good use of company resources.

LEARNING OBJECTIVE 2

Explain the components within a statement of cash flows.

Preparing a statement of cash flows involves calculating cash flows from operating, investing, and financing activities. Operating activities involve the day-to-day transactions that generate revenues, expenses, gains, and losses in the company's primary line of business. Investing activities involve the purchase and sale of long-term assets and investments. Financing activities concern debt or stockholders' equity.

Preparing a statement of cash flows involves four basic steps:

1. Calculate cash flows from operating activities.
2. Calculate cash flows from investing activities.
3. Calculate cash flows from financing activities.
4. Add the results of the above three steps to obtain net changes in cash for the period.

LEARNING OBJECTIVE 3

Prepare a statement of cash flows.

The statement of cash flows can be prepared using either the indirect method or the direct method. The indirect method makes adjustments to only selected income statement items, which are necessary to convert net income into net cash flows from operating activities. The direct method makes adjustments to all items on the income statement by converting them from the accrual basis to the cash basis, to obtain net cash flows from operating activities.

Adjustments to net income for operating activities include depreciation, changes in current assets, and changes in current liabilities. Adjustments to investing activities include investments and the purchase and sale of plant assets. Adjustments to financing activities include activities involving notes payable, debt, and stockholders' equity.

LEARNING OBJECTIVE 4

Demonstrate how to use the statement of cash flows to analyze a company's financial situation.

The statement of cash flows is helpful for evaluating a company's free cash flow and cash-generating capacity. Free cash flow is how much cash is left over after subtracting the funds necessary to maintain a company's planned operations. The cash flow yield measures the company's ability to generate operating cash flows in relation to net income.

¶1207

Glossary

Cash flow yield

Cash flow yield is the ratio of a company's net cash flows from operating activities to its net income.

¶1207

Financing activities

Financing activities are transactions involving debt or stockholders' equity.

Free cash flow

Free cash flow is how much cash is left over after subtracting the funds necessary to maintain a company's planned operations.

Investing activities

Investing activities are transactions involving long-term assets and investments.

Operating activities

Operating activities involve the day-to-day transactions that generate revenues, expenses, gains, and losses in the company's primary line of business.

Statement of cash flows

The statement of cash flows shows the company's cash receipts and cash payments, that is, the inflows and outflows of cash.

¶1208

Appendix: Direct Method for Preparing the Statement of Cash Flows

This appendix examines how to prepare a statement of cash flows using the direct method. In contrast to the indirect method, the direct method takes each income statement item and converts it to its cash equivalent. For example, sales revenue is converted to cash receipts from sales. Purchases are converted to cash payments for purchases, and so on. As a result, the section on cash flows from operating activities does not start with net income to which adjustments are made. Instead, the section shows the direct cash flows resulting from cash receipts into the company and cash payments from the company.

Using the information from Exhibits 12.4 and 12.5, we will look at each line item on BLT's income statement and convert it to its cash equivalent. First, let's consider sales revenue.

¶1208.01

CASH RECEIPTS FROM SALES

Sales revenue is earned when sales are made, but cash may not be collected immediately. Cash is collected immediately from cash sales, but cash is not collected until a future time from credit sales. A credit sale results in an account receivable, not cash. Later, customers send in cash to pay off their accounts receivable. Thus, on the schedule of operating activities, net cash flows are a result of cash receipts from sales and collections on accounts receivable. Cash receipts from sales is calculated as follows:

$$\text{Cash Receipts from Sales} = \text{Sales} \pm \begin{cases} + \text{ Decrease in Accounts Receivable} \\ \qquad\qquad\text{OR} \\ - \text{ Increase in Accounts Receivable} \end{cases}$$

Based on BLT's Sales (Exhibit 12.5) and change in Accounts Receivable (Exhibit 12.4), BLT's cash receipts from sales is determined as shown:

$$\text{Cash Receipts from Sales} = \$380,000 \text{ (Sales)} + \$500 \text{ (Decrease in A/R)}$$

¶1208.02

INTEREST INCOME

Next, BLT's income statement shows interest income of $8,000. For simplicity, it is assumed that BLT received cash for all its interest income. Thus, this amount is a cash inflow.

¶1208.03 CASH PAID FOR PURCHASES

The next amount to be converted is cost of goods sold. Cost of goods sold is not the same as cash paid for purchases. Cash payments for purchases is calculated from one income statement account, Cost of Goods Sold, and two balance sheet accounts, Inventory and Accounts Payable, are as shown:

$$\text{Cash Payments for Purchases} = \text{Cost of Goods Sold} \pm \left\{ \begin{array}{c} + \text{ Increase in Inventory} \\ \text{OR} \\ - \text{ Decrease in Inventory} \end{array} \right. \pm \left\{ \begin{array}{c} + \text{ Decrease in Accounts Payable} \\ \text{OR} \\ - \text{ Increase in Accounts Payable} \end{array} \right.$$

Referring to the items in Exhibit 12.4 and 12.5, BLT's cash payments for purchases is determined as shown:

$$\begin{aligned} \text{Cash Payments for Purchases} &= \$270{,}000 - \$27{,}400 - \$30{,}000 \\ &= \$212{,}600 \end{aligned}$$

¶1208.04 CASH PAID FOR WAGES, SUPPLIES, AND OTHER

The next item on BLT's income statement is operating expenses. Operating expenses are calculated based on accruals as well as actual amounts paid. Thus operating expenses are adjusted for three items to determine the cash paid, as shown:

$$\text{Cash Payments for Operating Expenses} = \text{Operating Expenses} \pm \left\{ \begin{array}{c} + \text{ Increase in Prepaid Expenses} \\ \text{OR} \\ - \text{ Decrease in Prepaid Expenses} \end{array} \right. \pm \left\{ \begin{array}{c} + \text{ Decrease in Accrued Liabilities} \\ \text{OR} \\ - \text{ Increase in Accrued Liabilities} \end{array} \right. - \text{ Depreciation and other Noncash Expenses}$$

Referring to the items in Exhibits 12.4 and 12.5, BLT's cash payments for operating expenses is determined as shown:

$$\begin{aligned} \text{Cash Payments for Operating Expenses} &= \$89{,}000 + \$3{,}500 - \$20{,}000 - \$45{,}800 \\ &= \$26{,}700 \end{aligned}$$

¶1208.05 CASH PAID FOR INCOME TAX

Finally, we convert income tax expense to its cash equivalent. Income tax expense is almost never the same as income tax payable. Cash paid for income tax expense is determined as shown:

$$\text{Cash Payments from Income Tax} = \text{Income Tax Expense} \pm \left\{ \begin{array}{c} + \text{ Decrease in Income Tax Payable} \\ \text{OR} \\ - \text{ Increase in Income Tax Payable} \end{array} \right.$$

Referring to the items in Exhibits 12.4 and 12.5, BLT's cash payments for income tax is determined as shown:

$$\begin{aligned} \text{Cash Payments for Income Tax} &= \$8{,}800 + \$6{,}000 \\ &= \$14{,}800 \end{aligned}$$

¶1208.06   **THE DIRECT METHOD**

Based on the above calculations, the statement of cash flows for BLT can now be prepared using the direct method; this is shown in Exhibit 12.A. The net cash flows from operating activities, $134,400, is shown in the top section of the statement of cash flows.

Exhibit 12.A BLT CORPORATION
Statement of Cash Flows (Using the Direct Method) For Year Ended December 31, 20Y2

Cash Flows from Operating Activities		
Cash Receipts from:		
Sales	$380,500	
Interest Received	8,000	$388,500
Cash Payments for:		
Purchases	$212,600	
Operating Expenses	26,700	
Income Tax	14,800	254,100
Net Cash Flows from Operating Activities		$134,400
Cash Flows from Investing Activities		
Purchase of Investments	$(104,200)	
Sale of Investments	56,000	
Purchase of Plant Assets	(20,000)	
Sale of Plant Assets	10,000	
Net Cash Flows from Investing Activities		(58,200)
Cash Flows from Financing Activities		
Repayment of Notes	$(60,000)	
Issue of Common Stock	20,000	
Dividends Paid	(9,200)	
Net Cash Flows from Financing Activities		(49,200)
Net Increase (Decrease) in Cash		$27,000
Cash at Beginning of Year		38,000
Cash at End of Year		$65,000
Schedule of Noncash Investing and Financing Transactions		
Issue of Notes for Plant Assets		$40,000
Reconciliation of Net Income to Net Cash Flows from Operating Activities		
Cash Flows from Operating Activities		
Net Income		$13,200
Adjustments to Reconcile Net Income to Net Cash Flows from Operating Activities		
Depreciation	$45,800	
Gain on Sale of Plant Assets	(7,000)	
Loss on Sale of Investments	14,000	
Changes in Current Assets and Current Liabilities		
Decrease in Accounts Receivable	500	
Decrease in Inventory	27,400	
Increase in Prepaid Expense	(3,500)	
Increase in Accounts Payable	30,000	
Increase in Accrued Liabilities	20,000	
Decrease in Income Tax Payable	(6,000)	121
Net Cash Flows from Operating Activities		$134,400

Whether the indirect method or direct method is used, the resulting amount for net cash flows from operating activities is the same. When the direct method is used, the statement of cash flows must include a section at the bottom showing the reconciliation of net income to net cash flows from operating activities.

¶1209   # Chapter Assignments

QUESTIONS

1. **[Obj. 1]** Why is it important for management to have current information regarding the company's cash flows?

2. **[Obj. 1]** Why is the statement of cash flows useful to investors?

3. **[Obj. 2]** How does the statement of cash flows provide further insight into the balance sheet?

4. **[Obj. 2]** What are the four basic steps involved in preparing a statement of cash flows?

5. **[Obj. 2]** List and define the three major types of activities of a business.

6. **[Obj. 2]** Give examples of a company's operating activities.

7. **[Obj. 2]** Give examples of a company's investing activities.

8. **[Obj. 2]** Give examples of a company's financing activities.

9. **[Obj. 3]** Describe the two methods for preparing a statement of cash flows.

10. **[Obj. 3]** Compare and contrast the indirect and direct methods of statement of cash flows preparation.

11. **[Obj. 3]** How does depreciation affect the statement of cash flows?

12. **[Obj. 3]** How do gains and losses affect the statement of cash flows?

13. **[Obj. 3]** What is the purpose of the Schedule of Noncash Investing and Financing Transactions which is shown at the bottom of the statement of cash flows?

14. **[Obj. 3]** When a company issues notes for plant assets, where does it report this activity on the statement of cash flows? Why?

15. **[Obj. 4]** Define "free cash flow."

16. **[Obj. 4]** Define "cash flow yield." What does it measure?

SHORT EXERCISES – SET A

Building Accounting Skills

1. **[Obj. 3]** Adjustments to the Statement of Cash Flows: The following items are adjustments needed for preparation of the operating activities section of the statement of cash flows using the indirect method. Indicate whether the adjustment for each item has a positive (+) or negative (–) impact on cash flows:
   __ Depreciation expense
   __ Loss on sale of plant assets
   __ Gain on sale of plant assets
   __ Increases in current assets other than cash
   __ Decreases in current assets other than cash
   __ Increases in current liabilities
   __ Decreases in current liabilities
   __ Payment of dividends

2. **[Obj. 3]** Preparing the Schedule of Cash Flows from Operating Activities: Using the indirect method and the data for the current year ended December 31 (shown below), prepare the Cash Flows from Operating Activities section of the cash flow statement for Magnus Robotics Corporation (similar to that of Exhibit 12.6).

Net Income	$22,000
Depreciation	34,000
Loss on Sale of Investments	10,000
Gain on Sale of Plant Assets	4,000
Decrease in Accounts Receivable	2,000
Decrease in Inventory	18,600
Increase in Prepaid Expenses	3,200
Increase in Accounts Payable	24,000
Increase in Accrued Liabilities	16,000
Decrease in Income Tax Payable	3,000

3. **[Obj. 3]** Preparing the Schedule of Cash Flows from Investing Activities: Using the indirect method and the data for the current year ended December 31 (shown below), prepare the Cash Flows from Investing Activities section of the cash flow statement. Refer to Exhibit 12.7.

Net Income	$22,000
Purchased Investments	96,000
Sold Investments	228,000
Purchased Plant Assets	108,000
Sold Plant Assets	168,000

4. **[Obj. 3]** Preparing the Cash Flows from Financing Activities section: Using the indirect method and the data for the current year ended December 31 (shown below), prepare the Cash Flows from Financing Activities section of the cash flow statement. Refer to Exhibit 12.7.

Net Income	$22,000
Repaid Notes at Face Value at Maturity	120,000
Issue of Common Stock	40,000
Paid Cash Dividends	60,000

5. **[Obj. 4]** Computing Free Cash Flows: Use the information below to compute free cash flow for Marquis Newspaper Company.

Net Cash Flows From Operating Activities	$210,000
Dividends	8,000
Purchase of Plant Assets	30,000
Sale of Plant Assets	20,000

6. **[Obj. 4]** Making Decisions Based on Free Cash Flow: Free cash flow is how much cash is left over after subtracting the funds necessary to maintain a company's planned operations. Assume the following information regarding the Washington Post:

Cash Flows From Operating Activities	$630,000
Dividends	21,000
Sale of Plant Assets	80,000

The company is also considering the sale of $73,000 in plant assets. If the company decides not to sell the plant assets, what is its free cash flow? If the Washington Post does sell the plant assets, what is its free cash flow?

7. **[Obj. 4]** Computing Cash Flow Yield: Use the information below to compute cash flow yield for JJJ Media Corporation.

Net Income	$44,000
Net Cash Flows From Operating Activities	413,600

8. **[Obj. 4]** Interpreting Cash Flow Yield: Cash flow yield is the ratio of a company's net cash flows from operating activities to its net income. Assume Colonial Souvenirs reported net income of $110,000 and net cash flows from operating activities of $800,000.
   a. Compute cash flow yield.
   b. Assume Colonial Souvenirs' cash flow yield was 7.8 last year. Comparing last year with this year, is the company more or less efficient at producing cash from its earnings?

9. **[Appendix]** Computing Cash Receipts from Sales: Master Movers uses the direct method in preparing its statement of cash flows. At the end of the year, sales equaled $40,000 and accounts receivable decreased by $10,000. Compute the company's cash receipts from sales.

10. **[Appendix]** Computing Cash Payments for Purchases: Elsie's Shakes uses the direct method in preparing its statement of cash flows. At the end of the year, cost of goods sold equaled $50,000. The company had an increase in inventory of $7,000 and a decrease in accounts payable of $2,000. Compute the company's cash payments for purchases.

SHORT EXERCISES – SET B

Building Accounting Skills

1. **[Obj. 3]** Adjustments to the Statement of Cash Flows: The following items require adjustment on the statement of cash flows using the indirect method. Indicate whether the adjustment for each item has a positive (+) or negative (–) impact on cash flows:

 ___ Sales of plant assets (e.g., investments, land, building, and equipment)
 ___ Purchases of plant assets
 ___ Collections of long-term receivables
 ___ Long-term loans to others
 ___ Issuance of stock
 ___ Sale of treasury stock
 ___ Purchase of treasury stock
 ___ Borrowing (issuing notes or bonds payable)
 ___ Payment of notes or bonds payable

2. **[Obj. 3]** Preparing the Schedule of Cash Flows from Operating Activities: Using the indirect method and the data for the current year ended December 31 (shown below), prepare the Cash Flows from Operating Activities section of the cash flow statement for Home Depot (similar to that of Exhibit 12.6).

Net Income	$44,000
Depreciation	68,000
Loss on Sale of Investments	20,000
Gain on Sale of Plant Assets	8,000
Decrease in Accounts Receivable	4,000
Decrease in Inventory	37,200
Increase in Prepaid Expenses	6,400
Increase in Accounts Payable	48,000
Increase in Accrued Liabilities	32,000
Decrease in Income Tax Payable	6,000

3. **[Obj. 3]** Preparing the Schedule of Cash Flows from Investing Activities: Using the indirect method and the data for the current year ended December 31 (shown below), prepare the Cash Flows from Investing Activities section of the cash flow statement. Refer to Exhibit 12.7.

Net Income	$44,000
Purchased Investments	60,000
Sold Investments	155,000
Purchased Plant Assets	80,000
Sold Plant Assets	104,000

4. **[Obj. 3]** Preparing the Cash Flows from Financing Activities section: Using the indirect method and the data for the current year ended December 31 (shown below), prepare the Cash Flows from Financing Activities section of the cash flow statement. Refer to Exhibit 12.7.

Net Income	$44,000
Repaid Notes at Face Value at Maturity	80,000
Issue of Common Stock	10,000
Paid Cash Dividends	35,000

5. **[Obj. 4]** Computing Free Cash Flow: Use the information below to compute the free cash flow for Florida Orange Company.

Net Cash Flows From Operating Activities	$250,000
Dividends	9,000
Purchase of Plant Assets	40,000
Sale of Plant Assets	30,000

6. **[Obj. 4]** Making Decisions Based on the Statement of Cash Flows: Free cash flow is how much cash is left over after subtracting the funds necessary to maintain a company's planned operations. Assume the following information regarding the *Wall Street Journal*.

Cash Flows From Operating Activities	$420,000
Dividends	16,000
Sale of Plant Assets	40,000

The company is also considering the purchase of $60,000 in plant assets. If the company does not purchase plant assets, what is its free cash flow? If the Wall Street Journal makes the purchase, what is its free cash flow?

7. **[Obj. 4]** Computing Cash Flow Yield: Use the information below to compute the cash flow yield for Maine Lobster Corporation.

| Net Income | $65,000 |
| Net Cash Flows From Operating Activities | 209,000 |

8. **[Obj. 4]** Interpreting Cash Flow Yield: Cash flow yield is the ratio of a company's net cash flows from operating activities to its net income. Assume Music Mountain reported net income of $74,000 and net cash flows from operating activities of $550,000.
   a. Compute cash flow yield.
   b. Assume Music Mountain's cash flow yield was 6.8 last year. Comparing last year with this year, is Music Mountain more or less efficient at producing cash from its earnings?

9. **[Appendix]** Computing Cash Receipts from Sales: Storage-for-U uses the direct method in preparing its statement of cash flows. At the end of the year, sales equaled $100,000 and accounts receivable increased by $5,000. Compute the company's cash receipts from sales.

10. **[Appendix]** Computing Cash Payments for Purchases: Archie's Hamburgers uses the direct method in preparing the statement of cash flows. At the end of the year, cost of goods sold equaled $180,000. The company had an increase in inventory of $10,000 and an increase in accounts payable of $5,000. Compute the company's cash payments for purchases.

PROBLEMS – SET A

Applying Accounting Knowledge

1. **[Obj. 3]** Preparing the Schedule of Cash Flows from Operating Activities: The information shown below was derived from the income statement and balance sheets of Digital Vacation Company. Use this information to prepare a schedule of cash flows from operating activities (using indirect method) for the current year ended December 31.

	($ Thousands)
Net Income	$240
Depreciation	75
Loss on Sale of Investments	15
Gain on Sale of Plant Assets	90
Decrease in Accounts Receivable	30
Decrease in Inventory	12
Increase in Prepaid Expenses	60
Increase in Accounts Payable	50
Increase in Accrued Liabilities	13
Decrease in Income Tax Payable	10

Required:
a. Prepare the schedule of cash flows from operating activities.
b. How much are net cash flows from operating activities?
c. Evaluate: Change the increase in accounts payable from $50,000 to $100,000. Now how much are net cash flows from operating activities?

2. **[Obj. 3]** Preparing the Schedule of Cash Flows from Operating Activities: The information shown below was derived from the income statement and balance sheets of Mexico City Diamond Company. Use this information to prepare a schedule of cash flows from operating activities (using indirect method) for the current year ended December 31.

	($ Millions)
Net Income	$460
Depreciation	20
Loss on Sale of Investments	15
Gain on Sale of Plant Assets	280
Decrease in Accounts Receivable	90
Decrease in Inventory	30
Increase in Prepaid Expenses	120
Increase in Accounts Payable	40
Increase in Accrued Liabilities	22
Decrease in Income Tax Payable	32

Required:
a. Prepare the schedule of cash flows from operating activities.
b. How much are net cash flows from operating activities?
c. Evaluate: Change the increase in prepaid expenses from $120,000 to $20,000. Now how much are net cash flows from operating activities?

3. **[Obj. 3]** Preparing the Schedule of Cash Flows from Operating Activities: The information shown below was derived from the income statement and balance sheets of Madrid Manufacturing Corporation. Use this information to prepare a schedule of cash flows from operating activities (using indirect method) for the current year ended December 31.

	($ Thousands)
Net Income	$2,400
Depreciation	42
Loss on Sale of Investments	330
Gain on Sale of Plant Assets	1,200
Decrease in Accounts Receivable	48
Decrease in Inventory	40
Increase in Prepaid Expenses	220
Increase in Accounts Payable	180
Increase in Accrued Liabilities	140
Decrease in Income Tax Payable	260

Required

a. Prepare the schedule of cash flows from operating activities.
b. How much are net cash flows from operating activities?
c. Evaluate: Change the gain on sale of plant assets from $1,200,000 to $2,200,000. Now how much are net cash flows from operating activities?

4. **[Obj. 3]** Preparing the Statement of Cash Flows: Use indirect method to prepare a statement of cash flows for Southwest Oil Corporation. The necessary information is taken from the current year ended Dec. 31:

Cash, Beginning of Year	$24,000
Cash Flows from Operating Activities	
Net Income	33,000
Depreciation	26,000
Loss on Sale of Investments	8,000
Gain on Sale of Plant Assets	5,000
Decrease in Accounts Receivable	3,000
Decrease in Inventory	16,000
Increase in Prepaid Expenses	4,400
Increase in Accounts Payable	18,000
Increase in Accrued Liabilities	12,000
Decrease in Income Tax Payable	2,600
Cash Flows from Investing Activities	
Purchased Investments	52,000
Sold Investments	34,000
Purchased Plant Assets	22,000
Sold Plant Assets	14,000
Cash Flows from Financing Activities	
Repaid Notes at Face Value at Maturity	36,000
Issued Common Stock	18,000
Paid Cash Dividends	4,000
Noncash Investing and Financing Transactions	
Issued Notes at Face Value in a Noncash Exchange for Plant Assets	$20,000

Required

a. Prepare a statement of cash flows.
b. Evaluate: What impact would an increase of repayment of notes at face value at maturity from $36,000 to $100,000 have on the statement of cash flows, specifically on cash at end of year?

5. **[Obj. 3]** Preparing the Statement of Cash Flows: Use the indirect method to prepare a statement of cash flows for Rapid Transit Corporation. The necessary information is taken from the current year ended December 31:

Cash, Beginning of Year	$99,000
Net Income	48,000
Depreciation	44,000
Loss on Sale of Investments	19,000
Gain on Sale of Plant Assets	3,500
Decrease in Accounts Receivable	8,000
Decrease in Inventory	39,000
Increase in Prepaid Expenses	13,200
Increase in Accounts Payable	15,000
Increase in Accrued Liabilities	6,300
Decrease in Income Tax Payable	5,700
Purchased Investments	57,000
Sold Investments	19,000
Purchased Plant Assets	54,000
Sold Plant Assets	11,000
Repaid Notes at Face Value at Maturity	27,000
Issued Common Stock	10,000
Paid Cash Dividends	21,000
Issued Notes at Face Value in a Noncash Exchange for Plant Assets	47,000

Required:
a. Prepare a statement of cash flows.
b. Evaluate: What impact would an increase of repayment of notes at face value at maturity from $27,000 to $90,000 have on the statement of cash flows, specifically on cash at end of year?

6. **[Obj. 3]** Preparing the Statement of Cash Flows: Use indirect method to prepare a statement of cash flows for Tankers 'R' Us Corporation. The necessary information is taken from the current year ended Dec. 31:

Cash, Beginning of Year	$10,800
Cash Flows from Operating Activities	
Net Income	44,000
Depreciation	19,000
Gain on Sale of Investments	33,000
Gain on Sale of Plant Assets	12,400
Decrease in Accounts Receivable	21,000
Increase in Inventory	16,000
Decrease in Prepaid Expenses	36,200
Increase in Accounts Payable	7,500
Increase in Accrued Liabilities	12,700
Increase in Income Tax Payable	9,200
Cash Flows from Investing Activities	
Purchased Investments	24,000
Sold Investments	57,000
Purchased Plant Assets	27,300
Sold Plant Assets	42,000
Cash Flows from Financing Activities	
Repaid Notes at Face Value at Maturity	80,000
Issued Common Stock	10,000
Paid Cash Dividends	40,000
Noncash Investing and Financing Transactions	
Issued Notes at Face Value in a Noncash Exchange for Plant Assets	56,000

Required:
a. Prepare the statement of cash flows.
b. Evaluate: What impact would an increase of cash dividends paid from $40,000 to $70,000 have on the statement of cash flows, specifically on cash at end of year?

7. **[Obj. 4]** Computing Free Cash Flow and Cash Flow Yield: The Jones Newspaper Company reported the following financial information at the end of their fiscal year:

Net Income	$30,000
Dividends	15,000
Purchase of Plant Assets	27,000
Sale of Plant Assets	10,000
Net Cash Flows From Operating Activities	48,000

Required:
a. Compute free cash flow.
b. Compute cash flow yield.

8. **[Obj. 4]** Computing Free Cash Flow and Cash Flow Yield: The Norman Electronics Company reported net income of $11,000 for the current fiscal year. The company purchased plant assets of $32,000 and sold plant assets for $12,000. Dividends of $17,000 were paid. Net cash flows from operating activities were reported at $49,000.

Required:
a. Compute free cash flow.
b. Compute cash flow yield.

9. **[Obj. 4]** Computing Free Cash Flow and Cash Flow Yield: Use the following information to compute the free cash flow and cash flow yield for Thompson Computer Company:

Net Income	$5,000
Dividends	25,000
Purchase of Plant Assets	11,000
Sale of Plant Assets	6,000
Net Cash Flows From Operating Activities	35,000

Required:
a. Compute free cash flow.
b. Compute cash flow yield.

10. **[Obj. 4]** Making Decisions Based on the Statement of Cash Flows: Southeast Seed Corporation reported a net income of $22,000 in the current year. Net cash flows from operating activities were $330,000. The company paid $10,000 in dividends and $33,800 for new plant assets. $27,200 was received for the sale of plant assets.

Required:
a. Based on its strategic plan, the company's goal is to keep at least $300,000 in free cash flow. Did the company meet this goal? If not, by what amount was the goal missed?
b. What was the company's cash flow yield this year? How does it compare to last year's cash flow yield of 9.8?

PROBLEMS – SET B

Applying Accounting Knowledge

1. **[Obj. 3]** Preparing the Schedule of Cash Flows from Operating Activities: The information shown below was derived from the income statement and balance sheets of Computer Games Galore. Use this information to prepare a schedule of cash flows from operating activities (using indirect method) for the current year ended December 31.

	($ Thousands)
Net Income	$480
Depreciation	150
Loss on Sale of Investments	30
Gain on Sale of Plant Assets	180
Decrease in Accounts Receivable	60
Decrease in Inventory	24
Increase in Prepaid Expenses	120
Increase in Accounts Payable	100
Increase in Accrued Liabilities	26
Decrease in Income Tax Payable	20

Required:
a. Prepare the schedule of cash flows from operating activities.
b. How much are net cash flows from operating activities?
c. Evaluate: Change the increase in accounts payable from $100,000 to $200,000. With the new amount, how much are net cash flows from operating activities?

2. **[Obj. 3]** Preparing the Schedule of Cash Flows from Operating Activities: The information shown below was derived from the income statement and balance sheets of Tennessee Music Company. Use this information to prepare a schedule of cash flows from operating activities (using indirect method) for the current year ended December 31.

	($ Thousands)
Net Income	$230
Depreciation	10
Loss on Sale of Investments	8
Gain on Sale of Plant Assets	140
Decrease in Accounts Receivable	45
Decrease in Inventory	15
Increase in Prepaid Expenses	60
Increase in Accounts Payable	20
Increase in Accrued Liabilities	11
Decrease in Income Tax Payable	16

Required:

a. Prepare the schedule of cash flows from operating activities.

b. How much are net cash flows from operating activities?

c. Evaluate: Change the increase in prepaid expenses from $60,000 to $20,000. With the new amount, how much are net cash flows from operating activities?

3. **[Obj. 3]** Preparing the Schedule of Cash Flows from Operating Activities: The information shown below was derived from the income statement and balance sheets of Oregon Tree Farm. Use this information to prepare a schedule of cash flows from operating activities (using indirect method) for the current year ended December 31.

	($ Thousands)
Net Income	$1,200
Depreciation	21
Loss on Sale of Investments	165
Gain on Sale of Plant Assets	600
Decrease in Accounts Receivable	24
Decrease in Inventory	20
Increase in Prepaid Expenses	110
Increase in Accounts Payable	90
Increase in Accrued Liabilities	70
Decrease in Income Tax Payable	130

Required:

a. Prepare the schedule of cash flows from operating activities.

b. How much are net cash flows from operating activities?

c. Evaluate: Change the loss on sale of investments from $165,000 to $100,000. With the new amount, how much are net cash flows from operating activities?

4. **[Obj. 3]** Preparing the Statement of Cash Flows: Use indirect method to prepare a statement of cash flows for Ben & Jerry's. The necessary information is taken from the current year ended Dec. 31:

Cash, Beginning of Year	$48,000
Cash Flows from Operating Activities	
Net Income	66,000
Depreciation	52,000
Loss on Sale of Investments	16,000
Gain on Sale of Plant Assets	10,000
Decrease in Accounts Receivable	6,000
Decrease in Inventory	32,000
Increase in Prepaid Expenses	8,800
Increase in Accounts Payable	36,000
Increase in Accrued Liabilities	24,000
Decrease in Income Tax Payable	5,200
Cash Flows from Investing Activities	
Purchased Investments	104,000
Sold Investments	68,000
Purchased Plant Assets	44,000
Sold Plant Assets	28,000
Cash Flows from Financing Activities	
Repaid Notes at Face Value at Maturity	72,000
Issued Common Stock	36,000
Paid Cash Dividends	8,000
Noncash Investing and Financing Transactions	
Issued Notes at Face Value in a Noncash Exchange for Plant Assets	40,000

Required:

a. Prepare a statement of cash flows.

b. Evaluate: What impact would an increase of repayment of notes at face value at maturity from $72,000 to $100,000 have on the statement of cash flows, specifically on cash at end of year?

5 . **[Obj. 3]** Preparing the Statement of Cash Flows: Use indirect method to prepare a statement of cash flows for The Party Shop. The necessary information is taken from the current year ended Dec. 31:

Cash, Beginning of Year	$50,000
Cash Flows from Operating Activities	
Net Income	24,000
Depreciation	22,000
Loss on Sale of Investments	10,000
Gain on Sale of Plant Assets	2,000
Decrease in Accounts Receivable	4,000
Decrease in Inventory	20,000
Increase in Prepaid Expenses	7,000
Increase in Accounts Payable	8,000
Increase in Accrued Liabilities	3,000
Decrease in Income Tax Payable	2,600
Cash Flows from Investing Activities	
Purchased Investments	28,000
Sold Investments	10,000
Purchased Plant Assets	27,000
Sold Plant Assets	6,000
Cash Flows from Financing Activities	
Repaid Notes at Face Value at Maturity	14,000
Issued Common Stock	5,000
Paid Cash Dividends	11,000
Noncash Investing and Financing Transactions	
Issued Notes at Face Value in a Noncash Exchange for Plant Assets	24,000

Required:

a. Prepare a statement of cash flows.

b. Evaluate: What impact would an increase of repayment of notes at face value at maturity from $14,000 to $25,000 have on the statement of cash flows, specifically on cash at end of year?

6. **[Obj. 3]** Preparing the Statement of Cash Flows: Use indirect method to prepare a statement of cash flows for Tuxedo Rental. The necessary information is taken from the current year ended Dec. 31:

Cash, Beginning of Year	$20,000
Cash Flows from Operating Activities	
Net Income	22,000
Depreciation	38,000
Gain on Sale of Investments	66,000
Gain on Sale of Plant Assets	24,000
Decrease in Accounts Receivable	42,000
Increase in Inventory	36,000
Decrease in Prepaid Expenses	72,000
Increase in Accounts Payable	15,000
Increase in Accrued Liabilities	24,000
Increase in Income Tax Payable	18,000
Cash Flows from Investing Activities	
Purchased Investments	48,000
Sold Investments	114,000
Purchased Plant Assets	54,000
Sold Plant Assets	84,000
Cash Flows from Financing Activities	
Repaid Notes at Face Value at Maturity	160,000
Issued Common Stock	20,000
Paid Cash Dividends	80,000
Noncash Investing and Financing Transactions	
Issued Notes at Face Value in a Noncash Exchange for Plant Assets	112,000

Required:
a. Prepare a statement of cash flows.
b. Evaluate: What impact would a decrease of cash dividends paid from $80,000 to $40,000 have on the statement of cash flows, specifically on cash at end of year?

7. **[Obj. 4]** Computing Free Cash Flow and Cash Flow Yield: Use the following information to compute the free cash flow and cash flow yield for The New York Times ($ in thousands):

Net Income	$60,000
Dividends	30,000
Purchase of Plant Assets	54,000
Sale of Plant Assets	20,000
Net Cash Flows From Operating Activities	96,000

Required:
a. Compute free cash flow.
b. Compute cash flow yield.

8. **[Obj. 4]** Computing Free Cash Flow and Cash Flow Yield: Use the following information to compute the free cash flow and cash flow yield for The Shop Around the Corner:

Net Income	$30,000
Dividends	21,000
Purchase of Plant Assets	60,000
Sale of Plant Assets	25,000
Net Cash Flows From Operating Activities	98,000

Required:
a. Compute free cash flow.
b. Compute cash flow yield.

9. **[Obj. 4]** Computing Free Cash Flow and Cash Flow Yield: Use the following information to compute the free cash flow and cash flow yield for Trains Galore:

Net Income	$10,000
Dividends	5,000
Purchase of Plant Assets	19,000
Sale of Plant Assets	9,000
Net Cash Flows From Operating Activities	40,000

Required:
a. Compute free cash flow.
b. Compute cash flow yield.

10. **[Obj. 4]** Computing Free Cash Flow and Cash Flow Yield: Use the following information to compute the free cash flow and cash flow yield for The Bridal Shop:

Net Income	$44,000
Dividends	20,000
Purchase of Plant Assets	66,000
Sale of Plant Assets	54,000
Net Cash Flows From Operating Activities	260,000

Required:
a. Compute free cash flow.
b. Compute cash flow yield.

CROSS-FUNCTIONAL PERSPECTIVES

Discussion Questions

1. **[Obj. 3]** How can various departments help promote effective usage of cash within a company?

2. **[Obj. 1 and 4]** How is the statement of cash flows helpful to investors?

3. **[Obj. 1 and 4]** How is the statement of cash flows helpful to lenders?

Cross-functional Case: Sky Photography Corporation

Sky Photography Corporation is a multi-million dollar company that takes aerial photographs of houses, business buildings, city parks, zoos, lakes, engineering projects, and other sites. Customers include individuals, business firms, and government agencies. The company has been in business for five years. Total plant assets amount to $10 million, mostly aircraft. The company purchased new aircraft of $400,000 in 20Y5. The company has earned a profit every year: $340,000 in Year 20Y1 and most recently, $1.4 million in 20Y5. Even so, the company's cash balance has steadily declined every year, from $500,000 at the end of 20Y1 to only $38,000 at the end of 20Y5. The company's CEO is perplexed. She is frustrated that the company has consistently earned a profit but cash has decreased each year. If this continues, the company will not have cash to pay its bills. As a result of the company's cash flow problems, you have been hired as a business consultant to help each department come up with ways to improve cash flows. The most recent statement of cash flows is shown below:

SKY PHOTOGRAPHY CORPORATION Statement of Cash Flows For Year Ended December 31, 20Y5		
Cash Flows from Operating Activities		($ Thousands)
Net Income		$1,400
Adjustments to Reconcile Net Income to Net Cash Flows from Operating Activities		
Depreciation	$360	
Changes in Current Assets and Current Liabilities		
Increase in Accounts Receivable	(580)	
Increase in Inventory	(190)	
Decrease in Accounts Payable	(85)	
Increase in Accrued Liabilities	75	
Increase in Income Tax Payable	50	(370)
Net Cash Flows from Operating Activities		$1,030
Cash Flows from Investing Activities		
Purchase of Investments	$(220)	
Sale of Investments	50	
Purchase of Plant Assets	(400)	
Sale of Plant Assets	290	
Net Cash Flows from Investing Activities		(280)
Cash Flows from Financing Activities		
Repayments of Notes	$(500)	
Dividends Paid	(300)	
Net Cash Flows from Financing Activities		(800)
Net Increase (Decrease) in Cash		$(50)
Cash at Beginning of Year		88
Issued Notes at Face Value in a Noncash Exchange for Plant Assets		$38

Required: Review the statement of cash flows and offer suggestions where different departments in the company might be able to help improve cash flows?
a. Accounting
b. Finance
c. Production (Pilots and Photographers)
d. Marketing

EXCEL ASSIGNMENTS

1. **[Obj. 3]** Preparing the Schedule of Cash Flows from Operating Activities: The information shown below was derived from the income statement and balance sheets of Tokyo Flower Company. Use this information to prepare a schedule of cash flows from operating activities (using indirect method) for the current year ended December 31.

	($ Millions)
Net Income	$740
Depreciation	60
Loss on Sale of Investments	220
Gain on Sale of Plant Assets	50
Decrease in Accounts Receivable	94
Decrease in Inventory	120
Increase in Prepaid Expenses	86
Increase in Accounts Payable	94
Increase in Accrued Liabilities	208
Decrease in Income Tax Payable	320

Required: Prepare a worksheet of the schedule of cash flows from operating activities.

2. **[Obj. 3]** Preparing the Schedule of Cash Flows from Operating Activities: The information shown below was derived from the income statement and balance sheets of Paraguay Bulldozer Corporation. Use this information to prepare a schedule of cash flows from operating activities (using indirect method) for the current year ended December 31.

	($ Millions)
Net Income	$125
Depreciation	25
Loss on Sale of Investments	18
Gain on Sale of Plant Assets	24
Decrease in Accounts Receivable	16
Decrease in Inventory	36
Increase in Prepaid Expenses	24
Increase in Accounts Payable	5
Increase in Accrued Liabilities	17
Decrease in Income Tax Payable	12

Required: Prepare a worksheet of the schedule of cash flows from operating activities.

3. **[Obj. 3]** Preparing the Statement of Cash Flows: Use the information shown below and prepare a statement of cash flows (using indirect method) for Choctaw Canoe Corporation. This information is taken from the current year ended December 31:

Cash, Beginning of Year	$22,000
Cash Flows from Operating Activities	
Net Income	34,000
Depreciation	12,000
Gain on Sale of Investments	42,800
Gain on Sale of Plant Assets	12,600
Decrease in Accounts Receivable	42,000
Increase in Inventory	9,000
Decrease in Prepaid Expenses	14,800
Increase in Accounts Payable	22,000
Increase in Accrued Liabilities	19,000
Increase in Income Tax Payable	5,000
Cash Flows from Investing Activities	
Purchased Investments	14,000
Sold Investments	37,000
Purchased Plant Assets	17,300
Sold Plant Assets	32,000
Cash Flows from Financing Activities	
Repaid Notes at Face Value at Maturity	40,000
Issued Common Stock	6,000
Paid Cash Dividends	36,000
Noncash Investing and Financing Transactions	
Issued Notes at Face Value in a Noncash Exchange for Plant Assets	26,000

Required:
a. Prepare a worksheet that shows the statement of cash flows.
b. Evaluate: What impact would an increase of cash dividends paid from $36,000 to $56,000 have on the statement of cash flows?

4. **[Obj. 3]** Preparing the Statement of Cash Flows: Use the information shown below, and prepare a statement of cash flows (using indirect method) for Peking Shoe Corporation. This information is taken from the current year ended December 31:

Cash, beginning of year	$39,000
Cash Flows from Operating Activities	
Net Income	17,000
Depreciation	15,000
Loss on Sale of Investments	34,000
Gain on Sale of Plant Assets	20,000
Decrease in Accounts Receivable	12,000
Increase in Inventory	44,000
Decrease in Prepaid Expenses	15,200
Decrease in Accounts Payable	43,600
Increase in Accrued Liabilities	18,200
Increase in Income Tax Payable	10,000
Cash Flows from Investing Activities	
Purchased Investments	16,000
Sold Investments	18,000
Purchased Plant Assets	25,000
Sold Plant Assets	44,400
Cash Flows from Financing Activities	
Repaid Notes at Face Value at Maturity	48,600
Issued Common Stock	12,000
Paid Cash Dividends	10,000
Noncash Investing and Financing Transactions	
Issued Notes at Face Value in a Noncash Exchange for Plant Assets	18,000

Required:
a. Prepare a worksheet that shows the statement of cash flows.
b. Evaluate: What impact would an increase of cash dividends paid from $10,000 to $30,000 have on the statement of cash flows?

5. **[Obj. 3]** Preparing the Statement of Cash Flows: Use the information shown below, and prepare a statement of cash flows (using indirect method) for Vermont Ski Equipment. This information is taken from the current year ended December 31:

Cash, Beginning of Year	$35,000
Cash Flows from Operating Activities	
Net Income	60,000
Depreciation	25,000
Gain on Sale of Investments	67,000
Gain on Sale of Plant Assets	31,000
Decrease in Accounts Receivable	64,000
Increase in Inventory	10,000
Decrease in Prepaid Expenses	23,000
Increase in Accounts Payable	34,000
Increase in Accrued Liabilities	22,000
Increase in Income Tax Payable	6,000
Cash Flows from Investing Activities	
Purchased Investments	34,000
Sold Investments	60,000
Purchased Plant Assets	40,000
Sold Plant Assets	25,000
Cash Flows from Financing Activities	
Repaid Notes at Face Value at Maturity	55,000
Issued Common Stock	8,000
Paid Cash Dividends	27,000
Noncash Investing and Financing Transactions	
Issued Notes at Face Value in a Noncash Exchange for Plant Assets	42,000

Required:
a. Prepare a worksheet that shows the statement of cash flows.
b. Evaluate: What impact would an increase of cash dividends paid from $27,000 to $40,000 have on the statement of cash flows?

WEB ASSIGNMENTS

1. **[Obj. 3]** Go to the website for Yahoo, or do a Web search, and find Yahoo's Statement of Cash Flows. For December 31 of most recent year, what are Yahoo's net cash flows from: operating activities, investing activities, and financing activities?

2. **[Obj. 3]** Find Yahoo's Statement of Cash Flows from its website or use a Web search. For December 31, two years previous, what are Yahoo's net cash flows from: operating activities, investing activities, and financing activities?

3. **[Obj. 4]** Go to the website for Yahoo, or do a Web search, and find Yahoo's annual reports from last year. Compute Yahoo's cash flow yield by finding its Net Income from the Income Statement and its Net Cash Flows from Operations from the Statement of Cash Flows (Cash Flow Yield = Net Cash Flows from Operations / Net Income).

4. **[Obj. 4]** Go to the website for Yahoo, or do a Web search, and find Yahoo's annual reports from 2006. Compute Yahoo's cash flow yield by finding its Net Income from the Income Statement and its Net Cash Flows from Operations from the Statement of Cash Flows (Cash Flow Yield = Net Cash Flows from Operations / Net Income).

¶1210

Test Prepper

Use this sample test to gauge your comprehension of the chapter material.

True/False Questions

___ 1. While the balance sheet shows the account balance of cash, it is the statement of cash flows that explains what caused the change in the account balance of cash from one year to the next.

___ 2. Depreciation is one of the adjustments to net income required when preparing the statement of cash flows.

___ 3. Since the issue of notes payable for plant assets does not affect cash flows for investing and financing, it is not reported on the statement of cash flows.

___ 4. Reporting investing and financing activities is one of the purposes of the statement of cash flows.

___ 5. Repayment of notes and the payment of dividends are examples of investing activities.

___ 6. Cash flows from operating activities include purchases and sales of plant assets.

___ 7. The statement of cash flows can be prepared using either the indirect method or the direct method.

___ 8. Free cash flow measures the company's ability to generate operating cash flows in relation to net income.

___ 9. Cash flow yield is the ratio of a company's net cash flows from operating activities to its net income.

___ 10. Cash flow yield is the amount of cash remaining after deducting funds needed for planned operations.

Multiple-Choice Questions

— 1. Which of the following is NOT included in a statement of cash flows?
  a. Cash flows from operating activities.
  b. Cash flows from investing activities.
  c. Cash flows from financing activities.
  d. Cash flows from industry averages.
  e. All of the above.

— 2. Which of the following represent the day-to-day transactions that generate revenues, expenses, gains, and losses for a company?
  a. Operating activities
  b. Investing activities
  c. Financing activities
  d. Free flow activities
  e. Cash yield activities

— 3. Which of the following represent transactions concerning debt and stockholders' equity?
  a. Operating activities
  b. Investing activities
  c. Financing activities
  d. Free flow activities
  e. Cash yield activities

— 4. Which of the following include gains and losses related to purchasing and selling of plant assets?
  a. Operating activities
  b. Investing activities
  c. Financing activities
  d. Free flow activities
  e. Cash yield activities

— 5. On the statement of cash flows, items that reduce net income, but do not reduce cash, are treated as positive adjustments. Which of the following is NOT a positive adjustment?
  a. Depreciation
  b. Loss on sale of plant assets
  c. Increases in current liabilities
  d. Decreases in current liabilities
  e. Decreases in current assets other than cash

— 6. Which of the following shows the company's cash receipts and cash payments?
  a. Income statement
  b. Statement of stockholders' equity
  c. Statement of cash flows
  d. Balance sheet
  e. All the financial statements

— 7. Which method for preparing a statement of cash flows makes adjustments to all items on the income statement, converting them from the accrual basis to the cash basis, resulting in net cash flows from operating activities?
  a. Select method
  b. Conversion method
  c. Cash flow method
  d. Indirect method
  e. Direct method

— 8. Which method for preparing a statement of cash flows makes adjustments to only select income statement items, those necessary to convert net income into net cash flows from operating activities?
  a. Select method
  b. Conversion method
  c. Cash flow method
  d. Indirect method
  e. Direct method

— 9. Major Corporation has the following: $200,000 net cash flows from operating activities, $50,000 in dividends, $60,000 in purchases of plant assets, and $40,000 in sales of plant assets. What is Major Corporation's free cash flow?
  a. $50,000
  b. $90,000
  c. $130,000
  d. $150,000
  e. $300,000

— 10. Which of the following is the ratio of a company's net cash flows from operating activities to its net income.
  a. Free cash flow
  b. Petty cash
  c. Cash flow ratio
  d. Cash flow yield
  e. Cash dividend

Chapter

13

Financial Statement Analysis

LEARNING OBJECTIVES

After studying Chapter 13, you should be able to do the following:

1. Describe the importance of financial statement analysis to people within and outside the business.
2. Explain why financial analysis is performed.
3. Calculate and interpret financial ratios.
4. Prepare a vertical analysis of the financial statements for a business.
5. Prepare a horizontal analysis of the financial statements for a business.
6. Prepare a trend analysis of the financial data for a business.
7. Explain how comparative analyses are performed.

CHAPTER CONTENTS

Financial Statement Analysis

¶1301

Financial statement analysis is an evaluation of a company's financial statements in order to identify significant trends or relationships among the items.

Applications to People Within and Outside the Firm

LEARNING OBJECTIVE 1: Describe the importance of financial statement analysis to people within and outside the business.

Financial statement analysis is an evaluation of the financial statements to identify significant trends or relationships among the items contained within them. It is a tool for evaluating a company's success or failure. Various financial ratios are used in financial statement analysis. A financial ratio shows the relationship of a number on the financial statements to another number. Financial ratios are designed to assess different aspects of the firm's financial situation.

¶1301.01   ## INTERNAL USERS

Within the firm, management personnel analyze the company's financial statements as part of the evaluation of their own management performance. The financial statements are similar to a report card of a company's management. Management can evaluate whether its planning and control activities are having the desired impact on the company's operations and financial performance.

For example, the marketing manager at a Ford dealership wants to know how quickly vehicles are being sold off the lot. Using information from the financial statements, he or she can compute inventory turnover, which indicates the number of times the average amount in inventory is sold in a year. Perhaps the finance manager wants to know if the collections personnel are doing a good job managing Ford's accounts receivable. He or she can compute receivables turnover, which measures a company's ability to collect cash from customers who bought on credit.

¶1301.02   ## EXTERNAL USERS

Outside the firm, financial analysts, investors, lenders, and other parties analyze the financial statements to determine how well the company is performing, and how well it is likely to do in the future. Positive trends in financial performance are indicators that the company has positive future prospects. This is good news for investors, and typically leads to higher stock prices. Negative trends suggest a difficult future for the firm. In the worst case, the firm might even face financial ruin and bankruptcy.

Could financial analysis be a useful tool in your future job?

Positive trends in financial performance are equally good news for lenders, as positive trends provide comfort that loans will be repaid. For example, suppose Ford applies for a loan from Wells Fargo Bank. In deciding whether to loan the money, Wells Fargo may look at Ford's financial statements in order to compute its interest coverage ratio, which shows Ford's ability to make interest payments. Wells Fargo may also look at Ford's debt to assets ratio, which shows the proportion of total assets financed by the business firm's creditors. These and other financial ratios will be discussed in this chapter.

¶1302   Analyzing Financial Performance

LEARNING OBJECTIVE 2: Explain why financial analysis is performed.

Measuring financial performance begins with the information provided directly on the financial statements. On the surface, financial statements provide answers to key questions asked by management, investors, lenders, and other parties interested in a firm's performance. For example, the income statement answers the question: How much did the firm earn or lose from operations during the period? The statement of stockholders' equity answers the question: In what way did the firm's retained earnings and other stockholders' equity accounts change during the period? The balance sheet answers the question: What is the firm's financial position at a designated point in time? The statement of cash flows answers the question: What amount of cash was received and disbursed during the period?

Questions that are not answered by simply reviewing a single year's financial statement, include the following:

- What change has occurred in revenue over the past few years?
- Has the company improved its capacity to pay back its current liabilities with current assets?
- Is the amount of net income generated from each dollar of net sales increasing or decreasing from one year to the next?
- How does the gross profit of one company compare to another company within the same industry?

Have you ever analyzed your own financial situation? What problems or goals did the analysis help you identify?

Several techniques can be used to further explore a company's financial performance. In this chapter, we will examine analysis techniques including:

- Financial Analysis Ratios,
- Vertical Analysis,
- Horizontal Analysis,
- Trend Analysis, and
- Comparative Analysis.

¶1303   Financial Ratios

LEARNING OBJECTIVE 3: Calculate and interpret financial ratios.

A financial ratio is the relationship of one number on the financial statements to another number.

Examining individual numbers such as revenues and net income is a good starting point for financial statement analysis. In addition to individual numbers, financial performance analysis should also look at **financial ratios,** which show the relationship of one number on the financial statements to another number.

Consider that a company's reported net income is $350,000. While this is important information, deeper insight may be gained on the company's profitability by comparing net income to another amount, like net sales, during that same fiscal period. This comparison gives investors an idea of the proportion of net income created from each dollar of sales. Financial ratios are key tools for measuring financial performance, because they are designed to assess various aspects of a company's financial condition.

Financial ratios help evaluate a company's financial performance over time. For example, an increase in net income from year to year is a good trend. However, if the ratio of net income to net sales is declining, this is a cause for concern, regardless of the fact that net income is increasing. Furthermore, financial ratios enable meaningful comparisons among companies of different sizes, to assess which are performing better or worse. For example, when comparing two companies, the total dollar amount of debt is less important than the ratio of total debt to total assets. The company with the most debt may be in better financial condition because it has proportionately much more in total assets. Financial ratios put companies of different sizes on equal footing for comparison of financial performance.

Financial ratios can be categorized as follows:

- Liquidity ratios: Measure firm's ability to pay short-term debts.
- Profitability ratios: Measure firm's ability to earn a satisfactory net income.
- Long-Term Solvency ratios: Measure firm's ability to pay long-term debt.
- Stock Performance ratios: Measure firm's ability to attract investors.

¶1303.01 LIQUIDITY RATIOS

Liquidity ratios indicate the firm's ability to obtain cash and pay short-term liabilities.

Liquidity ratios indicate the firm's ability to obtain cash and thereby pay short-term liabilities as they come due. Liquidity ratios include the following: current ratio, acid-test ratio, receivable turnover, and inventory turnover.

¶1303.01.01 Current Ratio

Current ratio shows the firm's ability to pay its current liabilities using current assets.

The most frequently-used liquidity ratio is the **current ratio**, which is calculated as current assets divided by current liabilities. Thus, the current ratio shows the firm's ability to pay its current liabilities using current assets.

$$\text{Current Ratio} \; = \; \frac{\text{Current Assets}}{\text{Current Liabilities}}$$

Exhibit 13.1 shows the comparative income statement and balance sheet for Ford Motor Company for three recent years, 20Y1, 20Y2, and 20Y3. The current ratios of Ford Motor Company at December 31, 20Y3 and 20Y2 are calculated as follows:

Ford's current ratio for 20Y3   = $58,921 / $52,676   =   1.12

Ford's current ratio for 20Y2   = $58,536 / $49,970   =   1.17

Exhibit 13.1 COMPARATIVE FINANCIAL STATEMENTS FOR FORD MOTOR COMPANY

Ford Motor Company Income Statement For Year Ended Dec. 31	($ Millions)		
	20Y3	**20Y2**	**20Y1**
Net Sales	$171,652	$164,338	$162,258
Cost and Expenses			
Cost of Goods Sold	135,856	129,685	125,027
Interest Expense	7,071	7,643	8,801
Other Costs and Expenses	23,872	25,671	27,366
Earnings Before Taxes	$4,853	$1,339	$1,064
Tax Expense (Benefit)	937	123	342
Discontinued Op. & Other Adjustments	429	721	1,702
Net Income	$3,487	$495	$(980)

Ford Motor Company Balance Sheet Dec. 31	($ Millions)		
Assets	**20Y3**	**20Y2**	**20Y1**
Cash	$23,511	$23,208	$12,221
Marketable Securities	9,507	10,439	18,271
Accounts Receivable	15,137	15,738	19,683
Inventory	10,766	9,151	6,977
Total Current Assets	58,921	58,536	57,152
Long-Term Assets	233,733	240,861	219,970
Total Assets	$292,654	$299,397	$277,122
Liabilities & Stockholders' Equity			
Current Liabilities	$52,676	$49,970	$43,995
Other Liabilities	223,933	237,776	227,537
Total Liabilities	$276,609	$287,746	$271,532
Total Stockholders' Equity	16,045	11,651	5,590
Total Liabilities & Stockholders' Equity	$292,654	$299,397	$277,122

Ford's current ratio decreased slightly from 20Y2 to 20Y3. The current ratio is tracked by financial analysts, investors, lenders, and company managers. Normally a higher current ratio indicates a better financial position. A higher current ratio implies that a company has adequate liquidity to carry out business operations.

What is a good current ratio? To evaluate any financial ratio, a comparison should be made using one or more past years of a company's data and benchmarking it against industry averages and similar ratios from key competitors. Ford's largest competitor, General Motors, had a current ratio of 1.37 in 20Y3, which was somewhat better than Ford's current ratio of 1.12. A rule of thumb is that companies should have a current ratio between 1 and 2.

The current ratio is often important in debt covenants. When a company borrows money, the lender will specify certain requirements to maintain the loan. These lending requirements, also called "debt covenants," may indicate that the borrower must maintain a specified minimum current ratio, such as 2.5. This helps to ensure that the borrower will have the money necessary to pay its interest obligations and later repay the loan.

¶1303.01.02 Acid-Test Ratio (Quick Ratio)

The acid-test ratio indicates whether a company is able to quickly pay its current liabilities.

A second measure of liquidity is the acid-test ratio. The **acid-test ratio**, also called the "**quick ratio**," is calculated by dividing the *most* liquid current assets (cash and marketable securities and receivables) by current liabilities. The acid-test ratio indicates whether a company is able to quickly pay its current liabilities, if required to do so.

$$\text{Acid-Test Ratio} = \frac{\text{Cash} + \text{Marketable Securities} + \text{Receivables}}{\text{Current Liabilities}}$$

Ford's acid-test ratios for 20Y3 and 20Y2 are calculated as follows:

Ford's acid-test ratio for 20Y3 = ($23,511 + $9,507 + $15,137) / $52,676 = 0.91

Ford's acid-test ratio for 20Y2 = ($23,208 + $10,439 + $15,738) / $49,970 = 0.99

Like Ford's current ratio, the acid-test ratio declined slightly from 20Y2 to 20Y3. The company's most liquid current assets are 0.91 times as much as its current liabilities. For most industries, an acid-test ratio of 0.90 is considered satisfactory.

¶1303.01.03 Receivables Turnover

The receivable turnover ratio shows how many times the average amount in accounts receivable is collected during a period.

A third measure of liquidity is receivable turnover. **Receivable turnover** is calculated by dividing net credit sales by average accounts receivable.

$$\text{Receivable Turnover} = \frac{\text{Net Credit Sales}}{\text{Average Accounts Receivable}}$$

The receivable turnover ratio shows how many times the average amount in accounts receivable is collected during a period. The receivable turnover ratio measures a company's ability to manage its accounts receivable and collect cash from credit customers. Consequently, the ratio is a report card on the effectiveness of the company's credit policies.

Ford's receivable turnover ratios for 20Y3 and 20Y2 are calculated as follows:

Ford's receivable turnover for 20Y3 = $171,652 / (($15,137 + $15,738) / 2) = 11.12

Ford's receivable turnover for 20Y2 = $164,338 / (($15,738 + $19,683) / 2)) = 9.28

A simple way to calculate the average accounts receivable is by adding the end-of-the-year balance to the start-of-the-year balance in accounts receivable and then dividing the sum by two.

Ford's 20Y3 receivable turnover is an improvement over the prior year's receivable turnover. Ford's receivable turnover increased from 9.28 in 20Y2 to 11.12 in 20Y3. In addition, Ford's 20Y3 receivable turnover of 11.12 is better than General Motor's 20Y3 receivable turnover of 9.27. This suggests that Ford is more effectively managing its credit policies.

¶1303.01.04 Inventory Turnover

The inventory turnover ratio is the number of times the average amount in inventory is sold in a year.

A fourth measure of liquidity is inventory turnover. **Inventory turnover** is calculated by dividing cost of goods sold by average inventory.

$$\text{Inventory Turnover} = \frac{\text{Cost of Goods Sold}}{\text{Average Inventory}}$$

The inventory turnover ratio is the number of times the average amount in inventory is sold in a year. Thus, inventory turnover measures a company's ability to manage its inventory.

The challenge of inventory management is keeping exactly the right amount of inventory on hand. Keeping too much inventory on hand leads to high warehouse and storage costs. On the other hand, if a company fails to keep enough inventory on hand, then the company may run out. Running out of inventory and being unable to fill customer orders is called a "stock out." When a stock out occurs, customers are dissatisfied and take their business elsewhere. Marketing research shows that when stock outs cause customers to go to competitors, those customers often continue doing business with the competitors indefinitely.

Ford's inventory turnover ratios for 20Y3 and 20Y2 are calculated as follows:

Ford's inventory turnover for 20Y3 = $\$135,856 / (\$10,766 + \$9,151) / 2)) = 13.64$

Ford's inventory turnover for 20Y2 = $\$129,685 / ((\$9,151 + \$6,977) / 2)) = 16.08$

The inventory turnover declined from 16.08 in 20Y2 to 13.64 in 20Y3. The slower turnover in 20Y3 might indicate a buildup in inventory due to an unexpected decline in auto sales. Alternatively, the increase in inventory might be planned, as production could be increased to meet anticipated higher future sales. Regarding comparisons to key competitors, Ford's inventory turnover of 13.64 in 20Y3 is comparable to General Motor's inventory turnover of 13.41 for the same year.

Inventory turnover is a particularly critical ratio for auto manufacturing firms and must be carefully monitored. When new model year autos are introduced, typically in the summer months, the older model year autos are not nearly as desirable. At that point, retail auto dealers are not too interested in buying the older model year autos from the manufacturer. If inventory builds up, prices might have to be deeply discounted to stimulate sales, which then reduces profitability.

The necessary data to compute liquidity ratios initially comes from various departments within the company. For instance, the finance department supplies information regarding marketable securities for the acid-test ratio. The marketing department provides information regarding credit sales for the receivables turnover ratio and inventory amounts for the inventory turnover ratio. The accounting department gathers the data and provides financial statement analysis that will assist management in making better-informed decisions.

¶1303.01.05   Summary of Liquidity Ratios

Liquidity ratios help the departments within a company monitor the effectiveness of their various functions. For instance, the current ratio and acid-test ratio help the finance department focus on whether the amount of debt the company has incurred is manageable. Better decisions can be made regarding the firm's liquidity and potential need for financing. The production department benefits from the inventory turnover ratio, which indicates whether inventory is under- or over-stocked. Inventory turnover also assists the marketing department in understanding whether it is producing enough sales volume. Exhibit 13.2 provides a summary of the liquidity ratios.

Exhibit 13.2 LIQUIDITY RATIOS

Ratio	Purpose	Formula
Current ratio	Measures ability to pay current liabilities out of current assets.	Current assets / Current liabilities
Acid-test ratio	Measures ability to quickly pay current liabilities out of the most liquid current assets.	(Cash + marketable securities + receivables) / Current liabilities
Receivables turnover	Measures ability to collect cash from accounts receivable.	Net credit sales / Average accounts receivable
Inventory turnover	Measures ability to manage and sell inventory.	Cost of goods sold / Average inventory

¶1303.02   PROFITABILITY RATIOS

Profitability ratios indicate a firm's ability to make a satisfactory profit.

Profitability ratios indicate a firm's ability to make a satisfactory profit. Profitability is essential for a company to be able to provide investors a return on their investment and to pay back loans received from lenders. If a company fails to achieve a reasonable profitability, investors and lenders will be unwilling to provide the company with additional capital. Profitability ratios include the following: earnings per share, profit margin, asset turnover, return on assets, and return on common stockholders' equity. With the exception of asset turnover, the profitability ratios include net income (profit) in their formulas.

¶1303.02.01 Earnings Per Share

The earnings per share (EPS) ratio shows the firm's earnings per common share of stock.

The most frequently-quoted profitability ratio is **earnings per share (EPS)**. EPS is calculated by dividing the firm's net income, less preferred dividends, by average common shares outstanding. EPS shows the firm's earnings per common share of stock.

$$\text{EPS} = \frac{\text{Net Income – Preferred Dividends}}{\text{Average Common Shares Outstanding}}$$

Unlike other ratios, EPS is unique because it must be included on the income statement. Ford's EPS ratios for 20Y3 and 20Y2 are calculated as follows:

Ford's EPS ratio for 20Y3	=	($3,487 – $0) / 1,830	=	1.91
Ford's EPS ratio for 20Y2	=	($495 – $0) / 1,832	=	0.27

Ford's earnings per share (EPS) increased significantly from 20Y2 to 20Y3. This increase in EPS was the result of a significant increase in net income. As shown in the formula, Ford has no preferred dividends. The average common shares outstanding decreased slightly from 1,832 to 1,830 million. Average common shares can be calculated by adding the common shares at the beginning of the year to the common shares at the end of the year, and dividing the sum by two.

Financial analysts, investors, lenders, and company management are interested in changes in EPS from year to year. However, EPS alone is not meaningful when comparing one company to another. Instead, the comparative power of EPS is used in calculating the PE ratio, where EPS is divided into a company's stock price. (The result is called the "price to earnings" (P/E) ratio and is described in ¶1303.04.05 below, "Summary of Stock Performance Ratios.")

¶1303.02.02 Return on Sales (Profit Margin)

Return on sales or profit margin shows the proportion of net income created from each dollar of net sales.

A second measure of profitability is return on sales, also called "sales profit margin" or simply "profit margin." **Return on sales** or **profit margin** is calculated by dividing net income by net sales. Thus, return on sales shows the proportion of net income created from each dollar of net sales.

$$\text{Return on Sales or Profit Margin} = \frac{\text{Net Income}}{\text{Net Sales}}$$

Ford's return on sales (profit margin) ratios for 20Y3 and 20Y2 are calculated as follows:

Ford's profit margin for 20Y3	=	$3,487 / $171,652	=	0.02
Ford's profit margin for 20Y2	=	$495 / $164,338	=	0.003

The profit margin increased substantially from .003 to .02, that is, 0.3% to 2.0% between 20Y2 and 20Y3. This compares favorably with Ford's competitor, General Motors, which had a profit margin of 1.4% in 20Y3. Every company seeks a high return on sales, since this yields more income that can be reinvested in company operations or paid out as dividends to stockholders.

¶1303.02.03 Asset Turnover

Asset turnover shows how efficiently assets are able to generate sales.

A third measure of profitability is asset turnover. **Asset turnover** is calculated by dividing net sales by average total assets. The asset turnover shows how efficiently assets are able to generate sales.

$$\text{Asset Turnover} = \frac{\text{Net Sales}}{\text{Average Total Assets}}$$

Ford's asset turnover ratios for 20Y3 and 20Y2 are calculated as follows:

Ford's asset turnover for 20Y3   = $171,652 / (($292,654 + $299,397) / 2)   =   0.580

Ford's asset turnover for 20Y2   = $164,338 / (($299,397 + $277,122) / 2)   =   0.570

Going from 20Y2 to 20Y3, Ford marginally improved its asset turnover, which means that the company produced more sales revenue per dollar of assets in 20Y3 than in 20Y2. Ford's asset turnover was better than its competitor, General Motors, in 20Y3, whose asset turnover ratio was 0.417.

¶1303.02.04   Return on Assets

Return on assets (ROA) shows how efficiently a company uses its assets to generate income for the owners and creditors of the company.

A fourth measure of profitability is return on assets. **Return on assets (ROA)** is calculated by dividing the sum of net income and interest expense less tax savings, by average assets.

$$\text{Return on Assets} \;=\; \frac{\text{Net Income} + \text{Interest Expense} - \text{Tax Savings}}{\text{Average Assets}}$$

ROA indicates how efficiently a company uses its assets to generate income for the owners and creditors of the company. Shareholders are the owners of the company and net income is the return on their investment. The creditors loan the company money, and interest expense is the return on their loan, that is, their investment. Thus, the sum of net income and interest expense is the return to the two groups who have financed the assets used in the company operations.

Return on assets (ROA) ratios for Ford Motor Company for 20Y3 and 20Y2 are calculated as follows:

Ford's ROA 20Y3   =   ($3,487 + $7,071 – $2,828) / (($292,654 + $299,397) / 2)   =   0.026

Ford's ROA 20Y2   =   ($495 + $7,643 – $3,057) / (($299,397 + $277,122) / 2)   =   0.018

As shown in the ROA formula, the tax savings resulting from interest expense is subtracted from the interest expense. For example, in 20Y3, Ford's interest expense was $7,071. The interest expense of $7,071 is before taxes. The company's tax rate is 40%. Thus, tax savings from interest expense is $2,828 ($7,071 × .40). Interest expense less tax savings is $4,243 (($7,071 – $2,828).

Improving from 20Y2 to 20Y3, Ford's ROA in 20Y3 of 0.026, or 2.6%, compares favorable with its competitor, General Motors, which has an ROA of 0.022, or 2.2%. Companies strive to generate as high a return on assets as possible, thereby benefiting shareholders and lenders.

¶1303.02.05   Return on Equity

Return on equity (ROE) shows how much profit is earned for each dollar invested by the common shareholders.

A fifth measure of profitability is return on equity (ROE). **Return on equity (ROE)** is calculated as follows: net income minus preferred dividends (if any), divided by average common stock equity.

$$\text{Return on Equity} \;=\; \frac{\text{Net Income} - \text{Preferred Dividends}}{\text{Average Common Stockholders' Equity}}$$

ROE shows how much profit is earned for each dollar invested by the common shareholders. For this reason, return on equity is also called "return on common shareholders' equity" or "return on common stock equity." Almost always, the ratio is simply referred to as "return on equity" (ROE), and it is understood to refer to the equity of common shareholders.

Return on equity (ROE) ratios for Ford Motor Company for 20Y3 and 20Y2 are calculated as follows:

Ford's ROE for 20Y3   =   ($3,487 – $0) / (($16,045 + $11,651) / 2)   =   0.252

Ford's ROE for 20Y2   =   ($495 – $0) / (($11,651 + $5,590) / 2)   =   0.057

As shown in the ROE formula, Ford's preferred dividends are $0, as Ford has no preferred stock. If Ford did have preferred stock, the preferred dividends would be subtracted from net income in the ROE formula. In addition, if Ford had preferred stock, then preferred stockholders' equity would be subtracted from total stockholders' equity to compute common stockholders' equity.

In 20Y3, ROE of 0.252 or 25.2% is much higher than its return on assets (ROA) of 0.026 or 2.6%. This is a result of positive leveraging, which occurs when the return on borrowed money is higher than the cost of borrowing. Achieving an ROE higher than its ROA occurs when a company borrows at one rate, such as 7%, and invests funds to yield a higher rate, such as the firm's 25.2% ROE. Ford's 20Y3 ROE compares favorably to its competitor, General Motors, whose 20Y3 ROE was 10.6%.

¶1303.02.06 Summary of Profitability Ratios

Profitability ratios provide information that can assist department managers in performing their jobs more effectively. For instance, profitability ratios that show positive trends help the finance department secure loans for the company, since these positive trends provide reassurance that loans will be repaid. Good profitability ratios also help the production or marketing department obtain suppliers, since they are indicators that the company is in good financial condition with the ability to pay its bills. Exhibit 13.3 provides a summary of the profitability ratios.

Exhibit 13.3 PROFITABILITY RATIOS

Ratio	Purpose	Formula
Earnings per share (EPS)	Shows the firm's earnings per common share of stock.	(Net income – pref. dividends) / Avg. common shares outstanding
Return on sales (Profit margin)	Shows the proportion of net income created from each dollar of net sales.	Net income / Net sales
Asset turnover	Shows how efficiently assets are able to generate sales.	Net sales / Average assets
Return on assets (ROA)	Indicates how efficiently a firm uses its assets to generate income for owners and creditors.	(Net income + interest exp. – tax savings) / average assets
Return on equity (ROE)	Shows how much profit is earned from each dollar invested by the common shareholders.	(Net income – pref. dividends) / Average common stock equity

¶1303.03 LONG-TERM SOLVENCY RATIOS

Long-term solvency ratios indicate the business firm's ability to meet its long-term obligations.

Long-term solvency ratios indicate the business firm's ability to meet its long-term obligations. Being able to pay off long-term debt is essential to successful operations in future years. Poor long-term solvency ratios may be a warning sign that the firm is in danger of future bankruptcy. The two key long-term solvency ratios are debt to assets ratio and times-interest-earned ratio

¶1303.03.01 Debt to Assets Ratio

The debt to assets ratio shows the proportion of total assets financed by the business firm's creditors.

The most common measure of long-term solvency is the debt to assets ratio. The **debt to assets ratio** is calculated by dividing the firm's total liabilities by its total assets.

$$\text{Debt to Assets Ratio} = \frac{\text{Total Liabilities}}{\text{Total Assets}}$$

The debt to assets ratio shows the proportion of total assets financed by the business firm's creditors. Thus, the debt to assets ratio is a measure of the firm's capital structure. The ratio is also referred to as simply the "debt ratio."

The debt to assets ratios for Ford Motor Company for 20Y3 and 20Y2 are calculated as follows:

Ford's debt to assets for 20Y3	=	$276,609 / $292,654	=	0.945
Ford's debt to assets for 20Y2	=	$287,746 / $299,397	=	0.961

In 20Y3, Ford's debt to assets ratio is marginally better than its ratio in 20Y2. The debt to assets declined from 96.1% in 20Y2 to 94.5% in 20Y3. This means Ford used debt to finance 94.5% of its assets in 20Y3. Ford's debt to assets ratio is comparable to its competitor, General Motors, whose debt to assets ratio in 20Y3 is 94.1%. Generally, less debt to assets is regarded as less risky. You may question why a business firm takes on any debt, if that increases risk. The answer relates to the leveraging concept. As long as the firm earns a return on assets that is higher than the cost of interest, the firm makes a profit.

¶1303.03.02 Times-Interest-Earned Ratio

Times-interest-earned ratio, also called the "interest-coverage ratio," shows the ability of the firm to make interest payments.

A second measure of long-term solvency is the times-interest-earned ratio. **Times-interest-earned ratio,** also called the "**interest coverage ratio,**" is calculated by dividing earnings before interest and taxes (EBIT) by interest expense.

$$\text{Times-Interest- Earned Ratio} \ = \ \frac{\text{Net Income + Interest Expense + Tax Expense}}{\text{Interest Expense}}$$

The debt to assets ratio shows the proportion of assets financed by debt, but that ratio does not specifically address the firm's ability to pay interest expense. A firm with a higher times-interest-earned ratio has a greater ability to pay its interest expense. As a result, creditors to the firm are more secure, since the firm is less likely to default on interest payments.

Times–interest-earned ratios for Ford Motor Company for 20Y3 and 20Y2 are calculated as follows:

Ford's times interest earned for 20Y3   =   ($3,487 + $7,071 +$937) / $7,071   =   1.63

Ford's times interest earned for 20Y2   =   ($495 + $7,643 + $123) / $7, 643   =   1.08

As shown, Ford's times-interest-earned ratio strengthened from 1.08 in 20Y2 to 1.63 in 20Y3. A stronger times-interest-earned ratio is good news to creditors because this means that Ford is better able to pay its interest expense. Ford's 20Y3 times interest earned of 1.63 compares favorable to General Motors' 20Y3 times interest earned of 1.158.

¶1303.03.03 Summary of Long-Term Solvency Ratios

Exhibit 13.4 provides a summary of the long-term solvency ratios.

Exhibit 13.4 LONG-TERM SOLVENCY RATIOS		
Ratio	**Purpose**	**Formula**
Debt to assets ratio	Shows the proportion of total assets financed by the firm's creditors.	Total liabilities / Total assets
Times-interest-earned ratio	Shows the proportion of assets financed by debt.	Net income + taxes + interest expense / Interest expense

¶1303.04   STOCK PERFORMANCE RATIOS

Stock performance ratios help investors evaluate the current and potential future value of a company's stock.

Stock performance ratios help investors evaluate the current and potential future value of a company's stock. When investors purchase stock, they hope to obtain a return on their investment. The return on investment can take two forms: (1) gains or losses from selling the stock for more or less than the price paid, and (2) dividends. The market price of a company's stock is the amount investors are willing to pay at a specific point in time. It is the price at which the stock is bought and sold.

The stock performance ratios, which are related to the stock's market price, include the following: price to earnings, dividend yield, book value per share, and market price to book value.

¶1303.04.01 Price to Earnings Ratio

The price to earnings (P/E) ratio indicates the confidence of investors in a company.

The price to earnings (P/E) ratio indicates the confidence of investors in a company. The **price to earnings (P/E) ratio** is calculated by dividing the market price per share by the earnings per share (EPS).

$$\text{Price to earnings ratio} \quad = \quad \frac{\text{Market Price Per Share}}{\text{Earnings Per Share}}$$

When investors anticipate that a company's future earnings will grow faster than average, they are willing to pay a higher price relative to current earnings, thus, resulting in a higher than average P/E ratio. The P/E ratio is usually shown in stock listings in newspapers such as The Wall Street Journal, and financial websites, like Yahoo! Finance (www.finance.yahoo.com) and NYSE.com.

The P/E ratios for Ford Motor Company for 20Y3 and 20Y2 are calculated as follows:

Ford's P/E ratio for 20Y3	=	$14.64 / $1.91	=	7.66
Ford's P/E ratio for 20Y2	=	$16.00 / $0.27	=	59.26

Ford's P/E ratio decreased from 59.26 in 20Y2 to 7.66 in 20Y3. The large decrease was the result of a large increase in the ratio's denominator; Ford's earnings increased from $0.27 to $1.91 per share. The current decrease in the P/E ratio indicates that investors do not believe that earnings will continue to grow in future years sufficiently to merit a high P/E ratio of 59.26. Investors are willing to pay 7.66 times the earnings, which indicates that investors expect earnings to grow only at a moderate pace. Ford's 20Y3 P/E ratio is comparable to General Motors' 20Y3 P/E ratio of 8.07.

As with other ratios, what is considered a good or bad P/E ratio varies from industry to industry. P/E ratios larger than 50 are common among high tech firms (such as Google), while P/E ratios ranging from six to ten are prevalent among utility companies (such as Texas Utilities). Investors often regard stocks with higher P/E ratios as having higher downside risk, that is, the risk that the market price will decline. For that reason, a sudden jump in the P/E ratio will cause some investors to sell the stock.

¶1303.04.02 Dividend Yield

The dividend yield indicates the proportion of a stock's market price that the company pays to an investor in the form of dividends.

A second measure of stock performance is dividend yield. **Dividend yield** is calculated by dividing the dividends per share of stock by the market price per share.

$$\text{Dividend Yield} \quad = \quad \frac{\text{Dividends Per Share of Stock}}{\text{Market Price Per Share}}$$

The dividend yield indicates the proportion of a stock's market price that the company pays to an investor in the form of dividends. For stockholders who are interested in cash flow from their investments, the dividend yield is especially important.

The dividend yield for Ford Motor Company for 20Y3 and 20Y2 are calculated as follows:

Ford's dividend yield for 20Y3	=	$0.40 / $14.64	=	2.7%
Ford's dividend yield for 20Y2	=	$0.40 / $16.00	=	2.5%

Ford's dividend yield increased in 20Y3 because the market price per share decreased from $16 to $14.64, while the dividend remained constant at $0.40 per share. A stockholder of Ford Motor Company who pays $14.64 per share for the company stock would expect to receive 2.7% of the investment in annual dividends. In 20Y3, General Motors' yield was 5%, nearly double the dividend yield of Ford. Of course, dividend yield is only one aspect of a stock's return on investment; the change in the stock's market price is the other aspect.

Many older, established companies pay substantial dividends each year to their stockholders. Auto companies such as Ford, DaimlerChrysler, General Motors, and Toyota, typically pay dividends ranging from 2% to 6%. Technology companies emphasizing company growth, such as Amazon, EBay, Yahoo, and Google, typically pay little or no dividends. Depending on the investors' need for cash flow, an investor will buy stocks with relatively high or low dividend yields.

¶1303.04.03 Book Value Per Share

Book value per share shows the recorded accounting amount per share.

A third measure of stock performance is book value per share. **Book value per share** is calculated by dividing common stockholders' equity by the number of common shares outstanding.

$$\text{Book Value Per Share} \quad = \quad \frac{\text{Common Stockholders' Equity}}{\text{Common Shares Outstanding}}$$

Common stockholders' equity is total stockholders' equity less preferred stockholders' equity. Book value per share shows the recorded accounting amount per share.

The book value per share for Ford Motor Company for 20Y3 and 20Y2 are calculated as follows:

Ford's book value per share for 20Y3   = $16,045 / 1,830   = $8.77

Ford's book value per share for 20Y2   = $11,651 / 1,832   = $6.36

The increase in Ford's book value per share from $6.36 in 20Y2 to $8.77 in 20Y3 is the result of a large increase in Ford's common stockholders' equity and a small decrease in common shares outstanding. Ford's competitor, General Motors, has a 20Y3 book value per share of $49.06. Comparing book values per share of different companies is not meaningful for investment analysis unless the book value is compared to the stock's market price. Thus, many financial analysts use the ratio of market price to book value in their investment analysis.

¶1303.04.04 Market Price to Book Value

Market price to book value is the ratio of what investors are willing to pay compared to the recorded accounting amount per share of stock. Low market price to book value stocks are sometimes regarded as "value" stocks.

A fourth measure of stock performance is market price to book value. The **market price to book value** is calculated by dividing the market price per share by the book value per share.

$$\text{Market Price to Book Value} \quad = \quad \frac{\text{Market Price Per Share}}{\text{Book Value Per Share}}$$

Market price to book value is the ratio of what investors are willing to pay compared to the recorded accounting amount per share of stock. Many investors regard companies with low market price to book value ratios to be desirable investments. Investors who prefer stocks with low market to book ratios are referred to as "value" investors. Investors who prefer stocks with high market to book ratios are referred to as "growth" investors. Growth investors choose companies at which earnings are expected to increase significantly each year.

The market price to book value for Ford Motor Company for 20Y3 and 20Y2 are calculated as follows:

Ford's market price to book value for 20Y3   = $14.64 / $8.77   =   1.67

Ford's market price to book value for 20Y2   = $16.00 / $6.36   =   2.52

The decrease in Ford's market price to book value ratio, from 2.52 in 20Y2 to 1.67 in 20Y3, makes the stock more attractive to value investors. Similar to Ford, General Motors also has a low market price to book value ratio, 0.82 in 20Y3. Of course, investors should consider more than just one financial ratio in making investment decisions.

¶1303.04.05   Summary of Stock Performance Ratios

Exhibit 13.5 provides a summary of the stock performance ratios. By using these ratios, investors and analysts evaluate the current and potential future value of a company's stock.

Exhibit 13.5 STOCK PERFORMANCE RATIOS

Ratio	Purpose	Formula
Price to earnings (P/E)	Indicates the confidence of investors in a company.	Market price per share / Earnings per share (EPS)
Dividend yield	Indicates the proportion of a stock's market price that the company pays to an investor in the form of dividends.	Dividends per share of stock / Market price per share
Book value per share	Shows the recorded accounting amount per share.	Common stockholders' equity / Common shares outstanding
Market price to book value	The ratio of what investors are willing to pay compared to the recorded accounting amount per share of stock.	Market price per share / Book value per share

¶1303.05   HOW GAAP AFFECTS RATIOS

Financial ratios provide useful information for evaluating a company's financial performance. The ratios are derived from the information provided on the company's financial statements, which are prepared according to GAAP. You will recall that GAAP sometimes allows for more than one method to account for an item. Consequently, calculation of financial ratios may yield different results, depending on which accounting method is used.

Let's consider two examples: inventory methods and depreciation methods. Acceptable inventory methods include FIFO, LIFO, weighted average, and the specific identification method. (For further discussion of acceptable inventory methods, see Chapter 7, "Accounting for the Merchandising Firm.") The inventory method selected will affect the dollar amount in inventory. The amount in inventory is used in the computation of the inventory turnover ratio. Thus, depending on which inventory method is used, the inventory turnover ratio will be higher or lower. Inventory is also included in the calculation of the current ratio, so that ratio would also be affected by the inventory method used.

Depreciation, like inventory, can be accounted for using different GAAP-approved methods. Depreciation methods include straight-line, units-of-production, and double-declining-balance method. (For further discussion of depreciation methods, see Chapter 8, "Plant Assets, Intangibles, and Long-Term Investments.") The depreciation method selected will affect amounts shown on the financial statements, which in turn will affect the financial ratios. For example, if depreciation expense is reduced, then net income is increased. As a result, most of the profitability ratios will be enhanced.

Company managers may be tempted to change accounting methods for the purpose of manipulating financial ratios. To change accounting methods solely for the purpose of improving ratios is unacceptable. Furthermore, investors, lenders, and financial analysts would eventually see through such deception. This, in turn, would lead to lower trust and lower stock prices.

¶1303.06   RATIO ANALYSIS OF A SMALL BUSINESS

Using some of the financial ratios that we have just discussed, let's evaluate how well our small business, JK Productions, is doing. The financial statements previously shown in Chapter 4, "Measuring Profitability and Financial Position on the Financial Statements" (Exhibit 4.11), are used to calculate the following ratios.

¶1303.06.01   Current Ratio

Measuring the company's liquidity, its current ratio is 6.18 ($46,100 current assets / $7,460 current liabilities). Since this is the first operating year for JK Productions, a comparison should be made with industry averages and competitors to determine if this is a good current ratio. However, for many industries, a current ratio of 2.0 is regarded as satisfactory. Thus, we can say that our company appears to be in good shape regarding its ability to pay its current liabilities out of its assets.

¶1303.06.02 Earnings Per Share

Measuring profitability, JK Productions' earnings per share (EPS) is $0.96 ($9,640 net income / 10,000 average common shares outstanding). Another measure of profitability is the company's return on sales of 0.62 ($9,640 net income / $15, 400 net sales). Thus, $0.62 of net income is created from each dollar of net sales. JK Productions' profit margin is very positive.

¶1303.06.03 Debt to Assets Ratio

Measuring long-term solvency, JK Productions' debt to assets ratio is 0.0642 ($7,460 total liabilities / $116,100 total assets). This means the company uses debt to finance 6.44% of its assets. It is less risky for a small company to have a low debt to assets ratio, such as the one that JK Productions shows.

¶1303.06.04 Price to Earnings Ratio

Regarding your personal finances, do you have a good debt to assets ratio?

JK Productions issued 10,000 shares of stock to finance the business. How is that stock performing for the stockholders? If the market price is assumed to be $10.00 per share, then the price to earnings (P/E) ratio is 10.42 ($10.00 stock price / .96 EPS). Investors are willing to pay 10.42 times the earnings. Assume that JK Productions pays a $0.10 dividend per common share. The dividend yield is 0.01 ($0.10 dividend per share / $10.00 market price of stock). Thus, 1% of the stock's market price was paid in dividends to investors. For a somewhat risky investment in a new company, investors should be pleased with the stock performance. Overall, JK Productions' financial analysis shows promising signs of future growth and profits.

¶1304   Vertical Analysis

LEARNING OBJECTIVE 4: Prepare a vertical analysis of the financial statements for a business.

Vertical analysis shows the proportional relationships of the items in a financial statement.

Common-size statements result from vertical analysis and show percentages of a total figure that is set at 100%, such as net sales on the income statement.

In addition to ratio analysis, the use of vertical analysis is often useful to highlight relative changes of financial statement items. **Vertical analysis** shows the proportional relationships of the items included in a financial statement. In vertical analysis, a total figure on the statement is designated as 100% and all other items are shown as a component of this total figure.

The result of vertical analysis is a statement of percentages that is referred to as a "**common-size statement.**" For example, in preparing a vertical analysis of the income statement, the net sales amount is set at 100% and all other items are shown as a percentage of net sales.

The common-size income statements for Ford Motor Company for 20Y3 and 20Y2 are shown in Exhibit 13.6. As you can see, net sales is shown as 100% and all other income statement items are reflected as a percentage of net sales.

Exhibit 13.6 COMMON-SIZE INCOME STATEMENTS

Ford Motor CompanyCommon-Size Income Statement For Year Ended Dec. 31

	20Y3*	20Y2*
Net Sales	100.0%	100.0%
Cost and Expenses		
Cost of Goods Sold	79.1	78.9
Interest Expense	4.1	4.7
Other Costs and Expenses	13.9	15.6
Earnings Before Taxes	2.8%	0.8%
Tax Expense (Benefit)	0.5	0.1
Discontinued Op. & Other Adjustments	0.2	0.4
Net Income	2.0%	0.3%

*****Note:** Due to rounding, additions and subtractions do not always total precisely.

Using the common-size income statements, relative changes in income statement items are more obvious. For example, cost of goods sold as a percentage of sales increased from 78.9% in 20Y2 to 79.1% in 20Y3. Net income as a percentage of sales, which is called the "sales profit margin," increased from 0.3% in 20Y2 to 2.0% in 20Y3.

In preparing a vertical analysis of the balance sheet, the total assets amount and the total liabilities and stockholders' equity amount are set at 100%. Common-size balance sheets for Ford Motor Company are shown in Exhibit 13.7. As a percentage of total assets, cash increased slightly from 7.8% in 20Y2 to 8.0% in 20Y3. Total liabilities as a percentage of total assets decreased slightly from 96.1% in 20Y2 to 94.5% in 20Y3. The vertical analysis reveals that Ford uses a great amount of debt financing to pay for its assets. Using debt financing, as opposed to equity financing (issuing stock), results in greater financial risk for the company. On the other hand, debt financing also creates leverage that can be beneficial to return on equity.

Exhibit 13.7 COMMON-SIZE BALANCE SHEETS

Ford Motor Company Common-Size Balance Sheet December 31

Assets	20Y3*	20Y2*
Cash	8.0%	7.8%
Marketable Securities	3.2	3.5
Accounts Receivable	5.2	5.3
Inventory	3.7	3.1
Total Current Assets	20.1	19.6
Long-Term Assets	79.9	80.4
Total Assets	100.0%	100.0%
Liabilities & Stockholders' Equity		
Current Liabilities	18.0	16.7
Other Liabilities	76.5	79.4
Total Liabilities	94.5	96.1
Total Stockholders' Equity	5.5	3.9
Total Liabilities & Stockholders' Equity	100.0%	100.0%

*Note: Due to rounding, additions and subtractions do not always total precisely.

Have you ever performed a vertical analysis of your monthly budget? What amount would you designate as 100 percent in this analysis?

As you can see, vertical analysis shows the proportional relationships of the items in a financial statement and can reveal if one item is out-of-balance with the rest. For example, vertical analysis revealed that Ford uses a great amount of debt financing to pay for its assets.

FOCUS ON TECHNOLOGY

Using Microsoft Excel
Creating Common-Size Income Statements

Using Excel, we will recreate Exhibit 13.6, which shows the common-size income statements for Ford. In writing the necessary formulas, we will use relative and absolute addressing. With **relative** addressing, cell addresses within a formula will automatically change as you copy the formula from one cell to another. For example, suppose a cell contains the formula "=C5." If you copy this formula into the next row, the formula will automatically increase the row number by one and become "=C6."

With **absolute** addressing, the cell address will not change. To make a cell address absolute, put dollar signs ($) before the letter and the number of the cell; e.g. $C$5.

1. File Identification Area: Enter the appropriate information.
2. Input Area: Type the following into the designated rows and columns.

	20Y3*	20Y2*
Net Sales	100.0%	100.0%
Cost and Expenses		
Cost of Goods Sold	79.1	75.6
Interest Expense	4.1	4.5
Other Costs and Expenses	13.9	15.0
Earnings Before Taxes	2.8%	0.8%
Tax Expense (Benefit)	0.5	0.1
Discontinued Op. & Other Adjustments	0.2	0.4
Net Income	2.0%	0.3%

3. Output Area: Set up your headings to resemble Exhibit 13.6. Put the heading for 20Y3 in column C and the 20Y2 heading in column D. Set Net Sales equal to 100% for both years. With the help of relative and absolute addressing, you only need to type in one formula; this formula can be copied into the remaining cells. Using the addresses in the input area above, the formula for 20Y3 Cost of Goods Sold in the output area is =C21/$C$19*100. (Cost of Goods Sold / Net Sales* 100.) Since every item of the income statement will be divided by Net Sales, we want the Net Sales address to remain the same; thus we enter it as absolute with dollar signs. However, we want the first address within the formula (Cost of Goods Sold) to change as we copy it into the cells for Interest Expense, etc. For Interest Expense on the next row, the row number within the formula will change from C21 to C22 (=C22/$C$19*100).

The 20Y3 Cost of Goods Sold formula can also be copied into the column containing the 20Y2 Cost of Goods Sold. Using relative addressing, the column letter within the formula will automatically change from C21 to D21 (=D21/$C$19*100).

¶1305   Horizontal Analysis

LEARNING OBJECTIVE 5: Prepare a horizontal analysis of the financial statements for a business.

Horizontal analysis shows the percentage changes in financial statement items from one year to the next.

Horizontal analysis shows the percentage changes in financial statement items from one year to the next. Usually the change in dollars and percentages is shown. Investors are more interested in the percent change than the dollar change. For example, knowing that net income increased by 50% is more useful than knowing that the increase in net income is $50,000.

There are two steps in horizontal analysis.

1. Compute the dollar change from the base (earlier) period to the later period. The base period in any set of data is the first time period being studied.

$$\text{Percentage Change} \ = \ 100 \ \times \ \frac{\text{Amount of Change}}{\text{Base Period Amount}}$$

2. Second, divide the dollar amount of change by the base-period amount. The percentage change is calculated as shown:

Exhibit 13.8 shows the comparative income statements of Ford Motor Company with horizontal analysis.

Exhibit 13.8 COMPARATIVE INCOME STATEMENTS WITH HORIZONTAL ANALYSIS

Ford Motor Company Income Statement For Years Ended Dec. 31, 20Y3 and 20Y2 ($ Millions)	20Y3	20Y2	Increase (Decrease) Amount	Increase (Decrease) Percentage
Net Sales	$1717,652	$164,338	$7,314	4.5
Cost and Expenses				
Cost of Goods Sold	135,856	129,685	6,171	4.8
Interest Expense	7,071	7,643	(572)	(7.5)
Other Cost and Expenses	23,872	25,671	(1,799)	(7.0)
Earnings Before Taxes	$4,853	$1,339	$3,514	262.4
Tax Expense (Benefit)	937	123	814	661.8
Discontinued Op. & Other Adjustments	429	721	(292)	(40.5)
Net Income	$3,487	$495	$2,992	604.4

A horizontal analysis of comparative income statements for 20Y2 and 20Y3 reveals an increase in net sales from $164,338 million to $171,652 million. This is a dollar amount increase of $7,314 million or 4.5%. The change in net income is more significant, a dollar amount increase of $2,992 million or 604.4%. This very positive change was attained because net sales increased, while interest expense and other costs and expenses decreased.

Comparative balance sheets with horizontal analysis are displayed in Exhibit 13.9. As shown, several balance sheet accounts show a decrease from 20Y2 to 20Y3. However, the most notable change was an increase in stockholders' equity from $11,651 million in 20Y2 to $16,045 million in 20Y3, an increase of 37.7%.

Exhibit 13.9 COMPARATIVE BALANCE SHEETS WITH HORIZONTAL ANALYSIS

Ford Motor Company Balance Sheet Dec. 31, 20Y3 and 20Y2 ($ Millions)	20Y3	20Y2	Increase (Decrease) Amount	Increase (Decrease) Percentage
Assets				
Cash	$23,511	$23,208	$303	1.3
Marketable Securities	9,507	10,439	(932)	(8.9)
Accounts Receivable	15,137	15,738	(601)	(3.8)
Inventory	10,766	9,151	1,615	17.6
Total Current Assets	$58,921	$58,536	$385	0.7
Long-Term Assets	233,733	240,861	(7,128)	(3.0)
Total Assets	$292,654	$299,397	$(6,743)	(2.3)
Liabilities & Stockholders' Equity				
Current Liabilities	$52,676	$49,970	$2,706	5.4
Other Liabilities	223,933	237,776	(13,843)	(5.8)
Total Liabilities	$276,609	$287,746	$(11,137)	(3.9)
Total Stockholders' Equity	16,045	11,651	4,394	37.7
Total Liabilities & Stockholders' Equity	$292,654	$299,397	$(6,743)	(2.3)

[?] *If you performed a horizontal analysis of your yearly income, or your annual living expenses, what would you find?*

Using horizontal analysis, management can monitor the company's yearly progress, showing the percentage changes in financial statement items from one year to the next.

¶1306 Trend Analysis

LEARNING OBJECTIVE 6: Prepare a trend analysis of the financial data for a business.

Trend analysis shows percentage changes of key financial statement items for several time periods.

Examining financial statements from only one year is insufficient to adequately evaluate a business firm's performance. Analysis of financial statements from several years will provide a more complete understanding of the current situation and future outlook of a business firm. Typically, the best predictor of future performance is past performance. A trend analysis is an extension of horizontal analysis. **Trend analysis** shows percentage changes of key financial statement items for several time periods.

Exhibit 13.10 shows Ford Motor Company's total revenues for three years, 20Y1 to 20Y3. The exhibit also shows the company's net income. Ford displays a positive trend in both total revenues and net income.

Exhibit 13.10 FINANCIAL INFORMATION OF FORD MOTOR COMPANY

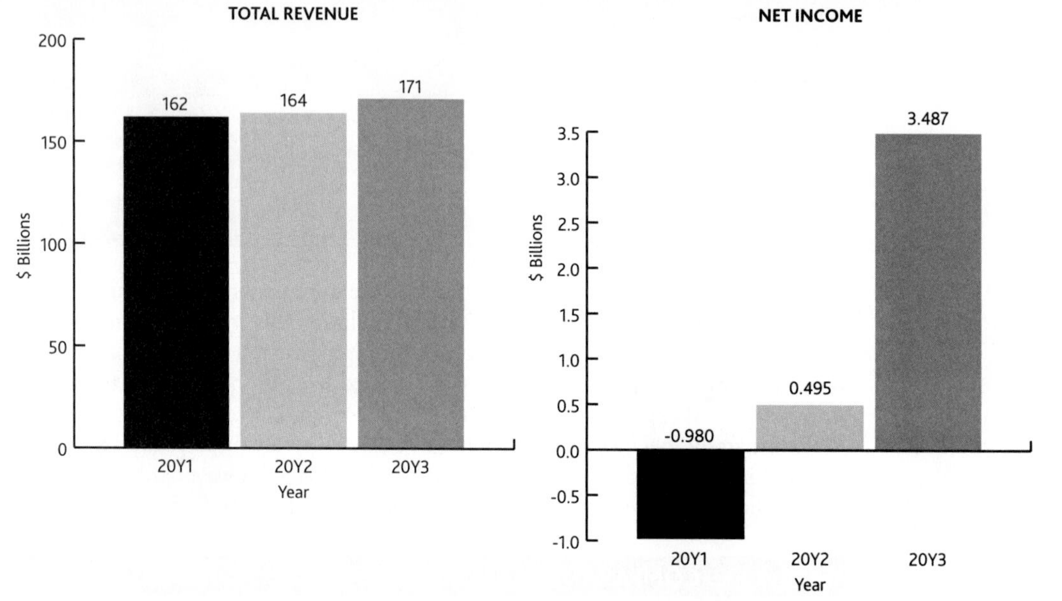

Revenues and net income both increased over the three-year period. Revenues went from $162.2 billion to $171.7 billion. Even more significantly, net income increased from a net loss of $0.98 billion to a net income of $3.48 billion. Based on the trend of these three years, you would expect Ford's revenues and net income to increase in the future.

Suppose an investor wants to see how sales for the Ford Motor Company have changed over the past three, four, or more years. A trend analysis can be presented in table form (as in Exhibit 13.11) or in a graphical presentation (as in Exhibit 13.12).

Exhibit 13.11 TREND ANALYSIS

Ford Motor Company Net Sales for Four Years

Year	Dollar Amount ($ Millions)	Percentage
20Y0	$160,652	100.0
20Y1	$162,258	101.0
20Y2	$164,338	102.3
20Y3	$171,652	106.8

Exhibit 13.12 TREND ANALYSIS PRESENTED GRAPHICALLY

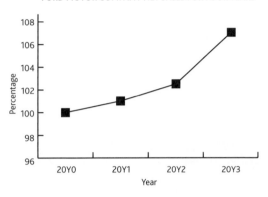

FORD MOTOR COMPANY NET SALES FOR FOUR YEARS

FOCUS ON ETHICS

Cooking the Books to Manipulate Trend Analysis

Trend analysis helps individuals evaluate a company's financial performance. As a general rule, a consistent growth in sales revenue and net income is a positive indicator of a company's current financial performance and its likely future success. Thus, company managers try to achieve this steady upward trend in revenue and net income. Most managers do so in an ethical manner and follow the rules of GAAP. If this were not true, investors would have little confidence in the stock market. However, there are some unethical managers who may attempt to violate GAAP and "cook the books" for the purpose of making earnings falsely appear to grow in a consistent fashion. Such efforts are referred to as "abusive earnings management" or "income smoothing."

The SEC has investigated companies that violate GAAP to varying degrees for the purpose of managing earnings. In the worst cases, the company managers were guilty of fraud and subject to criminal penalties. The independent auditors of some companies were held liable for failing to catch and correct the deceptive accounting practices. Major financial scandals such as Enron, Worldcom, Lucent, Cendant, and MicroStrategy involved questionable earnings management practices or outright fraud. Investors in these companies lost billions of dollars. Furthermore, many other people were negatively affected — from lenders whose loans were not paid back to employees who lost their jobs.

In some cases, warning signs of abusive earnings management are apparent. One such warning sign is when cash flows do not closely match earnings. If cash flows fall far behind revenues, that could signal that the company is overstating revenues by recognizing sales in inappropriate periods, making sales to non-creditworthy customers, or recording fictitious sales.

Another indicator that a company may be improperly recognizing receivables is the lack of a close correlation between receivables with revenues. If receivables increase much faster than revenues, that is an indicator that the company might be recording fictitious sales or otherwise inflating revenues and accounts receivable.

Source: Lorraine Magrath and Leonard G. Weld. Abusive Earnings Management and Early Warning Signs. The CPA Journal, Website: *http://www.nysscpa.org/cpajournal/2002/0802/features/f085002.htm* (August 1, 2006).

The Form 10-K is an annual report that most U.S. publicly-traded corporations must file with the SEC. The Form 10-K provides a comprehensive overview of the corporation's business and financial condition and includes audited financial statements.

Trend information is included in the annual financial report that publicly-traded corporations must file each year with the Securities and Exchange Commission (SEC). Most U.S. publicly-traded corporations must submit annual reports to the SEC on Form 10-K. The **Form 10-K** provides a comprehensive overview of the corporation's business and financial condition and includes audited financial statements. The Form 10-K includes trend information, such as a description of company's business development in the last five years, and five years of specified key financial information.

¶1307

Comparative Analysis

LEARNING OBJECTIVE 7: Explain how comparative analyses are performed.

To gain a better understanding of one company's financial performance, it is helpful to compare the company to a competitor or to industry averages. To evaluate Ford's financial performance, let's compare its financial ratios to those of one of its major competitors, General Motors Corporation. Exhibit 13.13 shows the total revenue and net income of General Motors for the same three-year period as shown for Ford.

Exhibit 13.13 FINANCIAL INFORMATION OF GENERAL MOTORS COMPANY

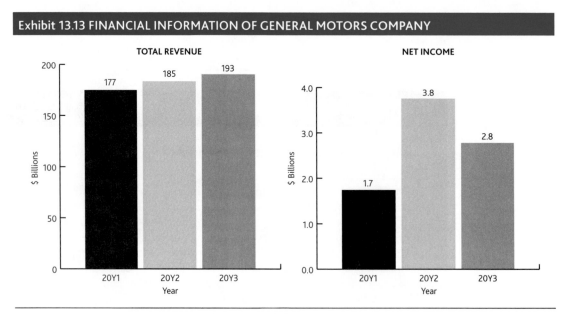

Like Ford, General Motors has a positive trend in total revenues. Unlike Ford, General Motors has a mixed trend in net income, an increase from 20Y1 to 20Y2 and a decrease from 20Y2 to 20Y3. Will net income go up or down in the next year? The mixed trend makes a future prediction more uncertain. Based on this one measure of financial performance, Ford compares favorably to General Motors, as Ford's trend in net income is steadily upward.

In addition to comparing a company's financial data and ratios to its competitors, comparing ratios of a company to industry averages can be beneficial. Ford is in the industry of major auto manufacturers, which includes companies such as GM, Toyota, and DaimlerChrysler. Industry averages can be obtained from financial websites such as Yahoo! Finance, E-trade, and VentureLine.

Exhibit 13.14 shows a comparison of selected financial ratios for Ford along with the industry averages. Ford's profit margin of 0.02, or 2.0%, is very close to the industry average of 0.019, or 1.9%. Ford's dividend yield of 0.027, or 2.7% is higher than the industry average of 0.011, or 1.1%.

Exhibit 13.14 COMPARISON OF FORD TO INDUSTRY AVERAGES OF MAJOR AUTO MANUFACTURERS

		Ford	Industry Average
Profit Margin (Return on Sales)	=	0.020	0.019
Return on Equity	=	0.252	0.091
Price to Earnings	=	7.683	22.500
Dividend Yield	=	0.027	0.011
Market Price to Book Value	=	1.670	1.700

Source: Yahoo! Finance website: *http://finance.yahoo.com/*.

In a general way, perhaps you have made a trend analysis of the cost of going to the movies, or the cost of DVDs. What does your trend analysis indicate?

In addition to comparative analysis, the information in the financial statements can be used in a variety of specialized analyses. For example, there have been numerous efforts to develop a bankruptcy prediction model using financial statement data. Bankruptcy prediction models are referred to as "measures of financial distress." Edward Altman, Professor of Finance at the Stern School of Business, New York University, developed one of the first and most well-known measures of financial distress: Altman's z-score or zeta model. Evaluating a firm's potential for bankruptcy is important to investors, lenders, and auditors, among others.

¶1308   Concluding Remarks

At the beginning of this chapter, we wondered whether Ford's P/E ratio of 7.66 was good or bad. You learned that the P/E ratio indicates the confidence of investors in a company and is calculated by dividing market price per share by the earnings per share. One way of determining if a financial ratio is good or bad is to compare it with competitors or industry averages. Since Ford's P/E ratio of 7.66 was comparable to General Motors' P/E ratio of 8.07, we concluded that the ratio is adequate.

We also wondered whether Ford stock was a good investment based on its dividend yield of 2.7%. If a stockholder is interested in cash flow from the investment, the dividend yield is especially important. The dividend yield indicates the proportion of a stock's market price that the company pays to an investor in the form of dividends. Auto companies typically pay dividends ranging from 2% to 6%. Thus, Ford's dividend yield is on the low end and GM may be a better investment with a dividend yield of 5%. However, you also learned there are other financial ratios to consider when evaluating an investment or a stock's performance.

Now we will expand our horizons, and explore the international marketplace in the next chapter. Let's learn how financial accounting and reporting is affected by global commerce.

¶1309

Chapter Review

LEARNING OBJECTIVE 1

Describe the importance of financial statement analysis to people within and outside the business.

Financial statement analysis is an evaluation of financial statements to identify significant trends or relationships among the items contained in the financial statements. To the people outside the firm, such as financial analysts, investors, and lenders, financial statement analysis is a tool for evaluating a company's success or failure. Within the firm, managers analyze the company's financial statements as part of the evaluation of their own managerial performances.

LEARNING OBJECTIVE 2

Explain why financial analysis is performed.

Measuring financial performance begins with the information provided directly on the financial statements. Analysis of financial statements helps users understand more fully the relationships of different financial amounts to others. It can be used to compare the performance of one company to another or identify trends in financial data.

LEARNING OBJECTIVE 3

Calculate and interpret financial ratios.

A financial ratio is the relationship of a number on the financial statements to another number. Financial ratios can be categorized as follows: (1) liquidity ratios, (2) profitability ratios, (3) long-term solvency ratios, and (4) stock performance ratios.

Liquidity ratios measure a firm's ability to pay short-term debts. Liquidity ratios include current ratio, acid-test ratio, receivables turnover, and inventory turnover. The current ratio shows the firm's ability to pay its current liabilities out of its current assets. The acid-test ratio indicates whether a company is able to quickly pay its current liabilities. The receivables turnover ratio shows how many times the average amount in accounts receivable is collected in a year. The inventory turnover ratio is the number of times the average amount in inventory is sold in a year.

Profitability ratios measure a firm's ability to earn a satisfactory net income. Profitability ratios include earnings per share, return on sales, asset turnover, return on assets, and return on common stockholders' equity. The earnings per share (EPS) ratio shows the firm's earnings per common share of stock. Return on sales or profit margin shows the proportion of net income created from each dollar of net sales. Asset turnover shows how efficiently assets are able to generate sales. Return on assets (ROA) shows how efficiently a company uses its assets to generate income for the owners and creditors of the company. Return on equity (ROE) shows how much profit is earned for each dollar invested by the common shareholders.

Long-term solvency ratios measure a firm's ability to pay long-term debt. The two key long-term solvency ratios are debt to assets ratio and times-interest-earned ratio. The debt to assets ratio shows the proportion of total assets financed by the business firm's creditors. The times-interest-earned ratio, also called the "interest-coverage ratio," shows the ability of the firm to make interest payments.

Stock performance ratios measure a firm's ability to attract investors. The stock performance ratios include price to earnings ratio, dividend yield, book value per share, and market price to book value. The price to earnings (P/E) ratio indicates the confidence of investors in a company. The dividend yield indicates the proportion of a stock's market price that the company pays to an investor in the form of dividends. Book value per share shows the recorded accounting amount per share. Market price to book value is the ratio of what investors are willing to pay compared to the recorded accounting amount per share of stock.

LEARNING OBJECTIVE 4

Prepare a vertical analysis of the financial statements for a business.

Vertical analysis shows the proportional relationships of the items included in one financial statement. In vertical analysis, a total figure on the statement is designated as 100% and all other items are shown as a component of this total figure. The result of vertical analysis is a statement of percentages called a "common-size statement."

LEARNING OBJECTIVE 5

Prepare a horizontal analysis of the financial statements for a business.

Horizontal analysis shows the percentage changes in financial statement items from one year to the next.

LEARNING OBJECTIVE 6

Prepare a trend analysis of the financial data for a business.

Trend analysis shows percentage changes of key financial statement items for several time periods. A trend analysis is an extension of horizontal analysis.

LEARNING OBJECTIVE 7

Explain how comparative analyses are performed.

A comparative analysis compares the financial data or ratios from one company to another, or to industry averages.

¶1310

Glossary

Acid-test ratio

The acid-test ratio, also called the "quick ratio," is calculated by dividing the most liquid current assets (cash and marketable securities and receivables) by current liabilities. This ratio is one of the liquidity ratios and indicates whether a company is able to quickly pay its current liabilities.

Asset turnover

Asset turnover shows how efficiently assets are able to generate sales. The formula is net sales divided by average total assets.

Book value per share

Book value per share shows the recorded accounting amount per share. It is calculated by dividing common stockholders' equity by the number of common shares outstanding.

Common-size statement

A common-size statement results from vertical analysis and shows individual financial statement components expressed as percentages of a total figure, such as net sales on the income statement (set at 100%).

Current ratio

The current ratio, computed by dividing current assets by current liabilities, is one of the liquidity ratios. Current ratio shows the firm's ability to pay its current liabilities using current assets.

Debt to assets ratio

The debt to assets ratio, also referred to as simply "debt ratio," shows the proportion of total assets financed by the business firm's creditors. It is calculated by dividing the firm's total liabilities by its total assets.

Dividend yield

The dividend yield indicates the proportion of a stock's market price that the company pays to an investor in the form of dividends. It is calculated by dividing the dividends per share of stock by the market price per share.

Earnings per share (EPS)

EPS is calculated by dividing the firm's net income, less preferred dividends, by the average common shares outstanding. EPS shows the firm's earnings per common share of stock.

Financial ratio

A financial ratio shows the relationship of a number on the financial statements to another number. Financial ratios are designed to assess different aspects of the firm's financial condition.

Financial statement analysis

Financial statement analysis is an evaluation of the financial statements to identify significant trends or relationships among the items contained in the financial statements.

Form 10-K

Form 10-K is an annual report that most U.S. publicly-traded corporations must file with the SEC. The Form 10-K provides a comprehensive overview of the corporation's business and financial condition, and includes audited financial statements.

Horizontal analysis

Horizontal analysis shows the percentage changes in financial statement items from one year to the next.

Interest coverage ratio

The interest coverage ratio, also called the "times-interest-earned ratio," shows the ability of the firm to make interest payments. It is calculated by dividing earnings before interest and taxes (EBIT) by interest expense.

Inventory turnover

Inventory turnover is calculated by dividing cost of goods sold by average inventory. This ratio is one of the liquidity ratios and indicates the number of times the average amount in inventory is sold in a year.

Liquidity ratios

Liquidity ratios indicate the business firm's ability to obtain cash and thereby pay short-term liabilities as they come due.

Market price to book value

Market price to book value is the ratio of what investors are willing to pay for a stock (market price) as compared to the recorded accounting amount per share (book value). This ratio is calculated by dividing the market price per share by the book value per share.

Price to earnings ratio (P/E)

The P/E ratio is calculated by dividing the market price per share by the earnings per share (EPS). The P/E ratio indicates the confidence of investors in a company.

Profit margin

Profit margin, also called "return on sales," shows the proportion of net income created from each dollar of net sales. It is calculated by dividing net income by net sales.

Quick ratio

The quick ratio, also called the "acid-test ratio," is calculated by dividing the most liquid current assets (cash and marketable securities and receivables) by current liabilities. This ratio indicates whether a company is able to quickly pay its current liabilities

Receivable turnover

Receivable turnover is calculated by dividing net credit sales by average accounts receivable. This ratio is one of the liquidity ratios and measures a company's ability to manage its accounts receivable and collect cash from credit customers.

Return on assets (ROA)

Return on assets (ROA) indicates how efficiently a company uses its assets to generate income for the owners and creditors of the company. ROA is calculated by dividing the sum of net income and interest expense less tax savings, by average assets.

Return on equity (ROE)

Return on equity (ROE) shows how much profit is earned for each dollar invested by the common shareholders. ROE is calculated as follows: net income minus preferred dividends (if any), divided by average common stock equity.

Return on sales

Return on sales, also called "profit margin," shows the proportion of net income created from each dollar of net sales. It is calculated by dividing net income by net sales.

Times-interest-earned ratio

Times-interest-earned ratio, also called the "interest coverage ratio," shows the ability of the firm to make interest payments. It is calculated by dividing earnings before interest and taxes (EBIT) by interest expense.

Trend analysis

Trend analysis shows percentage changes of key financial statement items for several time periods.

Vertical analysis

Vertical analysis shows the proportional relationships of the items within a financial statement.

¶1311 # Chapter Assignments

QUESTIONS

1. **[Obj. 1]** What is financial statement analysis and who uses it?

2. **[Obj. 2]** Why would an analyst want to look at a company's past financial statements in addition to the current year statements?

3. **[Obj. 2]** Define financial ratios, vertical analysis, and horizontal analysis.

4. **[Obj. 3]** What is the purpose of liquidity ratios? Describe four types of liquidity ratios.

5. **[Obj. 3]** Give the formulas for these liquidity ratios: current ratio, acid-test ratio, receivables turnover ratio, and inventory turnover ratio.

6. **[Obj. 3]** What does the receivables turnover ratio tell you about the company's credit policies?

7. **[Obj. 3]** How do you determine if a ratio is positive or negative regarding a company's financial condition?

8. **[Obj. 3]** What is the purpose of profitability ratios? Describe five types of profitability ratios.

9. **[Obj. 3]** Give formulas for these profitability ratios: earnings per share, return on sales, asset turnover, return on assets, and return on equity.

10. **[Obj. 3]** What is unique about earnings per share (EPS)?

11. **[Obj. 3]** Why are the shareholders and creditors of a company especially interested in the company's return on assets (ROA)?

12. **[Obj. 3]** What is the purpose of long-term solvency ratios? Describe two types of long-term solvency ratios.

13. **[Obj. 3]** Give formulas for these long-term solvency ratios: debt to assets ratio and times-interest-earned ratio.

14. **[Obj. 3]** What is the purpose of stock performance ratios? Describe four types of stock performance ratios.

15. **[Obj. 3]** Give formulas for these stock performance ratios: price to earnings (P/E), dividend yield, book value per share, and market price to book value.

16. **[Obj. 4]** What is vertical analysis and why use it?

17. **[Obj. 4]** What is a common-size statement and what is its purpose?

18. **[Obj. 5]** What is horizontal analysis and why use it?

19. **[Obj. 5]** Describe the two steps involved in horizontal analysis.

20. **[Obj. 6]** What is trend analysis?

SHORT EXERCISES – SET A

Building Accounting Skills

1. **[Obj. 1]** Analyze Financial Statement Information: Mastermind Media Company is entering its fourth year of business. Sales Revenues for its first three years were as follows: Year 1: $25 million; Year 2: $30 million; and Year 3: $40 million. Based on the sales revenue, analyze Mastermind's financial situation. Provide answers to the following questions:
   a. What kind of trend is this? Positive, negative, or mixed?
   b. What does this trend suggest to investors and lenders?
   c. How should company management react to this trend?

2. **[Obj. 2]** Measuring Financial Performance: On their surface, the financial statements provide answers to key questions asked by management, investors, lenders, and other parties interested in a firm's performance. Required: Identify the key question addressed by each of the following financial statements:
   a. Income statement
   b. Statement of stockholders' equity
   c. Balance sheet
   d. Statement of cash flows

3. **[Obj. 3]** Defining Financial Ratios: Match the following financial ratios to their descriptions.
   ___ 1. Receivables turnover
   ___ 2. Acid-test ratio
   ___ 3. Inventory turnover
   ___ 4. Current ratio
   ___ 5. Debt to assets ratio
   a. Measures ability to pay current liabilities out of current assets.
   b. Measures ability to manage and sell inventory.
   c. Measures ability to quickly pay current liabilities out of the most liquid current assets.
   d. Shows the proportion of total assets financed by the firm's creditors.
   e. Shows how many times the average amount in accounts receivable is collected in a year.

4. **[Obj. 3]** Defining Financial Ratios: Match the following financial ratios to their descriptions.
   ___ 1. Asset turnover
   ___ 2. Earnings per share (EPS)
   ___ 3. Return on assets (ROA)
   ___ 4. Profit margin
   ___ 5. Return on equity (ROE)
   a. Shows the firm's earnings per common share of stock.
   b. Shows the proportion of net income created from each dollar of net sales.
   c. Shows how efficiently assets are able to generate sales.
   d. Shows how much profit is earned from each dollar invested by the common shareholders.
   e. Indicates how efficiently a firm uses its assets to generate income for owners and creditors.

5. **[Obj. 3]** Calculate Current Ratio and Acid-Test Ratio: Use the information below to calculate current ratio and acid-test ratio. Current assets and current liabilities are as follows:

Cash	$4,000
Marketable securities	9,000
Receivables	12,600
Inventory	20,000
Total current assets	$45,600

Accounts payable	$7,300
Short-term notes payable	2,200
Total current liabilities	$9,500

   a. Compute current ratio; show calculations.
   b. Compute acid-test ratio; show calculations.

6. **[Obj. 3]** Calculate Current Ratio and Acid-Test Ratio: Use the information below to calculate current ratio and acid-test ratio. Current assets and current liabilities are as follows:

Cash	$21,000
Marketable securities	15,800
Receivables	37,500
Inventory	77,000
Total current assets	$151,300
Accounts payable	$45,900
Short-term notes payable	16,600
Total current liabilities	$62,500

a. Compute current ratio; show calculations.

b. Compute acid-test ratio; show calculations.

7. **[Obj. 3]** Calculate Receivables Turnover and Inventory Turnover: Use the information below to calculate receivables turnover and inventory turnover. Account balances are given for the following: Net credit sales, accounts receivable at year-end and start of the year, cost of goods sold, and inventory at year-end and start of the year.

Net credit sales	$55,000
Accounts receivable, end of year	$3,200
Accounts receivable, start of year	$3,400
Cost of goods sold	$39,000
Inventory, end of year	$4,200
Inventory, start of year	$4,000

a. Compute receivables turnover; show calculations.

b. Compute inventory turnover; show calculations.

8. **[Obj. 3]** Calculate Receivables Turnover and Inventory Turnover: Use the information below to calculate receivables turnover and inventory turnover. Account balances are given for the following: Net credit sales, accounts receivable at year-end and start of the year, cost of goods sold, and inventory at year-end and start of the year.

Net credit sales	$15,000
Accounts receivable, end of year	$3,000
Accounts receivable, start of year	$3,200
Cost of goods sold	$10,000
Inventory, end of year	$2,400
Inventory, start of year	$2,000

a. Compute receivables turnover; show calculations.

b. Compute inventory turnover; show calculations.

9. **[Obj. 3]** Calculate Earnings Per Share and Profit Margin: Use the information below to calculate earnings per share (EPS) and profit margin:

Net sales	$75,000
Net income	$15,000
Preferred dividends	$5,000
Avg. common shares outstanding	1,000

a. Compute EPS; show calculations.

b. Compute profit margin; show calculations.

10. **[Obj. 3]** Calculate Earnings Per Share and Profit Margin: Use the information below to calculate earnings per share (EPS) and profit margin:

Net sales	$124,000
Net income	$9,600
Preferred dividends	$4,800
Avg. common shares outstanding	2,000

a. Compute EPS; show calculations.

b. Compute profit margin; show calculations.

11. **[Obj. 3]** Calculate Asset Turnover, Return on Assets, and Return on Equity: Use the information below to calculate asset turnover, return on assets (ROA), and return on equity (ROE):

Net sales	$375,000
Net income	$75,000
Interest expense	$18,000
Preferred dividends	$25,000
Total assets, start of year	$250,000
Total assets, end of year	$300,000
Com. stock equity, start of year	$180,000
Com. stock equity, end of year	$220,000
Tax rate	40%

a. Compute asset turnover; show calculations.
b. Compute ROA; show calculations.
c. Compute ROE; show calculations.

12. **[Obj. 3]** Calculate the Long-Term Solvency Ratios: Use the information below to calculate debt to assets ratio and times-interest-earned ratio.

Total assets	$424,000
Total liabilities	$68,000
Net income	$99,000
Taxes	$39,000
Interest expense	$8,800

a. Compute debt to assets ratio; show calculations.
b. Compute times-interest-earned ratio; show calculations.

13. **[Obj. 3]** Calculate the Stock Performance Ratios: Use the information below to calculate price to earnings (P/E) ratio, dividend yield, book value per share, and market price to book value:

Market price per share	$12.00
Earnings per share (EPS)	$4.80
Dividends per share	$3.00
Common stock equity	$80,000
Common shares outstanding	10,000

a. Compute P/E ratio; show calculations.
b. Compute dividend yield; show calculations.
c. Compute book value per share; show calculations.
d. Compute market price to book value; show calculations.

14. **[Obj. 3]** Compare a Company to Industry Averages: Selected ratios for Southwest Technology Company are shown below, along with industry averages. Evaluate the company's ratios in relation to industry averages.

	Company	Industry Average
Profit margin	0.040	0.025
Return on equity (ROE)	0.325	0.440
Price to earnings (P/E)	12.500	8.600
Dividend yield:	0.050	0.100
Market price to book value:	6.880	5.500

SHORT EXERCISES – SET B

Building Accounting Skills

1. **[Obj. 1]** Analyze Financial Statement Information: Jones Burger Company is entering its fifth year of business. Sales Revenues for its first four years were as follows: Year 1: $10 million; Year 2: $12 million; Year 3: $9 million; and Year 4: $6 million. Based on the sales revenue, analyze the company's financial situation. Provide answers to the following questions:
   a. What kind of trend is this? Positive, negative, or mixed?
   b. What does this trend suggest to investors and lenders?
   c. How should company management react to this trend?

2. **[Obj. 2]** Measuring Financial Performance: Assume you are a financial analyst and many investors are depending on the analysis you provide, so that they can make wise investment decisions. You have financial statements for two companies, Deluxe Pizza Corporation and Midwest Mortgage Company. Deluxe has been in business for only one year. Midwest is starting its fifth year. Provide answers to the following:
   a. How will the time that these companies have been in business affect your analysis?
   b. In addition to a company's financial statements, what else can a financial analyst do to gain an understanding of the company's financial performance?

3. **[Obj. 3]** Defining Financial Ratios: Match the following financial ratios to their descriptions.
   ___ 1. Times–interest-earned ratio
   ___ 2. Book value per share
   ___ 3. Price to earnings (P/E)
   ___ 4. Dividend yield
   ___ 5. Market price to book value
   a. Indicates the confidence of investors in a company.
   b. Indicates the proportion of a stock's market price that the company pays to an investor in the form of dividends.
   c. Shows the ability of the firm to make interest payments.
   d. The ratio of what investors are willing to pay compared to the recorded accounting amount per share of stock.
   e. Shows the recorded accounting amount per share.

4. **[Obj. 3]** Defining Financial Ratios: Match the following four categories of financial ratios to their descriptions.
   ___ 1. Profitability ratios
   ___ 2. Stock performance ratios
   ___ 3. Liquidity ratios
   ___ 4. Long-term solvency ratios
   a. Measure a firm's ability to pay short-term debts.
   b. Measure a firm's ability to earn a satisfactory net income.
   c. Measure a firm's ability to pay long-term debt.
   d. Measure a firm's ability to attract investors.

5. **[Obj. 3]** Calculate Current Ratio and Acid-Test Ratio: Use the information below to calculate current ratio and acid-test ratio. Current assets and current liabilities are as follows:

Cash	$8,000
Marketable securities	18,000
Receivables	25,200
Inventory	40,000
Total current assets	$91,200

Accounts payable	$10,600
Short-term notes payable	4,400
Total current liabilities	$15,000

a. Compute current ratio; show calculations.
b. Compute acid-test ratio; show calculations.

6. **[Obj. 3]** Calculate Current Ratio and Acid-Test Ratio: Use the information below to calculate current ratio and acid-test ratio. Current assets and current liabilities are as follows:

Cash	$11,000
Marketable securities	7,500
Receivables	17,500
Inventory	34,000
Total current assets	$70,000

Accounts payable	$25,400
Short-term notes payable	8,000
Total current liabilities	$33,400

a. Compute current ratio; show calculations.
b. Compute acid-test ratio; show calculations.

7. **[Obj. 3]** Calculate Receivables Turnover and Inventory Turnover: Use the information below to calculate receivables turnover and inventory turnover. Account balances are given for the following: Net credit sales, accounts receivable at year-end and start of the year, cost of goods sold, and inventory at year-end and start of the year.

Net credit sales	$105,000
Accounts receivable, end of year	$6,400
Accounts receivable, start of year	$6,800
Cost of goods sold	$70,000
Inventory, end of year	$8,400
Inventory, start of year	$8,000

a. Compute receivables turnover; show calculations.
b. Compute inventory turnover; show calculations.

8. **[Obj. 3]** Calculate Receivables Turnover and Inventory Turnover: Use the information below to calculate receivables turnover and inventory turnover. Account balances are given for the following: Net credit sales, accounts receivable at year-end and start of the year, cost of goods sold, and inventory at year-end and start of the year.

Net credit sales	$30,500
Accounts receivable, end of year	$6,000
Accounts receivable, start of year	$6,400
Cost of goods sold	$22,000
Inventory, end of year	$4,800
Inventory, start of year	$4,000

a. Compute receivables turnover; show calculations.
b. Compute inventory turnover; show calculations.

9. **[Obj. 3]** Calculate Earnings Per Share and Profit Margin: Use the information below to calculate earnings per share (EPS) and profit margin:

Net sales	$160,000
Net income	$40,000
Preferred dividends	$10,000
Average common shares outstanding	2,000

a. Compute EPS; show calculations.
b. Compute profit margin; show calculations.

10. **[Obj. 3]** Calculate Earnings Per Share and Profit Margin: Use the information below to calculate earnings per share (EPS) and profit margin:

Net sales	$190,000
Net income	$20,000
Preferred dividends	$9,000
Average common shares outstanding	2,000

a. Compute EPS; show calculations.
b. Compute profit margin; show calculations.

11. **[Obj. 3]** Calculate Asset Turnover, Return on Assets, and Return on Equity: Use the information below to calculate asset turnover, return on assets (ROA), and return on equity (ROE):

Net sales	$750,000
Net income	$140,000
Interest expense	$35,000
Preferred dividends	$45,000
Total assets, start of year	$510,000
Total assets, end of year	$590,000
Com. stock equity, start of year	$250,000
Com. stock equity, end of year	$290,000
Tax rate	40%

a. Compute asset turnover; show calculations.
b. Compute ROA; show calculations.
c. Compute ROE; show calculations.

12. **[Obj. 3]** Calculate the Long-Term Solvency Ratios: Use the information below to calculate debt to assets ratio and times-interest-earned ratio.

Total assets	$630,000
Total liabilities	$108,000
Net income	$155,000
Taxes	$60,000
Interest expense	$13,000

a. Compute debt to assets ratio; show calculations.
b. Compute times-interest-earned ratio; show calculations.

13. **[Obj. 3]** Calculate the Stock Performance Ratios: Use the information below to calculate price to earnings (P/E) ratio, dividend yield, book value per share, and market price to book value:

Market price per share	$21.00
Earnings per share (EPS)	$9.60
Dividends per share	$6.00
Common stock equity	$160,000
Common shares outstanding	10,000

a. Compute P/E ratio; show calculations.
b. Compute dividend yield; show calculations.
c. Compute book value per share; show calculations.
d. Compute market price to book value; show calculations.

14. **[Obj. 3]** Compare a Company to Industry Averages: Selected ratios for Corner Grocery Company are shown below, along with industry averages. Evaluate the company's ratios in relation to industry averages.

	Company	Industry Average
Profit margin	0.015	0.025
Return on equity (ROE)	0.220	0.440
Price to earnings (P/E)	7.000	8.600
Dividend yield:	0.095	0.100
Market price to book value:	4.900	5.500

PROBLEMS – SET A

Applying Accounting Knowledge

1. **[Obj. 3]** Calculate Liquidity Ratios: Use the information below for Southern Carpet Corporation regarding end-of-year balances and start of year balances to calculate the liquidity ratios.

End-of-Year Balances:		
Cash	$17,000	
Marketable securities	3,000	
Accounts receivable	10,100	
Inventory	3,900	
Total current assets		$34,000
Accounts payable	$3,300	
Short-term notes payable	7,700	
Total current liabilities		$11,000
Net credit sales	$122,000	
Cost of goods sold	40,000	
Start of Year Balances:		
Accounts receivable, start of year	5,400	
Inventory, start of year	6,000	

Required:

a. Show your calculations for the following: Current ratio, Acid-test ratio, Receivables turnover, and Inventory turnover.

b. Evaluate: Compare the company's ratios to the following industry averages: Current ratio 2.5, Acid-test ratio 1.5, Receivables turnover 20.5, and Inventory turnover 12.7.

2. **[Obj. 3]** Calculate Liquidity Ratios: Use the information below for Johnson Motor Corporation regarding end-of-year balances and start of year balances to calculate the liquidity ratios.

End-of-Year Balances:		
Cash	$43,200	
Marketable securities	17,600	
Accounts receivable	43,200	
Inventory	20,000	
Total current assets		$124,000
Accounts payable	$23,400	
Short-term notes payable	17,600	
Total current liabilities		$41,000
Net credit sales	$542,000	
Cost of goods sold	270,000	
Start of Year Balances:		
Accounts receivable, start of year	54,400	
Inventory, start of year	42,600	

Required:

a. Show your calculations for the following: Current ratio, Acid-test ratio, Receivables turnover, and Inventory turnover.

b. Evaluate: Compare the company's ratios to the following industry averages: Current ratio 4.1, Acid-test ratio 3.7, and Receivables turnover 9.4, and Inventory turnover 5.5.

3. **[Obj. 3]** Calculate Two Profitability Ratios: Use the information below to calculate earnings per share (EPS) and profit margin:

Net sales	$390,000
Net income	$27,000
Preferred dividends	$6,000
Average common shares outstanding	10,000

Required:

a. Compute EPS; show calculations.

b. Compute profit margin; show calculations.

c. Evaluate EPS: Last year, the company's EPS was $1.25, and the year before it was $0.75.

d. Evaluate profit margin: Last year the company's profit margin was 0.058 (5.8%), and the year before it was 0.024 (2.4%).

4. **[Obj. 3]** Calculate Two Profitability Ratios: Use the information below to calculate earnings per share (EPS) and profit margin:

Net sales	$490,000
Net income	$53,600
Preferred dividends	$18,000
Average common shares outstanding	5,000

Required:
a. Compute EPS; show calculations.
b. Compute profit margin; show calculations.
c. Evaluate EPS: Last year, the company's EPS was $8.50, and the year before it was $10.55.
d. Evaluate profit margin: Last year the company's profit margin was 0.145 (14.5%), and the year before it was 0.155 (15.5%).

5. **[Obj. 3]** Calculate Three Profitability Ratios: Use the information below to calculate asset turnover, return on assets (ROA), and return on equity (ROE):

Net sales	$640,000
Net income	$96,000
Interest expense	$24,000
Preferred dividends	$40,000
Total assets, start of year	$445,000
Total assets, end of year	$475,000
Com. stock equity, start of year	$320,000
Com. stock equity, end of year	$300,000
Tax rate	40%

Required:
a. Compute asset turnover; show calculations.
b. Compute ROA; show calculations.
c. Compute ROE; show calculations.
d. Evaluate asset turnover, ROA, and ROE relative to industry averages, which are 1.75, 0.355, and 0.246, respectively.

6. **[Obj. 3]** Calculate the Long-Term Solvency Ratios: Use the information below to calculate debt to assets ratio and times-interest-earned ratio:

Total assets	$226,000
Total liabilities	$84,000
Net income	$21,600
Taxes	$8,400
Interest expense	$4,000

Required:
a. Compute debt to assets ratio; show calculations.
b. Compute times-interest-earned ratio; show calculations.
c. Evaluate the debt to assets ratio and times-interest-earned ratio relative to industry averages, which are 0.453 and 6.755, respectively.

7. **[Obj. 3]** Calculate the Stock Performance Ratios: Use the information below to calculate price to earnings (P/E) ratio, dividend yield, book value per share, and market price to book value:

Market price per share	$48.00
Earnings per share (EPS)	$12.00
Dividends per share	$6.00
Common stock equity	$300,000
Common shares outstanding	20,000

Required:
a. Compute P/E ratio; show calculations.
b. Compute dividend yield; show calculations.
c. Compute book value per share; show calculations.
d. Compute market price to book value; show calculations.
e. Evaluate company ratios relative to the following industry averages: P/E 2.40, Dividend yield 0.25, Book value per share $18.00, and Market price to book value 1.95.

8. **[Obj. 3]** Calculate Stock Performance Ratios: Use the information below to calculate price to earnings (P/E) ratio, dividend yield, book value per share, and market price to book value:

Market price per share	$50.00
Earnings per share (EPS)	$8.00
Dividends per share	$5.00
Common stock equity	$100,000
Common shares outstanding	10,000

Required:

a. Compute P/E ratio; show calculations.

b. Compute dividend yield; show calculations.

c. Compute book value per share; show calculations.

d. Compute market price to book value; show calculations.

e. Evaluate company ratios relative to the following industry averages: P/E 4.00, Dividend yield 0.08, Book value per share $15.00, and Market price to book value 4.00.

9. **[Obj. 4]** Prepare a Vertical Analysis: Vertical analysis shows the proportional relationships of the items included in one financial statement. For example, on the income statement, the net sales amount is shown as 100% and all other items are shown as a percentage of net sales. Shown below is the income statement for Branson Ball Bearings Corporation, which includes two years, 20Y2 and 20Y1. Use this information to prepare a common-size income statement, showing both years.

Branson Ball Bearings Corporation
Income Statements
For Years Ended December 31

	20Y2	20Y1
Net Sales	$88,000	$75,200
Costs and Expenses		
Cost of Goods Sold	49,400	47,700
Interest Expense	5,500	2,200
Other Expenses	22,600	21,400
Earnings Before Taxes	$10,500	$3,900
Tax Expense (Benefit)	4,200	1,560
Net Income	$6,300	$2,340

Required:

a. Prepare the common-size income statement.

b. Evaluate: Discuss the relative changes in the income statement items.

10. **[Obj. 5]** Prepare a Horizontal Analysis: Horizontal analysis shows the percentage changes in financial statement items from one year to the next. Shown below is the income statement for Midwest Motor Company, which includes two years, 20Y4 and 20Y3. Use this information to prepare a horizontal analysis of the income statement.

Midwest Motor Company
Comparative Income Statements
For Years Ended December 31, 20Y4 and 20Y3

	20Y4	20Y3
Net Sales	$119,900	$104,600
Costs and Expenses		
Cost of Goods Sold	66,300	59,400
Interest Expense	11,400	9,900
Other Expenses	19,800	20,300
Earnings Before Taxes	$22,400	$15,000
Tax Expense (Benefit)	14,600	8,500
Net Income	$7,800	$6,500

Required:

a. Prepare the comparative income statements with horizontal analysis.

b. Evaluate: Discuss the changes in the income statement items.

11. **[Obj. 6]** Prepare a Trend Analysis: Trend analysis is an extension of horizontal analysis. Trend analysis shows percentage changes of key financial statement items for several time periods. Shown below are the net sales for Downtown T-Shirt Company for the past five years, 20Y1 to 20Y5.

Downtown T-Shirt Company
Net Sales for Past Five Years

Year	Dollar Amount
20Y1	$194,500
20Y2	$211,300
20Y3	$236,200
20Y4	$293,300
20Y5	$416,700

Required:

a. Prepare the trend analysis of net sales.

b. Evaluate: Discuss the trend.

12. **[Obj. 6]** Prepare a Trend Analysis: Trend analysis is an extension of horizontal analysis. Trend analysis shows percentage changes of key financial statement items for several time periods. Shown below are the net sales for Boudreaux Crawfish Restaurant for the past five years, 20Y1 to 20Y5.

Boudreaux Crawfish Restaurant Net Sales for Past Five Years	
Year	Dollar Amount
20Y1	$546,400
20Y2	$492,600
20Y3	$524,900
20Y4	$487,200
20Y5	$616,600

Required:
a. Prepare the trend analysis of net sales.
b. Evaluate: Discuss the trend.

PROBLEMS – SET B

Applying Accounting Knowledge

1. **[Obj. 3]** Calculate Liquidity Ratios: Use the information below for Southern Fried Chicken Corporation regarding end-of-year balances and start of year balances to calculate the liquidity ratios.

End-of-Year Balances:		
Cash	$5,000	
Marketable securities	1,000	
Accounts receivable	2,000	
Inventory	3,000	
Total current assets		$11,000
Accounts payable	$2,000	
Short-term notes payable	4,000	
Total current liabilities		$6,000
Net credit sales	$60,000	
Cost of goods sold	30,000	
Start of Year Balances:		
Accounts receivable, start of year	2,500	
Inventory, start of year	1,500	

Required:
a. Show your calculations for the following: Current ratio, Acid-test ratio, Receivables turnover, and Inventory turnover.
b. Evaluate: Compare the corporation's ratios to the following industry averages: Current ratio 2.5, Acid-test ratio 1.5, Receivables turnover 20.5, and Inventory turnover 12.7.

2. **[Obj. 3]** Calculate Liquidity Ratios: Use the information below for Speedy Boats Corporation regarding end-of-year balances and start of year balances to calculate the liquidity ratios.

End-of-Year Balances:		
Cash	$70,000	
Marketable securities	35,000	
Accounts receivable	90,000	
Inventory	180,000	
Total current assets		$375,000
Accounts payable	$10,000	
Short-term notes payable	35,000	
Total current liabilities		$45,000
Net credit sales	$950,000	
Cost of goods sold	400,000	
Start of Year Balances:		
Accounts receivable, start of year	90,000	
Inventory, start of year	80,000	

Required:
a. Show your calculations for the following: Current ratio, Acid-test ratio, Receivables turnover, and Inventory turnover.
b. Evaluate: Compare the corporation's ratios to the following industry averages: Current ratio 4.1, Acid-test ratio 3.7, and Receivables turnover 11.4, and Inventory turnover 5.5.

3. **[Obj. 3]** Calculate Two Profitability Ratios: Use the information below to calculate earnings per share (EPS) and profit margin:

Net sales	$600,000
Net income	$50,000
Preferred dividends	$12,000
Average common shares outstanding	20,000

Required:
a. Compute EPS; show calculations.
b. Compute profit margin; show calculations.
c. Evaluate EPS: Last year, the company's EPS was $1.25 and the year before it was $0.75.
d. Evaluate profit margin: Last year the company's profit margin was 0.058 (5.8%) and the year before it was 0.024 (2.4%).

4. **[Obj. 3]** Calculate Two Profitability Ratios: Use the information below to calculate earnings per share (EPS) and profit margin:

Net sales	$250,000
Net income	$25,000
Preferred dividends	$9,000
Average common shares outstanding	2,500

Required:
a. Compute EPS; show calculations.
b. Compute profit margin; show calculations.
c. Evaluate EPS: Last year, the company's EPS was $8.50 and the year before it was $10.55.
d. Evaluate profit margin: Last year the company's profit margin was 0.145 (14.5%) and the year before it was 0.155 (15.5%).

5. **[Obj. 3]** Calculate Three Profitability Ratios: Use the information below to calculate asset turnover, return on assets (ROA), and return on equity (ROE):

Net sales	$560,000
Net income	$82,000
Interest expense	$21,000
Preferred dividends	$34,000
Total assets, start of year	$415,000
Total assets, end of year	$435,000
Com. stock equity, start of year	$300,000
Com. stock equity, end of year	$280,000
Tax rate	40%

Required:
a. Compute asset turnover; show calculations.
b. Compute ROA; show calculations.
c. Compute ROE; show calculations.
d. Evaluate asset turnover, ROA, and ROE relative to industry averages, which are 1.75, 0.355, and 0.246, respectively.

6. **[Obj. 3]** Calculate the Long-Term Solvency Ratios: Use the information below to calculate debt to assets ratio and times-interest-earned ratio:

Total assets	$200,000
Total liabilities	$78,000
Net income	$18,000
Taxes	$8,500
Interest expense	3,000

Required:
a. Compute debt to assets ratio; show calculations.
b. Compute times-interest-earned ratio; show calculations.
c. Evaluate the debt to assets ratio and times-interest-earned ratio relative to industry averages, which are 0.255 and 8.755, respectively.

7. **[Obj. 3]** Calculate the Stock Performance Ratios: Use the information below to calculate price to earnings (P/E) ratio, dividend yield, book value per share, and market price to book value:

Market price per share	$42.00
Earnings per share (EPS)	$9.00
Dividends per share	$4.00
Common stock equity	260,000
Common shares outstanding	15,000

Required:
a. Compute P/E ratio; show calculations.
b. Compute dividend yield; show calculations.
c. Compute book value per share; show calculations.
d. Compute market price to book value; show calculations.
e. Evaluate company ratios relative to the following industry averages: P/E 2.40, Dividend yield 0.25, Book value per share $18.00, and Market price to book value 1.95.

8. **[Obj. 3]** Calculate Stock Performance Ratios: Use the information below to calculate price to earnings (P/E) ratio, dividend yield, book value per share, and market price to book value:

Market price per share	$60.00
Earnings per share (EPS)	$7.50
Dividends per share	$4.50
Common stock equity	$100,000
Common shares outstanding	9,000

Required:
a. Compute P/E ratio; show calculations.
b. Compute dividend yield; show calculations.
c. Compute book value per share; show calculations.
d. Compute market price to book value; show calculations.
e. Evaluate company ratios relative to the following industry averages: P/E 5.00, Dividend yield 0.05, Book value per share 15.00, and Market price to book value 8.50.

9. **[Obj. 4]** Prepare a Vertical Analysis: Vertical analysis shows the proportional relationships of the items included in one financial statement. For example, on the income statement, the net sales amount is shown as 100% and all other items are shown as a percentage of net sales. Shown below are the 20Y2 and 20Y1 income statements for The Lollipop Corporation. Use this information to prepare a common-size income statement, showing both years.

The Lollipop Corporation Income Statements For Years Ended December 31		
	20Y2	**20Y1**
Net Sales	$66,000	$50,500
Costs and Expenses		
Cost of Goods Sold	34,000	27,000
Interest Expense	4,000	1,700
Other Expenses	16,000	14,000
Earnings Before Taxes	$12,000	$7,800
Tax Expense (Benefit)	4,800	3,120
Net Income	$7,200	$4,680

Required:
a. Prepare the common-size income statement.
b. Evaluate: Discuss the relative changes in the income statement items.

10. **[Obj. 5]** Prepare a Horizontal Analysis: Horizontal analysis shows the percentage changes in financial statement items from one year to the next. Shown below is the income statement for Fast Cars Company, which includes two years, 20Y2 and 20Y1. Use this information to prepare a horizontal analysis of the income statement.

Fast Cars Company
Comparative Income Statements
For Years Ended December 31, 20Y2 and 20Y1

	20Y2	20Y1
Net Sales	$240,000	$210,000
Costs and Expenses		
Cost of Goods Sold	130,000	120,000
Interest Expense	22,000	19,000
Other Expenses	40,000	41,000
Earnings Before Taxes	$48,000	$30,000
Tax Expense (Benefit)	29,000	17,000
Net Income	$19,000	$13,000

Required:
a. Prepare the comparative income statements with horizontal analysis.
b. Evaluate: Discuss the changes in the income statement items.

11. **[Obj. 6]** Prepare a Trend Analysis: Trend analysis is an extension of horizontal analysis. Trend analysis shows percentage changes of key financial statement items for several time periods. Shown below are the net sales for Vintage Clothing Company for the past five years, 20Y1 to 20Y5.

Vintage Clothing Company
Net Sales for Past Five Years

Year	Dollar Amount
20Y1	$280,500
20Y2	$342,000
20Y3	$415,000
20Y4	$502,000
20Y5	$590,500

Required:
a. Prepare the trend analysis of net sales.
b. Evaluate: Discuss the trend.

12. **[Obj. 6]** Prepare a Trend Analysis: Trend analysis is an extension of horizontal analysis. Trend analysis shows percentage changes of key financial statement items for several time periods. Shown below are the net sales for Georgia Peach Restaurant for the past five years, 20Y1 to 20Y5.

Georgia Peach Restaurant
Net Sales for Past Five Years

Year	Dollar Amount
20Y1	$274,000
20Y2	$250,500
20Y3	$267,000
20Y4	$246,500
20Y5	$303,000

Required:
a. Prepare the trend analysis of net sales.
b. Evaluate: Discuss the trend.

CROSS-FUNCTIONAL PERSPECTIVES

Discussion Questions

1. **[Obj. 1]** Outside the firm, who is interested in financial statement analysis?

2. **[Obj. 3]** How do departments within a company contribute to the computation of liquidity ratios?

3. **[Obj. 3]** How do different departments in a company benefit from liquidity ratios?

4. **[Obj. 3]** How do different departments in a company benefit from profitability ratios?

5. **[Obj. 3]** How does the finance department benefit from long-term solvency ratios?

6. **[Obj. 4 & 5]** How does management benefit from vertical and horizontal analysis?

Cross-functional Case:
Improving Ford's Financial Condition

Suppose top management at Ford Motor Company is concerned over the company's stock price because it is not as high as they would like. Stock price increases when demand for the stock increases. Before buying stock, investors usually look for good financial ratios along with positive trends that indicate the company has promising future prospects. Management wants suggestions from various internal departments on how to improve the company's financial ratios for the purpose of attracting more investors and achieving a higher stock price.

Required: What are possible actions that each of the following departments can implement to help improve Ford's financial ratios?
a. Marketing
b. Finance
c. Purchasing
d. Human resources
e. Production

EXCEL ASSIGNMENTS

1. **[Obj. 4]** Vertical Analysis: Vertical analysis shows the proportional relationships of the items included in one financial statement. For example, on the income statement, the net sales amount is shown as 100% and all other items are shown as a percentage of net sales. Shown below are the comparative income statements for Years 20Y2 and 20Y1 for Midwest Mortgage Corporation. Use Excel to prepare the common-size income statements, 20Y2 and 20Y1.

Midwest Mortgage Corporation Income Statements For Years Ended December 31 ($ Thousands)		
	20Y2	**20Y1**
Net Sales	$745	$699
Costs and Expenses		
Cost of Goods Sold	372	399
Interest Expense	54	49
Other Expenses	182	179
Earnings Before Taxes	$137	$72
Tax Expense (Benefit)	55	29
Net Income	$82	$43

2. **[Obj. 4]** Vertical Analysis: Vertical analysis shows the proportional relationships of the items included in one financial statement. For example, on the income statement, the net sales amount is shown as 100% and all other items are shown as a percentage of net sales. Shown below are the comparative income statements for Years 20Y6 and 20Y5 for Thompson Car Repair Company. Use Excel to prepare the common-size income statements, 20Y6 and 20Y5.

Thompson Car Repair Company Income Statements For Years Ended December 31 ($ Thousands)		
	20Y6	20Y5
Net Sales	$95	$89
Costs and Expenses		
Cost of Goods Sold	50	44
Interest Expense	12	10
Other Expenses	23	18
Earnings Before Taxes	$10	$17
Tax Expense (Benefit)	4	7
Net Income	$6	$10

3. **[Obj. 5]** Horizontal Analysis: Horizontal analysis shows the percentage changes in financial statement items from one year to the next. Shown below are comparative income statements for Western Internet Provider, Inc., which includes two years, 20Y2 and 20Y1. Use Excel to prepare a horizontal analysis of the income statement.

Western Internet Provider, Inc. Comparative Income Statements For Years Ended December 31, 20Y2 and 20Y1 (Amounts in $ Millions)		
	20Y2	20Y1
Net Sales	$99	$88
Costs and Expenses		
Cost of Goods Sold	65	62
Interest Expense	14	12
Other Expenses	9	6
Earnings Before Taxes	$11	$8
Tax Expense (Benefit)	4	3
Net Income	$7	$5

4. **[Obj. 5]** Horizontal Analysis: Horizontal analysis shows the percentage changes in financial statement items from one year to the next. Shown below are comparative income statements for Enchanting Tours Corporation, which includes two years, 20Y3 and 20Y2. Use Excel to prepare a horizontal analysis of the income statement.

Enchanting Tours Corporation Comparative Income Statements For Years Ended December 31, 20Y3 and 20Y2 (Amounts in $ Millions)		
	20Y3	20Y2
Net Sales	$124	$114
Costs and Expenses		
Cost of Goods Sold	62	58
Interest Expense	5	5
Other Expenses	37	35
Earnings Before Taxes	$20	$16
Tax Expense (Benefit)	4	3
Net Income	$16	$13

5. **[Obj. 6]** Trend Analysis Using a Bar Chart: Stampede Rodeo Company has been in business for four years. Total revenue and net income for Years 1 to 4 are shown below. Use Excel to prepare a bar chart of total revenue and a bar chart of net income.

Year	Total Revenue ($ Millions)	Year	Net Income ($ Millions)
20Y1	$250	20Y1	$16
20Y2	370	20Y2	24
20Y3	480	20Y3	31
20Y4	650	20Y4	52

6. **[Obj. 6]** Trend Analysis Using a Bar Chart: Car Design Corporation has been in business for six years. Total revenue and net income for Years 1 to 6 are shown below. Use Excel to prepare a bar chart of total revenue and a bar chart of net income.

Year	Total Revenue ($ Millions)	Year	Net Income ($ Millions)
20Y1	$5	20Y1	$1.5
20Y2	7	20Y2	1.7
20Y3	10	20Y3	2.1
20Y4	9	20Y4	1.6
20Y5	12	20Y5	2.4
20Y6	16	20Y6	3.2

WEB ASSIGNMENTS

1. **[Obj. 3]** Go to Yahoo's financial website, or do a search on Google, to find some of Ford's recent financial ratios. Find the following for Ford Motor Company: return on assets, return on equity, current ratio, book value per share, and market price to book value. Note: Ford's ticker symbol in the stock market is "F.")

2. **[Obj. 3]** Go to Ford's website, or do a search on Google, to find the current stock quote for Ford Motor Company. Is this price an increase or decrease from the previous closing price?

3. **[Obj. 3]** Go to Ford's website, or do a search on Google, to find the company's most recent dividend announcement. What is Ford's dividend yield?

4. **[Ethics]** Go to the Ford's website, or do a search on Google, for Ford's corporate governance. Write a paragraph summarizing their code of ethics for senior financial personnel.

¶1312 Test Prepper

Use this sample test to gauge your comprehension of the chapter material.

True/False Questions

__ 1. The current ratio shows the firm's ability to pay its current liabilities out of current assets.

__ 2. The acid-test ratio shows how many times the average amount in accounts receivable is collected in a year.

__ 3. Earnings per share (EPS) shows the firm's earnings per common share of stock.

__ 4. Asset turnover shows the proportion of net income created from each dollar of net sales.

__ 5. Return on assets (ROA) shows how much profit is earned for each dollar invested by the common shareholders.

__ 6. The debt to assets ratio shows the proportion of total assets financed by the business firm's creditors.

__ 7. Vertical analysis shows the percentage changes in financial statement items from one year to the next.

__ 8. Horizontal analysis shows the proportional relationships of the items included in one financial statement.

__ 9. Common-size statements result from vertical analysis and show percentages of a total figure that is set at 100%.

__ 10. Low market price to book value stocks are sometimes regarded as "value" stocks.

Multiple-Choice Questions

___ 1. Which of the following measures a firm's ability to attract investors?
    a. Liquidity ratios
    b. Profitability ratios
    c. Long-Term Solvency ratios
    d. Stock Performance ratios
    e. All of the above

___ 2. Which of the following measures a firm's ability to pay long-term debt?
    a. Liquidity ratios
    b. Profitability ratios
    c. Long-Term Solvency ratios
    d. Stock Performance ratios
    e. All of the above

___ 3. Which of the following measures a firm's ability to earn a satisfactory net income?
    a. Liquidity ratios
    b. Profitability ratios
    c. Long-Term Solvency ratios
    d. Stock Performance ratios
    e. All of the above

___ 4. Which of the following measures a firm's ability to pay short-term debt?
    a. Liquidity ratios
    b. Profitability ratios
    c. Long-Term Solvency ratios
    d. Stock Performance ratios
    e. All of the above

___ 5. Which of the following is calculated by dividing the market price per share by the earnings per share?
    a. Price to earnings (P/E)
    b. Dividend yield
    c. Book value per share
    d   Market price to book value
    e. None of the above

___ 6. Which of the following is calculated by dividing the market price per share by the book value per share?
    a. Price to earnings (P/E)
    b. Dividend yield
    c. Book value per share
    d. Market price to book value
    e. None of the above

___ 7. Which of the following is calculated by dividing the dividends per share of stock by the market price per share?
    a. Price to earnings (P/E)
    b. Dividend yield
    c. Book value per share
    d. Market price to book value
    e. None of the above

___ 8. Which of the following is calculated by dividing common stockholders' equity by the number of common shares outstanding?
    a. Price to earnings (P/E)
    b. Dividend yield
    c. Book value per share
    d. Market price to book value
    e. None of the above

___ 9. Which of the following shows the percentage changes of key financial statement items for several time periods?
    a. Horizontal analysis
    b. Vertical analysis
    c. Long-term solvency ratios
    d. P/E ratio
    e. Trend analysis

___ 10. Which of the following shows the proportion of net income created from each dollar of net sales?
    a. Return on assets
    b. Return on equity
    c. Return on sales
    d. Profit margin
    e. c and d

Chapter

14

Accounting for Global Commerce

LEARNING OBJECTIVES

After studying Chapter 14, you should be able to do the following:

1. Describe the importance of accounting for a global marketplace to people within and outside a business.
2. Explain the role of accounting in global commerce.
3. Describe the development of international financial reporting standards.
4. Describe the objectives of international standards on auditing.
5. Restate a foreign subsidiary's financial statements in U.S. dollars.
6. Explain how cultural factors affect the accountant's workplace.

CHAPTER CONTENTS

Accounting for Global Commerce

FOCUS ON BUSINESS

Coca-Cola Around the World

The Coca-Cola Company operates in more than 200 countries around the world. Operations outside the United States generate approximately 70% of its revenues. Because more than 95% of the world's population resides outside the U.S., substantial profits can be generated from global sales. Every day, consumers enjoy more than 1.3 billion servings of Coca-Cola products. This is a function of the company's quality products, good management, and unrivaled distribution network that Coke has put into place over the past 100 years.

Coke's accountants face several challenges when operating in global markets, such as: (1) fluctuations in currency exchange and interest rates; (2) distinctive tax rates and laws; (3) cost and deployment of capital; (3) differing food, labor, and operating costs; and (4) diverse accounting policies and practices. For example, financial reporting in the U.S. values assets according to the historical cost (the amount paid). However, in Mexico where inflation is much higher, asset values are adjusted for the impact of inflation.

As a multinational business, The Coca-Cola Company must comply with the rules and regulations of the countries in which it operates. International accounting standards have been developed that can be utilized by business firms around the world; however, adherence to these standards is up to individual nations. The United Nations is concerned that globalization of business makes it difficult for external stakeholders, including governments, to verify a multinational firm's data. The problem is considered, at least partly, the result of a lack of uniform reporting requirements and standards. How do you compare the financial statements of a U.S. firm with a firm in India or Germany? Within this chapter, you will learn about the challenges of accounting for international operations and what accountants do to solve the problems.

Source: *Coca-cola.com*

¶1401 — Applications to People Within and Outside the Firm

The International Accounting Standards Board (IASB) establishes financial reporting standards for international companies.

LEARNING OBJECTIVE 1: Describe the importance of accounting for a global marketplace to people within and outside a business.

Advances in electronic media and the Internet, the prevalence of mass media in our culture, and the accessibility of air travel, continue to break down the traditional barriers among world populations. As a result, global business operations are increasingly competitive, and in an economic sense, the world is shrinking.

Along with the evolution of the international business environment, changes in the accounting industry are also underway. Efforts of the International Accounting Standards Board (IASB), the organization that establishes international accounting standards, continue to drive a trend towards the use of international accounting standards by firms around the world. As companies expand into new markets, recruit employees from foreign countries, and report on their international operations, parties within and outside the business seek information regarding the global economy.

¶1401.01 — INTERNAL USERS

International trade has significant challenges such as exchange rates, tariffs, and different accounting standards. Managers within a business need specific accounting information related to global operations in order to assess the profitability associated with those operations. For example, when the accountants at Coke prepare the financial statements of its foreign subsidiaries, the accounts must be translated into U.S. dollars and reported according to U.S. GAAP. Remember, accounting is the language of business. A key component in the success of multinational business is the ability to communicate data in a common format.

¶1401.02   EXTERNAL USERS

Have you ever purchased a product from another country using the Web? Think about what kinds of tools you used to make the purchase, such as currency conversions, online payment systems, or language translators.

Outside a business, investors, lenders, financial analysts, government agencies, and other stakeholders are interested in the firm's involvement in international trade. These stakeholders want to know if the firm is successfully participating in the global marketplace. They may be interested in how the business affects other cultures or natural environments. Government agencies must ensure that international operations adhere to laws and regulations related to trade, human resources, and the environment. Thus, accounting for global commerce can have significant economic implications for the firm, sometimes leading to its success or failure.

¶1402   Accounting for Global Commerce

> **LEARNING OBJECTIVE 2:** Explain the role of accounting in global commerce.

From the beginning of recorded history, people have engaged in global commerce. For as long as international trade has occurred, accounting has been necessary to record and report the results. Today, international operations are increasingly important to every type of business. Many multinational firms are either expanding international operations or becoming part of other multinational firms via mergers or acquisitions.

¶1402.01   THE CHALLENGES OF ACCOUNTING FOR GLOBAL OPERATIONS

Peculiarities of international trade periodically lead to specialized accounting treatment. For example, during the 17th century, Elizabethan England expanded its overseas business opportunities, which led to a new type of corporate entity. Merchants faced various difficulties, including encounters with pirates, hostilities between trading nations, and dangerous journeys to transport goods. Consequently, trade was an expensive and risky undertaking. In order to be successful in these new business opportunities, merchants joined together to share the risks and increase productivity.

In 1600, Queen Elizabeth chartered the first joint-stock company, the East India Company. The charter legally established one corporate body to manage approximately 220 adventurers. The charter also provided for corporate succession with power to admit and expel members; to receive, hold, and grant property; to sue and be sued in the corporate name; and to use a common seal. Funds were collected from a broad array of investors, including earls, dukes, merchants, and tradesmen. Management directed business operations and ensured that shareholders received their portion of the profits.

Transactions of the East India Company sometimes created awkward financial reporting problems. The accountants and auditors of that time complained of the difficulty in keeping accounts up-to-date. The most difficult accounting problem resulted when operations of several voyages overlapped in the same time period. Much to its own confusion and embarrassment, the firm was unable to segregate the accounting for the activities of individual trading voyages.

Business firms today rarely need armed ships to fight off pirates, but international trade still has significant challenges including tariffs, language barriers, cultural differences, and incompatible equipment standards. The accounting information system provides crucial information to management for evaluating the viability of a firm's international operations. For example, marketing relies on information about sales volume, distribution costs, manufacturing costs, profitability analysis, and tax costs in international markets. The production department relies on accounting for information on raw material costs, start-up costs for new facilities, and inventory storage expenses. The cost of labor in international markets is of great interest to the human resources department. In the following sections, we will explore particular topics that require special accounting attention when dealing with international operations.

¶1402.02 RECORDING FOREIGN SALES

When a company sells its goods or services to a customer in a different country, the company can bill the customer to pay in the company's domestic currency or in the foreign currency of the customer. For example, assume that on June 1, a U.S. company sells $10,000 of merchandise to a German customer. If the customer is billed in U.S. dollars, the transaction is recorded in the same manner as for a U.S. customer:

June 1	Accounts Receivable	10,000	
	Sales		10,000
	To record sale to German customer.		

When the German customer pays the bill on June 30 the company records the cash receipt as follows:

June 30	Cash	10,000	
	Accounts Receivable		10,000
	To record German customer's payment.		

In contrast, some U.S. companies conduct business in the currency of the foreign customer. In this case, invoices will be billed and payment is received in the foreign currency. It is important to note that, even though a U.S. company might bill its customers in another currency, the company must still keep its accounting records in one currency, usually the U.S. dollar.

Using the previous example, assume the German customer is billed in euros instead of 10,000 U.S. dollars. The euro is the currency used by countries of the European Union (EU). If the dollar-to-euro exchange rate at the time of the sale is 2.00 ($2 per euro), the customer would be billed for 5,000 euros. The U.S. company indicates that the transaction was denominated in the foreign currency (FC) and records the transaction as shown:

June 1	Accounts Receivable (FC)	10,000	
	Sales		10,000
	To record sale to German customer, sale denominated in euros: 5,000 euros × $2 = $10,000.		

Between the time the sale is made and payment is received, the foreign currency may go up or down in value relative to the domestic currency, in this case, the U.S. dollar. In other words, the exchange rate has changed. Most currencies are traded on the free market and the forces of supply and demand determine their relative values. For example, if Americans increase their demand for European products and services, assuming all other factors stay the same, then the value of the euro, relative to the dollar, would increase. In the same way, if tourism by Americans to Japan increases, then demand for the yen would increase relative to the dollar; consequently, the value of the yen, relative to the dollar would increase.

In our example, assume the German customer makes payment on June 30. On that date, the exchange rate of dollars to euros has changed to 1.90 ($1.90 per euro). The U.S. company will receive 5,000 euros in payment, which are now worth $9,500 (5,000 × 1.90). Thus, the company incurs an exchange loss of $500. The 5,000 euros were valued at $10,000 at the time of the sale but only $9,500 at the time payment is made. The difference of $500 is recorded as an exchange loss. The payment transaction is recorded as shown:

June 30	Cash	9,500	
	Exchange Loss	500	
	Accounts Receivable (FC)		10,000
	To record payment from German customer: 5,000 euros × $1.9 = $9,500.		

As you can see, the U.S. company suffered an exchange loss because the euro decreased in value relative to the U.S. dollar and the company was paid in euros. On the other hand, the U.S. company could have incurred an exchange gain if the euro had increased in value relative to the U.S. dollar. Suppose that on June 30, the dollar to euro exchange rate increased to 2.2 ($2.20 per euro). In that case, the company would record the exchange gain as shown:

June 30	Cash	11,000	
	Exchange Gain		1,000
	Accounts Receivable (FC)		10,000
	To record payment received from German customer: 5,000 euros × $2.2 = $11,000.		

¶1402.03   RECORDING FOREIGN PURCHASES

In today's economy, businesses often purchase goods from suppliers all over the world. Recording purchases from foreign suppliers follows the same methodology as recording purchases from domestic suppliers. If the purchase transaction is denominated or paid in the domestic currency, that is payment is made in domestic currency, then the journal entry is identical to the entry for a purchase from a domestic supplier. For example, if a U.S. company purchases $50,000 of goods from a Mexican company on August 1, and payment is to be made in U.S. dollars on August 31, the transaction is recorded as shown:

Aug. 1	Purchases	50,000	
	Accounts Payable		50,000
	To record purchase from Mexican company.		

When payment is made on August 31, the transaction is recorded as follows:

Aug. 31	Accounts Payable	50,000	
	Cash		50,000
	To record payment to Mexican company.		

If the Mexican company requires payment in Mexican currency, pesos, then the U.S. company may experience an exchange gain or loss. The exchange gain or loss on a purchase is computed in the same manner as with exchange gains and losses on sales, except of course the relationship of exchange rates to the gain or loss is reversed.

Suppose the purchase from the Mexican company is denominated in pesos. The U.S. company must pay pesos, not dollars, to the Mexican company. Assume the U.S. company purchases $50,000 dollars worth of goods. The dollar-to-peso exchange rate on August 1 is 0.10 ($0.10 per peso). The transaction is recorded as shown:

Aug. 1	Purchases	50,000	
	Accounts Payable (FC)		50,000
	To record purchase from Mexican company, purchase denominated in pesos: 500,000 pesos × $0.10 = $50,000.		

On August 31, the U.S. company makes payment to the Mexican company. Since the purchase transaction is denominated in pesos, the U.S. company must make payment in pesos, not dollars. On August 31, the dollar-to-peso exchange rate has decreased to 0.09. This results in an exchange gain to the U.S. company. The payment transaction is recorded as shown:

Aug. 31	Accounts Payable (FC)	50,000	
	Exchange Gain		5,000
	Cash		45,000
	To record payment to Mexican company: 500,000 pesos × $0.09 = $45,000.		

Have you ever purchased a product from a foreign company over the Internet? In what currency was the transaction handled?

In this case, the U.S. company pays 500,000 pesos to the Mexican supplier. The 500,000 pesos were worth 50,000 dollars on August 1 at the time of the purchase. On August 31, the 500,000 pesos were worth 45,000 dollars. Thus, the U.S. company incurs an exchange gain of $5,000.

¶1402.03   INTERNATIONAL FINANCIAL REPORTING STANDARDS

> **LEARNING OBJECTIVE 3:** Describe the development of international financial reporting standards.

Throughout this book, you have learned that accounting is the language of business. When business activities become complex, accounting for those activities is usually an equally complex process. The complexity of accounting merely reflects the complexity of modern-day business. In the same way, generally accepted accounting principles reflect the nation or culture in which the accounting principles are developed. For this reason, U.S. GAAP differs from Egyptian GAAP, which differs from Japanese GAAP.

¶1403.01   DIFFERENCES IN THE EVOLUTION OF GAAP FROM COUNTRY TO COUNTRY

A nation's cultural heritage is a key factor in the development of that nation's accounting and financial reporting practices. The success of the U.S. economic system can be traced to the business environment established at the very beginning of the nation. The American Republic was founded on principles of individual liberty and free enterprise. Any person had the opportunity to start a business, with minimum interference from the government. Buying and selling stock of publicly-traded corporations has been part of the American culture almost from the beginning. The New York Stock Exchange was created in 1792, just sixteen years after the creation of the United States.

Because the development of the U.S. business culture included many publicly-traded corporations, the development of GAAP accommodates the special accounting needs for the publicly-traded corporation. For countries in which publicly-traded corporations are not prevalent, GAAP naturally evolved in a different manner. The need for financial transparency and full disclosure is less important in cultures that do not have widespread public ownership of major corporations.

The fact that GAAP may be different between two countries does not necessarily mean that one country has a better GAAP than the other. For example, the development of accounting in Germany took a path different from the U.S. In Germany, banks largely own corporations and prefer less financial disclosure to the public, which includes their competitors. Since stock for these corporations are not publicly traded to the extent that they are in the U.S., GAAP in Germany did not need or require the same provisions as U.S. GAAP. Germany, along with the rest of the European Union, has since adopted IFRS. This shows the constant evolution of standards as financial reporting needs of countries change.

¶1403.02   ADHERING TO GAAP FOR THE MULTINATIONAL CORPORATION

Most foreign stock exchanges allow U.S. companies to file their financial statements using U.S. GAAP. However, many foreign governments require companies operating in their countries to submit reports using IFRS or that country's GAAP for regulatory or tax purposes. This can be challenging for multinational corporations which must prepare some financial reports according to the GAAP of the various countries in which they do business. We will discuss this further through an example with Coke later in this chapter.

The accounting activities at multinational firms would be greatly simplified if there were only one GAAP or one set of accounting standards, which were used in all countries of the world. There has been an effort to create such a GAAP and to encourage all countries to adopt it.

IASB: International Accounting Standards Board

As stated earlier, the International Accounting Standards Board (IASB) establishes international accounting standards. The current structure and organization of the IASB came about as a result of a strategy review undertaken by its predecessor body, the Board of the International Accounting Standards Committee. The IASB publishes its standards in a series of pronouncements called "International Financial Reporting Standards" (IFRS). The IFRS are the generally accepted accounting principles required or voluntarily used in many countries around the world.

IFRS: International Financial Reporting Standards

IAS: International Accounting Standards

The IASB has also adopted the body of standards issued by the Board of the International Accounting Standards Committee. Those pronouncements continue to be designated as the **International Accounting Standards (IAS)**. The IAS are the accounting standards that provided the initial foundation to which the International Financial Reporting Standards (IFRS) are now being added. The IAS remain in effect until they can be replaced by an IFRS.

¶1403.03 MORE DETAILS ABOUT THE IASB

The IASB is an independent, privately funded, accounting standard-setter based in London. Most projects require a minimum of three years from formation to standard issuance. Each IASB member has one vote. The publication of a Standard, Exposure Draft, or final SIC Interpretation requires approval of the majority of the board members. The organization structure of the IASB is shown in Exhibit 14.1.

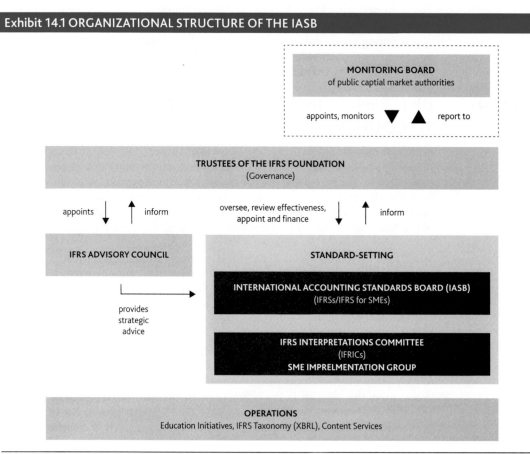

Exhibit 14.1 ORGANIZATIONAL STRUCTURE OF THE IASB

MONITORING BOARD
of public captial market authorities

appoints, monitors ▼ ▲ report to

TRUSTEES OF THE IFRS FOUNDATION
(Governance)

appoints ↓ ↑ inform   oversee, review effectiveness, ↓ ↑ inform
appoint and finance

IFRS ADVISORY COUNCIL   **STANDARD-SETTING**

provides → **INTERNATIONAL ACCOUNTING STANDARDS BOARD (IASB)**
strategic   (IFRSs/IFRS for SMEs)
advice

IFRS INTERPRETATIONS COMMITTEE
(IFRICs)
SME IMPRELMENTATION GROUP

OPERATIONS
Education Initiatives, IFRS Taxonomy (XBRL), Content Services

Source: IFRS.org

As an example of the IASB's standard setting process, let's consider the timeline of events leading to adoption of IFRS 2: Share Based Payment. The term "share based payment" refers to payments to employees in the form of shares of stock, in this case, via stock options. IFRS 2 requires that employee stock options be expensed at their fair value at the time they are awarded to employees. The project was added to the IASB agenda in July 2001. Comments were invited on the discussion paper in September 2001. An exposure draft was issued in November 2002. IFRS 2 was issued in February 2004 with an effective date of January 1, 2005.

The IASB Board members come from various countries and have a variety of functional backgrounds. It is interesting that five members on the IASB board are from the U.S. That is the most representation from one country, even though the U.S. has yet to adopt IFRS. The Board is committed to developing, in the public interest, a single set of high quality, understandable and enforceable global accounting standards that require transparent and comparable information in general purpose financial statements. In addition, the Board cooperates with national accounting standard setters to achieve convergence in accounting standards around the world.

¶1403.04 OBJECTIVES OF INTERNATIONAL FINANCIAL REPORTING STANDARDS

The goal of the IASB is to formulate and publish standards to be used in audited financial statements and to promote worldwide acceptance and recognition of these standards for a harmonized approach to accounting and reporting. It is, therefore, important that these standards are designed to reflect the needs of the professional and business communities throughout the world. More specifically, the objectives of the IASB include:

- Developing a single set of high quality, understandable, enforceable and globally-accepted international financial reporting standards (IFRSs) through its standard-setting body, the IASB;
- Promoting the use and rigorous application of those standards;
- Taking account of the financial reporting needs of emerging economies and small- and medium-sized entities (SMEs); and
- Bringing about convergence of national accounting standards and IFRSs to high quality solutions.

The IFRS encompass the most frequently-encountered business transactions. Accounting issues such as joint ventures, inventory and depreciation, are addressed in the standards. Though international accounting standards are constantly evolving, Exhibit 14.2 provides a list of the standards currently in effect.

Exhibit 14.2 INTERNATIONAL FINANCIAL REPORTING STANDARDS CURRENTLY IN EFFECT	
IAS 1:	Presentation of Financial Statements
IAS 2:	Inventories
IAS 7:	Cash Flow Statements
IAS 8:	Net Profit or Loss for the Period, Fundamental Errors and Changes in Accounting
Practices	
IAS 10:	Events After the Balance Sheet Date
IAS 11:	Construction Contracts
IAS 12:	Income Taxes
IAS 16:	Property, Plant and Equipment
IAS 17:	Leases
IAS 18:	Revenue
IAS 19:	Employee Benefits
IAS 20:	Accounting for Government Grants and Disclosure of Government Assistance
IAS 21:	The Effects of Changes in Foreign Exchange Rates
IAS 23:	Borrowing Costs
IAS 24:	Related Party Disclosures
IAS 26:	Accounting and Reporting by Retirement Benefit Plans
IAS 27:	Consolidated Financial Statements
IAS 28:	Investments in Associates
IAS 29:	Financial Reporting in Hyperinflationary Economies
IAS 31:	Financial Reporting of Interests in Joint Ventures
IAS 32:	Financial Instruments: Disclosure and Presentation
IAS 33:	Earnings per Share
IAS 34:	Interim Financial Reporting
IAS 36:	Impairment of Assets
IAS 37:	Provisions, Contingent Liabilities and Contingent Assets
IAS 38:	Intangible Assets
IAS 39:	Financial Instruments: Recognition and Measurement
IAS 40:	Investment Property
IAS 41:	Agriculture
IFRS 1:	First-time Adoption of International Financial Reporting Standards
IFRS 2:	Share-based Payment
IFRS 3:	Business Combinations
IFRS 4:	Insurance Contracts
IFRS 5:	Non-current Assets Held for Sale and Discontinued Operations
IFRS 6:	Exploration for and Evaluation of Mineral Resources
IFRS 7:	Financial Instruments: Disclosures
IFRS 8:	Operating Segments
IFRS 9:	Financial Instruments

Source: IFRS.org

A country's accounting rules and regulations result from its cultural, economic, political, and legal systems. These four factors have the potential to restrict economic development and international trade. The acceptance and implementation of international accounting standards have been impeded by cultural and ethnic differences. The IASB seeks to resolve these differences in a manner that benefits everyone.

IFRS often provide two or more options of accounting methods or techniques. The number and variety of accounting choices were reviewed and reduced, under a project titled, "The Comparability and Improvements Project." This project was designed to revise current international accounting standards, permitting fewer alternatives of accounting treatments of the same transaction. The revised standards provide better implementation guidelines, resulting in more uniform interpretation by accountants, auditors, and standards-setting boards across the globe. IFRS are required in many countries, such as Bahamas, Costa Rica, Egypt, Russia, South Africa, and countries of the European Union.

¶1403.05   ACCEPTANCE OF INTERNATIONAL STANDARDS

Whether or not the U.S. decides to fully adopt IFRS, the standards are becoming more visible in the U.S. The Securities and Exchange Commission (SEC) allows foreign companies' financial statements to be based on IFRS. This change, effective in 2008, eliminated the need for foreign companies using IFRS to reconcile their financial statements to U.S. GAAP. While it does cause issues with comparability between companies, it is viewed by many as a step closer to the U.S. adopting IFRS.

The domestic U.S. economy may have much to gain from the acceptance of international accounting standards. The use of these standards may be the most cost-efficient and cost-effective method of utilizing international capital markets.

At present, many U.S. companies are already in compliance with international standards. For many accounting issues there is no significant difference between U.S. GAAP and the IFRS. Where significant differences exist, the IASB is working with the Financial Accounting Standards Board (FASB) and the Government Accounting Standards Board (GASB) to reconcile differences and move toward harmonization.

The Norwalk Agreement is a joint commitment by the FASB and IASB to develop compatible accounting standards that can be used for both domestic and cross-border financial reporting.

At a meeting in 2002, the FASB and the IASB made a joint commitment to develop compatible accounting standards that could be used for both domestic and cross-border financial reporting. Both the FASB and IASB pledged their best efforts to make existing financial reporting standards fully compatible, as soon as practicable, and to work to ensure that once achieved, compatibility would be maintained. This collaboration between the FASB and IASB is referred to as the "**Norwalk Agreement**," because it took place in Norwalk, Connecticut.

One of the key differences between U.S. GAAP and IFRS is that IFRS are generally regarded as "principles-based" standards with limited application guidance. U.S. GAAP is generally regarded as "rule-based" standards with more specific application guidance. Examples of specific differences between U.S. GAAP and IFRS are shown in Exhibit 14.3. The impact of these differences will fluctuate among individual companies depending on factors such as the industry in which the company operates, the company's specific operations, and the company's accounting policies. Understanding the specific differences in U.S. GAAP and IFRS requires knowledge of the underlying accounting standards and relevant national regulations.

Exhibit 14.3 EXAMPLES OF DIFFERENCES BETWEEN IFRS AND U.S. GAAP		
IAS 2	The use of LIFO for determining inventory cost:	
	IFRS: LIFO is prohibited.	
	U.S. GAAP: LIFO is permitted.	
IAS 2	Measuring inventory at net realizable value even if above cost:	
	IFRS: Permitted only for producers' inventories of agricultural and forest products and mineral ores and for broker-dealers' inventories of commodities.	
	U.S. GAAP: Similar, but not restricted to producers and broker-traders.	
IAS 7	Classification of interest received and paid in the cash flow statement:	
	IFRS: May be classified as an operating, investing, or financing activity.	
	U.S. GAAP: Must be classified as an operating activity.	
IAS 12	Classification of deferred tax assets and liabilities:	
	IFRS: Always non-current.	
	U.S. GAAP: Classification is split between the current and non-current components based on the classification of the underlying asset or liability.	
IAS 14	Basis of reportable segments:	
	IFRS: Lines of business and geographical areas.	
	U.S. GAAP: Components for which information is reported internally to top management, which may or may not be based on lines of business or geographical areas.	
IAS 16	Basis of property, plant, and equipment:	
	IFRS: May use either: (a) revalued amount, or (b) historical cost with depreciation and impairment. Revalued amount is fair value at date of revaluation less subsequent accumulated depreciation and impairment losses.	
	U.S. GAAP: Generally required to use historical cost with depreciation and impairment.	
IFRS 5	Definition of a discontinued operation:	
	IFRS: A reportable business or geographical segment or major component thereof.	
	U.S. GAAP: A reportable segment, operating segment, reporting unit, subsidiary, or asset group (less restrictive than the IASB definition).	

Source: Deloitte Touche Tohmatsu. 2008. IAS Plus. Website: http://www.iasplus.com/usa/ifrsus.htm (August).

As the FASB and the IASB work together to converge standards, sometimes the IASB follows the lead of the FASB, and sometimes the FASB follows the lead of the IASB. For example, shortly after the IASB's adoption of IFRS 2, the U.S. followed the IASB's lead and adopted essentially the same accounting approach. The U.S. FASB issued a revised standard, SFAS 123(R): Share-Based Payment, which became effective for most U.S. companies in 2006; thus, U.S. GAAP and IFRS are now in congruence on this accounting issue.

IFRS are gaining increased adoptions. More than 100 countries either require or accept IFRS for corporate financial reporting purposes. Many more countries are considering adoption of IFRS. These countries may move to recognize the international financial documents of foreign companies operating within their boundaries. Additionally, many underdeveloped countries that have insufficient resources to develop domestic standards, may choose to adopt the international standards, and thus facilitate their national economic progress.

The International Organization of Securities Commissions (IOSCO) and the individual securities commissions, which make up the IOSCO, may ultimately determine global acceptance of the IFRS. Approximately 115 securities regulatory agencies worldwide comprise the IOSCO, including the SEC, with over 85 other countries affiliated with the organization. A major objective of the IOSCO is to facilitate cross-border securities offerings and multiple listings without compromising the financial statement information provided.

¶1403.06   CONTRIBUTIONS FROM THE UNITED NATIONS

The United Nations has also been concerned with international standards of accounting and reporting. In July 1972, the UN Economic and Social Council, in a unanimous resolution, asked the Secretary-General to appoint a Group of Eminent Persons (GEP) to study the role of multinational business firms. The concern was that complexity of accounting for international operations makes it increasingly difficult for external stakeholders, including governments in the home and host countries, to monitor and verify a multinational firm's data. The study focused on the potential to hide profits, falsify cost data, or transfer funds as part of a strategy of maximizing consolidated returns. The problems were partially attributed to a lack of uniform reporting requirements and standards.

The UN Economic and Social Council unanimously decided to establish appropriate permanent machinery to address the full range of issues related to multinational firms, including the enactment of international standards of accounting and reporting. The GEP determined that governments and other external stakeholders would benefit from financial information, such as asset valuation issues related to different currencies, inventories, R&D expenditure, start-up expenses, transfer prices, pension and other reserves, sources and timing of income, and wages and other workers' benefits. Accordingly, the GEP recommended that an expert group on international accounting standards be convened.

In collaboration with the private sector, including the big accounting firms, a working group of the UN sought to develop universally-acceptable standards of accounting and reporting. The UN was not alone in recognizing the need for standardization, and it became marginalized as other professional groups, like the America Institute of Certified Public Accountants (AICPA) in the U.S. and the IASB in the U.K., began to examine the issue. While the IFRS issued by the IASB are the premier international standards, the UN's International Standards on Accounting and Reporting (ISAR) have made meaningful contributions to accounting and reporting around the world. Exhibit 14.4 lists some of the applications of the ISAR.

Exhibit 14.4 APPLICATIONS OF INTERNATIONAL STANDARDS ON ACCOUNTING AND REPORTING

The United Nations Conference reported the following cases on Trade and Development (UNCTAD) related to the impact of its work on international accounting and reporting:

- In 2001, UNCTAD assisted the Russia Federation in developing and introducing national standards for accounting and reporting that were consistent with international accounting principles, and made recommendations for accounting at small- and medium-sized enterprises.

- The International Chamber of Commerce found ISAR's guideline for national requirements on the qualification of professional accountants useful for strengthening accounting education in developing countries and countries in transition.

- Stock exchanges, governments, regulatory bodies, professional associations, institutes and universities have used ISAR guidelines on environmental accounting and professional qualifications. The objective of the project is to improve environmental financial accounting and reporting by enterprises for users of the annual reports and financial statements, providing standard-setter direction, as well as preparer and user guidance. Over 220 accounting practitioners, financial analysts, and standard setters from 29 countries and 32 trainers from 17 countries were trained in five workshops.

- The guidelines and training materials were adopted and incorporated in the syllabi of 10 accounting institutions in India and Malaysia, and by the Arab Society of Chartered Accountants and the Eastern Central and Southern African Federation of Accountants.

- The European Union draft recommendation on environmental issues in the annual accounts and annual reports of companies was influenced by the ISAR guidelines.

- A Thai bank said it would incorporate environmental screening in project finance, and the Bank of Thailand broadened banking regulations and supervision to incorporate environmental reporting similar to the ISAR guidelines.

- The Ministry of Finance of China advised the workshop, which would help shape the Chinese Accounting Standards.

- Universities in the Czech Republic, Bahrain, Gaza, and Egypt introduced the training materials into their curricula. Universities in the Czech Republic and Thailand translated the training materials for their use.

? In your travels, have you benefited from standardization of some type? Perhaps you have used a credit card or cell phone internationally.

¶1404   International Standards on Auditing

LEARNING OBJECTIVE 4: Describe the objectives of international standards on auditing.

ISA: International Standards on Auditing

The **International Standards on Auditing (ISA)** are a set of standards that provide guidance on auditing. Auditing is the examination of a company's financial statements to determine if the statements have been presented fairly and prepared according to generally accepted accounting principles. The International Auditing and Assurance Standards Board (IAASB), a committee of the International Federation of Accountants, issues ISA. The IAASB works to improve the uniformity of auditing practices and related services throughout the world by issuing pronouncements on a variety of audit and assurance functions, and by encouraging their acceptance around the world.

FOCUS ON ETHICS

Culture Varies, Ethics Don't

Around the world people have different ways of doing things. In some countries, people customarily greet each other with a kiss; in other places people bow or shake hands. In some countries, people observe formal dining etiquette requiring the proper use of multiple forks, knives, and spoons. In other countries, the use of your hands while eating may be appropriate. These are examples of cultural differences.

Some people confuse cultural differences with ethics. Ethical values have to do with right and wrong. Whatever the source of ethics, whether derived from religious principle, history and literature, or personal observation, there are some basic ethical values to which everyone must agree. These fundamental ethical values are universally accepted around the world. No nation survives for long without citizens who share common values such as honesty, courage, devotion to duty, respect for other people's lives and property, and a willingness to sacrifice personal interests for a greater cause. People around the world, in every culture, share a basic set of ethical values, sometimes called "universal values" or "moral absolutes." The extent to which citizens of a nation actually put these values into practice will determine the success or failure of that nation.

The mission of the IAASB is to foster internationally-recognized standards of auditing. However, the implementation or adherence to the international standards is a decision for individual nations and their auditing regulatory agencies.

The International Standards on Auditing include basic principles and essential procedures for auditing, along with related guidance in the form of explanatory and other material. The basic principles and essential procedures are to be interpreted in the context of the explanatory and other material that provide guidance in their application.

ISA cannot override national regulations or pronouncements governing the audit of financial information in a particular country. In the U.S., compliance with domestic auditing standards usually results in compliance with the international standards. Where significant differences exist between U.S. and international standards, the Public Company Accounting Oversight Board will give consideration to the differences with a purpose of achieving harmonization. Exhibit 14.5 lists the International Standards on Auditing.

Exhibit 14.5 INTERNATIONAL STANDARDS ON AUDITING

100	—	Assurance Engagements
120	—	Framework of International Standards on Auditing
200	—	Objective and General Principles Governing an Audit of Financial Statements
210	—	Terms of Audit Engagements
220	—	Quality Control for Audit Work
230	—	Documentation
240	—	The Auditor's Responsibility to Consider Fraud and Error in an Audit of Financial Statements
240A	—	Fraud and Error
250	—	Consideration of Laws and Regulations in an Audit of Financial Statements
260	—	Communications of Audit Matters with Those Charged with Governance
300	—	Planning
310	—	Knowledge of the Business
320	—	Audit Materiality
400	—	Risk Assessments and Internal Control
401	—	Auditing in a Computer Information Systems Environment
402	—	Audit Considerations Relating to Entities Using Service Organizations
500	—	Audit Evidence
501	—	Audit Evidence-Additional Considerations for Specific Items
505	—	External Confirmations
510	—	Initial Engagements — Opening Balances
520	—	Analytical Procedures
530	—	Audit Sampling and Other Selective Testing Procedures
540	—	Audit of Accounting Estimates
545	—	Auditing Fair Value Measurements and Disclosures
550	—	Related Parties
560	—	Subsequent Events
570	—	Going Concern
580	—	Management Representations
600	—	Using the Work of Another Auditor
610	—	Considering the Work of Internal Auditing
620	—	Using the Work of an Expert
700	—	The Auditor's Report on Financial Statements
710	—	Comparatives
720	—	Other Information in Documents Containing Audited Financial Statements
800	—	The Auditor's Report on Special Purpose Audit Engagements
810	—	The Examination of Prospective Financial Information
910	—	Engagements to Review Financial Statements
920	—	Engagements to Perform Agreed-Upon Procedures Regarding Financial Information
930	—	Engagements to Compile Financial Information

IFAC: International Federation of Accountants

The parent organization of the IAASB, the **International Federation of Accountants (IFAC),** is the world's largest accounting organization. The IFAC is an organization of national professional accountancy organizations that represents accountants employed in public practice, business and industry, the public sector, and education, as well as some specialized groups that interface frequently with the profession. Currently, it has 167 member bodies in 127 countries, representing 2.5 million accountants. IFAC's structure and operations provide for representation of its diverse member organizations. IFAC strives to develop the accounting profession and harmonize auditing standards worldwide so that accountants can provide services of consistently high quality in the public interest.

As U.S. citizens, we benefit from having some uniformity of laws among the 50 states. Can you imagine the obstacles that would exist if each state had its own currency?

For effective and efficient functioning of the global marketplace, uniformity in accounting and auditing standards is beneficial. However, international subsidiaries of a given company may use different accounting procedures that affect financial results. People within the company must recognize and interpret these different procedures. When making decisions concerning the viability of an international operation, top management must assess these differences. Outside businesspersons, financiers, and investors must also consider the differences that exist. Such differences curtail the development of international business activity. Harmonization of standards has the potential to benefit economic activity around the globe.

FOCUS ON GLOBAL TRADE

Corporate Social Responsibility Reporting

Global Reporting Initiative (GRI) is the most extensively used international standard for corporate social responsibility reporting. Numerous companies around the world, including the Coca-Cola Company, use GRI to guide preparation of their corporate social responsibility reports. To meet the needs of top corporate managers and stakeholders, worldwide efforts to better define corporate responsibility gained attention during the late 1980s and early 1990s. Business firms began accepting responsibility for at least some of their impacts on natural and social systems. These natural and social systems have been traditionally excluded from accounting and financial reporting.

In 1997, the Coalition for Environmentally Responsible Economies (CERES) and the United Nations Environment Programme (UNEP) jointly created the Global Reporting Initiative. While various organizations have developed guidelines for corporate governance or principles for social responsibility, the GRI is the most widely-accepted set of guidelines among international businesses, non-profit advocacy groups, accounting organizations, and other stakeholder groups for enhancement of quality, rigor, and utility in corporate social responsibility reporting.

The GRI Sustainability Reporting Guidelines are a set of voluntary guidelines that assist business firms reporting in three areas of sustainability – economic, environmental, and social performance. The Guidelines provide reporting principles that help business firms show a balanced and credible picture of their sustainability actions in a manner that can be consistently applied across different organizations and over time.

Economic indicators relate to economic impact on customers, suppliers, employees, capital providers and the public. Environmental indicators include materials, energy, water, biodiversity, emissions, effluents, waste, suppliers, products, services, compliance, and transport. Social indicators include labor practices, human rights, societal, and product responsibility.

¶1405 Restating Foreign Subsidiary Financial Statements

LEARNING OBJECTIVE 5: Restate a foreign subsidiary's financial statements in U.S. dollars.

Many U.S. companies have multinational operations with foreign subsidiaries around the globe. For example, the Coca-Cola Company owns a number of foreign subsidiaries. The company employs approximately 55,000 people; over three-fourths of these employees are located outside the United States. Exhibit 14.6 provides a breakdown of employees by geographic location.

Exhibit 14.6 THE COCA-COLA COMPANY'S GLOBAL WORKFORCE

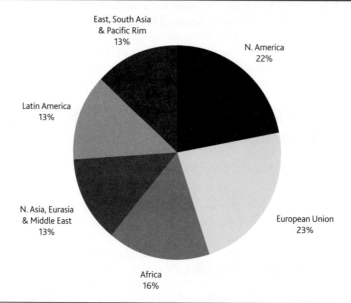

Source: The Coca-Cola Company Corporate Responsibility Review, Published July 2006.

FOCUS ON TECHNOLOGY

Using Microsoft Excel: Preparing a Pie Chart

Using Excel, we will recreate the pie chart in Exhibit 14.6, which shows the breakdown of Coca-Cola employees by geographic location.

1. Enter the necessary data onto your Excel worksheet in the following format:

East, South Asia & Pacific Rim	0.13
Latin America	0.13
N. Asia, Eurasia & Middle East	0.13
Africa	0.16
European Union	0.23
N. America	0.22

2. Highlight the data range that contains the information to be charted (i.e., the cells containing all the descriptions and amounts you just entered). The descriptions are being included so that Chart Wizard can incorporate them into the chart.
3. Click on the Chart Wizard icon, which will immediately launch into a four-step process to create your chart.
4. In step one, you select a specific chart type. Select Pie Chart. Choose any of the pie chart variations. Click on "Next" to go to the next step.
5. In step two, Chart Wizard is simply confirming the data range that you previously highlighted. There is a display showing what your chart currently looks like. Click "Next."
6. Several chart-enhancing options are made available in step three. To add percentages and/ or labels to the pie slices, select the "Data Labels" tab and click on the option you prefer. These options can also be accessed after the chart is completed by right clicking on the chart. Click "Next."
7. Click "Finish" and the chart will appear on your worksheet. Like any other object, clicking on the chart or items within the chart will enable you to move or revise them.

A parent company is an investing company that owns a controlling interest in another company.

Consolidated financial statements are two or more sets of financial statements combined into one set.

Currency of books and records (CBR): currency of foreign financial statements.

Functional currency (FC): currency in which the subsidiary buys, sells, borrows, repays, and generally conducts business.

Reporting currency (RC): currency of consolidated financial statements.

When a U.S.-based multinational corporation such as the Coca-Cola Company owns more than 50% of the voting stock of a foreign company, a parent-subsidiary relationship exists. The **parent company** is the investing company and is usually required to prepare consolidated financial statements. Combining two or more sets of financial statements into a single set of statements results in **consolidated financial statements**. Before this can be done, the financial statements of the foreign subsidiary must be recast using U.S. generally accepted accounting principles (GAAP). Next, the foreign accounts must be re-measured (translated) from the foreign currency into U.S. dollars. To translate financial statements from the foreign currency to the U.S. dollar, three currencies must be identified:

- Currency of books and records (CBR) — The CBR is the currency in which the foreign subsidiary's financial statements are denominated.
- Functional currency (FC) — The FC is the one in which the subsidiary buys, sells, borrows, repays, and generally conducts business.
- Reporting currency (RC) — The RC is the one in which the consolidated financial statements are denominated.

Three methods can be used to translate foreign currency: (1) the current rate method, (2) the temporal rate method, and (3) the use of both methods. The following rules are used to determine the appropriate method of translation:

Rule 1: If the functional currency (FC) is hyper-inflationary (i.e., 100% cumulative inflation within three years), ignore the FC and re-measure the currency of books and records (CBR) into the reporting currency (RC) using the temporal rate method.

Rule 2: If the CBR is different from the FC, re-measure the CBR into the FC using the temporal rate method.

Rule 3: Translate from the FC into the RC using the current rate method.

You must apply the rules in sequence, stopping when the subsidiary's financial statements have been converted into the parent company's reporting currency (RC). Review the following examples.

- Example 1: When the functional currency (FC) is hyper-inflationary, then Rule 1 applies. The financial statements that are denominated in the CBR are translated into the RC using the temporal rate method. Rules 2 and 3 are not used.
- Example 2: If the CBR is British pounds, the FC is Japanese yen (not hyper-inflationary), and the RC is U.S. dollars, then skip Rule 1 and apply Rule 2, translating the CBR (pounds) into the FC (yen) using the temporal rate method. Since the FC (yen) is not the RC (dollars), apply Rule 3 to translate the FC (yen) into the RC (dollars) using the current rate method.
- Example 3: When the CBR and the FC are the same, go directly to Rule 3.

¶1405.01   CURRENT RATE METHOD

Using the current rate method, all assets and liabilities are translated using the current rate (i.e., exchange rate on the balance sheet date). Owners' equity and dividends are translated at historical rates (exchange rate at the time the asset was acquired, the liability was incurred, or when the element of paid-in capital was issued or reacquired). Income statement items can be translated using the average exchange rate (the average of the exchange rate at the beginning of the accounting period and the current rate).

Exhibit 14.7 provides an example of how a foreign firm's financial statements would be translated from British pounds to U.S. dollars using the current rate method.

Exhibit 14.7 FOREIGN CURRENCY TRANSLATION USING THE CURRENT RATE METHOD

ADJUSTED TRAIL BALANCE
in British Pounds (BP) December 31, Year 5

	Debit	Credit
Cash	20,000	
Accounts Receivable	35,000	
Inventory	105,000	
Equipment	60,000	
Accumulated Depreciation		15,000
Accounts Payable		40,000
Bonds Payable		50,000
Revenues		120,000
General Expenses	108,000	
Depreciation Expense	8,000	
Dividends	4,000	
Common Stock		62,000
Paid-in Capital in Excess of Par		44,000
Retained Earnings		9,000
Total	340,000	340,000
Exchange Rates		1 BP = $___
Current Exchange Rate		1.900
Average Exchange Rate		2.000
At July 31, 20Y5		2.200
At June 30, 20Y2		1.800

Other: All common stock was issued on June 30, Year 2 (i.e. 6/30/Y2)
Dividends were declared and paid on July 31, 20Y5.
Translated Retained Earnings at December 31, 20Y5 $3,000

TRANSLATION FROM BRITISH POUNDS TO DOLLARS

CURRENT RATE METHOD

Debits:	BPs	Exchange Rates	U.S. Dollars
Cash	20,000	1.900	38,000
A/R	35,000	1.900	66,500
Inventory	105,000	1.900	199,500
Fixed Assets	60,000	1.900	114,000
General Expenses	108,000	2.000	216,000
Depreciation Expense	8,000	2.000	16,000
Dividends (7/31/Y5)	4,000	2.200	8,800
Total	340,000		658,800
Credits:			
Accumulated Depreciation	15,000	1.900	28,500
A/P	40,000	1.900	76,000
Bonds Payable	50,000	1.900	95,000
Revenues	120,000	2.000	240,000
Common Stock (6/30/Y2)	62,000	1.800	111,600
Paid-in Cap. (6/30/Y2)	44,000	1.800	79,200
Retained Earnings	9,000	n.a.	3,000
Cum. Translation Adjustment			25,500
Total	340,000		658,800

¶1405.02   TEMPORAL RATE METHOD

The objective of the temporal rate method is to measure the transactions of each subsidiary as though the parent had made the transaction. Monetary items (e.g. cash, receivables, inventories at market value, payables, and long-term debt) are re-measured using the current exchange rate. Other items (e.g. prepaid expenses, inventories carried at cost, fixed assets, and stock) are re-measured using historical exchange rates.

Exhibit 14.8 provides an example of how a foreign firm's financial statements would be translated from Mexican pesos to U.S. dollars using the temporal rate method.

Exhibit 14.8 FOREIGN CURRENCY TRANSLATION USING THE TEMPORAL RATE METHOD

Debits:	Mexican Pesos	Exchange Rates	U.S. Dollars
Cash	32,000	0.100	3,200
A/R	50,000	0.100	5,000
Inventory (10/31/Y3)	40,000	0.110	4,400
(7/31/Y4)	160,000	0.088	14,080
Fixed Assets (6/30/Y1)	13,000	0.170	2,210
(12/31/Y1)	65,000	0.160	10,400
(7/31/Y2)	52,000	0.140	7,280
General Expense	189,000	0.090	17,010
Depreciation Exp. (6/30/Y1)	1,500	0.170	255
(12/31/Y1)	7,500	0.160	1,200
(7/31/Y2)	6,000	0.140	840
Dividends (7/31/Y4)	10,000	0.088	880
Total	626,000		66,755
Credits: Accum. Depreciation (6/30/Y1)	8,000	0.170	1,360
(12/31/Y1)	40,000	0.160	6,400
(7/31/Y2)	32,000	0.140	4,480
A/P	43,000	0.100	4,300
Bonds Payable	160,000	0.100	16,000
Revenues	214,000	0.090	19,260
Common Stock (6/30/Y1)	28,000	0.150	3,300
(1/31/Y2)	22,000	0.150	3,300
Paid-in Capital (6/30/Y1)	30,000	0.170	5,100
(1/31/Y2)	20,000	0.150	3,000
Retained Earnings	29,000	n.a.	10,700
Cum. Translation Adjustment			(11,905)
Total	626,000		66,755
Exhange Rates:	1 peso = $__		
Current Exchange Rate	0.100		
Average Exchange Rate	0.090		
At July 31, Year 4	0.088		
At October 31, Year 3	0.110		
At July 31, Year 2	0.140		
At January 31, Year 2	0.150		
At December 31, Year 1	0.160		
At June 30, Year 1	0.170		

Other: Regarding common stock, 60% was issued 6/30/Y1; 40% on 1/31/Y2.
Regarding inventory, 20% was acquired 10/31/Y3; 80% on 7/31/Y4.
Dividends were declared and paid on 7/31/Y4.
Regarding fixed assets, 10% were acquired 6/30/Y1; 50% on 12/31/Y1; and 40% on 7/31/Y2.
Revenues and expenses were accrued evenly throughout the year.
Translated retained earnings at 12/31/Y4 was $10,700

¶1405.03 CUMULATIVE TRANSLATION ADJUSTMENT

The cumulative translation adjustment is the debit or credit required to bring the dollar-denominated accounts into balance after applying different exchange rates to the accounts.

Since different exchange rates are applied to different accounts, the resulting dollar-denominated trial balance will not likely balance. The debit or credit required to bring the dollar-denominated accounts into balance is the **cumulative translation adjustment**. The change in the cumulative translation adjustment during the current accounting period results in a translation gain or loss. Under the current rate method, the translation gain or loss is accumulated on a separate line in the owner's equity section of the balance sheet and has no impact on the income statement. Under the temporal rate method, the translation gain or loss is shown on the income statement.

¶1406 Working in a Different Culture

Have you ever translated U.S. dollars into another currency?

LEARNING OBJECTIVE 6: Explain how cultural factors affect the accountant's workplace.

Accountants, business managers, and other employees of multinational businesses may be asked to work outside their native countries. Since preparation is key to successful international job assignments, many companies provide training and orientation programs to their employees bound for international assignments. The multinational oil and gas company, Royal Dutch Shell, provides a cross-cultural workshop for all of its graduate trainees, whether they are assigned to work abroad or not. Exhibit 14.9 lists some of the cultural differences employees might encounter while conducting business in other countries. The purpose is to familiarize the employee with the customs and business practices of other cultures.

Exhibit 14.9 CONDUCTING BUSINESS IN VARIOUS CULTURES

Business Hours

- Stores in Spain typically close from 1:00 pm to 4:00 pm for lunch.
- Stores in Italy usually close for lunch from noon to 3:00 pm, even in the resorts.
- While Italian stores usually close at 7:00 pm on weekdays, they close early (1:00 pm) on Saturday and are closed all day on Sunday.
- In most West European nations, almost all of the workers receive four weeks paid vacation plus several paid holidays each year.

Product Names

- Was Chevrolet's Nova a good name for a car? In Spanish, "no va" means "it doesn't go."
- In Japanese, General Motors' "Body by Fisher" translates as "Corpse by Fisher."

Gifts

- In England, apparel and soap are considered too personal for gifts.
- In Saudi Arabia, a man should never offer a gift to another man's wife, and never offer anyone alcoholic beverages as a gift.
- In Mexico, yellow flowers symbolize death. In Brazil, purple is a death color.

Source: L.M. Smith, K.T. Smith, and D. Kerr. 2003. Accounting Information Systems, 4th Ed., Boston, Mass.: Houghton Mifflin.

Accounting for the costs of the international job assignment is an important task of the accounting department. As with all business activities, accounting can help the other departments determine whether benefits outweigh costs. Suppose the direct costs of sending an employee on an overseas assignment include $5,000 for preparation and orientation, $30,000 for relocating and moving expenses, and $40,000 for training and developing job skills at the international location. After relocation, the employee's compensation and other benefits are $80,000 per year. Thus, the company will incur $155,000 in total costs sending an employee abroad in the first year. Suppose the employee's work contributes $200,000 to the firm's profits. Thus, the benefits outweigh the costs of sending the employee overseas. This would be an example of a positive international job assignment that the firm would want to pursue.

On the other hand, if the employee is unable to work effectively in the foreign location, then the employee may have to be returned home prior to fulfilling his or her responsibilities. Costs would then exceed benefits. In the worst case, the employee may actually damage relations with customers at the foreign location. At a minimum, the money spent on the international job assignment is wasted. The additional cost and risk is why multinational companies are very careful in selecting employees for international job assignments.

When people travel and conduct business outside their home cultures, lack of sensitivity to cultural differences may lead to unintentionally offending someone. Understanding these cultural differences helps all the various departments within a business firm operate more effectively.

The most obvious example may be marketing; knowing how to appeal to the customer is fundamental to selling a product. Understanding the preferences and taboos of a culture can determine the success or failure of a new venture.

Another function within the firm that is very dependent upon knowledge of the culture is human resources. That department must know how to relate to the foreign workforce in order to hire and retain competent personnel. The production department cannot operate if it is not familiar with the resources available to that department. All departments within the firm must be acquainted with the rules of their host government. As the saying goes, "You're not in Kansas anymore," so learn about your new environment if you want to be successful. The boxed insert on Cultural Differences provides some cultural differences that are helpful to be aware of.

FOCUS ON GLOBAL

Cultural Differences

Power Distance. Large versus small power distance indicates the extent to which the members of a society accept the fact that power in organizations is unequally distributed. People in large power-distance societies accept a hierarchical order in which everybody has a place that needs no further justification. The U.S. scores relatively low on power distance. The citizens who formed the U.S. emphasized equality of persons and strongly opposed the system of nobles that was then prevalent in Europe.

Uncertainty Avoidance. Strong versus weak uncertainty avoidance is the degree to which members of a society feel uncomfortable with uncertainty. Strong uncertainty avoidance cultures have very strict guidelines and do not tolerate deviation from these standards. Weak uncertainty avoidance cultures have more flexible rules and are more accepting of differences. The U.S. scores on the weak side.

Individualism versus Collectivism. The individualism versus collectivism dimension indicates whether the focus is on the individual or the group. It relates to one's self-concept: "I" or "we." This affects the degree of interdependence a society maintains among individuals. The average person in the U.S. is more individualistic than the average person in other cultures.

Masculinity versus Femininity. Masculinity versus femininity (achievement orientation) represents traits traditionally associated with male and female genders. Masculinity indicates the preference in society for achievement, heroism, assertiveness, and material success. Its opposite, femininity, stands for the preference for relationships, caring for the weak, and the quality of life. The U.S. is relatively balanced regarding achievement orientation.

Time Orientation. Time orientation relates to long-term versus short-term time orientation. The short-term orientation emphasizes social and status obligations, and spending rather than saving. A long-term orientation has greater emphasis on a virtuous approach to life, large savings levels, sacrifice for long-term goals and the greater good. The average American tends to have a relatively short-term time orientation.

Source: Geert Hofstede. 1984. *Culture's Consequences*. Sage Publications, Inc., Beverly Hills, CA. and G. Hofstede and M. Bond. 1988. "The Confucius Connection: From Cultural Roots to Economic Growth." *Organizational Dynamics*, Vol. 16, No. 4.

Here What situations have you been involved in that required sensitivity to cultural differences? How did you become aware of the cultural differences in your situation? and now

¶1407 Concluding Remarks

How do you compare the financial statements of a U.S. firm with a firm in India or Germany? That was this chapter's opening question. You learned that The International Accounting Standards Board (IASB) establishes uniform international accounting standards that facilitate the comparison of financial statements of companies from different countries. These standards are required or voluntarily used by companies in many countries around the world. The goal of the IASB is to formulate internationally-recognized standards of accounting and reporting that will be accepted by all countries.

Chapter Review

LEARNING OBJECTIVE 1

Describe the importance of accounting for a global marketplace to people within and outside the business.

Managers within a business need specific accounting information related to global operations in order to assess profitability associated with those operations. Efforts of the International Accounting Standards Board (IASB), the organization that establishes international accounting standards, continue to drive a trend toward the use of international accounting standards by firms around the world.

LEARNING OBJECTIVE 2

Explain the role of accounting in global commerce.

International trade has significant challenges such as tariffs, language barriers, cultural differences, and incompatible equipment standards. Multinational businesses must comply with the rules and regulations of the countries in which they operate. The accounting information system provides crucial information to management for evaluating the viability of a firm's international operations.

When a company sells its goods or services to a customer in a different country, the company can request payment in the company's domestic currency or in the foreign currency of the customer. An exchange gain or loss occurs when the exchange rate changes from the time a sale takes place to the time payment is received. Depending on whether the exchange rate changes favorably or unfavorably, the company can incur a gain or loss.

LEARNING OBJECTIVE 3

Describe the development of international financial reporting standards.

The International Accounting Standards Board (IASB) establishes international accounting standards. IASB publishes its Standards in a series of pronouncements called "International Financial Reporting Standards" (IFRS). The IFRS are the generally accepted accounting principles required, or voluntarily used, in many countries around the world. The International Accounting Standards (IAS) are the accounting standards that provided the initial foundation to which the International Financial Reporting Standards (IFRS) are now being added. The IAS remain in effect until they are replaced by an IFRS. The goal of the IASB is to formulate internationally-recognized or harmonized standards of accounting and reporting.

Currently, foreign companies that sell securities in the U.S. must reconcile their financial statements to U.S. GAAP. The use of international standards may be the most cost-effective method of utilizing international capital markets. The United Nations is concerned that globalization of business makes it difficult for external stakeholders, including governments, to verify a multinational firm's data.

LEARNING OBJECTIVE 4

Describe the objectives of international standards on auditing.

International standards on auditing (ISA) are issued by the International Auditing and Assurance Standards Board (IAASB), a committee of the International Federation of Accountants. The IAASB's mission is to foster internationally-recognized standards of auditing; however, adherence to the international standards is a decision for individual nations and their auditing regulatory agencies.

LEARNING OBJECTIVE 5

Restate a foreign subsidiary's financial statements in U.S. dollars.

When a parent company in the U.S. prepares consolidated financial statements, the financial statements of the foreign subsidiary must be recast using U.S. GAAP. The foreign accounts must be translated into U.S. dollars. Three currencies must be considered: (1) currency of books and records (CBR) in which the foreign financial statements are denominated; (2) functional currency (FC) in which the subsidiary generally buys, sells, borrows, repays, and generally conducts business; and (3) reporting currency (RC) in which the consolidated financial statements are denominated.

The current rate method, the temporal rate method, or the use of both methods may be utilized for currency translation. The cumulative translation adjustment is the debit or credit required to bring the dollar-denominated accounts into balance after applying different exchange rates to the accounts.

LEARNING OBJECTIVE 6

Explain how cultural factors affect the accountant's workplace.

Many multinational companies provide orientation programs to their employees bound for international assignments in order to prepare them for differences in culture, laws, and the marketplace. Accounting can help determine whether benefits outweigh the costs of sending an employee overseas. Besides salary, the first-year cost of sending an employee abroad may include training and moving expenses. The financial benefit of having the employee abroad must exceed these additional costs in order to make the assignment worthwhile for the firm.

¶1409

Glossary

Consolidated financial statements

Consolidated financial statements are two or more sets of financial statements that have been combined into one set of statements.

Cumulative translation adjustment

The cumulative translation adjustment is the debit or credit required to bring the dollar-denominated accounts into balance after applying different exchange rates to the accounts.

Currency of books and records (CBR)

The CBR is the currency in which the foreign financial statements are denominated.

Functional currency (FC)

The FC is the currency in which the subsidiary buys, sells, borrows, repays, and generally conducts business.

International Accounting Standards (IAS)

The IAS are the accounting standards that provided the initial foundation to which the International Financial Reporting Standards (IFRS) are now being added. An IAS remains in effect until they are replaced by an IFRS.

International Federation of Accountants (IFAC)

The IFAC is an organization of national professional accountancy organizations that represents accountants employed in all different sectors in countries around the world.

International Standards on Auditing (ISA)

The ISA are a set of standards that provide guidance on auditing. The ISA are issued by the IAASB, a committee of the International Federation of Accountants.

Norwalk Agreement

This agreement is a joint commitment by the FASB and IASB to develop compatible accounting standards that can be used for both domestic and cross-border financial reporting.

Parent company

An investing company that owns a controlling interest in another company.

Reporting currency (RC)

The RC is the currency in which the consolidated financial statements are denominated.

¶1410   # Chapter Assignments

QUESTIONS

1. **[Obj. 1]** How does international trade affect individual businesses?

2. **[Obj. 2]** What was the name of the first joint-stock company? What were the benefits to its members? Where did operating funds come from?

3. **[Obj. 2]** What financial reporting problems did the East India Company encounter?

4. **[Obj. 2]** When a company sells its goods or services to a customer in a country with a different currency, in which currency is the transaction recorded?

5. **[Obj. 2]** What is an exchange gain or loss?

6. **[Obj. 3]** What is the International Accounting Standards Board (IASB)?

7. **[Obj. 3]** How are the International Financial Reporting Standards (IFRS) and the International Accounting Standards (IAS) connected?

8. **[Obj. 3]** List four objectives of the international accounting standards board.

9. **[Obj. 3]** What is the status of the acceptance of International Financial Reporting Standards (IFRS) around the world?

10. **[Obj. 3]** What is a concern of the United Nations regarding the lack of international standards of accounting?

11. **[Obj. 4]** What are the international standards on auditing? Can they override a country's national regulations?

12. **[Obj. 4]** What is the function and mission of the International Auditing and Assurance Standards Board (IAASB)?

13. **[Obj. 4]** What is the International Federation of Accountants (IFAC)?

14. **[Obj. 5]** What is the first step in translating foreign currency into U.S. dollars?

15. **[Obj. 5]** Explain the current rate method to currency translation.

16. **[Obj. 5]** Explain the temporal rate method to currency translation.

17. **[Obj. 6]** Describe the five primary differences among cultures identified by Hofstede in the boxed insert on Cultural Differences.

SHORT EXERCISES – SET A

Building Accounting Skills

1 . **[Obj. 2]** Recording Foreign Sales: Assume that on April 1, Ford Motor Company sells $100,000 of products to a customer in Japan and the customer is billed in U.S. dollars. The customer pays the bill on April 30.
   a. Record the sale on April 1.
   b. Record the customer payments received by Ford on April 30.

2. **[Obj. 2]** Recording Foreign Sales: Assume that on April 1, Ford Motor Company sells $100,000 of products to a customer in Japan. Unlike the previous exercise, the customer is billed in Japanese yen, not U.S. dollars. The customer pays the bill on April 30. Between April 1 and April 30, the dollar to yen exchange rate changes. The U.S. dollar to Japanese yen exchange rates are as follows:

| April 1: dollar / yen = .010 |
| April 30: dollar / yen = .009 |

   a. Record the sale on April 1.
   b. Record Ford's receipt of the customer payment on April 30.

3. **[Obj. 2]** Recording Foreign Sales: Same as Exercise A2, except the dollar to yen exchange rate increases instead of declining. Assume that on April 1, Ford Motor Company sells $100,000 of products to a customer in Japan. The customer is billed in Japanese yen. The customer pays the bill on April 30. Between April 1 and April 30, the dollar to yen exchange rate changes. The U.S. dollar to Japanese yen exchange rates are as follows:

April 1: dollar / yen = .010
April 30: dollar / yen = .011

    a.   Record the sale on April 1.
    b.   Record Ford's receipt of the customer payment on April 30.

4. **[Obj. 2]** Recording Foreign Purchases: Assume that on June 1, General Electric Corporation purchases $1,000 of goods from a company in France and the payment is to be made in U.S. dollars. On June 30, General Electric pays the bill.
    a.   Record GE's purchase transaction on June 1.
    b.   Record GE's payment on June 30.

5. **[Obj. 2]** Recording Foreign Purchases: Assume that on June 1, General Electric Corporation purchases $1,000 of goods from a company in France. GE is billed in EU euros at the time of the sale, not U.S. dollars. On June 30, General Electric pays the bill. Between June 1 and June 30, the dollar to euro exchange rate changes. The U.S. dollar to EU euro exchange rates are as follows:

June 1: dollar / euro = 1.25
June 30: dollar / euro = 1.20

    a.   Record GE's purchase transaction on June 1.
    b.   Record GE's payment on June 30.

6. **[Obj. 2]** Recording Foreign Purchases: Same as Exercise A5, except the dollar to euro exchange rate increases instead of declining. Assume that on June 1, General Electric Corporation purchases $1,000 of goods from a company in France. GE is billed in EU euros at the time of the sale, not U.S. dollars. On June 30, General Electric pays the bill. Between June 1 and June 30, the dollar to euro exchange rate changes. The U.S. dollar to EU euro exchange rates are as follows:

June 1: dollar / euro = 1.25
June 30: dollar / euro = 1.50

    a.   Record GE's purchase transaction on June 1.
    b.   Record GE's payment on June 30.

7. **[Obj. 2]** Impact of Exchange Rates on a Sale: Suppose a U.S.-based company makes a credit sale to a customer in Austria. The sale is denominated in EU euros. At the time of the sale, the exchange rate is 1.7 ($1.70 per euro). Between the time of the sale and the customer payment in euros, the dollar to euro exchange rate fluctuates. Indicate whether an exchange gain or loss occurs for the U.S. company in each case:

Dollar to euro exchange rate	Exchange gain or loss
Increases to 1.9	?
Decreases to 1.4	?

8. [Obj. 3&4] International Organizations: Select answers to the following questions from the choices below:
   1. International Auditing and Assurance Standards Board (IAASB)
   2. United Nations (UN)
   3. International Federation of Accountants (IFAC)
   4. International Accounting Standards Board (IASB)
   a. __ issues International Financial Reporting Standards (IFRS).
   b. __ is an organization of national professional accountancy organizations that represent accountants employed in public practice, business and industry, the public sector, and education.
   c. __ is an independent, privately funded standard-setter based in London.
   d. __ issues International Standards on Accounting and Reporting (ISAR).
   e. __ issues International Standards on Auditing (ISA).

9. [Obj. 5] Business Currencies: Select answers for the following currency descriptions from the choices below:
   1. Reporting currency
   2. Functional currency
   3. Currency of books and records
   a. __ is the currency in which the foreign subsidiary's financial statements are denominated.
   b. __ is the currency in which the consolidated financial statements are denominated.
   c. __ is the currency in which the subsidiary buys, sells, borrows, repays, and generally conducts business.

10. [Obj. 5] Foreign Currency Translation: The following are rules used to determine the method of currency translation:
    1. Translate from the functional currency (FC) into the reporting currency (RC) using the current rate method.
    2. If the functional currency (FC) is hyper-inflationary (i.e., 100% cumulative inflation within three years), then ignore the FC and re-measure the currency of books and records (CBR) into the reporting currency (RC) using the temporal rate method.
    3. If the CBR is different from the FC, then re-measure the CBR into the FC using the temporal rate method.

    What is the correct order in which the rules are applied?

11. [Obj. 5] Foreign Currency Translation: Suppose that a subsidiary of IBM is located in Zimbabwe. The functional currency of the subsidiary is hyper-inflationary. What method of currency translation should be used to restate the subsidiary's financial statements? Explain your answer.

12. [Obj. 5] Foreign Currency Translation: Suppose that a subsidiary of Ford Motor Company uses Japanese yen as the currency of books and records (CBR) and EU euro as the functional currency (FC). The euro is not hyper-inflationary. The reporting currency (RC) of Ford is the U.S. dollar. What method of currency translation should be used to restate the subsidiary's financial statements? Explain your answer.

13. [Obj. 5] Foreign Currency Translation: Suppose that a subsidiary of Coca-Cola Company is located in Cardiff, Wales in the United Kingdom. The functional currency (FC) and currency of books and records (CBR) is Great Britain pounds. Great Britain pounds are not hyper-inflationary. The reporting currency of Coca-Cola is the U.S. dollar. What method of currency translation should be used to restate the subsidiary's financial statements? Explain your answer.

14. [Obj. 5] Foreign Currency Translation: Contrast the current rate method with the temporal rate method.

SHORT EXERCISES – SET B

Building Accounting Skills

1. **[Obj. 2]** Recording Foreign Sales: Assume that on October 1, Best Buy sells $200,000 of products to a customer in Mexico and the customer is billed in U.S. dollars. The customer pays the bill on October 31.
   a. Record the sale on October 1.
   b. Record the customer payments received by Best Buy on October 31.

2. **[Obj. 2]** Recording Foreign Sales: Assume that on October 1 Best Buy sells $200,000 of products to a customer in Mexico. Unlike the previous exercise, the customer is billed in Mexican pesos, not U.S. dollars. The customer pays the bill on October 31. Between October 1 and October 31, the dollar-to-peso exchange rate changes. The U.S. dollar to Mexican peso exchange rates are as follows:

October 1: dollar / peso = .010
October 31: dollar / peso = .009

   a. Record the sale on October 1.
   b. Record Best Buy's receipt of the customer payment on October 31.

3. **[Obj. 2]** Recording Foreign Sales: Same as Exercise A2, except the dollar-to-peso exchange rate increases instead of declining. Assume that on October 1, Best Buy sells $200,000 of products to a customer in Mexico. The customer is billed in Mexican pesos, not U.S. dollars. The customer pays the bill on October 31. Between October 1 and October 31, the dollar-to-peso exchange rate changes. The U.S. dollar to Mexican peso exchange rates are as follows:

October 1: dollar / peso = .010
October 31: dollar / peso = .011

   a. Record the sale on October 1.
   b. Record Best Buy's receipt of the customer payment on October 31.

4. **[Obj. 2]** Recording Foreign Purchases: Assume that on September 1, Walden Books purchases $2,000 of goods from a company in Japan and the payment is to be made in U.S. dollars. On September 30, Walden Books pays the bill.
   a. Record Walden Books' purchase transaction on September 1.
   b. Record Walden Books' payment on September 30.

5. **[Obj. 2]** Recording Foreign Purchases: Assume that on September 1, Walden Books purchases $2,000 of goods from a company in Japan. Unlike the prior exercise, Walden Books is billed in Japanese yen at the time of the sale, not U.S. dollars. On September 30, Walden Books pays the bill. Between September 1 and September 30, the dollar to yen exchange rate changes. The U.S. dollar to yen exchange rates are as follows:

Sept 1: dollar / yen = 1.25
Sept 30: dollar / yen = 1.20

   a. Record Walden Books' purchase transaction on September 1.
   b. Record Walden Books' payment on September 30.

6. **[Obj. 2]** Recording Foreign Purchases: Same as Exercise B5, except the dollar to yen exchange rate increases instead of declining. Assume that on September 1, Walden Books purchases $2,000 of goods from a company in Japan. Walden Books is billed in Japanese yen at the time of the sale, not U.S. dollars. On September 30, Walden Books pays the bill. Between September 1 and September 30, the dollar to yen exchange rate changes. The U.S. dollar to yen exchange rates are as follows:

Sept 1: dollar / yen = 1.25
Sept 30: dollar / yen = 1.50

   a. Record Walden Books' purchase transaction on September 1.
   b. Record Walden Books' payment on September 30.

7. **[Obj. 2]** Impact of Exchange Rates on a Purchase: Suppose a U.S.-based company makes a credit purchase from a supplier in Finland. The purchase is denominated in EU euros. At the time of the sale, the exchange rate is 2.0 ($2 per euro). Between the time of the sale and the payment in euros, the dollar to euro exchange rate fluctuates. Indicate whether an exchange gain or loss occurs for the U.S. company in each case:

Dollar to euro exchange rate	Exchange gain or loss
Increases to 2.3	?
Decreases to 1.8	?

8. **[Obj. 3&4]** International Organizations: Select answers to the following questions from the choices below:
   1. International Auditing and Assurance Standards Board (IAASB)
   2. United Nations (UN)
   3. International Federation of Accountants (IFAC)
   4. International Accounting Standards Board (IASB)
   a. __ is an independent, privately funded standard-setter based in London.
   b. __ issues International Standards on Auditing (ISA).
   c. __ issues International Financial Reporting Standards (IFRS).
   d. __ is an organization of national professional accountancy organizations that represent accountants employed in public practice, business and industry, the public sector, and education.
   e. __ issues International Standards on Accounting and Reporting (ISAR).

9. **[Obj. 5]** Business Currencies: Select answers for the following currency descriptions from the choices below:
   1. Reporting currency
   2. Functional currency
   3. Currency of books and records
   a. __ is the currency in which the subsidiary buys, sells, borrows, repays, and generally conducts business.
   b. __ is the currency in which the foreign subsidiary's financial statements are denominated.
   c. __ is the currency in which the consolidated financial statements are denominated.

10. **[Obj. 5]** Foreign Currency Translation: The following are rules used to determine the method of currency translation:
    1. If the functional currency (FC) is hyper-inflationary (i.e., 100% cumulative inflation within three years), then ignore the FC and re-measure the currency of books and records (CBR) into the reporting currency (RC) using the temporal rate method.
    2. Translate from the functional currency (FC) into the reporting currency (RC) using the current rate method.
    3. If the CBR is different from the FC, then re-measure the CBR into the FC using the temporal rate method.
    What is the correct order in which the rules are applied?

11. **[Obj. 5]** Foreign Currency Translation: Suppose that a subsidiary of Walt Disney Company uses Japanese yen as the currency of books and records (CBR) and EU euro as the functional currency (FC). The euro is not hyper-inflationary. The reporting currency (RC) of Walt Disney is the U.S. dollar. What method of currency translation should be used to restate the subsidiary's financial statements? Explain your answer.

12. **[Obj. 5]** Foreign Currency Translation: Suppose that a subsidiary of London Fog Company is located in Stirling, Scotland. The functional currency (FC) and currency of books and records (CBR) is Great Britain pounds. Great Britain pounds are not hyper-inflationary. The reporting currency of London Fog is the U.S. dollar. What method of currency translation should be used to restate the subsidiary's financial statements? Explain your answer.

13. **[Obj. 5]** Foreign Currency Translation: Suppose that a subsidiary of ChevronTexaco is located in Zimbabwe. The functional currency of the subsidiary is hyper-inflationary. What method of currency translation should be used to restate the subsidiary's financial statements? Explain your answer.

PROBLEMS – SET A

Applying Accounting Knowledge

1. **[Obj. 5]** Foreign Currency Translation using the Current Rate Method: Use the exchange rates and the trial balance shown below, and translate the account balances from EU euros to US dollars using the current rate method.

    Required:
    a. Show account balances for the debit accounts and credit accounts, in both euros and dollars.
    b. Evaluate: Why is it helpful to managers within a firm when account balances are translated from euros to dollars?

Adjusted Trial Balance In Euros December 31, Year 4	Debit	Credit
Cash	$5,000	
Accounts Receivable	25,000	
Inventory	208,000	
Equipment	60,000	
Accumulated Depreciation		$5,000
Accounts Payable		25,000
Bonds Payable		150,000
Revenues		215,000
General Expenses	203,000	
Depreciation Expense	8,000	
Dividends	4,000	
Common Stock		64,000
Paid-in Capital in Excess of Par		47,000
Retained Earnings		7,000
Total	$513,000	$513,000
Exchange Rates:		1 Euro = $____
Current Exchange Rate		0.510
Average Exchange Rate		0.480
At July 31, Year 4		0.495
At June 30, Year 1		0.460

Other: All common stock was issued on June 30, Year 1 (i.e., 6/30/Y1). Dividends were declared and paid on July 31, Year 4. Translated Retained Earnings at 12/31/Y4 was $4,000.

2. **[Obj. 5]** Foreign Currency Translation using the Current Rate Method: Same as previous assignment, except the exchange rates are as follows:

Current Exchange Rate	0.710
Average Exchange Rate	0.680
At July 31, Year 4	0.695
At June 30, Year 1	0.600

Required: Show account balances for the debit accounts and credit accounts, in both euros and dollars.

3. **[Obj. 5]** Foreign Currency Translation using the Current Rate Method: Use the exchange rates and the trial balance shown below, and translate the account balances from Great Britain pounds to US dollars using the current rate method.

    Required:
    a. Show account balances for the debit accounts and credit accounts, in both pounds and dollars.
    b. Evaluate: Why is it helpful to U.S. investors and lenders when account balances are translated from euros to dollars?

Adjusted Trial Balance In British Pounds December 31, Year 8	Debit	Credit
Cash	$42,000	
Accounts Receivable	30,000	
Inventory	76,000	
Fixed Assets	80,000	
Accumulated Depreciation		$46,000
Accounts Payable		20,000
Bonds Payable		50,000
Revenues		142,000
General Expenses	128,000	
Depreciation Expense	10,000	
Dividends	4,000	
Common Stock		58,000
Paid-in Capital in Excess of Par		28,000
Retained Earnings		26,000
Total	$370,000	$370,000
Exchange Rates:		1 BP = $____
Current Exchange Rate		1.750
Average Exchange Rate		1.600
At July 31, Year 8		1.850
At June 30, Year 1		1.200

Other: All common stock was issued on June 30, Year 1 (i.e., 6/30/Y1).
Dividends were declared and paid on July 31, Year 8.
Translated Retained Earnings at 12/31/Y8 was $35,500.

4. **[Obj. 5]** Foreign Currency Translation using the Current Rate Method: Same as previous assignment, except the exchange rates are as follows:

Current Exchange Rate	3.000
Average Exchange Rate	2.500
At July 31, Year 8	2.750
At June 30, Year 1	1.500

Required: Show account balances for the debit accounts and credit accounts, in both pounds and dollars.

5. **[Obj. 5]** Foreign Currency Translation using the Temporal Rate Method: Use the exchange rates and the trial balance shown below, and translate the account balances from Great Britain pounds to US dollars using the temporal rate method.

Required:

a. Show account balances for the debit accounts and credit accounts, in both pounds and dollars.

b. Evaluate: What causes changes in the relative value of one currency to another currency, such as the British pound to the US dollar?

Adjusted Trial Balance
In British Pounds December 31, Year 4

	Debit	Credit
Cash	$12,000	
Accounts Receivable	30,000	
Inventory (10-31-Y3)	40,000	
(7-31-Y4)	160,000	
Fixed Assets (6-30-Y1)	33,000	
(12-31-Y1)	55,000	
(7-31-Y2)	42,000	
Accumulated Depreciation (6-30-Y1)		$6,000
(12-31-Y1)		18,000
(7-31-Y2)		23,000
Accounts Payable		46,000
Bonds Payable		120,000
Revenues		184,000
General Expenses	156,000	
Depreciation Expense (6-30-Y1)	7,000	
(12-31-Y1)	8,000	
(7-31-Y2)	7,000	
Dividends (7-31-Y4)	6,000	
Common Stock (6-30-Y1)		45,000
(1-31-Y2)		29,000
Paid-in Capital in Excess of Par		
(6-30-Y1)		25,000
(1-31-Y2)		38,000
Retained Earnings		22,000
Total	$556,000	$556,000
Exchange Rates		1 BP = $___
Current Exchange Rate		0.400
Average Exchange Rate		0.410
At July 31, Year 4		0.406
At October 31, Year 3		0.391
At July 31, Year 2		0.385
At January 31, Year 2		0.386
At December 31, Year 1		0.390
At June 30, Year 1		0.380

Other: Regarding common stock, 60% was issued 6/30/Y1; 40% on 1/31/Y2.
Regarding inventory, 20% was acquired 10/31/Y3; 80% on 7/31/Y4.
Dividends were declared and paid on 7/31/Y4.
Regarding fixed assets, 10% were acquired 6/30/Y1; 50% on 12/31/Y1; and 40% on 7/31/Y2.
Revenues and expenses were accrued evenly throughout the year.
Translated retained earnings at 12/31/Y4 was $2,800.

6. **[Obj. 5]** Foreign Currency Translation using the Temporal Rate Method: Same as previous assignment, except the exchange rates are as follows:

Exchange Rates	1 BP = $___
Current Exchange Rate	1.400
Average Exchange Rate	1.410
At July 31, Year 4	1.406
At October 31, Year 3	1.391
At July 31, Year 2	1.385
At January 31, Year 2	1.386
At December 31, Year 1	1.390
At June 30, Year 1	1.380

Required: Show account balances for the debit accounts and credit accounts, in both pounds and dollars.

PROBLEMS – SET B

Applying Accounting Knowledge

1. **[Obj. 5]** Foreign Currency Translation Using the Current Rate Method: Use the exchange rates and the trial balance shown below, and translate the account balances from EU euros to US dollars using the current rate method.

    Required: Show account balances for the debit accounts and credit accounts, in both euros and dollars.

Adjusted Trial Balance In Euros December 31, Year 4	Debit	Credit
Cash	$17,000	
Accounts Receivable	14,000	
Inventory	108,000	
Equipment	40,000	
Accumulated Depreciation		$5,000
Accounts Payable		37,000
Bonds Payable		35,000
Revenues		319,000
General Expenses	303,000	
Depreciation Expense	8,000	
Dividends	8,000	
Common Stock		44,000
Paid-in Capital in Excess of Par		47,000
Retained Earnings		11,000
Total	$498,000	$498,000
Exchange Rates:		1 Euro = $___
Current Exchange Rate		0.810
Average Exchange Rate		0.780
At July 31, Year 4		0.795
At June 30, Year 1		0.760

Other: All common stock was issued on June 30, Year 1 (i.e., 6/30/Y1).
Dividends were declared and paid on July 31, Year 4.
Translated Retained Earnings at 12/31/Y4 was $2,200.

2. **[Obj. 5]** Foreign Currency Translation Using the Current Rate Method: Same as previous assignment, except the exchange rates are as follows:

Current Exchange Rate	0.910
Average Exchange Rate	0.880
At July 31, Year 4	0.895
At June 30, Year 1	0.860

Required:

a. Show account balances for the debit accounts and credit accounts, in both euros and dollars.

b. Evaluate: Why is it helpful to managers within a firm when account balances are translated from euros to dollars?

3. **[Obj. 5]** Foreign Currency Translation Using the Current Rate Method: Use the exchange rates and the trial balance shown below, and translate the account balances from Great Britain pounds to US dollars using the current rate method.

Required: Show account balances for the debit accounts and credit accounts, in both pounds and dollars.

Adjusted Trial Balance In British Pounds December 31, Year 8	Debit	Credit
Cash	$12,000	
Accounts Receivable	10,000	
Inventory	66,000	
Fixed Assets	20,000	
Accumulated Depreciation		$16,000
Accounts Payable		10,000
Bonds Payable		30,000
Revenues		142,000
General Expenses	128,000	
Depreciation Expense	10,000	
Dividends	4,000	
Common Stock		28,000
Paid-in Capital in Excess of Par		18,000
Retained Earnings		6,000
Total	$250,000	$250,000
Exchange Rates:		1 BP = $____
Current Exchange Rate		1.250
Average Exchange Rate		1.200
At July 31, Year 8		1.220
At June 30, Year 1		0.900
Other: All common stock was issued on June 30, Year 1 (i.e., 6/30/Y1). Dividends were declared and paid on July 31, Year 8. Translated Retained Earnings at 12/31/Y8 was $11,500.		

4. **[Obj. 5]** Foreign Currency Translation Using the Current Rate Method: Same as previous assignment, except the exchange rates are as follows:

Current Exchange Rate	1.750
Average Exchange Rate	1.700
At July 31, Year 8	1.720
At June 30, Year 1	1.400

Required:

a. Show account balances for the debit accounts and credit accounts, in both pounds and dollars.

b. Evaluate: Why is it helpful to U.S. investors and lenders when account balances are translated from euros to dollars?

5. **[Obj. 5]** Foreign Currency Translation Using the Temporal Rate Method: Use the exchange rates and the trial balance shown below, and translate the account balances from Great Britain pounds to US dollars using the temporal rate method.

Required: Show account balances for the debit accounts and credit accounts, in both pounds and dollars.

**Adjusted Trial Balance
In British Pounds December 31, Year 4**

	Debit	Credit
Cash	$62,000	
Accounts Receivable	10,000	
Inventory (10-31-Y3)	25,000	
(7-31-Y4)	95,000	
Fixed Assets (6-30-Y1)	63,000	
(12-31-Y1)	99,000	
(7-31-Y2)	12,000	
Accumulated Depreciation (6-30-Y1)		$16,000
(12-31-Y1)		28,000
(7-31-Y2)		53,000
Accounts Payable		6,000
Bonds Payable		104,000
Revenues		44,000
General Expenses	16,000	
Depreciation Expense (6-30-Y1)	7,000	
(12-31-Y1)	8,000	
(7-31-Y2)	7,000	
Dividends (7-31-Y4)	6,000	
Common Stock (6-30-Y1)		45,000
(1-31-Y2)		29,000
Paid-in Capital in Excess of Par (6-30-Y1)		25,000
(1-31-Y2)		38,000
Retained Earnings		22,000
Total	$410,000	$410,000
Exchange Rates		1 BP = $___
Current Exchange Rate		2.400
Average Exchange Rate		2.410
At July 31, Year 4		2.406
At October 31, Year 3		2.391
At July 31, Year 2		2.385
At January 31, Year 2		2.386
At December 31, Year 1		2.390
At June 30, Year 1		2.380

Other: Regarding common stock, 60% was issued 6/30/Y1; 40% on 1/31/Y2.
Regarding inventory, 20% was acquired 10/31/Y3; 80% on 7/31/Y4.
Dividends were declared and paid on 7/31/Y4.
Regarding fixed assets, 10% were acquired 6/30/Y1; 50% on 12/31/Y1; and 40% on 7/31/Y2.
Revenues and expenses were accrued evenly throughout the year.
Translated Retained Earnings balance at 12/31/Y4 was $33,000.

6. **[Obj. 5]** Foreign Currency Translation Using the Temporal Rate Method: Same as previous assignment, except the exchange rates are as follows:

Exchange Rates	1 BP = $___
Current Exchange Rate	1.400
Average Exchange Rate	1.410
At July 31, Year 4	1.406
At October 31, Year 3	1.391
At July 31, Year 2	1.385
At January 31, Year 2	1.386
At December 31, Year 1	1.390
At June 30, Year 1	1.380

Required:
a. Show account balances for the debit accounts and credit accounts, in both pounds and dollars.
b. Evaluate: What causes changes in the relative value of one currency to another currency, such as the British pound to the US dollar?

CROSS-FUNCTIONAL PERSPECTIVES

Discussion Questions

1. **[Obj. 2]** What information can the accounting information system provide concerning global operations that will help other departments within a firm?

2. **[Obj. 3]** How does a business, as a whole, benefit from standardized accounting procedures?

3. **[Obj. 4]** How do non-standardized accounting and auditing standards hinder a firm's operations in the global marketplace?

4. **[Obj. 6]** How do various departments within a business firm benefit from learning about the culture in which their firm operates?

Cross-functional Case: Increasing Coke's Revenue in Germany

The Coca-Cola Company has sold its products in Germany since 1929. It was the company's first marketing success outside North America. Germany was the birthplace of a new soft drink for the company. Unable to obtain Coca-Cola ingredients during WWII, German-born Coca-Cola executive Max Keith began marketing a new drink in 1940 called "Fanta." Today, the Coca-Cola system employs over 12,000 associates in Germany.

Germany is currently one of the largest markets for The Coca-Cola Company in the world. Top management at Coca-Cola believes there are still untapped markets in Germany that present the potential for new products and increased sales of existing products. They also believe costs can be streamlined in the German market.

Required: From each of the following department's perspective, provide top management with ideas to increase revenue. Go to the company's website, Coca-Cola.com, to gather information that will help you.
a. Accounting
b. Marketing
c. Production

EXCEL ASSIGNMENTS

1. **[Obj. 5]** Foreign Currency Translation Using the Current Rate Method: Use the exchange rates and the trial balance shown below, and translate the account balances from EU euros to U.S. dollars using the current rate method.

    Required: Show account balances for the debit accounts and credit accounts, in both euros and dollars.

Adjusted Trial Balance In Euros December 31, Year 4	Debit	Credit
Cash	$20,000	
Accounts Receivable	35,000	
Inventory	105,000	
Equipment	60,000	
Accumulated Depreciation		$20,000
Accounts Payable		35,000
Bonds Payable		50,000
Revenues		120,000
General Expenses	108,000	
Depreciation Expense	8,000	
Dividends	4,000	
Common Stock		62,000
Paid-in Capital in Excess of Par		44,000
Retained Earnings		9,000
Total	$340,000	$340,000
Exchange Rates:		1 Euro = $____
Current Exchange Rate		0.520
Average Exchange Rate		0.490
At July 31, Year 4		0.505
At June 30, Year 1		0.470

Other: All common stock was issued on June 30, Year 1 (i.e., 6/30/Y1).
Dividends were declared and paid on July 31, Year 4.
Translated Retained Earnings balance at 12/31/Y4 was $5,500.

2. **[Obj. 5]** Foreign Currency Translation Using the Current Rate Method: Same as previous assignment, except the exchange rates are as follows:

Current Exchange Rate	1.200
Average Exchange Rate	1.250
At July 31, Year 4	1.300
At June 30, Year 1	1.000

    Required: Show account balances for the debit accounts and credit accounts, in both euros and dollars.

3. **[Obj. 5]** Foreign Currency Translation Using the Current Rate Method: Use the exchange rates and the trial balance shown below, and translate the account balances from Great Britain pounds to US dollars using the current rate method.

Required: Show account balances for the debit accounts and credit accounts, in both pounds and dollars.

Adjusted Trial Balance In British Pounds December 31, Year 8	Debit	Credit
Cash	$72,000	
Accounts Receivable	60,000	
Inventory	136,000	
Fixed Assets	130,000	
Accumulated Depreciation		$76,000
Accounts Payable		50,000
Bonds Payable		90,000
Revenues		172,000
General Expenses	158,000	
Depreciation Expense	10,000	
Dividends	4,000	
Common Stock		58,000
Paid-in Capital in Excess of Par		98,000
Retained Earnings		26,000
Total	$570,000	$570,000
Exchange Rates		1 BP = $____
Current Exchange Rate		2.100
Average Exchange Rate		2.000
At July 31, Year 8		2.050
At June 30, Year 1		1.500
Other: All common stock was issued on June 30, Year 1 (i.e., 6/30/Y1). Dividends were declared and paid on July 31, Year 8. Translated Retained Earnings balance at 12/31/Y8 was $22,600.		

4. **[Obj. 5]** Foreign Currency Translation Using the Current Rate Method: Same as previous assignment, except the exchange rates are as follows:

Current Exchange Rate	3.100
Average Exchange Rate	2.900
At July 31, Year 8	2.950
At June 30, Year 1	4.000

Required: Show account balances for the debit accounts and credit accounts, in both pounds and dollars.

5. **[Obj. 5]** Foreign Currency Translation Using the Temporal Rate Method: Use the exchange rates and the trial balance shown below, and translate the account balances from Great Britain pounds to US dollars using the temporal rate method.

Required: Show account balances for the debit accounts and credit accounts, in both pounds and dollars.

Adjusted Trial Balance In British Pounds December 31, Year 4		
	Debit	**Credit**
Cash	$52,000	
Accounts Receivable	60,000	
Inventory (10-31-Y3)	40,000	
(7-31-Y4)	160,000	
Fixed Assets (6-30-Y1)	13,000	
(12-31-Y1)	65,000	
(7-31-Y2)	52,000	
Accumulated Depreciation (6-30-Y1)		$8,000
(12-31-Y1)		40,000
(7-31-Y2)		32,000
Accounts Payable		43,000
Bonds Payable		160,000
Revenues		214,000
General Expenses	189,000	
Depreciation Expense (6-30-Y1)	1,500	
(12-31-Y1)	7,500	
(7-31-Y2)	6,000	
Dividends (7-31-Y4)	10,000	
Common Stock (6-30-Y1)		48,000
(1-31-Y2)		32,000
Paid-in Capital in Excess of Par (6-30-Y1)		30,000
(1-31-Y2)		20,000
Retained Earnings		29,000
Total	$656,000	$656,000
Exchange Rates		1 BP = $___
Current Exchange Rate		0.600
Average Exchange Rate		0.610
At July 31, Year 4		0.606
At October 31, Year 3		0.591
At July 31, Year 2		0.585
At January 31, Year 2		0.586
At December 31, Year 1		0.590
At June 30, Year 1		0.580

Other: Regarding common stock, 60% was issued 6/30/Y1; 40% on 1/31/Y2.
Regarding inventory, 20% was acquired 10/31/Y3; 80% on 7/31/Y4.
Dividends were declared and paid on 7/31/Y4.
Regarding fixed assets, 10% were acquired 6/30/Y1; 50% on 12/31/Y1; and 40% on 7/31/Y2.
Revenues and expenses were accrued evenly throughout the year.
Translated Retained Earnings balance at 12/31/Y4 was $16,400.

6. **[Obj. 5]** Foreign Currency Translation Using the Temporal Rate Method: Same as previous assignment, except the exchange rates are as follows:

	1 BP = $____
Current Exchange Rate	2.000
Average Exchange Rate	2.400
At July 31, Year 4	2.300
At October 31, Year 3	2.150
At July 31, Year 2	2.200
At January 31, Year 2	2.180
At December 31, Year 1	2.250
At June 30, Year 1	2.100

Required: Show account balances for the debit accounts and credit accounts, in both pounds and dollars.

WEB ASSIGNMENTS

1. **[Obj. 3]** Identify the mission statement of the International Accounting Standards Board using the IASB website or a search on Google.

2. **[Obj. 3]** Prepare a diagram showing the structure of the International Accounting Standards Board. Find the IASB structure at its website, or do a search on Google.

3. **[Obj. 3]** Prepare an overview of International Financial Reporting Standards (IFRS). Find the information at the IFRS website, or do a search on Google.

4. **[Obj. 4]** What is the objective of the International Auditing and Assurance Standards Board? Find the answer on the IAASB website, or do a search on Google.

5. **[Obj. 6]** Go to the Coca-Cola website, or do a search on Google, and prepare a ½-page report on global expansions, challenges, or events for Coca-Cola.

¶1411   Test Prepper

Use this sample test to gauge your comprehension of the chapter material.

True/False Questions

__ 1. The International Financial Reporting Standards (IFRS) are the generally accepted accounting principles required or voluntarily used in many countries around the world.

__ 2. The International Business Organization establishes international accounting standards.

__ 3. The International Accounting Standards Board (IASB) is a government-run accounting standard-setter based in London, UK.

__ 4. The goal of the International Accounting Standards Board (IASB) is to formulate and publish standards to be observed in the presentation of audited financial statements and to promote their worldwide acceptance and observance.

__ 5. International Financial Reporting Standards (IFRS) often provide two or more options or choices for selection of accounting methods or techniques.

__ 6. Currently, the Securities Exchange Commission requires that financial statements either be based on U.S. GAAP or be reconciled to U.S. GAAP.

__ 7. The implementation or adherence to international standards on auditing is mandatory.

__ 8. The cumulative translation adjustment is the debit or credit required to bring the dollar-denominated accounts into balance after applying different exchange rates to the accounts.

__ 9. The cultural environment influences and shapes the values of a society, which in turn affect attitudes and behavior.

__ 10. A company keeps the record of each transaction in the currency of the customer.

Multiple-Choice Questions

__ 1. Which of the following poses a problem for international trade?
   a. Tariffs
   b. Language barriers
   c. Cultural differences
   d. Incompatible equipment standards
   e. All of the above

__ 2. Which of the following establishes international accounting standards?
   a. International Government Reporting Standards (IGRS)
   b. International Economic Standards (IES)
   c. International Accounting Standards Board (IASB)
   d. International Law
   e. Federal Trade Commission

__ 3. Which of the following is published by the International Accounting Standards Board (IASB)?
   a. International Financial Reporting Standards (IFRS)
   b. International Economic Standards (IES)
   c. Government Trade Rules
   d. International Law
   e. Federal Trade Commission

__ 4. Which of the following is an international set of standards that provide guidance on auditing?
   a. U.N. auditing standards
   b. International standards on auditing (ISA)
   c. Financial reporting standards
   d. U.S. auditing standards
   e. Microsoft auditing guidelines

__ 5. When restating foreign subsidiary financial statements, which of the following is the currency in which the consolidated financial statements are denominated?
   a. Currency of books and records (CBR)
   b. Functional currency (FC)
   c. Reporting currency (RC)
   d. Denominated currency (DC)
   e. Marginal currency (MC)

__ 6. When restating foreign subsidiary financial statements, which of the following is the currency in which the foreign financial statements are denominated?
   a. Currency of books and records (CBR)
   b. Functional currency (FC)
   c. Reporting currency (RC)
   d. Denominated currency (DC)
   e. Marginal currency (MC)

__ 7. When restating foreign subsidiary financial statements, which of the following is the currency in which the subsidiary generally buys, sells, borrows, repays, and generally conducts business?
   a. Currency of books and records (CBR)
   b. Functional currency (FC)
   c. Reporting currency (RC)
   d. Denominated currency (DC)
   e. Marginal currency (MC)

__ 8. If the exchange rate changes unfavorably for the seller from the time the sale is made to the time payment is received, then the seller will incur a(n):
   a. Exchange gain
   b. Exchange loss
   c. Denominated rate
   d. Delayed payment
   e. Back order

__ 9. Which group is interested in a firm's involvement in international trade?
   a. Financial analysts
   b. Lenders
   c. Government agencies
   d. Investors
   e. All of the above

__ 10. Which of the following is an objective of the IASB in formulating international accounting standards?
   a. Increase harmonization of accounting standards and disclosures to meet the needs of the global market.
   b. Provide an accounting basis for underdeveloped or newly industrialized countries.
   c. Increase the compatibility of domestic and international accounting requirements.
   d. Promote worldwide acceptance of these standards for a harmonized approach to accounting and reporting.
   e. All of the above.

Topical Index

References are to paragraph (¶) numbers

References are to paragraph (¶) numbers

References are to paragraph (¶) numbers

References are to paragraph (¶) numbers

References are to paragraph (¶) numbers

References are to paragraph (¶) numbers

H

I

References are to paragraph (¶) numbers

References are to paragraph (¶) numbers

References are to paragraph (¶) numbers

References are to paragraph (¶) numbers